Beginning WAP, WML, and WMLScript

Soo Mee Foo

Wei Meng Lee

Karli Watson

Ted Wugofski

Wrox Press Ltd. ®

Beginning WAP, WML, and WMLScript

Published by Wrox Press Ltd,
Arden House, 1102 Warwick Road, Acock's Green,
Birmingham, B27 6BH, UK
Printed in Canada

ISBN 1861004583

Trademark Acknowledgements

Credits

Authors
Soo Mee Foo
Wei Meng Lee
Karli Watson
Ted Wugofski

Additional Material
Jon Hill
Chanoch Wiggers

Category Manager
Jan Kolasinski

Technical Architects
Jon Hill
Victoria Hudgson

Technical Editors
Howard Davies
Chris Mills
Karli Watson
Chanoch Wiggers

Author Agent
Marsha Collins

Project Administrator
Avril Corbin

Technical Reviewers
Terry Allen
Stuart Brown
Trei Brundrett
Humphrey Chiu
Armand Datema
Simon Ellis
Costantinos Hadjisotiriou
Mark Harrison
Chris Houston
Kamran Kordi
Kenneth Lo
Chris Neale
Mike Nowlin
Iztok Polanic
Srinivasa Sivakumar
Gavin Smyth
Pascal Van Geest

Production Coordinator
Pip Wonson

Figures
Shabnam Hussain

Cover
Shelley Frazier

Index
Martin Brooks

About the Authors

Soo Mee Foo

Soo Mee is currently lecturing at Ngee Ann Polytechnic, Singapore. She lectures in web application development, networking, and security. She also conducts workshops on web and WAP application development for IT professionals.

Soo Mee is actively involved in developing web sites for industry and in-house web-based learning and assessment software. She is also involved in supervising projects that develop WAP services for enterprises. During her leisure time, she messes around with intelligent agents built into her home network. You can contact her at soomee_foo@hotmail.com.

I would like to express my utmost thanks to the great team of people at Wrox. Specifically, I would like to thank Victoria for the opportunity to participate in this book-writing project. I would also like to thank Jon Hill and the great editorial staff of the Wrox Mobile/Wireless team for their valuable suggestions and comments that helped to make this book a better one. Also, many thanks to Avril and Marsha for their efforts in getting things coordinated, and their patience in taking care of me along the way to the completion of my writing.

Thanks also go to David Buckland and Leslie Lim of TransQuest, without whom my involvement in this project may not have been possible. And not forgetting my colleague, Wei Meng, who made this project a fun one.

Most of all, I would like to thank my beloved family members for their support and encouragement at all times.

Wei Meng Lee

Wei Meng graduated from the National University of Singapore in 1996 with a degree in Computer Science. His interest is in web technologies, and he conducts training for XML and web developers. Wei Meng has recently caught the WAP fever and is intrigued by the ability to surf the Internet using a telephone. When not writing, you can find him lazing in Borders.

Wei Meng spoke at the Wrox Professional Wireless Developer Conference, held in Amsterdam, July 2000. He is also a regular contributor to magazines and online publications. You can reach him via email at wei_meng_lee@hotmail.com. He is currently lecturing at Ngee Ann Polytechnic, Singapore.

First of all, I would like to express my most sincere thanks to the editorial team at Wrox for their expert guidance. Thanks to Victoria, for trusting in me, and to Jon and Chanoch for their invaluable advice and attention to detail. Thanks must also go to Marsha and Avril for their patience in dealing with such an impatient author. Without the Mobile/Wireless team at Wrox, this book would never have been possible.

Next I would like to thank Way Kiat, Wee Kwan, Sudhir and Seok San from StarHub Singapore for their gracious help and support. Special thanks go to Sudhir of the Mobility division for taking time out to share with us his vast experience in WAP technology. I am also grateful to Kai Loong and Teck Kim from Ericsson for their support.

Also, not forgetting Leslie and David from TransQuest Publishers, who have been more like friends to me than business associates – you know that this book would not have been possible without your help! And to Joycelyn, who never fails to make fun of my photo.

Finally, my deepest gratitude to my family for enduring all the late nights at work. Now that the book is out, I think I can come back home earlier...

Karli Watson

Karli Watson is an in-house author for Wrox Press, with a penchant for multicolored clothing. He started out with the intention of becoming a world famous nanotechnologist, so perhaps one day you might recognize his name as he receives a Nobel Prize. For now, though, Karli's computing interests include all things mobile, and upcoming technologies such as C#. He can often be found preaching about these technologies at conferences, as well as after hours in drinking establishments. Karli is also a snowboarding enthusiast, and wishes he had a cat.

Thanks go to the Wrox team, both for helping me get into writing, and then dealing with the results when I started. Particular thanks to all in the Mobile group for their ideas, enthusiasm, and WAP cocktails. Finally, and most importantly, thanks to my wife Donna for continuing to put up with me.

Ted Wugofski

Ted Wugofski is a technologist for Phone.com. He is active within the Wireless Application Protocol (WAP) Forum, World Wide Web Consortium, and ECMA, focusing on the convergence of traditional web technologies with non-traditional computing environments.

Prior to Phone.com, Ted worked for Gateway and several other computer manufacturers. He provided technical leadership in the application of a variety of emerging technologies: artificial intelligence, computer telephony, and digital television.

Ted spends his days and nights in Fort Worth Texas with his wife, Ana, and their three children: Sofia, Bianca, and David. Ted can be contacted at ted.wugofski@ieee.org.

Table of Contents

Table of Contents

Table of Contents

Table of Contents

Table of Contents

Table of Contents

Introduction

Surveys and predictions may vary in the detail, but they all seem to agree that the astonishing growth of the mobile telephone industry is the precursor to an equally successful mobile *information* industry, in which people can request data and services from wherever they are. For all those with an interest in telecommunications, and for programmers in all fields, it's an exciting time: the 'killer' mobile application is yet to be developed, and as is typical in a new area, the opportunities are significant.

Right now, however, mobile devices don't have enormous processing power, run a range of diverse, proprietary operating systems, and are constrained by the low speeds at which they can receive and transmit data. WAP, the Wireless Application Protocol, has emerged as an important technology in this area because it has answers to all three problems. The WAP Specification, as defined by the WAP Forum (www.wapforum.org), can be implemented on top of existing operating systems, and places few processing demands on the devices that use it. Also, while it reuses much of the existing Internet architecture for the transmission of information, it adds some new ideas that make the process more streamlined.

It's with this last point that we'll largely be concerning ourselves in this book. Within the WAP specification are specifications for two new programming languages: WML, the Wireless Markup Language, and its companion WMLScript. Used well together, these two can create compelling applications that can be delivered to mobile devices quickly and efficiently, with many of the features users have come to expect from their experiences with the Internet.

Beginning WAP, WML and WMLScript provides a complete tutorial in the use of these languages to best effect, from the fundamentals of syntax and structure, through dealing with the constraints of mobile devices, to the development of complex applications that use technologies like ASP, XML, and XSLT to provide the best possible end-user experience.

Who Is This Book For?

This book has been structured carefully to appeal to a number of different readers. First, if you're interested in the burgeoning potential of the telecommunications industry, but have no knowledge of programming, this book will teach you from scratch how to create applications that run on mobile devices. Second, if you have some 'traditional' programming experience, this book will provide you with the information and techniques you need to get started in this exciting new area. Finally, if you're already involved in WAP development, the advice in the second half of the book on usability and interoperability should prove invaluable, especially when we detail the differences between current microbrowser implementations.

What's Covered In This Book

In this book, each chapter builds upon its predecessor, and new information is presented in logical order. Because nothing is taken for granted, introductions to new technologies are interwoven with the broad sweep of the tutorial in WML and WMLScript. Here's how things will pan out:

❑ Chapter 1 describes the birth of WAP and associated technologies, and examines the motivation for designing a new system for delivering content over the Internet. Specifically, we look at the differences between WAP and the Web, and cover installation of the tools you need to follow the numerous examples provided in the book. You also get to try out your very first WAP application.

❑ Now armed with knowledge of what we're working towards, Chapter 2 examines the history of markup languages, including SGML, HTML, and XML, on which the Wireless Markup Language (WML) is based. We also discuss why HTML was not chosen as the markup language to be used for WAP application development. Chapter 3 then contains a more detailed introduction to XML, including such things as syntax, well formedness, and validity.

❑ Chapters 4 thru 10 are concerned entirely with WML. We explain the format, structure and syntax of WML by example, covering all you need to know in order to write 'static' WML sites. The chapters in this section describe WML's facilities for text handling, navigation, displaying images and tables, using variables, and requesting information from the user – with sample code and applications at every stage.

❑ On its own, WML is extremely limited when it comes to handling mathematical processes such as addition, subtraction, multiplication, etc. The next three chapters – 11, 12, and 13 – introduce and explain WAP's scripting language, WMLScript, which allows us to interact meaningfully with users, and add complexity to our sites. We discuss the situations in which it's most appropriate, lay down its syntax, and provide numerous samples.

❑ Chapter 14 discusses events, which allow our WML applications to perform tasks in direct response to a timer expiring or users' actions, while in Chapter 15 we look at some extensions to the WML specification that Phone.com provides in its microbrowser. If you can be sure that your clients will be using devices that support them, these facilities are useful additions to the WML developer's arsenal.

❑ The final part of the book, from Chapter 16 to Chapter 20, is concerned with the exposition of some advanced techniques for adding professional touches to your WAP applications. They may also inspire you to explore more deeply into one of the numerous new technologies that we introduce here.

In Chapter 16, we look at ways of making WAP sites attractive and easy to use. Then, in Chapter 17, we examine the differences between browsers from the various vendors, and work out some ways of minimizing the effects of incompatibilities between them.

In Chapter 18, we look at the dynamic creation of WAP sites, using ASP to create WML applications on the fly. Chapter 19 revisits XML, with the focus this time on XSLT and how it allows you to target your content to different devices. The final chapter then combines the lessons learned from its four precursors to create a truly usable, dynamic WAP application.

The book's appendices include complete references for WML elements, the syntax of WMLScript, and the WMLScript Standard Libraries. They also cover the installation and use of the WAP emulators provided by all the major implementers.

What You Need To Use This Book

The following is a list of all the software we used in the projects documented in this book, and we provide download and installation instructions for many of them when they first appear in the text. Apart from the operating systems, all of these tools are available for download without charge.

- ❏ **Platform:** The code has been developed and tested on Windows 9x, Me, NT 4, and 2000. Any machine capable of running these operating systems is suitable for WAP development. While there's no technical reason for preferring Microsoft solutions, there are compelling practical ones − most of the simulators are only available for Windows. If you're interested, www.freaklabs.com includes an installation guide for the Nokia toolkit on the Linux OS.

- ❏ **WAP development kit and simulator:** For the reasons that will become clear, we've chosen to use Phone.com's UP.SDK for the creation of most of the examples in this book. A detailed download and installation guide for this package is provided in Chapter 1. Other toolkits and simulators are available from companies including Benefon, Ericsson, Motorola, and Nokia, and installation guides for these are provided in Appendix A.

- ❏ **Web server:** While many of the examples in this provided in this book can be tested without a web server, the more advanced demonstrations do require one. Because of their convenience, we cover Microsoft's Internet Information Server (IIS) and Personal Web Server (PWS), which ship with the operating systems listed above.

- ❏ **XML:** For Chapters 19 and 20, you will need an XML parser and an XSLT processor. We've used two in this book, namely MSXML (which comes as a part of Internet Explorer 5.5), and James Clark's xt. The latest version of MSXML can also be downloaded separately from Microsoft's web site, while xt can be downloaded from www.jclark.com

All of the source code developed in this book is available for free download from the Wrox Press web site at www.wrox.com

Conventions

To help you get the most from the text and keep track of what's happening, we've used a number of conventions throughout the book.

For instance:

> **These boxes hold important, not-to-be forgotten information that is directly relevant to the surrounding text.**

While this style is used for asides to the current discussion − useful information that is not always directly related to the current discussion, but nevertheless has bearing on it.

As for styles within the text:

> When we introduce important words, we **highlight** them
>
> We show keyboard strokes like this: *Ctrl-A*
>
> We show filenames and code within text like so: `books.wml`
>
> Text in user interfaces is shown like this: Menu

When we list code, or the contents of files, we'll use the following conventions:

```
Lines that show concepts directly related to the surrounding text are shown on a
gray background.
But lines that do not introduce anything new, or which we have seen before, are
shown on a white background.
```

Finally, we show commands typed at the command line like this:

```
> xt document.xml stylesheet.xsl output
```

These formats are designed to make sure that you know what it is you're looking at. We hope they make life easier.

Tell Us What You Think

We've worked hard on this book to make it useful. We've tried to understand what you're willing to pay for, and we've tried to make it live up to your expectations. Please let us know what you think: tell us what we did wrong, and what we did right. We'll answer, and we'll take what you say on board for future editions. The easiest way is to use e-mail:

feedback@wrox.com

If you find a mistake in the text, or need help with something that's been written, please refer to Appendix E, which explains our commitment to you via the errata and support service we offer. Come and join our Peer to Peer™ lists on http://p2p.wrox.com, and get advice and help from the authors and editors of the book, other experts in WAP, and your peers as they begin to put into practice the knowledge they have learned in this book.

An Introduction
to Wireless Technologies

The world in which we live is an increasingly wireless one. If the human eye were able to see the full electromagnetic spectrum, we'd be faced with the sight of a mind-blowing quantity of information being exchanged. In some places – in most major cities, in fact – it seems as though *everyone* has a mobile phone, including the children. Despite the constant background noise that's made up of tinny melodies and people apparently conversing with thin air, consumers have accepted mobile telecommunications with open arms, and their enthusiasm shows no signs of abating.

Running a parallel course with this wireless revolution, the Internet has also been expanding at a remarkable rate, in terms of the number of people using it, the amount of information stored on it, the business being done on it, and the speed with which we can access it. In less than ten years, it has gone from being the realm of academics and enthusiasts, through a period of widening acceptance, to a stage where market analysts are beginning to report people proclaiming themselves 'bored' of it – or at least, of the hype that sometimes surrounds it. The Internet is now 'just another resource' that they have become used to using in their everyday lives.

Without any doubt, these are two stories of outstanding success, but some of the statistics involved can still make for interesting reading. For example, in the USA, Japan, and Western Europe, where penetration is highest, somewhere between a third and a half of the population are Internet users. Mobile phone use, on the other hand, is highest in the countries of Northern Europe, where around *three quarters* of the people – and still rising – own a handset. Although fears about safety are yet to be conclusively disproved, consumers have demonstrated that they're willing to pay for the ability to send and receive information while they're on the move. Right now, that "information" is overwhelmingly in the form of spoken conversation and text messages, but the future holds some exciting possibilities.

What happens when a means of communication like the Internet is extended to the wireless world? What sorts of information are people likely to need wherever they are? The confluence of these technologies raises the prospect of a range of services – some familiar, some new – specifically tailored to the needs of the mobile user. In this book, we're going to tell you how to create them.

Mobile Access to Information

When the public or the media talk about "the Internet", they are almost always talking about the World Wide Web – in everyday parlance, the two have become practically synonymous, and it's fair to say that without the Web, the number of Internet users wouldn't be as high as it is. In its present form, however, there are two significant barriers to its further adoption:

❑ Using the Web requires at least some proficiency in the art of using a computer. Even the set-top boxes that allow web pages to be displayed on a TV screen come with a mouse and a keyboard, and the authors of web pages tend to create user interfaces that are similar to those used in PC applications.

❑ The hardware required is still relatively expensive, so if you don't already own a computer, the entrance costs are high.

If we're serious about creating wireless information services that will gain mass-market acceptance, they can't be allowed to fall at either of these hurdles. At the same time, however, it would be foolish in the extreme to ignore the Internet; as a means for the transportation of data, it's unsurpassed. We need to find a way of reusing the infrastructure – even some of the data it contains – in a way that appeals to consumers in the same way that mobile phones have. The best candidate we have for fulfilling that joint role is WAP: the Wireless Application Protocol.

What is WAP?

WAP is an effort, with broad industry support, to define a standard for communicating Internet-type information to devices that have roughly the same form factor and processing power as the average mobile telephone. In fact, the majority of WAP-enabled devices in people's pockets right now *are also* mobile phones. Straight away, then, we can list some characteristics of these devices that must be taken into account by both the creators of WAP, and the people who will use it as a means of providing information.

❑ They have small screens, so they can't display a lot of information at once

❑ They don't have the powerful processing ability of a desktop computer, so they are unlikely to have the same multimedia capabilities

❑ They may not have a keyboard, so user input is likely to be more awkward than on a desktop computer

As we'll see, these restrictions necessarily mean that the appearance of information on a WAP-enabled device is less rich than a typical web page, and the writers of the WAP specification have been able to make the parts of it that deal with presentation considerably simpler than the equivalent constructs for the Web. The most important thing to be dealt with, though, is the one we've left until last:

❑ Wireless networks have much less bandwidth for transmitting information than the fixed-line networks of desktop computers

Currently, wireless Internet connection speeds are around 9600 bits per second, which translates to around 1200 text characters per second. To put that in context, you've already read around four times that many characters in this chapter! A typical web page on the Internet is likely to be at least five times as long as that, and once you start adding graphics and sounds into the mix, you can be looking at another factor of ten or twenty.

By comparison, for a modest price you can set up your desktop computer to connect to the Internet six times faster than current mobile devices, over a standard phone line. Corporate solutions enable connection speeds an order of magnitude higher than this.

It doesn't take a huge leap of understanding to see that on its own, this bandwidth limitation requires an approach to transferring and presenting information that's different from the techniques used on the Internet in the past. We'll spend much of the book discussing how WAP deals with the second of these issues, but for now, let's take a look at the first.

How Does the Web Work?

Because they use the same infrastructure, you need to know how the Web works before you can understand how WAP works. We can start by saying that in order to specify communication over *any* system, you must have all of the following:

❑   A technological understanding of the data bearer – in other words, the medium that's used to transmit information. For the Web, this concerns cables and their properties; wireless networks make use of the electromagnetic properties of air.

❑   A method of transmitting information over the bearer.

❑   Ways of encoding information so that it can be transferred over the bearer.

❑   Methods of creating secure links for information transfer.

On the Web, all of this detail is wrapped up inside the Hypertext Transfer Protocol (HTTP). Simply put, it works like this: when you enter the name of a web page into your web browser (the client in the diagram below), an HTTP request for that page is sent to the web server. In reply, the server retrieves the page from its store, and sends it to you via an HTTP response.

This is why, if you type (say) www.wrox.com into your browser, the prefix http:// is added to it automatically. When you send a request to a server, you're supposed to specify a protocol. With no reason to believe otherwise, the browser assumes you want to use HTTP.

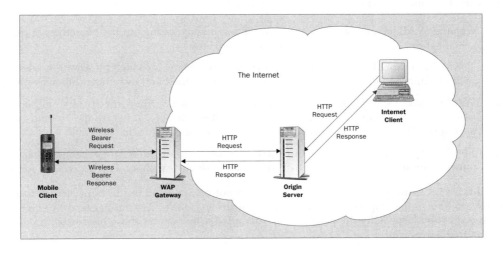

How Does WAP Work?

The differences between wireless and web systems are such that HTTP is not ideal as a transport protocol for wireless communication – it's not optimized for the low bandwidth we've been discussing. WAP's solution, though, is not to abolish HTTP altogether, but to replace it for the 'wireless' stage of a document's journey.

WAP-enabled devices do not connect directly to the server that holds the information they've requested. Instead, they communicate with a **WAP gateway** that's positioned at the 'edge' of the Internet, using protocols that are defined in the WAP specification. The gateway acts like an ordinary Internet client: it requests and receives documents from the server, on behalf of the device, using HTTP.

This clever arrangement enables us to store WAP content on existing web servers, with only a small amount of configuration required in order to do so. The programming languages in which this content is written, however, are not the same as those used elsewhere on the Web. So-called **WAP applications** are programmed in WML (Wireless Markup Language) and WMLScript. As you'd expect, we'll be seeing more of these two very soon.

> *Don't be misled by the above diagram: you don't need to set up your own gateway in order to provide WAP content to mobile devices. WAP gateways will normally be owned by wireless network operators (and a few other institutions, like banks) – you just need to place your content on a web server, and connect your WAP-enabled device to a gateway (contact the institution concerned if you don't know how to do this). The gateway will deal with the situation from then on.*

The WAP Specification

The current WAP specification can be downloaded from http://www.wapforum.org. At the time of writing, the most recent version is WAP 1.2, which was last updated in June 2000. This is the specification that we have used in the development of this book.

A glance at the list of documents that comprise the WAP specification will tell you that there are quite a lot of them! To summarize, the WAP specification includes documents relating to:

❑ General WAP technologies – a selection of documents setting out the objectives of the WAP specification, and the various enabling technologies.

❑ The WAP protocol stack and WAP gateways – the means by which information is exchanged with the Internet, optimized to be as efficient as possible in a low bandwidth environment.

❑ WAP language specifications, including WML and WMLScript – specifically on the way in which applications may be created for WAP-enabled devices. It is with the contents of this part of the specification that we'll be spending most of our time in this book.

❑ The WAP push specification – information on server-initiated WAP exchanges (that is, how information may be transmitted to WAP enabled devices without a direct request for it).

Much of this specification is quite advanced, and will not be discussed in this book, which focuses primarily on how to develop WAP applications. In order to do this, it is not necessary to digest the entire specification (especially the parts that are intended primarily for those interested in developing WAP-enabled hardware).

Enabling WAP Development

Before we reach the end of this chapter, we'll have written our first WAP application using WML. Once it's complete, we *could* test it (and the other examples in the book) on a WAP-enabled mobile device, but it is far easier (not to mention cheaper!) to use a PC-based emulator – that is, a program that runs on your desktop machine and *behaves like* such a device. Emulators enable you to write WAP applications without any additional hardware, confident in the knowledge that they will work on a WAP-enabled device when the time comes.

Most of the major mobile phone manufacturers distribute applications that emulate the devices they produce. (Often, the emulators' interfaces even look like the real devices!) In Appendix A, we describe how to download, install, and use the emulators available from Benefon, Ericsson, Motorola, and Nokia; and we'll look at them in some detail in Chapter 17; but we're not going to use them for the greater part of the book, for a couple of reasons.

When we started to assemble the tome you have before you, we soon began to discover differences in how the various emulators implemented the WAP (or more pertinently, the WML) specification. We certainly didn't want to spend every chapter saying "...but in this other emulator..." so we knew that we'd have to specialize in just one – for most of the time, at least. Given these inconsistencies, however, we were also worried about giving the impression that any one of them used the 'right' approach – so we took a different tack.

For the first fourteen chapters of the book, we decided to stick to the letter of the WML specification: what *it* says is correct, what *it* says is wrong, and how *it* says things should be done. Only then would we 'break out' and examine the foibles of particular implementations. In the end, of course, we've had to compromise a little – after all, we had to have *some* way of demonstrating the examples – but we tried to stay true to the specification, and for the most part we've managed that.

So what emulator did we choose? In the end, we decided on the one that we've found easiest to use, and which best enabled us to follow the specification. Phone.com's UP.Simulator is popular among WAP developers, and while it certainly has departures from WML 1.2 (we'll examine those in Chapter 15), it handles the basics pretty well. Shortly, we will see where you can obtain this simulator, how to install it, and how to use it. First, though, we'll look at serving WAP content from your computer.

> *In case you're wondering, Phone.com used to be called Unwired Planet, hence the "UP" that features in the names of a number of its products.*

Serving WAP Content

The UP.Simulator is capable of viewing WAP content in three different ways. It can:

❑   Load files that are stored in the PC's file system directly

❑   Access files stored on web servers by using the HTTP protocol and 'pretending' also to be a gateway

❑   Access files via a real WAP gateway

Some of examples we'll look at in this book (though none of the simpler ones) will *require* content to be stored on a web server in order to execute correctly. If you don't have access to a web server, you'll be fine to start off with, and you'll certainly be able to learn all the basic principles, but you'll miss out on some of the more interesting functionality that WAP offers. For that reason, we recommend that you use a web server if you can.

A consequence of choosing the UP.Simulator is that you're tied to the Windows platform – at present, Phone.com doesn't support any other operating system. We're aware that opinions about Microsoft tend to be polarized, but the truth is that if you want to develop WAP applications, Windows is the sensible choice right now. There are WAP emulators for Macintosh and flavors of UNIX, but the majority are Windows-only.

The good news is that acquiring and using a web server is fairly simple. You can even run one on the same computer as the UP.Simulator, enabling you to write, test, and debug your WAP applications on a single machine – you don't need access to a network, for example. If you're using Windows NT or 2000, you can choose to install Microsoft Internet Information Server (IIS) as part of your operating system. If you're using Windows 9x or ME, you can use Microsoft Personal Web Server (PWS), which may be downloaded from its web site at http://www.microsoft.com/ntserver/web/exec/feature/PWS.asp.

The link on this page says Download the Windows NT Option Pack. Don't worry about this: it's the right thing to do, even though you're not running Windows NT!

We're not going to cover installing the web servers here – in tests, we found the default settings perfectly adequate for our needs, and the documentation on the Microsoft web site should be able to help with any problems you have. Regardless of which web server you choose, however, a small amount of *additional* setting up is necessary. In order for the web server to send files to the emulator in the correct format, you need to configure your MIME types.

Setting up the WAP MIME Types

MIME stands for **Multipurpose Internet Mail Extensions**; the standard that's used to differentiate between different types of content stored on the Internet. To see why such a thing might be necessary, consider the example of downloading a picture into a browser. If we're not able somehow to tell the browser what's coming next (text, an image, an audio file, etc.), we're likely to end up with a mess.

The problem we face is that while the browser is expecting to be told what MIME type is about to be sent to it, the web server doesn't hold that information on a per-file basis. Instead, we have to create a list of associations between the file types on the server, and the MIME types demanded by the browser. A list of this sort will have been created when you installed the web server, but we need to add to it in order to handle files containing WAP application content.

All files stored on a PC have an **extension** as part of their name that's used in helping to determine the file type. A filename is constructed in the following way:

```
name.extension
```

so that files with names like these:

```
news.doc
flower.bmp
connery.html
```

have extensions of .doc, .bmp, and .html respectively.

Note that the period is mandatory and not technically part of the extension, although extensions are often written with the period included (as above).

The MIME types that need to be set up for serving WAP content are as follows:

Description	MIME Type	Associated Extension
Plain WML file	text/vnd.wap.wml	.wml
Compiled WML file	application/vnd.wap.wmlc	.wmlc
WMLScript file	text/vnd.wap.wmlscript	.wmls
Compiled WMLScript file	application/vnd.wap.wmlscriptc	.wmlsc
Wireless Bitmap Image	image/vnd.wap.wbmp	.wbmp

In the next two sections, we'll look at how to set up these MIME types for serving content from IIS and PWS web servers. If you're using a different web server, you should find instructions on setting up MIME types in its documentation.

Internet Information Server

MIME type configuration in IIS is available through the Internet Services Console. Here you have the choice of setting MIME types for either the entire server, for individual web sites, or even for specific directories. In our case, setting them for the entire server is fine. To do this, right click on the server in the left hand window, and select Properties:

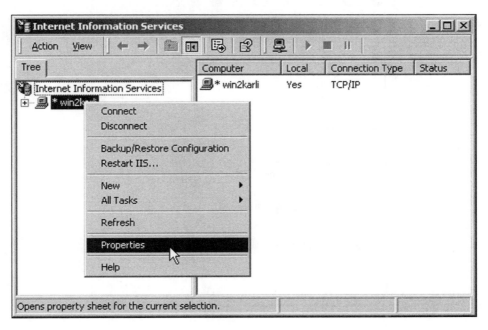

13

Next, select the **Edit...** button in the **Computer MIME Map** section of the dialog that appears:

Finally, for each WAP MIME type, select **New Type...** and enter the details in the dialog that appears:

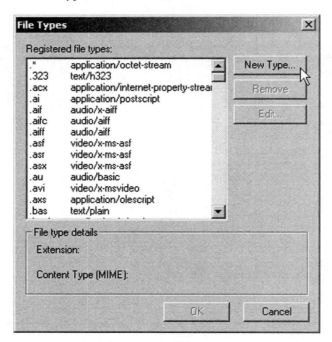

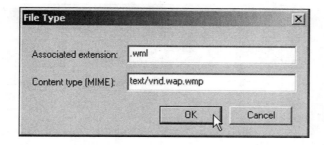

Personal Web Server

Unfortunately, PWS doesn't have a friendly interface for setting up MIME types. Instead, it stores its settings in the **registry** – a special database that Windows and its applications can use for many different purposes. The easiest and safest way to add information to the registry is with a **registry script**, and we've provided one of these in the source code for this book that you can download from the Wrox web site. Alternatively, you can open Notepad and enter the following:

```
REGEDIT4

[HKEY_CLASSES_ROOT\.wml]
"Content Type"="text/vnd.wap.wml"

[HKEY_CLASSES_ROOT\.wmlc]
"Content Type"="application/vnd.wap.wmlc"

[HKEY_CLASSES_ROOT\.wmls]
"Content Type"="text/vnd.wap.wmlscript"

[HKEY_CLASSES_ROOT\.wmlsc]
"Content Type"="application/vnd.wap.wmlscriptc"

[HKEY_CLASSES_ROOT\.wbmp]
"Content Type"="image/vnd.wap.wbmp"
```

Notice in particular the extra, empty line of code. It's important to end the final line of code with a return character. This file is interpreted line-by-line, and this 'extra' character is used to signify that a line is complete.

The file in the source code is called `wapmime.reg`, so if you've typed it in yourself, it's probably sensible to save it with the same name. Then, however you've acquired the file, double click on it. Finally, **OK** the two dialogs that appear, and we're done: your web server is ready to do the job we require of it.

The Phone.com UP.Simulator

The first step in using the UP.Simulator is to download it. You can do this for free, the only proviso being that Phone.com requires you to register on its web site before allowing you to do so. Point your web browser at http://developer.phone.com and you should see the following (or something very like it):

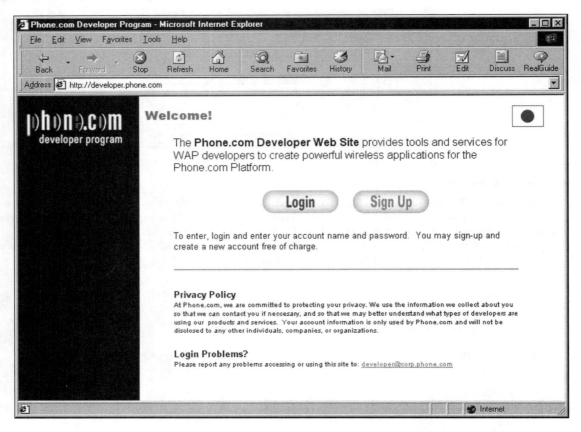

On the first occasion you visit this site, you'll need to follow the Sign Up link. After you've filled in all your details, you'll be able to Login by entering your user name and password in the dialog box that appears:

When you hit OK, you will enter the Phone.com developer site. Clicking the UP.SDK Downloads link (in the left-hand toolbar) will take you to a page where you can download the latest version of the UP.SDK, which at the time of writing was 4.0:

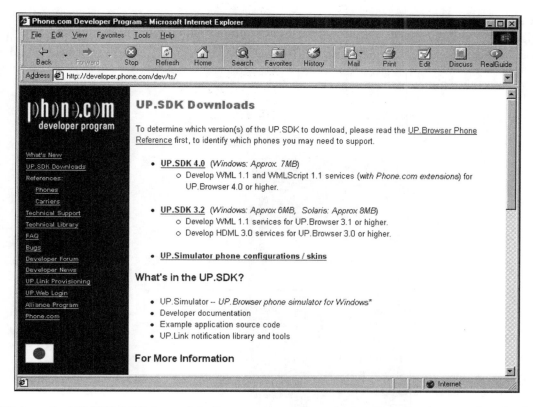

Click on the UP.SDK 4.0 link, read the license agreement, and select Download to start downloading the 7MB installation file, `upsdkW40e.exe`:

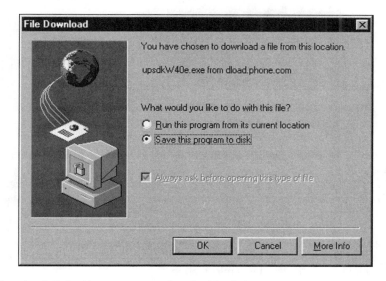

Once you've downloaded the file, you just need to double click on its icon to start the installation procedure.

Installing the UP.Simulator

Installation couldn't be easier: you just need to accept all the default settings, agree to the license, and confirm that you are not installing on top of a beta version of the simulator. Once this has completed, you can start the simulator through your Start menu (it will be under Programs | UP.SDK 4.0 | UP.Simulator). If all has gone to plan, you should be greeted with a window containing a picture of a phone:

This window contains the device simulator, and it functions in much the same way as a real WAP-enabled device, except of course that we can operate it on-screen using a mouse!

> *The information in the display area shown above is the 'home' WAP site on the Phone.com web server. This will only be displayed if your computer is connected to the Internet, and only then if you don't require an HTTP proxy – if you do, further configuration is required. (This setting is accessible through the Settings | UP.Link Settings... menu item. If this causes confusion, speak to your network administrator.)*

Launching the application will also cause the appearance of a second window that will start its life minimized in your taskbar. This window, of which we'll see a great deal more later on in the book, is used by the UP.Simulator to display status information.

Using the UP.Simulator

We'll see more and more of the functionality provided by the UP.Simulator throughout the book, but we should look at the basics here so that we start from a level playing field. Keep the labels in the previous diagram in mind as we proceed.

Most operation of WAP applications is achieved via the directional and softkey buttons on the phone. On the screen shown in the last section, clicking on the up and down directional buttons moves the cursor among the options listed (the left and right buttons won't do anything here), while clicking the softkey marked OK will select the option. The UP.Simulator also allows us to select options using the numeric keypad – pressing the number shown to the left of the option is equivalent to moving the cursor to the option and pressing OK.

For example, if we press the button labeled 1, we will be taken to the following screen:

Just in passing, note that it's possible to have images in WAP applications – although only in black and white.

There's more information here than can fit in the display area, and we can use the up and down directional buttons to scroll the display. If we scroll down to the bottom, we see the following:

19

Although there are more items to see, the list doesn't continue because there are only nine numeric keys that can be assigned to them. Clicking on the More... entry would take us to a different screen containing further options.

This site also makes use of the second softkey, labeled Menu above, allowing you to get to a further list of options:

As well as allowing us to select numbered options, the numeric keypad is also the primary tool for user input. If you select the Go to... option from the above screen, you get to this one:

This particular screen allows you to type in a web address, and will take you to that address when you click on OK. However, entering text using the numeric keypad is tricky. In general, each key is responsible for several different characters – key 4, for example, allows you to enter g, h, i, and 4. All of these are printed on the key in question, but you can't take this for granted – key 3 can select d, e, f, É, and 3!

In addition, the *range* of characters that each key selects can be changed. The * key, for example, changes the case of all subsequent characters. To give a visual hint of this, the alpha label in the bottom right changes to ALPHA. Other character sets are available via the second softkey, including symbol and numeric entry modes. We can also move the cursor left and right through the text to insert missing characters, and delete the character to the left of the cursor using the CLR button.

When it comes down to it, this is a very awkward way of entering data, although it does get easier with practice. To enter the web address wap.h2g2.com, for example, requires the following key presses:

927144222222224222222221222666 <pause> 6

The pause is necessary because the last two characters ('o' and 'm') are located on the same key. Incidentally, you can also use the PC keyboard for input, which can save a lot of time during WAP application development! Always remember, though, that real users won't have this luxury – slow and cumbersome user input is most definitely the norm!

We're almost through: the simulator has three remaining function buttons that we haven't looked at yet: HOME, MENU, and BACK. The first of these takes us to the 'home' WAP site for the simulator, which can be changed in the Settings | Up.Link Settings... menu item. MENU calls up some standard phone setup menu items and utilities, which aren't of much interest to us. BACK, on the other hand, is a very useful key: it allows us to switch to the last screen we looked at – something that's not always possible using the built in functionality of the WAP sites we visit.

Viewing WAP Applications

Perhaps the most common thing we'll need to do is view WAP application files. Obviously, the method of entering URLs we just described is hardly ideal, so the designers have provided an alternative: the Go entry box just above the device display. To load a file, we just need to type its name and location into the box (just as you would for a web page in a web browser), and hit *Return*.

We can also use the Go box to load application files from the hard disk. The simulator comes with some example WML files that (by default) are stored in c:\Program Files\Phone.com\UPSDK40\ examples\wml\, so let's try one of those. Type the following into the Go box, and hit *Return*:

file://c:/Program Files/Phone.com/UPSDK40/examples/wml/news.wml

If you've typed the location in correctly, you should see the following:

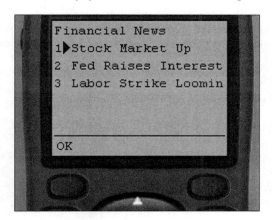

Clearing the Cache

One last thing to be aware of is that the UP.Simulator stores all of the files it loads in memory, even if you've subsequently looked at different ones. If you go back to look at a file you loaded earlier, the emulator will use the version stored in memory, which can cause problems if the file in question has been updated – you won't see the new version.

Luckily, we can get round this quite easily. All we need to do is select the Edit | Clear Cache menu option, or just press *F12*, to remove any files stored in memory. In fact, we recommend doing this fairly frequently during development, and when testing the numerous examples contained in this book!

Your First WAP Application

As we progress through the chapters to come, we'll be building a number of small WAP applications that demonstrate the things you've learned. However, there will also be a 'running' example that we'll be adding to throughout the course of the book, augmenting it with new functionality as we discover it. This case study will feature the WAP site of a fictitious travel agent, and it starts right here.

Try It Out — Your First WAP Application

1. In terms of their content, WML files are extremely simple, and it's possible to create them using any text editor. The most readily available of these – and therefore the one we'll use here – is Windows' Notepad. Open this application, and type in the following exactly as you see it.

```
<?xml version="1.0"?>
<!DOCTYPE wml PUBLIC "-//WAPFORUM//DTD WML 1.2//EN"
                     "http://www.wapforum.org/DTD/wml_1.2.xml">

<wml>
    <card>
        <p>Wrox Travel</p>
        <p>Welcome to our WAP site!</p>
    </card>
</wml>
```

2. Now we need to save the file somewhere sensible. If you've installed (or you already had) a web server, it will have created a directory on the installation drive called inetpub. (Use Windows' Find function if it's not immediately apparent.) Inside *that* is a subdirectory called wwwroot, and that's where this file needs to go. Give it the name travel.wml.

   If you're not using a web server, this decision is less important – you can put the file more or less where you like. For this example, we'll use c:\wap\travel.wml.

3. Next, open the UP.Simulator (if it wasn't already open), type either http://localhost/travel.wml or file://c:/wap/travel.wml (if you have or do not have a server, respectively) into the Go box, and hit *Return*. You should see the following:

The name 'localhost' that you typed in order to view the application on the web server is the name of your computer, as far as the web server is concerned. If your applications will be stored on a different computer, you will need to use the name of that machine instead.

Congratulations! You've just created your first WAP site! Soon, we will examine what the code you have typed in all means, and from then on we will begin to learn more about the possibilities that WAP provides, and adding functionality to this application.

Summary

At the start of this chapter, we discussed the world of wireless communication and saw where WAP fits into it. We then took a brief look at the mechanics of WAP – or at least, enough of it for you to be comfortable while developing WAP applications. We also talked about what the WAP specifications contain, and where they may be obtained: http://www.wapforum.org.

Next, we went through the process of preparing for WAP application development, which meant first configuring the MIME types of a web server, and then installing Phone.com's UP.Simulator. We'll be using this emulator for the rest of this book, so we also had a quick tour of its main features.

Finally, we put together our first WAP application: the first page of the Wrox Travel example that will be developed in subsequent chapters.

In order to instill you with confidence for your future forays into WML, the next chapter is going to take a small sidestep away from WAP application development. WML is a recent addition to a long, distinguished line of markup languages, and to understand it properly, it's enormously helpful to know something of that history. That's where we're headed next.

Markup Languages

In Chapter 4 of this book, we're going to begin a run of seven chapters in which you'll find out all about the Wireless Markup Language (WML), which is used in the creation of WAP applications. If we wanted to do so, we could probably start that discussion right now and achieve the same goal just as quickly, but you'd have to take more information on trust, and you'd be less well equipped to exploit future changes in the technology. Instead, we're going to spend the next two chapters talking about **markup languages** in general, and **XML** in particular, with the aim of teaching you not just how to use WML, but how it works.

Knowing how to structure a chapter on this subject is tricky, because while it would be possible to start with, "What is a markup language?" and arrive eventually at XML and WML, to do so would be to miss out on some interesting sidelines. There are a few places in which the development of markup languages has split in two, and while the pursuit of our goal will always take us one way, there are places where the other way is also intriguing. When this happens, we'll try to give you at least a taster of what lies down the road not taken.

What is Markup?

Before we start talking about markup *languages*, we should first be clear on what's meant by **markup**. In the broadest terms, markup is anything added to a (text) document that 'describes' the original content. In the first sentence of this paragraph, for example, we put the word "languages" in an italic font to describe where we wanted the emphasis to fall. Similarly, according to our conventions, putting "markup" in a bold face identified it as a word that was about to be defined.

Markup is not, therefore, exclusive to the world of computing; but it *is* used extensively in electronic documents, such as the word processor file that contained this chapter while it was being written and edited. In *that* document, those same two words — "markup" and "languages" — will have been marked up (using codes of some kind) in a way that described how they should be represented on the screen and the printed page.

What is a Markup Language?

Markup languages *are* a product of the computer age. They are a formalization of the codes used to mark up the content of electronic documents – a set of conventions defining things such as:

❑ What marks (or **elements**) are allowed

❑ Where elements may occur

❑ Whether any or all of the elements *must* occur somewhere in a document to which the language has been applied.

It's probably about time that we had a more explicit example of the kinds of thing we're talking about here, and it's at this early stage that we get our first 'split'. There are two types of markup (and therefore two types of markup language): **procedural** and **generalized**. The Wireless Markup Language belongs to the second of these two groups, so we'll take a quick look at the first, and move on.

Procedural Markup Languages

Procedural markup is typified by its use in typesetting and publishing systems, including word processors. The elements are placed right in the flow of the text, and the markup languages that define them have the following characteristics:

❑ Documents marked up with procedural markup languages contain clear instructions (procedures) for the document-rendering program, so that it produces output of the original content in a particular format and style.

❑ The formatting instructions are likely to be specific to the output medium, so the document containing the original content interspersed with markup is not portable across different output media.

A common procedural markup language is the Rich Text Format (RTF) that's available as an option in most modern word processors. You don't see it while you're editing a document, but it's there in the files you save to disk. Take a look at this screenshot:

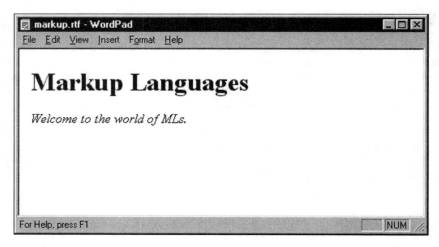

To see the formatting instructions contained within this document, you need to open it using an editor that doesn't support RTF, such as Notepad:

```
markup.rtf - Notepad
File   Edit   Search   Help
{\rtf1\ansi\ansicpg1252\deff0\deflang2057{\fonttbl{\f0\fnil\fcharset0 Times New Roman;}}
\viewkind4\uc1\pard\f0\fs24\par
\b\fs48 Markup Languages\par
\b0\i\fs24\par
Welcome to the world of MLs.\b\i0\fs48\par
}
```

We're not about to get into a discussion of what everything here means, but you should be able to see the eight words of our tiny document being surrounded by markup elements. Notice the typeface being specified in the top line, and it's probably safe to assume that `\par` means 'paragraph', `\b` means 'bold', `\i` means 'italic', and `\fs` means 'font size'. The markup describes exactly how the document should appear.

Sometimes, control like this is just what you want. If you know that your documents are always destined for the printed page (or any other single medium), procedural markup languages are well suited to the task of formatting them – PostScript and TeX are also popular examples of this type. However, if you ever intend to perform any other kind of processing on the document – to extract information from it, perhaps – you'd be well advised to use a generalized markup language instead.

Generalized Markup Languages

Imagine that, without being able to see its representation in a word processor, you were asked to list the section headings in an RTF-encoded document. Maybe you could look for bold characters – but what if bold were also used for emphasis in ordinary text? Perhaps you'd try to find font sizes that seemed larger than normal – but how could you be sure that something wasn't a chapter title? In this particular instance, it's likely that you'd eventually come up with a set of rules, but that wouldn't always be the case, and the task would never be easy.

A **Generalized Markup Language** (**GML**) addresses requirements like these by marking up documents in a different way. The characteristics of these markup languages are:

❑   The elements have 'logical' names, rather than expressing detailed formatting instructions. An element in a generalized markup language called H1, for example, might be used to mark up text that is intended to be a first-level header.

❑   Applications that can read documents marked up using a GML are free to present them as they see fit, using formatting rules for particular elements that are either defined internally, or specified elsewhere. When being output to the screen, our H1 element could be associated with a particular combination of font size and weight.

One of the most commonly used markup languages for Web content publishing is HTML, which we'll treat in the same way as we handled RTF. Here's a screenshot of Microsoft Internet Explorer displaying a familiar document:

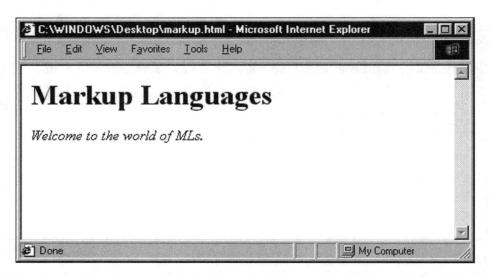

Although it's been marked up using HTML rather than RTF, this document looks the same on screen as our earlier example. If we take a look at the document itself, however, you'll see that it's rather different:

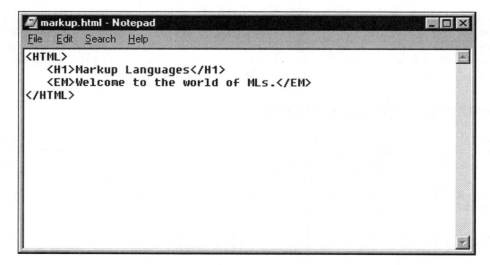

Again, it is not our objective in this chapter to teach you the syntax and elements of HTML, but there are definitely some things that we can say about this document. For a start, it's much easier to read, because the elements of the markup language are more clearly delimited. GML elements usually involve **start** and **end tags**, so that the original content is effectively 'contained' by an element.

Second, there is no hint about how this document should be presented. You've probably guessed that <H1> means a first-level heading, and <EM> means emphasis, but while Internet Explorer has chosen sensible ways to reflect the meanings of these elements, that had nothing to do with us.

Generalized Markup Rule-sets

As we said at the beginning of the previous section, WML is a generalized markup language. Clearly, HTML is one as well, and there are numerous others. However, that's not the end of the story. Each GML has its own elements, its own rules, and its own particular area of application – and in order for the language to function properly *as* a language, those must all somehow be defined.

GMLs are themselves written using **Generalized Markup Rule-sets** (**GMRS**), which are sometimes called **meta-languages** (a meta-language is a language that describes another language). The two that we'll be concerning ourselves with are the Standard Generalized Markup Language (SGML), and the Extensible Markup Language (XML). In fact, the latter is a subset of the former; it is also the one from which WML is derived, and our subject in the next chapter. Here, we'll look at the past and present of SGML.

The Standard Generalized Markup Language

Markup languages are not a new idea. In the late 1960s, proposals for such things were being put forward by a number of individuals and groups, but we shall start our story with the milestone erected by Charles Goldfarb, Edward Mosher, and Raymond Lorie. In 1969, these three IBM researchers were faced with the task of integrating disparate law office information systems that stored documents in different proprietary formats. To enable sharing of documents among the text editing, formatting, and retrieval subsystems, they proposed the use of a common formatting system that all the documents must follow. This system was given the name **Generalized Markup Language** (**GML**) – and can those letters really be a coincidence?

> *Don't confuse this GML with the other GMLs we've been talking about so far! Prior to this paragraph, we've been using GML as a collective term, and we'll continue to do so from here on.*

Charles Goldfarb continued to lead in the development work on GML, with support from both the Graphic Communications Association (GCA) and the American National Standards Institute (ANSI) committee. Their concerted efforts eventually led to the publication of the Standard Generalized Markup Language (SGML) in 1986, also known as ISO 8879. SGML is an international standard approved by the International Standards Organization.

As mentioned briefly above, SGML is not used to mark up a document; it is a meta-language that's used to *create* markup languages that suit different application domains. In this section, we will first present the design principles of SGML, and then examine a few markup languages that have been created using it.

Design Principles of SGML

The basic design principles of SGML emphasize the importance of separating formatting instructions from content, as we've been discussing. When Internet Explorer displayed the HTML document that contained <H1> and <EM> elements, it did so by using an internal **stylesheet** that specified how those elements ought to be represented on the screen. In general, it's possible to create several stylesheets that contain instructions for outputting the content of a marked up document to a variety of output devices, as shown overleaf.

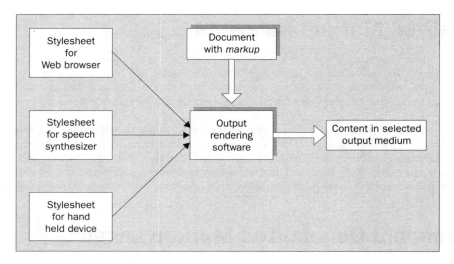

Another principle of SGML is that when markup languages are created, it's expected that the names of the elements will describe what their content represents in the application domain. In other words, if a language has an element that represents a book, then it ought to be *called* <book> rather than, say, <elephant>.

A **Document Type Definition** (**DTD**) is used to define the set of valid elements for a particular GML, as well as the **content model** of each element. To facilitate electronic processing, documents marked up using GMLs are highly structured, and the notion of elements being able to 'contain' other elements is a powerful one in SGML. For example, we could use a content model to specify that our <book> element must always contain one or more <chapter> elements, which in turn would contain many <paragraph> elements.

Rules of Using SGML

Just before we look at some languages created with SGML, here's a quick list of rules that apply to all such languages:

- ❑ The elements in SGML-based languages are not case sensitive, unless explicitly specified as such in the DTD. The two tags <h1> and <H1>, for example, are deemed identical.

- ❑ Element tags may be omitted. To simplify document creation, SGML allows the omission of certain end tags, as long as there are rules to define the location of an end tag implicitly.

  For example, if the occurrence of a 'new paragraph' tag, <p>, also means the end of the previous paragraph, then there is no ambiguity in the following code regarding the boundaries of the two paragraphs:

```
<p>
   This is the first paragraph.
<p>
   This is the second paragraph, even though
   the first is not closed with an end tag.
</p>
```

❑ A DTD is required, because all SGML documents must be **valid**. This means that documents may not use elements that don't appear in the DTD defining the language they're written in. Documents must also conform to the correct structure of elements, as specified in the DTD.

Applications of SGML

Markup languages defined using SGML – often referred to as **applications** of SGML – abound across different communities, including publishers, academic institutions, the aircraft industry, and government sectors. The following list gives some examples of document structures that are maintained as public standards, in the form of SGML DTDs:

❑ DocBook – an SGML application designed by the Association of American Publishers (AAP) for books, articles, and journals. The association started their work in 1983, and this specification was probably the first major application of SGML.

❑ Computer-aided Acquisition and Logistic Support (CALS) – a DTD for technical manuals in the format required by the Department of Defense (DoD). The publication of the military standard, MIL-M-28001, took place in 1988.

❑ Hypertext Markup Language (HTML) – the DTD used to describe content in a web document.

The story behind the last of these is particularly interesting. HTML is now nearly ten years old, during which time (apart from the small matter of enabling the World Wide Web) it has been out of and then in phase with SGML, and is shortly to move away once again.

The Evolution of HTML

While working at CERN (Conseil European pour la Recherche Nucleaire) in 1989, Tim Berners-Lee and Robert Caillau encountered similar problems to those that had been faced by the GML team at IBM two decades earlier. Research materials at CERN were documented in incompatible formats, which made sharing and porting of documents a tremendously difficult task. Often, one had to access and view data stored in different systems using different terminals and software!

Their solution to the incompatibility problem emerged in 1992 as the first version of HTML. However, although it was developed using SGML's rule-set, there was no HTML DTD, and so it was never recognized as a 'true' SGML application. That recognition came in 1994, when a DTD was developed for HTML version 2.

With the emergence of HTML document viewers such as Mosaic by Marc Andreesen (and others), later versions of HTML came with a plethora of elements to satisfy the requirements of presenting information in graphical browsers. Those efforts culminated in HTML 3.2, which became a recommendation of the World Wide Web Consortium (W3C) in 1996.

It's worth noting that this version in particular had strayed from the 'ideal' of a generalized markup language, due to the proliferation of elements concerned purely with visual display. We'll have more to say on this subject in the next section.

Bringing things further up to date, HTML 4.0 was first released in late December 1997, while HTML 4.01 appeared in 1999 to resolve a few issues in the previous version. The motivation for these releases was to tidy up some elements used in previous versions – particularly 3.2 – in order to minimize the use of presentation-related markup within a document.

For more information about the latest version of HTML, you should point your web browser at http://www.w3.org/TR/html401.

Where is HTML Heading?

HTML was originally created with the humble objective of allowing users to describe documents residing on disparate systems, to facilitate the sharing of information. However, the ease with which it could be used to publish content on the Web has been the driving force behind a desire to squeeze HTML for more features that satisfy publishing needs, but for which it was never originally designed. For example, the <font> element allowed the specification of colors and styles in text presentation from within the document itself.

In the latest versions of HTML, a conscious effort was made to adhere to the original design philosophy of SGML. One of the notable inclusions in HTML 4 is the stylesheet, which (as we've discussed) provides a mechanism to separate information from presentation. Most of the elements that specify presentation information such as fonts, alignment and colors are deprecated in HTML 4, in favor of the stylesheet. Also, HTML 4 supports a set of **media descriptors**, such as 'screen' for computer screen display, 'projection' for projectors, 'handheld' for handheld devices, 'aural' for speech synthesizers, and 'braille' for Braille tactile feedback devices. Device-dependent formatting information can now be handled in separate stylesheets.

The last chapter in this story is that the W3C Working Groups have now recommended *X*HTML 1.0 as the version of HTML that should be used for future development. We will discuss what XHTML 1.0 is soon, but not until after we've introduced our second meta-language: **XML**.

The Extensible Markup Language

HTML has been an excellent standard for web publishing. It has been developed into a powerful tool that provides a wealth of well-defined presentation elements for marking up web documents. However, this strength is also its limitation in some other respects. For instance, we cannot make use of elements that are specific to another application domain to structure our document content. In other words, we are confined to the set of HTML elements in all application domains, be it a memo or an insurance claim.

What we need is the ability to create elements that SGML provides, but without many of its more abstract features, and this is the role that XML is intended to fill. The W3C XML Working Group states the goal for XML as: *To bring SGML to the Web.* Development work on XML started in 1996, and it became a W3C standard in 1998.

Design Principles of XML

The basic design principles of XML are largely governed by its intended goal: allowing easy exchange of information on the Internet:

❑   XML is intended to retain SGML's ability to define new sets of elements. That is, XML is a language for defining markup languages, and you are able to extend your defined languages as and when the need arises.

❑   XML documents contain markup that describes precisely what the marked up content is. This means that an XML document can simply use text to store data, making delivery of information over the Internet easy, fast, and independent of any particular platform.

- XML should support document publishing as strongly as HTML. Unlike the latter, however, the goal of separating presentation from data is to be upheld. As you may guess, stylesheets are once again involved in this process, and you'll learn more about the **Extensible Stylesheet Language** (**XSL**) in Chapters 19 and 20.

- XML places stricter rules on its applications than does SGML. While tag omission, cross-element nesting and mixed-case element names are all permissible with SGML, they are not allowed in XML-based languages.

The more stringent rules adopted by XML mean that processing an XML document is a less complex procedure, resulting in better performance. Consider the use of some HTML element tags in the following example:

```
<H1><CENTER> Welcome to Markup Languages! </H1></CENTER>
<p> This is the first paragraph in this section...
<p> This is the second paragraph in this section...
```

The tags for the <H1> and <CENTER> elements are not properly nested – XML would require the start and end tags for <CENTER> to be completely enclosed within the start and end <H1> tags. Also, a </p> tag is required to indicate the end of a paragraph explicitly.

If the above elements were to be used in an XML document, the three lines of code could be made compliant by modifying them in the manner shown below:

```
<h1><center> Welcome to Markup Languages! </center></h1>
<p> This is the first paragraph in this section... </p>
<p> This is the second paragraph in this section... </p>
```

There's still a great deal more to say about XML than this, and we'll be looking at it hard in the next chapter. For now, though, we're going to look a one particular application to which XML is being put.

Transition from HTML to XHTML

Before we get carried away with the promise of XML, you'll remember that we broke off our discussion about the future of HTML. Now that you have a little knowledge of XML under your belt, we're able to close out this chapter by giving you a clearer picture of where HTML is heading in the world of markup languages.

Why do we Need XHTML?

As mentioned earlier, **XHTML** (**Extensible HTML**) is a reformulation of HTML 4 in XML. To understand why we'd want to do that, let's review the undesirable features of HTML we want to avoid, and assess the advantages that moving towards XML offers:

- HTML defines a fixed set of elements that any HTML document can use. There is no flexible mechanism to extend the set of elements as the needs arise in our application domain. For example, <p> is a valid tag, but more descriptive tags such as <paragraph>, or domain-specific tags such as , are not acceptable. HTML does not provide a mechanism to expand the valid element set to include tags such as these.

- HTML documents cannot be used for data processing by other software.

❑   Presentation-oriented elements such as <font> are unable to cope with the growing number of browsers that are quite different from traditional web browsers. Variations in the level of support for HTML and stylesheets make rendering information with the format you intended harder to achieve.

All of the above issues can be addressed by using XML. However, we are definitely not ready to throw away the investment we have put into writing HTML pages for the past decade! XHTML is proposed as a means of tidying up the familiar HTML vocabulary to conform to the syntactical structure of an XML document, *and* as a way of allowing the language to expand by providing a mechanism to add new elements.

For more information about XHTML 1.0, please refer to www.w3.org/TR/xhtml1. If you're intrigued by the future plans for *this* technology, try the HTML Working Group at www.w3.org/TR/xhtml-roadmap.

Summary

This chapter has been quite short, but we've managed to cover quite a lot of subjects at a fairly high level. We began by explaining markup and markup languages, and explained that there were two types. Procedural markup is targeted squarely at a single task (often, specifying how a document should be presented), but its elements say nothing about the content of a document. Generalized markup, on the other hand, conveys information about the content and structure of a document, but nothing about how it should be presented. That task is left to stylesheets, which can be used to specify how content marked up with particular elements should be rendered on a given device.

Next, we talked about the languages that are used to *create* markup languages: generalized markup rule-sets, or meta-languages. We examined SGML in a little detail, and looked quickly at XML, as a preview of what's to come in the next chapter. You learned that XML is actually a simplified version of SGML, created with the specific aim of enabling the exchange of information over the Internet.

Amid these discussions, we also examined the evolution of HTML. Although it's not the subject of this book, it is certainly the most visible markup language, and the factors that have affected its development are those that also drive the evolution of markup languages in general. XML was born from the limitations of HTML, and while it's now being used in a very wide variety of situations, it's significant that it's also being used to set HTML's future direction.

A lot of the discussion in this chapter has been quite descriptive. We've talked about SGML, and XML, and DTDs, and validity, but there's been no detail about *how* markup languages are defined, or how to make sure that the documents you write conform with them properly. We also need to keep sight of the fact that one of the languages defined using XML is the Wireless Markup Language. In the next chapter, we'll go into greater depth on XML, and look at all of these subjects more carefully. After that, we'll be ready to press on with WML.

An Introduction to XML

In Chapter 2, you learned about markup languages: what they are, what they're for, and a little detail about some of the more prevalent (and relevant) ones. When we leave this chapter, we'll begin a lengthy exposition of WML that will keep us busy for some time, but here we're going to look more closely at the **Extensible Markup Language** (**XML**) that we started to talk about in Chapter 2.

To open this discussion, we'll list some facts about XML that we've already introduced; it will be the goal of the remainder of the chapter to expand on these subjects. Quite apart from the applications to which it can be put, XML is an interesting technology in its own right, and a good understanding of it will be of benefit in your future WML development efforts. Here's what you know about it so far:

- ❏ XML is a meta-language, used to create generalized markup languages (so-called "applications" of XML). It's a subset of SGML, the Standard Generalized Markup Language.

- ❏ XML was designed to allow easy exchange of information on the Internet. XML allows data to be stored in plain text files, which are easy to create and fast to transfer.

- ❏ The set of valid elements in an XML language is defined in a Document Type Definition (DTD)

- ❏ To aid with the task of processing the data they contain, XML places tight rules on the structure of documents. For example, the elements of XML applications are case sensitive, and any nesting of elements must be approached with great care.

- ❏ The elements of a language created with XML generally have logical names that describe the data they contain.

- ❏ Nothing about the presentation of data is implied by the elements of an XML-based language. Rules governing how languages based on XML should be displayed can be specified using stylesheets.

- ❏ As its name so clearly implies, XML is extensible – there is no limit on the number of elements in an XML application, and nothing to prevent you from adding elements to applications you've created earlier.

Of this list, the two ideas that will recur most frequently in this chapter are the importance of structuring XML documents correctly (a document that obeys these rules is said to be **well-formed**), and being able to check the elements in a document against a DTD (a process called **validation**). Before we can raise those subjects again, though, we'd better look at an XML document!

An XML Document

There's a limit to what you can say about XML before things start sounding repetitive, or the concepts involved become too abstract. What's the *point* of extensibility? What *kind* of data might we use XML to store? How do we *use* the data we've stored? Things tend to become a little clearer when you start to look at examples of XML documents – like this one:

```
<?xml version="1.0"?>
<Books>
    <Book ISBN="1-861003-41-2">
        <Title>Beginning XML</Title>
        <Author>David Hunter</Author>
        <Pages>823</Pages>
        <Price>39.99</Price>
        <PublicationDate>2000</PublicationDate>
        <Synopsis>
            This book explains and demonstrates XML and related technologies.
        </Synopsis>
    </Book>
    <Book ISBN="1-861004-04-4">
        <Title>Professional WAP</Title>
        <Author>Various</Author>
        <Pages>1000</Pages>
        <Price>59.99</Price>
        <PublicationDate>2000</PublicationDate>
        <Synopsis>
            This book explains and demonstrates WAP programming.
        </Synopsis>
    </Book>
</Books>
```

Without indulging in any further explanation, you can already see that this document conforms to many of the ideas we've discussed:

- ❑ The author of this document was freely able to 'invent' tags that were appropriate to the task in hand, and to use them to mark up this data.

- ❑ From the names of the elements, it's completely clear that this XML document contains information about books.

- ❑ From the structure of the document, it's equally obvious that this particular file contains information about *two* books.

It says something about the ease with which humans can interpret XML files like this one that we've been able to come to these conclusions about the first XML file we've seen! However, although this is a useful fringe benefit, the important thing is that *computers* are able to read them easily, and that depends on a consistent set of rules for the various parts of the markup, and their relationships with one another. In the remainder of this section, we'll examine in depth what those are.

Elements and Tags

An XML document is composed of a number of **elements**. As we saw in the 'books' example, each element begins with a descriptive **tag**. Tags are indicated by a pair of angled brackets: they start with the < character, and end with the > character. Between the angled brackets is the **tag name**. Consider the following example:

```
<Title>Professional WAP</Title>
```

In this case, we have an element that represents the title of a book, so we've chosen Title as a suitable tag name. <Title> is known as a **start tag** because it begins the data element, while </Title> is known as an **end tag** because it appears at the end of the element. Notice that the tag name is the same for both start and end tags, but the end tag is identified as such by the inclusion of a forward slash before the tag name.

Naming Tags

The next rules we'll consider are the naming conventions for tags. The first character in a tag name, which must immediately follow the opening <, must be a letter or underscore. After that, numbers, dashes, and periods are also allowed. Tag names must not start with any upper or lower case variation of "xml".

An XML element is defined as being the collection of the start tag, its matching end tag, and *everything* in between. Similarly, everything between the end of the start tag and the start of the end tag is known as the **element content**. Elements can contain text (the data itself, also known as the element's **value**), or other elements. In our example, the content of the <Title> element *is* just text, in one case with a value of Professional WAP. For reasons that will become clear later, text data is also sometimes referred to as **parsed character data**, or **PCDATA**.

Matching Tags

In almost all cases, XML start tags must have a matching end tag. Remember that XML is case sensitive, so <PRICE> does not match </Price>, and in the following example the two tags do not mark the beginning and end of an element:

```
<PRICE>... ...</Price>
```

Sometimes, however, it *is* possible to use just a single tag, like this:

```
<Price/>
```

With this syntax, the element is effectively starting and ending itself, and expressing clearly the fact that there's no content – in other words, it's an **empty element**. In the context of this example, we might use an empty <Price> element in the data of a book still being written, and for which the price has not yet been decided. The element could be written like this:

```
<Pages>1000</Pages>
<Price/>
<PublicationDate>2001</PublicationDate>
```

Or like this:

```
<Pages>1000</Pages>
<Price></Price>
<PublicationDate>2001</PublicationDate>
```

These representations of an empty element are both allowed, according to the rules of XML.

Nesting Elements

The elements in most XML documents form a **hierarchy** that reflects the structure of the data they contain. In our 'books' example, the `<Book>` element is a **parent** element, with **child** elements of `<Title>`, `<Author>`, `<Pages>`, `<Price>`, `<PublicationDate>`, and `<Synopsis>`. These children are **siblings** because they are all at the same level in the hierarchy.

```
<Book>
    <Title>Professional WAP</Title>
    <Author>Various</Author>
    <Pages>1000</Pages>
    <Price>59.99</Price>
    <PublicationDate>2000</PublicationDate>
    <Synopsis>This book explains and demonstrates WAP programming.</Synopsis>
</Book>
```

Another rule of XML is that the elements in a document must be properly nested – they may not overlap one another. This (abbreviated) form of the above listing is therefore incorrect:

```
<Book><Title>Professional WAP</Book></Title>
```

Whereas this line obeys the rules nicely:

```
<Book><Title>Professional WAP</Title></Book>
```

In general, XML permits this nesting to continue indefinitely, with elements containing other elements to the extent required to reflect the data structure being portrayed. In our document, the `<Author>` element could contain a `<Surname>` and `<Forename>`, or a list of `<Name>`s, rather than plain text.

The Root Element

Lastly, every XML document must have a **root element**. This must be the first element in the document, and it must be unique in the document – in other words, the same element cannot be used anywhere else. Our 'books' document has a unique root element called `<Books>`, and therefore complies with this rule.

Attributes

But for a couple of fleeting appearances, our work with markup languages so far has yet to expose us to **attributes**, but we'll be making good that shortcoming here. Attributes provide a second way – that is, in addition to containing other elements – of associating additional information with an element. An attribute is a name-value pair separated by an = symbol, and they are always specified in the *start* tag:

```
<Book ISBN="1-861004-04-4">

   Element content here

</Book>
```

The first line in the above section of code associates the ISBN attribute (and the value it contains) with *this* <Book>. An element can have multiple attributes, so the element in the next example contains two attributes: ISBN and Price

```
<Book ISBN="1-861004-04-4" Price="59.99">

   Element content here

</Book>
```

The same naming rules that apply to tags also apply to attributes. You can't use the same attribute name twice in the same element, so this would not be allowed:

```
<Book ISBN="1-861004-04-4" Price="49.99" Price="59.99">

   Element content here

</Book>
```

Specifying Attributes

In XML, all attribute values must be enclosed either by a pair of single quotes (' '), or a pair of double quotes (" "). The quotes must match, so you can't use ' " or " '. An attribute in a start tag must *always* have a value, even if that value is "empty", which can be specified by a pair of matching quotes with nothing in between.

Attributes or Elements?

Any information we choose to specify in attributes could be represented equally well by elements, so we could just as soon have written the highlighted line above as:

```
<Book>
   <ISBN>1-861004-04-4</ISBN>
   <Price>59.99</Price>
</Book>
```

Clearly, that gives us something of a dilemma, as we now have two ways of doing essentially the same thing. Although the final choice may come down to personal preference, it can be a good idea to use the following guidelines when deciding whether to use elements or attributes:

❑   Imagine attributes to be the 'properties' of an element. For instance:

```
<Product color="red" id="9876-44">
```

❑   Imagine elements as 'belonging' to another element. For example:

```
<Address>
    <Add1>Blk 123</Add1>
    <Add2>Bukit Timah</Add2>
    <Add3>Singapore</Add3>
    <Postal>873443</Postal>
<Address>
```

In fact, the argument over the relative merits of attributes and elements is still in progress, and shows few signs of achieving a resolution. Point your web browser to the following URL to see the various arguments regarding the use of elements and attributes: www.oasis-open.org/cover/elementsAndAttrs.html

Well-formed XML

In the light of all the things we've just discussed, let's look again at the XML document we saw at the beginning of the chapter:

```
<?xml version="1.0"?>
<Books>
    <Book ISBN="1-861003-41-2">
        <Title>Beginning XML</Title>
        <Author>David Hunter</Author>
        <Pages>823</Pages>
        <Price>39.99</Price>
        <PublicationDate>2000</PublicationDate>
        <Synopsis>
            This book explains and demonstrates XML and related technologies.
        </Synopsis>
    </Book>
    <Book ISBN="1-861004-04-4">
        <Title>Professional WAP</Title>
        <Author>Various</Author>
        <Pages>1000</Pages>
        <Price>59.99</Price>
        <PublicationDate>2000</PublicationDate>
        <Synopsis>
            This book explains and demonstrates WAP programming.
        </Synopsis>
    </Book>
</Books>
```

You should be able to see that this document obeys all the rules we've just described, and that we've explained everything it contains – except, that is, for the very first line:

```
<?xml version="1.0"?>
```

This is called the **XML declaration,** and it indicates that this document conforms to XML version 1.0. All XML documents should contain a declaration like this one right at the beginning – it is an error even for white space (spaces, return characters) to come before it.

An XML document that adheres to all the rules we've set out above is said to be **well-formed**, and in fact well-formedness is the minimum requirement on an XML document for it to be described as such. Newcomers to XML are sometimes surprised at how strict the rules are, but luckily the reason for this situation is also the means by which we can ensure our documents *are* well-formed.

The software that's used to process and extract information from an XML document is called a **parser**, and the rules of well-formedness exist in order to make the job of this program simpler. The converse of this, however, is that we can use a parser to tell us whether our documents *are* well-formed, and perhaps even give us a clue as to what's wrong.

So where do we find a parser at this time of night? Well, in the spirit of XML being a product of the Internet age, both Microsoft and Netscape have built XML parsers into the most recent versions of their web browsing software (Internet Explorer 5.*x* and Netscape 6 respectively), so all we have to do is load our document into those applications, and see what happens. Here's what Netscape makes of it:

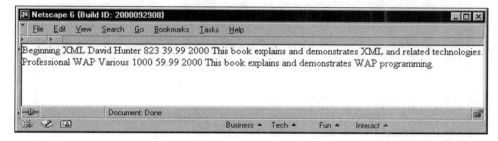

And this is the same document, as seen in Internet Explorer:

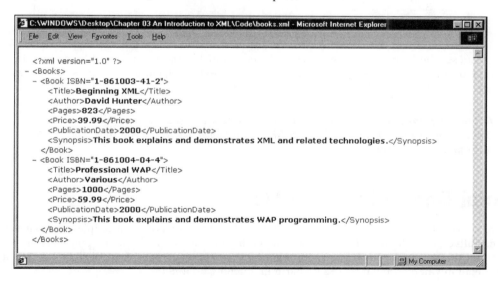

Clearly, these are two very different interpretations of the data, with the Microsoft browser in particular going to some lengths to present the XML file in a readable format. Remember, though, that neither of these is 'correct' – the XML file says absolutely nothing about how the data should be presented, and Internet Explorer's efforts are a convenience for the user, nothing more.

If you're skeptical that either browser is *really* parsing the XML, try introducing a deliberate error into the file and see what happens. Changing `<PublicationDate>` to `<PublicationData>` should do the trick:

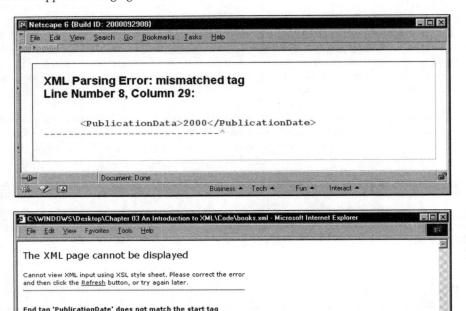

As you can see, both applications pounce on the error quickly and unambiguously, disagreeing only about the position in the line at which it occurs. On this evidence, either browser is suitable as a tool for checking the well-formedness of any XML files you write.

Just in case you're interested, the upper case 'P' that both browsers are pointing at is the 30th character in the row – but it could be that Netscape is numbering its columns from zero, in which case both would be right!

Special Characters in XML

Before we switch subject for the second half of this chapter, there are just a couple more issues to cover that can affect the well-formedness of a document, if you're not careful. Simply put, there are some characters that can cause XML parsers problems if they appear in your data. We'll be looking at this in more detail in Chapter 5, but there's no harm in touching on it here.

Sometimes, you'll want to put characters such as the ampersand (&) in the content of an XML element. Consider the example on the next page, `movies.xml`.

```
<?xml version="1.0"?>
<MovieClubMembers>
    <Member ID="S756436">
        <Name>Henry Cheng</Name>
        <Favorites>
            <Movie>MI2</Movie>
            <Movie>Tom & Jerry</Movie>
        </Favorites>
    </Member>
</MovieClubMembers>
```

Despite first appearances, this document is not well formed, as an attempt to load it into Netscape will soon demonstrate. The reason for this is that it contains the & character, which has a special meaning in XML. You can see the error below:

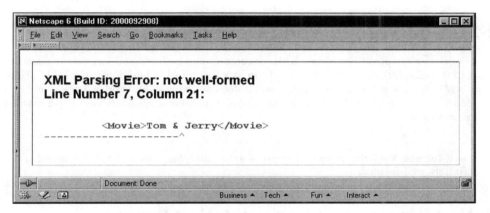

To insert characters that have special meanings (like the & you've just seen) into our XML documents, we have to replace them with **character entities**. In this case, that means simply substituting & with & as shown:

```
<Movie>Tom &amp; Jerry</Movie>
```

As you can see, the reason why & is a special character is that it's used to help with inserting special characters like... itself! We'll look at some other special characters when we confront this subject from a WML point of view in Chapter 5.

PCDATA and CDATA

Earlier in this chapter, we mentioned that text data in XML content is usually referred to as PCDATA, which stands for parsed character data. Simply put, this means that by default, the XML parser will parse any and all characters contained in elements. To understand this better, consider the following example:

```
<Statement> 2 is < 3 </Statement>
```

45

Within the `<Statement>` element, we have another special character: `<`. When an XML parser processes a document containing it, the above element will generate an error, because the XML parser interprets the less-than sign as the start of a tag. To resolve this problem, you can use a character entity again, or you can enclose the problem statement within a **CDATA** (**character data**) **section**. For example:

```
<Statement> <![CDATA[ 2 is < 3 ]]> </Statement>
```

The format of the CDATA string type is:

```
<![CDATA[ text ]]>
```

The XML parser will not parse any text contained within a CDATA statement, and you'll find that whatever they contain, CDATA statements will never be the cause of a document's failure to be well-formed.

Well-formed versus Valid Documents

As we've said on a couple of occasions, XML documents can be both well-formed (as discussed over the first part of this chapter), and valid (they conform to a specification laid down in a DTD). However, while an XML document has to be well-formed, it does not have to be valid – there is no compulsion on developers to create DTDs for their documents, although there are some very good reasons to do so, as we'll soon discover.

> **A well-formed XML document is not necessarily valid, but a valid XML document is definitely well-formed.**

Validating Parsers and Non-validating Parsers

So far, we've been using Microsoft Internet Explorer and Netscape 6 to check the well-formedness of our XML documents, but if we want to check for validity as well, we need to take an extra step. A **validating parser** is one that validates the content of an XML document against a DTD, but while the MSXML parser that comes with Internet Explorer 5.01 is capable of this task, it doesn't do it by default, and you can only make it do so programmatically.

However, if you go to the Microsoft web site (http://www.microsoft.com) and search for XML Validator, you'll get to a page from which you can download the "IE Tools for Validating XML and Viewing XSLT Output". Once installed, these tools add items to Internet Explorer's context menus that allow you to validate any XML document, on the spot. We'll be using these tools in the second half of the chapter.

Document Type Definition (DTD)

Allowing everyone in the world to make up their own elements in an extensible markup language is all very well, but a situation in which everyone goes out and does exactly that clearly isn't. Remember: our goal here is to allow the easy *interchange* of data, but if the company down the hall has decided on a completely different set of tags, elements and attributes from the one you're using, we haven't really made any progress toward that goal.

Bringing order to this state of affairs are **Document Type Definitions** (**DTD**s), which *describe* the content of an XML document. They provide a way for an XML document to adhere to a predefined structure.

To understand *how* a DTD is used to define the structure of an XML document, imagine that you have a pile of product information that needs to be marked up using XML. The following information, for example, describes some of the properties of a single product:

```
<?xml version="1.0"?>
<Products>
    <Product>
        <ID>S-9836</ID>
        <Name>Keyboard</Name>
        <Colors>
            <Color>Black</Color>
            <Color>Beige</Color>
        </Colors>
        <Price>12.50</Price>
        <Qty>30</Qty>
    </Product>
    <Product>


    ...


    </Product>
</Products>
```

Now imagine that you've also instructed a colleague at another branch to do likewise. Your colleague has just learned about the flexibility and usefulness of XML, and enthusiastically marks up their products using XML too:

```
<?xml version="1.0"?>
<Products>
    <Product ID="T-8674" Price="24.00">
        <ProductName>Keyboard</ProductName>
        <Color>Green</Color>
        <Qty>30</Qty>
    </Product>

    <Product>

    <!-- Details omitted -->

    </Product>
</Products>
```

When you receive the XML document, you realize that you forgot to tell him about the elements you're using, and how he should stick to your convention. In this situation, there's nothing else for it: one of you is going to have to enter the information all over again!

If only you'd sent a DTD to your colleague along with your request, you could have specified what elements should be present, how many of each were required, what kind of element content was permitted, and in what order the elements should appear. Then, when you'd both finished creating your documents, you could have used the DTD with a validating parser to check their validity – in other words, to make sure they both conformed to the required format.

47

Let's turn back the clock, and imagine that before you asked your colleague to mark up the products, you *had* created a DTD, which is shown below:

```
<!ELEMENT Products (Product)*>
<!ELEMENT Product  (ID, Name, Colors, Price, Qty)>
<!ELEMENT ID       (#PCDATA)>
<!ELEMENT Name     (#PCDATA)>
<!ELEMENT Colors   (Color)+>
<!ELEMENT Color    (#PCDATA)>
<!ELEMENT Price    (#PCDATA)>
<!ELEMENT Qty      (#PCDATA)>
```

We'll look at the syntax of this in more detail as we progress, but this DTD simply states that:

❑ <Products> is the root element, and it can contain zero or more <Product> elements

❑ The <Product> element further contains one each of the <ID>, <Name>, <Colors>, <Price>, and <Qty> elements, in the sequence specified

❑ The <ID> and <Name> elements contain only parsed character data (that is, text)

❑ The <Colors> element contains one or more <Color> elements

❑ The <Color>, <Price> and <Qty> elements contain only text

Defining Elements in a DTD

To create a document type definition, you have to know the syntax for defining elements and attributes – but more fundamentally even than that, you have to know how to specify that what you're creating *is* a DTD. As we'll see, DTDs can coexist in the same file as an XML document, or they can be stored in separate files. In the latter case, XML documents that want to use a particular DTD must include references to it.

DTDs invariably begin with the **document type declaration**:

```
<!DOCTYPE rootelement [
   declaration of elements and attributes
]>
```

Yes, "document type declaration" is a lot like "document type definition", and yes, it's very easy to get them confused. One way of keeping them apart in your mind is to refer to the definition always as a DTD, and the declaration always in longhand.

The rootelement specified in this declaration is the name of the root element in the XML document to which this DTD will apply.

Now we can define elements in the DTD. For this, we use the **element type declaration**, specifying the name of the element and the content model for that element:

```
<!ELEMENT elementname (.. content model ..)>
```

The content model is made up of various items, depending on whether the element content is other elements, text, or a mixture of the two.

Occurrences

For elements that contain other elements, we need to list the elements to be contained, and specify how many of each should be included. Consider the following example, which has the DTD at the top of the document and the XML data at the bottom (this file is in the source code as `address.xml`):

```
<?xml version="1.0"?>

<!DOCTYPE Address [
    <!ELEMENT Address (Address1, Address2, Address3, Postal)>
    <!ELEMENT Address1 (#PCDATA)>
    <!ELEMENT Address2 (#PCDATA)>
    <!ELEMENT Address3 (#PCDATA)>
    <!ELEMENT Postal (#PCDATA)>
]>

<Address>
    <Address1>Blk 123</Address1>
    <Address2>Tampines</Address2>
    <Address3>Singapore</Address3>
    <Postal>123456</Postal>
</Address>
```

The `<Address>` element contains four elements – `<Address1>`, `<Address2>`, `<Address3>`, and `<Postal>` – and each element must appear once and only once.

Now let's add a new element, `<Telephone>`:

```
<?xml version="1.0"?>

<!DOCTYPE Address [
    <!ELEMENT Address (Address1, Address2, Address3, Telephone+, Postal)>
    <!ELEMENT Address1 (#PCDATA)>
    <!ELEMENT Address2 (#PCDATA)>
    <!ELEMENT Address3 (#PCDATA)>
    <!ELEMENT Telephone (#PCDATA)>
    <!ELEMENT Postal (#PCDATA)>
]>

<Address>
    <Address1>Blk 123</Address1>
    <Address2>Tampines</Address2>
    <Address3>Singapore</Address3>
    <Telephone>460-6872</Telephone>
    <Postal>123456</Postal>
</Address>
```

Here, the + sign in the element type declaration indicates that the `<Telephone>` element can occur one or more times, but it *must* appear at least once.

49

For example, you could have multiple occurrences of the `<Telephone>` element in the XML document:

```
<Telephone>460-6872</Telephone>
<Telephone>587-5673</Telephone>
```

Replacing the + sign with * would make the `<Telephone>` element completely optional – it could appear zero, one, or many times.

The final symbol of this sort is the ? character, which means that the element can appear either once, or not at all. Multiple appearances of the element are not permitted.

Symbol	Meaning
+	Element must appear once; but can appear more than once
*	Element is optional; but can appear more than once
?	Element can appear either once or never
(none)	Element must appear once and only once

Composition

Sometimes, we might want to specify that any one of a number of elements should be included – in other words, we want to provide a list of *options* of elements that may appear:

```
<?xml version="1.0"?>

<!DOCTYPE Payment [
    <!ELEMENT Payment (Check | VISA | Mastercard)>
    <!ELEMENT Check (#PCDATA)>
    <!ELEMENT VISA (#PCDATA)>
    <!ELEMENT Mastercard (#PCDATA)>
]>

<Payment>
    <Check>123-9867-3334</Check>
</Payment>
```

The | sign indicates that any one of the three elements in parentheses can appear. In the above case, only *one* of the elements (`<Check>`, `<VISA>` or `<Mastercard>`) can appear inside the `<Payment>` element.

To declare an element that must always be empty, we use the EMPTY keyword, as follows:

```
<?xml version="1.0"?>

<!DOCTYPE Paragraph [
    <!ELEMENT Paragraph (Content, NewLine*)*>
    <!ELEMENT Content (#PCDATA)>
    <!ELEMENT NewLine EMPTY>
]>
```

```
<Paragraph>
    <Content>123-9867-3334</Content>
<NewLine/>
    <NewLine/>
    <Content>123-9867-3334</Content>
</Paragraph>
```

Defining Attributes in a DTD

To see how to define attributes in a DTD, we can make a couple of quick modifications to the one we were developing to represent a list (in fact, two lists) of products. Having changed a couple of elements into attributes, here's what that DTD looks like:

```
<!ELEMENT Products (Product)>
<!ELEMENT Product (Name, Color, Qty)>
<!ATTLIST Product ID CDATA #REQUIRED>
<!ATTLIST Product Price CDATA #REQUIRED>
<!ELEMENT Name (#PCDATA)>
<!ELEMENT Color (#PCDATA)>
<!ELEMENT Qty (#PCDATA)>
```

It will come as no surprise that to define an attribute in a DTD, you use the `<!ATTLIST>` element. For example, consider the following section of the DTD:

```
<!ATTLIST Product ID CDATA #REQUIRED>
<!ATTLIST Product Price CDATA #REQUIRED>
```

A structure like this would enable the document to contain the following:

```
<Product ID="T-8674" Price="24.00">
```

The `#REQUIRED` keyword indicates that the attribute is required whenever the element is used. If an attribute declared in this way is not used with the element in a document, the XML parser will generate an error when it attempts to validate the document

Literals and Tokens

If we wanted to, we could combine the two `ATTLIST` elements shown above into one:

```
<!ATTLIST Product ID    CDATA #REQUIRED
                  Price CDATA #REQUIRED>
```

In situations like this, the `CDATA` keyword indicates the type of value that can be supplied to the attribute. Here, it means a **string literal**, which is basically just a sequence of characters – letters, numbers, words, whatever you like. A more restrictive type would be `NMTOKEN`, which stands for **name token**; this also contains text, but it comes with some restrictions. Name tokens cannot begin with the letters "xml", and the only non-alphanumeric symbols they can contain are the underscore, dash, period and colon. If `NMTOKEN` is used, the attribute value of `ID` must not contain any spaces.

For example, if this was the entry in the DTD:

```
<!ATTLIST Product ID NMTOKEN #REQUIRED>
```

Then the following would not be valid, because the ID attribute contains a space:

```
<Product ID="12 34" Price="24.00">
```

To have multiple tokens within the attribute, you should use the NMTOKENS keyword; with this in place, the above Product element would be valid:

```
<!ATTLIST Product ID NMTOKENS #REQUIRED>
```

Optional Attributes

To specify an attribute that's optional, we use the #IMPLIED keyword:

```
<!ATTLIST Product Weight CDATA #IMPLIED>
```

Fixed Attributes

You can use the #FIXED keyword to denote an attribute that should always be set at a given value, or not at all. To see its use, consider the following:

```
<!ATTLIST Product Available #FIXED "yes">
```

The attribute Available is optional. If it is used, it will always have a value of "yes". If it is left out, it will not have a value.

Fixed Set of Attributes

From our earlier discussion, <Color> is probably more appropriate as an attribute than as an element, so let's see how easy it is to switch from one the other. In making this change, we'll also be able to restrict the range of colors that can be specified in a document based on this DTD. It would probably go something like this:

```
<!ELEMENT Products (Product)>
<!ELEMENT Product (Name, Qty)>
<!ATTLIST Product ID CDATA #REQUIRED>
<!ATTLIST Product Price CDATA #REQUIRED>
<!ATTLIST Product Color (red | blue | green | black | white) "white">
<!ELEMENT Name (#PCDATA)>
<!ELEMENT Qty (#PCDATA)>
```

Here, the Color attribute can take on a value of red, blue, green, black or white. If the attribute were not specified in the element, the *default* color would be white.

Confusion Between CDATA Sections and CDATA Attributes

We mentioned earlier that the XML parser would not parse CDATA sections, so you might be tempted to define an attribute using the CDATA keyword, and then set its value to contain a pair of tags or some other special characters. The following line of code attempts to use this technique in order to store some layout information:

```
<Markup text="<B>Hello</B>" />
```

However, the XML parser will complain about this, just as it did the last time it found a less-than symbol in a place where it wasn't expecting one.

Don't confuse the CDATA *section* and the CDATA *keyword* in attributes. They do not represent the same functionality. The CDATA keyword in an attribute indicates that the attribute may contain text. The CDATA section is used to tell the parser not to parse the included characters.

References Between Attributes

Before leaving the discussion of attributes, we should also examine the ID, IDREF and IDREFS keywords. Consider the following XML document, examination.xml, as an example:

```
<?xml version="1.0"?>

<!DOCTYPE Examination [
    <!ELEMENT Examination (Grade+, Maths, Previous)>
    <!ELEMENT Grade EMPTY>
    <!ATTLIST Grade g ID #REQUIRED>
    <!ELEMENT Maths EMPTY>
    <!ATTLIST Maths grade IDREF #REQUIRED>
    <!ELEMENT Previous EMPTY>
    <!ATTLIST Previous grade IDREFS #REQUIRED>
]>

<Examination>
    <Grade g="a1" />
    <Grade g="a2" />
    <Grade g="b3" />
    <Grade g="b4" />
    <Maths grade="a1"/>
    <Previous grade="a1 a1 a2"/>
</Examination>
```

In the above, the attribute g is defined to be an ID in the third line of the document type declaration. To see the effect of ID, look at the <Maths> and <Previous> elements. First, the former:

```
<Maths grade="a1"/>
```

53

For this document to be valid, the value of the `grade` attribute in the `<Maths>` element must come from the g attribute of a `<Grade>` element. This referral is indicated by the `IDREF` keyword. If you have:

```
<Maths grade="c5"/>
```

An error will result, because c5 is not a value in the g attribute in any of the `<Grade>` elements. Valid values in this example are a1, a2, b3 and b4.

Looking ahead to the `<Previous>` element (if you'll pardon the expression), this can contain multiple IDs. This referral is indicated by the `IDREFS` keyword. In this case, all the IDs are separated by a space.

Associating a DTD with a Document

At this stage, we've already seen a number of small examples featuring internal DTDs, and there isn't a great deal more to say about that technique here – it really is just a matter of inserting the `DOCTYPE` declaration after the XML declaration. What we could demonstrate, however, is the Microsoft tool for XML validation we mentioned earlier.

Internal DTD Example

The document we'll be using for this example is shown below. It's called `products.xml`:

```
<?xml version="1.0"?>

<!DOCTYPE Products [
<!ELEMENT Products (Product)*>
<!ELEMENT Product  (ID, Name, Colors, Price, Qty)>
<!ELEMENT ID       (#PCDATA)>
<!ELEMENT Name     (#PCDATA)>
<!ELEMENT Colors   (Color)+>
<!ELEMENT Color    (#PCDATA)>
<!ELEMENT Price    (#PCDATA)>
<!ELEMENT Qty      (#PCDATA)>
]>

<Products>
    <Product>
        <ID>S-9836</ID>
        <Name>Keyboard</Name>
        <Colors>
            <Color>Black</Color>
            <Color>Beige</Color>
        </Colors>
        <Price>12.50</Price>
        <Qty>30</Qty>
    </Product>
</Products>
```

You can see that the document is well-formed almost by inspection, and loading it into Internet Explorer proves it beyond doubt – we've seen that before. However, look what happens now if you right-click on the document, having installed the Microsoft tools:

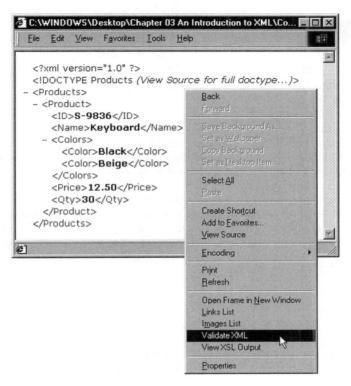

Choosing the highlighted option will then result in a dialog box confirming that the XML document is valid:

If you wish, you can experiment with breaking the code in a number of different ways, to see what kinds of results you get. We found that the tool took the deletion of one of the element type declarations in its stride, simply complaining: "The element 'Qty' is used but not declared in the DTD/Schema."

External DTD Example

We can use our favorite example as our first demonstration of using an external DTD, too – although we do need to do a little preparatory work beforehand. For a start, we need to strip out all of the element type declarations into a separate document, calling it `products.dtd`, and saving it in the same location as the other files from this chapter.

After that, we need to tell the `products.xml` document where to find its document type definition, which requires a small modification to the document type declaration:

```
<?xml version="1.0"?>
<!DOCTYPE Products SYSTEM "products.dtd">

<Products>
    <Product>
        <ID>S-9836</ID>
        <Name>Keyboard</Name>
```

The code now states that this document will have a root element called `<Products>`, and will be validated by a DTD that's available on the local machine as `products.dtd`. The two-line combination of XML declaration and document type declaration at the top of the document is a common one in XML development, and is often referred to as the **document prolog**.

The word `SYSTEM` in the document type declaration just means that the parser will go straight for the URL of the specified file. This is what you'll use most of the time for your own work with XML. The alternative to `SYSTEM` is `PUBLIC`, which allows the parser to look for the DTD it requires in a local 'repository', rather than going straight to a URL. You'll tend to find yourself using this form when employing a well-known, widespread DTD – say, the one that defines WML! Almost every WML file you write will have the following prolog:

```
<?xml version="1.0"?>
<!DOCTYPE wml PUBLIC "-//WAPFORUM//DTD WML 1.2//EN"
                     "http://www.wapforum.org/DTD/wml_1.2.xml">
```

This provides the path to the WML DTD, with a URL in case the file is not stored in the specified local path. If you're already intrigued, you'll find version 1.2 of the WML DTD in Appendix B.

Internal and External DTDs

It's not inconceivable that sometimes, we'll want to use a mixture of internal and external DTDs. For example, there may be elements we want to add into *our* XML documents but don't require from our colleagues; or we might want to add a few more elements without having to update a shared DTD. Consider the following example, `products2.xml`:

```
<?xml version="1.0"?>
<!DOCTYPE Products SYSTEM "Products2.dtd" [ <!ELEMENT Comments (#PCDATA)> ] >

<Products>
    <Product>
        <ID>S-9836</ID>
        <Name>Keyboard</Name>
        <Colors>
            <Color>Black</Color>
            <Color>Beige</Color>
        </Colors>
        <Price>12.50</Price>
        <Qty>30</Qty>
        <Comments>Water-proof keyboard</Comments>
    </Product>
</Products>
```

And the following DTD, `products2.dtd`:

```
<!ELEMENT Products (Product)*>
<!ELEMENT Product  (ID, Name, Colors, Price, Qty, Comments)>
<!ELEMENT ID       (#PCDATA)>
<!ELEMENT Name     (#PCDATA)>
<!ELEMENT Colors   (Color)+>
<!ELEMENT Color    (#PCDATA)>
<!ELEMENT Price    (#PCDATA)>
<!ELEMENT Qty      (#PCDATA)>
```

In this example, there is both an internal and an external DTD. The latter does not contain the definition of the `<Comments>` element, which is defined in the internal DTD. This approach allows flexibility in designing how the `<Comments>` element can be defined. You may create further elements within the `<Comments>` element without affecting the external DTD at all, like this:

```
<?xml version="1.0"?>
<!DOCTYPE Products SYSTEM "Products2.dtd" [
    <!ELEMENT Comments (Line1, Line2)>
    <!ELEMENT Line1 (#PCDATA)>
    <!ELEMENT Line2 (#PCDATA)>
]>

<Products>
    <Product>
        <ID>S-9836</ID>
        <Name>Keyboard</Name>
        <Colors>
            <Color>Black</Color>
            <Color>Beige</Color>
        </Colors>
        <Price>12.50</Price>
        <Qty>30</Qty>
        <Comments>
            <Line1>Water-Proof keyboard</Line1>
            <Line2>No stocks</Line2>
        </Comments>
    </Product>
</Products>
```

Advantages of Using Internal and External DTDs

So when do you use an internal DTD, and when do you use an external DTD? In general, you'd use an external one when:

- ❑ You are creating a *set* of XML documents, all following the same format.
- ❑ A group of co-workers are creating a common set of XML documents.
- ❑ You are creating an application that is based on XML – such as WML!

And you'd use an internal DTD when:

- ❑ You're creating only a single XML document.

- ❑ You want your XML document to be standalone, containing all the data as well as the validating instructions.

If you're ever concerned about the validity of your XML documents, you need to make use of DTDs to enforce the document structure.

Entities

For the final two sections in this chapter, we're going to take a look at a couple of slightly more advanced XML topics that are particularly relevant to the remainder of this book: **entities**, which pepper the WML DTD, and **namespaces**, which will come into their own when we begin to look at the Extensible Stylesheet Language (XSL) in Chapter 19.

Entities are used to define shortcuts to commonly used text. They are defined using the <!ENTITY> element. Consider the following XML document, entity.xml, as an example:

```
<?xml version="1.0"?>
<!DOCTYPE Company [ <!ENTITY Company "XML Incorporated"> ] >

<Company>
    <Name>&Company;</Name>
    <Address>Singapore</Address>
</Company>
```

Here, we've defined an entity called Company, and specified that it should represent the text XML Incorporated. When the document is parsed, &Company; will be replaced with XML Incorporated wherever it occurs. The screenshot shows how Internet Explorer parses this document:

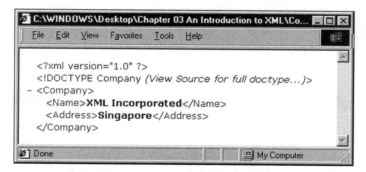

We have declared an entity *within* the XML document, so it is known as an **internal entity**. A much more useful approach is to declare the entity in an *external* file, so that it can be shared by others. Take a look at the following example DTD, entity.dtd:

```
<!ENTITY Company "XML Incorporated">
```

Now our XML document needs to refer to the DTD, but then it can use the entity just as we did before:

```
<?xml version="1.0"?>
<!DOCTYPE Company SYSTEM "Entity.dtd">

<Company>
    <Name>&Company;</Name>
    <Address>Singapore</Address>
</Company>
```

By declaring the entities in an external file, they can be shared. Obviously, this was quite a trivial example, but using entities for incorporating large strings of text or special items can save time and storage space, and provide for 'once-only' updating of information.

Namespaces

XML **namespaces** are a means of qualifying the element and attribute names used in XML documents. They provide a mechanism to identify elements distinctly that are identical in name but possess different contextual meaning.

As so often, the best way to understand namespaces is to look at an example. The following XML document shows details about a member of staff at a university, and the courses he teaches:

```
<?xml version="1.0"?>

<StaffInfo>
    <Staff>
        <Title>Mr</Title>
        <Name>Lee Wei Meng</Name>
        <Tel>460-6872</Tel>
    </Staff>
    <Courses>
        <Title>WAP Programming</Title>
        <Title>Web Programming</Title>
    </Courses>
</StaffInfo>
```

This example uses `<Title>` elements in two different contexts: one is used to describe the title of a *person*, while the other is used to describe the titles of *courses*. Now, imagine that you're writing an application to parse this document and retrieve all the course titles that a trainer is teaching. In this case, you must have a way to differentiate between the title of a trainer, and the title of a course.

To differentiate the `<Title>` elements and create uniqueness, we use namespaces. We will leave the elements that relate to courses as they are, but add a prefix to those that relate to staff:

```
<?xml version="1.0"?>

<StaffInfo>
    <Staff>
        <people:Title>Mr</people:Title>
```

```
          <people:Name>Lee Wei Meng</people:Name>
          <people:Tel>460-6872</people:Tel>
     </Staff>
     <Courses>
        <Title>WAP Programming</Title>
        <Title>Web Programming</Title>
     </Courses>
   </StaffInfo>
```

Next, we need to add a couple of `xmlns` attributes to the root element. These attributes are used to define the namespaces:

```
<?xml version="1.0"?>
```

```
<StaffInfo xmlns="www.abc.com/courseinfo"
           xmlns:people="www.abc.com/staff">
    <Staff>
       <people:Title>Mr</people:Title>
       <people:Name>Lee Wei Meng</people:Name>
       <people:Tel>460-6872</people:Tel>
    </Staff>
    <Courses>
       <Title>WAP Programming</Title>
       <Title>Web Programming</Title>
    </Courses>
</StaffInfo>
```

What's going on here? Well, the first attribute defines a **default namespace**, into which all the elements without a prefix have now been placed. The second attribute has defined a second namespace called `people`, into which have gone all the elements with a `people:` prefix.

Why couldn't we just have added the prefixes without the `xmlns` attributes? Well, once you've started down the road, you might as well go the whole way! The URLs supplied as values to the attributes have nothing to do with the Internet – they're just text that we can more-or-less guarantee to be unique, since we own the domain names. Even if another developer were to come along and create a `people` namespace, the chances of them associating it with the same text as ours are absolutely tiny, so what we have is a unique namespace for life.

Summary

This chapter has followed on from the previous one in giving you a no-frills introduction to XML. We covered the rules for creating well-formed XML documents, and then talked about using DTDs as a way of standardizing and validating their structure.

Armed with this basic knowledge of XML, we're at last ready to begin looking at WML. In the next chapter, we'll cover the structure of typical WAP applications, which will never change much from the first time you read about them. Then we'll really be on our way to bigger, better things.

Fundamentals of WML

We've reached Chapter 4 of a book on WAP, WML and WMLScript, and yet it's been quite some time since we talked about any of those subjects in any depth. The last two chapters, though, have laid some important foundations; after reading them, you should have a clear understanding of WML's place in the family of markup languages, and an appreciation of just why XML remains the cause of so much enthusiasm in the developer community. The latter is particularly important to us here, not only because we'll be able to use WML's relationship with XML to explain some of its characteristics, but also because we'll be meeting some more XML-related technologies later, for which a reasonable knowledge of XML will be required.

In this chapter, however, we're going to set about the task that will keep us occupied for the first two-thirds of the book: learning about WML and WMLScript. We'll start to do that by revisiting the first example you created in Chapter 1, picking it apart to see how it works, and dealing with some other subjects that arise as we do so. Our list of topics comprises the following:

❑   The formal structure of a WML document

❑   Why WML needs to be compiled, and what happens when it is

❑   Adding comments to the code of a WML application

❑   The common attributes of a great many WML elements

❑   An introduction to the problems of writing code to be viewed on many different devices

Let's begin by reminding ourselves what we know about WAP and WML from Chapters 1 and 2, adding a few new insights and observations as we go.

What is WML?

The Wireless Markup Language is a markup language that was designed expressly for the purpose of creating **applications** to be sent over wireless networks to small devices, such as mobile telephones. The Wireless Markup Language is an open standard that was developed by the Wireless Application Protocol Forum, and the WML specification forms a part of the broader WAP specification. WML is an application of XML, which means that it's defined in a document type definition.

Taken together, these three facts – and the assumptions they imply – can be used to answer many of the "Why does it do it like *that*?" questions that often seem to be thrown at WML. The Wireless Markup Language has differences from other markup languages because it's aimed at a different target from other markup languages. If its behavior ever seems strange, that's usually down to decisions that have been made in order for it to succeed in that aim.

The Structure of a WML Application

If you've used the World Wide Web, you don't need to understand HTML in order to form an impression of how the thing works. Each web site (of which there are many tens of millions) is composed of a number of pages (of which, in total, there are literally billons). Depending on the site in question, each page will contain some information, or a set of tasks for the user to perform, or a combination of the two. In all but a very few cases, it will provide ways of moving to other pages on the same web site, and often to pages on other sites too. HTML is well suited to these purposes, and it has been an enormous success.

At face value, WML looks quite like HTML, but there are differences in the intentions of their creators. WML was designed for creating *applications*, whereas HTML was really designed for creating *documents*. The line between the two is not clean, but in general an application tends to be designed around user interaction, while documents tend to be designed around the display of information.

Another key difference between WAP and the Web lies in the hardware and software typically in use for accessing the Internet in each case. In general, the Web is accessed from powerful desktop computers that have large displays and fast, cheap, reliable network connections. The web browsing software itself is a sophisticated program that offers every possible convenience to its users. Contrast that with the relatively slow, unreliable, expensive networks available to users on the move; and then compound it with the fact that the **microbrowsers** (also called **user agents**) on WAP-enabled devices are basic by necessity, and have very small displays in which to present information to the user.

Faced with these restrictions, WML needs a different metaphor from HTML for both the type of information being sent to the user, and the way in which it's sent. Users of WAP-enabled devices are not likely to be willing to read long tracts of text in order to find what they're looking for – seldom has the adage "Time is money" been more appropriate than in the world of mobile communications. These people will come to your site seeking specific pieces of information, and they'll expect to be able to find it quickly. In those circumstances, the 'browsing' model of the Web doesn't fit the bill. More suitable is a high degree of interaction, with the user reading short 'menu' pages and answering quick questions in order to find what they need.

Cards and Decks

WML's first step toward addressing these needs is to abolish the idea of a 'page'. Instead, WML applications are composed of one or more **decks** containing collections of **cards**. Each card typically contains some content that is displayed to the user, and some other content that is used by the microbrowser to control how the user moves from one card to the next. The following diagram represents this situation, with the addition of **documents**, which are the files called `something`.wml that we'll create as we write our applications. Each of these houses a single deck.

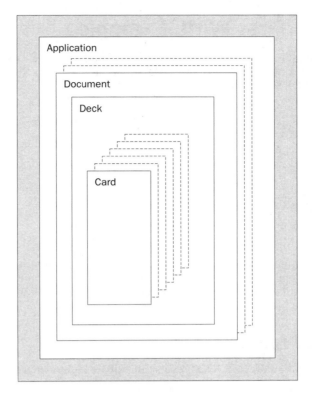

In terms of the concept (rather than the content), a WML card is similar to an HTML page, but there is no standard way in HTML to bundle a collection of pages together. This extra facility that decks provide is important for wireless Internet applications: by bundling related cards, we can send several of them to the microbrowser at once, so that it doesn't have to ask for new cards from the server every time the user tries to move from one to another. This has the potential to save a great deal of time, and if you design your applications carefully it's possible to reduce the decks that must be transferred to a very small number indeed.

Using Multiple Decks in an Application

When designing your applications, you will need to decide whether your cards need to be split into separate decks, and if so how best to do that. To some extent, this will be governed by the structure or function of your application, as discussed above, but there is another significant factor that will also affect your decision.

We'll discuss this in more depth shortly, but there is a maximum permitted size for a WML deck. If your deck is too large, you *must* split it up in the most logical way you can. Try not to think of this as a problem, however, but as the creators of WAP lending you a hand. You need to play off the benefits of having many cards on the WAP-enabled device at once, against the time it takes for a very large deck to be transferred from the server. Getting this balance wrong in either direction is likely to frustrate your users.

Revisiting Our First WML Example

Now that we've talked more about the makeup of a WML application, let's see how the things we've just discussed map to a real, albeit simple, example. The file we used back in Chapter 1 to test that installation of the UP.SDK had worked correctly looked like this:

```
<?xml version="1.0"?>
<!DOCTYPE wml PUBLIC "-//WAPFORUM//DTD WML 1.2//EN"
                     "http://www.wapforum.org/DTD/wml_1.2.xml">

<wml>
   <card>
      <p>Wrox Travel</p>
      <p>Welcome to our WAP site!</p>
   </card>
</wml>
```

This application consists of a single deck that contains a single card, and is therefore defined in a single document. It really is about as basic as a WML document can ever be, and therefore the things it contains are those that will be shared by all other documents. It's so short that we can take the time to examine it line by line.

The Document Prolog

Since WML is an application of XML, you'd expect the file to begin with a document prolog, and of course it does:

```
<?xml version="1.0"?>
<!DOCTYPE wml PUBLIC "-//WAPFORUM//DTD WML 1.2//EN"
                     "http://www.wapforum.org/DTD/wml_1.2.xml">

<wml>
   <card>
      <p>Wrox Travel</p>
      <p>Welcome to our WAP site!</p>
   </card>
</wml>
```

The highlighted lines just state that WML is based on XML version 1.0, and give the location of the document type definition against which this document will be validated. In particular, the document type declaration identifies the DTD for version 1.2 of the WML specification, which is reproduced in the Appendices.

The Deck

The document type declaration also states that the root element in this document will be <wml>, which is precisely what we find:

```
<?xml version="1.0"?>
<!DOCTYPE wml PUBLIC "-//WAPFORUM//DTD WML 1.2//EN"
                     "http://www.wapforum.org/DTD/wml_1.2.xml">
```

```
<wml>
    <card>
        <p>Wrox Travel</p>
        <p>Welcome to our WAP site!</p>
    </card>
</wml>
```

The <wml> element defines a WML deck, and you'll find a single pair of start and end tags in every WML file: one document, one deck. If required, <wml> elements can contain <head> elements (which we'll meet in Chapter 15), and <template> elements (Chapter 14). However, they *always* contain <card> elements.

The Card

It doesn't take a leap of intuition to understand that WML cards are defined by the <card> element, and in keeping with what you already know, decks may contain one or many pairs of <card> tags, representing one or many cards. Our document contains just the one:

```
<?xml version="1.0"?>
<!DOCTYPE wml PUBLIC "-//WAPFORUM//DTD WML 1.2//EN"
                     "http://www.wapforum.org/DTD/wml_1.2.xml">

<wml>
    <card>
        <p>Wrox Travel</p>
        <p>Welcome to our WAP site!</p>
    </card>
</wml>
```

Cards may contain a variety of other elements, alone or in combination, and the examples we'll write over the course of the book will involve all of them. At their simplest, though, cards contain paragraphs.

The Content

Technically, there are a couple of ways to mark data for output in WML, but the one that's used in virtually all cases is the paragraph element, <p>, which we'll look at in the next chapter.

```
<?xml version="1.0"?>
<!DOCTYPE wml PUBLIC "-//WAPFORUM//DTD WML 1.2//EN"
                     "http://www.wapforum.org/DTD/wml_1.2.xml">

<wml>
    <card>
        <p>Wrox Travel</p>
        <p>Welcome to our WAP site!</p>
    </card>
</wml>
```

In the form we have them here, the two <p> elements simply specify a couple of lines of text that should be displayed in the microbrowser, and you've already seen that in action in Chapter 1.

Sometimes, in the interests of saving space, we'll present 'snippets' of code that don't feature <wml> or <card> elements. If you find yourself wanting to give them a try, just place them in a 'frame' like the one holding the <p> elements above.

Compiled WML

When we loaded that first WML example into the UP.Simulator, we really only paid attention to what happened in the window containing the 'phone':

However, there were things going on in the text window at the same time, and we need to investigate that now. We're going to start building on the example in this chapter, so make a copy of the WML file, name it `ex4_1.wml`, and load it into the UP.Simulator. In the Phone Information window, this is what you should see:

From our point of view, the important information here lies between the two horizontal lines. The UP.Simulator locates the file and reports its size (244 bytes), examines its content (you should recognize the MIME type `text/vnd.wap.wml` from our table in Chapter 1), and then announces that the `Compiled WAP binary is 151 bytes`. It's that last line in particular that we're going to focus on.

The WAP Binary XML (WBXML) Content Format

We've spoken already, several times, about the importance of keeping data transfer sizes to a minimum when dealing with wireless networks, and this process of **compilation** is another means by which the WAP specification helps you to do that. When the word "compilation" is used in relation to computer programming, it usually refers to a process in which the instructions in a programming language are converted into codes that a computer can understand, and that's not a bad description of what's going on here.

WML files are sent to microbrowsers in a compact representation called **WAP Binary XML** (**WBXML**), and this is as true for the UP.Simulator on your desktop computer as it is for the WAP-enabled mobile phone in your jacket pocket. The difference is that under 'normal' circumstances, the WML files you write are compiled by the WAP Gateway on their way to the phone. (We talked about the WAP Gateway in Chapter 1.) On your PC, the UP.Simulator steps into that role.

The compilation of WML files is mostly a process of **tokenization**, in which the names of the tags and elements in your files are replaced by predefined, single-character codes. You can probably imagine that this represents a significant size saving when performed over a whole file, as names that can be up to ten characters in length are reduced to just one. When the compiled deck reaches the user agent, it is 'uncompiled', and your cards appear as you intended them to be displayed. Of course, all of this occurs without the user knowing (or needing to know) anything about it. They just get the benefit of decks appearing on their devices more quickly.

> **Earlier in the chapter, we mentioned the existence of a size limit for WML decks. In fact, the limit applies to *compiled* decks, and stands at 1400 bytes. If you see the UP.Simulator reporting a compiled size greater than that, you need to split the deck.**

White Space

When we said that WML compilation is "mostly" a process of tokenization, we did so because of two other things that are affected by compilation: white space, which we'll look at here; and comments, which we'll save for the next section.

White space is a generic term for characters in your WML code that serve to break it up visually, but have no meaning as far as WML is concerned. By this, we mean things like spaces, tabs, line breaks, and so forth. As an XML application, WML inherits its parent's rules for handling white space, which are to ignore it before and after an element, and to compress all other sequences of white space into a single space between two words.

To see what this means, here once again is our sample WML document, which we've gone to some lengths to make easy-to-read. (Notice in particular the indentation before each element, the line break and space in the document type declaration, and the line breaks in the deck itself.)

```
<?xml version="1.0"?>
<!DOCTYPE wml PUBLIC "-//WAPFORUM//DTD WML 1.2//EN"
                     "http://www.wapforum.org/DTD/wml_1.2.xml">

<wml>
    <card>
        <p>Wrox Travel</p>
        <p>Welcome to our WAP site!</p>
    </card>
</wml>
```

As far as WML is concerned, however, we might just as well have written the code like this:

```
<?xml version="1.0"?><!DOCTYPE wml PUBLIC "-//WAPFORUM//DTD WML 1.2//EN"
"http://www.wapforum.org/DTD/wml_1.2.xml">
<wml><card><p>Wrox Travel</p><p>Welcome to our WAP site!</p></card></wml>
```

It might not look pretty, but it conveys exactly the same information, and it's 54 bytes smaller than our original version. If you load it into the UP.Simulator, however, you'll find that it compiles to exactly the same size: 151 bytes.

This means we can write our code so that it's easy to read, without worrying about increasing the amount of data being sent to the WAP-enabled device. (You can't assume that you'll always be given the job of maintaining and updating the WML you write, and even when it *is* you, it's a lot easier to make sense of code that's been laid out neatly.) The process of compilation applies XML's rules about white space as it proceeds.

Comments in WML

As you begin writing WML decks, it is a very good idea to add comments to your code. **Comments** are a feature that WML has inherited directly from XML, and they allow programmers to insert plain text in their WML files, to describe what's going on at any given point – they will never be seen by users of your applications. Of course, comments will become more valuable as our code becomes more complex, but we can see how they work here:

```
<wml>
    <card>
        <!-- Say hello to the users -->
        <p>Wrox Travel</p>
        <p>Welcome to our WAP site!</p>
    </card>
</wml>
```

This single line of code tells you almost everything you need to know about WML comments. They start with the sequence '<!--', end with '-->', and you're free to put anything you like between these two delimiters – over multiple lines, if you need to. Better yet, comments are completely ignored by the WML compiler, so files containing them are no larger (when they're sent to user agents) than ones that don't.

You shouldn't use comments to state the obvious – that's a waste of effort (and probably disqualifies the one we've used above!) – but if there's anything in your code that may cause confusion, there's no reason not to include them. And when one helps you to decipher an otherwise mysterious section of code, you'll be glad that you did.

Common Attributes for WML Elements

At this point, we've pretty much exhausted the things there are to say about our sample WML file, so it must be time to start thinking about extending it. Assuming for now that we're not going to create any more decks at this stage, and since WML is based on XML, we're left with two possibilities: adding more elements to our existing deck, or adding attributes to the elements that already exist. In a moment, we'll look at an example that features both of these operations, but we need just a little more theory before we do so.

In WML, there are three attributes that can be used with almost all elements: `xml:lang`, `class`, and `id`. The first of these, `xml:lang`, is optional, and its value defines the (human) language of any data that may be presented to the user, so that the user agent can modify its behavior if need be (to display text in a different direction, perhaps, or to change hyphenation rules). We won't be giving any further coverage to the attribute in this book.

By specifying a `class` attribute with the same value to several different elements, you make them all part of the same class. This fact has no direct relevance to the microbrowser, or to the users of your applications, but it could be used by some external program that was tasked with processing your decks in some way, as a way of dealing with many elements together. The WML specification states that user agents should ignore this attribute, so we won't spend any more time on it here.

Finally, the `id` attribute is used to provide an element with a unique name within a single deck, so that it's possible programmatically to tell two elements of the same type apart. This functionality is absolutely essential when your deck contains more than one card, as we're about to discover.

When we introduce more WML elements in the chapters to come, we'll often enumerate the attributes they support, but we won't list these three – it would rapidly become very repetitive. With the exception of using the `id` attribute with the `<card>` element, we won't be needing them.

The `<card>` Element

Although it's true that WML applications are made up of decks, the latter seldom function as much more than containers for cards, and it's in *these* that you'll spend the majority of your development time. A card can contain text and images to be displayed to the user, controls that enable the user to make selections, and input fields for the user to enter data.

By convention, WAP-enabled devices will display a single card at a time. If a card is too large to fit the display all at once, the device may split the card and show it as a sequence of screens, or use some other mechanism (such as scroll bars). It is important, therefore, that you keep your cards small and test them across a range of devices to ensure that what gets displayed is coherent.

The `<card>` Element's id Attribute

As you build a WML application, you will want the user to be able to navigate from one card in the deck, to another. This means that we need a card to be able to *refer* to another card in the deck, which in turn means that we need some way of distinguishing cards uniquely. Is this starting to sound familiar?

The `<card>` element's `id` attribute specifies a name for a card, and looks like this:

```
<card id="name">
   content
</card>
```

With that in mind, let's see what happens if we attempt a slightly more sophisticated example.

Try It Out — Using the id Attribute to Name Cards

1. Open the `ex4_1.wml` file in your text editor, and make the following changes:

```wml
<wml>
   <card id="splash">
      <p>Wrox Travel</p>
      <p>Welcome to our WAP site!</p>
      <p><a href="#menu">Enter</a></p>
   </card>
   <card id="menu">
      <p>Check out our new unbeatable offers,
         our full vacation listings,
         and our competitive vacation insurance scheme.
         You can also read reviews of our vacations in
         our features section. For more information,
         you can search the site, or follow our links,
         which include up to the minute weather reports.
         If you have any queries don't hesitate to contact us!
      </p>
   </card>
</wml>
```

2. Save the file as `ex4_2.wml`.

3. Load the file into the UP.Simulator, and you should see something like this:

4. Press the *Down* (cursor) key on your keyboard until the line saying Enter is highlighted (an arrow will appear next to it, and the word OK at the bottom left will change to Link). Press the left softkey, and this is what you should see:

How It Works

We've made three changes to this code, with varying degrees of complexity. The first one is the shortest, and the simplest:

```
<wml>
    <card id="splash">
        <p>Wrox Travel</p>
```

We've assigned the value `splash` to the `id` attribute of our original card. This card can now be identified uniquely in the deck, because there are no other cards whose `id` attributes have been set to the same value. From here on, we will often refer to a `<card>` element by the value assigned to its `id` attribute. This one, therefore, is the "splash" card.

The third change we made looks like a big one, but it's actually just another card containing a single, albeit longer, paragraph. Among other things, this "menu" card demonstrates once again that white space is irrelevant as far as WML is concerned. The line breaks that appear in the text of the WML paragraph bear no relation to the breaks seen by the user in the microbrowser.

Finally, the second change to the deck, which involved the addition of a new paragraph to the "splash" card. This is what it looked like:

```
        <p>Welcome to our WAP site!</p>
        <p><a href="#menu">Enter</a></p>
    </card>
```

To allow users to move between the two cards in our deck, we've had to use an element that we won't be introducing formally until Chapter 6. The `<a>` element allows you to place a 'link' on a card, and to specify what card should be displayed when a user selects that link. By inspection, it must be that the destination card is somehow controlled by the `href` attribute – and it's actually fairly obvious that the value assigned here is just the name of the card, prefixed with a # symbol. More interesting is an explanation of *why* this is the case.

When we started using the UP.Simulator in Chapter 1, we told it what deck to look at by providing a Uniform Resource Locator (URL), just as we would if we were using a web browser. If you're using a local web server for testing your WML files, for example, the URL of the deck we're looking at now is http://localhost/ex4_2.wml. The values we assign to the `href` attribute are *also* URLs, although you'd be justified in thinking that #menu doesn't look much like one.

URLs of the form http://... are termed "absolute", because they specify their target wherever it happens to be. It's quite possible to supply URLs of this form to the `href` attribute. However, if you know that the file you want is in the same directory as the current file, you can use a "relative" URL and simply provide the filename – the other details will be assumed from your location. The last thing you need to know in order to understand what's going on in this example is that an individual card can be specified in a URL by adding its `id`, prefixed with #, to the end. Because the card we want is in the same *deck* as the current card, the rules of relative URLs allow us to specify only this part of the absolute URL to the `href` attribute.

To test this idea, try typing http://localhost/ex4_2.wml#menu into the UP.Simulator – you'll find that you're taken straight to the "menu" card. We'll have much more to say on the issues raised here in Chapter 6.

The <card> Element's title Attribute

As a final example in this chapter, we'll take a look at another of the <card> element's attributes: title. The WML specification states that this attribute provides information about the card that may be used by the microbrowser in any way that it chooses.

```
<card title="value">
    content
</card>
```

If you want the title to be "Menu", for example, you would write:

```
<card title="Menu">
```

Let's see what happens when we add a title attribute to the second card in our simple deck.

Try It Out — Adding a Title to a Card

1. Open the ex4_2.wml file in your text editor and make the following change:

```
<wml>
    <card id="splash">
        <p>Wrox Travel</p>
        <p>Welcome to our WAP site!</p>
        <p><a href="#menu">Enter</a></p>
    </card>
    <card id="menu" title="Wrox Travel">
        <p>Check out our new unbeatable offers,
            our full vacation listings,
            and our competitive vacation insurance scheme.
            You can also read reviews of our vacations in
            our features section. For more information,
            you can search the site, or follow our links,
            which include up to the minute weather reports.
            If you have any queries don't hesitate to contact us!
        </p>
    </card>
</wml>
```

2. Save the file as ex4_3.wml.

3. Load the file into the UP.Simulator, and this is what you'll see:

We appear to have achieved absolutely nothing at all! This one's going to need some explaining.

How It Works (or, Why It Fails)

This is our first example (and there will be many) of an instance in which the user agent is conforming perfectly to the WML specification, but failing to do what you expected. We'll be looking at the reasons for this in the next chapter, but there are a number of places where the specification states that microbrowsers are free to deal with attributes (and even some elements) as they see fit – and that can include ignoring them altogether!

With that in mind, some devices will display the `title` attribute's value as the first line in the display, some may place it in another location, and others – of which the UP.Simulator is clearly one – don't display the value at all. This means that you should be wary of putting critical information in the value you provide to the `title` attribute, as not all users will see it!

> We strongly encourage you to test your WML applications on as many devices and emulators as you can find — microbrowser implementations vary significantly. This subject will raise its head throughout the book, but we'll be dealing with it in detail in Chapter 17.

Summary

In this chapter, you've learned about the basic components of a WML application: cards and decks. You saw that WML's root element, `<wml>`, is used to define a deck, and that the `<card>` element is used to define a card. We also examined what happened when we specified some attributes to our cards: `id`, to uniquely identify the card, and `title`, to provide some additional description.

Elsewhere in the chapter, we took a look at compilation – the process by which your WML code is converted into WBXML for delivery to a microbrowser – and at how to comment your deck so that you and other programmers can clearly understand your intentions. This will become increasingly important as the size of your applications increases.

In the next chapter, we are going to start focusing on how best to present information to the user. Our subject will be the writing and formatting of text-based content.

Writing and Formatting Text

In the previous chapter, we outlined the general makeup of a WML application. We showed that it consists of one or more **decks**, any one of which will contain a collection of **cards**. We also introduced the `<card>` element's id attribute, which specifies a name for the card, and its `title` attribute, which hints at what the card does.

In this chapter, we will begin to explore some of the elements a card may contain, looking at how to place text inside a card, and how to format text for display. As part of our discussion, we will discover that the creators of WML have deliberately left some parts of the specification open to interpretation. We'll examine why they've done that, and what it means for us as WML developers. More specifically, then, we'll cover the following:

- ❏ How to break the text within a card into paragraphs
- ❏ Ways of formatting a paragraph relative to the borders of the screen
- ❏ Controlling how and when long lines of text are 'wrapped'
- ❏ Including symbols and special characters in your text
- ❏ Specifying when line breaks should occur, and when they shouldn't
- ❏ Applying styles like bold, italics, and underline

Paragraphs

In the overwhelming majority of applications, text is the kind of information you will want to display most frequently. Now, while you *could* just fill your cards with text and hope for the best, it's unlikely that your users would thank you for doing so: unformatted text is difficult to read even in ideal circumstances, and the small screens of WAP-enabled devices are far from that.

As a first step to improving this situation, we can break text up into paragraphs using the `<p>` element. In fact, WML *requires* that all text in a card be contained in paragraphs, which take the general form shown overleaf.

```
<p>
   content
</p>
<p>
   more content
</p>
```

We should say here that the *content* of a `<p>` element is not restricted to text – it's possible to include a variety of other elements between the `<p>` start tag and the `</p>` end tag, as we shall see – but the paragraph construct allows us to display whatever it contains in a more pleasing way. The paragraphs in this book, for example, break information into sections and (hopefully) make things easier for the reader. `<p>` elements can certainly do that, but there's a little more to them: WML paragraphs demarcate blocks of text, to which specific formatting can then be applied.

To see why that could be important, imagine that your document contains a list of numbers. Usually, you'd want to align such a list with the right-hand edge of the screen, like this:

```
         147
         180
          42
           3
        1024
```

We'll see in a moment that WML provides a way of doing precisely this, but you probably wouldn't want the rest of your text to appear this way. By breaking content into paragraphs, you can apply such formatting to *sections* of your cards, without affecting everything else.

The `<p>` Element's align Attribute

The alignment options in WML are quite simple, and echo those you might find in any word processing package: right alignment, left alignment, and centering. You saw in the last chapter that if text alignment is not specified, left alignment is the default. If you want text to be centered or aligned to the right (as in the case suggested above), you need to use the `<p>` element's `align` attribute:

```
<p align=value>
   content
</p>
```

The `align` attribute has three possible values: `left`, `center`, and `right`. Therefore, if you want a paragraph to be centered, you would write:

```
<p align="center">The paragraph</p>
```

As an example, and to reprise the point about displaying numbers that we made earlier in this discussion, here's some WML code that doesn't use the `align` attribute:

```
<p>
   Prices are listed below:
</p>
```

```
<p>
    365.42
</p>
<p>
    2.95
</p>
<p>
    12.18
</p>
```

View this in your microbrowser, and you'd see something like the following:

If we now change the alignment using the `align` attribute:

```
<p>
    Prices are listed below:
</p>
<p align="right">
    365.42
</p>
<p align="right">
    2.95
</p>
<p align="right">
    12.18
</p>
```

You'll surely agree that the information in the card is more easily readable:

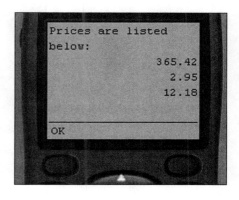

In this second example, we have changed the layout so that the last three paragraphs are right aligned, displaying the prices in a more natural way. If you like, you can try left aligning and centering text, to prove that works too.

Try It Out — Aligning Text

Let's apply this new knowledge to the Wrox Travel application we started in the last chapter. As we progress through this chapter, we will develop the application to be more appealing to look at, and – importantly – easier to use.

1. Open the `ex4_3.wml` file from the last chapter, and make the following changes:

```wml
<wml>
    <card id="splash">
        <p align="center">Wrox Travel</p>
        <p>Welcome to our WAP site!</p>
        <p align="center"><a href="#menu">Enter</a></p>
    </card>
    <card id="menu" title="Wrox Travel">
        <p>Check out our new unbeatable offers,
            our full vacation listings,
            and our competitive vacation insurance scheme.
            You can also read reviews of our vacations in
            our features section. For more information,
            you can search the site, or follow our links,
            which include up to the minute weather reports.
            If you have any queries don't hesitate to contact us!
        </p>
    </card>
</wml>
```

2. Save the file with the name `ex5_1.wml`.

3. Run the `ex5_1.wml` file in the UP.Simulator. You should see something like this:

How It Works

By changing the alignment of the first and third paragraphs in the "splash" card, we have moved the text into the center of the card:

```
<p align="center">Wrox Travel</p>
<p>Welcome to our WAP site!</p>
<p align="center"><a href="#menu">Enter</a></p>
```

When viewed in the UP.Simulator, you can see that the text is now centered, and you'll probably agree that the text in a title page looks more natural in the center of the screen.

The `<p>` Element's mode Attribute

As well as the alignment of a paragraph, the `<p>` element can be used to configure its line wrap setting, which determines what happens when a paragraph is too long to fit on a single line of the display. By default, the behavior is much like the paragraph you're reading now: if there are too many words for one line, the remainder will be displayed on the next line – what else would you expect to happen on a piece of paper? On a screen though, there's an alternative: the words can continue off the edge, with some means of viewing them provided to the user.

The `<p>` element's mode attribute is used to specify the line wrap setting:

```
<p mode="wrapmode">
    content
</p>
```

The mode attribute has two possible values: `wrap` and `nowrap`. The former is the default setting: lines of text will span multiple lines of the display if they are too long. If mode is set to `nowrap`, paragraphs will appear on a single line of the display, no matter how long they are.

Try It Out — Changing the Line Wrap Mode for Paragraphs

It's left to the microbrowser to determine how `nowrap` paragraphs should be displayed. One possibility is that off-screen items could be viewed by means of a scroll bar; another is the technique employed by the UP.Simulator we've been using for our WML development so far. It's an interesting solution that we'll investigate in the following example.

1. To begin, make the following changes to ex5_1.wml:

```
<wml>
   <card id="splash">
      <p align="center">Wrox Travel</p>
      <p mode="nowrap">Welcome to our WAP site!</p>
      <p align="center" mode="wrap"><a href="#menu">Enter</a></p>
   </card>
   <card id="menu" title="Wrox Travel">
      <p>Check out our new unbeatable offers,
         our full vacation listings,
         and our competitive vacation insurance scheme.
         You can also read reviews of our vacations in
         our features section. For more information,
```

```
            you can search the site, or follow our links,
            which include up to the minute weather reports.
            If you have any queries don't hesitate to contact us!
        </p>
    </card>
</wml>
```

2. Save the file as `ex5_2.wml`.

3. Run the file in the UP.Simulator, and see what you get:

4. Select the second paragraph (Welcome to our WAP site!) in the browser, and you should see that the sentence scrolls horizontally:

How It Works

In Step 1, we made a couple of changes to the "splash" card:

```
        <p align="center">Wrox Travel</p>
        <p mode="nowrap">Welcome to our WAP site!</p>
        <p align="center" mode="wrap"><a href="#menu">Enter</a></p>
    </card>
```

To the second paragraph element, we added the `mode` attribute, setting its value to `nowrap`. Reasonably enough, this means that we are switching from the previous line wrap mode (the default: `wrap`) to `nowrap`. As you saw, this resulted in the line of text scrolling rather than wrapping.

An interesting aspect to note here is that we were compelled to add a `mode` attribute to the third paragraph as well, in order to restore the line wrap to its default setting. The WML specification states that on being set, the line wrap mode applies to the current paragraph, *and all subsequent ones*. This is a point well worth remembering, because if you do use `mode` and forget to reset it, you could find yourself with some very odd-looking cards!

Character Encoding

Before we can continue investigating WML's facilities for formatting text, we need to take a small step sideways. So far, all the text we've put in our cards has appeared faithfully in the microbrowser, but to some extent that's been down to a slightly careful choice of content. There are some characters that are intended to convey very specific information *to the microbrowser* (rather than to the readers of your cards), and making sure that they appear correctly requires a little extra effort on our part.

If that all sounds rather abstract, consider the following code fragment:

```
<p>x < y + z</p>
```

The intention here is to display the mathematical expression "x < y + z", but if you tried to show a card containing this paragraph in the UP.Simulator, you'd get an error message something like this:

The meaning isn't exactly crystal clear, but what's happening is that on encountering the < character immediately following the x, the microbrowser is expecting a tag to come next – a closing paragraph tag, perhaps, or some other type that we haven't yet met. However, as there are *no* tags whose names begin with a "y", this code is flagged as an error.

It is the responsibility of the WML user agent to display the content of our applications as we intended it to be displayed, but in cases like this there are good reasons why it can't do so. The less-than sign is an example of a **reserved character**, and outputting one of these requires us to find an alternative way of expressing them. In WML, reserved characters have two kinds of alternative representation: **numeric character entities**, and **named character entities**.

Numeric Character Entities

Numeric character entities are actually an alternative means of expressing *any* character, not just reserved ones. Every character that may be displayed has a number associated with it, and by referring to that number in your WML code, you can cause the corresponding character to be displayed. The numbers that WML uses to represent characters are borrowed from **Unicode**, an international standard that defines numbers to represent characters from many of the world's languages: upper and lower case letters, numerals, mathematical symbols, you name it. To see how it works, it's probably the right time for another example.

Try It Out — Using Numeric Character Entities

1. In our usual style, type the following WML code into your text editor, and save it with the name ex5_3.wml.

```
<?xml version="1.0"?>
<!DOCTYPE wml PUBLIC "-//WAPFORUM//DTD WML 1.2//EN"
                     "http://www.wapforum.org/DTD/wml_1.2.xml">

<wml>
   <card id="numeric">
      <p>&#72;&#101;&#108;&#108;&#111;&#32;&#119;&#111;&#114;&#108;&#100;</p>
   </card>
</wml>
```

2. Point the UP.Simulator to your new file, and you should see... this:

How It Works

When you don't know what you're looking for, the single paragraph in our card seems to bear very little relation to the eventual output, but examine it a little more closely and you can see a pattern emerging. The paragraph contains eleven items, each of which begins with an ampersand (&) and ends with a semicolon (;). Including the space between the words, the output consists of eleven characters – and of course, this is no coincidence. The items in the paragraph are being converted into characters before being displayed by the microbrowser.

In WML, *all* character entities (numeric and named) are bounded by & and ; characters. In this example, they're surrounding a # sign, followed by the number that represents the character we require. By inspection, you can see that 72 corresponds to 'H', 32 to a space, 114 to 'r', and so on. Of course, you wouldn't normally resort to numeric character entities in order to display non-reserved characters, but this does demonstrate their versatility. The table in the next section lists the numeric character entities associated with some common reserved characters.

Named Character Entities

Named character entities work in broadly the same way as numeric ones, but they're not defined for all characters. Instead, they serve as an easy way to remember the representations of some of the reserved characters you'll need to display most frequently – and as a side effect, they make your code easier to read, too! Here's the complete list, as defined by the WML specification:

Named Character Entity	Numeric Character Entity	Definition
&quot;	&#34;	Quotation mark (?)
&amp;	&#38;	Ampersand (&)
&apos;	&#39;	Apostrophe (')
&lt;	&#60;	Less than (<)
&gt;	&#62;	Greater than (>)
		Non-breaking space
&shy;	&#173;	Soft hyphen

Returning at last to the example with which we began this discussion, we can output our mathematical expression by replacing the < character with <, like so:

```
<p>x &lt; y + z</p>
```

Similarly, if you wanted to use quotes round a piece of test, like "Think out of the box", you could write:

```
<p>Bob says, &#34;Think out of the box.&quot;</p>
```

As you can see, it's possible to mix and match the way you refer to reserved characters, although for code readability and maintenance you should try to be consistent.

Controlling Line Breaks

What on earth does any of the preceding section have to do with our earlier theme? The clue to that question lies in the last two lines of the character entity table, which mentioned the non-breaking space and soft hyphen characters. These are just two of several mechanisms provided by WML for controlling when lines of text being displayed should and should not be broken, a subject that forms the topic for this part of the chapter. Don't forget about the character entities – they'll prove to be useful time and again – but for now we need to move on.

Different WAP-enabled devices have different screen sizes, so even if they use the same microbrowser, you can't guarantee that your applications will look the same wherever they're viewed. Sentences and paragraphs will wrap differently, depending on the number of characters that fit on a single line of the screen. There are occasions, though, when you'll want to have more control over this behavior. You may wish to force a line break between two words, prevent a line break from occurring between two words (so that they always occur on the same line), or suggest places where a word may be split across two lines (with the addition of a hyphen).

Adding a Line Break with the
 Element

The <br> element is used to force a line break between two words in a paragraph, regardless of the position in the current display line. The following changes, for example, would break the lines of our familiar paragraph in several places:

```
<p>Check out our new unbeatable offers,
    our full vacation listings,
    and our competitive vacation insurance scheme.<br/>
    You can also read reviews of our vacations in
    our features section.<br/> For more information,
    you can search the site, or follow our links,
    which include up to the minute weather reports.<br/>
    If you have any queries don't hesitate to contact us!
</p>
```

One of the first things you'll notice about this is that none of the <br> elements has any content. In fact, <br> elements are always empty – they *never* have any content. (What would it be sensible for them to contain?) Therefore, <br> elements are usually written as <br/>, although the equivalent notation
</br> is also correct.

Try It Out — Forcing Line Breaks

In terms of their direct effect on the appearance of text, there is little to choose between the <p> element and the <br> element: both end the current line, and force subsequent text to appear at the beginning of the next line. However, the <br> element carries none of the formatting information implied by the <p> element, and the WML specification does permit some differences in behavior when the elements appear in multiples. This example should demonstrate the point.

1. Load ex5_2.wml into your text editor and make the following changes:

```
<wml>
    <card id="splash">
        <p align="center">Wrox Travel</p>
        <p mode="nowrap">Welcome to our WAP site!</p>
        <p align="center" mode="wrap"><a href="#menu">Enter</a></p>
    </card>
    <card id="menu" title="Wrox Travel">
        <p>Check out our new unbeatable offers,
            our full vacation listings,
            and our competitive vacation insurance scheme.<br/>
            You can also read reviews of our vacations in
            our features section.
        </p>
```

```
        <p></p>
        <p>For more information,
            you can search the site, or follow our links,
            which include up to the minute weather reports.<br/><br/>
            If you have any queries don't hesitate to contact us!
        </p>
    </card>
</wml>
```

2. Save the updated file with the name ex5_4.wml.

3. Now, load this file into the UP.Simulator. Follow the Enter link, scroll to the bottom, and you should see something like this:

How It Works

We've changed the "menu" card in a number of places, adding new paragraphs and several line breaks. The screenshot above shows the effect of adding the double <br> element here:

```
        <p>For more information,
            you can search the site, or follow our links,
            which include up to the minute weather reports.<br/><br/>
            If you have any queries don't hesitate to contact us!
        </p>
```

You can see that we've successfully forced a completely blank line – a feat that was not achieved by the addition of an empty paragraph in this section of the code:

```
            You can also read reviews of our vacations in
            our features section.
        </p>
        <p></p>
        <p>For more information,
            you can search the site, or follow our links,
```

WML considers paragraphs containing nothing (or nothing but white space) to be insignificant, and they will be ignored by any microbrowser that implements the specification correctly.

Preventing a Line Break with the   Entity

The non-breaking space character entity ( ) is used to *prevent* a line break between two words. This is useful if there are particular things in your text that you want to keep together – the various sections of a mailing address, for example, or dashes like the one in the middle of this sentence:

```
<p>You can contact us by e-mail, or drop a
    letter in the post - our address is
    Arden House, 1102 Warwick Road,
    Birmingham, UK.
</p>
```

If you were to send a card containing this paragraph to the UP.Simulator, you'd see the following:

A word of warning, though: be wary of forcing, and especially of preventing, line breaks in your code. The microbrowser will do its best to satisfy your wishes, but it's possible to produce some undesirable results. For example, if you try to stop a section of text that's wider than the screen from breaking, the line will simply break at the edge of the screen, wherever that happens to fall in your text. As so often, the key is to be sensible, and to use these techniques in moderation.

Using the ­ Soft Hyphen Character Entity

One last layout control is worthy of further explanation. The ­ character entity is used to add a *discretionary* hyphen, which means that the microbrowser *may* add a line break at its location – and if it does, it should also add a hyphen. This is usually used in long words that would best be kept on a single line, but will often end up being wrapped, resulting in some rather ugly text. Look at the difference between these two:

```
Intel today announced        Intel today announced
two new additions to         two new additions to
its expanding                its expanding micro-
microprocessor               processor range
range
```

The addition of a soft hyphen to the word "microprocessor" has saved us a line on the 'screen', without overly compromising the readability of the text. However, the WML specification states quite clearly that user agents are free to ignore soft hyphens, so you shouldn't rely on support for them. If you like, you can think of them as a courtesy to users whose microbrowsers do support this feature.

Changing the Way Text is Displayed

The small amount of control available to the programmer for manipulating the appearance of content is a criticism often leveled at WML, but in fact this apparent shortcoming is rooted in good sense. By design, WML allows for the limitations of the devices it targets, and shuns features that could prove difficult to implement. The simplicity of WML design means we can guarantee that our applications will at least be viewable on any compatible device, and should look acceptable on all of them too.

The designers of WML have applied the same philosophy to the next set of elements we'll look at: the ones that perform the kinds of functions we talked about when we first started investigating markup languages. The following table lists the elements defined in WML for applying special formatting to sections of text that can vary in size from a single character, to a whole paragraph:

Element	Meaning	Example
`<b>`	Bold	`<p>This is <b>bold</b> text.</p>`
`<big>`	Large	`<p>This is <big>big</big> text.</p>`
`<em>`	Emphasized	`<p>This is <em>emphasized</em> text.</p>`
`<i>`	Italicized	`<p>This is <i>italicized</i> text.</p>`
`<small>`	Small	`<p>This is <small>small</small> text.</p>`
`<strong>`	Strongly emphasized	`<p>This is <strong>strong</strong> text.</p>`
`<u>`	Underlined	`<p>This is <u>underlined</u> text.</p>`

Some of these elements specify quite precisely how text should be displayed – the `<b>` element is used to make text use a bold font, while the `<i>` element is used to italicize text. Other elements are used to *describe* how their content should be displayed. For example, the `<em>` element says that the content should be "emphasized". It does not say exactly how the content should appear, only that the microbrowser should emphasize it in some way. The WML specification has this to say about the so-called "emphasis elements":

> *"Visual user agents must distinguish emphasized text from non-emphasized text. A user agent should make a best effort to distinguish the various forms of emphasized text as described above. It should distinguish text that has been emphasized using the `<em>` element from that using the `<strong>` element. User agents may use the same style for `<strong>`, `<b>`, and `<big>` emphasis. It may also use the same style for `<em>`, `<i>`, `<u>`, and `<small>` emphasis."*

There's only one "must" in that paragraph, reflecting once again the desire of the WML authors for their creation to work on even the most constrained of devices – they can eschew a number of features, but still remain compliant with the specification. Here, for example, is how the UP.Simulator we've been using performs when confronted with these elements:

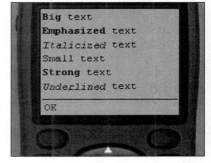

In the light of all this, it's probably best to avoid using text formatting to convey critical information. The sensible approach is only to use formatting to *supplement* meaning in the text. Stick to that advice, and your users will surely appreciate your efforts.

Summary

In this chapter, you have seen the fundamental features available for displaying text in WML, starting with the principal mechanism for doing so: the <p> element.

You also learned that a WML card has two formatting settings, controlled by the <p> element's align and mode attributes. The former specifies the alignment of lines in a paragraph relative to the borders of the display, while the latter specifies what line-wrapping mode to use.

Later, we introduced the notion that depending on the target device, what you type is not necessarily what you see. We demonstrated how character entities are used to display reserved symbols that would otherwise cause problems, and to achieve some particular effects.

Finally, you learned how to format your cards by using the <br> element and the   entity to control line breaks, and a bevy of character formatting elements including <b> and <small>.

In the next chapter, we'll move on to discuss another way of improving your application for its users. To be worthwhile, the information you supply must be sensibly structured, and it must be easy to navigate through it. WML allows the provision of that kind of functionality in a number of different ways, as you'll soon see.

Navigating Between Cards and Decks

Now that we can write a WML deck, and add and format text-based content through the use of paragraphs, elements and entities, we will look at how we can add a greater degree of interactivity to our applications. When we began to create the Wrox Travel application back in Chapter 4, and on the promise of future explanation, we added an element to our code that allowed us to move from one card to another in the same deck. You'll be pleased to know that's certainly one of the things we'll be covering here, but in fact there are a number of ways to implement similar functionality, and we'll be examining those too.

Allowing the user to make a choice, and to arrive at another card (in the same deck or in a different one) based on that choice, is an essential part of any non-trivial WML application. Your site will only provide an effective service to its users if it allows them easily to reach the information they require. The next step in developing our application, then, is to add more content and provide a path through it. Doing so will require us to cover the following in this chapter:

- ❑   Hyperlinks on the Web, and in WAP
- ❑   Using URLs to refer to cards in a deck
- ❑   Navigating to another card
- ❑   Navigating to another deck
- ❑   Navigating to the previous card in the deck
- ❑   Creating lists of options to present to the user

Hyperlinks

One of the things that make the Web so great, and such a useful resource, is that you can move from one document to another, related document by clicking on some text; a button; an image... you name it. When you click, a connection is made between the current document and a second document. This target document is then loaded into the web browser.

This connection between two documents is called a **hyperlink** (or just **link**, for short). When we move from one document to another, we are said to be **navigating** to a different document. The document that contains the link is called the **source**, and the document that you navigate to is called the **destination**. The starting point of a hyperlink (located in the source) is called the **anchor**. If that sounds like a lot of information all at once, the following figure should make things a little clearer:

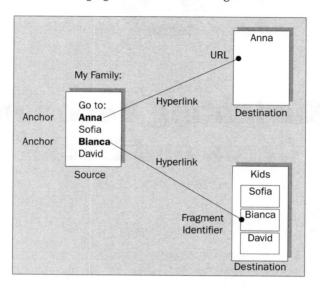

Looking at the diagram, you can see that we have a source document called "My Family". This source document has two anchors specified: one labeled "Anna", and the other "Bianca".

The anchor labeled "Anna" is the starting point of a hyperlink to the document called "Anna", while the anchor labeled "Bianca" is the starting point of a link to *a section* of a document called "Kids". This hyperlink uses a **fragment identifier** to specify the particular section of the document, and the anchor associated with it is termed a **fragment anchor**.

We'll have more to say about both of these items in the next section, and through the remainder of the chapter you'll discover that the scheme for creating links represented by the diagram is reproduced faithfully in WML.

Using URLs to Refer to Cards

In Chapter 4, we explained how Uniform Resource Locators (URLs) are used to name resources in WML, and defined two different types: absolute and relative URLs. We illustrated how URLs could be used to identify decks, but pointed out that they are not limited to this – we can also use URLs to identify the cards within a deck.

In the example of the deck we've been working with in our exercises so far (reproduced below), the first highlighted line contains a fragment identifier: #menu. This means that the <a> element (which we'll discuss in a moment) containing this identifier is a fragment anchor, and the starting point of a hyperlink to the "menu" card:

```
<wml>
  <card id="splash">
    <p align="center">Wrox Travel</p>
    <p mode="nowrap">Welcome to our WAP site!</p>
    <p align="center" mode="wrap">
      <a href="#menu">Enter</a>
    </p>
  </card>
  <card id="menu" title="Wrox Travel">
    <p>Check out our new unbeatable offers,
      our full vacation listings,
      and our competitive vacation insurance scheme.<br/>
      You can also read reviews of our vacations in
      our features section.
    </p>
    <p>For more information,
      you can search the site, or follow our links,
      which include up to the minute weather reports.<br/><br/>
      If you have any queries don't hesitate to contact us!
    </p>
  </card>
</wml>
```

In general, we specify a WML fragment anchor by suffixing the URL for a deck with a # symbol, and following that with the fragment identifier — that is, the destination <card> element's id attribute:

```
deck-url#card-id
```

For example, if you wanted to refer to the "menu" card in mydeck.wml, you would do so using an absolute URL such as http://www.wroxtravel.com/mydeck.wml#menu

In our example, we're referring to the "menu" card from within the same deck, enabling us to use a simpler, relative URL: #menu

The <a> Element

It's high time we got round to explaining the <a> element that's been lurking unexplained in our example since Chapter 4 — although it's likely that by now, you've already got a pretty good idea of how it works. The <a> element is the simplest way in WML of creating an anchor that links one document to another, and so far we've been using it in its simplest form. However, just like the other WML elements we've seen so far, <a> elements have a number of attributes that can be used to configure and customize their behavior.

In addition to the common attributes xml:lang, id, and class, the <a> element supports attributes called href (which you've seen), title, and accesskey.

The <a> Element's href Attribute

You've seen one particular example of using the href attribute already, but we can formalize its syntax here. href (an abbreviation of "hyperlink reference") is used to specify the destination of a hyperlink — in other words, the value of the attribute tells the microbrowser where to go when the link is selected:

```
<a href="destination">
   content
</a>
```

Here, the *destination* is an absolute or relative URL, with or without a fragment identifier, while the *content* is what will be displayed to the user to represent the link. This general format simply specifies that 'selecting' the content will cause the user to navigate to the destination. Let's look at the three most likely scenarios in which href may be used.

Navigating Within a Deck

This is precisely the scenario we've been involved in so far, and there's little to be gained by going through the description in detail again. Using the href attribute in this way is simply a matter of specifying the id of the destination card as the value of href, in the form of a fragment identifier. When the user selects the anchor, they navigate to the card concerned.

Navigating Within the Same Site

If you want the destination to be a card in another deck that's also on your site, you would specify the URL for the deck, and the id attribute of the desired <card> element within that deck. If you don't specify a card, or you supply an identifier that doesn't match a card, the microbrowser automatically navigates to the first card in the deck.

```
<a href="deck-url#card-id">
   content
</a>
```

So, if we're in a deck called history.wml, and the user wishes to navigate to the FAQ section in order to find out about the company's privacy policy, the architecture might look like this:

```
<!-- history.wml -->
<wml>
   <card>
      <p>
          Wrox.com was instituted in...
          <a href="faq.wml#privacy">
             FAQ
          </a>
      </p>
   </card>
</wml>
```

```
<!-- faq.wml -->
<wml>
   <card id="privacy">
      <p>
          As part of our policy, we do not
          release any information to parties
          outside Wrox.com departments.
      </p>
   </card>

   <!-- Other cards -->
</wml>
```

Because of the tight limits on the size of WML decks, you're likely to need this technique quite frequently in larger WML application. A typical way to proceed is for the first deck to display a menu that describes the contents of the other decks in the application, so that selecting one of items results in navigation to the appropriate secondary deck.

Navigation using Fully Qualified URLs

A fully qualified URL is one in which the destination has been defined completely: the server name, the deck to load, and the card within the deck to display:

```
<a href="http://www.wrox.com/faq.wml#privacy">FAQ</a>
```

The principal uses for this final URL format are to allow us to link to external resources, which might provide important additional functionality, or just more information on a similar theme.

Try It Out — Navigating to Another Deck

Now that we understand how anchors work rather better, let's add some more of them to our Wrox Travel application. We'll create a new deck containing a card with links to an external site, and back to the start of our original deck.

1. Enter the following into your text editor, and save the file with the name ex6_1links.wml:

```
<?xml version="1.0"?>
<!DOCTYPE wml PUBLIC "-//WAPFORUM//DTD WML 1.2//EN"
                     "http://www.wapforum.org/DTD/wml_1.2.xml">

<wml>
    <card id="links" title="Links">
        <p>
            <a href="http://www.pistoff.com/wap.wml">3 Valleys WAP Snow Report</a>
        </p>
        <p>
            <a href="ex6_1wrox.wml">Wrox Travel</a>
        </p>
    </card>
</wml>
```

2. Open ex5_4.wml file from the previous chapter and add the following hyperlink:

```
<p>For more information,
    you can search the site, or follow our
    <a href="ex6_1links.wml">links</a>,
    which include up to the minute weather reports.<br/><br/>
    If you have any queries don't hesitate to contact us!
</p>
```

3. Save the file with the name ex6_1wrox.wml.

4. Load the file ex6_1wrox.wml into the UP.Simulator, and select the Enter link to navigate to the "menu" card. Then, scroll down until you see the links hyperlink, as shown overleaf.

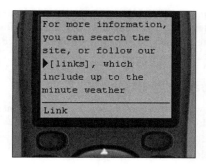

5. If you select the Link button, you should navigate to the "links" card in `ex6_1links.wml`, and see something like this:

If you have an Internet connection, you might like to try the top link – it's a live site giving snow reports for the French ski resorts Méribel, Courchevel and Val Thorens!

How It Works

In Step 1, we created a new deck with a single `<card>` element entitled `Links`. The card contains two `<p>` elements, with an anchor specified in each. The first anchor,

```
<a href="http://www.pistoff.com/wap.wml">3 Valleys WAP Snow Report</a>
```

specifies a hyperlink to an absolute URL named http://www.pistoff.com/wap.wml. The second anchor,

```
<a href="ex6_1wrox.wml">Wrox Travel</a>
```

specifies a hyperlink to a *relative* URL named `ex6_1wrox.wml`. Since this is a relative URL, the microbrowser will look for the file on the same server, and in the same directory, as the one the current deck was loaded from.

In Step 2, we modified a previously created file to include a hyperlink to the new file. This we did simply by wrapping an `<a>` element around some existing text:

```
you can search the site, or follow our
<a href="ex6_1links.wml">links</a>,
```

The `<a>` element's `href` attribute value is set to `ex6_1links.wml`, the name of the destination file. This means that when the user selects the word links (the `<a>` element's content), the microbrowser will navigate to the destination file.

What Can Be an Anchor?

In principle, text, images, and `<br>` elements can all appear in anchors – all you have to do is put the `<a>` start tag and `</a>` end tag around them. It's even possible to define an anchor with no content at all (although the value of such an anchor is highly questionable). The screenshot below shows the UP.Simulator displaying anchors containing an image and a couple of `<br/>` elements respectively:

We'll be looking at how to incorporate images into your WML applications, as well as some of the pitfalls this can entail, in the next chapter.

The `<a>` Element's title Attribute

The `<a>` element's `title` attribute is used to provide a brief description of the hyperlink:

```
<a href=destination title=label>
    content
</a>
```

Exactly how the `label` should be used is left for user agents to decide, and they may even choose to ignore it completely. Depending on the device in question, dynamically labeled keys, menus, tooltips, or even voice prompts might be appropriate.

> **In order to maintain a level of interoperability, the WML specification recommends that you keep the value of the `title` attribute to a length of six characters or fewer.**

Try It Out — Adding Titles to Links

Let's continue to work on the sample files we created earlier in this chapter, and add `title` attributes to the hyperlinks they contain.

1. Open `ex6_1wrox.wml` and make the following changes:

```
<wml>
    <card id="splash">

        <!-- Paragraphs omitted for brevity -->

        <p align="center" mode="wrap">
            <a href="#menu" title="Enter">Enter</a>
        </p>
    </card>
    <card id="menu" title="Wrox Travel">

        <!-- Paragraphs omitted for brevity -->

        <p>For more information,
            you can search the site or follow our
            <a href="ex6_2links.wml" title="Links">links</a>,
            which include up to the minute weather reports.<br/><br/>
            If you have any queries don't hesitate to contact us!
        </p>
    </card>
</wml>
```

2. Save the file with the name `ex6_2wrox.wml`.

3. Open `ex6_1links.wml`, make these changes, and save the file as `ex6_2links.wml`:

```
<wml>
    <card id="links" title="Links">
        <p>
            <a href="http://www.pistoff.com/wap.wml"
                title="Report">3 Valleys WAP Snow Report</a>
        </p>
        <p>
            <a href="ex6_2wrox.wml" title="Travel">Wrox Travel</a>
        </p>
    </card>
</wml>
```

4. Now let's see what effect this has had. Load `ex6_2wrox.wml` into the UP.Simulator and you should see the following:

5. Click the button labeled Enter, scroll down to the hyperlink, and you should get:

How It Works

In Step 1, we added `title` attributes to the two `<a>` elements in the deck. The first had its `title` attribute set to Enter, which corresponds to the text in the element's content. Similarly, the second anchor had its `title` attribute set to Links. Correlations like these between text and labels make your interface much friendlier for your users.

> *We also changed the "menu" card to link to our newly revised "links" URL. Forgetting to update links is a very common mistake, so be wary of this!*

When viewed, you can see that the Enter anchor has not changed – there are still square brackets around the text, and the solid triangle indicates that it is the currently selected hyperlink. What *has* changed is that one of the device's buttons has been relabeled with the selected `<a>` element's `title` attribute value:

In Step 5, you can see that the links anchor in the "menu" card has been similarly labeled.

The `<a>` Element's accesskey Attribute

The `<a>` element's third and final 'non-common' attribute is the optional `accesskey`, which the WML specification does not require user agents to support. If the attribute *is* supported, it provides a neat additional way of activating a hyperlink: it allows the user to select an anchor by pressing a key on the keypad of the WAP-enabled device.

To see how this might work, we could modify our "links" card still further:

```wml
<wml>
    <card id="links" title="Links">
        <p>
            <a accesskey="1" href="http://www.pistoff.com/wap.wml"
                title="Report">3 Valleys WAP Snow Report</a>
        </p>
        <p>
            <a accesskey="2" href="ex6_2wrox.wml" title="Travel">Wrox Travel</a>
        </p>
    </card>
</wml>
```

With this change in place, viewing the card in the UP.Simulator results in the following display:

The numbers specified as values to the accesskey attribute have appeared to the left of the hyperlinks, and pressing those keys on the UP.Simulator's keypad will result in immediate navigation, without the need to make a selection in any other way. On a different type of device, the number and names of the values that can be specified will vary – that aspect of the implementation will *always* be device-specific – but the principle will remain the same.

accesskey provides a way to navigate quickly, particularly for frequent users of your site, who would likely become used to pressing a sequence of keys to reach their destination. As such, it's a useful facility to add to the user interface of your applications.

The <anchor> Element

You just learned that the <a> element is used to create anchors in WML. You'd be forgiven for wondering, then, what the <anchor> element is for. In fact, the situation isn't quite as crazy as it might appear, because (as its name suggests) the <a> element is actually a shorter, more specialized form of <anchor>.

<a> elements *only* allow you to create hyperlinks to other cards or decks, while an <anchor> element is a more generic tool, broadening the scope of what may happen when the user selects it. <anchor> elements allow *you* to specify what action should take place when they are selected, as you'll begin to see in Chapter 9. For now, though, we'll just examine how to use <anchor> to perform straightforward navigation.

The <anchor> element supports the same attributes – with the same semantics – as <a>, with the exception of href (in other words, the list is xml:lang, id, class, title, accesskey). The reason why <anchor> doesn't support href is that a more versatile mechanism is provided for this purpose, as implied above. The <anchor> element can be used together with elements called <go> and <prev> to specify a destination for the hyperlink.

The <go> Element

The <go> element is used to specify a navigation action that occurs as a result of an **event**. We'll have a lot more to say about events later, especially in Chapter 14, but for now you only need to understand that they provide a way of reacting to 'things that happen' in your WML code. It's possible, for example, to detect when hyperlinks are selected, or when cards are displayed, and to do something in response to those events. It's also possible to start a countdown timer, and to do something when that timer expires.

> *One application of such an event would be to display a 'welcome' screen when a card is first requested, start a timer, and show the actual card a second or two later when the timer runs down. You may have seen a technique like this being used to display advertising on commercial WAP sites.*

The <go> Element's href Attribute

In this section, as an introduction to events, we will explore how the <go> element can be used with anchors to provide the same functionality as <a>. The <go> element has a number of attributes, and in time we'll cover them all, but for now we'll just use the familiar-looking href.

When used with the <anchor> element to perform simple navigation, the <go> element has the following general form:

```
<anchor>
    content
    <go href="destination" />
</anchor>
```

Here, destination is a URL that specifies where the browser should navigate to when the anchor is activated (causing an event to occur). For example, we could rewrite our previous "splash" card to use the <anchor> element:

```
<card id="splash">
    <p align="center">Wrox Travel</p>
    <p mode="nowrap">Welcome to our WAP site!</p>
    <p align="center" mode="wrap">
        <anchor title="Enter">
            Enter
            <go href="#menu" />
        </anchor>
    </p>
</card>
```

In the example, we've substituted this:

```
<a href="#menu" title="Enter">Enter</a>
```

with the completely equivalent:

```
<anchor title="Enter">
   Enter
   <go href="#menu" />
</anchor>
```

In future chapters, we'll be looking at more complex use of the <anchor> and <go> elements, but we've already created a dilemma: when creating hyperlinks, should we <a> or <anchor>? In general, the answer is to use <a> rather than <anchor> and <go> when it's possible to do so: the former is shorter, easier to optimize, and easier to write!

The <prev> Element

A new piece of functionality offered to us by the <anchor> element is the ability to navigate to the previous card, in the manner of the Back button in a web browser such as Microsoft Internet Explorer or Netscape Navigator. To achieve this feat, you need to use the <prev> element.

In order to understand how <prev> works, you need to know about WML's **navigational history model**, which the specification states all user agents must implement. A 'history' of the cards visited by the user during a single browsing session is kept by modeling navigation as a '**stack**' of URLs. When the user visits a new card, that card's URL is '**pushed**' onto the stack. When the user goes 'back', the current card's URL is '**popped**' off the stack, and the previous card becomes the current card:

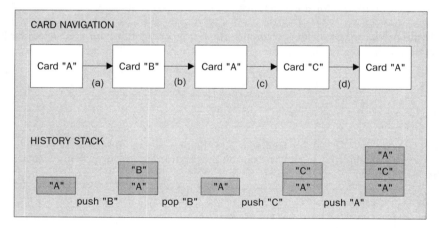

As illustrated in the figure above, if the user navigates from card "A" to card "B" (step a), the URL of the destination card is pushed onto the history stack. If the user then goes 'back' to the previous card (step b), the URL of the current card is popped off the history stack and discarded.

In step c, the user navigates to card "C", and its URL is pushed onto the history stack accordingly. In step d, the user navigates to card "A" using a link (rather than going 'back' to the previous card), and so its URL is pushed onto the stack for a second time, rather than popping that of the current card.

While we've been experimenting, you might have noticed that that the UP.Simulator has a dedicated **BACK** button, and in fact this works by providing direct access to the history stack. To see it in action, let's see what navigating back through the previous example would look like, starting with the browser pointing at the Pistoff.com home page:

Having entered this site, the user may wish to return to the Wrox Travel site without re-entering the URL. In this case, pressing the **BACK** button would once again present the user with the "links" page:

We can continue to navigate right the way back through the history stack, until we reach the very first card. When that has been done, selecting the **BACK** button will have no visible effect until we have built up a history again.

Navigation through history is useful functionality, and it's easy to see why the UP.Simulator has built-in support for it, but don't lose sight of the fact that it's a *non-standard* feature. The standard mechanism for moving to the previous element in the history stack is the `<prev>` element, as we'll demonstrate in the following example.

Try It Out — Going to the Previous Card

We're going to use an anchor containing a `<prev>` element to provide a means of navigating back from our "links" card in a way that doesn't rely on any non-standard features.

1. Open `ex6_2links.wml`, and make the following changes:

```
<wml>
    <card id="links" title="Links">
        <p>
            <a href="http://www.pistoff.com/wap.wml"
                title="Report">3 Valleys WAP Snow Report</a>
        </p>
        <p>
            <a href="ex6_3wrox.wml" title="Travel">Wrox Travel</a>
        </p>
        <p>
            <anchor>Back<prev/></anchor>
        </p>
    </card>
</wml>
```

2. Notice that we've changed the anchor to Wrox Travel to point at the new file
`ex6_3wrox.wml`, which we'll create in a moment. Save the file with the name
`ex6_3links.wml`.

3. Open `ex6_2wrox.wml` and make a single alteration to point the hyperlink back at the file we
created in Step 1. Save the file with the name `ex6_3wrox.wml`.

```
      <p>For more information,
          you can search the site, or follow our
          <a href="ex6_3links.wml" title="Links">links</a>,
          which include up to the minute weather reports.<br/><br/>
          If you have any queries don't hesitate to contact us!
      </p>
   </card>
</wml>
```

4. Load `ex6_3wrox.wml` into the UP.Simulator.

5. Selecting the links hyperlink as usual will result in the following screen:

6. Select the Back hyperlink to navigate to the previous card. You should see this:

How It Works

In Step 1, we added an `<anchor>` element:

```
              <anchor>Back<prev/></anchor>
          </p>
      </card>
```

This element contains some plain text (`Back`), and an empty `<prev>` element. What this means is that when the user activates the `<anchor>` element, the microbrowser will pop the URL of the current card off the history stack, and navigate to the previous card on the stack.

In Steps 5 and 6, you navigated to the "links" card and then returned to the previous card. If you were to watch how the history stack works, you would have seen the following:

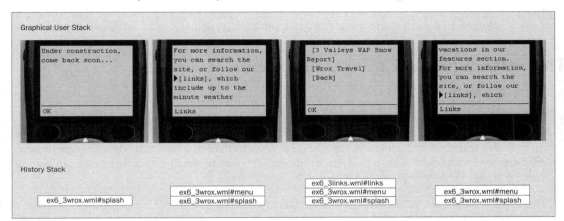

In the illustration above, we show the history stack at four points in time. At the first point (where t = 0), the user sees the "splash" card. The history stack contains the URL for that card (`ex6_3wrox.wml#splash`).

The user selects the Enter link (t = 1), and the microbrowser navigates to the "menu" card. Subsequently, the URL for the "menu" card (`ex6_3wrox.wml#menu`) is pushed onto the history stack.

When the user selects the links hyperlink, the microbrowser navigates to the "links" card, and its URL (`ex6_3links.wml#links`) is pushed onto the history stack.

In the final step, the user selects the Back link. The microbrowser pops the URL of the current card (`ex6_3links.wml#links`) from the history stack, and navigates to the new top URL in the history stack (`ex6_3wrox.wml#menu`).

The <do> Element

So far, you've learned how the `<a>` element is used for the simplest type of hyperlink – when you're linking to a named URL – and that the `<anchor>` element is more powerful, allowing you to link to a named URL, or back to a previous card. (That's not the limit of what `<anchor>` can do, but it's a start.) However, anchors of both types suffer from the same restrictions: they appear in the text flow, and they have a specific representation in the user interface (the text is underlined, or enclosed in brackets, or similar).

At first blush, that might not sound like a disadvantage, but there are a good many actions you might wish to offer your users that don't fit naturally in the flow of your text. Our Back hyperlink in the previous example was fine, but what if the card was longer? Would you really want people to have to scroll back and forth looking for the link? And how about providing a "help" page – at what position in the text would it be sensible to put that?

The <do> element provides a solution to these and other problems; it's a more general mechanism for canvassing and responding to a user action. Significantly, the representation of a <do> element is microbrowser dependent – you can't control *how* the element is presented to the user; you can only trust that the microbrowser will represent it in some way. That may involve a graphically rendered button, or a softkey, or voice operation, or anything else that need not be located in the flow of the text.

The <do> element's unique attributes are type, label, optional, and name. We'll be looking at name in Chapters 14 and 15, while the first three will be our topics for the remainder of this chapter.

The <do> Element's type and label Attributes

We've said that the user agent is in control of the way <do> elements are represented, but it's also true that it's sensible for different kinds of action to be presented to the user in different ways. The type attribute, which you must *always* specify when writing a <do> element, is used to provide a 'hint' to the microbrowser about the nature of the user action being defined. This hint may then be used by the user agent to determine how to represent the element. You can't enforce how this is done – one browser may offer a menu to represent a list of choices, while another may display buttons – but you can help to make sure that the user is presented with a sensible interface.

There are seven values for the type attribute that are defined in the WML specification, and that user agents are free to act upon or ignore, as they see fit:

Value	Definition
accept	Acknowledge or okay a piece information
prev	Navigate backwards in the history stack
help	Request help
reset	Clear the state of the card or deck
options	Request additional functions or actions
delete	Delete an item or choice
unknown or " "	A generic action

In addition to these seven types, there may be device-specific experimental and action types. If the browser does not recognize the type, it will treat it as though unknown was specified, which should protect other browsers from device-specific values. The examples later in this chapter will demonstrate the use of most of the predefined types, and we'll see the others as they become appropriate.

The label attribute has similar functionality to the anchor elements' title attribute: the microbrowser may use it to indicate the intention of the action to the user. As implied by the above discussion, the user agent uses the type attribute value to determine where, and how, to display the label attribute value. Once again, the WML specification recommends that you keep your labels to six characters or fewer, for the same reasons of interoperability.

Try It Out — Using the <do> Element

We're going to begin our demonstration of using the <do> element by adding a new feature to the Wrox Travel application: the ability to navigate between cards without relying on device-specific buttons, or hyperlinks in the text. At the same time, we'll add a brand new card, and tidy up our filenames a little.

1. Run your text editor, type in the following, and save it with the name `search.wml`:

```
<?xml version="1.0"?>
<!DOCTYPE wml PUBLIC "-//WAPFORUM//DTD WML 1.2//EN"
                     "http://www.wapforum.org/DTD/wml_1.2.xml">

<wml>
   <card id="search" title="Search">
      <p>
         Under construction, come back soon...
      </p>
      <do type="prev" label="Back">
         <prev/>
      </do>
   </card>
</wml>
```

2. Open `ex6_3links.wml`, make the following changes, and save it as `links.wml`:

```
<wml>
   <card id="links" title="Links">
      <p>
         <a href="http://www.pistoff.com/wap.wml"
            title="Report">3 Valleys WAP Snow Report</a>
      </p>
      <p>
         <a href="ex6_4wrox.wml" title="Travel">Wrox Travel</a>
      </p>
      <p>
         <anchor>Back<prev/></anchor>
      </p>
      <do type="prev" label="Back">
         <prev/>
      </do>
   </card>
</wml>
```

3. Open `ex6_3wrox.wml`, amend it as follows, and save as `ex6_4wrox.wml`:

```
<wml>
   <card id="splash">
      <p align="center">Wrox Travel</p>
      <p mode="nowrap">Welcome to our WAP site!</p>
      <p align="center" mode="wrap">
         <a href="#menu" title="Enter">Enter</a>
      </p>
```

```
      <do type="accept" label="Enter">
        <go href="#menu"/>
      </do>
    </card>
    <card id="menu" title="Wrox Travel">
      <p>Check out our new unbeatable offers,
        our full vacation listings,
        and our competitive vacation insurance scheme.<br/>
        You can also read reviews of our vacations in
        our features section.
      </p>
      <p>For more information, you can
        <a href="search.wml" title="Search">search</a>
        the site, or follow our
        <a href="links.wml" title="Links">links</a>,
        which include up to the minute weather reports.<br/><br/>
        If you have any queries don't hesitate to contact us!
      </p>
      <do type="accept" label="Search">
        <go href="search.wml"/>
      </do>
      <do type="accept" label="Links">
        <go href="links.wml"/>
      </do>
    </card>
  </wml>
```

4. Now let's walk through the new options we've added to our application and see how they're presented to the user. Running ex6_4wrox.wml in the UP.Simulator should result in the following, familiar-looking screen:

Look a little more closely, though, and you'll see that the Enter caption now appears above the left softkey, regardless of which line is currently selected in the display.

5. Select the left button or activate the Enter link to go to the "menu" card. Here's what you'll see:

This time, the new features to note are the words Search and Links, which appear at the bottom of the display above the left and right softkeys respectively. This is in addition to their appearance as anchors in the text.

6. Select the button located below the Search label to navigate to the "search" card. Unfortunately, as you probably suspected, it is currently under construction and there's nothing more we can do for now. We can recover from this by pressing either the BACK button, or the softkey labeled OK.

7. Once you're back to the "menu" card, select the Links button and navigate to the "links" card. After a moment or two, you should see our usual menu:

When none of the links is chosen, the left hand softkey will show OK, and selecting it will navigate back to the previous card. Alternatively, of course, we can still use the Back link provided by the <anchor> element.

8. There's just one more thing to see before we examine how all this works. When you return to the "menu" card (however you choose to get there), scroll down until you see the links hyperlink. With the cursor on that line, you'll see that the left and right softkeys are *both* labeled Links:

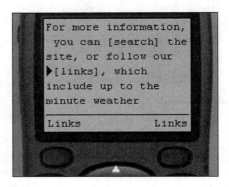

How It Works

In Step 1, you created a very simple deck that will serve as the basis for a means of searching our site. Of particular interest right now, though, is our usage of the <do> element:

```
<card id="search" title="Search">
   <p>
      Under construction, come back soon...
   </p>
   <do type="prev" label="Back">
      <prev/>
   </do>
</card>
```

We've set the <do> element's type attribute to prev, indicating to the user agent that the action associated with this element is related to navigating backwards in the history stack. The enclosed <prev> element clearly does just that! Furthermore, the <do> element's label attribute value is set to Back, meaning that *if* the microbrowser represents this action graphically, it *may* wish to use the label Back.

Unfortunately, you won't see this prev-type <do> element having any effect in the UP.Simulator. As we said when we introduced the type attribute, user agents are not compelled to act upon the "hints" you provide, and the UP.Simulator chooses to ignore the prev type completely!

In this case, the consequences aren't too bad because the UP.Simulator's default behavior in response to pressing the left softkey is to go back to the previous card – you may have seen this happening while experimenting with earlier examples. That's why, when you select the OK button, you go back to the "menu" card.

In Chapter 17, we'll be looking at some user agents that do take action in response to prev-type <do> elements.

In Step 3, you made some changes to the "splash" card and the "menu" card. Let's look at the "splash" card first:

```
<card id="splash">
  <p align="center">Wrox Travel</p>
  <p mode="nowrap">Welcome to our WAP site!</p>
  <p align="center" mode="wrap">
    <a href="#menu" title="Enter">Enter</a>
  </p>
  <do type="accept" label="Enter">
    <go href="#menu"/>
  </do>
</card>
```

We added a <do> element with the type attribute value set to accept, and the label set to Enter, so that it visually corresponds to the only link on the card. The <do> element contains a <go> element that links this task to the "menu" card.

> **If there is only one link on the card, it's usually a good idea to create an accept task that corresponds to that link. That way, the user does not have to scroll down to the link in order to select it. In addition, many users will assume this behavior anyway.**

We also made some changes to the "menu" card. We added a link to the "search" card:

```
<a href="search.wml" title="Search">search</a>
```

We updated the link to the "links" card:

```
<a href="links.wml" title="Links">links</a>,
```

And more importantly, we added two <do> elements:

```
<do type="accept" label="Search">
  <go href="search.wml"/>
</do>
<do type="accept" label="Links">
  <go href="links.wml"/>
</do>
```

Both of these <do> elements are accept types too: the first links to the "search" card, and the second to the "links" card. But was that an appropriate choice? Not including unknown, there are six possible types for the <do> element, and selecting the right one to use in a particular situation is often something of a compromise.

Have a look at the options available to us: accept represents the acceptance of a choice, or the recognition of a piece of information, which seems to fit. prev is clearly not appropriate, and neither is help – that would normally involve cards that give information about the site, or some similar details. We can eliminate reset and delete at face value, but it's not so easy to dismiss options – after all, couldn't the links on a card be considered as a set of options for the user? We'll see in the next section how that might pan out.

In Step 4, you ran the deck on the UP.Simulator. As we observed then, the Enter caption now appears above the left softkey permanently; this is the result of the <do> element being added to the "splash" card:

```
<do type="accept" label="Enter">
  <go href="#menu"/>
</do>
```

The accept-type <do> element has dissociated the act of entering the site from the rest of the text in this card, as we discussed at the very beginning of this section. The UP.Simulator uses the left button as the interface to the accept task, and will display the label for the task above that button. Other user agents are free to represent this task in other ways.

In Step 5, you navigated to the "menu" card, which contains *two* accept tasks labeled Search and Links. The UP.Simulator's behavior was to display the first label above the left button, and the second above the right button. This worked fine right until you reached Step 8, at which point the default action of selecting the links hyperlink replaced the accept-type <do> element on the left button, producing two rather unpleasant results. First, the user faces the confusing choice of two apparently identical options, and second, our efforts to provide an easy way of choosing to search are undone.

> **In order to avoid clumsy phrases like "accept-type <do> element", it's common to see these operations referred to as tasks. In other words, we talk about "accept tasks", "prev tasks", "options tasks", and so forth.**

Defining Multiple Tasks

The previous exercise illustrated how the accept task can be used to provide a default action when the user selects the OK button (or whatever acknowledgement mechanism the device uses). We also showed what happens on the UP.Simulator if you create multiple tasks of the same task type.

It's true the problems we observed are artifacts of the UP.Simulator, and may not be duplicated on other user agents, but the fact that they happen at all is another reason to experiment with an options-type <do> element, rather than the accept-types we've been using until now. Doing this makes it clear that the task is just one of several tasks that can be performed on the card, and hints that they can be grouped into a menu. The syntax of an options task looks like this:

```
<do type="options" label="name">
  content
</do>
```

As a rule, we recommend that you use accept tasks only to identify a default action; options can then be provided to identify additional features or functions on the card. This means that the user has a short path through the application in normal situations, while for additional functionality they need only inspect the menu of options. Separating navigational or other choices from the content also allows an experienced user to navigate to a service rapidly.

Try It Out — Creating options Tasks

Let's change our "menu" card to use `options` tasks rather than `accept` tasks, using the technique outlined above.

1. Modify `ex6_4wrox.wml` in the following way, and save it as `ex6_5wrox.wml`:

```
<card id="menu" title="Wrox Travel">

    <!-- Paragraphs omitted for brevity -->

    <do type="options" label="Search">
        <go href="search.wml"/>
    </do>
    <do type="options" label="Links">
        <go href="links.wml"/>
    </do>
    <do type="options" label="Wrox Menu">
        <go href="#menu"/>
    </do>
</card>
```

2. Run `ex6_5wrox.wml` in the UP.Simulator. You should see something like this:

3. Select the Menu button to display the list of optional tasks:

How It Works

We've changed the type of task from `accept` to `options`, and added a third option to return to the menu. This should mean that microbrowsers lacking a back button can still allow users to change their minds. Users that feel trapped into choices, unable to retrace their steps, are unlikely to persevere with your site for very long.

```
<do type="options" label="Search">
    <go href="search.wml"/>
</do>
<do type="options" label="Links">
    <go href="links.wml"/>
</do>
```

When you display the deck in the microbrowser, you can see that a Menu label appears above the right button, and that selecting it displays a list containing the options. Remember again, though, that just because the UP.Simulator creates a menu, it doesn't mean that all browsers will do the same. Is this warning starting to sound familiar?

Every decision we make regarding the structure of a site can affect its usability significantly. Because the WML specification allows so much flexibility in the way user agents should behave (and also because not all user agents implement the specification correctly), we will always need to make compromises in the design of our applications. Don't be discouraged: use the specification as your guide for now, and in Chapter 17 we'll say more about some particular limitations, and what you can do about them.

The <do> Element's optional Attribute

We have talked a lot about how the <do> element's `type` and `label` attributes provide presentational hints to the microbrowser, but we haven't addressed a more implicit assumption: that the browser should display the task to the user at all!

By default, unless it doesn't recognize the type, a user agent must present the task. However, if you specify the <do> element's `optional` attribute and set it to `true`, the microbrowser is free to ignore the element at its discretion. This could be useful (for example) if there is something about the content of the <do> element that is device-specific, or if the user interface would become too cluttered were the task to be represented.

Summary

In this chapter, you learned that hyperlinks are as fundamental to interactive WML applications as they are to interactive web applications. In examples, we created absolute hyperlinks that used the complete URL for a deck, as well as relative hyperlinks that resolved the name of a deck based on the current context.

You also learned how to use several different elements for linking between two cards, be they in the same deck, or in different decks:

❑ The <a> element is easy to use, and perfect for most of the hyperlinks you will ever create.

❑ The <anchor> element is slightly more expressive than the <a> element, providing you with a means of navigating to the previous card (via the <prev> element), as well as to any other card (via the <go> element).

❑ The <do> element is the most powerful of the three. It allows you to create links to other cards that are assigned to the user interface in a device-dependent manner.

In the next chapter, we'll continue our tour of WML's support for presenting information to the user by examining how to enliven our decks through the inclusion of images.

Displaying Images

In our exploration of WML so far, we've looked at how to add text to our cards, how to format text to our liking, and how to link our cards and decks together to form interactive applications. While examining these subjects, we haven't exactly courted controversy: the WML specification may allow for some differences in presentation, but there's no doubt that the content has to be displayed *somehow* – there wouldn't be much of an application if it weren't.

Images are another matter entirely. Because of the typical display size restrictions of WAP-enabled devices, and the comparatively large time it takes to transfer images to a mobile device, there is a school of thought that says images are *never* desirable in WML applications. However, the authors of the WML specification have gone to some considerable length to provide basic image support with the smallest possible impact on download times, and it's those efforts that we'll analyze in this chapter. By the end, you'll have enough information to decide whether and to what degree your applications should use images.

Specifically, we will cover the following:

❑ How to create images for display on WAP-enabled devices

❑ Basic image support through the <img> element

❑ Stipulating alternative representations for images

❑ Using microbrowsers' built-in images

❑ Aligning and resizing images

The Wireless Problem

The current WML specification supports a very limited set of facilities for displaying graphics on the user agent. Unlike the traditional web/PC environment, the WAP environment places some pretty tight constraints on the display of non-textual content:

❑ Due to their limited bandwidth, wireless networks can be relatively slow, making transmission of large images a tedious process.

❑   Not all devices have displays that support images, making it difficult to develop code that works across the board. In addition, it is impossible to 'draw' graphics in the client – images to be displayed on the client must have been created beforehand.

❑   Current devices have limited mathematical capability, making it impractical to display compressed images – there isn't enough processing power to uncompress them in reasonable time.

In response, the WAP Forum developed an optimized image format that would fill the gap created by wireless devices: the **wireless bitmap** (WBMP). The Wireless Application Environment (WAE) specification states that if a WAP-enabled device supports display of graphical images, it must at the very least support basic WBMP images.

What are Bitmaps?

The images displayed on digital devices are made up of small dots called **pixels** (it's an abbreviation of "picture elements"). Broadly speaking, there are two ways of representing the collection of pixels that go together to create an image: bitmaps, and vector graphics. The difference between the two is that while bitmaps contain information about every pixel in the image, vector graphics use mathematical equations that describe how to redraw the image. To understand how this might work, take a look at the line below:

This line is fourteen 'pixels' long. A bitmap representation would contain information about the color and position of all of these pixels, whereas a vector representation would contain the information for the first and last pixels only, plus an indication of how to get from one to the other (a straight line in this case, but it could be a curve). The vector format offers the potential for representing the image in less data, at the cost of higher processing requirements. However, because WAP-enabled devices are in general less able than desktop computers in this respect, there is no support in the WAP specifications for vector graphics.

Once we've elected to use bitmaps, another option presents itself: it's possible to reduce the amount of space required to represent an image by expressing the data in a more compact way. To describe the same line, you could say, "Black pixel, black pixel, black pixel..." a total of fourteen times – or you could just say, "Fourteen black pixels." Out in the real world, there are popular techniques for compressing image representations in several different ways (files whose names end with the extensions .gif, .png, and .jpg, for example, contain compressed images of various kinds), but what they have in common is that they require an encoding process to transform them from the original to the 'reduced' form, and a decoding process before they can be displayed. It's the latter that presents a problem for mobile devices, and once again, it's a question of processing power. The WAP specifications do not require microbrowsers to support compressed image formats, and therefore the WBMP format does not involve compression.

As a slightly more sophisticated example of a bitmap, take this logo that we've created for our Wrox Travel sample application. It's made up of a grid of size 16x12 pixels, some of which we intend to be colored black, and others of which we'd like to retain the background color of whatever screen it's displayed on:

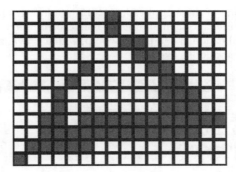

One way of storing this information in a file would be to represent the 'white' pixels with "0", and the 'black' pixels with "1". The data in such a file would then look something like this:

```
0 0 0 0 0 0 0 1 0 0 0 0 0 0 0 0
0 0 0 0 0 0 0 1 0 0 0 0 0 0 0 0
0 0 0 0 0 0 0 0 1 1 0 0 0 0 0 0
0 0 0 0 0 0 0 0 1 1 0 0 0 0 0 0
0 0 0 0 0 1 0 0 0 0 1 1 0 0 0 0
0 0 0 0 1 0 0 0 0 0 0 1 1 0 0 0
0 0 0 1 0 0 0 0 0 0 0 1 1 1 0 0
0 0 0 1 0 0 0 0 0 0 0 1 1 1 0 0
0 0 1 1 0 1 1 1 1 1 1 1 1 1 1 1
0 0 1 1 1 1 1 1 1 1 1 1 1 1 0 0
0 1 1 1 1 1 0 0 0 0 0 0 0 0 0 0
1 0 0 0 0 0 0 0 0 0 0 0 0 0 0 0
```

Note that we've broken this 'file' into lines simply to demonstrate the correlation with the original image. In a real file, the ones and zeros would appear in continuous sequence; provided that the file also contains an indication of the dimensions of the image, it's a simple matter for the user agent to present it in the manner required.

So: WBMP is a bitmap format, which implies that images are simple to display, but they're not as compact as they could be. The final feature of WBMP to consider (in the current version of the specification, at least) is that it's a monochrome format. Pixels can *only* be black or white, so there's no need for any additional information about color. This is a significant saving; it means that files containing images only ever have to contain information like that in the example above. Add in the fact that the small size of typical microbrowser displays places a practical limit on the dimensions of any image, and you should be able to see that WBMP files are unlikely to be very large. Just don't use too many of them at once!

Creating WBMP Files

At the time of writing, there are few tools available with built in support for creating WBMP images, but 'plug-ins' for existing applications are beginning to appear, and it's likely that future versions will include this functionality out-of-the-box. Right now, if you have Adobe Photoshop or JASC's Paintshop Pro, you can download a plug-in from www.rcp.co.uk/distributed/downloads that enables you to create WBMP files using those packages, with no additional fuss. In fact, that's the method we used for creating the images in our examples.

If you don't have access to one of these applications, all is not lost. It's possible to use a basic tool like MS Paint to create a "BMP" file, and then another to convert from that format to WBMP. One such tool that we've tried is a Java application called pic_2_wbmp, which is available from http://www.gingco.de/wap/, and looks like this:

This tool allows you to browse BMP files (in fact, it handles a number of formats), and then save them in WBMP format. The Nokia toolkit also features a tool that allows creation of WBMPs.

Displaying Images with the <img> Element

By one means or another, you've created an image and stored it in WBMP format, but how do you persuade a user agent to display it? The answer is that images are added to *paragraphs* using the <img> element:

```
<img src="url" alt="text" />
```

Like the <br> element, an <img> element is always empty, but unlike <br> it has a couple of attributes that you must always supply. Let's see why they're so important.

The <img> Element's src Attribute

The <img> element's src attribute specifies the URL of the image to be loaded. However, you need to be aware that while the WML specification says that microbrowsers must recognize and act upon <img> elements, they *don't* have to display the images identified in attributes – that would be to place too tight a restriction on user agents. If they choose, microbrowsers can use alternative representations, as we'll discuss shortly.

If the microbrowser supports images, it will download the image from the specified address, and render the image when the element containing it is displayed. For example, if the current deck is located at http://www.wrox.com/begwap/, and we have an image stored at the same location, we could simply refer to it in our WML code as follows:

```
<img src="myimage.wbmp" alt="my image"/>
```

We could also use the absolute address http://www.wrox.com/begwap/myimage.wbmp, but in general you should try to use relative URLs, since they make it easier to move your decks and their associated resources around. They also reduce the size of your compiled WML code!

The <img> Element's alt Attribute

The <img> element's alt attribute specifies a string that should be displayed by the microbrowser if it cannot display the image specified by the src attribute. This attribute is very important, because the alternative description it provides may be used if the device does not support images, *or* if the image resource cannot be found (that is, the image is not where the src attribute says it is).

Try it Out — Adding an Image to a Card

Let's improve the appearance of our Wrox Travel application a little by adding a small image to the top of our "splash" card.

1. Copy ex6_5wrox.wml from the previous chapter, amend it like this, and save it as ex7_1.wml:

```
<wml>
   <card id="splash">
      <p align="center">
         <img src="WTLogo.wbmp" alt="Wrox"/><br/>
      </p>
      <p align="center">Wrox Travel</p>
      <p mode="nowrap">Welcome to our WAP site!</p>
      <p align="center" mode="wrap">
         <a href="#menu" title="Enter">Enter</a>
      </p>
      <do type="accept" label="Enter">
         <go href="#menu"/>
      </do>
   </card>

   <!-- Rest of file omitted for brevity -->

</wml>
```

2. Copy the bitmap file WTLogo.wbmp from the archive on the Wrox web site to the same directory as your ex7_1.wml file.

3. Load the file into the UP.Simulator, and you should see the following:

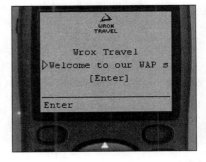

Note that this is our first example of code that will behave differently depending on whether we simply load the file into the UP.Simulator, or view it via a web server. In the former case, the image will not be displayed, and instead you'll see the value of the `alt` attribute, as described below.

How It Works

We have added an image to the "splash" card by inserting a `<p>` element containing an `<img>` element:

```
<p align="center">
   <img src="WTLogo.wbmp" alt="Wrox"/><br/>
</p>
```

This works exactly according to the guidelines for the `<img>` element we set out above. By setting the `src` attribute to `WTLogo.wbmp`, we instructed the microbrowser to search for (and find) the image in the same directory as the WML file. Setting the `alt` attribute to `Wrox` means that if the image cannot be displayed (for whatever reason), the microbrowser will display this value instead.

Predefined Images

In addition to the ability to load external images, as we did in the example above, WML provides a means of accessing and displaying *predefined* images that are stored permanently on the local device. The idea behind such a facility is that often-used images can be used by many applications without incurring the penalty of longer deck download times.

> Before we go any further, note that predefined images are highly device specific. Some devices will support them, some won't — and the way you get access to them is likely to vary too. You'll need to consult manufacturers' documentation to find out the state of play for a particular device.
>
> Because of this, you certainly can't count on client devices supporting any particular image. Fortunately, the WML specification has been designed to take factors like this into account.

You select a predefined image by using the `<img>` element's optional `localsrc` attribute, specifying an internal image. The behavior of the user agent is then to use the internal representation *if it is available*. On failure, the image at the location specified by the `src` attribute is downloaded instead.

For example, if we knew that some devices on which our card will be displayed support a 'traffic signal' icon, we could use the following element in our code:

```
<img localsrc="trafficsignal" src="trafficsignal.wbmp" alt="traffic signal" />
```

The `<img>` element specifies that if a local `trafficsignal` image is not available, the microbrowser should use the resource identified by the `src` attribute instead. If neither of these resources can be used, the microbrowser should display the alternative text specified by the `alt` attribute.

Try It Out — Using Predefined Icons

The UP.Simulator supports a total of 165 predefined images, all of which are listed in the documentation that comes with the UP.SDK. In this example, we'll use just one of them at the top of the "splash" card, in place of the icon we used in the last section.

1. Copy `ex7_1.wml`, make the following minor change, and save the new file as `ex7_2.wml`:

```
<wml>
    <card id="splash">
        <p align="center">
            <img localsrc="plane" src="WTLogo.wbmp" alt="Wrox"/><br/>
        </p>
        <p align="center">Wrox Travel</p>
        <p mode="nowrap">Welcome to our WAP site!</p>
        <p align="center" mode="wrap">
            <a href="#menu" title="Enter">Enter</a>
        </p>
        <do type="accept" label="Enter">
            <go href="#menu"/>
        </do>
    </card>

    <!-- Rest of file omitted for brevity -->

</wml>
```

2. Load `ex7_2.wml` into the UP.Simulator and wait for the result:

How It Works

Again, this example behaves as we hoped it would. By adding the `localsrc` attribute to the `<img>` element in Step 1:

```
<p align="center">
    <img localsrc="plane" src="WTLogo.wbmp" alt="Wrox"/><br/>
</p>
```

we requested that the user agent should use the `plane` icon, if it is available on the device. Displaying the deck in the UP.Simulator resulted in the appearance of the icon, in preference to the resource specified by the `src` attribute.

Aligning Images with the align Attribute

Rather than simply placing an image somewhere within a paragraph and hoping for the best, WML allows developers some control over the position and size of an image, and the effect it has on any surrounding text. This is achieved through three further sets of optional attributes to the `<img>` element, the first of which we'll examine in this section.

The `<img>` element's `align` attribute is used to align images in the *vertical* plane, relative to the current line of text. The `align` attribute can have one of the following values: `top`, `middle`, or `bottom`.

Alignment	Description
`top`	The image will be placed on the underside of an imaginary line that runs through the top of the text.
`middle`	The middle of the image will be placed on an imaginary line that runs through the middle of the text.
`bottom`	The bottom of the image will be placed on the baseline of a line of text. This is the default value.

The following figure will give you a better idea of what *ought* to happen, but you should also know that the user agents available at the time of writing are notoriously inconsistent in the way they interpret `align`:

Try It Out — Aligning Images

Let's test how well the UP.Simulator copes with the `<img>` element's `align` attribute, through an example that checks each of the possible values in turn.

1. Type the following in your text editor and save it with the name `ex7_3.wml`. If you intend to use the same code to test other user agents, make sure that there is a copy of `WTLogo.wbmp` in the same directory.

```
<?xml version="1.0"?>
<!DOCTYPE wml PUBLIC "-//WAPFORUM//DTD WML 1.2//EN"
                     "http://www.wapforum.org/DTD/wml_1.2.xml">

<wml>
   <card id="align">
      <p>
         Top
         <img align="top"    localsrc="plane" src="WTLogo.wbmp" alt="Top" />
         Top
      </p>
```

```
        <p>
            Middle
            <img align="middle" localsrc="plane" src="WTLogo.wbmp" alt="Middle" />
            Middle
        </p>
        <p>
            Bottom
            <img align="bottom" localsrc="plane" src="WTLogo.wbmp" alt="Bottom" />
            Bottom
        </p>
        <p>
            Default
            <img localsrc="plane" src="WTLogo.wbmp" alt="Default" />
            Default
        </p>
    </card>
</wml>
```

2. Load `ex7_3.wml` into the UP.Simulator. You'll see something like this:

How It Works

We have created four paragraphs. In the first, second, and third, the image ought to be aligned according to one each of the three possible values for the `align` attribute. The image in the fourth depends on the default alignment, which *should* be the same as `bottom`.

Looking at the screenshot above, you will see that the UP.Simulator has fared pretty well in the first three cases. The `bottom`-aligned image is perhaps a little lower than it might be, but that's a fairly minor concern. However, comparing lines two, three, and four seems to indicate that the creators of this user agent implemented `middle` alignment to be the default setting, rather than `bottom`. You may agree or disagree with them, but this is a violation of the WML specification. It's probably best, therefore, to avoid relying on default settings for this attribute.

Specifying Image Size

At this stage, we enter once again into the realm of attributes that user agents are, according to the WML specification, free to ignore if they so choose. The `width` and `height` attributes of the `<img>` element can be used to tell the microbrowser what area of the display should be occupied by an image, and as such they have a helpful and a not-so-helpful purpose.

When you tell the microbrowser how wide and high an image is in this way, you're allowing it to reserve space on the screen, but to continue rendering the rest of the data while the image is loading. In the WAP environment, where any image represents a significant download, this can significantly improve the performance of an application. However, if you specify `width` and `height` values that are different from those of the *actual* image, the microbrowser will attempt to scale the image to fit the size you've specified. That might sound attractive at first, but it's the kind of operation that takes a long time on a typical WAP-enabled device, resulting in unacceptable delays for the user. We recommend that if you use these attributes, you should always be sure to set them to the same size as the original image. If you're not happy with the size of an image, deal with it in a graphics application on your PC.

These attributes are used in the fashion `width="x" height="y"`, where x and y are integers that give the image's width and height in pixels. We could have reserved space for our Wrox Travel logo by adding the following code to the previous examples:

```
<card id="splash">
    <p align="center">
        <img src="WTLogo.wbmp" alt="Wrox" width="31" height="27" /><br/>
    </p>

    <!-- Rest of card omitted for brevity -->

</card>
```

In a microbrowser that supports these attributes of the `<img>` element (the UP.Simulator is not such a user agent), this code will have the effect described above.

Setting the Space Around an Image

The final pair of attributes that we can apply to an `<img>` element are `hspace` and `vspace`, which can be used to specify a 'border' around an image into which nothing else in the display may encroach. (A likely use for this functionality would be to improve the readability of a card by keeping text away from images.) Once again, microbrowsers are free to ignore these attributes if they wish.

Where they *are* supported, `hspace` is used to set the amount of space to the left and right of the image, while `vspace` is used to set the amount of space at the top and bottom. The value given to either of these attributes can be the number of pixels to use, or a percentage of the available horizontal or vertical space. For example, if we wanted to set a five-pixel margin around our logo, we would write:

```
<card id="splash">
    <p align="center">
        <img src="WTLogo.wbmp" alt="Wrox" vspace="5" hspace="5" /><br/>
    </p>

    <!-- Rest of card omitted for brevity -->

</card>
```

On the other hand, if we wanted to set a margin around our logo of 10% of the total available screen space, we would write:

```
<card id="splash">
   <p align="center">
      <img src="WTLogo.wbmp" alt="Wrox" vspace="10%" hspace="10%" /><br/>
   </p>

   <!-- Rest of card omitted for brevity -->

</card>
```

The default setting for both the hspace and the vspace attribute is zero. If you decide to try out any of this code, you should note that the UP.Simulator only supports the hspace attribute – setting the vspace attribute will have no effect.

Using Images

Before we leave this chapter, we'll return to a couple of issues that were raised right at the beginning: how best (and whether) to use images, and how to cater for the considerable leeway allowed by the WML specification with regard to image support.

In short, you should only use images when they make sense. Don't waste downloading time if there is no benefit of the image to the user – and using just one or two meaningful images is likely to be a more successful tactic than brandishing them left, right, and center. If you always set the <img> element's alt attribute to an intelligent value, you will ensure that *all* users will be happy with the displays they see.

Next, keep your images small. Most WAP-enabled devices have small displays, and if you fill them up with images, it will not always be clear to the user that there is more text below the screen.

Finally, stay away from fancy positioning: display your images as simply as you possibly can. It's a good idea to avoid having graphics and text on the same line, and then to put the text *above* the graphic. Since an image may fill up the screen, the user may not realize that there is more text below the image.

Summary

In this chapter, you learned the fundamentals of displaying images using WML. The mechanism for doing this is the <img> element, which allows us to include images in the WBMP format that was designed for precisely this purpose by the WAP Forum.

We explained that the <img> element has two mandatory attributes: src and alt. The src attribute identifies the resource containing the image, while alt provides alternate text that will be displayed if the image cannot be rendered. This is especially important because many WAP-enables devices do not have the capacity to display images. It is important to ensure that images are not vital to the functionality of your site, unless you can be sure that all of your users will be able to see them.

Some devices contain predefined images that come with a significant advantage: they don't need to be downloaded, so applications that use them suffer no performance penalty. You saw that images like these are specified using the localsrc attribute, provided of course that the microbrowser being used to view the card supports the images chosen. Because support for predefined images varies, you should be careful to use them advisedly.

Finally we discussed how the align, hspace, and vspace attributes can be used to position an image with respect to other elements on the display, and how the width and height attributes may be employed either to reserve some space for an image, or to resize it.

The overall picture is that well-chosen images are a powerful way to communicate information, but that it's impossible to guarantee support for them in all WML user agents. Use them with caution, make sure that you test your applications on as many different microbrowsers as you can find, and you should find that the ability to add images is a powerful tool for communicating using WML.

Tables

Our survey of WML's basic facilities for presenting information to the user comes to an end in this chapter, with an examination of its support for **tables**. As with so many of the other elements that are used to control the appearance of cards, the WML specification makes allowances for different user agents to render tables in different ways, and it's not hard to understand why. Tables can be an extremely useful way of laying out data, but they can also occupy a significant area – space that's likely to be a premium in the display of a WAP-enabled device. User agents need the freedom to display tables in a manner appropriate to the output facilities available.

Used with care, though, tables can be versatile tools for the WML developer, allowing quite precise control over layout, and interesting ways of presenting data. In this chapter, we will cover the following:

- ❏ Defining the structure of tabular data
- ❏ Labeling a table
- ❏ Aligning content inside a table
- ❏ Using tables for layout

Defining the Structure of a Table

The problem with a lot of data is that in the absence of context, it's difficult to interpret. Without prompting, it's tricky (for example) to see a relationship between every third number in a list, or to realize that each set of six numbers should be grouped together. Tables address situations like this by allowing us to arrange data in a collection of columns and rows, and by this means to highlight implicitly the relationships between groups of data. The technique works for applications as diverse as financial results and football leagues, and it's universally understood.

Tables would be worth having around if they were only useful for organizing data, but from the point of view of the WML developer, the row-and-column structure that they provide can be used to bring order to *any* data, related or not. Placing content in the regular, vertical columns of a table is an easier, more generic way of creating tidy output than, say, trying to align things by inserting extra spaces between them.

The <table> Element

Translating the above to our chosen medium, WML uses the <table> element to define a table as a whole, the <tr> element to define a row of data within a table, and the <td> element to define discrete data items within a row. A <table> element always appears inside a <p>, and it has a mandatory columns attribute that you must use to specify the number of data elements in each row:

```
<table columns="number">
   content
</table>
```

In WML, it is compulsory to specify the number of columns in a table right at the start; this helps the user agent to begin formatting the table straight away, without waiting to count the <td> elements that will come later on. number must always be a nonzero value, and if you try to exceed it by using too many <td> elements in your code, the microbrowser is obliged to aggregate the data in all surplus columns into the last column.

The <tr> and <td> Elements

You define a table's content by using the <tr> element to define each row ("tr" stands for table row). Unlike columns, we don't need to pre-specify the number of rows – you simply have to add a <tr></tr> tag pair for each row you require. A two-row table would therefore have the following structure:

```
<table columns="number">
   <tr>
      row 1 content
   </tr>
   <tr>
      row 2 content
   </tr>
</table>
```

To define the content of a row, you use the <td> element to contain each cell of data ("td" stands for table data). We've already explained what happens if you try to specify too many <td> elements, but WML is more forgiving if you supply too few: the row will be padded with empty columns. Adding three columns to our existing two-row table would require code like this:

```
<table columns="3">
   <tr>
      <td>row 1 column 1 content</td>
      <td>row 1 column 2 content</td>
      <td>row 1 column 3 content</td>
   </tr>
   <tr>
      <td>row 2 column 1 content</td>
      <td>row 2 column 2 content</td>
      <td>row 2 column 3 content</td>
   </tr>
</table>
```

`<td>` elements can contain images, text, and anchors, but they *can't* contain further `<table>` elements. Such so-called "nesting" of tables is *not* permitted by the WML specification.

Try It Out — Creating a Basic Table

Let's add to our burgeoning Wrox Travel application by adding a card that gives details of the "competitive vacation insurance scheme" in tabular format.

1. Run your text editor, enter the following, and save the file as `insure.wml`:

```
<?xml version="1.0"?>
<!DOCTYPE wml PUBLIC "-//WAPFORUM//DTD WML 1.2//EN"
                     "http://www.wapforum.org/DTD/wml_1.2.xml">

<wml>
    <card id="insurance" title="Insurance Offers">
        <p>Wrox Travel is pleased to be able to
            offer you the following insurance deals:
            <br/>
            <table columns="3">
                <tr>
                    <td>Type</td>
                    <td>Month</td>
                    <td>Year</td>
                </tr>
                <tr>
                    <td>Basic</td>
                    <td>$$20</td>
                    <td>$$100</td>
                </tr>
                <tr>
                    <td>Sports</td>
                    <td>$$30</td>
                    <td>$$150</td>
                </tr>
            </table>
        </p>
        <p>Contact us for more details, at:<br/>
            Insurance@WroxTravel.com
        </p>
        <do type="prev" label="Back">
            <prev/>
        </do>
    </card>
</wml>
```

You'll notice that where we've specified prices, we've used double dollar symbols ($$). This is because the dollar symbol is another of the reserved characters we first encountered back in Chapter 5, and doubling it is the way to make it display normally. We'll discuss why the symbol is reserved, and why this fix works, in the next chapter.

2. Open `ex7_2.wml` from the last chapter, make the following changes, and save as `ex8_1.wml`:

```
<card id="menu" title="Wrox Travel">
    <p>Check out our new unbeatable offers,
        our full vacation listings,
        and our competitive vacation
        <a href="insure.wml" title="Insure">insurance</a> scheme.<br/>
        You can also read reviews of our vacations in
        our features section.
    </p>
    <p>For more information, you can
        <a href="search.wml" title="Search">search</a>
        the site, or follow our
        <a href="links.wml" title="Links">links</a>,
        which include up to the minute weather reports.<br/><br/>
        If you have any queries don't hesitate to contact us!
    </p>
    <do type="options" label="Insure">
        <go href="insure.wml"/>
    </do>
    <do type="options" label="Search">
        <go href="search.wml"/>
    </do>
    <do type="options" label="Links">
        <go href="links.wml"/>
    </do>
    <do type="options" label="Wrox Menu">
        <go href="#menu"/>
    </do>
</card>
```

3. Run `ex8_1.wml` in the UP.Simulator. Select the Enter hyperlink and navigate to the "menu" card.

4. Select the insurance hyperlink and navigate to the "insurance" card. You should see something like this:

5. Finally, scroll down the "insurance" card until you see the table:

How It Works

We first create a basic table by putting a `<table>` element inside a `<p>` element. This table has three columns, as defined by the `<table>` element's `columns` attribute:

```
<table columns="3">
    <tr>
        <td>Type</td>
        <td>Month</td>


    ...
```

Looking at the `<table>` element more closely, you can see that there are three rows. Each row is identified by the `<tr>` elements whose start and end tags we have highlighted below:

```
<table columns="3">
  <tr>
      <td>Type</td>
      <td>Month</td>
      <td>Year</td>
  </tr>
  <tr>
      <td>Basic</td>
      <td>$$20</td>
      <td>$$100</td>
  </tr>
  <tr>
      <td>Sports</td>
      <td>$$30</td>
      <td>$$150</td>
  </tr>
</table>
```

Each of these rows contains three cells, defined by `<td>` elements. As is often the case, the first row contains the headings for the table's columns, while the other rows contain the data for the table.

137

The screenshot above demonstrates that the UP.Simulator makes a pretty good fist of displaying the table in a 'traditional' manner – its appearance is probably more or less what you were expecting. However, we've chosen our data pretty carefully; look what happens when we add a fourth column to the table:

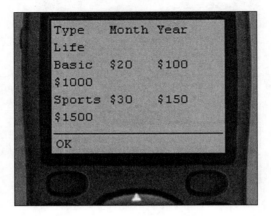

You'll probably agree that this is less impressive, and it's just another example of the care that needs to be taken whenever you create a WML application. Some microbrowsers might handle this situation better, and there are others that would have displayed our table quite differently in the first place – and they can do so while remaining compliant with the WML specification! We'll be looking at issues just like these when we consider usability and interoperability in Chapters 16 and 17.

Labeling a Table

You can label your tables using the <table> element's optional title attribute:

```
<table columns="number" title="label">
    content
</table>
```

The microbrowser *may* then use the value of the <table> element's title attribute when presenting the table – but the WML specification doesn't compel it to do so, and says nothing about how a title should appear. As usual, this means that you should refrain from using the title attribute to present critical information to the user.

Aligning Text Inside a Table

The <table> element's final optional attribute, align, can be used to set the alignment of the content in each of the columns in a table:

```
<table columns="number" align="alignment">
    content
</table>
```

The value of the `align` attribute should be a non-separated list of specifiers, one for each column of the table. Valid specifiers are `L`, `C`, `R`, and `D`, for left, center, right, and default alignment respectively. To set all three columns of our table to right alignment, for example, you'd use `align="RRR"`. If you don't provide a value for the `align` attribute, content is automatically left aligned (the default setting).

Tables Containing Images

As we mentioned earlier, WML tables are not restricted to displaying text; they can contain images and anchors too. Using tables to help with the positioning of images, in particular, is a good way of creating a clear user interface, as you'll see.

Along with demonstrating the things we've been discussing so far, the next two examples will involve the creation of several new cards for our Wrox Travel application, ready for plenty of functionality to be added in the forthcoming chapters. In particular, we'll be inserting descriptions of a couple of vacations, which will feature icons of the kind you often see in travel brochures – they indicate things like whether a vacation is suitable for families, and what recreational facilities are available.

Try It Out — Using Tables to Lay Out Images

The deck we'll create right now will contain a card bearing explanations of these 'vacation feature' icons, on the presumption that it will be possible to navigate to it from any vacation description card. As you'll soon see, this kind of information is ripe for tabular display.

1. Create a file called `ex8_2.wml`, containing the following code:

```
<?xml version="1.0"?>
<!DOCTYPE wml PUBLIC "-//WAPFORUM//DTD WML 1.2//EN"
                     "http://www.wapforum.org/DTD/wml_1.2.xml">

<wml>
   <card id="icons" title="Icon Explanation">
      <p>
         <img src="cat01.wbmp" localsrc="snowflake" alt="Wintersports" />
         Winter sports<br/>
         <img src="cat02.wbmp" localsrc="sparkle" alt="Sun" />
         Sun<br/>
         <img src="cat03.wbmp" localsrc="plus" alt="Accessible" />
         Accessible<br/>
         <img src="cat04.wbmp" localsrc="family" alt="Kids" />
         Kids<br/>
         <img src="cat05.wbmp" localsrc="baseball" alt="Water" />
         Watersports<br/>
         <img src="cat06.wbmp" localsrc="bolt" alt="Adventure" />
         Adventure<br/>
      </p>

      <!-- Only one action for this card, so use an 'accept'
           task to make the 'Back' option explicit -->
      <do type="accept" label="Back">
         <prev/>
      </do>
   </card>
</wml>
```

2. Make sure that the fourteen bitmap files cat01.wbmp thru cat14.wbmp, which are included in the code download from the Wrox web site, are present in the same location as the above file.

3. Run `ex8_2.wml` in the UP.Simulator:

4. It's not bad, but we can do better − that fourth line isn't all it could be. We'll amend the file slightly to use a table for presentation, and save it back as `icons.wml`:

```
<card id="icons" title="Icon Explanation">
    <p>
       <table columns="2" title="Icons">
          <tr>
             <td>
                <img src="cat01.wbmp" localsrc="snowflake" alt="Wintersports" />
             </td>
             <td>Winter sports</td>
          </tr>
          <tr>
             <td>
                <img src="cat02.wbmp" localsrc="sparkle" alt="Sun" />
             </td>
             <td>Sun</td>
          </tr>
          <tr>
             <td>
                <img src="cat03.wbmp" localsrc="plus" alt="Accessible" />
             </td>
             <td>Accessible</td>
          </tr>
          <tr>
             <td>
                <img src="cat04.wbmp" localsrc="family" alt="Kids" />
             </td>
             <td>Kids</td>
          </tr>
```

```
            <tr>
                <td>
                    <img src="cat05.wbmp" localsrc="baseball" alt="Water" />
                </td>
                <td>Watersports</td>
            </tr>
            <tr>
                <td>
                    <img src="cat06.wbmp" localsrc="bolt" alt="Adventure" />
                </td>
                <td>Adventure</td>
            </tr>
        </table>
    </p>
    <do type="accept" label="Back">
        <prev/>
    </do>
</card>
```

5. Run `icons.wml` in the UP.Simulator:

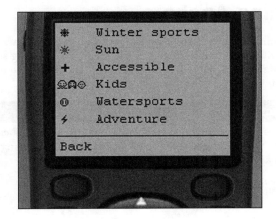

The descriptions are now nicely lined up, giving a page that's more pleasing to the eye.

How It Works

In Step 1, we created a card that contained a list of images and their textual definitions simply by using the `<br>` element to separate each image-text pair:

```
<img src="cat02.wbmp" localsrc="sparkle" alt="Sun" />
Sun<br/>
<img src="cat03.wbmp" localsrc="plus" alt="Accessible" />
Accessible<br/>
```

The problem with this approach was evident in our first test: if the images in a list like this are not the same size, the graphics and text will not be properly aligned.

In Step 4, we resolved this issue by placing each image-text pair in the row of a table:

```
<tr>
   <td>
      <img src="cat02.wbmp" localsrc="sparkle" alt="Sun" />
   </td>
   <td>Sun</td>
</tr>
<tr>
   <td>
      <img src="cat03.wbmp" localsrc="plus" alt="Accessible" />
   </td>
   <td>Accessible</td>
</tr>
```

In its implementation on the UP.Simulator, the `<table>` element provides us with a means of keeping the images in one column, and the text in another, resulting in the more neatly spaced layout we saw in our second test.

Tables Containing Anchors

Predictably, our final example in this chapter involves adding the two "vacation description" cards alluded to above, along with the plumbing that ties them in to the existing structure of the application (and to the new card we developed in the previous section). While we're doing that, we can also see how the `<table>` element can usefully be employed to contain anchors.

Try It Out — Putting Anchors in Tables

To achieve all of the above, we're going to create a card that lists our "unbeatable offers" in a table of links to other cards. There will also need to be a few changes to our existing code. Let's see how this might work, starting with a brand new deck.

1. Save the following code in a file named `offers.wml`:

```
<?xml version="1.0"?>
<!DOCTYPE wml PUBLIC "-//WAPFORUM//DTD WML 1.2//EN"
                     "http://www.wapforum.org/DTD/wml_1.2.xml">

<wml>
   <card id="offers" title="Special Offers">
      <p>Wrox Travel is pleased to be able to offer
         you the following amazing deals:
      </p>
      <p mode="nowrap">
         <table title="Vacations" columns="2">
            <tr>
               <td><a href="andorra.wml">Andorra</a></td>
               <td>$$200</td>
            </tr>
            <tr>
               <td><a href="london.wml">London</a></td>
               <td>$$300</td>
            </tr>
         </table>
      </p>
```

```
        <do type="prev">
            <prev/>
        </do>
    </card>
</wml>
```

2. Here's `andorra.wml`, which contains a description of the first of these offers:

```
<?xml version="1.0"?>
<!DOCTYPE wml PUBLIC "-//WAPFORUM//DTD WML 1.2//EN"
                     "http://www.wapforum.org/DTD/wml_1.2.xml">

<wml>
    <card id="vacation" title="Andorra Special">
        <p>Andorra - $$200</p>
        <p>What a price! Wrox Travel will have
            you up on the mountains in a flash,
            flying down the snow-laden slopes using
            whatever method of sliding transportation
            you desire!
        </p>
        <p>Accommodation type:<br/>
            Chalet<br/><br/>
            Details:<br/>
            <img src="cat01.wbmp" localsrc="snowflake" alt="Wintersports" />
            <img src="cat04.wbmp" localsrc="family"    alt="Kids" />
            <img src="cat09.wbmp" localsrc="football"  alt="Sports" />
            <img src="cat12.wbmp" localsrc="heart"     alt="Healthy" />
            <img src="cat13.wbmp" localsrc="present"   alt="Party" />
            <br/><br/>
            <a href="book.wml">Book now!</a>
        </p>

        <!-- The 'Options' menu will contain links to our card
             explaining the icons, and to a booking card -->
        <do type="options" label="Icons">
            <go href="icons.wml"/>
        </do>
        <do type="options" label="Book">
            <go href="book.wml"/>
        </do>
        <do type="prev">
            <prev/>
        </do>
    </card>
</wml>
```

3. And inevitably, this is `london.wml`, giving details of the second:

```
<?xml version="1.0"?>
<!DOCTYPE wml PUBLIC "-//WAPFORUM//DTD WML 1.2//EN"
                    "http://www.wapforum.org/DTD/wml_1.2.xml">

<wml>
   <card id="vacation" title="London Special">
      <p>London - $$300</p>
      <p>Treat yourself to a trip to one of the most
         famous cities on the planet. Enjoy the
         metropolitan sights and sounds, take in a
         show or two in one of the multitude of
         theaters, or just go shopping mad!
      </p>
      <p>Accommodation type:<br/>
         B&amp;B<br/><br/>
         Details:<br/>
         <img src="cat03.wbmp" localsrc="plus"     alt="Accessible" />
         <img src="cat04.wbmp" localsrc="family"   alt="Kids" />
         <img src="cat11.wbmp" localsrc="downtri2" alt="Cheap" />
         <img src="cat13.wbmp" localsrc="present"  alt="Party" />
         <br/><br/>
         <a href="book.wml">Book now!</a>
      </p>
      <do type="options" label="Icons">
         <go href="icons.wml"/>
      </do>
      <do type="options" label="Book">
         <go href="book.wml"/>
      </do>
      <do type="prev">
         <prev/>
      </do>
   </card>
</wml>
```

4. The last new deck, in `book.wml`, allows booking of the vacation (or at least, it will soon!):

```
<?xml version="1.0"?>
<!DOCTYPE wml PUBLIC "-//WAPFORUM//DTD WML 1.2//EN"
                    "http://www.wapforum.org/DTD/wml_1.2.xml">

<wml>
   <card id="book" title="Book">
      <p>Under construction...<br/>
         Come back soon.
      </p>
      <do type="prev">
         <prev/>
      </do>
   </card>
</wml>
```

5. Finally, we need to amend the application to include this new section. Open ex8_1.wml in your text editor, make the following changes, and save it as ex8_3.wml:

```
<card id="menu" title="Wrox Travel">
    <p>Check out our new unbeatable
        <a href="offers.wml" title="Offers">offers</a>,
        our full vacation listings,
        and our competitive vacation
        <a href="insure.wml" title="Insure">insurance</a> scheme.<br/>
        You can also read reviews of our vacations in
        our features section.
    </p>
    <p>For more information, you can
        <a href="search.wml" title="Search">search</a>
        the site, or follow our
        <a href="links.wml" title="Links">links</a>,
        which include up to the minute weather reports.<br/><br/>
        If you have any queries don't hesitate to contact us!
    </p>
    <do type="options" label="Offers">
        <go href="offers.wml"/>
    </do>
    <do type="options" label="Insure">
        <go href=" insure.wml"/>
    </do>
    <do type="options" label="Search">
        <go href="search.wml"/>
    </do>
    <do type="options" label="Links">
        <go href="links.wml"/>
    </do>
    <do type="options" label="Wrox Menu">
        <go href="#menu"/>
    </do>
</card>
</wml>
```

6. Run ex8_3.wml in the UP.Simulator, select the Enter hyperlink and navigate to the "menu" card. Choose the offers link, and at the bottom of the resulting card you should see the following:

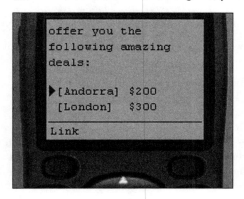

7. Select the Andorra hyperlink, and the following card will appear:

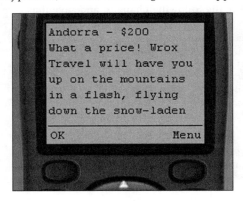

How It Works

We've added a lot of code to our application in this example, but much of it contained elements that should be familiar to you by now. The incorporation of anchors into tables took place in offers.wml, where we created a table containing two anchors:

```
<table title="Vacations" columns="2">
    <tr>
        <td><a href="andorra.wml">Andorra</a></td>
        <td>$$200</td>
    </tr>
    <tr>
        <td><a href="london.wml">London</a></td>
        <td>$$300</td>
    </tr>
</table>
```

Using the table construct with anchors in this way brought us the same advantages we saw when using it with images earlier in the chapter. Although they're different lengths, the labels are accommodated in cells of equal size, resulting in a more pleasing appearance.

> *Both of the decks linked to here contain a further link to a "book" card that displays an "under construction" notice for the time being. We'll start to add functionality to this card in the next chapter.*

The final thing of note that we added to the application was another options-type <do> element in the "menu" card:

```
<do type="options" label="Offers">
    <go href="offers.wml"/>
</do>
```

As we mentioned in Chapter 6, the options task is handy because you can use it to collect hyperlinks into a single menu. This is convenient for experienced users, who don't want to spend a lot of time reading text, and would rather jump to another topic straight away. On the downside, adding too many options adds to the size of the deck, and reduces the usability of the options menu. As so often, you need to reach a compromise that meets the needs and expectations of the majority of your users, and you can only do that reliably through a well-planned period of user testing.

Summary

There are two aspects to a table: its structural makeup (how the data is organized), and how it's presented. In this chapter, we looked at how tables are created in WML – including labeling and content alignment – and investigated their use in the UP.Simulator to clean up the user interface.

Like many other elements in WML, user agents have some freedom over their interpretation, in order that they may do the best job possible on a given device. The tables we created in the chapter complied with the WML specification, and worked well in the UP.Simulator. However, this is no guarantee of comparable results in other microbrowsers! We'll be looking at some approaches to tackling this problem of a flexible specification in Chapters 16 and 17.

It's time now to move away – for a little while – from the detail of presentation, and to introduce a feature of WML that will allow you (among other things) to customize cards as users navigate your site, depending on the route they've taken through your application. **Variables** are central to the process of bringing dynamism to your applications, and they're up for discussion in the next chapter.

Using Variables

The WML elements and techniques you've seen so far allow us to make WAP applications that are fine for most simple requirements, but often we'll want something more. Accepting and reacting to input, as a case in point, will greatly improve user interaction, and we will be looking at that later in the book. In order to use these techniques, however, we first need to learn about **variables**: what they are, how they work, and what we can do with them.

To this point, each deck we've built (and each card in each deck) has been independent of its fellows. Yes, some of them have been joined by hyperlinks to make up part of a larger application, but there has been no 'communication' between them. For example, in the Wrox Travel application, we have a selection of vacations that are each contained in a separate card. As yet, we haven't implemented a booking system, but to do so using what you've learned so far would require the creation of separate booking cards for each vacation too (to reflect different prices, etc.). This is clearly not ideal; it would be far better to have a *single* booking card that 'knew' what vacation had been selected, and customized itself accordingly. You'll soon see that variables allow us to do just that, providing a means of exchanging pieces of information between cards.

In this chapter, we'll take a long hard look at variables, enabling us to add new functionality to our WML applications straight away. In addition, it will provide a foundation for some more advanced techniques to be introduced later in the book, many of which rely on variable use. The topics included here are:

- ❑ What variables are, and how we can use them
- ❑ What variables mean to the WML developer
- ❑ Variable syntax
- ❑ A full example that brings all the concepts together

What is a Variable?

At heart, a **variable** is a mechanism for storing information temporarily. As an analogy, you can think of variables as a set of boxes on a shelf. In everyday life, when we want to store something, we can put it in a box and keep it on a shelf, ready for later retrieval. In a WML application, when we want to store some data, we put it in a variable until we need it again. In both cases, re-use is possible: we can empty the box and put something else in it, and we can just as easily replace the data in a variable.

*Variables are not an idea that's exclusive to WML development. Almost all programming languages support some means of storing data, and many differentiate between stores that can be filled once but then never change (so-called **constants**), and those whose content can be changed over time. It's this potential to vary their content that gives variables their name.*

Just as the boxes on the shelf would be labeled so that you could distinguish one from another, variables are identified by names that are given to them when they are created. When you want to find out what a particular variable contains, you ask for it by name. When you want to change what's being stored in a variable, you do the same thing.

This concept of variables begs some rather obvious, but fundamental, questions:

❑   What sort of things can we put in them?

❑   What do we use them for?

❑   How are they stored?

WML variables store **strings**: groups of letters, numbers, or symbols, in combinations of any length. This paragraph is a string, for example, as (taken individually) are all the sentences, words, and letters within it. When you've got a description as broad as that, it's important to be able to specify very clearly where you intend a string to start and end, and for this we use double quote characters. For example:

```
"This is a string."
"2-4-6-8"
"$!@?"
""
```

> **Take a look at some WML code from any of the examples in previous chapters, and you'll see that we've used this representation over and over again: every attribute we've used has been set with a string value!**

The final member in the list of example strings above contains no characters at all, and is termed an **empty string**. This is quite legitimate, and can actually be rather useful in a number of situations. Variables that contain an empty string are referred to as being 'empty' or 'unset'.

One example of a use for WML variables is to store information about the user, such as the choices they make as they navigate through your application. Cards can then share this information in order to customize what the user sees. For example, if you have the user's name stored in a variable, you can use it to address them as they browse around. (We'll investigate how to obtain this information in the next chapter.) Alternatively, you might build up a 'shopping basket' of the items a user has chosen to purchase.

Variables are stored in the memory of WAP-enabled devices. As you know from earlier discussions, however, the devices that run microbrowsers are limited (to a greater or lesser extent) when it comes to storage capacity. If we ignored this, and stored data with carefree abandon, we could quickly run into problems: the consequences of a device running out of memory are potentially disastrous. The message, then, is to employ variables judiciously; use them, but don't overuse them.

Setting Variables

There are three ways to store a string in a variable (the process is usually called 'setting' a variable):

- ❑ Using the `<setvar>` WML element
- ❑ By prompting for user input
- ❑ Through WMLScript functions

In this chapter, we'll concentrate on the first of these methods, which alone offers us plenty of opportunity to experiment. We'll examine the other possibilities in later chapters.

The <setvar> Element

The `<setvar>` element allows us to set a variable (that is, to store a string inside it), using the following syntax:

```
<setvar name="varname" value="mystring" />
```

If a variable called `varname` has already been created anywhere else in the WML application, its previous value will be discarded and replaced with `mystring`. If no variable with this name exists, a new one will be created and used to store the string you've specified. Regardless of the prevailing conditions, then, a piece of WML code such as the following:

```
<setvar name="var1" value="Scrumpy"/>
```

will result in the existence of a variable called `var1`, containing the string `Scrumpy`. Furthermore, this will remain the case until the `var1` variable is set again elsewhere in the application.

Predictably, the situation isn't *quite* as straightforward as we've presented it here. There are a couple of things that you need to bear in mind when using the `<setvar>` element, specifically:

- ❑ There are rules governing the composition of variable names – certain characters, and sequences of characters, are illegal
- ❑ There are rules governing where a `<setvar>` element can be placed – it can only be contained by certain other elements (just putting it in the middle of some display text, for example, is illegal)

Naming Variables

When you give a name to a variable, it can be useful if that name says something about the values it's likely to hold. Without knowing anything else about them, you'd quickly form an impression of the contents of variables called `greeting`, or `price`, or `color`, making code much easier to read from the developer's point of view. However, you're not free to call variables whatever you like – in WML, all variable names obey the following two rules:

- ❑ They *must* start with a letter, or an underscore character
- ❑ They *may* also contain additional letters, underscore characters, or numbers

The results of these rules are names consisting of strings of one or more characters, such as:

```
Name
xy1
_42
_NumberOfChairs
supercalifragilisticexpialidocious
HAL9000
```

A further consequence of the rules is that variable names *cannot* start with a number, so the following are not legal:

```
99RedBalloons
3Point14159
```

A final important point to note is that variable names are *case sensitive*:

```
carColor
CarColor
CARcolor
cArCoLoR
```

The names in the above list, for example, all refer to different variables. This is due to WML's origins in XML, which itself is case sensitive. Naming errors of this kind are definitely something to look out for when problems arise in your applications – certain combinations of letters can look similar, even though they are different!

Positioning the <setvar> Element

We can place the <setvar> element inside any of the following elements:

❏   <go>

❏   <prev>

❏   <refresh>

In turn, these can all be contained in <do> elements and <anchor> elements, which we met in Chapter 6. They can also be contained by certain other elements that you'll meet later in the book.

We didn't talk about <refresh> at the same time as we discussed <go> and <prev> because it didn't make sense to do so at that stage: the element updates card content due to changes in variable content. For example, we could have a <do> element that makes changes to variable content and updates the card accordingly, rather than causing a navigation action. These changes may occur as a result of <setvar> elements, or be due to other operations.

So, we could take the <setvar> example we saw earlier, and put it inside any one of these three elements. If we wanted to set the content of a variable at the same time as navigating backwards through the history stack, for example, we could put it in a <prev> element:

```
<prev>
    <setvar name="var1" value="Scrumpy"/>
</prev>
```

We could, in turn, place this inside a <do> element:

```
<do type="prev">
    <prev>
        <setvar name="var1" value="Scrumpy"/>
    </prev>
</do>
```

The result of this code would be that pressing the **Back** softkey from the card containing it would not only result in backwards navigation, but also set the value of the variable var1 to Scrumpy.

Try It Out — Setting a Variable

Let's take our new knowledge about <setvar> and put it into a proper example that will allow us to demonstrate that a variable is being created and set, as we've described.

1. Create a WML file called varset.wml, containing the following:

```
<?xml version="1.0"?>
<!DOCTYPE wml PUBLIC "-//WAPFORUM//DTD WML 1.2//EN"
                      "http://www.wapforum.org/DTD/wml_1.2.xml">

<wml>
    <card id="card1">
        <p>
            No variables set.<br/>
            <anchor>
                <go href="#card2">
                    <setvar name="var1" value="Scrumpy"/>
                </go>
                Set var1
            </anchor>
        </p>
    </card>
    <card id="card2">
        <p>
            var1 set
        </p>
    </card>
</wml>
```

2. Fire up the WAP browser and view this file.

3. Follow the **Set var1** link to set the variable var1 to Scrumpy.

How It Works

You shouldn't have been given any nasty surprises by the code in this example – there's nothing that wasn't detailed in the preceding sections. This deck involves just two cards: `card1` contains a single anchor that navigates to `card2`, while at the same storing a value in a variable called `var1`.

We'll examine how to make microbrowsers display the values stored in variables later on in this chapter, but in the meantime we need some other way to inspect their contents. In fact, this is a simple example of quite a common problem: when you're developing WML applications, it's often helpful to be able to check variables' values, in order to make sure that things are working correctly – an unexpected value could mean a problem with your code. This is one of the services usually offered to developers by toolkits like the UP.SDK, and we can use it here to test whether our code is behaving as advertised.

To look at variables on the UP.Simulator, we just have to select <u>V</u>ars from the <u>I</u>nfo menu (or hit *F10* on the keyboard):

When you do this, you'll see a report appear in the Phone Information window, listing the contents of any variables currently set. If you select it immediately after running the above code example as directed, you should see the following:

As you can see, the readout includes the name of the variable (`var1`), and its associated content (`Scrumpy`). The rest of the display (the word `vars`, the parentheses, the equals sign, the quotation marks, and the starred header and footer) is there purely to tell us we're looking at a variable content readout, and to make it easier for us to see what that content is. If there were no variables set, the output would consist of nothing but the two starred lines.

Using Variables

Now that you've learned something about variables – including one way to set them, and how to check that they have been set – it's time to start making proper use of them. Specifically, we'll look at how to write the values stored in our variables directly to the browser for display, or to other less visible WML code.

To get access to the value of a variable from within a WML program, you need simply to write its name, prefixed with a dollar symbol ($). On encountering such a combination, the user agent will replace it with the content of the variable so identified. To write out the value of a variable into display text, for example, all we need to do is type $, followed by the variable name, as in this code snippet:

```
<p>
   Variable var1 is set to $var1
</p>
```

If the value of var1 is still set to Scrumpy, this paragraph will display the following text:

Variable var1 is set to Scrumpy

Were you to try exactly the same thing using the name of a variable that *hasn't* been defined, you won't get an error – rather, an empty string will be inserted.

> *In the previous chapter, you saw that to output the dollar symbol to the screen, we needed to use $$ in our code. The reason for this strange requirement is now clear: in WML, the $ character alerts the user agent to the fact that what follows is the name of a variable; we have to double the symbol in order to dissuade the microbrowser from this point of view.*

An alternative notation for the same operation is to place the variable name in parentheses, like so:

```
<p>
   Variable var1 is set to $(var1)
</p>
```

In this instance, the variable's content will be output in exactly the same way as it was without parentheses. However, there are times when parentheses *are* mandatory, notably when passing parameters to WMLScript functions, as we'll begin to see in the next chapter. It's generally a good idea to use parentheses regardless of context, though, as it helps in keeping your code consistent, and in minimizing the possibility of errors of the kind mentioned. From this point on, we'll always include them.

Try It Out — Using Variables

Let's take a look at an example to try this out. Earlier in the chapter, we suggested that a possible use for variables would be to track the selections made by a user as they moved through your WML application. We're going to put that idea into practice, using the techniques you've learned so far.

1. Type in the following WML deck, or copy it from the source code that you can download from the Wrox web site. Save it as track.wml:

```
<?xml version="1.0"?>
<!DOCTYPE wml PUBLIC "-//WAPFORUM//DTD WML 1.2//EN"
                     "http://www.wapforum.org/DTD/wml_1.2.xml">

<wml>
   <card id="splash" title="Welcome!">
      <p>KarliSport: a portal for people who
         like the same sports as Karli!<br/>
```

```
              <anchor title="Enter">
                 Enter
                 <go href="#menu">
                    <setvar name="Visited1" value="No"/>
                    <setvar name="Visited2" value="No"/>
                    <setvar name="Visited3" value="No"/>
                    <setvar name="Visited4" value="No"/>
                 </go>
              </anchor>
        </p>
   </card>

   <card id="menu" title="Menu">
      <p>Choose from the following sports:<br/>
         <anchor title="F1">
            Formula 1
            <go href="#f1">
               <setvar name="Visited1" value="Yes"/>
            </go>
         </anchor>
         <anchor title="Snowbd">
            Snowboarding
            <go href="#snow">
               <setvar name="Visited2" value="Yes"/>
            </go>
         </anchor>
         <anchor title="TaiChi">
            Tai Chi
            <go href="#taichi">
               <setvar name="Visited3" value="Yes"/>
            </go>
         </anchor>
         <anchor title="Badmin">
            Badminton
            <go href="#badminton">
               <setvar name="Visited4" value="Yes"/>
            </go>
         </anchor>
      </p>
      <do type="options" label="Track">
         <go href="#track"/>
      </do>
   </card>

   <card id="f1" title="Formula 1">
      <p>Zoom!</p>
      <do type="prev" label="Back">
         <prev/>
      </do>
   </card>
```

```
      <card id="snow" title="Snowboarding">
        <p>Whoosh!</p>
        <do type="prev" label="Back">
          <prev/>
        </do>
      </card>
      <card id="taichi" title="Tai Chi">
        <p>Om!</p>
        <do type="prev" label="Back">
          <prev/>
        </do>
      </card>
      <card id="badminton" title="Badminton">
        <p>Thwack!</p>
        <do type="prev" label="Back">
          <prev/>
        </do>
      </card>

      <card id="track" title="User Tracking">
        <p>
          <b>Visited 1: </b>$(Visited1)<br/>
          <b>Visited 2: </b>$(Visited2)<br/>
          <b>Visited 3: </b>$(Visited3)<br/>
          <b>Visited 4: </b>$(Visited4)<br/>
        </p>
        <do type="prev" label="Back">
          <prev/>
        </do>
      </card>
</wml>
```

2. It's a little longer than our previous examples have tended to be, but once again there are no new constructs here – we're just using them in a slightly different way. Load the deck into the UP.Simulator:

3. Select the Enter link:

4. And select the Track softkey:

5. Go back to the "menu" card, and select any other link – for the sake of argument, we chose **Snowboarding**. Go back again, and then reselect the Track softkey. This time, one of the lines will read **Yes**, recording the fact that the link to a sport has been followed:

How It Works

When we select the **Enter** link from the first card, we initialize four variables (Visited1, Visited2, Visited3, Visited4) to No, and navigate to the "menu" card:

```
<anchor title="Enter">
    Enter
    <go href="#menu">
        <setvar name="Visited1" value="No"/>
        <setvar name="Visited2" value="No"/>
        <setvar name="Visited3" value="No"/>
        <setvar name="Visited4" value="No"/>
    </go>
</anchor>
```

Selecting the **Track** softkey from the "menu" card then takes us to the "track" card:

```
<do type="options" label="Track">
    <go href="#track"/>
</do>
```

Here, we display the values of the four variables that were created when we entered the site:

```
<p>
    <b>Visited 1: </b>$(Visited1)<br/>
    <b>Visited 2: </b>$(Visited2)<br/>
    <b>Visited 3: </b>$(Visited3)<br/>
    <b>Visited 4: </b>$(Visited4)<br/>
</p>
```

Before following any of the hyperlinks from the "menu" card, all these variables will be storing No, which explains the appearance of this card the first time you saw it. Activating any of the links changes the contents of one of the variables; the code below says that if the user chooses this link, the microbrowser should not only navigate to the "snow" card, but also set the value of Visited2 to Yes as it does so:

```
<anchor title="Snowbd">
    Snowboarding
    <go href="#snow">
        <setvar name="Visited2" value="Yes"/>
    </go>
</anchor>
```

The next time we navigate to the "track" card, we see that the value of the variable has been updated accordingly.

This tracking of users in your application may be useful in working out which areas are visited most frequently – although of course the code above makes no provision for passing this information to the site owner. A version released to your customers might still update variables in the same way, but instead of displaying them in a card, they could be transmitted to the server for further processing. The chapters at the end of this book will describe how that might be achieved.

More on Variable Use

Before we get ahead of ourselves, there are still plenty of avenues for us to explore here. Variables can be used in many other parts of WML, where previously we've just used ordinary text. Take a look at this <a> element, for example:

```
<a href="$(var1)">Go</a>
```

The hyperlink created by this WML code will be to whatever URL is currently stored in var1. As usual, this might be another WML deck, a card within a WML deck, etc. – the point is that the destination can change *while the application is executing*. One issue to be aware of when specifying URLs in this way, though, concerns 'escaping' strings.

Escaping Strings

As you know, URLs are built up in a very particular way, with strict syntax dependent on their target. In order to allow for different targets to use different syntaxes, while at the same time allowing for ease of transcription (both on computers and on paper), the characters that can appear in a URL are limited. The document that describes the standard for URLs (which can be found at http://www.ietf.org/rfc/rfc1738.txt) defines these characters in what's referred to as the **restricted set**. The set chosen consists of letters, numbers, and a few symbols.

The restricted set of characters is made up of two subsets: **reserved** and **unreserved** characters. The reserved set includes certain characters that are used for very specific purposes (such as the / character that is used to separate directories in web URLs). Problems can arise if these reserved characters are used in any other way (placing a / character in the middle of a directory name, for example). Unreserved characters include any other characters that are allowed in URLs but don't have a specific purpose, including all letters and numbers.

You'll surely have recognized parallels here with WML's reserved characters, which are defined for broadly similar reasons: in a particular context, they become something more than 'just another character'. Keep this comparison in mind as we continue this discussion; there are more similarities to come!

Back in Chapter 5, you saw that characters to be output in WML code have alternative representations in the form of numeric character entities, which use numbers from the Unicode standard to identify particular characters uniquely. These enabled us to send WML reserved characters to the user agent for display. Here, you'll see that we can use a comparable technique to 'disguise' characters in a URL. Each character in a URL that *isn't* being used as a delimiter can have two representations: **escaped** and **unescaped**.

'Escaping' a character in a URL also involves replacing it with a number that identifies it uniquely, but there are two changes from our earlier exploits with WML. First, the numbers don't come from Unicode — instead, they come from a different standard called ASCII (American Standard Code for Information Interchange). This defines a much smaller set of numbers than Unicode, although mercifully it uses the same numbers for the characters you're likely to use.

The second change is a little trickier: when you escape a character, you identify it not with a decimal number, but with a **hexadecimal** number. If you haven't come across it before, hexadecimal is a method of counting that uses sixteen digits, rather than the ten you'd normally expect. (To the digits 0 thru 9, hexadecimal adds the letters A thru F, so you count 1, 2, 3, 4, 5, 6, 7, 8, 9, A, B, C, D, E, F, 10.) The reasons for this system are to do with the way computers store numbers internally, but they needn't concern us here because we'll always tell you the representations of any characters you need. Hopefully though, you won't be confused when 'letters' start appearing in 'numbers'!

The complete syntax for escaping a character is to use a percentage symbol (%), followed by a two-digit hexadecimal number. For example, the character A has a hexadecimal value of 41 in ASCII, so it could be represented in a URL using either A or %41. One consequence of this encoding scheme is that the percentage character must *always* be represented as %25 — if it weren't, the browser would try to interpret the two characters following the symbol as a hexadecimal number, whatever they were.

At this stage, it would be entirely reasonable for you to ask where all this is headed. It's quite likely that you've never had to use a percentage symbol in a URL, let alone some of the other characters that need escaping (which include spaces, backspaces, and carriage returns, among others) in order to appear, so why start now? Why not make sure that the URLs of resources in your application never use these characters? The answer is that sometimes, URLs are used not only to request a resource, but also to send information to the server on which the resource is located. In cases like this, information is often encoded as a sequence of ASCII characters between delimiters, and from this it follows that escaping may be necessary.

Luckily for us as WML developers, the process of escaping (and later 'unescaping') characters shouldn't ever cause a problem. We don't even need to remember all of those awkward hexadecimal codes. The reason for this is that syntax exists for us to escape strings automatically. Not only that, but there are certain places where we don't even need to use this syntax — WML will do it for us.

To be more specific, when we place a reference to a variable in WML code, we can optionally specify a conversion scheme in the following way:

$(*varname*:*conversion*)

Here, *varname* is the variable name, and *conversion* is the scheme to use. The schemes available are:

conversion value	Meaning
e or escape	Replace non-alphanumeric characters with hexadecimal escape codes
u or unesc	Replace hexadecimal escape codes with the characters they represent
n or noesc	Output string with no replacement

Note that any conversion does not *affect the string stored by the variable. It only affects the string that's substituted into the WML code.*

Try It Out — Escape Codes

That's been quite a lot of new information, and it probably isn't quite clear in your mind just yet. The best way to provide some additional explanation is through an example that you can take away and experiment with.

1. Create the following WML file, called escape.wml:

```
<?xml version="1.0"?>
<!DOCTYPE wml PUBLIC "-//WAPFORUM//DTD WML 1.2//EN"
                     "http://www.wapforum.org/DTD/wml_1.2.xml">

<wml>
    <card id="card1">
        <p>
            <anchor>
                <go href="#card2">
                    <setvar name="var1" value="x%20= 3.2/y"/>
                </go>
                Set var1
            </anchor>
        </p>
    </card>
    <card id="card2">
        <p>
            <b>var1 noescaped:</b><br/> $(var1:noesc)<br/>
            <b>var1 escaped:</b><br/> $(var1:escape)<br/>
            <b>var1 unescaped:</b><br/> $(var1:unesc)<br/>
        </p>
    </card>
</wml>
```

2. Fire up the UP.Simulator and view this file.

3. Follow the Set var1 hyperlink, and look at the results:

How It Works

This example sets the value of the variable var1 to the string x%20= 3.2/y. When we view this string using the three different conversion schemes, we see the results above. We chose to use this particular string because it contains a mix of some characters that require an escaped representation, and some characters that don't:

Character	Escaping required?
x	No
%	Yes
2	No
0	No
=	Yes
" " (a space)	Yes
3	No
.	No
/	Yes
y	No

Just to stretch things to the limit, the string already contains %20, which is the escaped representation of a space. This means that escaping and unescaping should both have an effect on the string. Let's examine the results more carefully.

The output of the noesc'd version, using $(var1:noesc), looks like this:

x%20= 3.2/y

This is identical to the contents of var1, and also the default behavior when outputting variable content for display. We would have obtained precisely the same result had the line been simply:

```
<b>var1 noescaped:</b><br/> $(var1)<br/>
```

The escape'd version looks like this:

x%2520%3d%203.2%2fy

It may look confusing, but taken in small chunks it's quite straightforward. The x at the start of the string is unchanged, because the character doesn't need to be escaped. The % sign that followed in the original string has been converted into %25. The string 20, after that, is output unchanged, and so on.

> This escaping conversion is the default behavior when we supply variable content to the **href** attribute, so we don't have to remember to do this ourselves!

Finally, the unesc'd version looks like this:

x = 3.2/y

What's happened here? Well, as mentioned above, %20 is the escaped representation of a space. We can see this from the escaped string shown above, where %20 appears just before 3.2. We can use this facility in combination with the escaping procedure to convert strings back and forth.

Variable Context

Before we take all of our new knowledge and use it to improve the Wrox Travel application, we need to address one last issue. When we first started discussing variables, we warned against using them with abandon, for fear of exhausting the storage capacity of WAP-enabled devices. However, if you were to run application after application, you'd surely run out of space eventually, no matter how careful your programming – unless, of course, WML has some means of removing variables that are no longer in use.

For this purpose, WML uses the concept of **variable context**. When you create a variable, it becomes part of the current variable context, and it will stick around until a new context is initiated, or the device is switched off. A given context may span several cards, decks, or even whole applications.

To initiate a new variable context, you set the newcontext attribute of a <card> element to true:

```
<card id="newcard" newcontext="true">
    ...
</card>
```

When the user enters a card with this attribute, all variables will be deleted, and the browser's navigational history cleared. The result of this is pretty much the same as if the user had switched off the WAP-enabled device pointing at your application, then switched it back on and navigated back to it.

If your application uses variables, it is worth bearing in mind the possibility that whatever application the browser was looking at previously may have used variables with the same names – especially commonly used ones such as username or password. Because of this, it's probably a good idea to initialize a new context when the user first enters your site.

Extending the Wrox Travel Application

It's time to add some more functionality to the Wrox Travel application. The current state of play is that selecting **Book now!** from a vacation card gives us an "Under construction..." notice. In the new code here, we'll save the vacation the user has chosen in a variable, so that we can use these details later on in the booking process. For now though, we'll just display the price of the vacation in the booking form.

Try It Out — Variable Use Example

1. To start with, let's take our own advice and set a new context in the first card. This requires a single, simple modification. Open `ex8_3.wml`, and make the following change before saving the file as `wroxtravel.wml`:

```
<wml>
    <card id="splash" newcontext="true">
        <p align="center">
            <img localsrc="plane" src="WTLogo.wbmp" alt="Wrox"/><br/>
        </p>
        <p align="center">Wrox Travel</p>
        <p mode="nowrap">Welcome to our WAP site!</p>

        <!-- Rest of file as before -->
```

2. Next, we need to set variables from within our vacation decks, `andorra.wml` and `london.wml`. The method is the same for both, so we'll only show the former here:

```
<wml>
    <card id="vacation" title="Andorra Special">

        <!-- Paragraphs omitted for brevity -->

        <p>Accommodation type:<br/>
            Chalet<br/><br/>
            Details:<br/>
            <img src="cat01.wbmp" localsrc="snowflake" alt="Wintersports" />
            <img src="cat04.wbmp" localsrc="family"    alt="Kids" />
            <img src="cat09.wbmp" localsrc="football"  alt="Sports" />
            <img src="cat12.wbmp" localsrc="heart"     alt="Healthy" />
            <img src="cat13.wbmp" localsrc="present"   alt="Party" />
            <br/><br/>
            <anchor>
                <go href="book.wml">
                    <setvar name="V" value="Andorra"/>
                    <setvar name="P" value="$$200"/>
                </go>
                Book now!
            </anchor>
        </p>

        <do type="options" label="Icons">
            <go href="icons.wml"/>
        </do>
```

```
        <do type="options" label="Book">
           <go href="book.wml">
              <setvar name="V" value="Andorra"/>
              <setvar name="P" value="$$200"/>
           </go>
        </do>
        <do type="prev">
           <prev/>
        </do>
     </card>
  </wml>
```

Add the same two sections of code to london.wml, remembering to change the value of V to London, and P to $$300.

3. We can now make use of these variables in a significantly updated book.wml file:

```
<wml>
   <card id="book" title="Book">
      <p>
         <b>Destination:</b><br/>
         $(V)<br/>
         <b>Price:</b><br/>
         $(P)<br/>
      </p>
      <do type="prev" label="Back">
         <prev/>
      </do>
   </card>
</wml>
```

4. Load wroxtravel.wml into the UP.Simulator, and navigate to the book.wml card. (The sequence is Enter, offers, Andorra (or London), Book now!) You should now have the following on your screen:

How It Works

In Step 1, we set the newcontext attribute to true, as detailed earlier. Since we'll be using variables in the application, it makes sense to clear any that may be in memory – they could only cause harm.

The changes made in Step 2 result in two variables being set if the user navigates to book.wml: V is set to the destination name, and P to the relevant price.

Finally, book.wml displays the information we have saved in our variables. At the moment, all this does is to write out the destination and price of the chosen vacation. To complete a booking, we'll need to add a lot more interactivity, and this is detailed in the next section of the book.

Summary

In this chapter, we have discussed the concept of variables in detail; they crop up in the overwhelming majority of programming languages, but on the whole we stuck to considering their impact in WML. You've seen and experimented with the `<setvar>` element, and used it to extend the Wrox Travel application. We also took some time to introduce escaping, and variable contexts, both of which we'll find ourselves dealing with again.

The only thing holding us back now is a more complete knowledge of the rest of the capabilities that WML has to offer. In the next chapter, we'll see how to use variables in conjunction with user input, and really start to build on the lessons learned here. After that, we can start to look at WMLScript, a programming language that has the power to access variables and manipulate them in a multitude of ways. It won't be long before we start to see much more dynamic examples.

10

Acquiring User Input

In the last chapter, we introduced you to variables, and you saw that they quickly became useful in our Wrox Travel application by providing a means of 'carrying' information from one card to another. In truth, however, we don't begin even to scratch the surface of variables' full potential until we can fill them with data acquired directly from the user, and then manipulate that information.

Starting in this chapter, and continuing for the next four, we'll be looking at precisely those subjects. By the end of this run, you'll be in a position where you can accept input from the user, process it, and act upon it. To start the ball rolling, our subjects for this chapter are:

❑   Allowing users to input text

❑   Presenting lists of options for users to choose from

❑   Grouping input fields together in logical fashion

Allowing Users to Enter Text

You can request and accept text input from the users of your applications using WML's `<input>` element, which allows us to insert a text entry field into a WML card. In common with all the other elements that display information on the user agent, `<input>` elements are always contained inside `<p>` elements, like this:

```
<wml>
    <card>
        <p>
            some text
            <input attributes />
            some more text
        </p>
    </card>
</wml>
```

The `<input>` element is *always* empty (you'll get an error if you try to give it any content), but to make up for that it has a grand total of *ten* attributes. Of these, only one – the `name` attribute – is mandatory. The value supplied for this attribute should be a string specifying the name of a WML variable in which to store the user's input, so that we can use it later.

Try It Out — Entering Text

That's already enough information for us to be able to write our first WML application that prompts for input from the user. Let's see what happens when we try.

1. Enter the following code in your text editor, and save it as `textentry.wml`:

```
<?xml version="1.0"?>
<!DOCTYPE wml PUBLIC "-//WAPFORUM//DTD WML 1.2//EN"
                     "http://www.wapforum.org/DTD/wml_1.2.xml">

<wml>
   <card>
      <p>
         Please enter your name:
         <input name="var1"/>
         Thank you.
      </p>
   </card>
</wml>
```

2. Load `textentry.wml` into the UP.Simulator. You should see the following:

3. Now enter some text at the cursor. Note that the softkey labeled **ALPHA** can be used to change text entry mode from upper case alphabetic (**ALPHA**), to lower case alphabetic (**alpha**), to numeric (**NUM**), and to other modes. This feature is unique to the UP.Simulator.

4. If you press the **OK** softkey, you'll see this:

5. Finally, hit *F10* to display the current values of all variables, and observe the text written to the **Phone Information** window:

How It Works

The UP.Simulator renders the `<input>` element by placing a cursor on a new line in the window, and creating a mode-changing softkey. Notice that the other text in the paragraph (**Thank you.**) is not displayed until we select the **OK** softkey, when something that looks like a new card appears.

The other thing that happens when you hit **OK** is that the variable `var1` is set, as we saw by pressing *F10*.

> *So far, we've been trying hard to keep away from browser-specific features in this tutorial, but on this occasion the UP.Simulator behaves so differently from other user agents that it would be churlish not to mention it.*
>
> *None of the other microbrowsers we've tried – real or emulated – splits the card up in the way that the UP.Simulator does. Instead, they try to demarcate the input field in some way and continue the flow of text immediately afterwards. However, the core behavior of the `<input>` element is universal: by some means, it will obtain user input and place it in the variable specified.*
>
> *As you'd expect, we'll be raising this issue (and many others like it) when we discuss interoperability in Chapter 17.*

Once the user input has been stored, it becomes the content of a variable that's just like any other, and we have the same range of options for doing things with it. As well as being sent to the browser screen, user input can be processed by WMLScript, or sent to the server for further manipulation. We'll have more to say on this subject in the next chapter, and throughout the remainder of the book.

<input> Capabilities

Over the next few sections, we'll look at the various capabilities provided by the `<input>` element. Since it can't contain any other elements, these are all realized using its various attributes. Specifically, we'll look at:

- ❑ Default values for user input
- ❑ Entering passwords
- ❑ Controlling the appearance of input fields
- ❑ Specifying formats for text entry
- ❑ Other attributes

Default Values for User Input

Taking `name` as read, perhaps the simplest attribute that we can use with the `<input>` element is `value`. This attribute allows us to specify a default entry, so that the user can simply accept it if it's correct. Careful use of this attribute can be a great aid to WML applications, since entering text can be tricky using a numeric keypad. Any time saving techniques we can add are likely to make the user experience a whole lot friendlier – and where applications are concerned, "friendlier" is synonymous with "more popular"!

> *Although it's not possible without dynamic content generation, a natural extension of this idea is to store user-specific information on a server, and retrieve 'default' input in a context specific way. For example, you might store address details, to save users from having to enter this lengthy data more than once.*

To use the `value` attribute, we just need to assign a string to it:

```
<wml>
   <card>
      <p>
         Who is your favorite James Bond?
         <input name="bond" value="Sean Connery"/>
         Thank you.
      </p>
   </card>
</wml>
```

As long as the variable `bond` doesn't exist (or contains an empty string) when the code is executed, this `<input>` element will result in the input field being displayed, preset with the text Sean Connery.

However, if `bond` already contains a value – `Roger Moore`, perhaps – then this existing value will be displayed instead. It could be that you want this behavior, but if you don't, you should be sure to clear the variable before using the `<input>` element. In this case, simply setting `bond` to `" "` (the empty string) will do the trick.

Entering Passwords

If your computer is part of a network, or you have ever registered with one of the many web sites that offer some kind of personalization, you will be familiar with computer passwords. In almost all cases, when you enter a password into a dialog box or a text field, you will not see the characters you type – they'll be replaced by asterisks, or something similar. This feature exists for security reasons: it makes it harder for others to see what you're doing. To provide the same input-hiding feature on WAP-enabled devices, we have the <input> element's type attribute.

It can be argued – convincingly, in our opinion – that this functionality is unnecessary on a mobile device. Limited screen sizes and viewing angles make it very unlikely that someone else would see what you typed into a text field if you didn't want them to. Furthermore, text entry is difficult on many devices, and if you can't see what you've typed, it's easy to forget where you're up to. Facts like these lead us to question the value of the type attribute, but it is a part of the specification, and you can use it if you want to.

The type attribute accepts one of two values: text and password. The default value is text, which explains why we haven't had to use it so far: it just means, "Write all the input to the display." If we use this attribute in the form type="password", however, we get the input-hiding functionality discussed above. Let's give it a go in the UP.Simulator:

```
<wml>
    <card>
        <p>
            Enter password:
            <input name="pwd" type="password"/>
            Thank you.
        </p>
    </card>
</wml>
```

If you now enter a value using the keys on the simulated phone, you'll only see the character currently being entered:

So, we've made input more difficult, but what have we gained? The trouble is that although we couldn't see it on the screen, the value you typed is now stored – unencrypted – in a browser variable. Without further intervention from us, that's the way it's going to stay, and it may therefore be accessible to the unscrupulous. If we intend (say) to send this password to a server for validation, there's certainly a security issue, but it's not solved by the type attribute. The problem runs much deeper than that.

For an in-depth discussion of the security issues relating to WAP, WML, and WMLScript, take a look at Chapter 15 of Professional WAP *(Wrox Press, 1-861004-04-4).*

Controlling Input Field Appearance

Although text input fields appear differently on different browsers, there are a few 'hints' you can supply to specify simple presentation information. In this section, we'll take a look at the three attributes that allow you to do this.

Firstly, you can use the `title` attribute to *suggest* a title for the text input field. Depending on the browser, this may or may not be displayed. (The absence of a screenshot has probably led you to conclude already that the UP.Simulator belongs in the second camp!) We can use the `title` attribute in the following way:

```
<wml>
   <card>
      <p>
         Who is your favorite James Bond?
         <input name="bond" value="Sean Connery" title="Favorite Bond"/>
         Thank you.
      </p>
   </card>
</wml>
```

The next attribute we'll look at is `size`. The WML specification says that this attribute can specify the size, in characters, of the text entry field – but this too is only a suggestion. Once again, the UP.Simulator ignores this attribute, but other browsers can use it to format input fields in a more aesthetically pleasing way. We use it like this:

```
<wml>
   <card>
      <p>
         Who is your favorite James Bond?
         <input name="bond" value="Sean Connery" size="12"/>
         Thank you.
      </p>
   </card>
</wml>
```

Finally, we can specify the maximum number of characters that may be entered by using the `maxlength` attribute. The default value for this attribute allows text entry of unlimited length, but if you've some idea of the *kind* of data being entered, setting it shorter can be a useful 'sanity check' – a name, for example, is unlikely ever to be longer than thirty characters. Here's how `maxlength` works:

```
<wml>
   <card>
      <p>
         Who is your favorite James Bond?
         <input name="bond" value="Roger Moore" maxlength="11"/>
         Thank you.
      </p>
   </card>
</wml>
```

The above code would stop anyone entering Sean Connery, as this name is twelve characters long. It's up to you to decide whether this is a good thing!

Formats for Text Entry

Sometimes, only certain *types* of string can be taken as valid input in a text entry field. If we are asking for a name, for example, a string containing numbers is unlikely to be correct. In situations like this, it can be desirable to perform some validity checking not on the content of a string, but on its format.

There are two ways we can deal with this: we can reject invalid input *after* it has been entered, prompting the user for alternative data, or we can *force* the user to enter correct data in the first place. We'll look at the first of these options when we examine string manipulation using WMLScript in the next chapter. In the meantime, this section looks at the other technique – specifically, the use of **masks**.

Masks allow us to specify exactly what characters are allowed in an input string, and in what position. For example, we could specify a mask that said, "The input string must consist of two upper case characters, followed by a dash and 4 numeric characters." The browser would then prevent users from entering numbers for the first two characters, and so on.

To instruct the user agent to perform these checks, we use the `<input>` element's `format` attribute. We provide this attribute with a string that represents a template for the user input, and then it's up to the browser to act on it; a function that may vary. The browser may choose to limit the user to the correct input for each character, or it may stop the user from sending invalid input. Either way, this can occur without having to send any data to the server.

The masks we use are made up of codes that can specify:

- ❑ The values allowed for an individual character
- ❑ A fixed value for an individual character
- ❑ The values allowed for a number of characters at the end of a string

The codes for individual characters can specify that characters from one or more of the following sets may be used:

- ❑ Upper case alphabetic: characters from "A"-"Z"
- ❑ Lower case alphabetic: characters from "a"-"z"
- ❑ Numeric: characters from "0"-"9"
- ❑ Punctuation: characters such as ";"
- ❑ Mathematical: characters including "*", "+", "-", etc.
- ❑ Other: characters such as "$"

We've included this final group because the exact classification of certain characters seems to be unclear. "-" seems to be in both the punctuation and mathematical categories, but "=" is in neither, for example.

The codes, along with the sets of characters they allow, are:

Code	A	a	N	X	x	M	m
Upper case alphabetic	Yes	No	No	Yes	No	Yes*	Yes*
Lower case alphabetic	No	Yes	No	No	Yes	Yes*	Yes*
Numeric	No	No	Yes	Yes	Yes	Yes	Yes
Punctuation	Yes	Yes	No	Yes	Yes	Yes	Yes
Mathematical	No	No	Yes	Yes	Yes	Yes	Yes
Other	No	No	No	Yes	Yes	Yes	Yes

> *M and m are special cases, and allow the browser to change case in an interactive way. If these are used as the first character in a format string, the browser will automatically change to upper or lower case respectively. If several M codes are used, the browser will automatically change to lower case after the first character. This can speed typing is some situations, and the user is left with the ability to change case manually if desired.*

Taking all of the above on board, we can specify the rule we gave as an earlier example (two upper case letters, a dash, and four digits) using:

```
format="AAXNNNN"
```

However, this doesn't *explicitly* include the dash – the X code will allow the user to enter anything except lower case letters. Also, the A and N codes allow several other characters (punctuation, etc.) in places where they could cause problems. There is nothing we can do about the second of these here (the format codes aren't quite strict enough, and some script or server-side parsing may be necessary), but we *can* solve the first.

In order to fix individual characters absolutely, we can use another format code: "\". If we include this in our format value, the next character in the mask will be fixed, and will usually be filled in by the browser. To put our dash in, then, we need the following value for format:

```
format="AA\-NNNN"
```

Let's take a look at this in action.

Try It Out — Using the format Attribute

1. Enter the following code in your text editor:

```
<?xml version="1.0"?>
<!DOCTYPE wml PUBLIC "-//WAPFORUM//DTD WML 1.2//EN"
                   "http://www.wapforum.org/DTD/wml_1.2.xml">

<wml>
    <card>
```

```
    <p>
        Enter user code:
        <input name="code" title="User code" format="AA\-NNNN"/>
    </p>
  </card>
</wml>
```

2. Save this as `format.wml`, and open it in the UP.Simulator:

Note that it's impossible to change the mode to alpha *or* NUM, *as we have set the mask to upper case alphabetic.*

3. Use the phone keys to enter two characters. You'll find that a dash is added, the cursor advances one space, and the mode changes to NUM – all automatically:

4. Finally, use the phone keys to enter four numbers, and notice that the OK softkey only appears when the data input fits the mask supplied:

177

How It Works

The format code we supplied has given the microbrowser instructions as to what sort of input is acceptable, and it will accept nothing less. It forces the user to follow the mask.

This is something of a mixed blessing. It speeds input by selecting entry mode automatically, and filling in standard characters such as dashes; but it also stops the user from doing anything else until satisfactory input is obtained (there is no 'cancel' option), and there's no indication to the user of what the format should be (leaving users frustrated if they can't work it out).

The deciding factor, however, is the reduction in faulty input being sent to the server, which can save time and money in a situation where bandwidth is low and expensive. In Chapters 16 and 17, you'll see how we can address some of the negative issues listed, and how to allow for the slightly inconsistent implementation of this feature in the current generation of user agents.

Other Format Codes

The other kinds of format code we can use represent multiple characters in a sequence. We can only use one of these codes, and it must come at the end of the input mask. All we do is specify a number (between 1 and 9) of times to repeat a code, followed by the code itself. However, 6N doesn't work in quite the same way as NNNNNN. The former means, "Accept between 1 and 6 N-type characters," whereas the latter means, "Accept exactly 6 N-type characters." Alternatively, we can use * instead of a digit, which specifies that any number of the following type of character will be accepted. This is used by the default value of the format attribute, which is *M.

Before we look at other <input> attributes, there are a couple more points that need to be covered here. Firstly, what happens if we accidentally specify an invalid code? Well, it gets ignored and replaced with "*M". You won't get a compilation error, and invalid codes may well be difficult to spot – so make sure you test them out thoroughly! Secondly, what happens if the variable specified in the name attribute contains invalid data when the <input> element is encountered? Well, the variable either gets cleared, that is, an empty string is assigned to it, or gets set to the default input value if one has been specified. This ensures that the variable will only contain either an empty string or a valid one.

Other Attributes

There are three other optional attributes that we can apply to the <input> element: accesskey, emptyok and tabindex. The first of these works in the same way as it did for anchors when you saw it back in Chapter 6: it allows rapid selection of an <input> text field through keys on the WAP-enabled device's keypad. The second, emptyok, can be set to true to say that it's fine for a text field to be left blank: the empty string is valid 'input', and the application will not be compromised. The default value of this attribute is false.

Finally, tabindex specifies the position of the <input> element with respect to other <input> elements (and other elements that support this attribute) in terms of 'tabbing' between them. Given that current mobile phones don't have a 'tabbing' facility, the precise intention of this element is unclear, but perhaps future devices will allow users to perform this task? We can but wait and see!

Allowing Users to Select from a List

Versatile though it is, the `<input>` element is not always the best choice for user input. There are times when the freedom it allows – even when input masks are used – can lead to problems. For example, if the user is asked to answer Yes or No to a question, they might type "Yes", "No", "yes", "n", "Yes indeedy", or anything else that to them seems like a sensible positive or negative response. If you're writing the logic to interpret this input, you will quickly realize how tiresome it is first to try to anticipate all the possibilities, and then to code them.

A better method of obtaining user input in these situations is to present the user with a list of options to choose from. That way, there can be no misinterpretation of the result, and we get the additional advantage of avoiding data entry using the device's keypad, which can speed things up immensely. In WML, we can achieve this using the `<select>`, `<option>`, and `<optgroup>` elements, and over the next few sections we'll discuss how these and their attributes can combine to create a rich user interface.

Simple Lists Using `<select>` and `<option>`

The `<select>` element is used to embed a list selection field in text, rather like the way that we embedded text entry fields with `<input>`. Representations will vary, but the purpose of this element is first to convey to the user the fact that a list exists, and then to allow them to choose one or more items from it. The items in the list are specified by `<option>` elements contained within the `<select>` element; basic lists must contain at least one such element, and should really have two to be sensible.

> *Lists can have 'grouped' options, in which case `<select>` can contain no `<option>` elements, as long as it contains at least one `<optgroup>` element. We'll see how this works shortly.*

Neither `<select>` nor `<option>` has mandatory attributes; not even a variable name to store results in. This may seem strange, but the reason for it is that list selection fields can be used to provide a launch pad for events such as navigation, in which case there is no result to store. This enables you to provide, for example, a list of destination pages in a handy form. Functionality like this will be examined in Chapter 14.

If all attributes are optional, just what *is* the minimum structure necessary for a rudimentary list selection field? As discussed above, we should certainly specify a variable to store the result, but given that we're selecting from a list instead of entering text, this poses a pretty fundamental question: what should we store? The answer is best illustrated with an example.

Let's say that we're writing an application that allows guests to pre-order their food for a large dinner. For the main course, we have a list of fish for the user to choose from:

- Halibut
- Cod
- Salmon
- Plaice

When the user selects a fish, we have a number of choices. We could store:

❑ The *name* of the fish

❑ A *shorthand representation* of the fish, to save memory (H or P, for example)

❑ The *index* of the fish in the list, such as 1 or 4

WML allows any of these approaches. When we build up a list of `<option>` elements in a `<select>` element, the indices of these elements are implicit, and the browser can retrieve this information when the user chooses an option. Alternatively, we can specify a text representation of the option, which may be the full text, an abbreviation, or any other string. A text representation can be supplied using the `value` attribute of the `<option>` element, so a list of the above fish, with abbreviated values included, might look like this:

```
<option value="H">Halibut</option>
<option value="C">Cod</option>
<option value="S">Salmon</option>
<option value="P">Plaice</option>
```

With the contents of our list sorted out, we need to add the containing structure: the `<select>` element itself. We can identify the variable in which to store the chosen option using the `name` attribute, which works in much the same way as the `name` attribute of the `<input>` element. For example, we could write:

```
<wml>
    <card>
        <p>
            Select fish:<br/>
            <select name="fish">
                <option value="H">Halibut</option>
                <option value="C">Cod</option>
                <option value="S">Salmon</option>
                <option value="P">Plaice</option>
            </select>
            Done.
        </p>
    </card>
</wml>
```

If you try this in the UP.Simulator, you should find that the `fish` variable is assigned a string such as H or P, based on the chosen fish. The display will look something like this:

If you then press **OK** and examine the variables, the output should be fairly predictable:

> *As usual, the actual method of selection will vary depending on the emulator or device you try this out with. One thing worth noting here is that the UP.Simulator allows you to choose an item by typing its index on the keypad – a handy feature that's lacking in other user agents. However, the UP.Simulator only lets you have one list on screen, with no other content displayed until a selection is made. Other browsers allow multiple list selection fields on screen, with various methods of selection. See Chapter 17 for more on this subject.*

The other possibility we mentioned is to store the *index* of the user's choice, which we can do by specifying a variable not to `name`, but to a different attribute called `iname`:

```
<select iname="ifish">
```

In the case of our example, `ifish` will be assigned a value between 1 and 4.

Should you wish, it's quite legal to supply both of these attributes in a `<select>` element, creating variables containing the representation and the index of the selection:

```
<select name="fish" iname="ifish">
```

If we run this code and select **Salmon** in the same way as before, a look at the variables will show us:

List Selection Capabilities

Now you know how to create simple lists, the next sections will demonstrate additional functionality that WML can provide. We'll look at:

- ❑ Default selection
- ❑ Controlling list field appearance
- ❑ Selecting multiple list entries
- ❑ Grouping entries
- ❑ Other attributes

Default Selection

In the same way that we can suggest default input for text entry fields, we can specify default list selections, using either the value of the list item (as specified by the `value` attribute of the `<option>` element) or the index of the entry. To do this by value we use the `<select>` element's `value` attribute, and to do it by index we use the `ivalue` attribute.

Re-using the example from the previous section, we can specify cod to be the default fish using either:

```
<select name="fish" iname="ifish" value="C">
```

Or:

```
<select name="fish" iname="ifish" ivalue="2">
```

To avoid confusing the microbrowser, you should only use one or the other of these attributes to the `<select>` element. Also note that if you choose an illegal value for the default, it will be ignored.

Controlling List Field Appearance

Both the `<select>` and `<option>` elements have a `title` attribute, which as usual *may* be used by the user agent in the presentation of the list selection field. The UP.Simulator, for example, uses the `title` attribute of the `<option>` element, but ignores that of the `<select>` element. Specifying our fish list as follows:

```
<wml>
    <card>
        <p>
            Select fish:<br/>
            <select name="fish" iname="ifish" title="Fish">
                <option value="H" title="Fish 1">Halibut</option>
                <option value="C" title="Fish 2">Cod</option>
                <option value="S" title="Fish 3">Salmon</option>
                <option value="P" title="Fish 4">Plaice</option>
            </select>
            Done.
        </p>
    </card>
</wml>
```

Will result in the following display:

The `title` of the currently selected `<option>`, Fish 3, is shown, but the `<select>` title is invisible.

Selecting Multiple List Entries

The `<select>` element has another attribute called `multiple`, which allows us to say whether the user is allowed to select more than one entry from a list. It can be set to `false` (the default, giving us the behavior we've seen in previous sections) or `true` (allowing multiple selections).

Multiple selections can be thought of as 'check boxes', as seen on the Web and in countless desktop applications, and they will often be displayed as such in the microbrowser. Let's modify our fish list to allow multiple selections for very hungry diners:

```
<select name="fish" iname="ifish" multiple="true">
```

When we look at the card this time, we will be given the option of selecting multiple fish:

Here, the Pick softkey allows selection and de-selection of individual fish, and OK confirms the selection made. (Note that by cunningly making this example a choice of fish, we've avoided the singular/plural problem in the text!) If you take a look at the variables after making this selection, you should see the following:

The selections have been stored in semicolon-separated lists. To do anything meaningful with this data, we need somehow to process the lists and extract the individual items from them; that's a job for WMLScript, and in the next chapter we'll start to see how it can help us in situations like these. For now, we'll leave this section with a final observation about lists that permit multiple selections. Unlike their single-selection brethren, it's possible to OK a multiple-selection list without choosing *any* option. In that case, the `name` variable will be set to the empty string, and the `iname` variable will be set to zero. As you'll discover, this can be useful to know.

Grouping Entries

In this section, we'll look at the third of the elements involved in list selection. `<optgroup>` allows us to build up a hierarchy of entries in a list, giving two potential benefits: we don't have to display so much at once, and we can provide options in a more logical structure. It's not a panacea, as there will be times when a 'flat' arrangement makes more sense, but it can be extremely useful.

183

Let's change the list of fish on our menu a little, and provide some alternative ways of cooking them, like this:

- ❑ Battered halibut

- ❑ Battered cod

- ❑ Roasted monkfish

- ❑ Roasted cod

- ❑ Roasted trout

We might want to divide this up into two smaller lists, for battered and roasted fish respectively:

- ❑ Battered fish
  - ❑ Halibut
  - ❑ Cod
- ❑ Roasted fish
  - ❑ Monkfish
  - ❑ Cod
  - ❑ Trout

Programmatically, this would involve our `<select>` element containing two `<optgroup>` elements, each of which contains a number of `<option>` elements.

`<optgroup>` elements have only one attribute: `title`. This allows us to name the group, so the two `<optgroup>` elements we'll use for the above list need the titles `Battered` and `Roasted`. Adding these groups, and filling them with the appropriate `<option>` elements, results in the following WML code:

```
<wml>
    <card>
        <p>
            Select fish:
            <select name="fish" iname="ifish" multiple="true">
                <optgroup title="Battered">
                    <option value="BH">Halibut</option>
                    <option value="BC">Cod</option>
                </optgroup>
                <optgroup title="Roasted">
                    <option value="RM">Monkfish</option>
                    <option value="RC">Cod</option>
                    <option value="RT">Trout</option>
                </optgroup>
            </select>
            Done.
        </p>
    </card>
</wml>
```

Unfortunately, the WML specification is quite clear that user agents don't need to act upon `<optgroup>` elements, saying only that the `<option>` elements they contain must always be presented to the user. The UP.Simulator takes this advice to heart, and places everything in a single list:

Of course, `<optgroup>` does work on many other microbrowsers, which will display the `<optgroup>` elements separately, but it's interesting to note that none of them distinguishes between the lists in any way other than for display purposes. This means, for example, that the only way to tell whether cod has been selected from the 'battered' or 'roasted' lists is by manually assigning different `value` attributes to the two `<option>` elements, as we have here. It also means that if multiple selections are disabled, only one selection is allowed from all lists – that is, you couldn't have one roasted fish and one battered one.

`<optgroup>` elements can contain other `<optgroup>` elements, allowing you to have as many levels as you want in you hierarchy. Also, you can mix `<optgroup>` elements with `<option>` elements at all levels, so that you can either choose options from the current level, or navigate to the next one.

Other Attributes

The `<select>` element also comes equipped with a `tabindex` attribute that has exactly the same behavior as the `<input>` element's attribute of the same name, and the same points apply to its use.

`<option>` elements have an `onpick` attribute that can trigger events when selections are made. This behavior will be discussed in Chapter 14.

Grouping Fields and Other Card Content

The WML specification includes a `<fieldset>` element for grouping card content into logical sections. This gives you an additional layer of control over the display of a card, although once again the user agent governs the exact behavior and presentation. Consider, for example, the following WML code that poses several questions to the user:

```
<wml>
    <card>
        <p>
            Favorite movie:<br/>
            <input name="movie"/>
            Favorite actor:<br/>
            <input name="actor"/>
```

185

```
            Favorite actress:<br/>
            <input name="actress"/>
            Favorite food:<br/>
            <input name="food"/>
            Favorite drink:<br/>
            <input name="drink"/>
        </p>
    </card>
</wml>
```

The content here might be logically divided into two sections: movie preferences and culinary tastes. We can apply this logical structure to the WML code using <fieldset> elements, naming these using their title attributes:

```
<wml>
    <card>
        <p>
            <fieldset title="Movie Preferences">
                Favorite movie:<br/>
                <input name="movie"/>
                Favorite actor:<br/>
                <input name="actor"/>
                Favorite actress:<br/>
                <input name="actress"/>
            </fieldset>
            <fieldset title="Culinary Tastes">
                Favorite food:<br/>
                <input name="food"/>
                Favorite drink:<br/>
                <input name="drink"/>
            </fieldset>
        </p>
    </card>
</wml>
```

If you try this out using the UP.Simulator, you won't notice any difference when compared to the code without fieldsets. In both cases, each <input> element is displayed on a screen of its own, and must be dealt with in sequence. Other browsers *do* display fieldsets in more intelligent ways, as we'll see in Chapter 17.

Wrox Travel: More Advanced User Interaction

Until you know how to use WMLScript, which we'll begin to look at in the next chapter, it's difficult to make much practical use of text input from the user. However, there's plenty of new functionality from the other input techniques introduced in this chapter that we can use to enhance the Wrox Travel application.

This time, we're going to use the `<select>` and `<option>` elements we've now covered to improve the "book" card still further. At the moment, it just displays the destination and price of the vacation selected (more as a proof of concept, than anything else), but we want to be in a position where the user can tell us things like:

❑ Desired date (or dates if flexible) of departure

❑ Number of adult and child places required

❑ Special dietary requirement options

❑ Other specific vacation options required (additional tours, etc.)

Ideally, users should also be able to enter their personal details and payment instructions, and then just press a button to send the whole lot to us for processing. That's an awful lot of things to do, and it's going to be a little while before we can tackle sending information the server, in particular, but we can at least make a start. For now, we'll keep things simple, and ask for three things:

❑ Desired date of departure

❑ Number of places required

❑ User's e-mail address

At the end, in lieu of a link to the server, we'll simply display a new card containing all of the information we've now gathered.

Try It Out — Getting More Information from the User

Before we begin, it's worth reminding ourselves how far we'd got in the previous chapter. Our deck in `book.wml` had access to a couple of variables: `V`, which contains the destination, and `P`, containing the price. However, that's about *all* it had! Our new functionality is going to need a rewrite, rather than an update!

1. Let's start by adding the mechanism for choosing a departure date. For this, we could use either an `<input>` element with a format mask, or three list selection fields (one each for day, month, and year). The former approach is arguably neater, but even with the mask it would generate more faulty input. We'll go with the three-list approach, but for now we won't bother validating the day of the month (which would involve checking for leap years, etc.). Here, then, is how the new deck begins:

```
<wml>
    <card id="book" title="$(V) Booking">
        <p>
            Please enter your booking details:<br/>
            Departure date:<br/>
            Day:
            <select name="D" title="Day">
                <option value="01">1st</option>
                <option value="02">2nd</option>
                <option value="03">3rd</option>
                <option value="04">4th</option>
                <option value="05">5th</option>
                <option value="06">6th</option>
                <option value="07">7th</option>
                <option value="08">8th</option>
```

```
                <option value="09">9th</option>
                <option value="10">10th</option>
                <option value="11">11th</option>
                <option value="12">12th</option>
                <option value="13">13th</option>
                <option value="14">14th</option>
                <option value="15">15th</option>
                <option value="16">16th</option>
                <option value="17">17th</option>
                <option value="18">18th</option>
                <option value="19">19th</option>
                <option value="20">20th</option>
                <option value="21">21st</option>
                <option value="22">22nd</option>
                <option value="23">23rd</option>
                <option value="24">24th</option>
                <option value="25">25th</option>
                <option value="26">26th</option>
                <option value="27">27th</option>
                <option value="28">28th</option>
                <option value="29">29th</option>
                <option value="30">30th</option>
                <option value="31">31st</option>
            </select>
```

The above will store the day in a new variable called D, leaving us still to deal with the month, which uses M:

```
Month:
<select name="M" title="Month">
    <option value="Jan">January</option>
    <option value="Feb">February</option>
    <option value="Mar">March</option>
    <option value="Apr">April</option>
    <option value="May">May</option>
    <option value="Jun">June</option>
    <option value="Jul">July</option>
    <option value="Aug">August</option>
    <option value="Sep">September</option>
    <option value="Oct">October</option>
    <option value="Nov">November</option>
    <option value="Dec">December</option>
</select>
```

And the year, which (predictably) uses Y:

```
Year:
<select name="Y" title="Year">
    <option value="2000">2000</option>
    <option value="2001">2001</option>
    <option value="2002">2002</option>
    <option value="2003">2003</option>
    <option value="2004">2004</option>
    <option value="2005">2005</option>
</select>
```

2. A select list is also the most appropriate way to ask for the number of places required. We'll impose a limit on booking more than ten places at once, and store the selection in N:

```
Places:
<select name="N" title="Places">
    <option value="1">1</option>
    <option value="2">2</option>
    <option value="3">3</option>
    <option value="4">4</option>
    <option value="5">5</option>
    <option value="6">6</option>
    <option value="7">7</option>
    <option value="8">8</option>
    <option value="9">9</option>
    <option value="10">10</option>
</select>
```

3. The other thing we need is an e-mail address, for which we certainly *can* use an `<input>` element:

```
e-mail:
<input name="E" title="e-mail"/>
```

4. To provide at least a feel of authenticity, we'll add a Confirm hyperlink, which for now will simply take the user to another card:

```
<a href="details.wml" title="Confirm">Confirm</a>
```

5. And an additional Cancel link, which will take us back to the Wrox Travel home page:

```
<a href="WroxTravel.wml" title="Cancel">Cancel</a>
```

6. Finally, we conclude the WML code:

```
    </p>
  </card>
</wml>
```

7. The above code may appear quite lengthy, but we believe that it's justified by the added usability that list selection brings. The compiled size of the WML code is 1,181 bytes, which should fit in any of today's devices.

To give some indication that everything has gone as planned, the deck in `details.wml` is about as simple as it could be:

```
<?xml version="1.0"?>
<!DOCTYPE wml PUBLIC "-//WAPFORUM//DTD WML 1.2//EN"
                     "http://www.wapforum.org/DTD/wml_1.2.xml">

<wml>
    <card id="details" title="Details">
        <p>
            <b>Destination:</b><br/>
            $(V)<br/>
            <b>Price:</b><br/>
            $(P)<br/>
            <b>Departure date:</b><br/>
            $(D) $(M) $(Y)<br/>
            <b>Places:</b><br/>
            $(N)<br/>
            <b>e-Mail</b><br/>
            $(E)<br/>
        </p>
        <do type="prev" label="Back">
            <prev/>
        </do>
    </card>
</wml>
```

8. On running through the application with an arbitrary set of choices, we received the following output; you can expect to see something similar:

How It Works

Hopefully, this example shouldn't need a great deal of additional explanation; we've simply used some of the techniques you've seen over the course of this chapter to enhance the Wrox Travel application. Specifically, we added four `<select>` lists and an `<input>` field to the "book" card, and a new "details" card to display the information we've gathered.

The thing about our application that *doesn't* work is that we're still unable to 'do' anything with the data, other than present it right back to the user. Our task in the second part of the book is to put that right.

Summary

This chapter has covered all of the different ways in which we can use WML to obtain user input. To begin with, we looked at free-form text entry using the <input> element, and saw how we could fine-tune the response of the user agent to get exactly what we wanted from the user. Next, we looked at an alternative method of input: selecting one or more items from a list. By allowing selection from only a restricted set, we were able to reduce spurious input, and to introduce some handy hierarchical organization tricks.

We then saw how the <fieldset> element allows us to group input fields together with associated card content. This is the basis of creating 'forms' on a WAP-enabled device, although the support for this is, as yet, limited. Later on in the book, in the chapters on Usability and Interoperability, we'll return to some of the topics covered in this chapter and compare the functionality of various user agents.

Finally, as has become our tradition, we took some of the theory from the chapter and applied it to the Wrox Travel case study, greatly improving its interactivity.

An Introduction to WMLScript

Our investigations into WML so far have allowed us to assemble quite a complex application, and there are still some interesting WML elements to examine, as you'll see in Chapter 14. However, for a step change in functionality, and to perform even more complex operations, greater flexibility is required.

How to achieve this improvement? If we're to move away from cards that always appear exactly as they did when you wrote them, and applications that always behave in precisely the same way, there are only two places where we can possibly do anything about it. There's the server, where the application resides, and the client, where it's executed.

On the server, it's possible to generate WML cards dynamically, customizing their content according to user preferences, or the type of user agent, or any one of countless other reasons. The process involves the use of server-side logic, using technologies such as ASP and JSP, and we will be considering this option toward the end of the book. On the client, we can change the behavior of cards through the use of a programming language called **WMLScript**, which is defined as part of the WAP specifications.

> *Ostensibly, client-side logic is an advantage to low power, limited bandwidth systems − it can save the necessity of many round trips to the server by providing facilities like data validation on the WAP-enabled device. In practice, however, WMLScript isn't yet fully or robustly implemented on any device or emulator, so yet again you need to plan carefully before releasing an application that relies on support for WMLScript.*

With that guidance in mind, this chapter will explore:

- ❑ What WMLScript is
- ❑ The history of WMLScript
- ❑ How to use WMLScript from a WML card
- ❑ Basic WMLScript syntax
- ❑ Some of the functions WMLScript provides

The next chapter will analyze WMLScript in more depth, looking at some of the complex decision-making it's capable of. In the rest of the book, we'll be using WMLScript side by side with WML, allowing the creation of much more powerful WAP solutions. Let's start, though, by taking a look at the limitations of WML, and finding out why WMLScript gives us so much more power.

Why Do We Need WMLScript?

On its own, WML is extremely limited when it comes to handling mathematical processes such as addition, subtraction, multiplication, etc. We saw how to set and display variables in Chapter 9, and how to accept user input in the last chapter, but you can't do much more than that in WML alone. Of course, you might ask why this is an issue, and it's a perfectly valid question: not every WML application needs to be able to add two numbers together, or to make changes to a string. For even a modestly professional WAP site, however, being able to monitor users and validate input is a must.

WMLScript makes these things (and many others) possible, so while it's not essential for the running of all your WML decks, we strongly recommended that you know how to use it. As support for WMLScript in WAP-enabled devices becomes more consistent, WMLScript will be an increasingly important tool in your set.

The History of WMLScript

In 1995, Brendan Eich (then of Netscape Communications Corporation) developed a scripting language called LiveScript that was included in pre-release versions of Netscape Navigator 2.0. The idea behind this language was to make web pages more dynamic – until that time, they were largely just formatted text, and user interaction was minimal. LiveScript allowed web developers to carry out mathematical calculations, react to user input, and change how web pages looked without requiring the user to reload them.

Originally, Netscape had considering incorporating a full version of Sun Microsystems' Java platform, but it was deemed too 'heavyweight' at that time. Yes, Java would have provided powerful capabilities, but at quite a performance cost. To add to this, downloading and running full applications would have stretched the computing (and bandwidth) capabilities of the day, and would have been entirely unnecessary for the more simple tasks that were envisaged. The roots of the language came from that desire, though, and this is what moved them to rename LiveScript as JavaScript later that year.

The European Computer Manufacturers' Association (ECMA) and the International Standards Organization (ISO) soon adopted JavaScript, basing their ECMAScript standard on it in November 1996. This standard is still in development today.

> The current (third) edition of the specification for ECMAScript (ECMA-262) is available at http://www.ecma.ch/stand/ecma-262.htm.

When the WAP Forum sat down and considered the structure of its new technology, the decision to incorporate some form of scripting must have been an easy one to make. With the experience of watching the Web evolve for several years, both semantically and technologically, they wanted to release a fully featured technology. Dynamic content has proved its worth time and again, and is a natural extension of the ideas behind mobile access. WMLScript was born.

WMLScript is based on ECMAScript, although there have been some modifications to make it more suitable for low bandwidth communications and thin clients. One of the key additions is that (like WML itself) WMLScript can be compiled into a binary format that's more efficient for data transmission. To achieve this, some of the more advanced features of ECMAScript have been dropped, a side effect of which is that WMLScript is easier to learn than its big brother – so we shouldn't complain!

WMLScript Applications

Let's consider a few typical WML applications, and assess their suitability for being enhanced with the features WMLScript can provide. We'll consider where WMLScript would be essential, where it could be useful, and where it would be a waste of effort. Here's the list:

❑   A banking application

❑   An online train timetable

❑   A WML personal homepage

❑   A gallery of downloadable ringing tones

❑   A currency conversion site

We will take each one in turn, and give it a WMLScript 'applicability' rating (out of five stars).

A Banking Application

Mobile banking applications are responsible for a great deal of the current interest in WAP technology. The prospect of being able to check balances at any time (and from anywhere), and to perform tasks such as paying electricity bills at the touch of a button, is an attractive one. The emergence of these types of applications is not just a possibility; it's inevitable.

But would the developer of a banking application use WMLScript? In order to answer this question, we need to analyze the business case in more detail. The basic order of events in a typical user session might run something like this:

❑   A user connects to the banking service using a WAP-enabled device

❑   The user checks the balance of an account

❑   The user transfers some money to a credit card account

❑   The user leaves the banking service

There is no reason to use WMLScript to start off with, because the *server* needs to check all the details before we can carry out any requests, so processing must be done at the server's side. It might just be possible to perform some basic data validation, but that's certainly not essential, and the benefits are unlikely to be great.

Presumably, the bank would have all of its account data stored in a database. For all its merits, WMLScript is not the best way of accessing this sort of information – dynamically generating WML code using a technology such as ASP is a better option here, and we'll be looking at its potential later, starting in Chapter 18.

There are certainly places where WMLScript *could* be used, perhaps to give a quick estimated forecast of interest over the next year, or to calculate payments over one, two, or three years, but on the whole it doesn't appear to solve much in this scenario. For that reason, this application gets a middle-of-the-road three stars.

WMLScript applicability rating: ★ ★ ★

An Online Train Timetable

Picture the situation: you've just finished work, and you're sitting in a bar with a few friends. Suddenly, you realize that you've missed your 8:30 train home! Luckily, you have your WAP phone with you, and a few clicks takes you to a site where you can discover the time of the next train – all without struggling to hear an operator above the background noise. Like WAP banking, this is a highly plausible scenario, and applications such as this will surely be created.

Is this a place where WMLScript will find a home? Possibly. Large train operators might opt for a complex system linked to a large database, akin to the banking one discussed above, but a smaller outfit might just go for a scripting solution. If the scripting backend knew, for example, that trains left a given station at forty-minute intervals between 7:00 am and 11:00 pm, except at peak times where trains left at twenty-minute intervals, it would be relatively simple to query it for the time of the next train.

However, because this simple logic falls down for larger train networks, the application only gets two stars. Any scripting will have to be done hand-in-hand with dynamic generation.

WMLScript applicability rating: ★ ★

A WML Personal Homepage

If you've ever surfed the Web, you'll have noticed the proliferation of personal web sites. It's quite possible that their authors will want to impress their friends by supplying WAP versions of their homepages too. Will *they* use WMLScript?

The answer to this is simple, and relates to the spirit of the Internet as it is today. If a technology exists, people will use it. Without people sitting up all night in front of their computers, battling with the internals of the latest multimedia features, we wouldn't have the expertise that we see today. Of *course* these people will use WMLScript in their personal pages. They might not use it for anything useful, but use it they will, even if only to produce an animation of small dancing rodents. This application gets a four star rating here.

WMLScript applicability rating: ★ ★ ★ ★

A Gallery of Downloadable Ringing Tones

The ringing of mobile phones is one of the defining sounds of our age – you hear them wherever you go, from the train, to the office, to the cinema (if you're *really* unlucky). Unless vibrating call alerts suddenly increase significantly in popularity, the ringing tones are here to stay, ranging from the inoffensive (ring, ring), to the downright annoying (Star Wars).

Already, web sites exist that allow you to download new tunes for your phone. Would a WAP site along similar lines need WMLScript? No, it wouldn't. Sure, the site authors might manage a flourish or two in the user interface, but it's unlikely to be prevalent in a site of this nature. This one gets a single, lonesome, star.

WMLScript applicability rating: ★

A Currency Conversion Site

When you've been to a foreign country a few times, you become able to 'think' in the local currency. If you're an occasional traveler (or a real globetrotter), however, this isn't so simple. Remembering conversion factors, and continually updating them to reflect rates that can sometimes change significantly from one day to the next, can be a real chore. Perhaps one day there'll be a worldwide currency, and maybe we'll only have to worry about things when we visit relatives on Mars, but until then currency conversion will always be an issue.

What better way to deal with this then switching on your phone, keying in a price, and instantly being presented with the same value in a currency you're at home with? A mobile application of this nature would be able to use up-to-the minute financial information. Would we use WMLScript to achieve this? Certainly: simple mathematical operations of this nature are perhaps the key strength of a scripting language, and can be made very efficient. Five stars.

WMLScript applicability rating: ★ ★ ★ ★ ★

How Do We Use WMLScript?

We now have an idea of the areas where WMLScript can help us, but the question of how it is used remains. The basic concept is quite simple: we put script code in separate files from our WML decks, with names that have the extension `.wmls`. We can then use the WMLScript files by referring to them from our WML files.

The code in WMLScript files is broken up into **functions** – 'units' of script that each carry out a certain operation. For example, we might have a function that adds two numbers together, while another might capitalize the first letter of a word. Several functions may exist together in a single `.wmls` file.

Let's consider the first of these two examples, where the purpose of the WMLScript function is to add two numbers together, and return the result to the browser. The act of using a function is usually referred to as **calling** the function, and the sequence of events involved would look like this:

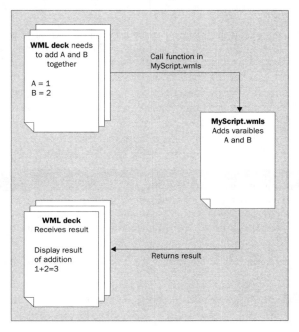

The WMLScript file has access to the WML variables currently in use, and can create new variables in the browser if it so requires. In the example above, we could create a variable C, and store in it the sum of A and B, from within the script. All we would then have to do in order to use it is refer to C (or more accurately, $(C)) from the WML deck.

As well as using browser variables, we can pass data to the function in the form of **parameters**. For the addition function above, the parameters would be the values of A and B. For the 'capitalizing' function mentioned, we would need to pass in the word we wished to have capitalized.

Parameters can be one of the following:

Parameter Type	Syntax	Example
String	String enclosed in single quotes	`'hello'`
Number	Numeric expression, no quotes	`-3`

Basic WMLScript

In practice, using WMLScript functions is actually fairly straightforward. Like variables, functions have names, making it possible to call a particular function in a WMLScript file by using a URL. The syntax for doing this is quite similar to that used for identifying a card within a deck: the URL points to the script file we want to use, and specifies the name of the function (along with any parameters we want to pass to it) as a fragment.

```
http://www.mydomain.com/MyScript.wmls#MyFunction(Param1, Param2)
http://www.mydomain.com/MyScript.wmls#MyOtherFunction(Param1)
```

As usual, the `http://www.mydomain.com/` part of the URL can be omitted for relative addressing (where the WMLScript file is in the same directory as the deck that requires it). A call to a function called `add()` in a file called `calc.wmls` could use URLs like these:

```
http://www.mydomain.com/calc.wmls#add(1, 2)
http://www.mydomain.com/calc.wmls#add($(A), $(B))
```

The difference between these two is that we've passed ordinary numbers to the function in the first call, and the values of the WML variables A and B in the second. Both of these calls are perfectly legal.

Try It Out — An add() Function

After all this, you're probably quite eager to see a WMLScript function at work. There's still some ground to cover before we can create fully-fledged applications that use WMLScript to its fullest, but we can at least get our hands dirty. The following demonstration puts the `add()` function discussed above into practice:

1. Type the following WML code into your editor, and save it in a file called `calc.wml`:

```
<?xml version="1.0"?>
<!DOCTYPE wml PUBLIC "-//WAPFORUM//DTD WML 1.2//EN"
                     "http://www.wapforum.org/DTD/wml_1.2.xml">
```

```
<wml>
  <card id="add" title="Add 2 Numbers">
    <p>This is a simple calculator.</p>
    <p>
      Please enter the first number<br/>
      X = <input name="var1" title="1st number" format="*N" /><br/>
      Please enter the second number<br/>
      Y = <input name="var2" title="2nd number" format="*N" /><br/>
      <a href="calc.wmls#add($(var1), $(var2))">Calculate</a>
    </p>
    <do type="accept">
      <go href="calc.wmls#add($(var1), $(var2))"/>
    </do>
  </card>
  <card id="result" title="Result">
    <p>X + Y = $(S)<br/></p>
  </card>
</wml>
```

2. Next, create another new file, enter the following WMLScript code, and save it in the same directory as `calc.wml`, with the name `calc.wmls`. Be careful to enter this *exactly* as shown; there is nothing more that needs adding to it for now.

```
extern function add(A, B)
{
    WMLBrowser.setVar("S", A + B);
    WMLBrowser.go("#result");
}
```

3. Load calc.wml into the UP.Simulator, and you should see the following:

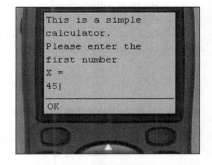

4. Enter a number and select OK. You will now be asked to enter a second number:

5. Enter a second number, choose OK again, and you'll be presented with the Calculate link. Selecting this will show the result on the screen:

How It Works

The first card in `calc.wml` allows the user to enter two numbers, and includes a Calculate link. Notice that we've used the `<input>` element's `format` attribute to restrict input to numbers of any length:

```
Please enter the first number<br/>
X = <input name="var1" title="1st number" format="*N" /><br/>
Please enter the second number<br/>
Y = <input name="var2" title="2nd number" format="*N" /><br/>
```

The next line contains a hyperlink that causes the `add()` function in `calc.wmls` to be called:

```
<a href="calc.wmls#add($(var1), $(var2))">Calculate</a>
```

From the results, you can see that the `add()` function creates a new variable called `S`, sets it to the sum of `var1` and `var2`, and displays the result. The issue we need to deal with, of course, is working out exactly how it does that. Just what is going on in that WMLScript file?

Looking at `calc.wmls`, there's not much to it – it's only five lines long! Let's examine it piece by piece, and see if we can come to any conclusions. Here's the first line:

```
extern function add(A, B)
```

This is called a **declaration**. The word `function` means that we're creating a function (no surprises there); the name of the function is `add`; and the two-item list between the parentheses (`A`, `B`) says that when this function is called, two parameters must be passed to it. Within the function, we'll be able to use the symbols `A` and `B` to refer to the two values passed in.

> *You can specify that a function should be called with any number of parameters, including none at all, but the parentheses after the function name must always be present in the declaration. That's why, when we refer to a function name in text, we follow it with a pair of parentheses, like so: `add()`.*

The word `extern` that appears at the start of the declaration means that this function is **externally accessible,** something about which we'll have more to say later on.

The rest of the script consists of the **body** of the function, enclosed between braces – that is, { and }:

```
{
    WMLBrowser.setVar("S", A + B);
    WMLBrowser.go("#result");
}
```

In the first line, we calculate the sum (that's the A + B part), and then send this result back to the microbrowser in a new variable called S. You can see that setVar() behaves rather like the <setvar> WML element – here, "S" is the name, and A + B is the value to assign to S. The second line directs the browser to navigate to the "result" card – the go() function, as you may have gathered, works in the same way as a <do> element with a <go> element in it.

Both of these lines of code demonstrate calls to **predefined functions** – these are included as standard in the browser, so we don't need to write them ourselves. WMLScript comes complete with a whole host of predefined functions, and we'll be seeing many more of them as we progress.

Structure of a WMLScript File

That's quite a lot to take in at once, so don't worry if you're not sure that you understand. Over the next few chapters, we're going to cover everything you've just seen more carefully, but some of the ideas and terminology we've discussed will help you on the way. The truth is that before you can write useful WMLScript functions, you first need to put in a fair amount of groundwork, and that's what we'll start to do now.

In this section, we will look at the main constituents of a typical WMLScript file, and discuss the essential facts about each. The four important topics we will examine are:

❑   Basic WMLScript syntax

❑   Functions – the building blocks of WMLScript files

❑   Variables

❑   Operators, and control of interactions between variables – the real strength of WMLScript

Basic Syntax

Like WML, a WMLScript file is just a text file, and it can be created using a text editor. However, there are rules that need to be followed in order for the text file to be interpreted correctly. The basic syntax of WMLScript follows that of ECMAScript:

❑   It is case sensitive, so myvariable is *not* the same as MyVariable.

❑   Spaces, tabs, and newline characters are ignored. Any amount of white space is treated the same way, be it one character or many. The only exception to this is the white space in strings.

❑   **Blocks** of code are enclosed in braces: '{' and '}'.

❑   Lines of code, also called **statements**, end in semicolons.

❑   Comments are denoted by starting a line of code with '//', and just like comments in WML, they're removed at compilation time.

Functions

WMLScript is a **procedural** language, which means that it is broken up into reusable portions called **procedures**, more commonly known as **functions**. A function is a block of code that can be called either externally (our add() function was called from outside the WMLScript file), or internally. Functions that are declared without the extern keyword can only be called by other functions in the same WMLScript file. The naming of WMLScript functions follows the same rules as naming WML variables.

Earlier on, we saw how to call WMLScript functions from within a WML page, using the URL format. Calling other functions from within WMLScript code is even easier: we just use the name of the function we want to call. For example:

```
extern function myFunc1()
{
   myFunc2(1, 2);
   // Script execution resumes here after myFunc2() finishes
}

function myFunc2(myParam1, myParam2)
{
   // Called from within myFunc1()
}
```

Here, myFunc1() includes a call to myFunc2(), passing parameters in the same was as we do from WML.

Return Values

To get the result of the add() function back to our WML code, we had to create a new WML variable by using the predefined setVar() function. Doing the equivalent between WMLScript functions is much easier: we can make use of **return values**, which are specified with the return keyword.

A return value can be thought of as the 'result' of a function, and it's effectively substituted for the function name in the code when the script is executed:

```
extern function myFunc1()
{
   WMLBrowser.setVar("S", myFunc2());
}

function myFunc2()
{
   return "Sorted!";
}
```

In this case, the browser variable S will be assigned with the return value of myFunc2(), which is just the string Sorted!. By default, functions return an empty string.

Being able to use return values like this allows a great deal of flexibility: we can split our code up into independent modules, according to functionality. If we wanted to execute a complex algorithm repeatedly, for example, we could split the algorithm code off into a separate function, making the rest of the code a lot shorter, not to mention more readable.

Function Libraries

As you gain more experience with WMLScript, you're likely to build up your own **library** of useful functions, which you can store in a separate file or files. WMLScript itself uses this concept of code libraries, and supplies several **standard libraries** of its own. In this way, it breaks off core functionality (basic syntax and operators) from code that performs more complex tasks. Specifically, the seven built-in libraries are:

Library	Purpose
Lang	Basic extensions to the WMLScript core, including some simple mathematical operations
Float	Advanced mathematical operations
String	String manipulation functions
URL	URL-specific string manipulation functions
WMLBrowser	Functions for interacting with the microbrowser and WML deck
Dialogs	User interface functions, such as pop-up windows
Crypto	Encryption functions for security purposes

You'll find a complete list of all the functions in the standard libraries in Appendix D.

Calling functions in the standard libraries follows another simple format: you simply specify the library to use, followed by a period, and then the function you want to call. Our first example used this syntax to set a variable in the microbrowser:

```
WMLBrowser.setVar("S", A + B);
```

This line of code calls the function called setVar() in the WMLBrowser library. We also used the following call, which caused the browser to navigate:

```
WMLBrowser.go(#result);
```

The following program provides some more examples of calling functions (user-defined and predefined) from various places in your code. It also uses a new function called refresh(), which again comes from the WMLBrowser library. refresh() causes the browser to redisplay the current card, so that any changes made to variable values are reflected. We will use this functionality to show the result of calculation in the example on the next page.

Try It Out — Using Return Values in Functions

1. Enter the following WMLScript code into your text editor, and save the file as `circle.wmls`:

```
extern function circle(radius)
{
   WMLBrowser.setVar("A", area(radius));
   WMLBrowser.setVar("P", perimeter(radius));
   WMLBrowser.refresh();
}

function area(radius)
{
   return Pi() * Float.pow(radius, 2);
}

function perimeter(radius)
{
   return 2 * Pi() * radius;
}

function Pi()
{
   return 3.14;
}
```

2. Now enter the following deck and save it as `circle.wml`:

```
<?xml version="1.0"?>
<!DOCTYPE wml PUBLIC "-//WAPFORUM//DTD WML 1.2//EN"
                     "http://www.wapforum.org/DTD/wml_1.2.xml">
<wml>
   <card>
      <p>Radius = 3<br/>
         Area = $(A)<br/>
         Perimeter = $(P)<br/>
      </p>
      <do type="accept" label="Calculate">
         <go href="circle.wmls#circle(3)"/>
      </do>
   </card>
</wml>
```

3. Try running this card in your microbrowser. You should see something like this:

4. Pressing Calculate will activate the <do> task that causes the script to execute, which in turn displays the newly calculated variable values:

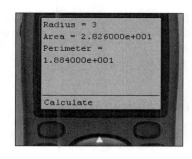

How It Works

The externally accessible function `circle()` sets two browser variables, A and P, based on the radius as supplied in the WML code. A and P are then calculated using the internal functions `area()` and `perimeter()`.

In the function, we use the `WMLBrowser.setVar()` library function that we've already seen, with the return values of our two internal functions as parameters. We also use another library function, `Float.pow()`, in the `area()` function to calculate the square of the radius.

Finally, we also define a function called `Pi()` that returns the (very approximate) value of π. We have to do this manually because mathematical constants like this aren't predefined anywhere in the WMLScript libraries.

Variables

When we used variables in WML, there was never any doubt over what *kind* of data was stored in them, because WML variables can only be used for storing string values. In WMLScript, however, variables can contain five different types of data:

❑ Integers

❑ Floating point numbers

❑ Strings

❑ Boolean values (`true` or `false`)

❑ Invalid data (none of the above and not empty – perhaps due to an error)

However, WMLScript is a **weakly typed** language, which means that you don't have to specify what type of data a given variable will contain – you can just assign a variable with a value, and the rest will be taken care of for you. There's not even a problem with assigning different types of data to a variable over the course of its lifetime, and as well shall see later, there are a number of ways of *converting* data from one type to another, implicit and explicit.

WMLScript variables must be **declared**, which means specifying that you wish to use a given identifier, or name, to represent a variable. This allows WMLScript to reserve memory to store the variable's value, and to check your code for simple errors, such as spelling a variable name wrongly. To declare a variable, you use the `var` keyword, like this:

```
var myVar;
```

205

Including this statement in a function enables you to use the variable `myVar` in any code that comes after it in the same function. You can declare multiple variables on consecutive lines:

```
var myVar1;
var myVar2;
```

Or on the same line, separated by commas:

```
var myVar1, myVar2;
```

If you wish, you can choose to initialize variables at the same time as declaring them. The line below, for example, would assign the value 3 to `myVar`:

```
var myVar = 3;
```

The next thing you need to know is that unlike browser variables, which (once defined) can be used from anywhere in WML or WMLScript code, the variables that you create have local **scope**. This means that, from a programming perspective, they only exist in the block of code in which they were defined (say, a function, or one of the looping structures we'll be discussing in the next chapter). Look at this:

```
extern function myFunc1()
{
   var myVar = 902;
}

extern function myFunc2()
{
   myVar = 904;
}
```

Calling `myFunc2()` from a WML deck will fail, even if `myFunc1()` has been called on an earlier occasion. `myVar` is created inside `myFunc1()`, and destroyed when that function ends. The variable is not 'in scope' in `myFunc2()`.

Finally, you should know that there are some **reserved identifiers**: strings that are either part of the WMLScript language already, or reserved for future use. You can't give your variables any of these names, as doing so would confuse WMLScript. The following is a list of these reserved identifiers:

access	extern	public
agent	false	return
break	finally	sizeof
case	for	struct
catch	function	super
class	header	switch
const	http	this
continue	if	throw
delete	import	true
div	in	try
debugger	invalid	typeof
default	isvalid	url
do	lib	use

```
domain      meta       user
else        name       var
enum        new        void
equiv       null       while
export      path       with
extends     private
```

Don't worry: you don't need to memorize all of these! WMLScript will soon complain if you try to use one of these identifiers by mistake.

Literals

Numbers and strings that appear in WMLScript code in their 'normal' form (that is, they're not stored in variables) are called **literals**. Integer literals can be written in decimal, hexadecimal (base 16), or octal (base 8) form. Hexadecimal numbers are prefixed with 0x, while octal numbers have a leading zero, so watch out for decimal numbers in your code with leading zeros, or you'll get a surprise!

Integers can be any number in the range −2147483648 to 2147483647, and to choose one from somewhere near the middle of that range at random, the number 17 (in decimal form) can be represented in the following ways:

```
17   // Decimal
0x11 // Hexadecimal
021  // Octal
```

Floating point literals are also possible:

```
3.1416
56392.5
```

As is scientific notation, where numbers are represented in mantissa-exponent form. To specify such a number in WMLScript, we can represent an exponent using the character "E" (or "e"). The following representations of 1.9754×10^3 are therefore equivalent:

```
1975.4
1.9754E3
```

The maximum number that can be represented in this fashion is 3.40282347E38, while the minimum is 1.17549435E-38.

Finally, string literals within WMLScript code can be specified by enclosing characters in single or double quotes, such as "Orinoco" or 'Orinoco'. We saw in Chapter 9 that we often need to 'escape' certain characters in strings for interpretation purposes, and WMLScript includes escape codes for encoding reserved and white space characters. For example, if you wanted to specify the following string:

```
"I understand your so-called "logic", and say that it's deeply flawed."
```

You would have problems. Enclosing this string in quotes, single or double, will lead to possible misinterpretations − as it stands, the string will be deemed to end just before logic, and then you'll get a syntax error because WMLScript doesn't know what to do with the remaining character sequence.

The solution to this problem is to use the escape codes for the offending characters. In this case, we can use \ ' for a single quote, and \ " for a double quote:

```
"I understand your so-called \"logic\", and say that it\'s deeply flawed."
```

This may not look attractive, and it's certainly less readable, but it will be interpreted correctly. The full list of possible escape codes is given in the table below:

Escape Code	Represents
\ '	Single quote
\ "	Double quote
\ \	Backslash
\ /	Forward slash
\b	Backspace
\f	Form feed
\n	Newline
\r	Carriage return
\t	Horizontal tab
\x*hh*	Character *hh* from the Latin-1 character set (ISO 8859-1), specified in hexadecimal format as two digits
ooo	Character *ooo* from the Latin-1 character set (ISO 8859-1), specified in octal format as three digits
\u*hhhh*	Character *hhhh* from the Unicode character set, specified in hexadecimal format as four digits

The last three entries in this table are the most general, allowing pretty much any character from any language to be inserted into a string. To give an example, we could insert a © (copyright) symbol into a string using any of the following:

```
"\xA9 Karli Watson, 2000"
"\251 Karli Watson, 2000"
"\u00A9 Karli Watson, 2000"
```

All of which would give us the result:

```
© Karli Watson, 2000
```

Bear in mind that if you try inserting character 0F93 (Tibetan subjoined letter GHA, apparently), for example, you'd better make sure that your target device supports it!

Operators

Operators allow us to manipulate and compare variables and literals. That sounds like a grand description, but in fact you've seen things like these thousands of times before. +, for example, is an operator: it adds together the values on either side of itself. (The values upon which an operator operates are sometimes called **operands**.) In WMLScript, operators fall into the following categories:

- ❏ The assignment operator
- ❏ Arithmetic and string operators
- ❏ Logical operators
- ❏ Bitwise operators
- ❏ 'Special' operators

The Assignment Operator

Perhaps the most basic operation we would ever want to perform with variables is assigning values to them. As we've seen, we use the assignment operator, =, to do that:

```
myVar = 3;
```

In general, this operator simply takes the value on its right hand side and places it in the variable on the left hand side. The value on the right hand side needn't be as simple as the one above – it could also be a mathematical expression, or another variable:

```
myVar2 = myVar1;
```

After execution of this line, the contents of myVar1 and myVar2 will be identical – they will contain whatever myVar2 contained before this assignment occurred. Other possibilities include assigning a variable with the return value of a function, or setting it to the result of an operation such as addition or division.

Arithmetic and String Operators

Now things start to get more interesting. Using the arithmetic and string operators, we can construct more complex mathematical operations, using multiple variables and/or literals. The usual mathematical operators are provided, including the add (+) operator we used in the first example:

```
myVar = 4 + 5;
```

As you'd expect, this adds the two numbers on each side of the operator together – but you can use the + operator on strings too. For example, this combination:

```
myVar = "It's time";
myVar = myVar + " to eat bananas";
```

would result in myVar containing the string "It's time to eat bananas".

We can use the subtract (–), multiply (*), and divide operators in the same way (for numbers, not for strings!), although the last of these isn't completely straightforward, because there are three operators for division: /, div, and %.

209

The first of these behaves as you would expect it to:

```
myVar = 10 / 4;
```

This will result in myVar containing 2.5. On the other hand, the div operator carries out integer division, losing any fractional part:

```
myVar = 10 div 4;
```

In the example above, 2 is stored in myVar – you're really asking, "How many times does the whole of 4 go into 10?" The remainder of this division can be calculated using %:

```
myVar = 10 % 4;
```

Here, the value 2 is stored in myVar, because 4 goes into 10 twice, leaving 2 as the remainder.

Try It Out — Extending the Calculator Application

There are many things that we could include to improve on the 'add-only' functionality of our calculator application. We could consider the various geometric operations (sine, cosine, tangent, etc.); the different numeric bases (octal and hexadecimal numbers); and numerous others. For the rest of the chapter, however, we'll just extend our calculator to allow the four basic operators, and we'll discuss ways of making the application more robust.

1. Make the following changes to calc.wml, and save the file as calc2.wml:

```
<?xml version="1.0"?>
<!DOCTYPE wml PUBLIC "-//WAPFORUM//DTD WML 1.2//EN"
                     "http://www.wapforum.org/DTD/wml_1.2.xml">
<wml>
    <card id="add" title="Calculate" newcontext="true">
        <p>This is a simple calculator.</p>
        <p>
            Please enter the first number<br/>
            X = <input name="var1" title="1st number" format="*N" /><br/>
            Please enter the second number<br/>
            Y = <input name="var2" title="2nd number" format="*N" /><br/>
            <a href="calc2.wmls#add($(var1), $(var2))">Add</a>
            <a href="calc2.wmls#sub($(var1), $(var2))">Subtract</a>
            <a href="calc2.wmls#mul($(var1), $(var2))">Multiply</a>
            <a href="calc2.wmls#divide($(var1), $(var2))">Divide</a>
        </p>
        <do type="accept">
            <go href="calc2.wmls#add($(var1), $(var2))" />
        </do>
    </card>
    <card id="result" title="result">
        <p>X $(P) Y = $(S)<br/></p>
    </card>
</wml>
```

2. We will also add three functions to calc.wmls that carry out the additional operations now available to the user. Modify the file according to the listing opposite, and save it as calc2.wmls.

```
extern function add(A, B)
{
    WMLBrowser.setVar("P", "+");
    WMLBrowser.setVar("S", A + B);
    WMLBrowser.go("#result");
}

extern function sub(A, B)
{
    WMLBrowser.setVar("P", "-");
    WMLBrowser.setVar("S", A - B);
    WMLBrowser.go("#result");
}

extern function mul(A, B)
{
    WMLBrowser.setVar("P", "*");
    WMLBrowser.setVar("S", A * B);
    WMLBrowser.go("#result");
}

extern function divide(A, B)
{
    WMLBrowser.setVar("P", "/");
    WMLBrowser.setVar("S", A / B);
    WMLBrowser.go("#result");
}
```

3. Load `calc2.wml` into your browser. As before, you should get the following screen:

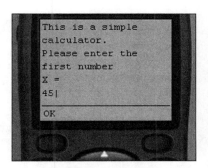

4. Enter 45 and 23 as your two numbers, after which you'll get the following:

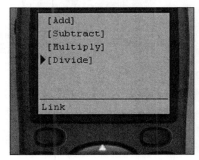

5. For the sake of argument, we'll choose Divide, resulting in the output below:

How It Works

We've amended our WML deck so that it now contains additional links allowing the user to perform the other basic operations on the numbers input by the user. We call each function in the same way, including the function name together with the input parameters:

```
<a href="calc2.wmls#add($(var1), $(var2))">Add</a>
<a href="calc2.wmls#sub($(var1), $(var2))">Subtract</a>
<a href="calc2.wmls#mul($(var1), $(var2))">Multiply</a>
<a href="calc2.wmls#divide($(var1), $(var2))">Divide</a>
```

We've also amended a line in the "result" card. As there are now four possible operations, we must alter the output to the user so that it reflects the operation carried out. We assign a variable P with the operator chosen: +, −, *, or /:

```
X $(P) Y = $(S)<br/>
```

This line simply outputs the operator assigned to P, so if the operation chosen was multiplication, * will be assigned to P, and the output will be:

```
X * Y = ...
```

Calc2.wmls is also quite straightforward. We have modified the add() function so that it now initializes the browser variable P with the value "+":

```
WMLBrowser.setVar("P", "+");
```

And the three new functions are identical to the first, with the exception of the operation carried out. We could easily add the remaining two operators (div and %), but things would start getting *very* repetitive!

More Arithmetic Operators

All of the operators we've just discussed have another form, in which they can be combined with the assignment operator to provide a 'shorthand' way of expressing certain operations. As an example, suppose that myVar has the value 10 stored in it. In that case, the following operation:

```
myVar = myVar * 4;
```

Is exactly equivalent to this one:

```
myVar *= 4;
```

Both of these will store the value 40 in myVar.

Another point concerning the arithmetic operators is the specialized use of two of them: + and –. These can be used to specify whether the following variable should be positive or negative (although the + sign is usually redundant). For example:

```
myVar1 = 5;
myVar2 = -myVar1;
```

This will result in myVar2 having the value minus 5. The – operator doesn't *force* a negative result, though; it just changes the sign of its operand:

```
myVar1 = -5;
myVar2 = -myVar1;
```

After these two lines, myVar2 will have the value 5.

The last two operators we need to consider here are unusual not only because they operate on just one operand, but also because they have two uses each (as we'll see in a moment), and they both permanently affect their operand.

++ increments (adds 1 to) its operand, while – – decrements (subtracts 1 from) its operand. These two operators can prefix or suffix their respective operands, and the relative location specifies *when* the incrementing or decrementing takes place. This needs an example for clarification!

```
myVar1 = 5;
myVar2 = ++myVar1;
```

In the situation above, both myVar1 and myVar2 will have the value 6 when the assignments are completed. The order of operations is as follows: myVar1 is assigned the value 5. It is then incremented, so its value is 6, whereupon that value is assigned to myVar2.

```
myVar1 = 5;
myVar2 = myVar1++;
```

This time, myVar1 will be 6, but myVar2 will be 5. Why? Well, myVar1 is first assigned the value 5, as before. This value is assigned to myVar2, and *then* myVar1 is incremented.

> *These two operators may look a little odd now, but they have a great many uses – especially when it comes to looping – as we shall see in the next chapter.*

Logical and Comparison Operators

The **comparison operators** add another level of control: they allow us to compare values, and the results of expressions, against one another. Is this variable's value less than ten? Is a given number equal to zero? We'll be making much use of these operators in the next chapter, when we look at **conditional logic**, but we can see how they work here.

Comparison operators all take two operands, and return a Boolean value indicating whether the comparison evaluates to true or false. The full list of these operators is shown in the table below:

Operator	Description
==	Equality
!=	Inequality
<	Less than
>	Greater than
<=	Less than or equal to
>=	Greater than or equal to

Using these operators is quite straightforward. If we wish to check whether myNumber is less than 10, we could write:

```
myVar = myNumber < 10;
```

myVar will be true if myNumber is less than 10.

The three **logical operators** work with Boolean values (such as those created by the comparison operators), and can be used to group expressions together – ideal when we need to check for several conditions at once. The logical operators can be used to determine whether one condition AND another are both true; whether one condition OR another is true; and whether a condition is NOT true. These operations are represented by the symbols &&, ||, and ! respectively.

For example, if we wanted to search a database for female patients over forty, we would need to test two conditions: that the patient was both female AND over forty. In code, this might look like the following:

```
myVar = (gender == "female") && (age > 40)
```

The logical OR operator (||) evaluates to true if either one of its operands is true. For example, to check if a child is too short OR too young to go on a ride:

```
myVar = (height < 94) || (age < 5)
```

The logical NOT operator (!) is slightly different in that it only takes one operand, which should immediately follow the operator. The result of the operation is simply the Boolean opposite of its operand, so that true will be returned if the operand is false, and vice versa.

An interesting situation occurs if the operands to the logical operators *aren't* Boolean values. Supplying the wrong kind of operand might sound like an error, but it can actually be quite useful, as we'll see. When this 'problem' arises, WMLScript automatically converts other data types to Boolean, using the rules in the following table.

Base type	Conversion Rule
Integer	0 converts to `false`, other values to `true`
String	"" (empty string) converts to `false`, other strings to `true`
Floating point	0.0 converts to `false`, other values to `true`
Invalid	Cannot be converted

So in the following expression:

```
myVar = myTest1 && myTest2
```

The value of `myVar` will be `true` if `myTest1` and `myTest2` are both any of the following: non-zero integers, non-zero floating-point values, non-empty strings, or `true` Boolean values. If either `myTest1` or `myTest2` contains anything else, `myVar` will be `false`. This means that we could, for example, use the `&&` operator with two string variables – it would be a way of ensuring that both the strings contained text, perhaps to ensure that the user had input some vital data.

The logical operators can be combined to make quite complex assignments, for example:

```
myVar = (myTest1 || !myTest2) && myTest3;
```

The results of this assignment can be summarized as follows:

myTest1 Value	**myTest2** Value	**myTest3** Value	**myVar** Value
true	true	true	true
true	true	false	false
true	false	true	true
true	false	false	false
false	true	true	false
false	true	false	false
false	false	true	true
false	false	false	false

What kind of situation might require logic like this? Well, maybe something like the following:

```
willGetWet = (forgotUmbrella || !carWorking) && itsRaining;
```

This ability to combine operators is *very* important in WMLScript programming, especially when we need conditional branching and testing. We'll be looking at these techniques in great detail in the next chapter, but there is another operator in this category that touches on these issues. The **tertiary** (or **conditional**) **operator**, which takes three parameters, returns a result based on a simple Boolean test.

The syntax is as follows:

```
<test> ? <result if true> : <result if false>
```

For example:

```
myVar = myTest ? "Yes indeedy!" : "Sorry, not this time!";
```

After this line of code is executed, the string that myVar contains will depend on the Boolean interpretation of myTest. If myTest evaluates to true, myVar will contain the string Yes indeedy!; otherwise, it will contain Sorry, not this time!.

Try It Out — A Car Purchase Advisor

Let's have a look at how we might combine these logical operators in a practical way. The following code dispenses purchasing advice for traveling arrangements, based on a questionnaire we'll ask the user to fill in.

1. Enter the following deck, and save the file as car.wml. This WML file will handle both the questionnaire and the result of evaluating the questionnaire.

```
<?xml version="1.0"?>
<!DOCTYPE wml PUBLIC "-//WAPFORUM//DTD WML 1.2//EN"
                     "http://www.wapforum.org/DTD/wml_1.2.xml">

<wml>
   <card id="distance">
      <p>Please answer the following questions:<br/>
         How many miles do you drive per week?
         <input name="miles" format="*N"/>
      </p>
      <p>I am single:
         <select name="single">
            <option value="true">True</option>
            <option value="false">False</option>
         </select>
      </p>
      <p>I have children:
         <select name="children">
            <option value="true">True</option>
            <option value="false">False</option>
         </select>
      </p>
      <p>I have a dog:
         <select name="dog">
            <option value="true">True</option>
            <option value="false">False</option>
         </select>
         <a href="car.wmls#advise($(miles), $(single), $(children), $(dog))">
            Advise me
         </a>
      </p>
```

```
            <do type="accept">
                <go href="car.wmls#advise($(miles), $(single), $(children), $(dog))"/>
            </do>
        </card>
        <card id="result">
            <p>You should consider buying a $(adv)<br/></p>
            <p>$(ext)</p>
        </card>
    </wml>
```

2. Now enter the WMLScript function below, and save it in a file called `car.wmls`. This code is more involved than any you've seen so far, but we've looked at everything it contains, and you can be assured that it will become clear shortly.

```
extern function advise(miles, single, children, dog)
{
    var advice = "";
    var extra = "";

    advice = (miles > 50) ? "bicycle for yourself." : "motorbike.";
    advice = !single ? "car" : advice;
    advice = children || dog ? "big car" : advice;
    advice = dog && children ? advice + " and hiring a chauffeur." : advice;

    extra = (miles > 250) && !single && children && dog ?
                "You should also get earplugs!" : "";

    WMLBrowser.setVar("adv", advice);
    WMLBrowser.setVar("ext", extra);
    WMLBrowser.go("#result");
}
```

3. Load `car.wml`, and enter your details. For this demonstration, I've answered the questions for myself – and it turns out that I do drive quite a lot:

4. I'm married, so I answer False to the next question:

217

5. I don't have children, but we do regularly look after a couple of kids:

6. The answer to the next question is the same – the neighbors have a German shepherd that we take for walks:

7. And the answer is:

How It Works

As usual, we'll start with the WML file. This is a fairly self-explanatory deck: the user must enter an approximation of the number of miles they drive, and True/False for subsequent questions. At the end of this stage, they will be presented with a link that calls the advise() function in car.wmls.

The advise() function is not as difficult as it may first appear. We know that it takes four parameters, so the declaration is easy to write:

```
extern function advise(miles, single, children, dog)
{
```

The first thing to do in the body of the function is to initialize two variables (advice and extra) that will eventually be used to send the result of the questionnaire back to the WML deck:

```
var advice = "";
var extra = "";
```

The next section of code is concerned with analyzing the details we've gathered – five lines of code that all use the tertiary operator. The first checks whether the user travels more than 50 miles per week, while the others tailor the advice given depending on some other aspects of the user's life.

If the user is traveling locally, they only need a bicycle. We test if `miles` is less than 50, and if so assign `advice` with the value `"bicycle for yourself."`. If they're traveling larger distances, they probably need something a little more powerful – a motorbike:

```
advice = (miles > 50) ? "bicycle for yourself." : "motorbike.";
```

The next question asks if the user is single. If they're not, they probably need a car.

```
advice = !single ? "car" : advice;
```

Notice the first operand here. If `single` is `true`, `!single` will evaluate to `false`. This means that the effective result of the code above will be the following:

```
advice = advice;
```

In other words, if the user is single, there will be no new value assigned to `advice`. We continue in this vein for the rest of the code: a `true` answer to one of the other questions will result in a new value being assigned to `advice`; otherwise the value remains unchanged.

```
advice = children || dog ? "big car" : advice;
advice = dog && children ? advice + " and hiring a chauffeur." : advice;
```

By now, you should be ready for the final test. The following statement checks whether the user travels quite significant distances, is not single, and has both children and a dog. If so, they should probably get some earplugs too!

```
extra = (miles > 250) && !single && children && dog ?
            "You should also get earplugs!" : "";
```

Now that we have the result of the questionnaire, we can save the values as browser variables. `adv` is assigned the value of `advice`, and `ext` holds the extra information:

```
WMLBrowser.setVar("adv", advice);
WMLBrowser.setVar("ext", extra);
WMLBrowser.go("#result");
}
```

When the browser navigates to the "result" card, this information is displayed. If there's no extra information, `ext` will contain an empty string, so it won't be shown on the screen.

```
<card id="result">
    <p>You should consider getting a $(adv)<br/></p>
    <p>$(ext)</p>
</card>
</wml>
```

Hopefully you can see how, with a little thought, we can apply the various logical operators to construct quite complex value checking.

Bitwise Operators

*The **bitwise operators** make changes to values at the binary level, and as such require some knowledge of the workings of binary numbers. We won't be used these operators in any other of the book's examples, but we've included this section for completeness. If you wish to skip this subject, you can do so without compromising the remainder of the book.*

The first operators we'll look at in this section allow us to **shift** the bit patterns of the values passed as their operands. If we were to shift the number 7 to the right twice, for example, we would get the number 1:

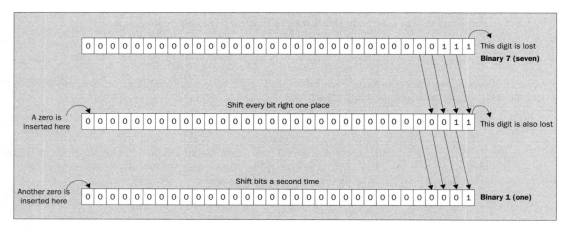

The shifting operators (<<, >>, and >>>) shift their left hand operand by the number of binary positions indicated by the right hand operand. This, for example:

```
myVar = 4;
myVar = myVar << 1;
```

results in `myVar` containing 8, as illustrated below:

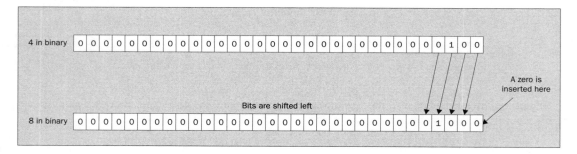

The binary representation of 4 is 100, so shifting left by one place gives you 1000 – the binary representation of 8 in decimal. In general, the effect of shifting the bits one place to the left is to multiply the value by 2, while shifting one place right results in the value being divided by two.

These operators have shorthand forms, too. If you consider the operation above:

```
myVar = myVar << 1;
```

It makes sense for us to be able to represent this operation as follows:

```
myVar =<< 1;
```

Finally, the &, |, and ^ operators (bitwise AND, bitwise OR, and bitwise NOT) take binary digits from the values passed to them, and perform logical operations on them. Logical operations on bit values work according to the following rules:

❑   Bitwise AND returns 1 only if both bit values are equal to 1

❑   Bitwise OR returns 1 if either bit value is 1

❑   Bitwise NOT returns the opposite bit value

To see what effect operators like these can have, here's an example:

```
myVar = 5 & 6;
```

Execution of this statement would result in myVar storing 4. Let's look at this in more detail.

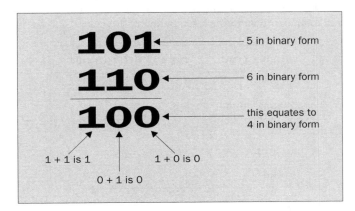

The bitwise operators have uses in the manipulation of 'flags' – variables that we have decided to treat not as number or strings, but as sets of ones and zeros in which a '1' usually means "on" or "true", while a '0' means "off" or "false". If you keep careful track of what each bit means, this can be a very compact alternative to (say) maintaining a large number of Boolean variables.

'Special' Operators

WMLScript contains a few other useful operators that we've chosen to group together under the blanket term 'special'. There are three of these operators, and we'll look at them in this section:

❑   The , (comma) operator

❑   The `typeof` operator

❑   The `isvalid` operator

The **comma operator** allows you to perform multiple operations at the same time – we simply separate them with commas. You saw this in action when we declared multiple variables simultaneously:

```
var myVar1, myVar2;
```

We can also use this operator to set the values of multiple variables in one go:

```
myVar1 = 2, myVar2 = 3;
```

This might not seem to bring any advantages right now (if anything, it makes code harder to read), but it does have its uses. When we look at looping in the next chapter, for example, you'll see this syntax again. The last thing you need to note for now is that when you use the comma operator, the 'result' of the expression is the rightmost part, so this statement:

```
myVar = 1, 2;
```

would result in `myVar` being equal to 2.

The **typeof operator** allows us to discover the type of any variable, as stored by WMLScript. We can use it to interrogate a variable to find out whether it's (say) a string. The return value of this operator is an integer value from 0 to 4, as shown in the table below:

Variable Type	**typeof** Return Value
Integer	0
Floating point	1
String	2
Boolean	3
Invalid	4

The following code shows an example of its use:

```
myVar = "Serre Chevalier";
myType = typeof myVar;
myTest1 = (myType == 1);
myTest2 = (myType == 2);
```

In this code snippet, `myType` will be 2, so the last two lines will result in `myTest1` being set to `false`, and `myTest2` being set to `true`.

The last operator we'll look at is the **isvalid operator**, which simply checks to see if a variable is invalid. If a variable to which this operator is applied has a value that has somehow been corrupted and become invalid, this will return `false`.

Look again at this extract from `calc2.wmls`:

```
        WMLBrowser.setVar("S", A / B);
```

If B contains a zero, this division will be illegal, and the value stored in S will be invalid. We can ensure that this is not the case by modifying the code as follows:

```
        var result = A / B
        var valid = isvalid result;
        WMLBrowser.setVar("S", valid ? result : "Please enter an non-zero divisor");
```

`valid` will be `false` if `myVal` is invalid and `true` otherwise, so S will be assigned the result of the division, or an error message.

Operator Precedence

From your high school math classes, you may remember that in an expression like this,

```
    6 + 4 x 10 - 2
```

the multiplication should be done 'first', so the value of the expression is 44 rather than 98 (which is the result you get by going from left to right). Multiplication has higher **precedence** than addition or subtraction operations.

In similar fashion, *all* of the operators in WMLScript have a precedence relative to one another that, in the absence of parentheses, will govern the order of execution. The following is a table of the various operators' comparative precedence.

Precedence	Operators
Highest	++ (prefix), -- (prefix), + (when not used for addition or string concatenation), - (when not used for subtraction), ~, !, typeof, isvalid
	*, /, div, %
	+ (when used for addition or concatenation), - (when used for subtraction)
	<<, >>, >>>
	<, <=, >, >=
	==, !=
	&
	^
	|
	&&
	||
	?:
	=, +=, -=, *=, /=, div=, %=, <<=, >>=, >>>=, &=, ^=, |=
Lowest	,

Note that the postfix operators ++ and -- don't really fit in this table. They will be used after the expression has been completely evaluated.

This order is not a very easy thing to memorize, so judicious use of parentheses can be very useful to aid the comprehensibility of the code you write. This, for example:

```
myVar = myNum1 * myNum2 <= 12 || !myBool && myNum3 >= 100;
```

looks very confusing, but this:

```
myVar = ((myNum1 * myNum2) <= 12) || (!myBool && (myNum3 >= 100));
```

makes it easier for the eye to follow the order of execution. Of course, if your expressions start to look as complex as the one above, it would be a better idea still to split them up onto several lines, storing intermediate results in temporary variables along the way. As with so many of these choices, it's your call, as it makes a negligible difference to the efficiency of the code.

Variable Management

Now that we've at least had a look at how to use variables and functions, let's consider some of the techniques that are involved in **variable management**. More specifically, we need to see how variables are converted from one type into another, both using WMLScript's built-in rules, and using some of the predefined library functions that can make our life easier. To start off with, though, we should consider why such conversions are necessary.

Earlier, we discussed the fact that every WMLScript variable you use has an associated type, which we can discover using the typeof operator. The type of a variable is set when we first assign it a value, but there are many occasions when we might want to reinterpret it, in order to use it in a different way. As an example, we might want to take a numeric value (perhaps the result of a calculation) and insert it into a string to be displayed in the user agent. WMLScript makes this easy: by taking the meaning of your code in context, it performs a lot of the conversions automatically. Consider the following code:

```
extern function result()
{
    var myNum = 2;
    var myString = "The result is ";
    var myResult = myString + myNum;
    WMLBrowser.setVar("R", myResult);
    WMLBrowser.refresh();
}
```

Here, myNum is an integer, as it was initialized with an integer literal, and myString is a string. However, WMLScript knows that it should return a string from the operation myString + myNum, and assign that string to myResult. This is because one of the variables is a string, the other can be *converted* into a string, and the + operator is able to work with strings. The upshot is that myResult becomes "The result is 2". If we changed the + operator into a – operator, myResult would become invalid; there is no – operator for strings, and myString can't be converted into a valid type for a numeric calculation, so returning an invalid result is quite reasonable.

What do you think might happen in this code?

```
extern function result()
{
    var myNum = 4;
    var myString = "10";
    var myResult = myString + myNum;
    WMLBrowser.setVar("R", myResult);
    WMLBrowser.refresh();
}
```

We've put a valid integer number into the string assigned to `myString`, so `myResult` becomes the *string* 104 using the + operator, and the integer 6 using the – operator, which probably isn't what you were expecting. This sort of thing can seem confusing, but the rules that are followed are quite straightforward.

WMLScript Internal Conversion

In performing its automatic conversions, WMLScript looks at three things:

❑ The type(s) of operand(s) that are required by a given operator (the target variables). For example, * only works on numeric (integer and float) values.

❑ The type(s) of the variable(s) that have been passed to that operator (the source variables). The interpreter checks whether the passed variables are already of the correct type.

❑ Whether the passed variable(s) can be converted into valid type(s)

Conversion of variables is only ever *im*possible in two situations:

❑ When the source variable is invalid

❑ When the target variable is numeric (integer or floating point), and the source variable is a string that cannot be converted into a numeric variable of the required type.

In both these cases, the result is an invalid variable. Otherwise, the interpreter will go ahead and try to convert the variable(s) to the required type(s).

The conversion of strings into numeric types is pretty much common sense, but if the string contains any *other* characters (even if they occur after the numeric part), the conversion is likely to fail. The following strings are all convertible:

```
"19"
"-3.67e3"
"   500.5 "
```

While the following are not:

```
"Number 7"
"3.5 rabbits"
"   11.4.6 "
```

Standard Library Conversion

The WMLScript standard libraries contain several functions that pertain to conversion in some way. These are shown in the following table, along with an explanation of their use:

Function	Explanation
Lang.parseInt(*source*)	Converts *source* into an integer. Follows the same rules as the standard WMLScript conversion, except that illegal characters are allowed in a string if they occur *after* interpretable characters. For example, the string 15.6 km will convert to the integer 15.
Lang.parseFloat(*source*)	Converts *source* into a floating-point number. Follows the same rules as the standard WMLScript conversion, except that illegal characters are allowed in a string if they occur *after* interpretable characters. For example, the string 15.6 km will convert to the floating point number 15.6.
Lang.isInt(*source*)	Returns Boolean true if Lang.ParseInt() would be able to convert *source* into a valid integer. Note that these semantics might not be quite what you'd expect from the function name, as (for example) Lang.isInt(2.5) would return true!
Lang.isFloat(*source*)	Returns Boolean true if Lang.ParseFloat() would be able to convert *source* into a valid floating point number.
String.toString(*source*)	Converts *source* into a string. Follows the same rules as the standard WMLScript conversion, except that if *source* is invalid, this function returns the string invalid.

These functions allow us to write more robust and readable code, in which conversion occurs explicitly. The Lang.Is*Xxx*() and String.toString() functions are particularly useful when it comes to avoiding invalid data before it causes errors. For example, we could use the isInt() library function to make the calculator program more robust by checking that the input entered by the user can be evaluated as integers. If the user were to enter invalid data, we would have a way of checking for this, and reporting an error. Remember that not all browsers will properly apply the format attribute of the <input> element.

Using WMLScript to Expand Wrox Travel

Over the next few chapters, we'll be using quite a lot of WMLScript to expand our Wrox Travel application. The first of these modifications (and probably the simplest) is to integrate scripting in the vacation insurance page. This makes sense: insurance details can change often, and they may need to be checked from several locations. Returning up-to-date values in a script helps keep maintenance low, since changing prices in one place will result in them being updated wherever they are needed.

To make things a bit more interesting, we'll also allow the functions in our script to return prices in US dollars or UK pounds, using a simple currency conversion function.

Insurance Script Overview

The first problem we have to overcome is exactly how we get data from the script file into the browser. So far in this chapter, we've called WMLScript functions using an embedded hyperlink, using the <a> element. Following this link has resulted in variables being set using WMLBrowser.setVar(), and displayed by refreshing the browser.

This situation isn't ideal for Wrox Travel – it means that an extra click would be required to get the insurance costs. There are several ways round this, probably the best of which is to force the microbrowser to call our script as soon as the insure.wml deck is entered. Schematically, the operation would look like this:

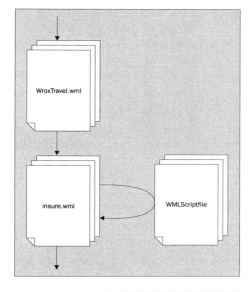

This works fine, but unfortunately it requires WML events, which we won't be looking at until Chapter 14! A quick fix for now is to modify WroxTravel.wml to call the WMLScript function – that is, we replace the link to insure.wml with a link to our script function. We can then set all the required variables in one go, and tell the browser to navigate to insure.wml from the script, using the WMLBrowser.go() function. *That* looks like this:

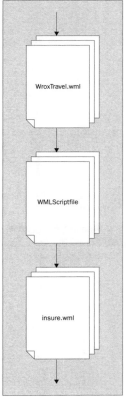

So, the only externally accessible function we require is the one that sets the required variables, and performs navigation. We'll call this function `getInsCosts()`, and we'll give it one parameter to represent the currency we want to use. In other words, calls will look like this:

```
getInsCosts(currency)
```

Where `currency` will be either 0 for US dollars, or 1 for UK pounds.

We need `getInsCosts()` to set four variables, to get the costs of insurance for either a month or a year, with or without extra sports cover. We'll do this using a more general function, `coverCost()`, which will accept parameters specifying the type of insurance required, and return a cost in the required currency. `coverCost()` can be called using the following:

```
coverCost(duration, sports, currency)
```

The three parameters are defined as:

Parameter	Meaning
duration	Integer value: the number of days of cover required. For now we'll accept two values: 28 for a month, 365 for a year.
sports	Boolean value: `true` if extra sports cover is required, `false` if it isn't.
currency	Integer value representing currency: 0 for US dollars, and 1 for UK pounds.

Note that both `duration` and `currency` have clear opportunity for expansion, and we'll be adding to them in the next chapter.

We'll store all of our insurance costs in US dollars, so we need a utility function (which needn't be externally accessible) to convert dollars into pounds. We'll call this function `toPounds()`, the syntax of which is:

```
toPounds(value)
```

Where `value` is the amount in dollars to convert. The return value of this function will be the value in pounds.

Try It Out — Expanding Wrox Travel Insurance

Now that we know the functions we need and how they'll work, we can start to write them.

1. Enter the following WMLScript code into your text editor, and save it as `insure.wmls`.

```
extern function getInsCosts(currency)
{
    WMLBrowser.setVar("A", coverCost(28, false, currency));
    WMLBrowser.setVar("B", coverCost(365, false, currency));
    WMLBrowser.setVar("C", coverCost(28, true, currency));
    WMLBrowser.setVar("D", coverCost(365, true, currency));
```

```
      WMLBrowser.go("insure.wml");
}

function coverCost(duration, sports, currency)
{
   var cost;
   cost = (duration == 365) ? 100 : 20;
   cost *= sports ? 1.5 : 1;
   return (currency == 0) ? ("$" + cost) : ("£" + toPounds(cost));
}

function toPounds(value)
{
   return value / 1.5;
}
```

2. Next we need to modify our existing cards to account for these new functions. Open up insure.wml, and make the following changes:

```
<table columns="3">
   <tr>
      <td>Type</td>
      <td>Month</td>
      <td>Year</td>
   </tr>
   <tr>
      <td>Basic</td>
      <td>$(A)</td>
      <td>$(B)</td>
   </tr>
   <tr>
      <td>Sports</td>
      <td>$(C)</td>
      <td>$(D)</td>
   </tr>
</table>
```

3. We only need to change two lines in wroxtravel.wml, replacing the links to insure.wml with insure.wmls#getInsCosts(0) in both cases. When you've done this, and you follow the link to insurance from wroxtravel.wml, you should see the following (after the text at the top):

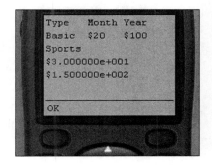

Admittedly, the emulated browser hasn't formatted the content very well here, but all the information is there!

How It Works

Since the `toPounds()` function is the simplest, we'll look at it first. All we need to do here is convert the value passed from US dollars to UK pounds. Ideally, we'd use an up-to-date value here, but right now we'll simply divide the value by 1.5:

```
function toPounds(value)
{
    return value / 1.5;
}
```

`coverCost()` is the function that calculates a price based on the specified parameters. We'll store this internally in a variable called `cost`, so the first task in this function is to declare this variable:

```
function coverCost(duration, sports, currency)
{
    var cost;
```

We calculate the insurance cost using a simple algorithm. First, we assign `cost` a base value that reflects the duration of the cover period: $20 for a month, and $100 for a year. We'll add 50% if sports cover is required, by multiplying `cost` by 1.5:

```
function coverCost(duration, sports, currency)
{
    var cost;
    cost = (duration == 365) ? 100 : 20;
    cost *= sports ? 1.5 : 1;
```

Here, we use the tertiary operator to test the values of `duration` and `sports`, assigning values to `cost` accordingly. In the first line, we check if the duration is 365 days, and if so add $100 to the cost. Otherwise, $20 is assigned. In the next line we simply check whether `sports` evaluates to `true`.

All that remains is for `coverCost()` to return a string representing the cost, in the correct currency. We decided earlier that 0 will prefix a $ sign, while 1 will prefix a £ sign. Again, we can use the tertiary operator to achieve this:

```
function coverCost(duration, sports, currency)
{
    var cost;
    cost = (duration == 365) ? 100: 20;
    cost *= sports ? 1.5 : 1;
    return (currency == 0) ? ("$" + cost) : ("£" + toPounds(cost));
}
```

Finally, the `getInsCosts()` function simply needs to call `coverCost()` four times, setting a browser variable on each occasion. We'll call the variables A, B, C, and D for simplicity:

```
extern function getInsCosts(currency)
{
    WMLBrowser.setVar("A", coverCost(28, false, currency));
    WMLBrowser.setVar("B", coverCost(365, false, currency));
    WMLBrowser.setVar("C", coverCost(28, true, currency));
    WMLBrowser.setVar("D", coverCost(365, true, currency));
```

With the browser variables set, we instruct the browser to navigate to `insure.wml`:

```
extern function getInsCosts(currency)
{
    WMLBrowser.setVar("A", coverCost(28, false, currency));
    WMLBrowser.setVar("B", coverCost(365, false, currency));
    WMLBrowser.setVar("C", coverCost(28, true, currency));
    WMLBrowser.setVar("D", coverCost(365, true, currency));
    WMLBrowser.go("insure.wml");
}
```

The last thing we need to consider is whether we've caused a problem for our 'back' option by adding an additional navigation step (the sequence is now `wroxtravel.wml` -> `insure.wmls` -> `insure.wml`).

The code to allow the user to navigate back through the decks is:

```
<do type="prev">
   <prev/>
</do>
```

Won't the `<prev/>` operation take us to `insure.wmls`, which automatically takes us to `insure.wml`? Actually, no: the `<prev/>` operation will return us to `wroxtravel.wml`, because `insure.wmls` isn't actually displayed in the browser – it's just an intermediate step. WMLScript files won't get into the browser history list, so everything will work fine.

Summary

WMLScript is a scripting language provided to supplement WML. We can use it to create more dynamic applications, and to customize applications to users' preferences without resorting to time-consuming and expensive trips to the server. We have discussed the power of WMLScript, and examined the types of use for which it's most suitable.

We also covered the origin of WMLScript, and its structure and syntax. You saw how to call WMLScript functions, pass values to carry out operations on, and obtain return values. We also listed the operators available to us, and introduced some standard library functions. As part of that, we examined how variable type conversion occurs, and how we can convert variables ourselves to suit our own purposes.

In the next chapter we will continue to expand our knowledge of the way WMLScript applications are typically structured, by adding decision-making and looping concepts to our repertoire.

WMLScript Control Structures

Given the quantity of material in the previous chapter, you might think —or even hope – that there's not much more to learn about WMLScript. However, the scripts we've written so far have been subject to two significant limitations. First, everything has happened in strictly sequential order: if we want to perform an operation more than once, we must include the same code more than once. By separating the code into functions, we can save on the *amount* of repetition by calling functions repeatedly, but there's a much better way. This chapter will explain what **loops** are, and how we can use them.

Second, the only decision-making tasks we've seen so far used the tertiary operator (? :). This operator allows us to perform a simple Boolean test and return one of two results, but it's rather crude, and somewhat limited. In this chapter, we'll see much better ways of doing things, by using the other **conditional execution** structures available to us.

Putting all of this information together will allow us a lot more freedom in the way we write WMLScript functions, and the examples in this chapter will illustrate this. With these new techniques, we'll be able to write more powerful, more readable scripts.

Conditional Execution: The if...else Structure

WMLScript provides us with *two* decision-making structures: the tertiary operator we looked at in the last chapter, and the if...else structure. Let's quickly recap the ? : operator, which has syntax like this:

```
returnValue = BooleanTest ? ValueIfTrue : ValueIfFalse
```

The *BooleanTest* parameter is evaluated, using whatever methods are necessary (this could involve function calls, complex algorithms, or simply looking at the value of a Boolean variable). If this parameter evaluates to true, then *ValueIfTrue* is the result of the operator; otherwise the result is *ValueIfFalse*. As a quick example, we could use this in an assignment:

```
Mood = DidMyTeamWinTheCup ? "Happy as can be" : "Depressed";
```

Now let's look at the syntax of the if...else structure, so that we can compare and contrast:

```
if (BooleanTest)
{
    // Code block 1
}
else
{
    // code block 2
}
```

In this case, we evaluate *BooleanTest* in exactly the same way as with ?:, but this time we execute one of two sections of code as a result. If *BooleanTest* evaluates to true, then we execute the code in block 1. If not, we execute the code in block 2.

The else statement, and the code block that follows it, is optional. You can also use the following syntax:

```
if (BooleanTest)
{
    // Code block 1
}
```

In this case, if *BooleanTest* evaluates to false, execution simply resumes at the end of the if...else structure.

As another demonstration, our earlier ?: example could be translated into an if...else structure like this:

```
if (DidMyTeamWinTheCup)
{
    Mood = "Happy as can be";
}
else
{
    Mood = "Depressed";
}
```

Admittedly, any improvement here is obscured by the fact that a one-line operation has spread onto several lines, but this simple example (which is really only intended to demonstrate the syntax) doesn't reveal the power that **nesting** structures like this can unlock. For example:

```
if (DidMyTeamWinTheCup)
{
    Mood = "Happy as can be";
}
else
{
    if (DidMyTeamFinishLast)
    {
        Mood = "Inconsolable";
    }
    else
    {
        Mood = "Depressed";
    }
}
```

The `Mood` variable here can take three different values, depending on two Boolean variables: `DidMyTeamWinTheCup`, and `DidMyTeamFinishLast`. In fact, it *is* possible to represent logic like this by using the tertiary operator, but it's extremely hard to follow, and definitely not recommended:

```
Mood = DidMyTeamWinTheCup ? "Happy as can be" :
          (DidMyTeamFinishLast ? "Inconsolable" : "Depressed");
```

Moreover, the tertiary operator can only assign a value to a variable as a result of the decision made. As we'll see in many other examples of using it, *any* legal WMLScript statements may be placed inside the blocks of the `if...else` structure. Before we begin, however, we should take a small aside. When we start using (and nesting) structures like the ones above, it can be very easy to fall into the trap of writing unreadable code. The next section suggests a technique to prevent this from happening.

Indentation

Indentation has been used in several of the code snippets we've seen so far, although you may not have been completely aware of it! What we mean by "indentation" is adding white space in front of code, in order to make it easier to read. (You may remember that we talked in Chapter 4 about doing something similar for WML decks.) To explain this better, let's take another look at the `if...else` structure from the last section, expanding it into a complete function and labeling different levels of indentation with comments:

```
function getMood(DidMyTeamWinTheCup, DidMyTeamFinishLast)      // Level 0
{                                                              // Level 0
   var Mood;                                                   // Level 1
   if (DidMyTeamWinTheCup)                                     // Level 1
   {                                                           // Level 1
      Mood = "Happy as can be";                                // Level 2
   }                                                           // Level 1
   else                                                        // Level 1
   {                                                           // Level 1
      if (DidMyTeamFinishLast)                                 // Level 2
      {                                                        // Level 2
         Mood = "Inconsolable";                                // Level 3
      }                                                        // Level 2
      else                                                     // Level 2
      {                                                        // Level 2
         Mood = "Depressed";                                   // Level 3
      }                                                        // Level 2
   }                                                           // Level 1
   return Mood;                                                // Level 1
}                                                              // Level 0
```

At execution time, the extra spacing doesn't affect the code in any way – it doesn't make it run any faster or slower. As we discussed in the last chapter, the code is compiled before transmission into a format that's not human-readable.

The size and syntax of the resultant code will be identical, whether we use code such as that above, or something like this:

```
function getMood(DidMyTeamWinTheCup, DidMyTeamFinishLast){
var Mood;
if (DidMyTeamWinTheCup){Mood="Happy as can be";}
else{
if (DidMyTeamFinishLast){Mood="Inconsolable";}
else{Mood = "Depressed";}}
return Mood;
}
```

Now that we know how the if...else structure works, it would be helpful to see another example of its use. Let's see how we can employ it to check the validity of the parameters passed to a function.

Parameter Validity Checking

Quite often, we'll have a function that expects, say, positive numbers less than 100 as parameters, or perhaps strings of fewer than 10 characters. Since the if...else structure allows us to execute blocks of code conditionally, we can handle situations where the parameters passed do not fulfill the conditions set, and perhaps return meaningful responses before the error causes more serious trouble.

As an example, let's look at some very simple code in which a WMLScript function obtains the square root of its parameter and sets a browser variable accordingly. This function will use the standard library function Float.sqrt(*value*), which returns the square root of *value*.

Try It Out — Another if...else Example

1. Enter the following function into your text editor and save it as root.wmls:

```
extern function sqroot(number)
{
    number = Lang.parseFloat(number);
    WMLBrowser.setVar("R", Float.sqrt(number));
    WMLBrowser.refresh();
}
```

2. Now, enter root.wml, the WML file that calls this function:

```
<?xml version="1.0"?>
<!DOCTYPE wml PUBLIC "-//WAPFORUM//DTD WML 1.2//EN"
                     "http://www.wapforum.org/DTD/wml_1.2.xml">
<wml>
    <card newcontext="true">
        <p>number = 3<br/>
            sqroot(number) = $(R)
        </p>
        <do type="accept" label="Calculate">
            <go href="root.wmls#sqroot('3')"/>
        </do>
    </card>
</wml>
```

3. Display this card, choose the Calculate softkey, and you should get the following:

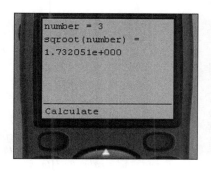

4. However, if we modify `root.wml` to use a negative number, like so:

```
<card newcontext="true">
    <p>number = -3<br/>
        sqroot(number) = $(R)
    </p>
    <do type="accept" label="Calculate">
        <go href="root.wmls#sqroot('-3')"/>
    </do>
</card>
```

Then we will see the following, no matter how many times we hit **Calculate**:

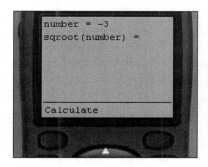

5. You can make the following modifications to `root.wmls` in order to return an error to cover the above situation (which is obviously flawed):

```
extern function sqroot(number)
{
    if (!Lang.isFloat(number))        // If number cannot be converted to a float
    {
        WMLBrowser.setVar("R", "Error - numeric value required.");
        WMLBrowser.refresh();
        return 0;
    }

    number = Lang.parseFloat(number);

    if (number < 0)
    {
        WMLBrowser.setVar("R", "Error - positive value required.");
    }
```

```
    else
    {
        WMLBrowser.setVar("R", Float.sqrt(number));
    }

    WMLBrowser.refresh();
}
```

In the new code above, the return *statement doesn't appear right at the end of the function, as it has on every previous occasion that we've seen it. In general,* return *can be used to exit a function and send a value back to the calling location from wherever it is sensible to do so.*

6. Now when we try to calculate using the value -3, we get a display like this:

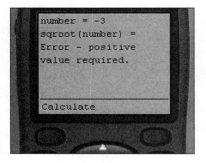

7. The following final modification can be made to the function to allow it to cope with negative numbers:

```
if (number < 0)
{
    WMLBrowser.setVar("R", Float.sqrt(Lang.abs(number)) + " x i");
}
```

8. Now when you run the card with a negative number, you will see the following result:

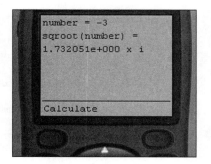

How It Works

In Step 1, we composed a rather abrupt version of the `sqroot()` function:

```
extern function sqroot(number)
{
    number = Lang.parseFloat(number);
    WMLBrowser.setVar("R", Float.sqrt(number));
    WMLBrowser.refresh();
}
```

This just extracts a floating point number from the parameter as well as it can, and saves the square root of this value in the browser variable R, before refreshing the browser. If the value returned from `Float.sqrt()` is invalid, as will happen with negative numbers, no discernable change will occur. This is lacking in some user friendliness!

We saw some possible improvements in the next few steps. In Step 5, we amended the function to give it a more sophisticated approach to parameter validation. The first `if` statement checks whether `number` can be converted to a floating point value:

```
if (!Lang.isFloat(number))       // If number cannot be converted to a float
```

If `number` cannot be converted, R is set with an error message. The browser is refreshed so that this error message is displayed, and the function exits:

```
        WMLBrowser.setVar("R", "Error - numeric value required.");
        WMLBrowser.refresh();
        return 0;
```

The other addition to `root.wmls` is a check that the value is positive – a negative value will set the browser variable R with another descriptive error message:

```
    if (number < 0)
    {
        WMLBrowser.setVar("R", "Error - positive value required.");
    }
```

Eventually, if all conditions have been met, we can safely calculate the square root of `number` to be stored in R, and refresh the browser.

```
    else
    {
        WMLBrowser.setVar("R", Float.sqrt(number));
    }

    WMLBrowser.refresh();
```

*The final modification depends on the concept of imaginary numbers, in which the square root of -1 is defined as i. As all negative numbers are equal to their absolute (positive) value multiplied by -1, we can say that the square root of S, where S is negative, is equal to the square root of abs(S), multiplied by the square root of -1. Therefore, sqrt(-3) = sqrt(3) * i.*

Loops

The easiest way to understand why **loops** are so useful is to illustrate them with an example straight away. Imagine, if you will, a function that calculates the total interest on a savings account over 10 years, with a fixed interest rate. We'll call this function `calcInterest()`:

```
calcInterest(bal, rate)
```

We'll pass in the account balance as a floating point dollar value in `bal`, the rate as a floating point percentage in `rate`, and return the balance after 10 years as the return value of the function. Using the expressions we've learned so far, we could program this as follows:

```
function calcInterest(bal, rate)
{
    bal *= (rate + 100) / 100;
    bal *= (rate + 100) / 100;
    bal *= (rate + 100) / 100;
    bal *= (rate + 100) / 100;
    bal *= (rate + 100) / 100;
    bal *= (rate + 100) / 100;
    bal *= (rate + 100) / 100;
    bal *= (rate + 100) / 100;
    bal *= (rate + 100) / 100;
    bal *= (rate + 100) / 100;
    return bal;
}
```

Just inspecting this code should be enough to make you think that there *must* be a better way of doing things. What if we wanted to calculate the interest over 15 years, or 20? Not only would we need multiple versions of this function (say, `calcInterest15()` and `calcInterest20()`), but some of them would be *huge* – can you imagine what `calcInterest100()` would look like?

What we'd *really* like to do is pass a parameter specifying the number of years' interest to calculate, and then repeat this line as many times as we need to:

```
    bal *= (rate + 100) / 100;
```

We can do this using a `for` loop.

for Loops

`for` loops are specifically designed for repeating tasks a fixed number of times. These tasks aren't limited to single lines of code, either – we can execute multiple instructions for each 'cycle' of the loop. Let's look at the syntax:

```
for (assignment; loopTest; increment)
{
    // Code to loop
}
```

The characteristics of the loop are defined by the three expressions *assignment*, *loopTest*, and *increment*. The code to be executed multiple times is placed in the body of the `for` structure – that is, between the braces.

The meanings of the three expressions are as follows:

❑ *assignment* – This statement is executed prior to the start of the loop, and never again. Its usual purpose is to initialize a **counter** variable, which will help to manage the loop. The counter variable may be declared as part of this statement.

❑ *loopTest* – This Boolean statement is evaluated at the *start* of each loop cycle. If it evaluates to `true`, the looping cycle will continue. Otherwise, the loop will end and script execution will continue after the closing brace. It is usually used to check the value of the counter variable.

❑ *increment* – This statement is executed at the *end* of every loop. It is usually used to increment the counter variable.

Try It Out — Building a Basic for Loop

1. Open a new file in your text editor, and add the following code: one external function to be called from WML, and one internal (general purpose) function. Save this file as `interest.wmls`.

```
extern function getNewBalance(bal, rate, years)
{
    WMLBrowser.setVar("balance", calcInterest(bal, rate, years));
    WMLBrowser.refresh();
}

function calcInterest(bal, rate, years)
{
    for (var loopCount = 0; loopCount < years; loopCount++)
    {
        bal *= (rate + 100) / 100;
    }
    return bal;
}
```

2. Now enter the following, which is the WML deck that will call our WMLScript code:

```
<?xml version="1.0"?>
<!DOCTYPE wml PUBLIC "-//WAPFORUM//DTD WML 1.2//EN"
                     "http://www.wapforum.org/DTD/wml_1.2.xml">

<wml>
    <card newcontext="true">
        <p>initial amount = $$1000<br/>
           final amount = $$$(balance)
        </p>
        <do type="accept" label="Calculate">
            <go href="interest.wmls#getNewBalance(1000, 5, 10)"/>
        </do>
    </card>
</wml>
```

You should call this file `interest.wml`. When this is run on the UP.Simulator, you get the following display, which shows what the balance will be after ten years of 5% interest:

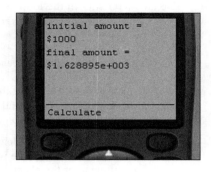

How It Works

In Step 1, we define two functions; one to be called from WML, and the other for use inside the script file:

```
extern function getNewBalance(bal, rate, years)
{
    WMLBrowser.setVar("balance", calcInterest(bal, rate, years));
    WMLBrowser.refresh();
}

function calcInterest(bal, rate, years)
{
    // More code to follow
```

`calcInterest()` first needs to declare and initialize a counter variable; we call this `loopCount`, and set its initial value to 0. We can do this as part of the `for` loop, which looks like this:

```
function calcInterest(bal, rate, years)
{
    for (var loopCount = 0;
```

Next, we decide how many times we want the loop to execute. For this example, we want to specify that number to be the value passed in the `years` parameter, which means that *loopTest* and *increment* need to be configured accordingly. The simplest way of doing this is to add one to `loopCount` at the end of each cycle, and test to make sure we only loop if `loopCount` is less than `years`. With these decisions in mind, we can complete the line:

```
function calcInterest(bal, rate, years)
{
    for (var loopCount = 0; loopCount < years; loopCount++)
```

Whatever we place inside braces after this line will be executed `years` times. In this case, it's just our interest calculation:

```
    for (var loopCount = 0; loopCount < years; loopCount++)
    {
        bal *= (rate + 100) / 100;
    }
```

The deck that we wrote to call the function in Step 2 contained nothing new, and just served as a way to call the `getNewBalance()` function. With a starting balance of $1000, an interest rate of 5% (per year), and an investment period of ten years, we'd get a final balance of $1628.89.

Making Better Use of the for Loop's Control Expressions

The three expressions that control the `for` loop allow us quite a bit of scope. One thing that wasn't immediately apparent in the last example is that the `loopCount` variable is accessible throughout the body of the loop. This means that we can use it not only as a counter, but also as part of our calculations. As a simple test of this, we could create a function that returns the factorial of its parameter.

*The factorial of a number is simply the result you get when you take the product of all the integers up to and including that number (3 factorial, for example, is 1 x 2 x 3 = 6). An operation like this allows us to make good use of the * = operator:*

```
function factorial(param)
{
   var result = 1;
   for (var loopCount = 2; loopCount <= param; loopCount++)
   {
      result *= loopCount;
   }
   return result;
}
```

Here, we loop for a number of times that's equal to the parameter passed to the function, adding another number to the multiplication sequence each time. (In fact, setting `loopCount = 2` means that we perform one cycle fewer than this, as multiplying a number by 1 is a waste of time.) The result we return in this case will be the result of the following equation:

```
result = 1 * 2 * ...* param
```

Another different way of using the `loopCount` variable is to change what we do with it in the third control expression. Take a look at the following code:

```
function multiAdd(limit)
{
   var result = 0;
   for (var loopCount = 1; loopCount <= limit; loopCount *= 2)
   {
      result += loopCount;
   }
   return result;
}
```

This time, we're not just adding 1 to `loopCount`; we're doubling it. There are no WMLScript rules that prevent us from doing this. The rest of this loop simply adds the current value of `loopCount` to a `result` variable, which is initialized to 0. We stop looping when the value of `loopCount` becomes greater than a specified limit.

When we start playing with the value of the loop counter like this, we need to be *very* careful with our end-of-loop test. The one we've used above, loopCount <= limit, is fine – but what if we used loopCount != limit? Then, the loop will only end if loopCount is *exactly* equal to limit, which will occur if you're simply incrementing, but may not if you're doing something more complex.

If loopTest never evaluates to true, the loop never ends. How this situation is handled will depend on the device or emulator you are using, which may report an error, show a warning, or simply become unresponsive. None of these results is particularly endearing to the user! For this reason, and because the standard method is to increment by 1, it is probably best not to change this behavior unless absolutely necessary.

Leaving Loops Prematurely

Waiting for the loopTest condition to be met isn't the only way to exit a loop. We can *force* a loop to exit by using the break statement. Put simply, as soon as the break statement is encountered, script execution will jump to the line of code immediately following the end of the loop.

Try It Out — Using break

The break statement is useful if we don't know at the start of the loop when we will be leaving it. For example, let's say we wanted a function to extract the first word from a string – we've no idea in advance how long that word's going to be. There are three standard library functions that will help us here, all from the String library:

❑ String.isEmpty(*string*) returns true if *string* is empty – that is, it contains ""

❑ String.length(*string*) returns an integer that gives the number of characters in the *string* parameter

❑ String.charAt(*string*, *position*) returns the character at *position* in the string, where *position* = 0 represents the first character in the string.

1. The functions we need for this demonstration are these, which you should put in a file called strlib.wmls:

```
extern function display()
{
   WMLBrowser.setVar("R", getFirstWord("Hang on lads, I've got an idea."));
   WMLBrowser.refresh();
}

function getFirstWord(myString)
{
   var firstWord = "";
   var strLength = String.length(myString);
   var currentChar = "";
   if (!String.isEmpty(myString))
   {
      for (var pos = 0; pos < strLength; pos++)
      {
          currentChar = String.charAt(myString, pos);
          if (currentChar == " ")
          {
             break;
```

```
            }
        firstWord += currentChar;
        }
    }
    return firstWord;
}
```

2. We will access this function from `fword.wml`:

```xml
<?xml version="1.0"?>
<!DOCTYPE wml PUBLIC "-//WAPFORUM//DTD WML 1.2//EN"
                    "http://www.wapforum.org/DTD/wml_1.2.xml">

<wml>
    <card newcontext="true">
        <p>
            Result = $(R)
        </p>
        <do type="accept" label="Show Result">
            <go href="strlib.wmls#display()"/>
        </do>
    </card>
</wml>
```

3. If you now view fword.wml in the UP.Simulator, you will have the following screen:

4. Pressing the left softkey will then extract the first word from the string, "Hang on lads, I've got an idea.":

How It Works

Aside from the `String` library functions we've already mentioned, the key component here is the `for` loop, reproduced overleaf.

```
                    for (var pos = 0; pos < strLength; pos++)
                    {
                       currentChar = String.charAt(myString, pos);
                       if (currentChar == " ")
                       {
                          break;
                       }
                       firstWord += currentChar;
                    }
```

Each cycle of this loop moves along the string, from one character to the next, checking whether the current character is a space. If it is, the `break` statement will be executed, and the loop will exit. Otherwise, the loop will continue right to the end of the string, copying characters from `myString` to `firstWord`. Given this description, the return value "Hang" is exactly what we'd expect.

Aborting Loop Cycles

Another important keyword in loop programming is `continue`. Whereas `break` causes the loop to abort completely, `continue` allows us to skip the rest of the current cycle. For example, if we were to replace `break` with `continue` in the previous example:

```
                    if (currentChar == " ")
                    {
                       continue;
                    }
```

Then the loop would *not* end when the first space in `myString` is encountered. Instead, the current *cycle* would end and the next would start, with `pos` being incremented as usual. The output of this function would be the original string, minus the spaces it contained. Using `fword.wml`, with the code otherwise identical to that in the last example, we will see:

In this case, we would probably want to rename the function — `getFirstWord()` hardly seems appropriate any more!

while Loops

We'll come back to `for` loops again later in the chapter, when we look at some more involved examples, but for the time being there's another type of loop in WMLScript that we need to talk about. The `while` loop is actually a little simpler than the `for` loop — for one thing, `while` loops require only a single parameter:

```
    while (condition)
    {
       // Code to loop
    }
```

Before each cycle of the loop, *condition* is evaluated for a Boolean result. If this expression is `true`, then a loop cycle ensues. If it is `false` or invalid, then the loop ends.

Once the test has been performed, the actual looping follows exactly the same pattern as it does in a `for` loop. In fact, we can emulate a `for` loop by maintaining our own counter variable – we need to initialize it before the loops starts, and increment it at the end of each loop. For example, the `for` loop we saw earlier:

```
for (var loopCount = 0; loopCount < 10; loopCount++)
{
    // Code to loop
}
```

Could be written using a `while` loop as follows:

```
var loopCount = 0;

while (loopCount < 10)
{
    // Code to loop
    loopCount++;
}
```

These two loops will do exactly the same thing. The only real advantage of using a `for` loop in this case is that all the parameters are set out together at the start of the loop, which can make it easier to see what's happening in the code, and easier to modify the loop.

Demonstrations such as this tend to prompt questions like, "Why do we need two kinds of loop?" To be honest, there's a certain amount of personal preference involved, but in general `for` loops are most useful when we *know* the number of times the loop must iterate. If we're iterating for an unknown number of times – that is, we are repeating a set of actions until a change occurs – a `while` loop is more suitable.

Try It Out — A while Loop Example

Let's illustrate this with an example. We'll create a function that simulates eating. When called from a WML card, it will set a variable (R) to display the current state of eating an enormous meal. It might sound a bit odd, but it's actually a reasonably sensible demonstration of `while` loops – honest!

1. Enter the following functions into your text editor, and save the file as `eat.wmls`:

```
extern function eat()
{
    var stillHungry = true;
    WMLBrowser.setVar("R", "");
    while (stillHungry)
    {
        stillHungry = eatSomeFood();
        WMLBrowser.refresh();
    }
}
```

```
function eatSomeFood()
{
   if (Lang.random(9) >= 8)
   {
      WMLBrowser.setVar("R", WMLBrowser.getVar("R") + "Full up!");
      return false;
   }
   else
   {
      WMLBrowser.setVar("R", WMLBrowser.getVar("R") + "Munch! ");
      return true;
   }
}
```

2. Next, enter `eat.wml`, the WML deck that causes the above functions to be called:

```
<?xml version="1.0"?>
<!DOCTYPE wml PUBLIC "-//WAPFORUM//DTD WML 1.2//EN"
                     "http://www.wapforum.org/DTD/wml_1.2.xml">

<wml>
   <card newcontext="true">
      <p>report = $(R)</p>
      <do type="accept" label="Show Result">
         <go href="eat.wmls#eat()"/>
      </do>
   </card>
</wml>
```

3. If you run this file in the UP.Simulator, you will initially get a screen that just contains the word report. Selecting the Show Result softkey will give a result similar to the one below, although the detail may differ because we're using a new library function: Lang.random().

How It Works

eat() is quite simple — it is the only external function in this file, and it has no parameters. It simply declares a variable named stillHungry, initializes it to true, and then enters a while loop that continues to execute until stillHungry is false. Within the loop it calls eatSomeFood(), whose return value is assigned to stillHungry and may therefore cause the loop to exit. Finally, eat() refreshes the browser so that any changes to variables will be visible in the user agent.

eatSomeFood() utilizes the Lang.random() function to obtain a random value between 0 and 9, inclusive. (The parameter passed to it specifies the range over which to obtain the random number.)

```
if (Lang.random(9) >= 8)
```

If the number returned is 8 or 9, the browser variable R is concatenated with the string "Full up!", and the value returned is false. This will cause the while loop to exit. For all other numbers (0 to 7), the code will add the string "Munch! " to the browser variable R. Notice in particular how we achieve this:

```
WMLBrowser.setVar("R", WMLBrowser.getVar("R") + "Munch! ");
return true;
```

We retrieve the contents of R using the getVar() function of the WMLBrowser library, which is fairly self explanatory. Then we add the string "Munch! " to it, and reassign the result to R. This means that for every iteration of the while loop, the string will grow. Finally, the function returns true, allowing a further iteration of the while loop.

Leaving while Loops, and Aborting while Loop Cycles

The two keywords we used in the last section – break and continue – can also be used with while loops, with identical effects. However, since while loops are dependent on a simple condition, you shouldn't be using break much, if at all. It's just as easy, and more appropriate, to set the exit condition accordingly. On the other hand, there will probably be the odd time when you want to leave a loop *cycle* prematurely, in which case continue may just be sensible.

Decision Making and Looping Examples

It's time to assemble what we've learned into a more involved application, to make sure the techniques are clear before using them to further our Wrox Travel project. To make this example a bit more interactive, we'll also use the standard library functions from the Dialogs library, so we'd better take a quick look at those before we dive in.

The Dialogs Library

The Dialogs library contains three functions that are used either to get quick responses from a WAP-enabled device user from within WMLScript, or to display short informational messages. They are very similar in operation to the pop-up dialogs you may be used to from graphical computing environments such as Microsoft Windows or the Macintosh OS.

Without further ado, the three functions (in order of increasing complexity) are:

- ❏ Dialogs.alert()
- ❏ Dialogs.confirm()
- ❏ Dialogs.prompt()

Let's look at each of these functions in detail, with illustrative examples.

Dialogs.alert()

This function displays a text message to the user, interrupting further script execution until the user chooses to continue. The mechanism of confirmation may vary between user agents, but it will often be a softkey labeled OK.

The syntax of this function is as follows:

```
Dialogs.alert(text)
```

Where *text* is the message displayed on the screen. For example, we could provide instant feedback on the parameter passed to a simple function like this:

```
extern function display(parameter)
{
    Dialogs.alert("The parameter is: " + parameter);
}
```

Calling `display(5747)` would then result in the following:

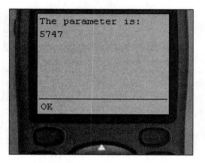

Clearly, the UP.Simulator displays the message as it would display any normal card, but as with so many other WML and WMLScript techniques, the detail of this operation is not determined in the specification. It's left for the implementers of user agents to decide what's most appropriate for their needs.

`Dialogs.alert()` has the default WMLScript function return value: an empty string. Pressing OK will return you to the calling deck.

Dialogs.confirm()

This function is just like `Dialogs.alert()`, except that it allows the user to choose one of two responses to the message displayed, instead of a simple confirmation. These two choices can be specified in the function call, or it can be left to the browser to fill in default values. The syntax is:

```
Dialogs.confirm(text, ok, cancel)
```

As before, *text* specifies the message to display, but this time there are two additional parameters: *ok* and *cancel* are the strings to be used as the two softkey options. If these two are left blank (using empty strings), the browser's default values will be used.

If we simply substitute this function into the last piece of code we looked at:

```
extern function display(parameter)
{
    Dialogs.confirm("The parameter is: " + parameter, "OK", "NotOK");
}
```

We will see the following:

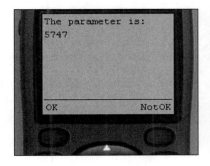

`Dialogs.confirm()` has a Boolean return value: if the user selects the *ok* option, then the function returns `true`; otherwise it returns `false`. We can use this value along with the `if...else` structure we looked at earlier, enabling the user to make simple decisions about the logical flow of script execution. For example:

```
extern function display(parameter)
{
    var choice = Dialogs.confirm("What now?", "Continue", "End");
    if (!choice)
    {
        return 0;                   // Stop further code from executing
    }

    // Rest of function...
}
```

`choice` will be `false` if the user selects **End**, forcing script execution into the `if` code block, which exits the function.

Dialogs.prompt()

The final function in the `Dialogs` library, `Dialogs.prompt()`, gives us a way to prompt the user for input from within a script file, rather than a WML card. The syntax of this function is as follows:

```
Dialogs.prompt(text, default);
```

Once again, *text* is the message displayed to the user, while *default* is the default response that will be provided for the user to accept or edit as appropriate (it can be left blank if desired). The string entered by the user then becomes the return value of the function. Let's try it out:

```
extern function display(parameter)
{
    var userName = Dialogs.prompt("Who are you?", "Pierce Brosnan");
    Dialogs.alert("Hello, " + userName + "!");
}
```

This code displays the following:

Once the user has finished editing the name, the rest of the script executes, displaying (on this occasion) **Hello, Timothy Dalton!**

Decision Making and Looping in Practice

For our example in this chapter, we'll put together a simple version of the traditional "hangman" game, which involves a player attempting to guess a hidden word that has a known number of letters. To begin with, this word is displayed as a sequence of underscore characters, informing the player how many letters the word has. "_ _ _ _ _" has five letters, for example.

The player can then guess a single letter from the alphabet, and if this letter occurs in the hidden word, they will be rewarded with a new string in which one or more of the underscores has been replaced with the letter in question, such as "_ _ Z Z _". If the letter guessed does not occur in the word, the player loses a 'life'.

Play continues either until the word is completed (success), or the player runs out of lives (failure). Full marks if you guessed that the example word used in this section was "P I Z Z A"!

To make things easier for ourselves, we'll limit the program to upper case letters – there is no easy way to convert between lower and upper case letters in WMLScript, so this restriction will make it a lot easier to find out if a given character occurs in the hidden word. Let's get down to writing some code!

Hangman: The Code

The WML decks that we've been using in these WMLScript chapters have been very simple indeed, and since we're continuing to focus on WMLScript, we're not going to change that here. Our WML deck will consist of a single card that displays the letters found so far, the number of lives remaining, and a link to follow to try another letter. In addition, there will be a softkey option to start a new game.

After that specification, the WML file practically writes itself. The only things we need to know are the relevant filenames, and the names of the functions to call. We'll take the easy naming option, calling the files `hangman.wml` and `hangman.wmls`, and the two functions `newgame()` and `guess()`.

Try It Out — Hangman

1. Enter the following deck into your text editor, and save it as `hangman.wml`:

```
<?xml version="1.0"?>
<!DOCTYPE wml PUBLIC "-//WAPFORUM//DTD WML 1.2//EN"
                     "http://www.wapforum.org/DTD/wml_1.2.xml">

<wml>
    <card newcontext="true">
        <p>word = $(W)<br/>
            lives = $(L)<br/>
            <a href="hangman.wmls#guess()">Guess</a><br/>
        </p>
        <do type="accept" label="New game">
            <go href="hangman.wmls#newgame()"/>
        </do>
    </card>
</wml>
```

2. We can now start to write our WMLScript file, `hangman.wmls`. This is by far the biggest script file we've used so far, but don't let that put you off: as usual, we'll be going through it step-by-step shortly:

```
extern function newgame()
{
    WMLBrowser.setVar("W", "_ _ _ _ _");
    WMLBrowser.setVar("A", "PIZZA");
    WMLBrowser.setVar("L", 6);
    WMLBrowser.setVar("G", "running");
    WMLBrowser.refresh();
}

extern function guess()
{
    // Check whether a game is running
    var state = WMLBrowser.getVar("G");
    if (state != "running")
    {
        Dialogs.alert("You must start a new game!");
        return 0;
    }

    var found = WMLBrowser.getVar("W");
    var answer = WMLBrowser.getVar("A");
    var lives = WMLBrowser.getVar("L");
```

```
// Request a letter from the user
var letter = "";
var letterOK = false;
while (!letterOK)
{
   letter = Dialogs.prompt("Choose a letter:", "");
   if (String.length(letter) != 1)
   {
      if (String.length(letter) == 0)
      {
         Dialogs.alert("You must enter a letter!");
      }
      if (String.length(letter) >= 2)
      {
         Dialogs.alert("You must enter a single letter!");
      }
   }
   else
   {
      if ((String.compare(letter, "A") < 0) ||
          (String.compare(letter, "Z") > 0))
      {
         Dialogs.alert("Letter must be upper case alphabetic!");
      }
      else
      {
         letterOK = true;
      }
   }
}

var pos;
var isInString = false;

// Iterate through each letter in answer
for (pos = 0; pos < String.length(answer); pos++)
{
   // Compare with guess character
   if (String.charAt(answer, pos) == letter)
   {
      // If it matches, replace the underscore with the letter
      isInString = true;
      found = String.replaceAt(found, letter, pos, " ");
   }
}

// Is the letter in the string?
var wonGame = false;
if (isInString)
{
   WMLBrowser.setVar("W", found);
   Dialogs.alert(letter + " found in hidden word!");
   wonGame = true;
```

```
        for (pos = 0; pos < String.length(found); pos += 2)
        {
            if (String.charAt(found, pos) == "_")
            {
                wonGame = false;
                break;
            }
        }
        if (wonGame)
        {
            WMLBrowser.setVar("G", "stopped");
            Dialogs.alert("You have won the game!");
        }
    }
    else
    {
        if (lives > 1)
        {
            WMLBrowser.setVar("L", Lang.parseInt(lives) - 1);
            Dialogs.alert(letter + " not found in hidden word! Lose a life...");
        }
        else
        {
            WMLBrowser.setVar("L", 0);
            WMLBrowser.setVar("G", "stopped");
            Dialogs.alert(letter + " not found in hidden word! Game over!");
        }
    }
    WMLBrowser.refresh();
}
```

3. A sample sequence of play will look something like this:

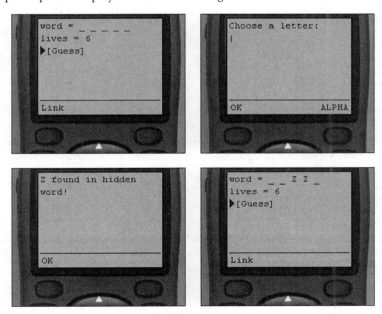

How It Works

The WML page is quite straightforward. It displays the letters guessed so far, and the number of lives (six, to begin with). It can be initialized using the left softkey, which calls `newgame()`:

```
<do type="accept" label="New game">
   <go href="hangman.wmls#newgame()"/>
</do>
```

`newgame()` itself is quite simple too: it just sets a few browser variables that hold our game details. In particular, note the use of W, which will store the letters of the word discovered so far, and L, which stores the number of lives remaining. For now, the hidden word is fixed in A as "PIZZA"; in a full version of the application, we'd want to vary this word between games.

```
extern function newgame()
{
    WMLBrowser.setVar("W", "_ _ _ _ _");
    WMLBrowser.setVar("A", "PIZZA");
    WMLBrowser.setVar("L", 6);
    WMLBrowser.setVar("G", "running");
    WMLBrowser.refresh();
}
```

The final browser variable set here, G, is a flag to say whether a game is in progress. We'll set G to `running` to signify a running game. At the end of this function, the browser is refreshed, showing the game values.

To understand what `guess()` does, we need to break it down into its component pieces. The first task that this function will perform is to check whether a game is running. We need to retrieve the game state in G from the browser, using the `WMLBrowser.getVar()` function, and check its contents. If G doesn't contain `running`, we'll exit the function immediately, with an appropriate error message:

```
extern function guess()
{
    // Check whether a game is running
    var state = WMLBrowser.getVar("G");
    if (state != "running")
    {
        Dialogs.alert("You must start a new game!");
        return 0;
    }
```

Assuming that all is well, we extract the letters found so far, the answer word, and the lives remaining, and store them in local variables named `found`, `answer`, and `lives`, respectively:

```
var found = WMLBrowser.getVar("W");
var answer = WMLBrowser.getVar("A");
var lives = WMLBrowser.getVar("L");
```

Next, we want to request a letter from the user, for which task we can use the `Dialogs.prompt()` function. `letter` represents the current guess, so we initialize it to an empty string and set a Boolean flag `letterOK` that indicates whether the entered text is acceptable.

There are a number of ways in which a user could enter an invalid guess, and we will continue to ask for input from the user until the entry is acceptable, through the use of a `while` loop:

```
// Request a letter from the user
var letter = "";
var letterOK = false;
while (!letterOK)
{
    letter = Dialogs.prompt("Choose a letter:", "");
```

Remember that the prompt dialog will return *any* entered data, which we will then store in `letter`, ready for validation. If `letter` isn't a string of exactly 1 character, we know for sure that the input is invalid, but we can be nice to the user by saying whether too many or too few characters were supplied. We do all our length checking with the `String.length()` function:

```
if (String.length(letter) != 1)
{
    if (String.length(letter) == 0)
    {
        Dialogs.alert("You must enter a letter!");
    }
    if (String.length(letter) >= 2)
    {
        Dialogs.alert("You must enter a single letter!");
    }
}
```

If there is only one character, we need to check that it is a letter, rather than a number or a special character. To do this, we need to use `String.compare()`, which takes two strings as parameters, and compares them based on their position in the current character set. If the strings are identical, this function returns 0. If the first string is 'less than' the second string, -1 is returned; if it is 'greater than' the second string, 1 is returned. In this character set, the letters A thru Z are in consecutive positions, which means that to limit the user to upper case letters, we just need to make sure the character entered is neither 'less than' A nor 'greater than' Z. If it is either of these, we return an error – otherwise, we have a valid character, and we can end the `while` loop by setting `letterOK` to true:

```
else
{
    if ((String.compare(letter, "A") < 0) ||
        (String.compare(letter, "Z") > 0))
    {
        Dialogs.alert("Letter must be upper case alphabetic!");
    }
    else
    {
        letterOK = true;
    }
}
}
```

The next thing that `guess()` needs to do is find out whether the chosen letter occurs in the hidden word. This is an ideal task for a `for` loop. We simply look at each character in `answer` (using the `String.charAt()` function we saw earlier), and compare it with `letter`. If we find a match, we can fill in the blank(s) in `found` and set a flag, `isInString`, to `true` ready for reporting back to the user. Because a letter might appear more than once, we need to make sure that we continue to test the remainder of the answer. The `pos` variable in the code below represents the position in the word of the character being tested.

In this next section of code, the item most worthy of note is the call to the `String.replaceAt()` function. Our `found` string can be interpreted as a series of elements (letters or underscores) broken up by separators (spaces). `String.replaceAt()` is able to replace a given element within a string by specifying the element index (pos) and the separator (" "). We'll be looking at this, and related string manipulation functions, in more detail in the next chapter. For now, it's enough to understand that this will replace the relevant underscore characters in `found` with the character in `letter`, filling in the blanks for us.

Of course, this might not happen. If `letter` *doesn't* occur in `answer`, then `String.replaceAt()` is never called, and `isInString` stays `false`.

```
var pos;
var isInString = false;

// Iterate through each letter in answer
for (pos = 0; pos < String.length(answer); pos++)
{
    // Compare with guess character
    if (String.charAt(answer, pos) == letter)
    {
        // If it matches, replace the underscore with the letter
        isInString = true;
        found = String.replaceAt(found, letter, pos, " ");
    }
}
```

We're nearly there! Next, we need to act on the contents of `isInString`. If this variable is `true`, we know that the chosen letter is in the hidden word, and we can report this to the user. We should also check whether the game has been won. To do this, we can look to see if `found` contains any underscore characters – if it doesn't, the game is over, and the user can have a pat on the back. In this situation, we also need to change the `G` variable to signify a non-running game state.

Note that when we look for underscore characters, we step through the string two characters at a time, as every other character is a space.

```
var wonGame = false;
if (isInString)
{
    WMLBrowser.setVar("W", found);
    Dialogs.alert(letter + " found in hidden word!");
    wonGame = true;
    for (pos = 0; pos < String.length(found); pos += 2)
    {
        if (String.charAt(found, pos) == "_")
        {
            wonGame = false;
            break;
        }
    }
    if (wonGame)
    {
        WMLBrowser.setVar("G", "stopped");
        Dialogs.alert("You have won the game!");
    }
}
```

If the user has not found a letter with their guess, they lose a life. We need to check whether they have any lives left, and if not declare the game over.

```
else
{
    if (lives > 1)
```

`parseInt()` is being used in the following code to convert the number of lives to an integer value. When it is stored, its value is a string, so we must convert it – if we don't, the browser will set L as invalid.

```
WMLBrowser.setVar("L", Lang.parseInt(lives) - 1);
```

When we are done, we cause the browser to refresh itself, so that the remaining lives will be shown. New letters found will be displayed, and the user will be given another guess if they have lives left:

```
    WMLBrowser.refresh();
}
```

And that's that: a sizable application has been cut down into bite-sized chunks, and hopefully this explanation has served to give you an understanding of what's going on, and an appreciation of the power of conditions and looping. If it hasn't all sunk in on a first read, take a break and look at it again later on, and try experimenting with the code: see if you can work out how to change the hidden word, or the number of lives per game.

The other point that you should take away from this example – the first we've written that's featured more than a token amount of user input – is the amount of code dedicated purely to input validation. This is actually typical of 'professional' code: in general, *users won't always give us the input we require*, and our applications must be written to act reasonably and appropriately when they don't.

Using WMLScript to Expand Wrox Travel

In the last chapter, we expanded the Wrox Travel application's ability to calculate insurance premiums. At the end of this one, we have a few more tools at our disposal, and we can make this section even better. In particular, we can use the Dialogs library to prompt for the type of insurance that the user wants, so that we can avoid displaying superfluous information.

Recall from the last chapter that our insurance script, insure.wmls, looked like this:

```
extern function getInsCosts(currency)
{
    WMLBrowser.setVar("A", coverCost(28, false, currency));
    WMLBrowser.setVar("B", coverCost(365, false, currency));
    WMLBrowser.setVar("C", coverCost(28, true, currency));
    WMLBrowser.setVar("D", coverCost(365, true, currency));
    WMLBrowser.go("insure.wml");
}
```

```
function coverCost(duration, sports, currency)
{
    var cost;
    cost = (duration == 365) ? 100 : 20;
    cost *= sports ? 1.5 : 1;
    return (currency == 0) ? ("$" + cost) : ("£" + toPounds(cost));
}

function toPounds(value)
{
    return value / 1.5;
}
```

For this chapter, make a copy of this file called `insure2.wmls`. We'll make all of our changes to this new file; the plan is to add the following capabilities to the Wrox Travel application:

- A dialog to choose the length of cover required
- A dialog to choose insurance type
- A dialog to choose the cover region
- A dialog to choose the currency

The only addition to the *calculation* here is the cover region, which will be either "National" or "Global" – basically, a selection of whether worldwide coverage is required.

We'll also split `insure.wml` into two cards:

- "insurance", which will give instructions and contain a link to commence quote calculation
- "quote", which displays the quote, along with personalization information

The "insurance" card will call `getInsCosts()` in `insure2.wmls`, which will do all the donkey work and then redirect the browser to "quote". Let's attack this expansion in the order that the user encounters it, starting with the "insurance" card.

The insurance Card

This card, and the card we'll look at later, is contained in `insure.wml`. We don't need the old contents of this deck at all, so we strip them out and replace them with the following:

```
<wml>
    <card id="insurance" title="Insurance Offers">
        <p>Wrox Travel is pleased to be able to offer you stunning insurance
            deals. To obtain your personalized quote, follow the link below to
            make your insurance choices.<br/>
            <a href="insure2.wmls#getInsCosts()">Go</a>
        </p>
        <do type="prev">
            <prev/>
        </do>
        <do type="accept" label="Quote">
            <go href="insure2.wmls#getInsCosts()"/>
        </do>
    </card>
</wml>
```

This card displays a paragraph of text telling the user what to expect next, and presents a link to `insure2.wmls#getInsCosts()`, which is where we'll perform the necessary calculations. Note that `getInsCosts()` has no parameters – in the last chapter, we passed it a currency parameter, but now we'll prompt the user for this information.

getInsCosts()

This function, in `insure2.wmls`, needs to change a lot. In the last chapter, we used it simply to get four specific insurance costs into four browser variables, using calculations from internal functions. Now we'll present the user with four personalization dialogs, and calculate a quote from the information supplied.

The first thing we'll ask for is the duration of the insurance cover, in days. This time we'll allow *any* number to be entered and calculate the cost accordingly, allowing the user more freedom. Of course, doing this means that we have to be careful, and make sure that the user enters valid data – that is, an integral number of days.

To perform this validation, we'll put the querying dialog in a `while` loop, and only exit it when the input is valid. We'll check validity by passing the input into `Float.parseInt()`, which will return invalid if its parameter can't be converted into an integer using WMLScript's conversion rules. A Boolean variable, `durOK`, will control the flow of the loop: as soon as we set it to `true`, the loop will exit.

All of this means that the first part of the (now parameterless) `getInsCosts()` function looks like this:

```
extern function getInsCosts()
{
   var duration;
   var durOK = false;
   while (!durOK)
   {
      duration = Lang.parseInt(Dialogs.prompt("Duration (days):", "365"));
      if (isvalid(duration))
      {
         durOK = true;
      }
      else
      {
         Dialogs.alert("Duration must be an integer number of days!");
      }
   }
```

Once a valid duration has been entered, we can go on and ask about winter sports cover, region required, and currency required. We'll restrict all of these questions to two answers, making it much easier to validate input:

```
   var sports = Dialogs.confirm("Winter sports cover?", "Yes", "No");
   var region = Dialogs.confirm("Region required:", "National", "Global");
   var currency = Dialogs.confirm("Currency:", "USD", "UKP");
```

Next, we'll assign some browser variables to reflect the user's choices (we'll be making use of these in the "quote" card):

```
WMLBrowser.setVar("A", duration);
WMLBrowser.setVar("B", sports ? "Yes" : "No");
WMLBrowser.setVar("C", region ? "National" : "Global");
WMLBrowser.setVar("D", currency ? "USD" : "UKP");
```

And we'll store the result of the calculation in a fifth variable:

```
WMLBrowser.setVar("E", coverCost(duration, sports, region, currency));
```

> Note that coverCost() now takes four parameters, as region is included. We'll deal with this in the next section.

Finally, we redirect the browser to the second card in insure.wml, "quote":

```
WMLBrowser.go("#quote");
}
```

Next, we need to make some modifications to coverCost().

coverCost()

Since we're allowing the user more freedom in insurance type, we need to make coverCost() a bit more general. For a start, we need to change its declaration to accept our new region parameter:

```
function coverCost(duration, sports, region, currency)
{
```

Then, we'll work out an insurance 'base rate' solely from the duration. We'll assume here that one month's basic cover costs $20, and that one month is equivalent to 28 days. This gives us a simple formula for our starting point:

```
var cost = duration * (20 / 28);
```

In earlier versions of this code, we gave a significant discount for a year's cover – it was only $100 basic. Associating this discount with 365 days gives us another quick formula to modify the cost (we'll give this discount on cover for 365 or more days):

```
if (duration >= 365)
{
    cost /= 2.607;
}
```

Next, we'll add 50% to the cost for sports cover, and 100% for global cover, in that order:

```
cost *= sports ? 1.5 : 1;
cost *= region ? 1 : 2;
```

Then we convert the currency (if necessary):

```
cost = currency ? cost : toPounds(cost);
```

And round the result to two decimal places, using the `Float.round()` function. This gets rid of fractions, but we need to shift the cost a couple of decimal places before and after this operation in order to get the required precision:

```
cost = Float.round(cost * 100) / 100;
```

Finally, we return the cost, with the correct currency symbol:

```
    return currency ? ("$" + cost) : ("£" + cost);
}
```

Assuming that there's been no fluctuation in the exchange rate while you've been reading this chapter, the `toPounds()` *function remains unchanged.*

The quote Card

The last-but-one thing we need to do is write the "quote" card and add it to the deck in `insure.wml`. It just needs to display the quote price, the options that led to the quote, and a contact address:

```
            <do type="accept" label="Quote">
                <go href="insure2.wmls#getInsCosts()"/>
            </do>
        </card>
        <card id="quote" title="Insurance Quote">
            <p>
                <b>Quote: $(E)</b><br/><br/>
                Quote personalized for:<br/>
                Duration: $(A) days<br/>
                Sports cover: $(B)<br/>
                Region: $(C)<br/>
                Currency: $(D)<br/>
                Contact us for more details, at:<br/>
                <u><b>Insurance@WroxTravel.com</b></u>
            </p>
            <do type="prev">
                <prev/>
            </do>
        </card>
    </wml>
```

Last of all, we need to rewrite the two links in `wroxtravel.wml` so that they point at `insure.wml`, otherwise we'll still see the primitive efforts from the last chapter:

```
            and our competitive vacation
            <a href="insure.wml" title="Insure">insurance</a> scheme.<br/>
            You can also read reviews of our vacations in
```

And:

```
<do type="options" label="Insure">
    <go href="insure.wml"/>
</do>
```

Insurance Quoting in Action

Now we've entered all this code, let's go ahead and try it out. Make your way through the application and follow the link from insure.wml:

You can see the selections we made in the last two screenshots here, and the quote is $150, give or take a little. Does that seem a bit steep to you as well?

Summary

In this chapter, we've looked at some of the more important structures we can use within our WMLScript applications to give more powerful processing. In particular, we've seen how to use:

-   if...else structures
-   for loops
-   while loops

In addition, we've seen these structures in action, both in the simple hangman-type game, and in a further extension of the Wrox Travel application.

Along the way, we encountered another way of accepting of user input: the Dialogs library. This has allowed us to prompt the user for input (either a simple two-choice decision, or free-form text entry), and to pop up quick informative dialogs without having to write WML in order to do so.

In the next chapter, we'll look at the rest of the facilities that WMLScript provides, along with some tips and tricks for effective WMLScript programming.

WMLScript Techniques

We now have enough knowledge to design and write some quite advanced WMLScript applications. We've covered all the basic syntax, operators, and structure that you can find in WMLScript files – but there are still some more techniques available to us to enhance and improve those applications.

So far, we have only covered a few of the available library functions, and (apart from some input validation) our applications generally accept that no errors will occur. In this chapter, we will discuss how we can make our WMLScript code more robust, and explore a few of the more advanced functions available through the code libraries in WMLScript. We will cover the following topics:

❑ **Pragmas** – these are commands that supply additional information to the WMLScript compiler, allowing us to specify such things as HTTP headers, and the use of external code.

❑ **WMLScript error handling** – including the kinds of errors we are likely to see and how to deal with them, whether they occur at compilation time, or are hidden in more obscure logic.

❑ **Advanced techniques** – looking in more detail at selected areas of the standard libraries that WMLScript supplies, so that we can build more advanced mathematical procedures and string handling into our functions.

These topics will again be accompanied by examples, in order to give you a better feel for the workings of WMLScript.

Pragmas

Pragmas are a type of statement that you can use in your WMLScript files to provide the browser with extra information of various kinds. They are unusual in that, unlike everything else in a WMLScript file, they *don't* make up part of a function – they stand alone, usually at the top of the file. WMLScript supports three types of pragmas, relating to:

❑ External file specification: 'use url' specifies the path to other WMLScript files whose content we want to use in our code.

❑ Access control: 'use access domain' can be used to restrict unauthorized access to functions.

❑   Meta-information: 'use meta' gives the WML engine ancillary information. The specifications provide this as a way of giving the compiler information that can be used to optimize code compilation.

All of these share a common syntax, the `use` keyword:

```
use <pragma and parameters>;
```

In the next sections, we'll look at each of these pragma types, along with potential applications for them.

Accessing External WMLScript Code

In previous chapters, we've said that it can be useful to separate your code into several smaller files, instead of having it all together in one place. This allows you to reuse code easily, and to build up your own libraries. Until now, however, we haven't been able to make calls between functions in different WMLScript files.

In the way that's similar to how we're able to call the functions of the standard libraries, we can assign a library name to a WMLScript file, and then call it in the following way:

```
ID#funcName(params);
```

The line of code above assumes that `ID` is the name we've given to the library, and `funcName()` is a function in that library. The library name is separated from the function name with the # character. A less obvious difference between this and using standard library functions is that `ID` is specific only to the current file. If your application uses many WMLScript files, and they all need access to your library, you'll need to make the association in all of them.

The association is performed using the 'use url' pragma, so the statement for the above WMLScript file might have taken the following form:

```
use url ID "http://www.somewhere.com/WMLScripts/script.wmls";
```

And to formalize this in a more generic way, the pragma for specifying external WMLScript files has the following syntax:

```
use url ID "URL";
```

Here, `ID` is the name by which we want to address the script file, and `URL` is (reasonably enough) its URL. As usual, local script files can use a relative URL, instead of a fully qualified one:

```
use url myScript "script.wmls";
```

The following example puts this concept into practice; although the application itself is quite trivial, the way of working doesn't change in more challenging contexts.

Try It Out — Accessing Remote Scripts

1. Create a new WML file, `caller.wml`, and add the following deck to it:

```
<?xml version="1.0"?>
<!DOCTYPE wml PUBLIC "-//WAPFORUM//DTD WML 1.2//EN"
                     "http://www.wapforum.org/DTD/wml_1.2.xml">

<wml>
    <card id="caller" title="Script caller">
        <p><a href="first.wmls#go()">Go</a></p>
    </card>
    <card id="done" title="Done">
        <p>Done</p>
        <do type="prev">
            <prev/>
        </do>
    </card>
</wml>
```

2. Save this deck, and create a new WMLScript file called `first.wmls`:

```
use url remote "remote.wmls";

extern function go()
{
    Dialogs.alert("first.wmls accessed.");
    var called = remote#remoteCall();
    if (called != true)
    {
        Dialogs.alert("Remote access failed.");
    }
    WMLBrowser.go("#done");
}
```

3. Save this file in the same directory as `caller.wml`, and create a third WMLScript file, `remote.wmls`:

```
extern function remoteCall()
{
    Dialogs.alert("remote.wmls accessed.");
    return true;
}
```

4. Save this file in the same directory, and then open `caller.wml` in your WML browser. Select **Go**, and then **OK** each dialog screen, observing the display. You should see the sequence shown overleaf:

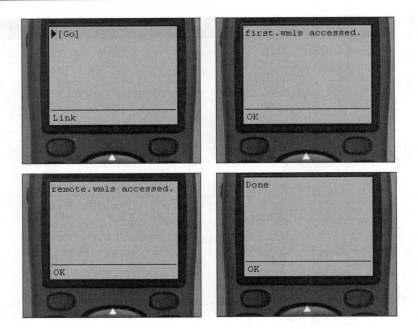

How It Works

`caller.wml` is quite simple. Its first card contains a hyperlink that when clicked, loads and executes `first.wmls#go()`.

```
<p><a href="first.wmls#go()">Go</a></p>
```

`first.wmls` begins with a pragma:

```
use url remote "remote.wmls";
```

This specifies that the name `remote` should be assigned to `remote.wmls`. We can now use any functions in `remote.wmls` by calling `remote#` plus the function name and any parameters required. The function notifies us that it has been called by using `Dialogs.alert()`, and then makes a call to the `remoteCall()` function in `remote`:

```
Dialogs.alert("first.wmls accessed.");
var called = remote#remoteCall();
```

We end the function by checking that the call was successful – the return value from `remoteCall()` is assigned to the variable `called` in the code above. We can use this to check that a successful call has been made, and otherwise give a warning using another `alert()`. When this has been done, we cause the browser to navigate to `caller.wml`'s "done" card:

```
if (called != true)
{
    Dialogs.alert("remote access failed.");
}
WMLBrowser.go("#done");
```

The code for `remoteCall()` is exceptionally simple – it just notifies the user that it has been called, using an `alert()`, and then returns `true`:

```
extern function remoteCall()
{
    Dialogs.alert("remote.wmls accessed.");
    return true;
}
```

The final step in this process is the "done" card. When we get there, we are presented with the text **Done**, and further backward navigation will return us to the first card. You will remember that WMLScript files don't appear on the history stack of the browser, so we'll immediately be transported to the "caller" card.

```
<card id="done" title="Done">
    <p>Done</p>
    <do type="prev">
        <prev/>
    </do>
</card>
```

Any use of a function from an external source will have the same semantics as this example, but for painless programming, there are two things that you should keep in mind. First, remember that the ID is separated from the function name by a # character, rather than the period that's used when dealing with the built-in libraries. Second, even though the call is WMLScript-to-WMLScript, the function you are calling *must* be declared as `external` – otherwise, you'll get an error.

Controlling Access to WMLScript Code

We've already seen one way to control access to our WMLScript code, simply by using the `extern` keyword. If we don't declare functions using this keyword, they will only be accessible to functions within the same code file.

The next WMLScript pragma, `access`, allows us finer access control over functions. In contrast with the previous one, this pragma is placed in the file containing the functions to be exported, and is supplied with a URL that specifies from where calls are allowed. The syntax is as follows:

```
use access domain "domain" path "path";
```

Furthermore, only one access control pragma is allowed in any given script. For example, we could write:

```
use access domain "wrox.com" path "";
```

Which would allow only files residing in the `wrox.com` domain to call functions in the WMLScript file.

The access conrol pragma on the previous page would include all of the following:

- ❏   www.wrox.com/caller.wml
- ❏   wap.wrox.com/BegWML/scripts/first.wmls
- ❏   www.wrox.com/wap/BegWML/Chapter11/test.wml

But it wouldn't include:

- ❏   www.microsoft.com/bill.wml
- ❏   www.wroxconferences.com/conference.wml

We can also fill in the *path* parameter:

```
use access domain "wrox.com" path "/BegWML/scripts";
```

with the result that we'd only be able to call this script from files in the `/BegWML/scripts` directory of the `wrox.com` domain (and subdirectories further down the hierarchy). Of our previous list, only the following file would now be allowed to call the script:

- ❏   wap.wrox.com/BegWML/scripts/first.wmls

Again, if you try to access a function in a script that doesn't give you access, you'll get a fatal error.

Meta-information

The **meta-information** pragmas we'll look at in this section allow additional information to be supplied alongside the code that represents the WMLScript file, in the form of headers. This information may be used and manipulated by the server, the gateway, or the user agent — or it may exist purely for informational purposes.

> *Much of this kind of functionality is beyond the scope of this book, but for completeness the syntax is detailed here.*

There are three forms that this meta-information can take, and there are three corresponding pragmas we can use. The basic syntax is the same for all three pragmas, and is as follows:

```
use meta "type" "property" "content" "scheme"
```

The primary attribute, *type* may be one of:

- ❏   name
- ❏   http equiv
- ❏   user agent

These represent the three different pragmas, and we'll look at the specific differences between them in a moment. To complete the group, *property* is the name of the header you wish to set, *content* (a string literal) specifies the value for this header, and the optional *scheme* parameter relates to the formatting of this value.

name

The name pragma allows you to specify headers intended to be used by web servers.

http equiv

This pragma is used to specify HTTP headers. These are a standard way of exchanging meta-information in the HTTP protocol, and have all manner of defined uses, ranging from authentication to specifying content type and its expiration date. Some of these headers are tagged onto your code automatically by the server; this pragma allows you to override those values and add additional information if required.

For a list of the standard HTTP headers and their usage, refer to http://www.w3.org/Protocols/rfc2616/rfc2616-sec14.html#sec14

user agent

The user agent will use headers specified with this pragma. Vendors may use these for their own proprietary extensions to the WMLScript language.

WMLScript Errors

There are three kinds of error that you are likely to encounter when developing WMLScript-enabled applications. The first kind, and perhaps the most obvious, occur at compilation time – that is, when WMLScript files are being converted for transmission to the target device. These will usually result in an interruption in compilation, such that the resultant code (if any) will be invalid and unusable.

The other kinds of error occur during WMLScript execution, and can be divided into fatal and non-fatal errors, where fatal errors are those that cause script execution to halt completely, rather than simply resulting in incorrect or unappealing output. We need to make sure that the likelihood of errors occurring is minimal, that users are not presented with confusing output if an error does occur, and that we are able to find the source of errors quickly through the use of error messages.

Compile-time Errors

More often than not, compile-time errors will be the result of simple problems with the syntax of your WMLScript files. However, this doesn't necessarily mean that they will be easy to find! As you look through the examples in this section, remember that the constraints of writing a book mean that we have to put the symptom and its cause quite close together, in the same code listing. Some of the problems we mention are much harder to pick up in longer tracts of code.

With that in mind, consider the following function:

```
extern function bad()
{
    Dialogs.alert("This won't work.")
}
```

If you can instantly tell why this code will not compile, give yourself a pat on the back – the trailing semicolons required by WMLScript are very easy to omit.

Furthermore, the error messages generated by the various WAP development environments will vary in quality – although in this case, the UP.SDK does a pretty good job:

```
Compiling WMLScript (4) : error: syntax error at "}"  missing ;
```

Another common sort of compilation error relates to variable declaration. Look at the following code:

```
extern function bad(var1, var2)
{
    var3 = var1 + var2;
}
```

Here, the variable var3 is used on the third line, but it is never declared. This goes against the rules we defined in Chapter 9, and will result in an error. The UP.SDK finds this error straight away, and reports:

```
Compiling WMLScript (3) : error: var3: undefined variable
```

Not only do we have to ensure that we declare variables, we also need to make sure we don't declare them more than once. This can occur when we accidentally re-declare a variable in one of the control expressions of a for loop, for example:

```
extern function bad()
{
    var var1;

    for (var var1 = 0; var1 < 10; var1++)
    {
        // Loop contents
    }
}
```

Which will prompt the following:

```
Compiling WMLScript (5) : error: var1: variable defined multiple times
```

The last type of error we'll look at in this section concerns function calls. Quite often, you'll find that you've either typed the name of a function wrongly, or used the wrong number of parameters. For example:

```
extern function bad()
{
    var var1 = 10;
    WMLBrowser.setVar("R");
}
```

In this case, we've omitted an important part of setVar(): the value we want to assign to the variable R! This time, the compiler says:

```
Compiling WMLScript (4) : error: Argument count mismatch in library call:
WMLBrowser.setVar
```

> *When discussing functions, the words "argument" and "parameter" are practically synonymous. Strictly speaking, a function that has been declared with three parameters is called with three arguments.*

All of these are errors that, no matter how much care you take over development, you will see time and again. Some care in the initial design stage, and in the subsequent implementation of that design, will improve matters a little – but as professional programmers know, these errors will always crop up. With a little practice, you'll become familiar with the errors generated by your preferred development environment, so that you'll be able to find and resolve them quickly when they occur.

Run-time Errors

There are times when code that compiles without a problem can produce errors further down the line. This can result in 'fatal' errors, where the script execution halts immediately, or some more subtle effects – perhaps an algorithm uses logic that is faulty, resulting in incorrect results without many clues as to their origin. The worst errors of all are those that occur intermittently – that is, they only occur under certain conditions that may be difficult to track down. We'll look at examples of all these situations in the next few sections.

Fatal Run-time Errors

As we said above, fatal errors cause an immediate break in *script* execution – but that doesn't *necessarily* mean the device or emulator user will be aware of this. In many cases, the only apparent problem will be that the WMLScript function called doesn't give the desired result. In order to explore this behavior (without knowing everything that can cause this kind of error) we can use the `Lang.abort(message)` standard library function. This causes a fatal error to occur, and passes the string *message* as an error report. Let's try it out:

```
extern function bad()
{
    var var1 = 10;
    WMLBrowser.setVar("R", var1);
    Lang.abort("Programmed abort");
    WMLBrowser.setVar("S", var1);
}
```

The "fatal error" we generate occurs on line 5. At this point, the script will exit immediately. This means that R will be set, but S won't be, as you can see from the Phone Information window:

The point to bear in mind here is that there was no indication in the microbrowser that anything had gone wrong, but there would certainly have been if we'd gone on to try to use S in the WML card that called this code! Of course, we've forced an error to occur here, so we knew what to look for. When fatal errors happen without being specified in this way, they can be extremely difficult to find.

File Access Errors

A number of fatal errors relate to external file access. Earlier in this chapter, we saw how to call functions in other WMLScript files, and also how to restrict access to these files to specific calling locations. Obviously, this isn't something that's easy for the compiler to validate, and even if it could, there might still be problems if the target file gets moved or deleted. There will almost certainly be times when an external function fails at runtime.

To be more specific, file-related fatal errors will occur if you try to call:

❑   A function in a non-existent WMLScript file

❑   A non-existent function in an existing WMLScript file

❑   A function in a file to which you do not have access, as specified by the access pragmas we discussed earlier

❑   A function with the incorrect number of parameters

In all of these cases, the error is fairly easy to avoid, and should be solved during application development. Of course, there may be times when files get accidentally deleted at a later date, but again these should be fairly easy to discover.

External Errors

Fatal errors may also be created by the user, or by the browsing device itself. This can occur when, for example, the user switches off their WAP-enabled device in the middle of script execution, or perhaps drops it in a cup of coffee. These errors can also happen due to device failure, whether due to bad design or battery exhaustion.

These errors are *not* something that you, as an application developer, can do anything about – and as the result of the failure won't matter much to the (now disconnected) user, there's not much motivation for you to attempt to help. You *might* want to maintain state between sessions (so that the user can return to the same place from which they were abruptly cut off), but to do that you need dynamically created content, which we'll cover later in the book.

Other Errors

Other errors that you are unlikely to encounter in normal conditions, but which also result in fatal errors, include:

❑   Bad code generation by a compiler

❑   Memory exhaustion

❑   Fatal error during library function execution

If you're unfortunate enough to encounter an error of one of these types, there is little you can do to avoid or handle them.

Non-fatal Run-time Errors

Non-fatal run-time errors won't cause your script to bail out immediately, but they are often the most difficult to track down. All non-fatal errors are related (in some way) to numeric operations, and they're often related to magnitude. Recalling our initial discussion of numbers from Chapter 9, both floating point and integer number in WMLScript have limits on the size of the value they contain.

To recap:

- ❏ Integers can be between -2147483648 and 2147483647

- ❏ The magnitude of a floating point number (positive or negative) must be between 1.17549435E-38 and 3.40282347E+38

If the result of any operation is an attempt to set a variable to a value beyond these limits, an error will occur. This error won't break the program, but it may well give unpredictable results – errors like this are handled in the following way:

- ❏ If the result is larger in magnitude than the limits specified (floating point or integer), then the variable will become invalid

- ❏ If the result is smaller in magnitude than the limits specified (floating point numbers), then the variable will become 0.0

These situations can arise either as part of a calculation, or during a conversion. When a calculation is in progress, it is possible that one or more of the operands are such that the result breaks the limits (adding two integers together such that the result is greater than 2147483647 would be a simple example). In response to the potential for problems such as this, you could check for the situation in your script and assign a more meaningful value (such as the string out of range), but whether that would help depends on the purpose of your code.

Conversion errors occur in exactly the same way. If you try to convert the *string* 2147483648 into an integer, you will get an invalid variable. The same will occur with string-into-floating-point conversions.

These errors are all fairly straightforward, and can easily be checked for – either by checking the operands you are about to use, or by having a close look at the result before you attempt to do anything with it.

Logical and Intermittent Errors

All of the above notwithstanding, logical and intermittent errors are the ones you will have to deal with most often. Small, unintentional errors in your scripts can lead to unforeseen problems, without causing immediately obvious flaws. In this section, we'll look at a couple of examples, and try to help you recognize and solve the problems you may have in future development.

Let's dive straight into the first of these. Consider the following WML and WMLScript files:

```
<wml>
   <card newcontext="true">
      <p>
         report = $(R)
      </p>
      <do type="accept" label="Show Result">
         <go href="test.wmls#bad()"/>
      </do>
   </card>
</wml>
```

```
extern function bad()
{
   var var1 = 10;
   WMLBrowser.setVar(var1, "R");
}
```

277

The error here is in the parameters of setVar() – they are in the wrong order. This will slip through the compiler, as it would be perfectly legal if var1 contained a string representing a variable name. In this case, however, var1 contains the number 10. When script execution reaches this line, and transfers to the setVar() function, an error will occur: the variable R will never be set. This will cause further errors later, and it is *these* that will be noticed. This 'removal' from the original cause is what makes it difficult to track these errors down.

Fixing this kind of error can be tricky, unless you know where to look. The two lines of code in the WMLScript file above may be embedded in a much larger code module, and it may not be apparent that var1 contains a number rather than a string, especially if that changes over the course of the application.

A common technique for tracking down bugs such as this one is to split the code into sections, adding temporary diagnostic calls along the way. In the above code, for example, you could check the value of the browser variable R at several points throughout your code – perhaps displaying it on screen with a function from the Dialogs library – along with a small section of informative text telling you what should be happening. You could write a simple function to do this, such that reporting just becomes a matter of inserting a single line of code wherever necessary.

Intermittent errors are most likely to occur due to inadequate validation of user input. Even experienced developers can forget to cover all of the possibilities, especially when only a simple response is required. As a simple example, consider the following code excerpt:

```
var carryOnLooping = true;
while (carryOnLooping)
{
    // Do something interesting, then...
    var userChoice = Dialogs.prompt("Interrupt?", "Y");
    if (userChoice == "Y")
    {
        carryOnLooping = false;
    }
}
```

If the user accepts the default input, the while loop will end; if they enter anything other than Y, then looping will continue. Unfortunately, this means that y and Yes are excluded, as are other ways of indicating acceptance. While testing this sort of code, it is all too easy to assume that the user will accept the default option and not add their own interpretation, leading to problems. In cases like this, it is far better to restrict input to certain values. In this example, it would make more sense to use Dialogs.confirm(), which doesn't require complex user input. Where other situations mandate more choices, you can use a <select> element.

However, there will always be cases where we can't restrict input in this way, and we will therefore need to be careful in our validation logic. It doesn't take *too* much effort to add comprehensive checking of this nature, and you can even stash the required code away in a library and re-use it.

Mathematical Techniques

Mathematical operations are an important requirement in many fields of programming, and the ability to perform them is a valuable resource to have at your disposal. Whether you need to use lengthy algorithms, or just a few lines of code to format columns, using the mathematical capabilities of WMLScript will soon become second nature to you.

By now, you'll probably have realized that WMLScript routines can be very useful for quick calculations that are impossible using WML, and for any even remotely advanced data validation. In this section, we will look at the standard library functions that are available to us for this purpose.

Standard Library Functions

We've used quite a lot of mathematics in the last few chapters, but we still haven't touched many of the capabilities that WMLScript supplies. We've divided this section up into the following parts:

❑   Numeric qualification

❑   Random number generation

❑   Other functions

Numeric Qualification

A lot of the operations that fall under this umbrella are really Boolean operations. We've already covered comparison operators (such as > and ==), so we won't repeat those here. Instead, we'll focus on the additional functions provided in the standard libraries.

The first two functions to examine are Lang.min() and Lang.max(). Both of these functions take two values and compare them – min() returns the lesser of the two values, max() the greater. Of course, if the two parameters have the same value, that value will be returned. For example:

```
Lang.min(-5, 3);
```

would return –5. If we wish to make a comparison based on magnitude (in which 3 would be treated as being 'less than' –5), we can use another function, Lang.abs(). This function takes one parameter and returns its absolute value, so:

```
Lang.abs(-5);
```

returns 5. We can then compare these numbers using the previous functions, so a generic way of determining the larger (by magnitude) of two variables would be this:

```
Lang.max(Lang.abs(myVal1), Lang.abs(myVal2));
```

In addition to obtaining absolute values for numbers, we can also convert floating point numbers into integers in a number of ways. The functions allowing us to do this are shown below, along with a brief description to highlight the differences between them (all of them take a single parameter):

❑   Float.int() returns the integer part of a floating point number, discarding the floating point part without attempting to perform rounding

❑   Float.floor() returns the integer that is closest to but less than its floating point parameter

❑   Float.ceil() returns the integer that is closest to but greater than its floating point parameter

❑   Float.round() returns the integer that is closest to the floating point parameter

Try It Out — A Rounding Application

To illustrate these properly, let's look at an example and see how these functions treat a couple of test parameters. We'll use a very simple application that comprises just two files, as shown below:

1. Enter the following text for `round.wml`:

```
<?xml version="1.0"?>
<!DOCTYPE wml PUBLIC "-//WAPFORUM//DTD WML 1.2//EN"
                     "http://www.wapforum.org/DTD/wml_1.2.xml">

<wml>
   <card id="round" title="Rounding">
      <p><a href = "round.wmls#go()">Go</a></p>
   </card>
   <card id="done" title="Done">
      <do type="prev">
         <prev/>
      </do>
   </card>
</wml>
```

2. `round.wmls` is as follows:

```
extern function go()
{
   var param = Dialogs.prompt("Enter a number:", "");
   var float = Lang.parseFloat(param);

   Dialogs.alert("int(" + param + ") = " + Float.int(float) +
            "\nfloor(" + param + ") = " + Float.floor(float) +
            "\nceil(" + param + ") = " + Float.ceil(float) +
            "\nround(" + param + ") = " + Float.round(float));

   WMLBrowser.go("#done");
}
```

3. We tried running the application three times, with the number 4.5, -8.75, and 1.2. Our results are shown below, and back up the theory presented before this example.

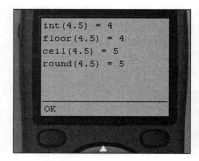
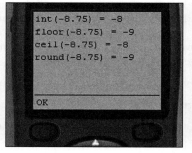

Random Number Generation

The `Lang` library also contains two functions related to random number generation, which can be useful for (among other things) simple WAP games, as we saw in the last chapter. `Lang.random()` takes a single, positive integer, and returns a random integer that's greater than or equal to zero, and less than or equal to the parameter supplied. It is also supposed to give a rectangular distribution – that is, an equal chance of each possible value appearing.

The generation of random numbers by computers is a strange process. Due to the precise way that computers work, it is almost impossible to find a truly random factor with which to calculate a random response. Historically, developers have worked round this by using a suitably complex formula that returns a sequence of numbers that *seem* random, but in fact are not. To all intents and purposes, however, you can expect the number you get from this function to be random.

The fact that these 'random' numbers are actually generated by a mathematical procedure means that at some stage, an initial value is used to 'kick off' the process. If we wish, we can determine what this initial value should be by using another of the functions in the `Lang` library relating to random numbers. The starting point of the random number sequence is called the **seed**, so the function (unsurprisingly) is called `Lang.seed()`, and takes an integer value as its single parameter.

For example, if we were to set the seed to 25 and look at the next 4 random numbers generated:

```
Lang.seed(25);
Dialogs.alert("result 1: " + Lang.random(10));
Dialogs.alert("result 1: " + Lang.random(10));
Dialogs.alert("result 1: " + Lang.random(10));
Dialogs.alert("result 1: " + Lang.random(10));
```

we'd get the same four numbers every time – on the UP.Simulator, we got 3, 6, 7, 10. Although the numbers will be different from place to place, you will find that the results on any given browser are reproducible across numerous invocations of this code.

One way of setting this seed randomly (a technique often used by game designers to ensure a convincing random number) is to initialize it with an integer that represents the current date and time. Unfortunately, this is impossible using plain WMLScript, but it can be done using, say, ASP functions. This is a topic that is covered later in the book.

Other Functions

There are six more standard library functions that may be of use to you in your development. Four of these simply return the maximum and minimum integer and floating point numbers supported by WMLScript; these functions are:

- ❑   `Lang.maxInt()`
- ❑   `Lang.minInt()`
- ❑   `Float.maxFloat()`
- ❑   `Float.minFloat()`

None of these functions takes any parameters, and they return the values we mentioned earlier in the chapter. It's possible that this may change in the future, when more powerful processors are used (an increase in size would be sensible in that case), but it may be some time before this happens.

Finally, there are two more mathematical functions. The first of these, `Float.pow()`, we have already seen in use – it allows us to raise one value to the power of another. Its syntax is as follows:

```
Float.pow(number, power);
```

The return value is *number* raised to the power *power*. To return four cubed, for example, we would use:

```
var result = Float.pow(4, 3);
```

We don't have to use integer values for *power* unless *number* is negative, so we could just as easily perform the above calculation in reverse, taking the cube root of 64:

```
var result = Float.pow(64, (1/3));
```

The final function in the `Float` library is `sqrt()`, which simply returns the positive square root of its parameter. However, this is really just shorthand for using `pow()` with *power* set to 0.5 – although using `sqrt()` instead may make for more readable code.

String Manipulation Techniques

In the final major section of this chapter, we will dissect string manipulation techniques in the same way as we did for the mathematical techniques above. Again, we've seen quite a lot of these functions in previous chapters, but here they will be assembled in a logical way, to make it easier to find exactly what you need for a given task.

First of all, we'll look at the more basic tasks. Then we'll move on to examine some slightly more advanced string formatting, including substrings, white space manipulation, and numeric formatting. Finally, we'll see how WMLScript provides limited support for arrays through the use of some `String` library functions.

Basic Manipulation

The `String` library offers all manner of functionality for handling and processing strings. The simplest of these is probably `String.isEmpty()`, which returns `true` if the string passed to it is an empty string (""), and `false` otherwise. There are a number of other ways in which you can check the same thing, but in the same way as (from the mathematical section) `Float.sqrt(myNum)` is easier to understand than `Float.pow(myNum, 0.5)`, so this function is handy in the explicit way it deals with the operation.

> *Note that passing non-string parameters to this function can lead to unpredictable results – it's possible that the browser will try to convert the parameter to a string, but it's equally possible that an error will occur, depending on the implementation.*

Once we know that a variable contains a non-empty string, we can start applying some of the other functions from the String library to it. It's quite common to see string manipulation done in a loop, analyzing the string a character at a time, and with that in mind the String.length() function returns the number of characters in the string that it takes as its only parameter. The function is often used in the control expressions of a for loop, so that every character in a string is iterated through:

```
for (var i = 0; i < String.length(myString); i++)
{
    // Do something with character i of myString
}
```

In common with many other programming languages, the first character of a string is deemed to be at position 0, so the last character in the string will be at position String.length() - 1.

Lastly, in order to access a given character in a string, we can use String.charAt(), the syntax of which is:

```
String.charAt(string, position);
```

This function returns the character at *position* in *string*, where a *position* of 0 represents the first character in the string, as mentioned above. If you attempt to access a character whose position is beyond the last character in the string, an empty string will be returned.

Substrings

In addition to getting at individual *characters* in a string, we can extract *portions* (or **substrings**) of a string by using the String.subString() library function, which has this syntax:

```
String.subString(string, position, length);
```

position and *string* specify a starting character in the same way as in charAt(), but we also specify the number of characters to extract. For example:

```
var mySubstring = String.subString(myString, 3, 4);
```

This statement would return a string containing the 4th to 7th characters of myString (bear in mind that in WMLScript, string positions start at 0). If we select a number of characters that would take us beyond the end of the original string, the substring from the position specified until the end of the string will be returned.

Alternatively, we might want to find out whether a string contains a particular sequence of characters. We can pass a string and a substring to search for into String.find():

```
String.find(string, substring);
```

This function returns a number indicating the position in the string of the first character of the substring, or -1 if it doesn't appear at all. If the substring occurs more than once in the string, this function will return the position of the first occurrence.

For example, if we had a string containing someone's genetic code, we could find out whether they possessed the gene for smelly feet (which is of course "TCGGAT") using the following call:

```
var doStevesFeetSmell = String.find(StevesGenes, "TCGGAT");
```

And then we could cure this horrible ailment using `String.replace()`:

```
String.replace(string, oldsubstring, newsubstring);
```

This returns a string in which all occurrences of *oldsubstring* have been replaced by *newsubstring*. Our little piece of WAP genetic engineering to remove the smelly foot gene would look like this:

```
var StevesNewGenes = String.replace(StevesGenes, "TCGGAT", "");
```

After this statement, all occurrences of the offending gene will have been replaced by "" – or in other words, deleted.

White Space

The `String` library contains two functions to help you deal with white space: `String.squeeze()` and `String.trim()`. The first of these functions takes a string parameter and returns it with any multiple adjacent white space characters replaced by a single space. The second one removes leading and trailing white space from a string.

For example, if we had a string declared as follows:

```
var myString = "   Paris in the      Spring.    ";
```

Then the following operations:

```
var mySqueezedString = String.squeeze(myString);
var myTrimmedString = String.trim(myString);
```

Would be equivalent to writing:

```
var mySqueezedString = " Paris in the Spring. ";
var myTrimmedString = "Paris in the      Spring.";
```

This could come in handy when formatting user input.

String Formatting

So far, whenever we have written out a number for display, we've relied on the default display options. Sometimes this is fine, but on other occasions (such as the vacation insurance cards of our Wrox Travel application) it's not so great. There are times when we want to limit the display to two decimal places (such as when outputting cash values), or to position several numbers so that their decimal points align vertically.

There's a handy function in the `String` library for specifying format instructions: `String.format()`. Despite its location, this function can be used for formatting strings *and* numbers; its syntax is as follows:

```
String.format(template, value);
```

The return value of this function is *value*, as a string formatted according to *template*. The *template* string is made up of the following:

❑   Zero or more 'hard-coded' characters

❑   A single formatting code that specifies the formatting required

The 'hard-coded' characters are returned in exactly the same way as they are written, but the formatting code is replaced with a formatted string representing *value*. This means that a typical call to the function might look like this:

```
var formattedString = String.format("force = fcode Newtons", myVal);
```

`formattedString` will then contain the string `"force = "`, followed by a formatted version of `myVal`. If `myVal` contained 3.1416, and *fcode* specified three decimal places (we'll see exactly how this is possible in a moment), `formattedString` would contain `"force = 3.142 Newtons"`. (Note that this value has been rounded up appropriately.) This kind of formatting can be quite useful, especially when you consider the display limitations that are inherent in WAP-enabled devices.

Now let's take a closer look at the possible formatting codes. The basic syntax for this code is:

```
%width.precisiontype
```

Taking this from left to right, the `%` symbol is mandatory, and is not output in the resultant string. If you wish to include a `%` character in the string, you need to write `%%`.

Next, *width*, which is optional, specifies the minimum number of characters that will be output. If you wish to format strings for display in a column, you can use this argument to specify how wide to make the columns, although because you are specifying a *minimum* you still have to be quite careful. The default value here is 0, meaning that no minimum is used.

Next, *.precision*, which is also optional, specifies different things depending on the *type* specified. If you use it, you must include the leading ".". If you don't use it, *precision* defaults to 1.

Finally, *type*, which is mandatory, specifies the type of formatting to use. This can be one of the following:

❑   d for integer formatting

❑   f for floating point formatting

❑   s for string formatting

The behavior for each *type* is shown in the next three sections, which are representative of how the function is supposed to work. Bear in mind that the behavior from browser to browser may differ.

type = d

In integer-type formatting, `.precision` specifies the minimum number of *digits* to display. This differs from `width` in that zeros are added to the left of a formatted integer in order to make up the minimum number of *digits*, but spaces are added to make up the minimum number of *characters*.

Let's look at a few examples of this `type`:

```
var myVal = 45;
var result1 = String.format("Result: '%d'", myVal);
var result2 = String.format("Result: '%1d'", myVal);
var result3 = String.format("Result: '%4d'", myVal);
var result4 = String.format("Result: '%4.3d'", myVal);
var result5 = String.format("Result: '%.6d'", myVal);
```

The results are as follows:

```
result1 = "Result: '45'"
result2 = "Result: '45'"
result3 = "Result: '  45'"
result4 = "Result: ' 045'"
result5 = "Result: '000045'"
```

The first and second results are identical, because the second line sets a minimum number of digits that's smaller than the parameter passed to the function. In the third example, two padding spaces will be added to make the minimum width 4 characters. The remaining examples follow in the same vein.

type = f

Here, `.precision` specifies the number of characters to output after the decimal place of the floating point number. If the given value contains more decimal places, it will be rounded to the nearest decimal place; if it has fewer, padding zeros will be added to the right of the number. The default value of this parameter is 6.

Here are some floating point-type formatting examples:

```
var myVal = 191.6;
var result1 = String.format("Result: '%f'", myVal);
var result2 = String.format("Result: '%1f'", myVal);
var result3 = String.format("Result: '%16f'", myVal);
var result4 = String.format("Result: '%4.3f'", myVal);
var result5 = String.format("Result: '%.4f'", myVal);
```

This time, the results are these:

```
result1 = "Result: '191.600000'"
result2 = "Result: '191.600000'"
result3 = "Result: '        191.600000'"
result4 = "Result: '191.600'"
result5 = "Result: '191.6000'"
```

As in the previous example, `result1` and `result2` will be identical, as they attempt to set minimum values for `width` that do not apply. It's possible for no decimal point (and subsequent digits) to be displayed if `.precision` is specified as 0.

type = s

For strings, `.precision` specifies the maximum number of characters to output. This may result in the string being truncated. Let's look at some string formatting examples:

```
var myVal = "Asparagus";
var result1 = String.format("Result: '%s'", myVal);
var result2 = String.format("Result: '%1s'", myVal);
var result3 = String.format("Result: '%16s'", myVal);
var result4 = String.format("Result: '%4.3s'", myVal);
var result5 = String.format("Result: '%.4s'", myVal);
```

The five results are as follows:

```
result1 = "Result: 'Asparagus'"
result2 = "Result: 'Asparagus'"
result3 = "Result: '        Asparagus'"
result4 = "Result: 'Asp'"
result5 = "Result: 'Aspa'"
```

Notice `result4` in particular: for strings, if `.precision` is smaller than `width`, then `width` will be ignored. By default, all characters are printed.

Try It Out — A Small Modification to the Wrox Travel Application

This new information allows us to fix a nasty problem with the Wrox Travel application that's been plaguing us for a couple of chapters now. At present, the quote for travel insurance appears in the UP.Simulator in mantissa-exponent format (the example in the last chapter produced $1.500100e+002), but now we're in a position to do something about that.

1. The problem lies in the `coverCost()` function, which is in `insure2.wmls`. The technique we've used allows us to quote in dollars and cents (or pounds and pence), but it has the display problems we've mentioned already.

```
function coverCost(duration, sports, region, currency)
{
    var cost = duration * (20 / 28);
    if (duration >= 365)
    {
        cost /= 2.607;
    }

    cost *= sports ? 1.5 : 1;
    cost *= region ? 1 : 2;

    cost = currency ? cost : toPounds(cost);
    cost = Float.round(cost * 100) / 100;

    return currency ? ("$" + cost) : ("£" + cost);
}
```

2. The solution to the problem is to add a single line of code that uses the `String.format()` function to force the quote to be displayed to two decimal places:

```
cost = currency ? cost : toPounds(cost);
cost = Float.round(cost * 100) / 100;
cost = String.format("%.2f", cost);

return currency ? ("$" + cost) : ("£" + cost);
```

3. With this change in place, the insurance quote page shows a considerable improvement (assuming all the same parameters that we used in the last chapter):

Strings as Arrays

Finally, rather than treating a given string as a sequence of characters, WMLScript makes it possible to treat it as a sequence of distinct elements of varying length. If you wish, this technique can be used to simulate **arrays**, which appear in many other programming languages.

Fundamentally, an array is a set of related elements, ordered in a logical way. You can think of an array as being a list of items, or perhaps a column of a spreadsheet. The key point is that you can ask to look at, say, item number ten without having to look at items one to nine first. WMLScript doesn't support arrays as such, but it does allow you to treat delimited strings as if they were arrays, and we'll look at some methods for achieving such a representation in this section.

The WMLScript technique for representing arrays involves the specification of a **separator**, or **delimiter**. This separator is a single character that separates the elements in a string array. You must choose a separating character that doesn't appear in any of the substrings you wish to separate, or you'll have breaks occurring in some very strange places! For example, if we had a string initialized as:

```
var myString = "cow,chicken,aardvark,ocelot";
```

We could specify the comma as our separator. This would give us the following four elements:

- ❑ cow
- ❑ chicken
- ❑ aardvark
- ❑ ocelot

However, we could just as easily specify "c" as our separator, giving us the following *five* elements:

- ❏   "" (an empty string)
- ❏   ow,
- ❏   hi
- ❏   ken,aardvark,o
- ❏   elot

Using the functions you already know about, and with judicious use of loops, you could implement the array scheme detailed above yourself without too much trouble. However, the creators of WMLScript have made things a little easier than that, and provided a suite of functions that perform many of the necessary tasks for you.

Standard Library String-Array Access Functions

The String library contains five string-array access functions, listed below:

- ❏   String.elements()
- ❏   String.elementAt()
- ❏   String.removeAt()
- ❏   String.replaceAt()
- ❏   String.insertAt()

Let's look at each of these in turn.

String.elements()

This function returns the number of elements in a string, given the specified separator. The syntax of this function is:

```
String.elements(array, separator)
```

The two parameters supply the string and the separator to be used respectively. The return value of the function is an integer specifying how many elements there are in the array. For example, taking the string defined in the last section:

```
var myString = "cow,chicken,aardvark,ocelot";

var result1 = String.elements(myString, ",");
var result2 = String.elements(myString, "c");
```

After these statements have been executed, result1 will contain 4, and result2 will contain 5.

If the separator supplied doesn't occur in the string, the return value will be 1 (the start and end of the string are treated as array terminators, and in this case these terminators will enclose a single element). An empty string also counts as an element, and the return value will still be 1.

String.elementAt()

This function allows you to get the value of the element specified. The syntax is:

```
String.elementAt(array, position, separator)
```

array and *separator* have the same meanings as before, while *position* is the **index** of the element to be returned as the function's return value. As with the positions of characters in strings, the index number of the first element is 0. If an index less than 0 is supplied, the first element is returned; if an index greater than that of the last element is supplied, the last element is returned. For example:

```
var myString = "cow,chicken,aardvark,ocelot";
var result1 = String.elementAt(myString, 0, ",");
var result2 = String.elementAt(myString, 1, ",");
var result3 = String.elementAt(myString, 2001, ",");
```

Results in:

```
result1 = "cow"
result2 = "chicken"
result3 = "ocelot"
```

String.removeAt()

`String.removeAt()` returns a string with the specified element removed. The syntax is:

```
String.removeAt(array, position, separator)
```

array, *separator*, and *position* have exactly the same meanings and semantics as before, so you should be able to guess what will happen here without too much trouble:

```
var myString = "cow,chicken,aardvark,ocelot";

var result1 = String.removeAt(myString, 2, ",");
var result2 = String.removeAt(myString, -99, ",");
```

After these operations, these strings will contain:

```
result1 = "cow,chicken,ocelot"
result2 = "chicken,aardvark,ocelot"
```

String.replaceAt()

This function, which you saw being used in our 'hangman' game in the last chapter, allows you to replace an element with a new value, and has this syntax:

```
String.replaceAt(array, newElement, position, separator)
```

array, *position*, and *separator* specify the element to be replaced, while *newElement* is the new value to replace it with.

For example:

```
var myString = "cow,chicken,aardvark,ocelot";

var result1 = String.replaceAt(myString, "turkey", 1, ",");
var result2 = String.replaceAt(myString, "lynx", 1975, ",");
```

Results in:

```
result1 = "cow,turkey,aardvark,ocelot"
result2 = "cow,chicken,aardvark,lynx"
```

String.insertAt()

Finally, you can add elements to a string array using `String.insertAt()`. This time, the syntax is:

```
String.insertAt(array, newElement, position, separator)
```

newElement is inserted into the array at the position specified by the other three parameters. For example:

```
var myString = "cow,chicken,aardvark,ocelot";

var result1 = String.insertAt(myString, "tiger", 1, ",");
var result2 = String.insertAt(myString, "hamster", 25, ",");
```

Would be equivalent to writing:

```
result1 = "cow,tiger,chicken,aardvark,ocelot"
result2 = "cow,chicken,aardvark,ocelot,hamster"
```

Note

There is no library function to return the index of a given element, but if you need functionality like that, it can be implemented using the functions we've seen already. For example:

```
var myString = "cow,chicken,aardvark,ocelot,chicken";
var positions = "";
var maxPos = String.elements(myString, ",");

for (var position = 0; position < maxPos; position++)
{
   if (String.elementAt(myString, position, ",") == "chicken")
   {
      positions = String.insertAt(positions, String.toString(position),
                                  maxPos, ",");
   }
}
```

This would result in `positions` containing "1,4" – a list of the indexes of the elements found. Notice the use of the `String.toString()` function in the assignment statement. We're inserting the current value of the loop counter into a string that we can later use as an array, if we choose to do so.

291

Summary

This chapter should have rounded off your WMLScript knowledge nicely. You started off with a whole lot of basic tools, and the extra techniques from this chapter should have sharpened them. The next step for you is to *practice* these new skills – it's the only way of gaining real experience.

The particular topics we looked at in this chapter were the following:

❑   Using pragmas

❑   Anticipating and dealing with errors

❑   The capabilities of the standard library mathematical functions

❑   String formatting

❑   Using strings as arrays

For the rest of this book, we'll be using WMLScript wherever it's required, or wherever it can make things a bit easier for you. Those sections should reinforce what you've already learned about the language, and will help to highlight the areas where you might want to use it.

Events

The WML and WMLScript techniques contained in the preceding chapters allow you to build quite complex WAP applications, with plenty of functionality and a rich user interface. However, WML has a few more tricks up its sleeve yet. It was back in Chapter 6 that we first mentioned **events** in conjunction with the `<go>` element, with a promise to discuss them in much greater detail later in the book. In this chapter, that time has come.

Especially in the world of programming, the word "event" can mean different things to different people, so to start with we need a definition of an event that we can all agree on:

> **A WML event is one of several specific occurrences on the user agent that we can detect and then act on by executing a task.**

Tasks that are triggered by events may occur *at any time* during execution of an application. They can lead to an interruption in WML interpretation, or some other sort of 'jump' outside of the normal flow of execution. This will become clear if we look at a couple of examples that further illustrate what events are and what they can do. Later on, we'll get into the finer points of implementation.

Uses for Events

The first time a user encounters our WAP application's home page, we might want to present them with a corporate logo, or 'splash screen'. The WML we've seen so far allows us to place this information in a separate card, along with a link to get to the first proper card of our deck. Events allow us a wider choice; we can use them to:

- ❏ Detect navigation into our site, providing a one-off redirection from our home page to a splash screen that won't be re-triggered if the user returns to the home page by going 'back'.

- ❏ Supply a splash screen with *no* user-activated link to our home page, where navigation occurs automatically after a set period of time.

We could even combine these techniques together to produce a one-off, timed splash screen, or hook in some WMLScript for additional manipulation at the client side.

Another example of event use concerns selecting items from a list. WML events allow us to detect the moment when the user *changes* the selected item – even before they select OK. We can act on this choice immediately (perhaps by navigating to a new card), resulting in speedier and more responsive applications.

> *Note that these events are a WML construct, not WMLScript. This is an important point to make, because it marks a big difference between WML and languages such as HTML, where separate scripting would be necessary to get event-like behavior.*

Over the course of this chapter, we will look at:

- ❑ What events are
- ❑ What types of events are available to us
- ❑ The sort of tasks that events can trigger
- ❑ How we associate events with tasks
- ❑ Examples of using all the different types of tasks
- ❑ Extensions to the Wrox Travel application

Hopefully, you'll soon see how judicious use of events can add a touch of sparkle to your applications – not to mention some significantly enhanced usability.

Types of Event

Broadly speaking, events fall into three notional categories:

- ❑ Events triggered directly by the user
- ❑ Events triggered indirectly by the user
- ❑ Events triggered by the user agent, through the use of a timer

We have already seen events directly triggered by the user – these are where softkeys on the phone are used to select tasks specified by <do> elements (as we first saw in Chapter 6). Indirectly triggered events occur as a side effect of other user activity, such as cards being entered or options in a list being chosen. Timer events are a different concept entirely; these are triggered by the user agent after a pre-set time has elapsed.

Types of Task

Events may be linked to (and therefore trigger) any of the following tasks:

- ❑ <go> – allows navigation (often redirection), information posting, and script calling
- ❑ <prev> – allows navigation backwards through the history stack
- ❑ <noop> – no action, often used to override default activities (see later)

❑   `<refresh>` – allows variables to be set, or refreshes the browser display to reflect updated variable content that has come about due to other processes

With the exception of `<noop>`, all of these tasks have been covered in previous chapters. Here, we'll just go ahead and use them, showing what is possible when they are linked to events. `<noop>` will come into play later when we talk about 'templated' activities, which are defined in deck-level `<template>` elements. These apply to all the cards in a deck, providing default tasks for certain actions.

Linking Tasks to Events

In order for an event to do anything, we have to link it to a task. One way of looking at this is to imagine that events are being triggered all the time in any WAP application, but that without linking them to a task they are simply ignored. The precise method of linkage varies from event to event, but in general you will use one of the two following methods:

❑   Specify the task using an attribute of the element that triggers the event

❑   Specify the task using an element contained by the element that handles the event

The main difference between these approaches is that specifying event-task linkage with attributes is limited – it's only possible to cause simple navigation this way. In the sections that follow, we'll look at the different tasks we can use, and see examples of linking them to events.

Events Triggered Directly by the User

As we've already mentioned, directly triggered events are specified using `<do>` elements, and triggered by the user via softkeys. `<do>` elements have been covered extensively already, but we'll have a quick recap here, as it will allow us to consider them in the context of events, and to compare their structure with those of other event types.

We specify the nature of a `<do>` user action using the `type` attribute – typically `type="accept"` for simply linking an action to a softkey. We can name a `<do>` element using the `name` attribute, which can be omitted – in which case it defaults to the value of the `type` attribute. Finally, we can provide it with a label for display purposes by using the `label` attribute.

We might, for example, specify a navigational menu option using the following WML code, which may be contained directly in a `<card>` element, or placed inside a `<p>` element:

```
<do type="accept" label="Timetable">
   <go href="#timetable"/>
</do>
```

`<do>` elements can contain `<go>`, `<prev>`, `<noop>`, and `<refresh>` elements – a list that's identical to the list of tasks we saw earlier. Now you know a little more about events, this makes perfect sense: the `<do>` element is specifying a type of event (a user-triggered one), and as such can be linked to any of the tasks that are possible for events.

Since we've covered `<do>` elements elsewhere, let's move on and look at the other events.

Events Triggered Indirectly by the User

Indirectly triggered events occur due to other actions being carried out by the user agent. This is easiest to explain by looking at the three indirectly triggered events that WML supports:

❑ `onenterforward` is triggered when a card is navigated to, except where the `<prev/>` operation is used to achieve this navigation

❑ `onenterbackward` is triggered when the `<prev/>` operation is used to navigate to a card

❑ `onpick` is triggered when an item is selected from a list selection field

The first two of these are related to navigation. When navigation occurs, one or the other of these events is triggered, and we can detect them if we have linked a task to them. The mechanics of this are explained below.

The third event, `onpick`, is the one we hinted at earlier; it can be used to execute tasks when the user selects an item from a list. This might be used to create some navigational options as an alternative to a list of links on a card – this would be especially powerful when combined with the UP.Simulator's list selection capabilities, allowing quick navigation using the keypad of a mobile device.

onenterforward

The `onenterforward` event may be specified using either of the two methods listed earlier: by an attribute, or by a separate element. In both cases, this event is associated with (triggered by) a `<card>` element. When navigation to a card occurs, a check is carried out, and if that navigation is in a 'forward' direction – that is, it *wasn't* achieved with a `<prev/>` element – the `onenterforward` event is triggered.

Specification by an Attribute

The attribute used to specify this event in a `<card>` element is, reasonably enough, `onenterforward`. All we need to do is supply it with the location to navigate to. For example:

```
<card id="first" onenterforward="#splash">
```

Of course, the target location doesn't have to be another card, or even another deck. If wanted to, we could use this event to execute a WMLScript function, perhaps setting a variable:

```
<card id="second" onenterforward="event.wmls#set()">
```

The point that bears reiteration is that redirection will only happen when the card is entered *forwards*. If this is the first card of the first deck, it will take place just once in the whole application. Let's have an example that demonstrates some of these issues.

Try It Out — onenterforward

Create the deck opposite, which consists of a "start" card with links to three other cards called "card1", "card2", and "card3". Save the file as `onenterfwd.wml`, and give it a spin in the UP.Simulator.

```
<?xml version="1.0"?>
<!DOCTYPE wml PUBLIC "-//WAPFORUM//DTD WML 1.2//EN"
                     "http://www.wapforum.org/DTD/wml_1.2.xml">

<wml>
    <card id="start">
        <p>
            Ready?<br/>
            <a href="#card1">First card</a><br/>
            <a href="#card2">Second card</a><br/>
            <a href="#card3">Third card</a>
        </p>
    </card>
    <card id="card1">
        <p>
            Here we are, happily in the first card.
        </p>
        <do type="prev" label="Back">
            <prev/>
        </do>
    </card>
    <card id="card2">
        <p>
            Now we're in the darkest depths of the second card.
        </p>
        <do type="prev" label="Back">
            <prev/>
        </do>
    </card>
    <card id="card3">
        <p>
            Warning! Now in the dangerous regions of the third card!
        </p>
        <do type="prev" label="Back">
            <prev/>
        </do>
    </card>
</wml>
```

You should have seen that all the cards (apart from the first one) contain a `prev`-type <do> element that allows us to get back to where we started. Next, add an `onenterforward` event to "card1", redirecting the user to "card2":

```
<card id="card1" onenterforward="#card2">
```

If you try the application again, the first card to be displayed still looks like this:

But if you follow *either* of the first two links from our "start" card, you will see the following screen:

How It Works

We can best understand the processes at work here by examining the behavior of the OK softkey. This carries the 'back' functionality that's also contained in the UP.Simulator's BACK key, and it will have a different effect depending on the link we followed from the "start" card. Remember: the <prev/> task moves us one stage back in history, and if we were redirected with onenterforward, that counts as two navigations (the first to "card1", the second to "card2").

So, if we choose First card and hit OK, we'll get "card1" because the onenterforward event isn't triggered by the <prev/> task. (Hitting OK a second time will take us back to the "start" card.)

But if we choose the link to Second card, the OK softkey will take us straight back to the "start" card because we've only navigated forward once. If you like, we can change that (and make things more complicated) by adding similar redirection to "card2":

```
<card id="card2" onenterforward="#card3">
```

And now any of the three links will take us to "card3":

The behavior is a little different, but the mechanisms are the same: from wherever we begin, the `onenterforward` events push us to the third card. Selecting OK will move us back up through the history stack, taking up to three tries to return to the "start" card.

As a final test, what do you think happens if we do this?

```
<card id="card3" onenterforward="#card1">
```

Try and resist the temptation to find out! This event will cause the user agent to enter an infinite loop of redirection, with unpredictable results. Admittedly, it's unlikely that you'd make a mistake like this in such a simple application, but it *could* happen in something more complex, and it's something you should be careful to avoid.

Specification by an Element

As we've said, events may also be specified and linked to tasks by using an element that's (directly) contained by the triggering element. The (contained) element we use for this is `<onevent>`, and it allows us a lot more freedom than specifying `onenterforward` using an attribute.

`<onevent>` has a single, mandatory attribute: `type`. This attribute specifies the name of the event for which `<onevent>` specifies the task, and in most cases this will be the type of the event. For an `onenterforward` event in a card, then, we need the following structure:

```
<card id="card1">
   <onevent type="onenterforward">

      <!-- Task specification -->

   </onevent>

   <!-- Card contents -->

</card>
```

In this case, `<card>` is the "triggering element" referred to in the discussion above.

The `<onevent>` element can contain any one of the 'task' elements (`<go>`, `<prev>`, `<noop>`, and `<refresh>`), so the following event specified by an attribute:

```
<card id="card1" onenterforward="event.wmls#set()">

   <!-- Card contents -->

</card>
```

Could be rewritten like this, with exactly the same effect:

```
<card id="card1">
   <onevent type="onenterforward">
      <go href="event.wml#set()"/>
   </onevent>

   <!-- Card contents -->
</card>
```

At first sight, that doesn't seem like much of an improvement – we've used more WML code to do the same thing – but handling events in this way allows us more flexibility. If you want to set a variable on card entry, for example, you can discard `event.wmls` and replace it with this:

```
<card id="card1">
    <onevent type="onenterforward">
        <refresh>
            <setvar name="A" value="Hello"/>
        </refresh>
    </onevent>

    <!-- Card contents -->

</card>
```

In Chapter 10, when we looked at user input, we saw how default values could be supplied to the `<input>` element. However, we *also* saw that if the variable being used for text input was already in use, *its* value would be used for the text field, regardless of the default value supplied. Setting this variable on entry to a card allows us to have a fresh default value every time the card is entered:

```
<card id="login" title="Login">
    <onevent type="onenterforward">
        <refresh>
            <setvar name="name" value="anonymous"/>
        </refresh>
    </onevent>
    <p>
        Enter name:<br/>
        <input name="name" title="Name"/>
        <a href="#card1">Login</a>
    </p>
    <do type="prev" label="Back">
        <prev/>
    </do>
</card>
```

Quite apart from being more versatile, the element method of event-task linkage is more explicit, and may make it easier for others to read your code. On the downside, however, it does use more memory for the same operations. If your decks start getting too big, and if you have the choice, you may want to use the attribute method for brevity.

onenterbackward

onenterbackward works in much the same way as onenterforward, except that its triggering conditions are different. This event is triggered when a card is entered by navigating backwards through the history stack – by using <prev/>, for example.

The main reason for handling this event is to prevent the user from having to move through pages that are no longer relevant. For example, the first page you reach after following a link might be a help message, a splash screen, or perhaps a disclaimer that you need to see before getting to the real content. In such a situation, it can be useful (and time saving) simply to bypass this superfluous information when the user is returning to a starting point.

Consider, for example, the following WML deck, `nuts.wml`:

```
<?xml version="1.0"?>
<!DOCTYPE wml PUBLIC "-//WAPFORUM//DTD WML 1.2//EN"
                     "http://www.wapforum.org/DTD/wml_1.2.xml">

<wml>
    <card id="start" title="Wrox Nuts">
        <p><a href="#buy">Buy nuts</a><br/>
            <a href="#about">About us</a>
        </p>
    </card>
    <card id="buy" title="Buy nuts">
        <p>Select a nut:<br/>
            <select name="nut" title="Select Nut">
                <option value="P">Peanuts</option>
                <option value="B">Brazil nuts</option>
                <option value="H">Hazelnuts</option>
                <option value="W">Walnuts</option>
            </select>
        </p>
        <do type="accept" label="Buy">
            <go href="buynuts.asp" method="post">
                <postfield name="nut" value="$(nut)"/>
            </go>
        </do>
        <do type="prev" label="Back">
            <prev/>
        </do>
    </card>
    <card id="about" title="Wrox Nuts">
        <p>Here at Wrox Nuts we aim to bring you nuts of
            the highest quality first time - every time.
        </p>
        <do type="prev" label="Back">
            <prev/>
        </do>
    </card>
</wml>
```

This WML application allows us to buy a variety of nuts online. The user can specify the type of nut, and ask to buy some through a `post` operation to an ASP file that we won't implement here. The nut selection screen looks like this:

As we saw in Chapter 6, the UP.Simulator doesn't act on prev-type <do> elements, relying instead on the BACK key. Since the latter just navigates through the history stack, this behavior isn't a problem for us here. Many other user agents would represent the <prev> task in some way.

To an application such as this, we can use the `onenterbackward` event to add a disclaimer card of the sort we discussed above:

```wml
<wml>
    <card id="start" title="Wrox Nuts">
        <p><a href="#disclaimer">Buy nuts</a><br/>
            <a href="#about">About us</a>
        </p>
    </card>
    <card id="disclaimer" title="Disclaimer">
        <onevent type="onenterbackward">
            <prev/>
        </onevent>
        <p>WARNING: Nuts bought from this site may contain nuts.<br/>
            <a href="#buy">Continue</a>
        </p>
        <do type="prev" label="Back">
            <prev/>
        </do>
    </card>
    <card id="buy" title="Buy nuts">
        <p>Select a nut:<br/>

        <!--Rest of code omitted for brevity -->
```

This disclaimer will now be displayed when the user follows the Buy nuts link. However, if the user navigates *backwards* from the "buy" card, they won't see the disclaimer a second time. Instead, they'll be returned to the first page of the application.

The `onenterbackward` event can also be used to run scripts, post information, or any of the other tasks that we can normally link to events.

It's possible to specify an `onenterbackward` attribute, but it again restricts the tasks you can perform. Furthermore, we have to be explicit about the destination of any redirection, because we can't specify the `<prev/>` task:

```wml
<card id="disclaimer" title="Disclaimer" onenterbackward="#start">
```

The trouble with this is that the history stack will retain the "disclaimer" card. Going back again from the "start" card won't take the device to the card displayed prior to "start", but to the "disclaimer" card again, resulting in automatic navigation to "start". In effect, 'back' functionality is disabled, and you run a high risk of annoying your users.

onpick

The third and final indirectly triggered event that WML supplies is `onpick`, and it too has attribute and element forms. As discussed briefly above, this event allows us to act on a user list selection *immediately*, thereby solving a problem that we first alluded to back in Chapter 10.

When we introduced the `<select>` and `<option>` elements, we found that they were great ways of presenting a set of choices to the user, and of storing information about the choices they made. With the knowledge we had then, though, there were a range of situations where list selection didn't seem appropriate, chief among which was navigation.

Without events, navigating as a result of a user's selection is a two-stage process: first you store the choice in a variable, then you act by passing it to a WMLScript function or using it to construct a URL. (If `V` contains either `London` or `Andorra`, then `<a href="$(V).wml"/>` represents a hyperlink to `London.wml` or `Andorra.wml` accordingly.) By specifying `onpick` attributes to `<option>` elements, we can get it down to a single, more compact action, as we'll see.

Try It Out — Quicker Vacation Navigation

At the moment, the Wrox Travel application's "offers" card contains details of only two vacations, but new deals come along all the time, and when they do it would be nice if we were able to present them to our users in a logical way. The `<table>` element has served us well, but it's time for a change.

1. Open `offers.wml`, remove the `<table>` element in the second paragraph, and substitute it with the following:

```
<card id="offers" title="Special Offers">
   <p>Wrox Travel is pleased to be able to offer
      you the following amazing deals:<br/>
   </p>
   <p mode="nowrap">
      <select title="Vacations">
         <optgroup title="Europe">
            <option onpick="andorra.wml">Andorra, $$200</option>
            <option onpick="birmingham.wml">Birmingham, $$250</option>
            <option onpick="london.wml">London, $$300</option>
         </optgroup>
         <optgroup title="Rest of World">
            <option onpick="cairo.wml">Cairo, $$400</option>
            <option onpick="lima.wml">Lima, $$500</option>
         </optgroup>
      </select>
   </p>
   <do type="prev">
      <prev/>
   </do>
</card>
```

We won't reproduce the three new files `birmingham.wml`, `cairo.wml`, *and* `lima.wml` *here. You can probably guess what they look like, and you can also download them from the Wrox web site.*

We've added three new holidays to our catalog, and arranged them into a `<select>`/`<optgroup>`/`<option>` structure. If you launch the Wrox Travel application now, and find your way to the "offers" card, this is what you should see:

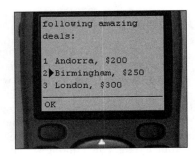

How It Works

The `<select>` element neatly replaces the `<table>` element, and when you select the links shown in the above figure, you'll find that navigation back and forth works as well as it did before. The `onpick` attribute can *only* be applied to the `<option>` element, and the value you supply must be a URL specifying the card, deck, or WMLScript function to be executed when the act of selection occurs. It's as simple as that.

With regard to the additional `<optgroup>` elements, you know from Chapter 10 that the UP.Simulator ignores them, but that's no reason to avoid them. In another user agent, the list *would* be split up, providing an even cleaner interface.

To complete this picture, `onpick` events can also be specified in `<onevent>` elements. When you do that, however, the structure can look a bit odd, and is significantly more verbose for even a few items. Our list of five holidays, for example, would look like this:

```
<select title="Vacations">
    <optgroup title="Europe">
        <option>
            <onevent type="onpick">
                <go href="andorra.wml"/>
            </onevent>
            Andorra, $$200
        </option>
        <option>
            <onevent type="onpick">
                <go href="birmingham.wml"/>
            </onevent>
            Birmingham, $$250
        </option>
        <option>
            <onevent type="onpick">
                <go href="london.wml"/>
            </onevent>
            London, $$300
        </option>
    </optgroup>
    <optgroup title="Rest of World">
        <option>
            <onevent type="onpick">
                <go href="cairo.wml"/>
            </onevent>
            Cairo, $$400
        </option>
```

```
                    <option>
                        <onevent type="onpick">
                            <go href="lima.wml"/>
                        </onevent>
                        Lima, $$500
                    </option>
                </optgroup>
            </select>
```

Still, this does allow us to attach tasks other than simple navigation to the `onpick` event. (But don't forget that if you want to set a variable, you might be able to use the `<option>` element's `value` attribute.) If extended functionality is what you need, then while it may not be pretty, it does work!

Events Triggered by a Timer

The final event we need to look at is `ontimer`, which (unsurprisingly) allows us to act on a timer. Any card may start a timer running when it is displayed, and after a specified interval the `ontimer` event occurs. At that point, we can act on the event.

Like the indirectly triggered events, we can use `ontimer` through either attribute or element syntax. For the former, we just need to set the `ontimer` attribute of the `<card>` element to the URL that should be navigated to when the timer elapses. Then, we specify the duration of the timer using a new element, `<timer>`.

```
<timer name="timername" value="duration" />
```

It's optional to specify the `name` attribute, but `value` is compulsory: it must be set to the number of tenths of seconds that should elapse before the `ontimer` event occurs. At that time, navigation will occur.

Try It Out — The ontimer Event

1. Let's look at a simple example: a splash screen that appears for a second before our WML application starts properly. Here's `splash.wml`:

```
<?xml version="1.0"?>
<!DOCTYPE wml PUBLIC "-//WAPFORUM//DTD WML 1.2//EN"
                    "http://www.wapforum.org/DTD/wml_1.2.xml">

<wml>
    <card id="splash" title="Splash!" ontimer="#start">
        <timer value="10"/>
        <p align="center">Welcome to our site!</p>
    </card>
    <card id="start" title="Application">
        <p>This is the first screen.</p>
        <do type="prev" label="Back">
            <prev/>
        </do>
    </card>
</wml>
```

When you load this deck into the UP.Browser, the splash screen will appear for a second, followed by the application proper. If you wish, you can repeat the process by navigating back to the first card.

Alternatively, we can use the `ontimer` event's element syntax, which has the same form we've seen in earlier examples:

```
<card id="splash" title="Splash!">
   <onevent type="ontimer">
      <go href="#start"/>
   </onevent>
   <timer value="10"/>
   <p align="center">Welcome to our site!</p>
</card>
```

Separating out the task like this allows us to do other things in response to the event, enabling the creation of some interesting display effects:

```
<?xml version="1.0"?>
<!DOCTYPE wml PUBLIC "-//WAPFORUM//DTD WML 1.2//EN"
                  "http://www.wapforum.org/DTD/wml_1.2.xml">

<wml>
   <card id="joke" title="A Joke!" newcontext="true">
      <onevent type="ontimer">
         <refresh>
            <setvar name="P" value="A stick!"/>
         </refresh>
      </onevent>
      <timer value="50"/>
      <p align="center">
         What's brown and sticky?<br/>
         <b>$(P)</b>
      </p>
   </card>
</wml>
```

The above code, for example, displays the feed line for a joke, followed five seconds later by the punchline.

The joke may be a bad one, but the concept is sound! When the card is first displayed, the P variable contains the empty string, so nothing appears on the third line of the display. Five seconds later, an ontimer event occurs and is handled by an <onevent> element. Here, a new value is assigned to P, and because the <setvar> element is contained by a pair of <refresh> tags, this change is represented in the user agent.

Before leaving this section, we need to say something about the <timer> element's optional name attribute, which allows us to specify the timer duration by using a named variable as its value. If the variable is unset, the default value (in the value attribute) is used. (If the variable is given an unusable value, such as a string with no numbers, the effect will be unpredictable.) We could use this to have a joke with a user-defined suspense period:

```
<wml>
    <card id="start" newcontext="true">
        <p>How much suspense do you want (in 1/10s)?<br/>
            <input name="time"/><br/>
            <a href="#joke">Go</a>
        </p>
    </card>
    <card id="joke" title="A Joke!">
        <onevent type="ontimer">
            <refresh>
                <setvar name="P" value="A stick!"/>
            </refresh>
        </onevent>
        <timer name="time" value="50"/>
        <p align="center">
            What's brown and sticky?<br/>
            <b>$(P)</b>
        </p>
    </card>
</wml>
```

You can now laugh at the same bad joke as many times as you like, but with slightly different comic timing.

Finally, it's worth noting that the value of the timer variable 'counts down' as the timer runs. If you check the value of time at the end of this demonstration, for example, you'll find that it's set to 0. However, if you were to leave the card before the timer had expired (by going 'back', perhaps), you'd find that time contains the number of tenths-of-seconds remaining on the clock.

Templated Decks

As we've gone along in this chapter – indeed, in this book – you've probably started to notice that certain segments of code crop up on a fairly regular basis. A lot of our cards, for example, have been equipped with a softkey for backward navigation, which has required the following lines of code:

```
<do type="prev" label="Back">
   <prev/>
</do>
```

> *As you know, the UP.Simulator ignores this particular construct, but including it in your cards is a good habit to get into – users of other microbrowsers will appreciate it. For the sake of illustration in this section, we'll use the following, which* does *have an effect in the UP.Simulator:*
>
> ```
> <do type="options" label="Back">
> </do>
> ```

It may not seem like a lot, but in decks with several cards it can soon add up, and we've spoken many times about the restrictions placed on deck size.

WML provides help with this problem by allowing you to specify items such as the Back softkey shown above *at the deck level.* Anything specified in this way will be common to all cards in a deck, so you don't need to repeat all that typing, and the size of the deck is smaller. This deck-level specification is carried out using the `<template>` element.

Creating a Template

The `<template>` element is contained by the `<wml>` element, so it sits on the same hierarchical level as `<card>` elements. It is similar to a `<card>` element in that it can contain event handlers, but it can't contain the other types of content that `<card>` can. It supports the following attributes:

- ❑ onenterforward
- ❑ onenterbackward
- ❑ ontimer

And it can contain the following elements:

- ❑ `<do>`
- ❑ `<onevent>`

To place a Back softkey in the template, then, we just need the following:

```
<wml>
   <template>
      <do type="options" label="Back">
         <prev/>
      </do>
   </template>

   <!-- Cards -->

</wml>
```

With this code in place, we can add cards to the deck, safe in the knowledge that they'll all benefit from the functionality we've specified in the `<template>` element:

```wml
<wml>
    <template>
        <do type="options" label="Back">
            <prev/>
        </do>
    </template>
    <card id="card1">
        <p>First card.<br/>
            <a href="#card2">Next</a>
        </p>
    </card>
    <card id="card2">
        <p>Second card.<br/>
            <a href="#card3">Next</a>
        </p>
    </card>
    <card id="card3">
        <p>Third card.<br/>
            <a href="#card4">Next</a>
        </p>
    </card>
    <card id="card4">
        <p>Fourth card.</p>
    </card>
</wml>
```

This is the simplest of simple four-card decks, with linear navigation from one card to the next. When we look at these cards in the UP.Simulator, we find that they all contain a **Back** option:

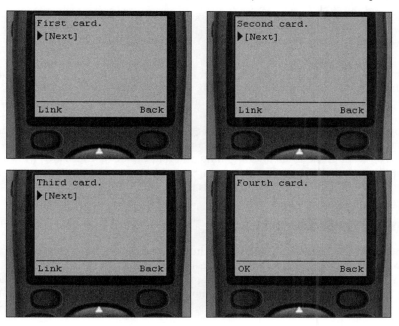

Overriding Templates

In the last example, the Back softkey was added to every card in our deck, but there are times when we might want to have exceptions to this sort of behavior. This is where the following rule becomes important:

> **Card-level event handlers always take precedence over deck-level event handlers.**

Put simply, if the same event has a handler at both the card and the deck level, it's the card that does the work. This is where the task we introduced at the beginning of the chapter comes into its own: the <noop> element (its name is short for "no operation") can be used to disable templated tasks.

In the previous example, it didn't make much sense for the first card to have a Back button (if it's the first card visited, there's nothing to go 'back' to), and we can use <noop> to get rid of it:

```
<wml>
   <template>
      <do type="options" label="Back">
         <prev/>
      </do>
   </template>
   <card id="card1">
      <p>First card.<br/>
         <a href="#card2">Next</a>
      </p>
      <do type="options" label=" ">
         <noop/>
      </do>
   </card>
```

The softkey in "card1" now performs no function, and we've labeled it with a space so that it's invisible to the user. (In the UP.Simulator, failing to specify a `label` results in the word options appearing above the softkey, which could also be confusing.) The other cards retain their Back softkeys, unchanged.

Of course, you don't have to use <noop> when you override. Templated event handlers can be disabled, but they can also be *replaced* by handlers that perform some other task. It could be, for example, that you want 'back' to mean something different in one of your cards (in which case you'd probably keep the same label), or you might want to make the same softkey change behavior completely (in which case you wouldn't). Either is perfectly possible.

Templating Other Events

We can template other events in the same way, and one that deserves special mention is the timer. The <template> element allows us to bind a timer using either the ontimer attribute or the <onevent> element, but it *doesn't* allow us to specify how long it lasts – <template> cannot contain the <timer> element. The result of this is that each card will have a timer event handler, but it will never trigger unless we specify the timer's duration on a card-by-card basis.

For example, one plausible use of the timer event is to jump to a help page if the user has been inactive for a certain period of time. We *could* use the template to specify this help page directly, but a friendlier technique would be to pop up a dialog telling the user that help is available, and where to get it. Let's take a look at the code for that, in `helptimer.wml`:

```
<?xml version="1.0"?>
<!DOCTYPE wml PUBLIC "-//WAPFORUM//DTD WML 1.2//EN"
                     "http://www.wapforum.org/DTD/wml_1.2.xml">

<wml>
    <template>
        <onevent type="ontimer">
            <go href="help.wmls#help()"/>
        </onevent>
        <do type="options" label="Back">
            <prev/>
        </do>
    </template>
    <card id="card1">
        <timer value="50"/>
        <p>First card.<br/>
            <a href="#card2" title="Next">Next</a>
        </p>
        <do type="options" label=" ">
            <noop/>
        </do>
        <do type="accept" label="Help">
            <go href="#help1"/>
        </do>
    </card>
    <card id="card2">
        <timer value="50"/>
        <p>Second card.</p>
        <do type="accept" label="Help">
            <go href="#help2"/>
        </do>
    </card>
    <card id="help1">
        <p>Help for first card.</p>
    </card>
    <card id="help2">
        <p>Help for second card.</p>
    </card>
</wml>
```

This deck consists of two main cards, and two context-specific help cards. The `<template>` element specifies **Back** softkeys, as it did in the last example, and also a timer event handler that calls a function called `help()` in `help.wmls`:

```
extern function help()
{
   Dialogs.alert("Select Help for more information.");
}
```

This function pops up a help message from both "card1" and "card2" after five seconds of inactivity, as specified in the <timer> elements contained in those two cards. The help() function will not be called from the "help1" or "help2" cards, as neither contains a <timer> element.

This **Help** option is specified in <do> elements in "card1" and "card2", and will take the user to "help1" and "help2" respectively, both of which have **Back** softkeys (as specified in the template) to return the user to the main cards. Although the content in this deck is minimal, the structure is sound, and it could readily form the backbone of a far more complex application.

Another use for this mechanism, for example, would be to log out a user after a specified time period. Although functionality like this would require more advanced WAP techniques in some areas, the underlying timer would need little modification.

Wrox Travel: A More Dynamic Application

We've already modified the Wrox Travel application once during this chapter, when we used the onpick attribute to speed navigation. Still, it wouldn't feel right if we finished without giving it another polish, which we'll do by using another of the events we discussed. In this short addition, we'll put a timer on the splash screen that causes automatic navigation to the first proper card in our deck after a specified period.

The Splash Screen

Currently, the code for the splash screen (in wroxtravel.wml) is:

```
<card id="splash" newcontext="true">
  <p align="center">
    <img localsrc="plane" src="WTLogo.wbmp" alt="Wrox"/><br/>
  </p>
  <p align="center">Wrox Travel</p>
  <p mode="nowrap">Welcome to our WAP site!</p>
  <p align="center" mode="wrap">
    <a href="#menu" title="Enter">Enter</a>
  </p>
  <do type="accept" label="Enter">
    <go href="#menu"/>
  </do>
</card>
```

Adding a timer couldn't be easier – we just insert the appropriate navigation instruction:

```
<card id="splash" newcontext="true" ontimer="#menu">
```

And give the timer a value:

```
<card id="splash" newcontext="true" ontimer="#menu">
   <timer value="20"/>
```

This will display the splash screen for two seconds, which might not seem like a long time, but sometimes every second counts! If your users still think it's an unbearable delay (and if they have speedy fingers), they can use the existing navigation options to get to the "menu" card more quickly.

Summary

This chapter has introduced you to WML events. We have seen what an event is, what a task is, and how we bind one to the other to create dynamic actions on the browser, streamlining our applications.

Although the <do> element has been covered in other chapters, this chapter has put it into its proper context as a user triggered event. We have also looked at the other types of event, including those that are indirectly triggered by the user, and those that rely on timed operation.

This chapter has also demonstrated how we can extract common deck-level tasks from the body of our code using the <template> element. This can save a considerable amount of memory if used correctly, allowing us to do more within the constraints of current specification.

Finally, we added features involving some of these new techniques to our Wrox Travel application, bringing it ever closer to completion.

Phone.com Extensions

So far, all the work we've done to understand WML and WMLScript has been with the stated aim of following the WAP specification as closely as possible. However, all of our development work has been done using Phone.com's tools, and we've mentioned on a couple of occasions that its microbrowser has some 'additional' features above and beyond those found in the specification. If you can be sure that the target audience for your applications will be using WAP-enabled devices that feature a Phone.com browser, some of these features are well worth considering, and we'll be looking at them in detail in this chapter.

It's interesting to note that Phone.com's WML extensions were first introduced alongside WAP version 1.1, since which time WAP 1.2 has incorporated some of them as part of the specification – an indication, perhaps, that we could see the same happen to some of the others in the future. Here's a list of the ones we'll be looking at in this chapter; for the others, you should refer to the documentation that comes with the UP.SDK.

Element	Purpose
`<reset>`	Clears all the variable values in the current browser context
`<spawn>`	Creates a child context (see the next section for a description of contexts)
`<exit>`	Exits current browser context and goes back to the parent context
`<send>`	Passes a value to the parent context
`<receive>`	Receives a value passed back from a child context
`<throw>`	Returns to the parent context and alerts the latter of an error or exceptional condition
`<catch>`	Acknowledges an alert raised regarding the occurrence of an error or exceptional condition

Using WML Extensions

We're two-thirds of the way through the book, and *every* WML file you've seen so far has begun with this prolog:

```
<?xml version="1.0"?>
<!DOCTYPE wml PUBLIC "-//WAPFORUM//DTD WML 1.2//EN"
                     "http://www.wapforum.org/DTD/wml_1.2.xml">
```

If you want to use any of Phone.com's WML extensions, you need to replace this document type declaration with a different one, containing the following:

```
<!DOCTYPE wml PUBLIC "-//PHONE.COM//DTD WML 1.1//EN"
                     "http://www.phone.com/DTD/wml11.dtd">
```

This is actually specifying a superset of the WML 1.1 DTD, for the reasons mentioned above. If you try to use a deck that uses Phone.com extensions but doesn't include the correct document type declaration, the Phone Information window will fill with error messages like the following

```
Phone Information                                              _ □ ×
------------------- DATA SIZE -------------------
Uncompiled data from HTTP is 2036 bytes.
...found Content-Type: text/vnd.wap.wml.
===================== WML Errors =====================
WML translation failed.
<15> : error: Invalid element 'spawn' in content of 'onevent'. Expected go : pre
v : noop : refresh
<21> : error: Element 'onevent' is not complete. Expected elements 'go' : 'prev'
: 'noop' : 'refresh'
<27> : error: Invalid element 'spawn' in content of 'onevent'. Expected go : pre
v : noop : refresh
<33> : error: Element 'onevent' is not complete. Expected elements 'go' : 'prev'
: 'noop' : 'refresh'
<39> : error: Invalid element 'spawn' in content of 'onevent'. Expected go : pre
v : noop : refresh
<45> : error: Element 'onevent' is not complete. Expected elements 'go' : 'prev'
: 'noop' : 'refresh'


===================== End Errors =====================

********************** Current WML ***********************************************
<?xml version="1.0"?>
<!DOCTYPE wml PUBLIC "-//WAPFORUM//DTD WML 1.1//EN"
        "http://www.wapforum.org/DTD/wml_1.1.xml">
```

In the above example, the complaints are mainly due to the lack of support for the `<spawn>` element (and any subsequent event handling) in the WAP Forum's document type definition.

User Agent Support

The Phone.com extensions are only supported by devices running the UP.Browser 4.0 or higher. This means that we're able to use the UP.SDK 4.0 and the UP.Simulator for illustration of all the examples used in this chapter. If you want to test them on a real device, Motorola's P7389 mobile phone is just one of a number of suitable platforms.

In the actual deployment, applications that make use of these extensions should include appropriate code to determine whether the target device is UP.Browser enabled. As we'll see in Chapter 18, this can be accomplished by capturing the HTTP_USER_AGENT header information that's embedded in an HTTP request to the server where the application resides.

Context

All of the Phone.com extensions we'll examine in this chapter will involve the idea of **context**, which we first came across back in Chapter 9, in our discussion about variables. We found that as the user navigates from card to card, the state of the history stack and any variables (and their values) are maintained *unless* the newcontext attribute is set to true in the <card> element of any card visited:

```
<card id="card1" newcontext="true">
```

The above specification causes the variables and the history stack of the current context to be cleared whenever the user navigates to "card1". Consider, then, a navigation path in which the first card loaded is "card1", followed by "card2", and finally "card3". Also, assume that "card3" has newcontext="true" as part of its attribute list. The diagrams below trace the history stack as navigation takes place.

When "card1" is loaded, it is the only entry in the history stack of the current context:

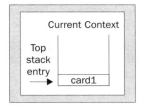

When the user navigates to "card2", the history stack is updated, with "card2" now becoming the top entry in the stack:

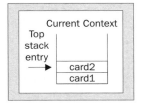

When the user continues to "card3", the current history stack is cleared – that is, "card3" starts with a fresh history stack. If there are any variables in the current context, they will also be removed. The history stack in the current context of the user agent will look like this:

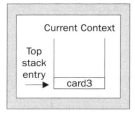

A slightly different navigation model, known as **nested context**, is more appropriate if we need to retain the history stack containing "card1" and "card2" when "card3" is loaded into a new context. If a nested context were used instead of the newcontext attribute, the following would be the final state:

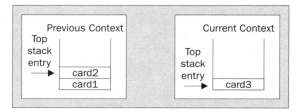

The "previous context" shown above is often called the **parent context**, while the "current context" is also known as the **child context**. Phone.com's WML extensions provide support for nested context, and we'll be discussing them soon, but first we need to look into the scoping issues of context-specific WML variables.

Scoping

WML variables are visible to all cards in the same context. In other words, any values defined for variables in one card are exposed to any other card – even those contained in different WML decks. We say that the variable has **global scope** with respect to the current context.

Try It Out — Variable Scope

1. Type the following into your text editor and save it as mydeck1.wml. Note that we're using the standard document prolog here, as we're not yet using any Phone.com extensions.

```
<?xml version="1.0"?>
<!DOCTYPE wml PUBLIC "-//WAPFORUM//DTD WML 1.2//EN"
                      "http://www.wapforum.org/DTD/wml_1.2.xml">

<wml>
    <card>
        <do type="accept" label="your card">
            <go href="yourdeck1.wml#yourcard" />
        </do>
        <p>
            Initial value of counter: <input name="counter" format="*N" />
        </p>
    </card>
</wml>
```

2. Then enter the next deck and save it as `yourdeck1.wml`.

```
<?xml version="1.0"?>
<!DOCTYPE wml PUBLIC "-//WAPFORUM//DTD WML 1.2//EN"
                     "http://www.wapforum.org/DTD/wml_1.2.xml">

<wml>
    <card id="yourcard">
        <p>
            Value of counter in your card: $(counter)
        </p>
    </card>
</wml>
```

3. Load the first deck into the UP.Simulator, and follow along with the walkthrough in the next section.

How It Works

When `mydeck1.wml` is first loaded and displayed, the following prompt is presented:

Enter 100 at the prompt, and click on the **your card** softkey. The single card in `yourdeck1.wml` is now displayed:

The value of the `counter` variable, which was assigned a value in `mydeck1.wml`, is also visible to another card in a different WML deck. While this sharing of variables across multiple cards and decks provides much convenience in some applications, it is a threat in others where exposing sensitive variable values would be undesirable. Another potential problem that may arise is the inability of a card to *preserve* its state. For example, if "yourcard" introduces another counter for local use, but unintentionally uses the same variable name as the one used in `mydeck1.wml`, the value of the latter will be overwritten.

321

Spawning

The <spawn> element, one of the Phone.com WML extensions, is able to provide variable scoping that counteracts the problems just highlighted. The function of <spawn> is to pass control to another card, referenced using an href attribute, *in a new child context*. When a child context is created, it is given a clean sheet for variables and a brand new history stack, without clearing the current context.

While the functionality of <spawn> is similar to that of the <go> element, the latter causes the current URL to be pushed onto the history stack, while the former does not. Instead, <spawn> creates a nested context, as described earlier.

We mentioned that using the <card> element's newcontext attribute also enables that card to be loaded into a clean context, but there are major differences:

❑   The <spawn> element creates a new context *without clearing the current context*. The current context is preserved and becomes the parent context, while the newly created child context becomes the current context. The parent context is temporarily saved when control is passed to the child context, and it will be restored to become the current context when control returns from the child context.

❑   Using the newcontext attribute to create a new context requires the *destination* card to set its newcontext attribute to true. <spawn>, on the other hand, empowers the *calling* card with the ability to grant the destination card a new context. The destination card does not need any special setting.

Attributes

The behavior of the <spawn> element may be customized through the use of the following six attributes:

❑   href – This is the only compulsory attribute for the <spawn> element. It specifies the URL of the location to navigate to, which may be a WML deck, a WMLScript function, etc.

❑   method – This attribute specifies the method used to send the request to the origin server. The default method is get, and the idea of request methods is discussed in Chapter 18.

❑   sendreferer – If this attribute has a true value, the user agent will supply the URL of the requesting deck to the server as the Referer in the HTTP request header. The target URL can then make use of this information if it wishes to do so.

❑   accept-charset – The value of this attribute can contain one or more character encodings (delimited by commas or spaces) to indicate the character sets supported by the user agent. For example, the character set ISO-8859-1 indicates ISO Latin-1, while IS-8859-7 indicates Modern Greek, UCS-2 indicates 2-byte Unicode encoding, etc.

❑   onexit – This attribute specifies the URL to be navigated to upon completion of the child context through the performing of an exit action, via Phone.com's <exit> extension.

❑   onthrow – This attribute indicates the URL to load when the child context terminates after it has reported the occurrence of an error or exceptional event – through the use of Phone.com's <throw> extension, for example.

href, onexit, and onthrow are covered in this chapter; method will be explained by information in Chapter 18; while sendreferer and accept-charset are beyond the scope of this book.

Embedded Elements

The elements that may be contained between the `<spawn>` and `</spawn>` tags are `<catch>`, `<onevent>`, `<postfield>`, `<receive>`, and `<setvar>`.

We've seen the `<setvar>` and `<onevent>` elements already: they're used respectively to set the value of a variable, and to specify the task to perform next upon the occurrence of a particular event.

The `<postfield>` element is used in conjunction with a request made to some executable program or script at the server, via the `href` attribute. Its usage will be discussed at length in Chapter 18.

The remaining two, `<catch>` and `<receive>`, are Phone.com extensions. Their function will be demonstrated later in this chapter.

Hiding Variable Values Using spawn

To demonstrate that variables defined in the parent context are not visible to the child, let us modify the previous example of displaying a counter value to use `<spawn>`:

Try It Out — Spawning

Make the following changes to `mydeck1.wml`, and save it as `mydeck2.wml`.

```
<?xml version="1.0"?>
<!DOCTYPE wml PUBLIC "-//PHONE.COM//DTD WML 1.1//EN"
                "http://www.phone.com/dtd/wml11.dtd">

<wml>
    <card>
        <do type="accept" label="spawn">
            <spawn href="yourdeck1.wml#yourcard" />
        </do>
        <p>
            Initial value of counter: <input name="counter" format="*N" />
        </p>
    </card>
</wml>
```

The other deck – `yourdeck1.wml` – can remain the same for this example.

How It Works

The results from this new code are shown below:

Note that the `counter` variable from the parent context is not visible in the child context. If you *need* some parent variables to be visible in the child, you can pass them explicitly using one of the following methods, depending on the child document type:

❑   Use `<setvar>` if the spawned context is another card

❑   Use `<postfield>` for spawned context such as a CGI program or an ASP script

Passing Variable Values When Spawning

A modified version of `mydeck2.wml`, in which a `<setvar>` element is inserted within the enclosing `<spawn>` and `</spawn>` tags, is presented below:

```
<wml>
    <card>
        <do type="accept" label="spawn">
            <spawn href="yourdeck1.wml#yourcard">
                <setvar name="counter" value="$counter" />
            </spawn>
        </do>
        <p>
            Initial value of counter: <input name="counter" format="*N" />
        </p>
    </card>
</wml>
```

As before, this card prompts the user for an initial value for `counter`. This time, however, the input value (say, 100) is passed to `yourcard` as well. (Or more accurately, a variable called `counter` is made visible in `yourcard`.) Here's what it looks like:

Navigation in a Spawned Context

In this section, we'll look at how navigation works when a 'back' key is clicked in a spawned child context. In order to understand it, you need to be aware of the two types of stacks involved:

❑   The context history stack – a stack of contexts

❑   The URL history stack for a given context – a stack of URLs

The UP.Simulator provides a way to view stacks. The History option under the Info menu displays the contents of both stack types in the Phone Information window, as we'll see through the next example.

Try It Out — Navigation and the History Stack

1. To do this properly, we're going to need a total of five decks! Enter the following into your text editor, and save it as `hello.wml`.

```
<?xml version="1.0"?>
<!DOCTYPE wml PUBLIC "-//PHONE.COM//DTD WML 1.1//EN"
                     "http://www.phone.com/dtd/wml11.dtd">

<wml>
   <card>
      <p>Hello!</p>
   </card>
</wml>
```

2. The second one is `startspawn.wml`, which uses a `<go>` element for navigation, as we've done so many times before:

```
<?xml version="1.0"?>
<!DOCTYPE wml PUBLIC "-//PHONE.COM//DTD WML 1.1//EN"
                     "http://www.phone.com/dtd/wml11.dtd">

<wml>
   <card>
      <do type="accept">
         <go href="grandparent.wml#card1"/>
      </do>
      <p>
         startspawn: Press OK to <b>go</b> to next card.
      </p>
   </card>
</wml>
```

3. Our next deck, `grandparent.wml`, is the first to use a `<spawn>` element to navigate to the next card:

```
<?xml version="1.0"?>
<!DOCTYPE wml PUBLIC "-//PHONE.COM//DTD WML 1.1//EN"
                     "http://www.phone.com/dtd/wml11.dtd">

<wml>
   <card id="card1">
      <do type="accept">
         <spawn href="parent.wml"/>
      </do>
      <p>
         grandparent: Press OK to <b>spawn</b> next card.
      </p>
   </card>
</wml>
```

4. Up fourth is `parent.wml`, which also uses a `<spawn>` element:

```
<?xml version="1.0"?>
<!DOCTYPE wml PUBLIC "-//PHONE.COM//DTD WML 1.1//EN"
                     "http://www.phone.com/dtd/wml11.dtd">

<wml>
   <card id="card2">
      <do type="accept">
         <spawn href="child.wml"/>
      </do>
      <p>
         parent: Press OK to <b>spawn</b> next card.
      </p>
   </card>
</wml>
```

5. Finally, `child.wml` simply invites the user to press the UP.Simulator's **BACK** button in order
to go to the previous card:

```
<?xml version="1.0"?>
<!DOCTYPE wml PUBLIC "-//PHONE.COM//DTD WML 1.1//EN"
                     "http://www.phone.com/dtd/wml11.dtd">

<wml>
   <card id="card3">
      <p>
         child: Press BACK to navigate to the <i>previous</i> card.
      </p>
   </card>
</wml>
```

How It Works

To examine what's going on at each point in this application, we'll navigate through the various cards
and keep a close eye on the history stacks in the **Phone Information** window. To start the ball rolling,
type in the URL of `hello.wml` to load it:

A new context is created when `hello.wml` is first loaded through explicit entry of its URL. This context is now the top element in the *context* history stack (HIST: 1). The *URL* history stack of this context has only one entry, namely the only card of `hello.wml`. Next, enter the URL of `startspawn.wml` to load that deck:

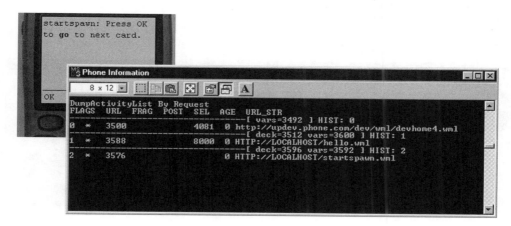

This time, a new context is created for `startspawn.wml`, which becomes the top element of the context history stack (HIST: 2). The URL history stack of the new and current context contains the only card in `startspawn.wml`. Press **OK** to navigate to the next card using a `<go>` element:

On this occasion, no new context is created. The URL history stack of the current context has two entries now, where card1 is on the top (AGE=0) of the stack. Press OK to navigate to the next card using a <spawn> element:

Another new context is created when "card2" of parent.wml is spawned, and a URL history stack consisting only of that card is allocated to the new current context. Press OK to navigate again:

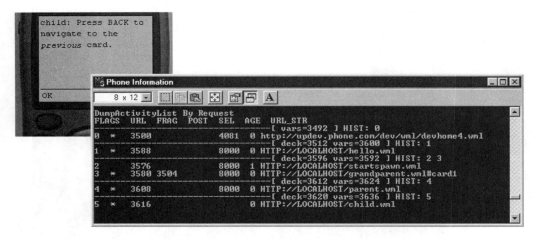

As in the previous step, a new context is created when "card3" of child.wml is spawned, and a URL history stack consisting only of "card3" is allocated to the new current context. Finally, press BACK, and you'll see the output opposite.

Is that what you were expecting? Well, you'll probably have noticed that the first deck (hello.wml) isn't related to the other four decks in any way – we just loaded it into the context history stack as a point of reference. When the URL of startspawn.wml was typed into the user agent, that deck was loaded. We then navigated to grandparent.wml via the <go> element, which kept the current context. The next two documents, however, involved **nested spawning** – that is, a child spawning another child before returning to its parent context.

Clicking the BACK key in any child context will trace the context history all the way back to the root of the nested spawning (in this case, "card1" of grandParent.wml). The entire ancestral tree of contexts is popped off the context history stack, and the top URL in the history stack of the new top context will be loaded. The diagram on the next page summarizes the navigation that we have just walked through.

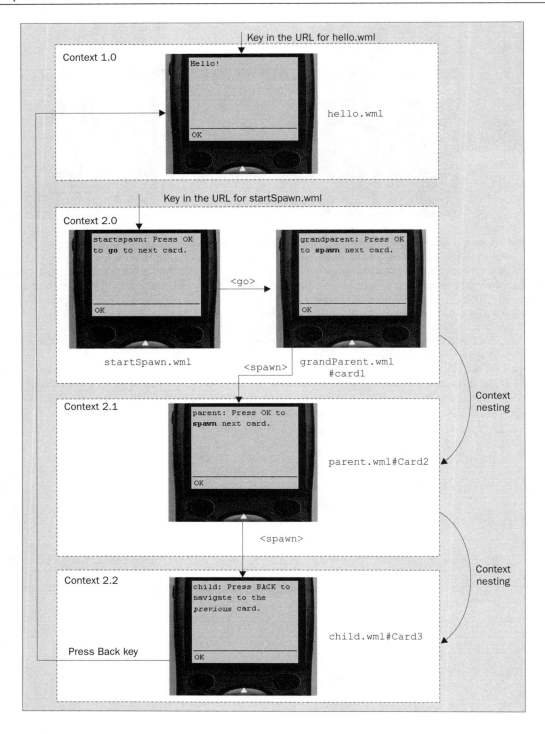

Exit Event Handling

In the example where `mydeck3.wml` was used as the parent context, the responses of the user agent to the left and right softkeys are as described below:

❑ Left: Displays the previous URL in the history stack (the default action)

❑ Right: Invalid key

It is not unfeasible that, upon terminating the child context, the application might want to load a card or script other than the previous URL in the history stack. In such circumstances, we can use an `exit` event bound to an 'accept' task as a way of deviating from the default action associated with the left softkey. Alternatively, you could bind the `exit` event to the right softkey by using an 'options' task.

The example code below shows how an `exit` event can bound to an 'accept' task:

```
<do type="accept" label="exit">
   <exit />
</do>
```

The `<exit>` and `</exit>` tags can be used if there are some statements to be executed during the exit event. For example, you might want to use the `<send>` element, through which values may be passed back to the parent context, as we'll discuss shortly.

When execution `exits` the card, control is passed to the parent that `spawned` it. If we want to use an event handler to navigate to the next appropriate destination when the `exit` event occurs, then we need to use the `onexit` attribute of the `<spawn>` element, or an `<onevent>` element of type `onexit` in the parent. If the parent doesn't make any specific provision to handle an `exit` event, the parent card will be loaded.

> *An `exit` event will always attempt to pop a context off the context stack, so if you use it without `<spawn>`, and if one is available, navigation will move to the context that was in effect before your application.*

Try It Out — Exit Event Handling

1. Make the following changes to `yourdeck1.wml`, and save it as `yourdeck2.wml`.

```
<?xml version="1.0"?>
<!DOCTYPE wml PUBLIC "-//PHONE.COM//DTD WML 1.1//EN"
                     "http://www.phone.com/dtd/wml11.dtd">

<wml>
   <card id="yourcard">
      <do type="accept" label="exit">
         <exit />
      </do>
      <p>
         Value of counter in your card: $(counter)
      </p>
   </card>
</wml>
```

2. Next, make the following changes to `mydeck3.wml`, and save it as `mydeck4.wml`.

```wml
<wml>
    <card id="mycard">
        <do type="accept" label="spawn">
            <spawn href="yourdeck2.wml#yourcard" onexit="#ackcard">
                <setvar name="counter" value="$counter" />
            </spawn>
        </do>
        <p>
            Initial value of counter: <input name="counter" format="*N" />
        </p>
    </card>

    <card id="ackcard">
        <p>
            Back to my deck - counter is $(counter)
        </p>
    </card>
</wml>
```

How It Works

As in `mydeck3.wml`, "mycard" spawns "yourcard". On exiting the latter through the **spawn** softkey, "mycard" retakes control and will proceed to "ackcard". In other words, the parent context will navigate to "ackcard" upon return from the child context.

Alternatively, an `<onevent>` element may be used within the `<spawn>` element to achieve the same purpose:

```wml
<spawn href="yourDeck2.wml#yourcard">
    <onevent type="onexit">
        <go href="#ackCard" />
    </onevent>
</spawn>
```

The sequence depicted below shows the navigation from "mycard" in `mydeck4.wml`, to "yourcard" in `yourdeck2.wml`, and finally to "ackcard" in the first deck:

Sending and Receiving

The `<send>` and `<receive>` elements are designed to provide a mechanism for passing information when spawning – typically, for passing data from the child to the parent when the child terminates. The syntax of `<send>` is very straightforward indeed:

```
<send value=VAL />
```

The value passed back may be a string enclosed within quotes, the evaluated result of an expression or variable name, or even an empty string. Some examples of values being passed back using `<send>` are shown below:

```
<send value="Invalid selection" />
<send value="300.50" />
<send value="$status" />
<send />
```

Notice in particular that no name is being assigned to the data sent. Any naming will take place on the recipient's side, at the time of receiving the incoming data. The counterpart of `<send>` is `<receive>`, with the following syntax:

```
<receive name=NAME />
```

The *NAME* value is the variable name to be assigned to the incoming data. For example, to receive the above four pieces of data, the following `<receive>` elements could be used:

```
<receive name="invalidMsg" />
<receive />
<receive name="status" />
<receive name="str" />
```

The above process would result in the following assignment of the received data to variable names:

Variable in Receiving Context	Value
invalidMsg	"Invalid selection"
status	Evaluated value of status in the sending context
str	Empty string

Note that the second piece of data was not assigned a variable name, which means that the receiving context cannot make subsequent use of that data.

Try It Out – Sending and Receiving

The following example demonstrates how "yourcard" can be modified to send data when it exits.

1. Make the following changes to `yourdeck2.wml`, and save it as `yourdeck3.wml`.

```wml
<wml>
   <card id="yourcard">
      <do type="accept" label="exit">
         <exit>
            <send value="$counter" />
            <send value="Normal termination" />
         </exit>
      </do>
      <p>
         Value of counter in your card: $(counter)
      </p>
   </card>
</wml>
```

2. Now make the following changes to `myDeck4.wml`, and save it as `myDeck5.wml`.

```wml
<wml>
   <card id="mycard">
      <do type="accept" label="spawn">
         <spawn href="yourdeck3.wml#yourcard" onexit="#ackcard">
            <setvar name="counter" value="$counter" />
            <receive name="returnedCounter" />
            <receive name="status" />
         </spawn>
      </do>
      <p>
         Initial value of counter: <input name="counter" format="*N" />
      </p>
   </card>

   <card id="ackcard">
      <p>
         Returned counter: $(returnedCounter)
         <br />
         $status
      </p>
   </card>
</wml>
```

How It Works

We will navigate through the cards involved in both `mydeck5` and `yourdeck3` to illustrate the effect of using the `<send>` and `<receive>` elements. First, enter the URL for `myDeck5.wml#myCard` into the UP.Simulator, and type a value at the prompt – say, 300:

If you then choose **spawn**, the value of `counter` is passed to "yourcard" via the `<setvar>` element:

When you then press **exit** to return from "yourcard" to "mycard", the two values sent are received into the variables `returnedCounter` and `status` respectively:

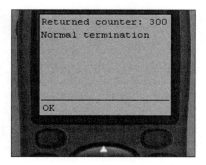

When `mycard` causes `ackcard` to be loaded (in the same context), the values of the variables remain visible to `ackcard`, and are displayed correctly as shown.

335

Exceptions

In computing, the term **exception** may be used to refer to an error, or to any exceptional condition occurring in an application. The inability to locate a file, for example, is often considered to be an input/output exception. In some applications, an unexpected negative input (for an age, say) may also be considered as an exception.

❑ **Throwing** an exception means raising an alert, or providing a reference to an exception.

❑ **Catching** an exception, on the other hand, refers to the addressing or handling of the exception with the necessary action.

Phone.com has introduced two WML extensions, <throw> and <catch>, to accomplish the functions of raising and handling an exception, as described above. In particular, they provide a means of creating events that can be triggered and handled in two different contexts – something that none of the other WML event types can do.

> **The card that handles an exception must be an ancestor (at least a parent, if not higher) of the card that throws the exception. That is, the parent context will take control to handle the exception, after the card that throws the exception terminates.**

Throwing Exceptions

The WML extension <throw> is designed to invoke a throw event, during which process a name may be given to the event invoked. It also supports the passing of information pertaining to the event to the context that will handle it. The attributes and elements that can be used within the <throw> element are shown below:

```
<throw name=NAME>
    <send>
</throw>
```

The name attribute is mandatory – it's used to identify the throw event uniquely, just as an id attribute is used to identify a card. With this identification mechanism, a context can include different throw events to indicate different exceptional cases.

The simplest way to throw an exception is:

```
<throw name="Full Booking" />
```

If more information needs to be sent to the card handling the event, one or more <send> elements can be used within the <throw> element tags:

```
<throw name="Full Booking">
    <send value="Summer holiday in London" />
</throw>
```

A `throw` event is initiated via a key press on the device, or the selection of an item in the display. The example below shows an 'options' task being used to trigger an unnamed throw event. The message "`Action aborted`" is passed back to the parent context:

```
<do type="options" label="abort">
   <throw>
      <send value="Action aborted" />
   </throw>
</do>
```

Catching Exceptions

The `<catch>` element is used within a `<spawn>` element to deal with a `throw` event that may occur in the child context being spawned. When a `throw` event occurs in the child context, the latter terminates and control will be passed to the parent context.

If there is no `<catch>` element in the parent context to handle it, the parent context will also cease, with control passed to the next context up. This process continues until either an exception handler is found, or all of the parents of the exception-originating context have been cleared away. In this case, an unrelated previous context that the user agent has visited before (or the home deck) will eventually take control.

Although none of them is mandatory, the attribute and elements that *can* be used within the `<catch>` element are:

```
<catch name=NAME onthrow=URL>
   <onevent>
   <receive>
   <reset>
</catch>
```

As with the syntax of `<throw>`, the name attribute is used to identify a particular exception. The `onthrow` attribute is used to specify the next URL to navigate to, in response to the exception in question being caught.

An alternative to using the `onthrow` attribute is to use the `<onevent>` element with a type of `onthrow`. The function of the `<receive>` element is to accept values passed in from a child using a `<send>` element, while the `<reset>` element is used to clear all of the variables in the current context, as described in the table at the beginning of the chapter.

The `<catch>` element can take different forms. The simplest of these specifies neither a particular `throw` event to catch, nor a URL to load. In this case, the `<catch>` element simply catches *any* exception that has no corresponding `<catch>` element to handle it, and control will pass to the top card in the URL history stack of the parent context.

```
<catch />
```

The next example shows the use of the `name` and `onthrow` attributes in a `<catch>` element. If the card observes that an exception named "Full Booking" has been raised via a `throw` event, it will navigate to the card called "waitinglist" in the same deck.

```
<catch name="Full Booking" onthrow="#waitinglist" />
```

If the parent card is expecting data from a `throw` event in the child context, then while the event is being caught, the `<receive>` element must be used to accept the data. For example, the `<catch>` below expects the `throw` event that raises the "invalid count" exception to send three pieces of data. However, only the first and last pieces are assigned a name.

```
<catch name="invalid count" onthrow="#waitinglist">
    <receive name="errorMsg" />
    <receive />
    <receive name="errorCode" />
</catch>
```

Scheduling Example

Before we close this chapter, we'll look at one last example that illustrates the various Phone.com extensions we've discussed. Imagine a WML card that allows the user to view a list of movies currently being shown at a cinema, in which selecting a name will give the performance times.

When that happens, a schedule screen is loaded via a `<spawn>` element from the previous card. In the schedule screen, the user is able to choose a course of action from several possible options. The parent card must carry out the chosen action when control returns from the child card.

Try It Out — A Cinema Schedule

1. Type this deck into a text editor, and save it as `cinema.wml`:

```
<?xml version="1.0"?>
<!DOCTYPE wml PUBLIC "-//PHONE.COM//DTD WML 1.1//EN"
                "http://www.phone.com/dtd/wml11.dtd">

<wml>
    <!-- Display current films available; set up navigation & error handling -->
    <card id="choosefilm">
        <do type="accept" label="Schedule">
            <spawn href="schedule.wml">
                <setvar name="film" value="$film" />
                <receive name="goodtime" />

                <onevent type="onexit">
                    <go href="#reserve" />
                </onevent>

                <catch name="fully booked" onthrow="#waitinglist">
                    <receive name="badtime" />
                </catch>
                <catch onthrow="#choosefilm" />
            </spawn>
        </do>
```

```
        <do type="options" label="Exit">
           <go href="#bye" />
        </do>
        <p>
           Pick a film to view its schedule:
           <select name="film">
              <option value="Prescott">Being John Prescott</option>
              <option value="Element">The 7th Element</option>
              <option value="Police">Police Academy XVI</option>
           </select>
        </p>
     </card>

     <!-- Will get here if everything proceeds correctly -->
     <card id="reserve">
        <do type="accept" label="Choose film">
           <go href="#choosefilm" />
        </do>
        <p>
           Reservation on $goodtime is successful.
        </p>
     </card>

     <!-- Will get here if user chooses a fully-booked performance -->
     <card id="waitinglist">
        <do type="accept" label="Choose film">
           <go href="#choosefilm" />
        </do>
        <p>
           Schedule on $badtime is full.
        </p>
     </card>

     <!-- Will get here if user decides to quit -->
     <card id="bye" newcontext="true">
        <p>
           Bye.
        </p>
     </card>
  </wml>
```

2. Then, type the following deck in a text editor and save it as `schedule.wml`:

```
<?xml version="1.0"?>
<!DOCTYPE wml PUBLIC "-//PHONE.COM//DTD WML 1.1//EN"
                     "http://www.phone.com/dtd/wml11.dtd">

<wml>
   <card id="schedule">
      <do type="accept" label="Book">
         <exit>
            <send value="$schedule" />
         </exit>
      </do>
      <do type="options" label="Cancel">
         <throw name="cancel" />
      </do>
```

```
        <p>
            Schedule - $film
            <select name="schedule">
                <option value="Fri 6pm">Friday 6pm</option>
                <option>
                    <onevent type="onpick">
                        <throw name="fully booked">
                            <send value="Fri 8pm" />
                        </throw>
                    </onevent>
                    Friday 8pm [full]
                </option>
                <option value="Sat 4pm">Saturday 4pm</option>
            </select>
        </p>
    </card>
</wml>
```

How It Works

First, we load the "choosefilm" card, where the user is able to select a film in order to view its schedule:

Then, the "schedule" card is loaded via a `<spawn>` element to list the available (as well as the currently unavailable) performance times:

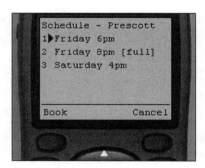

In this "schedule" card, the user can choose from the following possible courses of action:

- ❑ Choose an available performance, and click the **Book** button. When this happens, an `exit` event occurs and the value of the chosen screening is sent back to the parent card, `choosefilm`.

- ❑ Choose a performance time schedule that's currently full (and marked as such in the display). When the **Book** button is clicked, choosing the item causes a `throw` event to occur. The schedule is sent to the parent using the `<send>` element.

- ❑ Click the **Cancel** button to exit from the current page. This causes the invocation of a `throw` event. No additional information is sent back to the parent.

When the child (the "schedule" card) terminates, either via an `exit` or a `throw` event, the parent (the "choosefilm" card) will receive a `goodtime` value via the `<receive>` element inside the `<spawn>` tags. It will then perform one of the following, depending on the choice of the user:

- ❑ If the child terminates via an `exit` event, the calling card will navigate to the "reserve" card in the same deck.

- ❑ If the child throws an event with the name "`fully booked`", the calling card will receive the time (`badtime`) passed in via the `throw` event. It then navigates to the "waitinglist" card in the same deck.

341

❑ If the child terminates via any *other* throw events, the calling card will navigate to the "bye" card in the same deck, via <catch/>.

Summary

In this chapter, we've introduced some of Phone.com's extensions to WML – in particular, the following ones, which we examined in a fair amount of detail:

❑ <spawn>

❑ <exit>

❑ <throw>

❑ <catch>

❑ <send>

❑ <receive>

We demonstrated some of the problems that these extensions are intended to solve – among them, the scoping of variables in some applications where global visibility of variables is not desired. We also looked at the provision of nested context, which enables us to preserve previous context when navigating to a new card with a new context.

Remember that because these extensions are only supported by Phone.com browsers, any professional application intending to use them requires additional coding at the server side (an ASP script, for example) to check the type of user agent before sending WAP content containing them. Keep that in mind, and they can be very useful to have around.

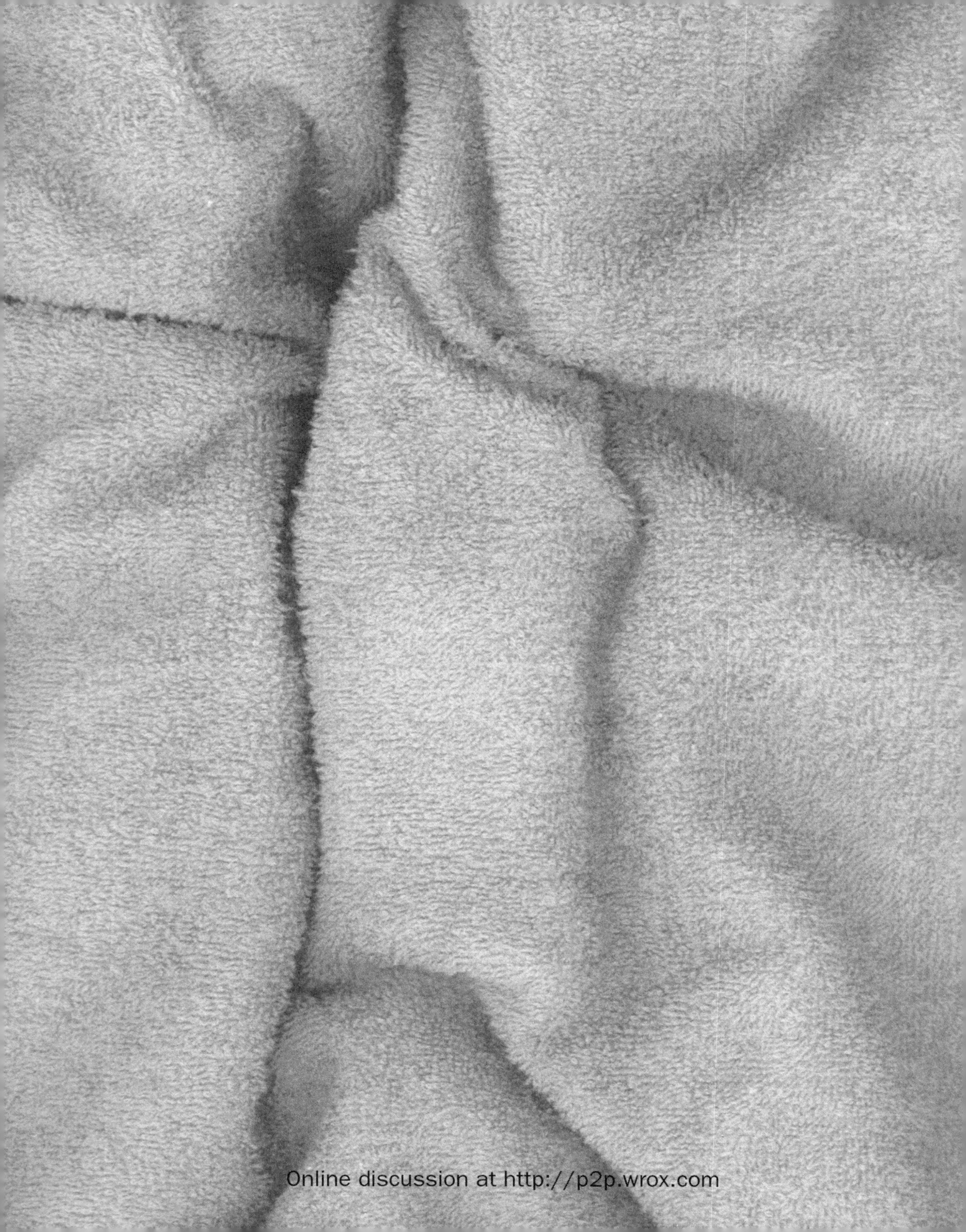
Online discussion at http://p2p.wrox.com

Usability

The chapters in this book so far have equipped you with the knowledge required to create WAP-enabled sites using WML and WMLScript. However, before we take a look at generating pages *dynamically* – a subject that has been mentioned on a few occasions in preceding text – it's worth taking a step back and looking at WAP applications from a different perspective. Specifically, the next two chapters will deal with **usability** and **interoperability**. Briefly, these refer to the general streamlining of your applications to make it easier for users to get the information they want, and making it possible for users to obtain this information regardless of the microbrowser they are using.

In this chapter, we will look at usability. We'll start with a more thorough explanation of the issues involved, and then go on to some more specific topics with practical examples to point you in the right direction.

What Do We Mean by Usability?

When we talk about "usability", we really mean "user-friendliness". It's quite possible to imagine a WAP site containing a vast amount of useful data, but the best and most comprehensive information store in the world is useless unless users can get at the items they want. Similarly, if it takes half an hour to find the time of the next train home, you might already have missed it.

In addition to this, usability also concerns the general look and feel of a WAP site. If you can convince users that your site is more "user-friendly" than others – even if the same information can be obtained elsewhere – then you're onto a winner. If you take care to consider the usability of your site, you'll get user loyalty, and that could make or break your business.

The above could be applied equally to WAP sites, traditional Internet sites, and even to non-connected applications; many of the general principles involved also apply to multiple methods of delivery. On the other hand, there are some aspects of usability that are quite unique to WAP-enabled devices. When dealing with mobile devices, a different design paradigm is required: one that, although similar in some ways to existing web design, differs in many crucial areas. It would be impossible to put, say, Wrox.com straight onto a small mobile phone screen and keep exactly the same graphical appearance and functionality.

In this chapter, we will look at two main aspects of usability in WAP applications:

❏   Considerations due to device constraints and capabilities

❏   General design tips

Together, these points will address most of the concerns that are shared by both developers and users, and hopefully help your WAP sites to be all the more successful.

Making a User-Friendly WAP Site

When it comes down to it, enhancing the usability of WAP sites and making them friendlier for your users really isn't that difficult. Although there are a number of areas we need to cover, most of the principles are simple, and you can dramatically enhance your applications with relatively little effort.

We'll start by looking at the general issues involved in usability, and then move on to look at specific areas of interest, with examples to illustrate the points made.

General Principles

Let's face it: not all web sites are everything they could be. In fact, it would be more realistic to say that intuitive, simple web sites, providing exactly what you are looking for with the minimum of effort, are few and far between. Inevitably, many of those responsible for these web sites will be applying their talents to the WAP arena too. This is worrying, because the restrictions imposed by WAP and microbrowsers make it even more important to design your applications carefully.

At the same time, though, these restrictions can actually make it *easier* to enforce good design rules and produce a streamlined product. The reasons for this are simple: without the ability to add things like enormous animated graphics and streaming audio, we are left with a clean and simple system for exchanging textual information. Of course, there will always be people who stretch the available facilities, and as technology improves we can expect to see capabilities improving too – hopefully at a time when network bandwidth has increased to the stage where this sort of thing won't result in appalling download rates.

What we need to identify are the key factors to be dealt with in order to keep things simple, and allow users quick and easy access to the information they require. In the next sections, we will examine specific issues and techniques for addressing precisely this issue. We'll look at:

❏   Keeping server round trips to a minimum

❏   Keeping user clicks to a minimum

❏   Keeping user input to a minimum

❏   Keeping text volume to a minimum

❏   Using images effectively

❏   Redundancy and content organization

❏   Testing

Most of these topics relate to two main themes:

❑ Getting information to the user as quickly as possible. As you're surely aware, current wireless communication is slow. Getting even the simplest WML deck onto a mobile device takes at least a few seconds – a very noticeable period of time. As we shall see, however, there are things we can do to minimize the performance hit that this results in.

❑ Structuring WAP services to maximize usability. WAP services need to be constructed in such a way as to make it easy for users to find their way around and get the information they need, without being held up by confusing navigation or obscure links. A well-designed site is a user-friendly site.

Keeping Server Round Trips to a Minimum

Given the memory constraints of current devices, we cannot hold more than a few cards in memory at one time. The upshot of this is that just about any useful WAP application will span several decks, contained in several separate files. (Remember that we have to contend with a 1400-byte limit for compiled WML files.) WAP applications may also use other files containing WMLScript functions or WBMP images, and each time we pull a new file from the server, there will be a significant unavoidable delay. The act of the browser getting a new file from the server, or interacting with the server in any other way that requires a response, is called a **server round trip**.

Second Guessing the User

One way of keeping down round trips to the server is to anticipate what the user is most likely to look at, and structure your decks accordingly. For example, let's say you have a deck with a selection of links to other decks:

```
<card id="menu" title="Main Menu">
    <p>
        Choose an option:<br/>
        <a href="introduction.wml">Introduction</a><br/>
        <a href="article.wml">Today's article</a><br/>
        <a href="register.wml">Registration</a><br/>
        <a href="links.wml">Links</a><br/>
    </p>
</card>
```

Navigation like this, to separate decks, will be slow: each deck will be loaded separately. It would be far quicker to link to cards within the deck that are already loaded in memory:

```
<card id="menu" title="Main Menu">
    <p>
        Choose an option:<br/>
        <a href="#introduction">Introduction</a><br/>
        <a href="#article">Today's article</a><br/>
        <a href="#register">Registration</a><br/>
        <a href="#links">Links</a><br/>
    </p>
</card>
```

However, the memory restrictions on WAP-enabled devices are likely to make this impossible – you just can't fit everything you want in one deck all of the time.

The solution is something of a halfway house. You need to put yourself in the place of the user and ask the question, "Which option am I most likely to choose?" In most cases, you will identify a route through your cards that will lead you to a more responsive card structure.

In the example above, the user will probably look at the "introduction" card just once (the first time they look at your site), as information here is unlikely to change. Similarly, "registration" and "links" are unlikely to be looked at as frequently as (today's) "article". If you're having problems with memory limitations, cards that will be viewed infrequently are probably better off in other decks, whereas cards that receive more traffic are better placed in the same deck as the main "menu" card shown above.

This would lead us to the following structure:

```
<card id="menu" title="Main Menu">
   <p>
      Choose an option:<br/>
      <a href="introduction.wml">Introduction</a><br/>
      <a href="#article">Today's article</a><br/>
      <a href="register.wml">Registration</a><br/>
      <a href="links.wml">Links</a><br/>
   </p>
</card>
```

Of course, it's quite possible that the full article wouldn't fit in the deck – if it's long, it might even require several decks. However, we should still consider putting as much of it in the first deck as we can, to speed up initial viewing. Alternatively, this might be the place for a short abstract, and a link to a deck containing the full article (or the first part of it).

So, is this the best structure for this simple example? Not necessarily! One more point to be borne in mind is that first impressions last. We've shifted the introduction card into a separate deck, which means that new users – the ones who are likely to read this information – will be greeted with an instant delay. This won't encourage them to carry on with your site!

Moving the introduction back into the deck will reduce the amount of space available for the first section of the article, but in terms of keeping users happy, it's probably the trade off to aim for:

```
<card id="menu" title="Main Menu">
   <p>
      Choose an option:<br/>
      <a href="#introduction">Introduction</a><br/>
      <a href="#article">Today's article</a><br/>
      <a href="register.wml">Registration</a><br/>
      <a href="links.wml">Links</a><br/>
   </p>
</card>
```

Caching

As an extension of the above discussion, **caching** is worth a brief mention. When a user agent accesses a WML deck, it will (by default in most cases) cache that deck – that is, it will store it in memory. When the user agent tries to look at a deck that exists in its cache, it will load its stored version without making any data transfers across the network. This has pros and cons, but it can be tweaked to give optimal performance according to the specific demands of your WAP site.

Note that this is distinct from caching on the server. Many web servers allow you to cache files, be they WML, HTML, or anything else. This simply means that they will be stored locally on the server, perhaps in memory rather than on disk, so that requests will get the files they require more quickly. In terms of wireless access, of course, this will still result in a delay because there's still communication with the server. The sort of caching we're discussing here is client-side caching.

It is very useful to cache cards containing static data, such as simple menus, but problems can arise if a card containing frequently updated information is cached. You might end up looking at yesterday's flight arrival times, for example, and accidentally miss meeting your mother-in-law at the airport. The standard way of dealing with this in WML is to use the facilities of an element we haven't met before: <head>.

The <head> Element

The WML <head> element is used to contain information relating to the deck as a whole. When we talk about data that describes other data (in this case, it's data that describes the rest of the deck), we call it **meta-data**. Now, since the content of the <head> element is *about* the deck (rather than part *of* it), the natural location for it is before the cards:

```
<wml>
   <head>
      meta-data
   </head>
   cards
</wml>
```

The <head> element has no attributes, but it can contain one <access> element, and several <meta> elements. It's the second of these that we need to use in order to control how cards are cached.

The <access> element has two mandatory attributes – domain and path – and controls access to WML files in much the same way as the access pragma in WMLScript. You can use it to permit access to WML files only to requests from within particular domains or sub-domains. We won't be looking at <access> any more closely in this book, but for details of the syntax and more information you can refer to the WML specifications.

The <meta> Element

The <meta> element provides a means of specifying names and supplying values for properties associated with a WML deck. These properties will frequently be exclusive to a particular user agent, and the WML specification makes no attempt to define them. However, some common, widely supported uses of <meta> elements have sprung up, and one such is the ability to specify HTTP headers.

Arriving finally at the purpose of this discussion, it's possible to use HTTP headers to specify that a WML deck should not be cached. From within WML, this is done by using a pair of `<meta>` elements:

```
<wml>
    <head>
        <meta forua="true" http-equiv="Pragma"
                           content="no-cache"/>
        <meta forua="true" http-equiv="Cache-Control"
                           content="no-cache, must-revalidate"/>
    </head>
    <card>
        ...
    </card>
    ...
</wml>
```

If the details are a little hazy, don't worry. Just take away the fact that decks containing the above code will never be added to the cache of the phone, allowing you to update content freely without worrying about users only seeing older versions of your cards.

> *There are some Phone.com extensions to WML that allow you to 'pre-load' multiple decks.*
> *Basically, you guess that the user is likely to navigate to a specific deck, and tell the browser to load*
> *this deck into its cache automatically. Then, if the user follows a link to this second deck, navigation*
> *will be much quicker – there will be no need to get it from the server, as it is already in memory.*
> *There are plans afoot to integrate this functionality into later versions of WML. Keep an eye on the*
> *WAP Forum web site (www.wapforum.org) for details.*

Client-side Processing

The computers that act as servers for your WAP applications will be doing quite a lot of work. In the busiest periods, WML decks will be sent out to many users at the same time. To relieve this load a little, we can perform some processing on the client device, using a method we've already seen: WMLScript.

For example, let's say we have a card that contains a date input field, and we're asking for a date between September and October 2001.

```
<wml>
    <card id="date" title="Date Entry">
        <p>
            Enter a date between September and October 2001 in MM/DD/YYYY format:
            <input name="date" format="NN\/NN\/\2\0\0\1"/>
            <do type="accept" label="Submit">
                <go href="date.wmls#validate('$(date:unesc)')"/>
            </do>
        </p>
    </card>
</wml>
```

We could then use this WMLScript code to validate the date before sending it to the server:

```
extern function validate(date)
{
   var isOK = false;
   var day = getDay(date);
   var month = getMonth(date);
   var year = getYear(date);

   if (year = 2001)
   {
      if (month = 9)
      {
         if ((day >= 1) && (day <= 30))
         {
            isOK = true;
         }
      }
      if (month = 10)
      {
         if ((day >= 1) && (day <= 31))
         {
            isOK = true;
         }
      }
   }
   if (isOK)
   {
      // Action if date OK
      Dialogs.alert("That's OK");
   }
   else
   {
      // Action if date invalid
      Dialogs.alert("That won't do");
   }
}

function getDay(date)
{
   if (String.subString(date, 3, 1) == "0")
   {
      return Lang.parseInt(String.subString(date, 4, 1));
   }
   else
   {
      return Lang.parseInt(String.subString(date, 3, 2));
   }
}

function getMonth(date)
{
   if (String.subString(date, 0, 1) == "0")
   {
      return Lang.parseInt(String.subString(date, 1, 1));
   }
```

```
      else
      {
         return Lang.parseInt(String.subString(date, 0, 2));
      }
   }

   function getYear(date)
   {
      return Lang.parseInt(String.subString(date, 6, 4));
   }
```

The `extern` function, `validate()`, uses three simple helper function to get the day, month, and year from the date string submitted by the user agent, checks to see if the date fits in the range expected, and then acts accordingly (the action lines are commented for clarity). All of this takes place on the client, so only a single round trip to the server is required (in order to load the WMLScript file). Any further validation won't require any server round trips, because the script is held in memory.

> *It would be relatively easy to make the above script more generic, perhaps by supplying cutoff dates for the range. This would mean that several dates could be requested – each with a different range – and a single cached script could be used to validate all of them.*

This is something that we'll really need to bear in mind later on, when we look in more depth at server side technologies such as ASP. There will be times when you're tempted to use ASP scripting to carry out tasks that would be easy to perform with WMLScript. In situations like that, WMLScript is definitely worth considering from the point of view of performance – assuming of course that your client devices support it!

Keeping User Clicks to a Minimum

One of the established guidelines for designing web sites is that for every 'click' users have to make in order to reach the information they're looking for, a proportion will simply give up – some surveys put the attrition rate as high as 50%. While a number as large as that sounds a little unlikely, the principle is sound, especially when applied to WAP systems where navigation between decks is usually accompanied by a substantial delay.

Let's look at a quick example. If the information required by the user – let's say, a train timetable – would be reached by following links in the following sequence:

Home Page • Travel • Trains • Timetable

then the above statistic would seem to suggest that only a small proportion of users would stick it out and get the required information. On the other hand, a site structured such that the user could follow a shorter path:

Home page • Train Timetable

is, when looked at in the same way, likely to get far more traffic, and happier users.

Of course, this sort of thing is always going to be a trade off in WAP development. Long lists of specific links and a basically flat tree structure may be just as annoying to users who have to scroll through everything in order to get exactly what they need. In contrast, web users can click on a link at any position in a list with ease, using a mouse. WAP devices equipped with touch sensitive screens are emerging, which would certainly ease navigation of this sort, but for now it's probably better to try and keep people without this capability on their devices happy.

When it comes down to it, the method you choose will be heavily dependent on the application, and optimizing it is something that you're only likely to be able to do through careful consultation with users (see the later section on testing).

Going Back

Whatever structure you end up with, you should keep the user's options open. Wherever possible, 'back' links should be included, and remember that this may mean using techniques other than <prev/> – when cards don't contain much content, or perform no function other than accepting user input, it isn't always logical to go back to the last card viewed. Links to a home page, and so forth, should also be included where appropriate.

For example, let's say that our application is an m-commerce site that allows you to buy DVDs. We might start off with a main menu with a link to a catalogue, a search function, features, etc. Presumably, navigating through these sections would eventually take you to a card representing a single item, which we could then choose to purchase. Perhaps we'd then display a quick warning page before allowing the user to make the purchase, then a confirmation. Let's look at the screens for the DVD ordering process, and see which cards would need what kind of 'back' links:

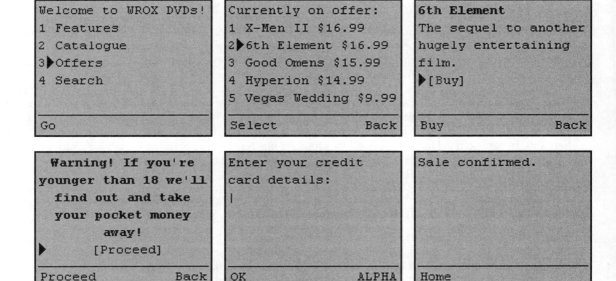

The first (menu) card has no 'back' link. From then on, all of the cards except the fifth have some sort of backward navigation functionality. The second, third, and fourth cards all allow the user to go back to the previous card, but the sixth card doesn't – it wouldn't make sense to order an item again, so a Home link is provided, which would take the user back to the main menu.

Because of the way the UP.Simulator works, the fifth card has no obvious way of navigating backwards. If we could include a back link here (other browsers do allow this, as we'll see in the next chapter), it wouldn't make sense to go to the previous card — seeing the warning once is enough! Instead, we could go back to the third card, effectively providing a sort of 'cancel' functionality, where the user is given the option of aborting the transaction.

Perhaps there is a case for adding Home links to more of the cards, to provide a speedy escape route for the user without having to look at the intermediate cards again. However, WAP browsers don't allow for many options to be provided at once, and it's better to limit the options to the most common ones (and have them readily available) than to hide a wider variety of options away in hard-to-reach submenus.

Keeping User Input to a Minimum

Most user agents won't have a QWERTY-style keyboard for user input, and entering text on a mobile phone keypad can be a bit of a chore (although I've seen teenagers writing text messages so quickly that their thumbs are little more than a blur!). The key points to bear in mind, then, are to avoid requiring user input wherever possible, and to keep it simple when it is necessary.

If a user is registering at your WAP site, for example, there is no real need to force them to enter a multitude of personal details: there are better ways of doing this. A method that seems to be catching on is to alert the user to the presence of a traditional web portal that they can access via their home computer, and enter lengthy data using a keyboard. This could then be accessible from the WAP site, and will certainly save the user a great deal of effort. Of course, this approach still requires the user to log in on their WAP-enabled device, but until different systems come up with a standard way of avoiding it, we're stuck with at least this small amount of user input.

Another issue here regards security. Whatever the facts, the Web is currently regarded as being more secure than WAP, so users may feel more secure entering their details that way. However, as some financial institutions are now launching their own gateways, so that no traffic ever gets outside of their secure internal networks, it's likely that some WAP transactions are at least as secure as Web ones, if not more so.

Where appropriate, format strings are also a good idea. If the user has to enter a date, then providing the required punctuation marks automatically will make them feel a lot more comfortable. (We saw an example of this earlier in the chapter.) As we'll see later on, though, there are interoperability issues here too. In some circumstances, option lists might be more suitable, providing an intuitive way of entering data and an assurance that invalid input is a lot less likely (although you'll still have to deal with things like entering the 31st of February, of course).

Keeping Text Volume to a Minimum

The small displays that are characteristic of WAP user agents really aren't suitable for lengthy passages of text. Can you imagine trying to read a novel on a mobile phone? Or, more importantly, how much it might cost you to do so? For a well-conceived WAP application, though, this shouldn't be a problem: the types of services that are most suitable for mobile devices tend to be those that aren't too verbose.

Keeping the volume of text down is something you should always consider when designing your WAP services. This doesn't just mean the body of your text, either — it also implies keeping list options and link text brief. Consider the next two screenshots, which demonstrate that simple, one-word links are generally a lot easier to use:

```
┌──────────────────────────┐  ┌──────────────────────────┐
│ might turn out much      │  │ and might turn out       │
│ like an octopus.         │  │ much like an octopus.    │
│ ▶[Go to the next page    │  │                          │
│ of this article.]        │  │ ▶[Next]                  │
│  [Go back to the home    │  │  [Home]                  │
│ page.]                   │  │                          │
├──────────────────────────┤  ├──────────────────────────┤
│ Link                     │  │ Link                     │
└──────────────────────────┘  └──────────────────────────┘
```

Of course, there are times where the body of text *does* need to be quite large – perhaps in a news article. In cases like this, it's often a good idea to keep such cards further down in the hierarchy; you certainly wouldn't want the first card encountered by a user to be packed full of text. See *Redundancy and Content Organization* (the next section but one) for more discussion of this topic.

One other method of keeping content volume down is to personalize your sites. Although this only applies to certain applications, and has the downside of requiring users to log in, it can dramatically reduce superfluous material. One method for doing this ties in with a point in the last section: you can provide a web front-end for users to choose what they want on their WAP service. Perhaps you might supply a list of categories for the user to choose from, which would then be converted into a selection of links on the WAP site. When users can simply choose not to see information about the sections they're not interested in, they're able to get to the sections they *are* interested in much more quickly.

As a final note, remember that space for softkeys is usually very limited – the WML specification says that they should be no more than six characters in length. This can be infuriating, as you scour the thesaurus hoping for brevity in communicating concepts. It *is* worth the effort, though, as many browsers will clip softkey entries to six letters even if you don't, leaving you with even more confusing phrases.

Using Images Effectively

As we have seen, it's quite easy to add graphical content to your applications using either WBMP files or built in images, but you need to take great care whenever you do so. If you add too many images to a card, you're risking problems in three nasty areas:

❑ Speed – each separate WBMP file you use in your cards needs to be obtained from the server, resulting in a noticeable pause.

❑ Confusion – when it comes down to it, WAP is optimized for text. Adding too many images can result in a confusing display, making it awkward for users to view the information they require and navigate around your site.

❑ Interoperability – as we'll see in the next chapter, support for images varies drastically. Some browsers have real trouble with image formatting, and will turn your carefully constructed cards into an unintelligible mess. Some browsers don't allow you to use images in anchors. As well as these annoying problems, you should also consider the fact that libraries of built-in images are likely to vary between devices; some might not even have any.

Of course, this doesn't mean that images should never be used. There are occasions when they really can add something to your application – although a lot of the time this will only be possible if you know what microbrowser your users have, or you design different pages for different user agents. For now, let's look at what's possible in the UP.Simulator, and come back to multi-browser issues in the next chapter.

One thing that's often seen on web and WAP sites is a logo, such as the one used in our Wrox Travel example. Don't be put off these – for an initial hit, you can make your site look more impressive. Another thing that can make sites look good is judicious use of bullet points, like the small boxes used in the list above. If you keep these small and simple, they can work – and they'll load quickly because the same image is used several times, which only requires a single graphic to be obtained from the server. You might end up with a list of points like this:

```
In Birmingham, you
might find:
▷ Buses
▷ Building sites
▷ Editors
▷ Pollution

OK
```

This makes a real change from dashes or other simple text bulleting, and it can be used to great effect. It is also simple to code:

```
<card id="main" title="Main">
    <p>
        In Birmingham, you might find:<br/>
        <img src="bullet.wbmp" alt="test" align="middle"/> Buses<br/>
        <img src="bullet.wbmp" alt="test" align="middle"/> Building sites<br/>
        <img src="bullet.wbmp" alt="test" align="middle"/> Editors<br/>
        <img src="bullet.wbmp" alt="test" align="middle"/> Pollution<br/>
    </p>
</card>
```

Another use of images is to provide icons for navigation:

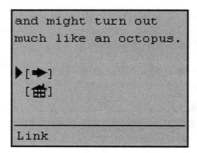

But is this really easier to understand? Do we genuinely get an advantage over using text? These are questions that you will have to answer for yourself, and they will depend on the site you are working on. Graphics may fit in very well with what you're aiming to achieve, but they may also make users wonder what to do next.

Finally, if you do use images, make sure that you also specify intelligible alternative text in the alt attribute: something that will help the user to understand why the graphic was needed, not just a random phrase. This will help the user if things go wrong and the images fail to load, or if they have images disabled. This may also be of use to those using a voice browser, where they'll 'hear' an image rather than see it. In cases such as this, the alt attribute will certainly be used.

Redundancy and Content Organization

Redundancy is a topic that can cause considerable disagreement among developers. In terms of user interface design, redundancy means allowing more than one way of doing the same thing. To illustrate this, consider using a word processor. Having written a paragraph, you might decide to add emphasis by changing the style of a single word to boldface. The word processor I'm using at the moment allows me to do this by:

❏ Highlighting the word, selecting Format | Font... from a dropdown menu, changing the font style to bold, and accepting my changes

❏ Highlighting the word and hitting the Bold icon on the toolbar

❏ Highlighting the word and pressing *Ctrl-B*

I can even get away with not highlighting the word – I just need to have my cursor somewhere among the letters that make it up.

There are several reasons why the developers of the word processor have done things this way:

❏ New users can usually find *some* way of accomplishing a task, even if it's not the quickest way of doing it.

❏ More experienced users can start to use shortcuts as they become accustomed to the software.

❏ Users migrating from other software are more likely to find that the methods they used before are supported, so they don't have to change the way they work.

❏ Power users who use many different products may well find that a single method works in all their chosen software. They can also program their own keys to accomplish such tasks, if need be.

The same principles have been built into many web sites. It isn't uncommon to have to enter some data in a field and click a Go button, but this requires a combination of typing on the keyboard and clicking on the mouse, which takes longer than just typing. Many web sites also allow you just to hit *Return* to submit data automatically, and even to use the *Tab* key to switch between input fields – a technique familiar to users of many graphical user interfaces. Options may also be available through icons, textual links, sidebar menus, drop down dynamic menus, etc., allowing you the freedom to use whatever method is most convenient.

Tactics like these are also valid when it comes to WAP-enabled devices, but (as mentioned above) they have invoked disagreement in the WAP community. The argument *against* adding redundancy to your WAP applications concerns their inherent simplicity: it is difficult to display a multitude of options on a mobile phone without running the risk of causing a great deal of confusion. However, we believe that redundancy *can* find a place in the WAP world, in the same way as it has found a place on the Web. Providing different ways of doing the same thing doesn't *necessarily* lead to confusion, as long as you're careful about it.

Let's get down to some specifics. Consider a WML card that contains quite a large amount of text – perhaps the news article we discussed earlier. To a card such as this, you will often want to add a link to a reference, such as the WAP site of an institution mentioned – but where do you *put* the link? Intuitively, you'd put it at the end of the text, because the reader is likely to want to finish the article before following it – but what about those that don't? What if they've been to this page before, and returned only because they want to use the link? In that case, scrolling all the way through the card to get to the bottom is a drag.

Should we put the link at the top of the article instead, then? In terms of navigation alone, that makes things easier, but it's completely counterintuitive: new readers would have to scroll past the link to get to the body of the article, then scroll back to follow it. "Softkeys," you say? Well, we could certainly provide a link in a <do> element, but would it be immediately obvious to the reader that it was there? Would the softkey link just look odd?

Here's a suggestion on how to handle the situation, based on the facts that:

❑ In terms of the order of interaction between the user and your site, placing the links at the end (or even throughout) an article makes sense

❑ Softkeys are accessible at any time, without requiring any scrolling

Bearing these in mind, it's a reasonable approach to keep the link(s) in their 'natural' positions in the article, and add a softkey called References (or Links, to conform to the six-character limit discussed earlier). This softkey will take the user to another card in the same deck (for speed of access) that just lists the links. Yes, that's a whole extra card that adds nothing to the information content of the deck, but it *does* make things a whole lot easier to use.

The sort of structure we're talking about is as follows:

```wml
<wml>
  <card id="article" title="Article">
    <p>
      A public awareness organization announced today that repeatedly
      banging your head against a brick wall is bad for your health.
      This has caused shock among programmers, who feel that it's
      something that they are forced to do every day, due to their job.
      The minister for health responded by saying that he "couldn't
      believe the stupidity of some people".<br/>
      <a href="link1.wml" title="MoH">Ministry of Health</a><br/>
      <a href="link2.wml" title="Dumb">Stupid people</a><br/>
    </p>
    <do type="accept" label="Links">
      <go href="#links"/>
    </do>
    <do type="prev">
      <prev/>
    </do>
  </card>
  <card id="links" title="Links">
    <p>
      <select title="Links">
        <option onpick="link1.wml" title="MoH">Ministry of Health</option>
        <option onpick="link2.wml" title="Dumb">Stupid people</option>
      </select>
    </p>
    <do type="prev">
      <prev/>
    </do>
  </card>
</wml>
```

The code on the previous page generates quite a long card. The top of it looks like this:

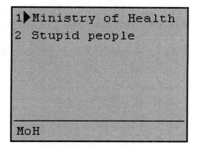

```
A public awareness
organization
announced today that
repeatedly banging
your head against a
brick wall is bad for
─────────────────────
Links
```

allowing the user to jump to the "links" card by pressing the Links softkey:

```
1▶Ministry of Health
2 Stupid people




─────────────────────
MoH
```

or to scroll to the bottom of the article and follow the links there:

```
responded by saying
that he "couldn't
believe the stupidity
of some people".
  [Ministry of Health]
▶[Stupid people]
─────────────────────
Dumb
```

which ought to give enough options for everyone!

Testing

The last thing to look at in this half of the chapter is the absolute necessity of testing. Testing is made up of three stages:

❑ **Integrity** (doing what you ought to do) – taking the application from the top, following every link, using every available option, and entering whatever data is necessary.

❑ **Stability** (doing what you shouldn't really do) – desperately trying to break your applications by using weird user input, such as negative numbers where positive ones are required, etc.

❑ **Usability** (doing what you think you should do) – performing 'cold tests' on people, who are given a brief description of the application and told to play with it for a while.

Each of these stages is likely to highlight areas where more work is needed – perhaps even total reorganization. Don't be afraid to do this! If it turns out that your application doesn't fulfill your initial requirements, then change it. You'll be happier in the long run.

Let's look at these stages in more detail by detailing a typical testing scenario for a WAP application.

Integrity

After many hours of coding, you decide that your application is ready. As yet, you've only seen the thing working on a PC simulator, but now you've uploaded the files to a server, made yourself a cup of coffee, and seated yourself down on the sofa ready to try it out on your WAP phone.

You connect. The splash screen shows up fine, and you can't help but smile to yourself with the satisfaction that comes from producing a working WAP site. The main menu appears, and you follow the first link... a "file not found" error occurs! Heading back to your computer, you quickly upload the file that you forgot about last time and try again. Success!

Later, after a few more teething troubles ("Curses! I forgot to set up the MIME type for WBMPs!"), you are satisfied that your application is working.

Points to note in this stage:

❑   Integrity testing is something you can usually do yourself – after all, who knows the options available in your application better than you do?

❑   Be prepared to be patient. Small problems *will* occur, especially if this is the first time you've made your application 'live', going through a real gateway onto a real device.

❑   Be thorough: try *everything*. In fact, try everything *twice*.

Stability

Tempted though you are to launch your site immediately, you call in 'Destructive Dan' from next door, sit him down, show him what you've achieved, how it all works, and tell him to break it... if he can!

You head off into the kitchen to fling together some cheese on toast while Dan has his fun. No sooner have you cut a single slice than Dan gives you a shout. He tried ordering minus 4 boxes of 'My Little Aardvark', and has apparently had them dispatched.

Looking at your code, you notice a small error in your WMLScript validation, so you make the changes and set Dan loose again. By midnight you've improved things greatly, so you settle down for pizza and videos.

Points to note in this stage:

❑   Stability testing is best done by someone else. After you've spent ages trying things out, you're likely to type in data that you've tried before, which is more likely to work. Other people will do things in a different way.

❑   For this stage, stability testers should know as much about the application as possible, short of actually telling them what to type. You want them to be quick at using it, in order that they can try as many weird things as possible.

❏ If serious errors are found, don't hesitate to go back to the integrity stage after you've made the changes. The more complicated the code, the more likely it is that this will be necessary.

❏ Make sure as many options are open as possible. Short of getting people actually to enter their credit card details, the site should be (or at least appear to be) fully functional, even if you don't actually carry out real transactions.

Usability

The next day, you try out your site on an unsuspecting group of volunteers. You equip them with WAP-enabled devices, tell them what the site is about, and let them play.

To get an objective view, you should set tasks. If it's a site for ordering CDs that you're creating, you could try something like, "Order 3 copies of *I Am A Jellyfish* by the Furry Humans," or, "Submit a review." You could even set an impossible one, to see what happens: "Delete your review."

Soon, one volunteer calls you over, telling you that it works but can be really annoying: it takes far too long to find the product they want to order. Another user complains that it's impossible to cancel a transaction, requiring them to leave and re-enter the site if they want to go back and try something else.

At the end of the session, you pass round a questionnaire, and go back to the drawing board. You've found plenty to change – things you never even thought of – and will have to start back at the beginning of the testing cycle. This time, though, you'll get it right!

Points to note in this stage:

❏ Obviously, you need people who haven't seen the site before, and preferably with a variety of backgrounds (some experienced WAP users, some who've never tried before).

❏ Setting tasks and getting people to note their successes and failures can help you to see if you've achieved your objectives.

❏ Don't be afraid to accept criticism – the people testing for you may well be the end users of your application, so keep them happy!

❏ Again, you may have to go back to the drawing board. This can be a little demoralizing, but in the end your application *will* be better.

Other Testing Notes

Remember that we've got a big advantage over web designers: we're designing for *mobile* devices. Take your WAP phone out with you at lunchtime and find suitable people on the street. Let them play (most people will be intrigued enough by a WAP phone to have a go), but above all listen to what they have to say. If they find it a chore to use, rethink your strategy. If they love it, that's great, but don't get too excited – the next person you meet might have completely the opposite opinion!

In a nutshell, there is no substitute for real, hands-on user involvement *before* products hit the streets. This isn't exactly a new idea, but after seeing some of the WAP (and web) sites out there, you'd think that it's a completely alien ideology to some people.

Summary

Hopefully, this chapter will have taught you something new about designing usable WAP sites. A lot of the information we have looked at may seem counterintuitive at first glance – it fact, it *is* counterintuitive until you start to consider the limitations that are inherent in WAP devices, at least for the time being. We've covered:

❑ General principles of usability

❑ Reducing the number of server round trips by tailoring our content and using a few tricks

❑ Making information simple to get to, and then as compact as possible when viewed

❑ Preventing too much user input

❑ Using images effectively

❑ The full testing cycle

Now here's the rub: all of the information in this chapter applies to the 'ideal' situation. Unfortunately, the variations among microbrowsers mean that our sites are inevitably a compromise between what would be best, and what's possible. We'll look at these variations in the next chapter, and provide suggestions as to how this seemingly disastrous situation can be resolved.

Interoperability

When WML was first devised, its creators employed what was thought to be an intelligent design concept: the separation of data content from display details. For example, the definition of a softkey is simply "something with a label that the user can access in some way to do whatever it's programmed to do". As we've seen, Phone.com's UP.Simulator renders these as labels above two buttons on the phone, but that's got nothing to do with the WAP specification – it is Phone.com's interpretation. Other vendors have effected their own interpretations.

From this, it follows that (as we've hinted a number of times) a given WML card may well look different on different WAP-enabled devices. However, it should always contain the same information, and provide the same functionality in terms of links to other cards and so on. The idea was that developers would *not* have to specify the exact locations of softkeys, etc. on the screen, allowing flexibility to device manufacturers.

This methodology is fine in principle, but it's led to a tricky situation. Device manufacturers have indeed created their own implementations of WML browsers, but they differ rather more than was intended by the designers of WML. The lack of a definitive standard for *browsers* (a standard for *WML*, of course, is well established) has resulted in several minor (and not so minor!) considerations that need to be borne in mind when designing WAP sites.

It is possible to design your applications such that they target specific devices, regardless of how they look on others. This is a valid approach when, for example, you're developing a solution for a company that will equip all its employees with the same hardware. It is equally possible to go for the 'lowest common denominator', such that your application looks reasonable on every device, but outstanding on none. The differences between web browsers from the various vendors have been a nuisance for web developers for some years now, and now WAP developers are faced with similar problems.

It's also possible to create different versions of your site that target different user agents, but this can mean a lot more work! An extension of this idea, and something we'll look at in the next chapter, involves generating content dynamically, depending on the browser being used.

Sadly, one of the issues that get tossed back into the melting pot as a result of these problems of interoperability is usability. In the last chapter, we saw how it's possible to tailor our content to achieve a much smoother user interface, and pointed out many of the common pitfalls along the way. Unfortunately, as different user agents handle WML in different ways, we are often forced to compromise many of these techniques. This means that the 'ideal' usability situations we've looked at may need slight modifications in order to work in the real world. Situations such as these will be pointed out throughout this chapter.

Targeting Different User Agents

It's time to get stuck in and look at some of the differences that we've been discussing. We'll start off by looking at some general principles, and then move on to more specific issues, as detailed in the next section.

General Principles

There is an increasingly wide range of WAP devices on the market, but contrary to popular belief, they don't all function in exactly the same way. Variations in screen size and softkey layout are not the big problem – we wouldn't *want* all WAP devices to look exactly the same, and these kinds of incompatibility aren't really a cause for concern. The trouble is that many existing WAP devices differ so much in other, more serious, areas that applications can be rendered practically unusable in some cases – even though they work fine on the device you tested them with.

Some of the problems stem from basic support for WAP being incomplete, with devices supporting only a subset of the WML elements. More problems stem from the built-in flexibility of the WML specification that we've discussed so often – two browsers sitting at either end of the range that the specification allows would be very different animals indeed. In this section, we'll discuss all of these issues, from those that are merely irritating to the real showstoppers. We'll look at:

❑ Text issues, including how to tackle different screen sizes and text formatting element support

❑ Graphical issues, including support, the `alt` attribute, sizes and alignment

❑ Different methods of navigation, where functionality and appearance vary a great deal

❑ Other issues, including lack of support for WMLScript, and other points of interest

For the purposes of illustration, the following WML development toolkits have been used. All of them are freely downloadable from the URLs indicated, and you'll find instructions on the installation and use of these toolkits in Appendix A:

❑ Phone.com UP.Simulator 4.0 (http://developer.phone.com/)

❑ Nokia Toolkit v2.0 simulating Nokia 7110 (http://www.forum.nokia.com/)

❑ Ericsson WapIDE SDK v2.1 simulating Ericsson R320 (http://www.ericsson.se/wap/)

❑ Ericsson R380 Emulator (http://www.ericsson.se/wap/)

❑ Microsoft Mobile Explorer Emulator Rev. 6 simulating Benefon Q (http://www.benefon.com/)

❑ Motorola MADK 2.0 Simulator (http://www.motorola.com/developers/wireless/tools/)

In addition, because (as we'll discover) these emulators do not always exactly reflect the functionality of the actual devices being simulated, this chapter also includes screenshots from the following real devices:

❑   Nokia 7110

❑   Motorola Timeport P7389

❑   Ericsson R320

All of the information in this chapter was correct at the time of writing (October 2000). Manufacturers are likely to change the specifications of their devices and emulators over time, and you should always check your code on every different device you can find before releasing your applications.

Text Issues

Perhaps the most immediately obvious difference between WAP-enabled devices is the variation in screen size. For current WAP phones, you can typically expect three to six lines of text (not including title bars and softkeys), with around twenty characters in each line (characters per line is difficult to characterize, if you'll forgive the pun, because proportionally spaced fonts are used in many browsers). Other WAP-enabled devices can allow far more text to be displayed; the WAP browsers that are now available for handheld computers, for example, come into this category.

The second thing to consider in this section is that devices support different subsets of the 'optional' text formatting instructions defined in the WML specification, and may give unpredictable results with other instructions. Let's take a look at both of these issues in more depth.

Different Screen Sizes (Aspects)

It's surprisingly difficult to find statistics about the screen sizes of WAP-enabled devices. Most manufacturers quote screen size in pixels, which will usually include the screen area taken up by the various icons and softkeys they use. One useful resource, at http://www.anywhereyougo.com/ayg/ayg/wap/devices/Index.po, contains of a list of devices along with their details, but (at the time of writing) there are a lot of gaps. The site runs on the submissions of contributors who own the devices listed, but it seems that hardly anyone has submitted screen size data!

Another point worth noting when talking about screen sizes in pixels is the aspect ratio of the pixels themselves. For example, the Nokia 7110 has a pixel aspect ratio of 1:1.3, which is far from square. This will result in slight distortions in text and graphics.

This compels us to follow more general guidelines, using the figures quoted above (3 to 6 lines of around 20 characters each) as a rule of thumb. Once again, the most important thing is to keep text volume to a minimum, but that's not all we have to contend with. Using too many line breaks can also cause problems, as this reduces still further the amount of information displayed on a single screen, so where you might otherwise use blank lines to space things out, this isn't something to be too strict about on WAP devices. You'll find that in most cases, the end result looks fine, and we'll be bearing that in mind over the coming sections.

Simple Text Display

We're going to start by taking a look at the displays of the WAP simulators and devices on test, comparing how they handle long sections of text. Before we begin, though, you'll see that we haven't included the document prolog in any of the listings in this chapter. This is because not all of the simulators and devices on test support WML 1.2 – some of them are only compatible with version 1.1. In case of any difficulty, the solution is to change from this:

```
<?xml version="1.0"?>
<!DOCTYPE wml PUBLIC "-//WAPFORUM//DTD WML 1.2//EN"
                     "http://www.wapforum.org/DTD/wml_1.2.xml">
```

to this, which includes the correct document type declaration for the older specification:

```
<?xml version="1.0"?>
<!DOCTYPE wml PUBLIC "-//WAPFORUM//DTD WML 1.1//EN"
                     "http://www.wapforum.org/DTD/wml_1.1.xml">
```

That danger dealt with, the abilities of the various browsers to handle passages of text can now be tested by means of the following deck:

```
<wml>
    <card id="card1" title="Lengthy Text">
        <p>
            We few, we happy few, we band of brothers;
            For he to-day that sheds his blood with me
            Shall be my brother; be he ne'er so vile,
            This day shall gentle his condition:
            And gentlemen in England now a-bed
            Shall think themselves accursed they were not here,
            And hold their manhoods cheap whiles any speaks
            That fought with us upon Saint Crispin's day.
        </p>
    </card>
</wml>
```

This excerpt from Shakespeare's Henry V should be long enough for our purposes. Let's see how it looks on the different toolkit microbrowser screens:

The Phone.com UP.Simulator

The Nokia 7110 simulator

The Benefon Q toolkit (using MME)   The Ericsson R320 simulator

The Ericsson R380 simulator:

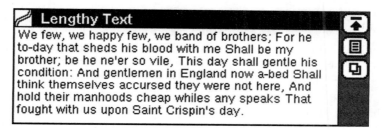

And finally, the Motorola ADK, simulating a Motorola P7389 device:

For comparison, let's look at the displays on some real phones:

The Nokia 7110

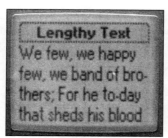

The Ericsson R320

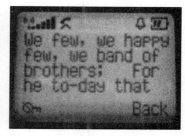

The Motorola Timeport P7389

As you can see, the aspects vary quite a lot, but the objective is achieved in all cases – the Ericsson R380 even manages to display the full text!

> *Note also that the Phone.com, MME, and Motorola browsers don't display the card's title. If a card isn't supplied with a title, then the Nokia will just have a blank line at the top, the R380 will show "(No Title)", and the R320 will display either the host name, or nothing at all.*

As this is the first time we've looked at the displays of *real* WAP-enabled devices, it's well worth raising a few points – especially as we have simulators for each of the devices in question too.

- ❑ Nokia 7110 – in this example, the Nokia 7110 simulator seems to do a very good job of showing what would appear on a real device, right down to the number of characters displayed and their positioning. The only difference in the display is the handset icon at the top left, showing that the phone is connected, but that seems quite minor.

- ❑ Ericsson R320 – the simulator's appearance here is slightly different from the real device. The latter has a dotted line around the title (not a solid one) and uses different fonts – it manages to fit more text on the screen than the simulator.

- ❑ Motorola P7389 – there's no escaping this one: the simulator display is completely different from that on the real device. The only thing they seem to have in common is the amount of text displayed on screen, although the amount of space on the simulator screen suggests that even this was more by chance than design. Also worth noting is the extra white space between the first and second lines of text on the device (between "brothers;" and "For"). The Motorola seems to interpret the end of line character as a 'different type' of white space, and includes three white space characters instead of one (one before end-of-line, one due to end-of-line, and one after end-of-line).

So far, these simulator-device differences are only cosmetic, and for as long as this remains the case, we won't show simulator and device screenshots for these three systems. However, if there is a significant difference worth noting, we will show the corresponding screenshots. It's useful to know *how* devices differ from their simulators, rather than simply being aware that they do differ. This also adds weight to the 'testing' discussion in the last chapter – real devices *are* different, and we need to test code out on them if at all possible!

Line Breaks

It's also worth considering the effect of line and paragraph breaks. As the text from the last section is a verse written in iambic pentameter, we have natural line breaks, but in order to illustrate the effects of line and paragraph breaks, we can also add an artificial paragraph break to the text:

```
<wml>
    <card id="card1" title="Lengthy Text">
        <p>
            We few, we happy few, we band of brothers;<br/>
            For he to-day that sheds his blood with me<br/>
            Shall be my brother; be he ne'er so vile,<br/>
            This day shall gentle his condition:
        </p>
        <p>
            And gentlemen in England now a-bed<br/>
            Shall think themselves accursed they were not here,<br/>
```

```
               And hold their manhoods cheap whiles any speaks<br/>
               That fought with us upon Saint Crispin's day.
          </p>
     </card>
</wml>
```

The results of this are quite interesting. `<br/>` elements are treated in the same way in all cases: a new line of text is begun. However, the different user agents interpret paragraph breaks in different ways. The UP.Simulator and the real and simulated Nokia 7110, Ericsson R320, and Motorola P7389 all treat paragraph breaks in exactly the same way as line breaks, while the MME and Ericsson R380 browsers add an extra bit of spacing to separate the lines of text slightly more. The displays on these two emulators look like this:

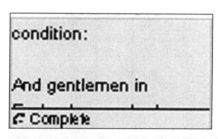

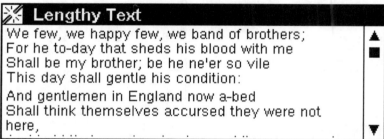

The MME browser adds a whole line break, which looks really quite big on such a small screen. The R380 just uses a slightly enlarged gap. This suggests that if we want to separate blocks of text in a way that produces similar results on all devices, we should use multiple `<br/>` elements rather than paragraph breaks.

Text Formatting

Next, let's try some text formatting:

```
<wml>
     <card id="card1" title="Text Formatting">
          <p>
               Normal,
               <em>Emphasis</em>,
               <strong>Strong</strong>,
               <i>Italic</i>,
```

```
            <b>Bold</b>,
            <u>Underline</u>,
            <big>Big</big>,
            <small>Small</small>
        </p>
    </card>
</wml>
```

This deck uses every formatting element defined by WML. The simulator results are as follows:

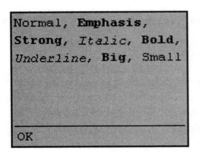

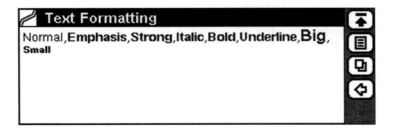

While the real devices gave the following results:

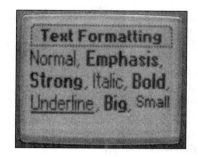

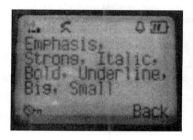

A mixed bag, you'll surely agree. Let's look at the results in tabular form:

Browser	Normal	Emphasis	Strong	Italic	Bold	Underline	Big	Small
Phone.com	OK	Bold	Bold	OK	OK	Italic	Bold	Normal
Nokia 7110 (simulated)	OK	Normal	Normal	Normal	Normal	Normal	Normal	Normal
Nokia 7110 (real)	OK	Normal	Normal	Normal	Normal	Normal	Normal	Normal
MME	OK	Italic	Bold	OK	OK	OK	OK	OK
R320 (simulated)	OK	Bold	Bold + Underline	Normal	OK	OK	Bold	Normal
R320 (real)	OK	Bold	Bold	Normal	OK	OK	Bold	OK
R380	OK	Bold	Bold	Bold	OK	Bold	OK	OK
Motorola (simulated)	OK	Underline	Bold	OK	OK	OK	Normal	OK
Motorola (real)	OK	Normal	Normal	Normal	Normal	Normal	Normal	Normal

We can see that *none* of the browsers examined here has a different font for every text style. Of course, this isn't *necessarily* a problem, although it can be useful to know how your styles will appear on various browsers if you are aiming for a particular look and feel. The Nokia 7110 (real and simulated) and real Motorola P7389, though, are significant underachievers here – they ignore text styles completely. In addition, the Nokia simulator strips out white space in between words of different styles.

In conclusion, it would be well worth referring to this table when designing your applications. In addition, if you know that your user base has Nokia 7110 or Motorola P7389 devices, it's worth considering avoiding these styles completely – or at least, using them in such a way as to make it unimportant if normal fonts are used instead.

Text Wrapping

Earlier in the book, we saw the effect of the `mode` attribute of the `<p>` element, which allowed us to specify that a line of text should not run onto any further lines. How is this handled on the devices on test? Let's go back to our earlier Shakespeare example, and try a really long line of non-wrapping text:

```wml
<wml>
    <card id="card1" title="Lengthy Text">
        <p mode="nowrap">
            We few, we happy few, we band of brothers;
            For he to-day that sheds his blood with me
            Shall be my brother; be he ne'er so vile,
            This day shall gentle his condition:
            And gentlemen in England now a-bed
            Shall think themselves accursed they were not here,
            And hold their manhoods cheap whiles any speaks
            That fought with us upon Saint Crispin's day.
        </p>
    </card>
</wml>
```

We won't display all the results here, but it's nevertheless interesting to know what they are. The Nokia 7110 and MME simulators (and the real Nokia 7110 device) completely ignore the `mode` attribute, and display text with wrapping regardless. The Ericsson R320 and Motorola simulators truncate the text to the first section, but don't allow any scrolling to get to the rest of it. The Motorola simulator, for example, leaves you with the following screen, allowing no further action:

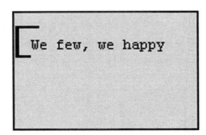

By contrast, the real Motorola P7389 *does* scroll a line of text, and highlights it to alert you to what it's doing. The screenshot at the top of the next page shows this scrolling in progress:

The real Ericsson R320 also supports scrolling text, although it appears from this test that there is a limit to how many characters can fit on a single line (around 125, it seems). The example resulted in three lines of text; the screenshot shows the first line in mid-scroll, and the other two lines at their leftmost positions:

The Phone.com and Ericsson R380 toolkits both behave correctly, albeit in slightly different ways. The Phone.com browser automatically scrolls selected text from right to left, and also allows manual control using the left and right directional buttons. The screenshot below shows it in mid-scroll:

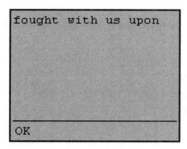

The R380 adds scrollbars to the screen, allowing the user to navigate to whatever area of text is required. The next screenshot shows the display when scrolled about a third of the way through the text:

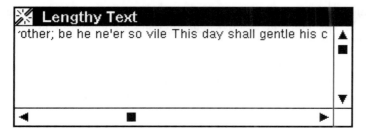

In conclusion, the `nowrap` attribute is probably another feature we should be reluctant to use if we want to keep our text readable on all devices. It might, however, be acceptable for limited use if you don't mind text being displayed over more than one line. The fact that some of the *simulators* resulted in text clipping shouldn't put us off too much – the real devices on test suggest that this is unlikely to happen in practice.

Text Alignment

The `<p>` element also has an `align` attribute that, as we have seen, allows you to specify the justification of your text: `left`, `right`, or `center`. The following code is a simple deck to test this:

```
<wml>
    <card id="card1" title="Alignment">
        <p align="left">
            Left
        </p>
        <p align="center">
            Center
        </p>
        <p align="right">
            Right
        </p>
        <p>
            Next
        </p>
    </card>
</wml>
```

The final `<p>` element uses the default alignment, `left`, and is in the deck to test that subsequent paragraphs have their alignment reset, and don't use that of the previous paragraph.

The results here were that all the devices on test handle this attribute correctly – except the Nokia 7110, which aligns everything to the left:

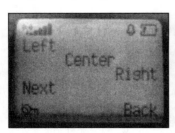  

Most of the simulators also coped well with this attribute, except the Nokia 7110 and (surprisingly) the Motorola P7389. It's becoming increasingly apparent that the emulator in the Motorola toolkit is a poor alternative to the real device.

Since majority support exists, it's probably OK to use this attribute – although you should always remember that the devices on test don't necessarily represent the devices owned by your users! It would probably be a good idea not to *rely* on this attribute, but to use it to enhance displays where supported.

Another point that relates to text alignment concerns the ­ entity, which (you may remember) specifies a position in a word where hyphenation is *possible* if the browser device requires a line break. None of the devices on test supported this entity correctly. The Nokia and Ericsson simulators ignored it completely, leaving out hyphens in all words, while the Phone.com and MME simulators added hyphens to all words, regardless of the space available for a line of text.

The real devices failed even more spectacularly. Using the simple test of a repeated word with ­ in it, with occasional random characters to space out the text, we got the following results:

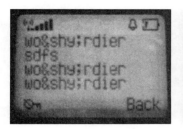

As you can plainly see, the results are quite disastrous, and certainly enough to recommend that you steer well clear of this entity! On a cheerier note, it's worth pointing out that the real Ericsson R320 device actually hyphenates words for you, without you having to specify anything. We've already seen evidence of this – although you might not have noticed it at the time:

It's quite reassuring to know that at least one vendor has put some thought into this, even if this functionality didn't get implemented in the simulator.

Tables

For a more challenging test, let's look at a table of moderate size:

```
<wml>
    <card id="card1" title="Big Table">
        <p>
            <table title="vegetables" align="CCC" columns="3">
                <tr>
                    <td>Vegetable</td>
                    <td>Color</td>
                    <td>Texture</td>
                </tr>
```

```
        <tr>
            <td>Cucumber</td>
            <td>Green</td>
            <td>Crisp</td>
        </tr>
        <tr>
            <td>Carrot</td>
            <td>Orange</td>
            <td>Crunchy</td>
        </tr>
        <tr>
            <td>Tomato</td>
            <td>Red</td>
            <td>Soggy</td>
        </tr>
        <tr>
            <td>Potato</td>
            <td>Brown</td>
            <td>Starchy</td>
        </tr>
      </table>
    </p>
  </card>
</wml>
```

On our emulators, this file appeared as:

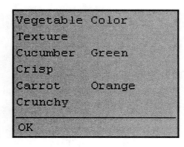

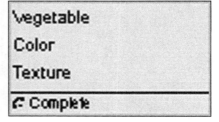

The MME and Nokia 7110 displays shown above are the tops of long, single columns.

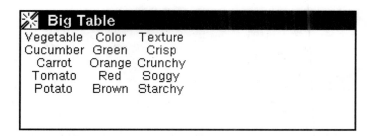

The Nokia 7110 and MME emulators have lost the table structure completely! The text has been extracted and placed in a single, long column – hardly ideal! The Phone.com browser has attempted to fit the table on the screen, but failed. To give it some credit, though, it has added line breaks at the ends of table rows.

Ericsson didn't do too badly. The R380 emulator has correctly formatted the whole table – although adding some lines to separate the cells would have been nice. The R320 allows you to scroll left and right to see the other columns, and it has added lines between the cells, but it might still cause confusion to the user. When it's scrolled over, it looks like this:

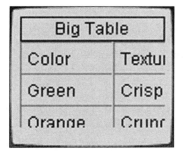

This is the limit of the scrolling – it is still impossible to see the whole of the third column on this emulator, which may also lead to confusion.

To finish off this discussion, the Motorola emulator has fitted the table onto its display, albeit with a total disregard for readability. The data is there, but it doesn't look very nice. One other point to note is that only the R380 aligned the text correctly: the `align` attribute in the WML code specified that the text should be centered in the columns.

Now let's look at how the actual devices perform:

The Motorola looks very similar to the UP.Simulator – it too has kept rows together, but run into problems with the text volume. Note that this is more evidence of the Motorola simulator being very different from the real device it simulates. The Nokia 7110 has lost the table structure, just like its emulator. The Ericsson R320 outperforms its emulator, displaying a nicely formatted table that can be easily scrolled to see all entries.

What can we learn from this? Right now, our strong suggestion is that you should rethink any plans to use the <table> element in your WAP sites, at least while this generation of devices proliferates. Unless you can be absolutely certain that your user base will use devices that show your data in the way you intended, it'll all end in tears!

If you've got data that really *needs* to be tabulated, then there are ways to get round device limitations, if you sit down and really think about it. The simplest way is to use plain text, physically writing out each row of the table, ending each with a <br/> element. Of course, this works, but the method is not without its concerns:

❑ Unless you use extra characters as delimiters, you won't have lines separating cells (although only some browsers add these lines anyway).

❑ Many browsers use a proportionally spaced font, which will result in columns not lining up properly.

❑ In order to add extra spaces where required, the <pre> element is necessary, which is only possible on WAP 1.2 capable browsers. Without this element, extra white space is likely to be truncated, leaving your columns unaligned, even in browsers with fixed-width fonts.

❑ The problem of not being able to fit whole rows on a single line remains. The nowrap attribute could be used to prevent rows ending up on multiple lines, but it isn't supported on all browsers, and where it *is* supported, it results in scrolling. If individual rows of your table scroll independently, it certainly won't be easy to decipher!

Another alternative is to structure your table in such a way that it looks acceptable, regardless of whether it is fully formatted or reorganized into a single column. We can do this by removing the heading row from the table and combining it with the data in the table. You'll still get problems if you have too much data to display, but for simple cases, this works fine. As an example, recall the insurance table from the Wrox Travel example we used earlier in the book:

```
<table columns="3" title="Insurance">
   <tr>
      <td>Type</td>
      <td>Month</td>
      <td>Year</td>
   </tr>
```

```
    <tr>
        <td>Basic</td>
        <td>$$20</td>
        <td>$$100</td>
    </tr>
    <tr>
        <td>Sports</td>
        <td>$$30</td>
        <td>$$150</td>
    </tr>
</table>
```

We can reorganize this as:

```
<table columns="3" title="Insurance">
    <tr>
        <td>Basic</td>
        <td>$$20/mo</td>
        <td>$$100/yr</td>
    </tr>
    <tr>
        <td>Sports</td>
        <td>$$30/mo</td>
        <td>$$150/yr</td>
    </tr>
</table>
```

Now we're including the header information in the cells themselves. On a browser that displays this information, such as the Phone.com simulator, it looks like this:

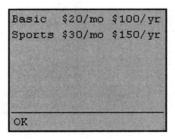

It's all formatted in such a way as to make the same information more readable. On a browser like the Nokia 7110 that doesn't format tables in this way, we get the following:

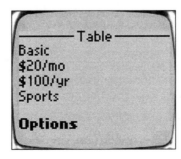

Each item in the table is separated from the rest, and its associated data is shown below its name. The values for the 'sports' item in the above screenshot are available if you scroll down the display.

381

Images

Now that we've completed our discussion of text issues, it is time to have a look at how images are handled. As we've seen, we can specify images in two ways: using custom WBMPs, and using built-in pictures. We'll take a look at support for both of these types in this section, as well as examining how the `alt` attribute works on different browsers. We'll also explore differences in image alignment, and the way in which text flows (or doesn't flow) around images.

WBMPs

To test out the graphical capabilities of the simulators and devices we're using, we'll return to one of our examples from Chapter 10. There, we asked the question, "Who is your favorite James Bond?"

The subject of Bond is a good fit with a chapter on interoperability – after all, the actors were trying to run the same Bond 'software' on different 'hardware'. The two images we'll use, `sean.wbmp` and `roger.wbmp`, are available with the downloadable code for this book, but for your reference here they are in glorious monochrome:

We'll display these using three decks (the images are too large to fit in a single one), the first being stored in `bond.wml`:

```
<wml>
    <card id="menu" title="Menu">
        <p>
            Who is your favorite Bond?<br/>
            <a href="sean.wml" title="Sean">Sean Connery</a><br/>
            <a href="roger.wml" title="Roger">Roger Moore</a>
        </p>
    </card>
</wml>
```

This calls `sean.wml` and `roger.wml`, shown below:

```wml
<wml>
   <card id="sean" title="Sean Connery">
      <p>
         <img alt="Sean" src="sean.wbmp"/>
      </p>
   </card>
</wml>
```

```wml
<wml>
   <card id="roger" title="Roger Moore">
      <p>
         <img alt="Roger" src="roger.wbmp"/>
      </p>
   </card>
</wml>
```

On our simulators, we got the following:

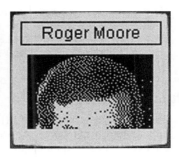

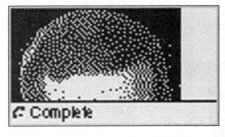

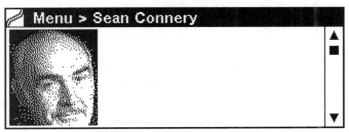

Note that scrolling down to see the rest of the image isn't possible on the Nokia and R320 simulators.

On our real phones, these were the results:

  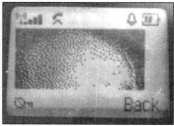

The images were displayed successfully on all three devices, but the Nokia 7110 did not allow scrolling, so the image shown above is all you could see.

Now we know that graphics work on all the browsers under test, although we do have to be careful with dimensions if we want users to be able to see the important parts. A glance at the screenshots above shows that pixel aspect also plays a part – our Bonds were stretched or compressed depending on the browser being used. We'll look differences in alignment and their effect on text flow in the *Graphic Alignment* section, below.

Built-in Images

As far as we were able to ascertain from the documentation, only the Phone.com microbrowser supports built-in images. However, although you might take this as a reason not to use built-in images, that's not the case. If one of the images provided by Phone.com is perfect for you, then use it – but make sure you have a suitable WBMP image for other phones!

To demonstrate, let's look at a brief example. One of the Phone.com built-in images is called 'clock', and is simply:

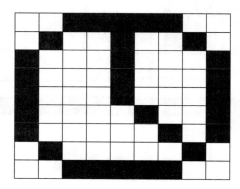

If you want to use this image, simply create an identical WBMP called `clock.wbmp`, and use the following code:

```wml
<wml>
    <card id="menu" title="Menu">
        <p>
            localsrc test, clock:<br/>
            <img localsrc="clock" alt="Clock" src="clock.wbmp"/>
        </p>
    </card>
</wml>
```

For illustrative purposes here, we made the WBMP file slightly different:

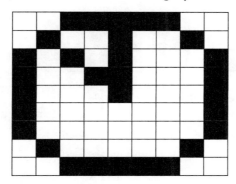

Loading this code into the Phone.com and Nokia simulators this looks like this:

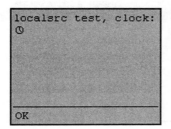 

An image is displayed in both cases (although it's positioned differently – see the *Graphic Alignment* section below), and as long as you plan things carefully, you can make them match. We've manufactured a situation in which the benefits of built-in images are realized if the user agent supports them, but there's no catastrophic failure if it doesn't.

The final thing to check, then, is whether this works on the Motorola P7389, which contains a Phone.com browser. (Note that simulator in the Motorola SDK *doesn't* support the Phone.com built-in images). The successful result from this device is as follows:

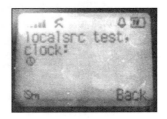

The alt Attribute

As we saw in Chapter 7, the `alt` attribute is used to substitute for images when (for whatever reason) they are unavailable. To make our browsers use this attribute, we can delete the `localsrc` attribute from the code we used in the previous example, and delete the `clock.wbmp` file. The results from our simulators are then as follows:

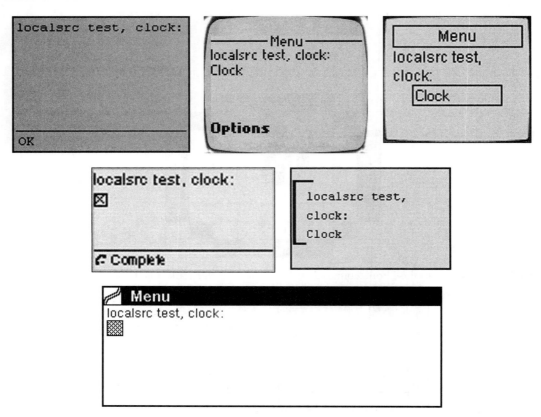

In fact, the UP.Simulator *did* display the value of the `alt` attribute; it just didn't do it for very long! If you watch it very closely, you'll see that this screen appears for a split second:

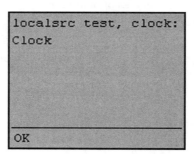

The real devices display the following:

  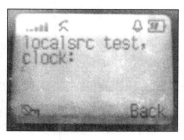

Like the UP.Simulator, the Motorola device also displayed the word Clock for a split second, then gave the above display – which does have some marks where the clock picture should be: a couple of dots.

So, we can summarize:

❑　The Nokia and Motorola simulators and Nokia 7110 device present the `alt` attribute as simple text.

❑　The R320 browsers present the `alt` attribute in a picture frame, signifying that a picture was intended.

❑　The MME and R380 simulators don't use the `alt` attribute at all. Instead, they provide a different image signifying that a picture was intended.

❑　The Phone.com simulator seems to have a bug – it displays the `alt` attribute briefly, and then clears it. The Motorola device did exactly the same thing, although it didn't clear the display completely.

Although there's not a great deal we can do about it, it's useful to know about these differences in behavior. The `alt` attribute is mandatory, but in most cases we won't see it apart from when images are being loaded.

Image Alignment and Sizing

The last topic to examine in this section on graphical interoperability is image alignment and sizing. Different devices handle images in slightly different ways, some placing them inline with text, others centering them on lines of their own. They also have varying support for the `align`, `height`, and `width` attributes. To test these, we'll use the clock image from the last section, and the following code:

```
<wml>
   <card id="card1" title="Lengthy Text">
      <p>
         -<img alt="Clock" src="clock.wbmp"/>
         <img alt="Clock" src="clock.wbmp" align="top"/>
         <img alt="Clock" src="clock.wbmp" align="middle"/>
         <img alt="Clock" src="clock.wbmp" align="bottom"/>-<br/>
         -<img alt="Clock" src="clock.wbmp"/>-<br/>
         -<img alt="Clock" src="clock.wbmp" align="top"/>-<br/>
```

```
            -<img alt="Clock" src="clock.wbmp" align="middle"/>-<br/>
            -<img alt="Clock" src="clock.wbmp" align="bottom"/>-<br/>
            -<img alt="Clock" src="clock.wbmp" height="18" width="18"/>-<br/>
        </p>
    </card>
</wml>
```

This first section of this code places four WBMPs with different `align` attributes (including a default test) together between two dashes, with no line breaks in between. Next, we look at each of these WBMPs again, this time on separate lines, each surrounded by dashes. Finally, we try resizing the clock WBMP to 18x18, which is twice its original size. The simulated results are as follows:

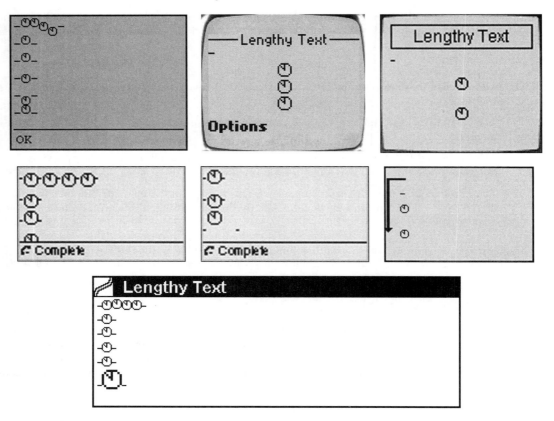

I've only included part of the displays from the Nokia, R320, and Motorola simulators, as the rest is pretty much the same. They place graphics on separate lines and seem to completely ignore the `align`, `height`, and `width` attributes.

The other simulators are much more interesting (note that there are two MME screenshots, as not all the data fitted into one screen), and we'll summarize those results shortly, but let's look at the real devices first:

 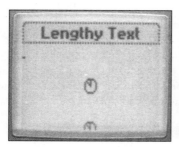 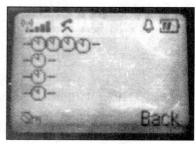

The Nokia and R320 devices behave just like their simulators – they ignore all attributes and just display images centered in a single column. The Motorola device, however, was rather more successful than its simulator.

For the browsers that didn't simply ignore the attributes on test, we can summarize:

❑ The UP.Simulator supports the align attribute, and keeps images in the text flow without adding extra line breaks. Note that the default align attribute for WBMPs is top, not middle as for built in graphics (which we saw in Chapter 7). height and width are not supported.

❑ The MME simulator keeps images inline with text, but ignores the align attribute for multiple images on a single line. Single images on lines of their own, on the other hand, *do* support this attribute. height and width cause a resizing of the space allotted for the image (the canvas), but they do not affect the image itself.

❑ The R380 simulator supports all attributes, although in this example the values middle and bottom for the align attribute resulted in the same display.

❑ The Motorola P7389 device seems to attempt alignment, but it's not very good at it. The screenshot shows that only the bottom alignment had any affect on the positioning of the clock image. The sizing attributes had no effect.

The recommendation, therefore, is that if you decide to use images, you should keep them on lines of their own, as this is the behavior of many existing browsers. This all adds weight to the recommendation of the usability chapter: use images sparingly!

Dealing with Different Methods of Navigation

The last sections have covered aesthetic issues, but what about the WML elements that have more functional intent? Unfortunately, these also have cross-browser problems. Almost every WAP application will involve some sort of navigation from one card to another, and there are several ways of achieving this from WML, as we have seen:

❑ Links using <anchor> or <a> elements containing text or images

❑ Softkeys linked to <go> elements

❑ onpick events in list selection elements

❑ Timed navigation

Apart from timed navigation, which works in exactly the same way on all the browsers tested (real and simulated), these methods can work quite differently on different phones – and look very different too. Let's look at some examples, starting with <anchor>-type links.

Anchor Links

WML hyperlinks can be specified using either <a> or <anchor> elements, the key difference being the additional versatility that <anchor> provides – if all you want is a basic link, just use <a>. In terms of *rendering* these two elements, we've found no differences between them on any browser. However, it's worth noting that some browsers include white space as part of a link, such that:

```
<a href="#destination" name="Go">Go</a>
```

Will be rendered differently from:

```
<a href="#destination" name="Go">
    Go
</a>
```

If you're using more complex links with the <anchor> element, it can be difficult to eliminate this additional white space and keep your code readable. Consistency is the key here: if one of your links is surrounded by white space, then make sure they all are – otherwise some browsers may make them look completely different from one another.

Anchor links, whether using <a> or <anchor>, can be used with plain text or images, simply by placing these items inside the anchor element. One thing we'd like to look at, then, is how the various browsers render text- and image-based links. In addition, the WML specification states that anchor links can occur *anywhere* in normal text flow. This is something else that we need to compare between devices.

Finally, both types of link can use the `title` attribute to provide a 'rendering suggestion' to the browser. As this is only a suggestion, it's worth seeing how the various vendors have approached it.

The deck we'll use to look at anchor links is structured to examine all of these points on our test browsers. The first three links are placed on separate lines, as a list of links. The next three links are placed in a body of text. The second and fifth links use an 8x8 WBMP image, `Link.wbmp`, which is simply:

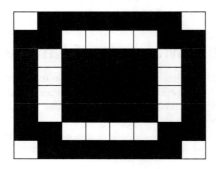

Finally, two links are placed closer together (separated by white space-dash-white space), to see if links can appear on the same line as each other on devices with small screens. The second of these links is surrounded by white space.

The code for the deck is as follows:

```
<wml>
   <card id="main" title="Anchor Links">
      <p>
         Now you've read this, try these:<br/>
         <a href="#link1" title="L1">Link1</a><br/>
         <a href="#link2"><img src="Link.wbmp" alt="Link2"/></a><br/>
         <a href="#link3">Link3</a><br/>
         <br/>
         text <a href="#link4" title="L4">Link4</a> text
         text <a href="#link5"><img src="Link.wbmp" alt="Link5"/></a> text
         text <a href="#link6">Link6</a> text<br/>
         <br/>
         <a href="#link7">L7</a>
         -
         <a href="#link8">
            L8
         </a>
      </p>
   </card>
</wml>
```

Note that the links in this deck won't work, because there are no destination cards defined. That's OK for this example, because we're really only worried about appearance – navigation works in all circumstances.

The results on the simulators are as follows, with screens artificially placed together for ease of viewing (screen size is not under investigation here):

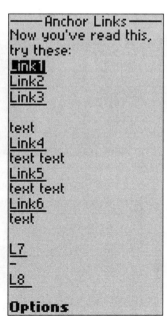

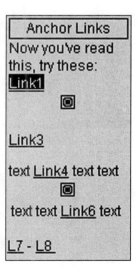

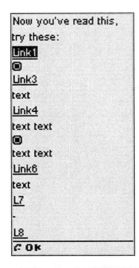
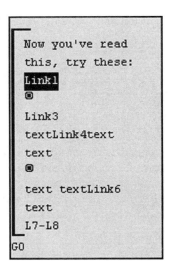

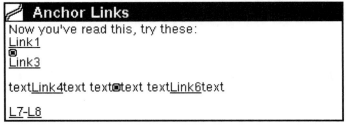

The real devices looked like this. First, the Nokia:

Next, the R320:

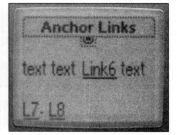

And finally, the Motorola:

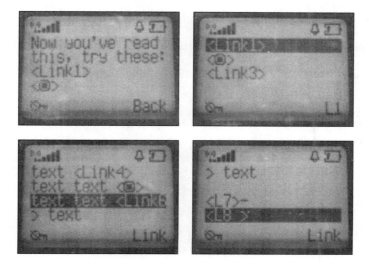

To summarize:

- ❑ Phone.com: each link is on a separate line (the cursor on the left requires this), but text is allowed to flow around links. Images work, although they are placed in slightly odd positions. The `title` attribute is used to label a softkey, which is labeled Link if the attribute isn't specified. White space included in the anchor element is transferred to the link display (although it's clipped to single characters) before and after the link text.

- ❑ Nokia 7110: the display is almost identical for both the simulator and real device. Each link is forced onto a line of its own, and images are not displayed (although, as we have seen, they *are* supported by the browser, and may be used elsewhere). Instead of images, the `alt` text is used for the link name. The `title` attribute is ignored. White space in anchor links is included after the link text.

- ❑ Ericsson R320: links appear in text, as specified in the WML file (this is possible because no vertical scrolling cursor is used). Linked images are placed in boxes centered on lines of their own. The `title` attribute is ignored. White space in anchor links is included after the link text in the emulator, although not in the real device.

- ❑ MME: each link is forced onto a line of its own, like the Nokia, but this time images are displayed (and function) correctly. The `title` attribute is ignored. White space in anchor links is included after the link text.

- ❑ Motorola P7389 simulator: textual links are placed in the flow of the text, although white space either side of them is clipped. Multiple textual links are allowed in single lines. Graphical links work, although selecting them doesn't result in a change of appearance. Graphical links appear on lines of their own. White space included in anchor links is clipped and not displayed on screen.

- ❑ Ericsson R380: links are placed in the text as specified in the WML, although white space is clipped either side of links. Images look fine and are functional. The `title` attribute is ignored. White space in anchor links is included before and after the link text.

393

❑ Motorola P7389 device: this looks a lot like the Phone.com simulator. The key difference is that angled brackets are used instead of square brackets to denote links (one of which has been forced onto a separate line, giving a slightly odd appearance).

So, if we want to present links in anchor form, we should (for acceptable functionality on current devices):

❑ Avoid images with links if possible, or at least supply sensible `alt` text

❑ Keep links out of body text

If we do this, we can expect to achieve a reasonable degree of consistency, although you might lose out in specific situations.

Softkey Links

Let's move on to a different method of navigation: links specified in `<do>` elements to be assigned to softkeys. We'll test this with the following code:

```
<wml>
   <card id="main" title="Softkey Links">
      <p>
         Now you've read this, try a link.
      </p>
      <do type="accept" label="Link1" name="link1">
         <go href="#link1"/>
      </do>
      <do type="accept" label="Link2" name="link2">
         <go href="#link2"/>
      </do>
      <do type="accept" label="Link3" name="link3">
         <go href="#link3"/>
      </do>
      <do type="accept" label="Link4" name="link4">
         <go href="#link4"/>
      </do>
   </card>
</wml>
```

Note that each of these `<do>` elements uses a different name *attribute. By default, the* name *attribute will use the value of the* type *attribute if unspecified. It is an error to specify multiple `<do>` elements with the same* name *attribute, which is what would happen if the* name *attributes were omitted from the above code. This error usually isn't fatal, but may cause some browsers to display only one of the `<do>` elements.*

The results are as follows (described for each device in turn, as multiple screens are often necessary).

The Phone.com browser chooses one link to display, and places the other links in a separate menu. Clicking on the Menu softkey gives access to these links. Note that the first link doesn't appear in the menu list:

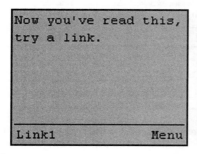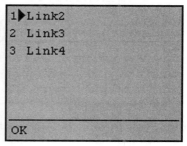

The Nokia 7110 places all these softkeys in an Options menu that, when accessed, lists the links along with other (phone specific) options. The user can then scroll down to the link desired, and select it:

The Ericsson R320 emulator gives no indication that the links exist at all! However, navigating to the phone menu shows that they are indeed there, mixed in with phone-specific options in a seemingly random order:

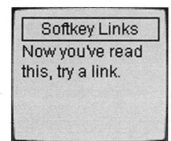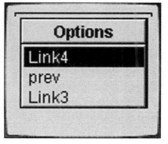

The MME browser displays the links in the form of buttons on the card:

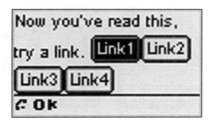

The Ericsson R380, like the MME device, displays the links in the form of buttons on the card:

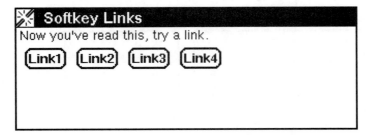

The Motorola P7389 has three softkeys. Two of them are used for the first two links; the other two are accessible through the third softkey, MENU. This is similar to the Phone.com simulator functionality shown above, which makes sense as the Motorola P7389 uses a Phone.com browser. Of course, as we have seen, the Motorola emulator doesn't normally provide such a good simulation as it does here:

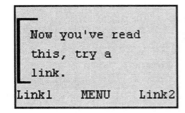 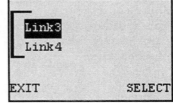

The real Nokia 7110 works just like its simulator:

As does the R320, although it appears to format the links better (they are ordered in the pop-up menu):

Finally, the Motorola P7389. Although this device has three softkeys, and the simulator used all three for <do> softkeys, the real device uses one for its 'non-secure connection' symbol, which doubles in most cases as a 'cancel' or 'back' option. The two other two softkeys function exactly like the Phone.com simulator:

 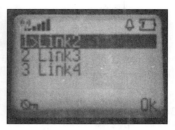

All the browsers on test treated multiple options-type *<do> elements in the same way as multiple* accept-type *ones. Changing one or all of the types in the WML file shown above will not affect the results.*

The Nokia 7110 and Ericsson R320 emulators and devices require two clicks to get to the next card, and don't give you any hints that these links exist! Yes, the 7110 has an Options menu, but it still doesn't explicitly mention that links exist here. If there is only *one* accept-type softkey, however, this *does* appear on screen, labeled appropriately. The Phone.com and Motorola browsers assign the first link to a softkey and the rest to a separate menu, although we can use this to our advantage in some circumstances by placing the most important link first. Again, though, there is no obvious clue as to what is contained in the menu.

The R380 and MME devices show the links as buttons, making for quite a nice user interface. However, this may cause confusion if other types of link are used as well – they will all appear in much the same place, but look different.

The recommendations here, then, are:

❑ Single softkeys can be used to good effect in most browsers, particularly in the Nokia and Phone.com browsers, as they will be easily selectable from anywhere in the card.

❑ Multiple softkeys can cause problems – but certainly have their uses. If you decide to use these, always place clues in the card text to make it clear that they exist (although, of course, doing this implies that your navigation system might be better served by more explicit links – see the later section).

Lists of Links

The third type of link to consider is a list entry field using onpick events. The code to do this is as follows:

```
<wml>
    <card id="main" title="List Links">
        <p>
            Now you've read this, try a link.
            <select title="Links">
                <option title="Link1" onpick="#link1">Link1</option>
                <option title="Link2" onpick="#link2">Link2</option>
```

```
                <option title="Link3" onpick="#link3">Link3</option>
                <option title="Link4" onpick="#link4">Link4</option>
            </select>
        </p>
    </card>
</wml>
```

Again, the results are varied. The Nokia 7110 shows a field that (when selected) gives a list of links. Selecting one of these links takes you directly to the target card:

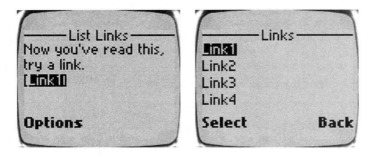

The Phone.com emulator shows the whole list straight away, allowing link selection either by scrolling to a link and selecting it, or by hitting the number assigned to the link. If you scroll to an option, the title attribute is used to label a softkey for selection:

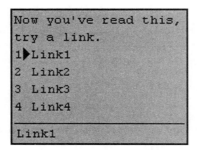

The MME emulator shows one item from the list in a field, and allows you to cycle through the available links using a **NEXT** softkey. Navigation is achieved by hitting the **SELECT** softkey:

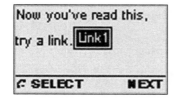

The R320 emulator shows a list entry field, along with its title (the word Select is used if no title is specified). Selecting this title pops up a menu for selecting and navigating to links:

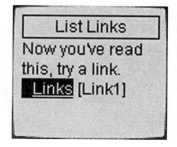 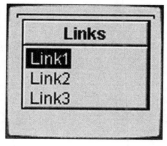

The R380 emulator shows a list selection field that conjures up a drop down list of links to select:

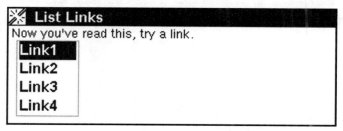

The Motorola emulator also supplies a field for selection, and then a list when this is selected. It uses the title attribute for the field in much the same way as the R320 emulator (if this attribute doesn't exist you'll see the text Select Item in the field). Also, similarly to the Phone.com simulator, links can be selected using their number when inside the field:

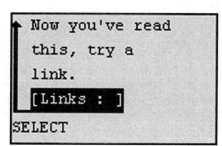 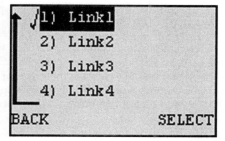

The real Nokia 7110 works just like its simulator:

As does the R320, although the appearance is again slightly different:

 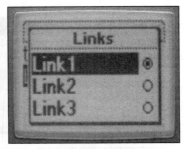

Once again, the Motorola P7389 works like the Phone.com simulator, not the Motorola one:

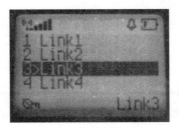

So, apart from the Phone.com emulator and the Motorola device, the results are all quite similar (this time, the R320 shows you that links are available): each device requires the user first to select the Links field, and then to select a link. The Phone.com interface is a dream: well laid out links, with quick access (for up to 10 links, at least) via a key press.

However, there are a couple of points to note regarding the UP.Browser. Firstly, as we saw in Chapter 10, the browser cannot display multiple selection fields, or a mix of list selection and user input fields, on the same card. In fact, *anything* that comes after the list field shown above will be placed on a separate card. Using lists like this may be great for navigation, but we'll have more decisions to make in the section on user input later in this chapter. Also, the UP.Browser places the cursor at the start of a list field on card entry, which might mean that text occurring earlier in the card does not get read.

> *One additional note on the way the Phone.com browser handles lists: it seems to ignore <do>-specified softkeys when the cursor is not positioned in the list. If you are in a body of text above the list, then no softkeys will appear!*

Should you choose this method of navigation? Well, it's not a bad choice for a series of links that can be grouped together logically, or for a menu of options, but it would hardly be suitable for a single link. Due to the way the Phone.com browser jumps to the start of the list, it is also not suitable if you have much information before the list starts, as it won't be seen by the user (unless they know to scroll upwards). At least this method works acceptably on all devices, though!

Navigation Summary

It seems as though each device manufacturer has decided what it thinks is the best way of navigating between cards, and made that method as easy as possible. Unfortunately, they didn't all choose the same method!

Perhaps it's slightly unfair to compare anchor links with the other two methods, since the underlying reasons for having links in the text are often different from having links in softkeys. Anchor links tend to be highly context-specific, occurring close to explanatory text, whereas softkey links are usually more general. Having said that, there is certainly some overlap: 'Home' links, for example, make sense both as a general link in a softkey, and as an anchor link at the end of a card.

The route you take when designing your sites is partly based on the data you want to present, but you should also take note of the information presented in the last sections. If you don't consider how things will look on multiple devices, then you *will* run into problems. We suggest the following:

❑ The majority of links in a card (especially independent ones – that is, contextual links that aren't part of a group) should be short, non-graphical anchor links (with `title` attributes).

❑ In general, softkeys should be kept to a minimum, as they can be difficult to find if there are a lot of them. If used for any means other than the very obvious, there should be notes in the text of the card telling the user that they exist.

❑ Groups of related links that occur either on a card of their own, or with little associated text, should be placed in list selection fields, making them easier to see and select than groups of softkeys. If anything else does appear on the card, it should be positioned *before* the list selection field, but keep this down to a couple of lines at most.

❑ Groups of related links that occur along with a larger amount of associated text should be placed in a series of short, non-graphical links – each on its own line, with a `title` attribute – or extracted onto a separate card.

❑ A small amount of redundancy is good in certain circumstances. For instance, a 'Home' link might be placed in a softkey *and* in an anchor at the end of a card.

This is better illustrated with an example. Let's imagine a gardening glossary site, the root card of which contains links to topics. One of these topics might be "Flowers", with some descriptive text, links to several specific flowers, and additional links to another topic ("Trees"), the home card, and a 'Back' softkey.

Let's take a look at the associated code, broken up into sections to explain the motivation for design choices:

```wml
<wml>
    <card id="flowers" title="Flowers">
        <p>
            Flowers are plants that have a specific flowering cycle and can
            often be pretty to look at. They are distinct from trees in that
            they are a lot smaller.
```

Here we want a cross-reference to `Trees.wml`, and as this is in context, the best solution is to use an anchor link. We also use a line break, as this will be forced on some browsers anyway:

```
<br/><a href="Trees.wml" title="Trees">(see Trees)</a>
```

After the anchor, we can continue the text, as this is supported on all browsers:

```
<br/>For more detailed information on specific flowers, choose one
from the list below. For other options see the options menu.
```

Next we come to our list of flowers. You might imagine that this would work best in a list selection field, but this will cause problems on Phone.com browsers (there is too much data before the list), so instead we use several anchor links on individual lines. We also need to limit the `title` attributes to six characters, to make sure they are displayable.

```
            <br/><a href="pansies.wml" title="Pansy">Pansies</a>
            <br/><a href="petunias.wml" title="Petun">Petunias</a>
            <br/><a href="roses.wml" title="Roses">Roses</a>
            <br/><a href="daffodils.wml" title="Daffs">Daffodils</a>
            <br/><a href="daisies.wml" title="Daisy">Daisies</a>
        </p>
```

It's always worth including a **Back** link:

```
        <do type="prev" label="Back">
            <prev/>
        </do>
```

Finally, we have some options that are accessible via softkeys – these are mentioned in the text, so the user should being able to find them. Because it's possible that the first one of these will be displayed while the rest are placed in a separate menu, we locate the most useful one, **Menu**, first:

```
        <do type="options" label="Menu" name="Menu">
            <go href="Menu.wml"/>
        </do>
        <do type="options" label="Weeds" name="Weeds">
            <go href="Weeds.wml"/>
        </do>
        <do type="options" label="Trees" name="Trees">
            <go href="Trees.wml"/>
        </do>
    </card>
</wml>
```

This code satisfies all the suggestions we made above, so how does it look? Here are some screenshots that, where appropriate, we've artificially stretched to show the complete content.

The Phone.com browser looks like this, allowing navigation to the Trees link and any flower from anchor links on the card, and to other links by following the Menu softkey:

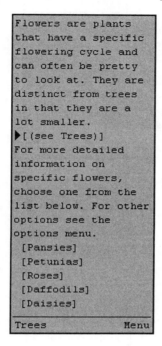
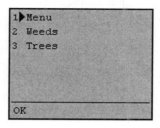

The Nokia 7110 works in pretty much the same way, although this time the Options softkey takes us to the extra links, which are mixed in with the standard Nokia options menu:

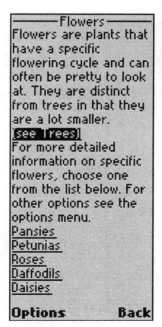
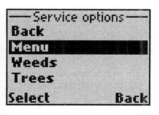

The R320 simulator is the same, although getting to the options menu is not obvious. This is aided by the fact that the text refers to the options available there:

> **Flowers**
> Flowers are plants that have a specific flowering cycle and can often be pretty to look at. They are distinct from trees in that they are a lot smaller. **(see Trees)** For more detailed information on specific flowers, choose one from the list below. For other options see the options menu.
> Pansies
> Petunias
> Roses
> Daffodils
> Daisies

> **Options**
> Back
> Menu
> Weeds

In this case, the Motorola simulator works quite well too, allowing simple selection of everything again:

> Flowers are plants that have a specific flowering cycle and can often be pretty to look at. They are distinct from trees in that they are a lot smaller. (see Trees) For more detailed information on specific flowers, choose one from the list below. For other options see the options menu.
> Pansies
> Petunias
> Roses
> Daffodils
> Daisies
> GO   MENU   Menu

> Weeds
> Trees
> Back
> EXIT   SELECT

The MME simulator contains all the links on a single card, with the softkeys formatted slightly differently from the anchor links, but functioning in the same way.

Flowers are plants that have a specific flowering cycle and can often be pretty to look at. They are distinct from trees in that they are a lot smaller.
see Trees
For more detailed information on specific flowers, choose one from the list below. For other options see the options menu.
Pansies
Petunias
Roses
Daffodils
Daisies
Back
Menu
Weeds
Trees
OK

Finally, the R380, which is similar to the MME simulator, but slightly better laid out:

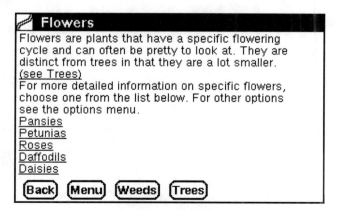

The Nokia 7110 works just like the simulator, but here are a few screenshots that prove the point. First, the main text and link screen:

Next, the options menu:

Screens from the Ericsson R320 show that once again, it's just like its simulator:

Finally, the Motorola, which again looks (and functions) a lot like the Phone.com simulator:

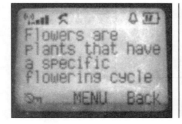  

In all cases, selection is simple, and options are readily available to take different navigation paths. The display is also simple throughout, with no problems in functionality between browsers.

Remember, if there wasn't so much text above the list of flowers it would be worth considering a list selection field, although non-Phone.com browsers would work slightly less efficiently here.

Additional Notes: Going Back

There are a couple of points to note concerning the use of 'Back' softkeys. First, only the Phone.com browser returns the user to *exactly* the right place – that is, the precise position in the previous card that was being viewed. For example, if the user had reached the end of a passage of text and followed an anchor link from the bottom, the <prev/> element (or other methods of going back through the history stack) will result in the display being returned to the end of this passage. This makes sense, but also makes it tricky for developers, as the behavior only occurs in the UP.Browser (and therefore, of the devices tested in this chapter, only the Motorola P7389).

In addition, different browsers place different requirements on developers when it comes to implementing 'Back' functionality. Using a Nokia 7110, it's sufficient to use this code:

```
<do type="prev">
    <prev/>
</do>
```

The Nokia automatically labels the softkey Back, and places it in a unique, accessible position. However, other browsers require you to enter the label attribute manually:

```
<do type="prev" label="Back">
    <prev/>
</do>
```

If you don't do this, they fail to label the softkey correctly. By default, the Phone.com browser labels a back softkey as OK (which isn't very helpful), although the Motorola implementation uses a key or crossed out key instead (doubling as an indication of connection security). The MME browser labels a softkey with SUBMIT (also not great), the R380 uses prev (better), and the R320 doesn't let you know there's a 'Back' option at all unless you pop up the built-in menu. Even with the second version of the code, the Phone.com browser still labels the softkey as OK, and the R380 still labels its one as prev. We can get the Phone.com browser to work 'correctly' by using a type="accept" softkey instead, but this doesn't work on the R380, and causes the Nokia to place the 'Back' option in its Options menu – so there doesn't seem to be an ideal solution.

Softkeys are not always the only way to navigate backwards. The real devices on test all had built-in ways of going back, either by using specific keys on the phone (in the case of the R320), or making this option available via menu options, without the need for additional code.

Other Issues

In addition to text and navigation issues, we have just a few other points to cover:

❑ WMLScript support

❑ User input

❑ Graphic alignment

WMLScript Support

Not all devices support WMLScript, which, having read through the WMLScript sections of this book, you will probably agree is a shame. The list of device characteristics mentioned earlier in this chapter, to be found at http://www.anywhereyougo.com/ayg/ayg/wap/devices/Index.po, includes this information and is worth a look if you are deciding whether to use WMLScript. This may well involve further consideration of your user base, as well as the pros and cons of using WMLScript in your specific application.

WMLScript is supported on all of the real devices under test in this chapter – we were able successfully to play the Hangman example from Chapter 12 on each of them. However, it behaved a little oddly on the Motorola – it seemed to freeze whenever a WMLScript function was called, and required hanging up and then viewing the card again to get to the next screen. This was quite quick, as both `Hangman.wml` and `Hangman.wmls` had been cached (so no reconnection was necessary), but very annoying. This would be far more serious if multiple script files were used in a large application, so we find it hard to recommend using WMLScript on the P7389.

In general, then, we can't rely on WMLScript support. The best recommendation here is not to use scripting for critical functionality unless you're sure that your users have appropriate devices.

User Input

Probably the main issue regarding user input is that the Phone.com browsers (including the one in the Motorola P7389 device) do not allow more than one input field (`<input>` or `<select>` element) to be displayed on screen at one time, as we have seen over the course or this book. Other browsers do.

Let's take a quick look at this situation, using the following simple deck:

```
<wml>
    <card id="card1" title="Enter Details">
        <p>
            Enter Name:
            <input name="username" title="Name"/>
            Choose Sex:
            <select name="sex" title="Sex">
                <option value="Male" title="Male">Male</option>
                <option value="Female" title="Female">Female</option>
                <option value="?" title="Not">Not saying</option>
                <option value="?" title="?">Don't know</option>
            </select>
            <a href="#card2" title="Next">Next</a>
        </p>
    </card>
    <card id="card2" title="Results">
        <p>
            Name: $(username)<br/>
            Sex: $(sex)
        </p>
    </card>
</wml>
```

On the Phone.com browser, we initially see only the first `<input>` field, and we can enter data into this field that is immediately displayed in the card:

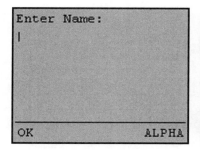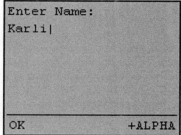

When we select **OK**, we move to the next field:

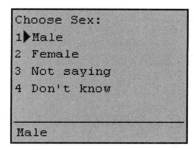

After making a selection here, we reach the end of the first card, containing a **Next** link. Following this takes us to the next card:

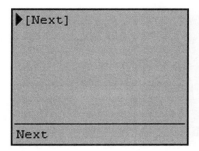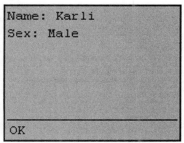

Most other browsers (for example, one in the Nokia 7110) show the whole first card. Let's look at the Nokia 7110 simulator (the actual device behaves identically):

Scrolling down, the Next link also appears on the same screen. We can select each of the fields in turn, adding details and returning to this card. First, the Name field:

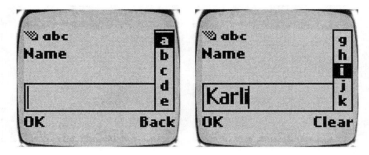

And then the Sex field:

Finally, we can follow the Next link, and reach the second card:

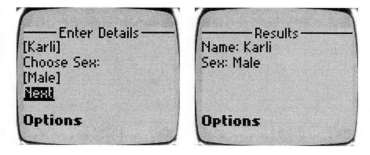

The Phone.com interface is perhaps simpler, but the Nokia interface allows you to go back and edit values in a more sensible fashion. As mentioned earlier, most browsers use the same system as the Nokia. If the UI you've designed is particularly bad on *any* device, it might be worth redesigning. In general though, as long as the information can always be entered without any major usability hitches, you should be all right.

On a similar note, it's worth looking briefly at support for the `format` attribute of the `<input>` element. In theory, this is a very useful tool, allowing implicit validation of entered data (to some degree), and accelerated data entry by restricting entry to (for example) numeric characters and adding standard symbols (like dashes in Social Security Numbers) automatically. Unfortunately, only the Phone.com and R320 browsers seem to handle this attribute correctly.

The other browsers allow you to enter data that doesn't fit the format attribute, and then proceed either to ignore input and leave the field blank, or to fill the field with the incorrect data without validation. Both of these behaviors can cause problems, especially as in all these cases there is no automatically provided clue to inform the user as to how the input *should* be formatted. The best solution is to provide extra information in the text containing the <input> element, detailing how the input should be formatted. We did this in the last chapter for a date entry:

```
<wml>
    <card id="date" title="Date Entry">
        <p>
            Enter a date between September and October 2001 in MM/DD/YYYY format:
            <input name="date" format="NN\/NN\/\2\0\0\1"/>
            <do type="accept" label="Submit">
                <go href="date.wmls#validate('$(date:unesc)')"/>
            </do>
        </p>
    </card>
</wml>
```

Specifying "MM/DD/YYYY" here lets the user know what is expected of them. We could make this even better by using the title attribute of the <input> element, which (as we saw above) is used in the text entry field on the Nokia 7110. Changing the above code to:

```
<input name="date" format="NN\/NN\/\2\0\0\1" title="MM/DD/YYYY"/>
```

Gives us the following on the Nokia 7110 (simulator and device):

This allows us to see very clearly what is necessary (even though the Nokia browser doesn't fill in the automatic characters for us). In this particular example, it might be worth changing the input field to require just a day and month (as the year is fixed), or even letting the user enter this data using <select> fields, but the above technique is definitely sound for general date entry.

Finally, it's worth pointing out the variation in the support for various elements and attributes on a few devices. In Chapter 10, we saw how we can include <optgroup> elements inside <select> fields, but noted that this didn't result in any change of behavior in the Phone.com browser. Other browsers *do* take note of this element. Let's take a look at the <select> element we used to look at this in Chapter 10 again.

```wml
<wml>
  <card>
    <p>
      Select fish:
      <select name="fish" iname="ifish" multiple="true">
        <optgroup title="Battered">
          <option value="BH">Halibut</option>
          <option value="BC">Cod</option>
        </optgroup>
        <optgroup title="Roasted">
          <option value="RM">Monkfish</option>
          <option value="RC">Cod</option>
          <option value="RT">Trout</option>
        </optgroup>
      </select>
      Done.
    </p>
  </card>
</wml>
```

The Nokia displays `<optgroup>` elements separately, allowing us to navigate down the option hierarchy, selecting fish in the groups they were meant to be in:

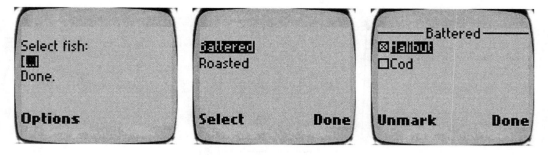

On the Ericsson R380 simulator, you get the whole list presented, including hierarchical headings, allowing simple selection of any fish:

Still, this isn't functionality you should rely on in your `<select>` elements, or you might be in for a surprise on a Phone.com browser!

Summary

In this chapter, we've looked at ways in which WML rendering differs between browsers, both simulated and real. We have seen that we can't always write exactly the code we want to. Sometimes, we need to compromise due to device-specific limitations.

Many of the sections in this chapter have provided tips to help you design code that will work acceptably on multiple devices, but this may leave you thinking that you are targeting the 'lowest common denominator', and missing out on the useful facilities provided by certain devices.

One way round this is to provide different WML cards for different devices, perhaps even providing different URLs. However, this hardly seems ideal, and would certainly make users think twice about visiting our sites.

In the next chapter, we will see some much better alternatives that are made possible by generating our WML content dynamically, using ASP. When we do this, it is possible to detect what type of browser is viewing our site. Armed with that knowledge, we can either send the browser to a WML file designed specifically for that browser (avoiding the need for multiple URLs), or even tailor the content of a single file based on the device that is displaying it. You could decide, for example, to send different content to devices equipped with the UP.Browser – perhaps using techniques that only work on these devices.

ASP and Dynamic WAP Sites

Over the course of this book, we have been using WML and WMLScript to develop WAP applications. However, the WML and WMLScript files we've used have been static, not dynamic: once we have created them, they stay the same. While WMLScript provides interactivity for the user, it does not allow dynamic content to be displayed.

To cite an example, you might be writing a WAP application that allows users to check on current stock prices. In this case, using WML and WMLScript, you would need to create a new card every time the stock prices change. As stock prices changes frequently, this is clearly not feasible.

In a truly dynamic WAP application, all the stock prices and other information would be stored in a database accessible to the web server. Based on user input, the web server could perform server-side processing and generate a deck containing the information that the user requires. A technology that allows us to do this is Microsoft's **Active Server Pages** (**ASP**).

In this chapter, we will take a look at:

❑ Microsoft's Active Server Pages (ASP) and its use in the development of dynamic WAP applications

❑ Using ActiveX Data Objects (ADO) together with ASP to access a database from the web server

❑ Extending the Wrox Travel application

Overview of Active Server Pages (ASP)

Internet access, as we have seen it so far in this book, has involved the following steps:

❑ A WAP browser asks for a file from the server

❑ The server sends this file to the browser

Dynamic content generation, such as is possible with ASP, introduces an additional step:

- ❑ A WAP browser asks for a file from the server
- ❑ *The server generates the file requested*
- ❑ The server sends this file to the browser

To request a deck that will be generated using ASP, the browser needs to ask the server for a file called *something*.asp, rather than *something*.wml. ASP files will contain some 'ordinary' WML, but they also contain script code (not WMLScript, but something similar) that, when executed, inserts the dynamic information into the file. Because this happens at the moment the .asp file is requested, the information being inserted can be completely up-to-date. When the deck leaves the server on its way back to the WAP-enabled device, it looks just like any other WML deck —it's what happens on the server that's different.

The last thing to add before we begin is that, provided you've installed one of the web servers we mentioned in Chapter 1 (Internet Information Server or Personal Web Server), you already have everything you need to create and use Active Server Pages. All the code in this chapter will be compatible ASP version 2.0; although more recent versions exist, there are no issues of backward compatibility.

By default, both servers create directories in your hard drive that correspond to the following file path:

```
c:\inetpub\wwwroot
```

This directory is where you should put the ASP files we will be creating here. Let's see some ASP in action.

Try It Out — Generating a WML File using ASP

1. Enter the following code using your text editor. ASP files can safely be placed in the same directory that we specified for WML files in Chapter 1 – inetpub\wwwroot – so save it there with the name hellowml.asp:

```
<%@ Language = "JScript"; %><% Response.ContentType = "text/vnd.wap.wml";
%><?xml version="1.0"?>
<!DOCTYPE wml PUBLIC "-//WAPFORUM//DTD WML 1.2//EN"
                    "http://www.wapforum.org/DTD/wml_1.2.xml">

<wml>
   <card>
      <p>
         My First WML application with ASP, generated:
<% Response.Write(Date()); %>
      </p>
   </card>
</wml>
```

2. Load this file into the Phone.com UP.Simulator using http://localhost/hellowml.asp. Note that ASP *requires* that you load it from the web server with an HTTP request, so if you try to enter a URL like file:///c:/inetpub/wwwroot/hellowml.asp, this example *will not work*.

The resulting file looks like this:

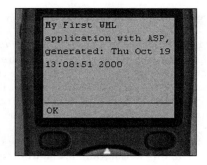

How It Works

As you can see, we've successfully viewed an ASP page on our browser, just as we would look at a WML deck. In fact, looking at the code we've used, we can see that it does indeed contain an entire WML deck. The only difference is the presence of the extra code that's delimited by `<%` and `%>` marks:

```
<%@ Language = "JScript"; %>
```

```
<% Response.ContentType = "text/vnd.wap.wml"; %>
```

```
<% Response.Write(Date()); %>
```

If the browser were actually to receive a WML file that started with '`<%`' instead of an XML declaration, it wouldn't work. What happens is that, as a server processes ASP files, these sections of code are processed and then removed or replaced. The file that reaches the browser is pure WML – in this case, as follows:

```
<?xml version="1.0"?>
<!DOCTYPE wml PUBLIC "-//WAPFORUM//DTD WML 1.2//EN"
                     "http://www.wapforum.org/DTD/wml_1.2.xml">

<wml>
    <card>
        <p>
          My First WML application with ASP, generated:
Thu Oct 19 13:08:51 2000
        </p>
    </card>
</wml>
```

The third piece of ASP code, `Response.Write(Date());`, has been replaced with the text "Thu Oct 19 13:08:51 2000" – but what happened to the rest?

The first section of ASP code specifies the language that the rest of the ASP code is written in. We'll see why this is necessary in the next section, but we will be using JScript.

The second section of ASP code tells the server what MIME type it should send to the browser. As you can see, we have used `text/vnd.wap.wml` — which is the type we associated with the `.wml` extension in Chapter 1. When the browser sees that it is receiving content of this type, it knows to expect WML code.

`Response.ContentType = "text/vnd.wap.wml";` is *the most important* line to remember when writing ASP generated WAP applications. When plain WML files are passed to the browser, the server sends the relevant MIME type automatically, which it gets from the configuration file we set up. The browser checks that it is able to read the file using this information. The MIME type that is sent when ASP files are requested is negotiable, but the default is usually set to `text/html` — HTML files. We override this using the code above; if we don't, the browser will report an error.

> **Note that the ASP file shown in this section contains no white space between the code specifying the content type and the XML declaration — not even an end of line character. This is important, because some gateways will simply refuse to process WML files if there is *anything* before the XML declaration.**

ASP Internals

What we've seen so far has shown that we can use ASP to embed executable script code in our files, and generate documents of the appropriate type by setting the MIME type to be transmitted. What we haven't looked at yet is the form that this extra processing takes, apart from being enclosed in `<%` and `%>` braces.

There is no specific 'ASP language' that we need to learn in order to write ASP files. In fact, it's possible to use a number of different scripting languages. By default, a language called VBScript is expected, but JScript can be used as well.

> *We're not going to go into detail about the scripting languages you can use; there are already plenty of books devoted to the subject. Here, we'll concentrate on the way in which ASP can be used in WAP applications, and the benefits it can provide. The details contained in other ASP books can then be used to build on this, even if they're not WAP-specific — you'll have enough grounding from this book to make use of the information.*

Like WMLScript, JScript is a derivative of ECMAScript, which we met (briefly) in Chapter 11. We'll be using JScript throughout this chapter, and you'll soon see that its syntax shares a lot of common features with the WMLScript you're familiar with. For example, each line of JScript code ends in a semicolon, the syntax for looping and decision-making structures is identical, and "`//`" is used to indicate a comment. One point worth noting, however, is that you don't have to declare variables using `var` in JScript. Instead, rather like WML variables, they come into being on the first occasion you use them.

One new thing we do have to discuss, though, is the concept of **objects**. Whatever language we use to put scripting code in ASP documents, they all make use of the **built-in objects** that ASP supplies. It is through these objects that much of the functionality of ASP is available. In fact, we've already used one of these objects – the `Response` object – when we set the content type for WML and wrote out the date and time in the example in the last section.

As you can see from the brevity of code in the last example, using objects isn't terribly difficult, but it is definitely an advantage to know what objects are, and how to use them. This knowledge applies to more than just the ASP objects; it will be essential when we look at database access later in the chapter.

Objects

Software 'objects', as a programming concept, have been around for some time now. They form the basis of modern object-oriented programming languages, which can be used to *create* objects. The language we will be using in this chapter, JScript, is not one of these, but we can still use it to *access* objects.

Object-oriented programming represents discrete processes as objects. Objects have **properties**, which describe the object, and **methods**, which are actions that you can carry out on the object. To understand what that means a little more clearly, consider the analogy of a car:

❏ You can *drive* a car, *reverse* it, *lock* it, and so on. Each of these actions could be described as a 'method' of a car object.

❏ A car has a *color*, it has *weight*, and it also has a *value*. Each of these characteristics is a 'property' of a car object.

The most important aspect of using a software object is that you're shielded from the details of the action you're requesting. You don't need to understand the mechanics of how a car works in order to drive from home to the office, and in the same way you don't need to know how objects work – merely how to use them.

Using objects in JScript is simple. It looks a lot like the way we accessed library functions in WMLScript, which isn't a bad analogy either – the objects of ASP are providing us with default functionality, just like WMLScript's libraries. We simply write the name of the object, a period, and then the name of the function or property we want to access, along with any parameters.

The ASP `Response` object that we used in the last section, for example, has a large number of methods and properties, including the ones we accessed in the example code. First, we set the `ContentType` *property* of the `Response` object:

```
Response.ContentType = "text/vnd.wap.wml";
```

And later, we called the `Write()` method of the `Response` object:

```
Response.Write(Date());
```

> *When talking about properties and methods, it is usual to include parentheses at the end of method names, to distinguish them from properties.*

The ASP Built-in Objects

Like the car object we considered in the last section, the built-in objects in ASP are designed to shield the developer from the underlying implementation of ASP. Rather, in order to develop ASP applications, the developer just needs to know how to manipulate the methods and properties of the objects provided.

ASP 2.0 supplies six built-in objects, and we'll use the following five over the course of this chapter:

❑ `Request` – stores the information received from the browser during an HTTP request

❑ `Response` – used to send information back to the browser

❑ `Application` – allows several files to be considered as a single 'application', allowing the sharing of information between them

❑ `Session` – allows information pertaining to a user session to be saved

❑ `Server` – controls the behavior of the script at the server

We couldn't possibly detail how all of these objects work in this chapter; we'll just see enough for you to get started making ASP WAP applications, dipping into the capabilities of the objects as and when necessary. The sixth object, `ObjectContext`, will not be covered at all – its use is quite advanced, and not required for the examples in this chapter.

Basic WML Generation with ASP

To start off with, let's look at how we can generate WML with ASP, building on the example from the first section of this chapter. The most useful method for this purpose is the one we used in the example above, `Response.Write()`. We can use this function to output the string it takes as a parameter into the WML content returned to the browser. For example:

```
<wml>
    <card id="hello">
        <p>
            <% Response.Write("Hello there!"); %>
        </p>
    </card>
</wml>
```

Which results in:

```
<wml>
    <card id="hello">
        <p>
            Hello there!
        </p>
    </card>
</wml>
```

Also, because no XML validation occurs until *after* the ASP code has been processed, we can also include elements in this method call:

```
<% Response.Write("<wml><card id="hello"><p>Hello there!</p></card></wml>"); %>
```

This would result in exactly the same WML as above, although it's not as nicely formatted. We can also use the `Write()` method to output the result of a function, as we saw earlier:

```
<% Response.Write(Date());
```

Here, the `Date()` function returns a string representing the current date and time, and the `Write()` function simply places this string into the WML content.

As we mentioned earlier, JScript has the same looping capabilities as WMLScript, and we can use these to generate large quantities of WML with just a few lines of code. In Chapter 10, for example, we had a data entry card in which the user was given the opportunity to select the number of places required in a vacation booking using a `<select>` element. This involved quite a lot of WML, as we needed to specify 10 `<option>` elements:

```
<select name="N" title="Places">
    <option value="1">1</option>
    <option value="2">2</option>
    ...
    <option value="10">10</option>
</select>
```

Using JScript in ASP, we could write:

```
<select name="N" title="Places">
<%
    for (place = 1; place <= 10; place++)
    {
        Response.Write("\n<option value=\"" + place + "\">" + place + </option>");
    }
%>
</select>
```

This would result in the same WML code – and the longer the list, the more efficient this method becomes! In another application, we could use JScript's decision-making structures, using `if...else`, to generate ordinals rather than cardinals. For example:

```
<select name="N" title="Places">
<%
    for (place = 1; place <= 10; place++)
    {
        if (place >= 4)
        {
            suffix = "th";
        }
        else
        {
            if (place == 1)
            {
                suffix = "st";
            }
```

```
        if (place == 2)
        {
            suffix = "nd";
        }
        if (place == 3)
        {
            suffix = "rd";
        }
    }
    Response.Write("\n<option value=\"" + place + "\">" + place +
                       suffix + "</option>");
    }
%>
</select>
```

This would result in the following list of options:

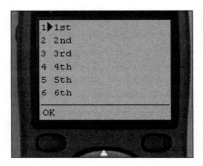

Sending Data to ASP Files

The one-line description of the `Request` object we saw earlier said that it stores the information received from the browser during an HTTP request. This includes some data that's always present – such as the name of the file being requested – but it's possible to send extra, custom information too, in effect transmitting data from the browser to the ASP file. We can then act on this data, perhaps using it for database access, decision-making, etc. In this section, we will look at the ways that we can use WML to send information to an ASP file, and the ways of extracting and using this data.

There are two ways to send data to an ASP file, depending on the **HTTP method** used in the request. The HTTP method specifies the format of the HTTP request, as well as the type of response that is required. There are several different methods available, but only two that we can use from WML: **GET** and **POST**. GET is the default, and therefore it's what we've been using in the book so far.

The main difference between GET and POST is that GET-type HTTP requests encode the data as part of the URL, whereas POST-type HTTP requests send data in the **message body**. The latter provides additional space for data to be sent to web servers, which is why we haven't looked at it until now – we haven't needed to send anything to the server.

> *At the time of writing, only GET requests are reliable in WAP-related software. It appears that vendors have been slow in implementing POST functionality in their devices and gateways. If you need to use POST requests, make sure you test them on as many devices and gateways as possible to make sure that they work.*

WML provides a simple way to send information to ASP files using either GET or POST requests, using `<postfield>` elements contained in `<go>` elements.

The *<postfield>* Element

The `<postfield>` element is used to specify the data to be transmitted as part of an HTTP request. Specifically, this data takes the form of name-value pairs. ASP files can then extract the values from this data, as we will see later.

`<postfield>` elements are always contained in `<go>` elements, and their syntax is identical to `<setvar>`, which also uses the name and value attributes.

The format in which data is sent to the server is determined by the method attribute of the `<go>` element that contains the `<postfield>` elements. This defaults to GET, so the following code will send two name-value pairs to login.asp

```
<go href="Login.asp">
   <postfield name="UserID" value="$(UserID)"/>
   <postfield name="Password" value="$(Password)"/>
</go>
```

Alternatively, we could write this:

```
<go href="Login.asp" method="post">
   <postfield name="UserID" value="$(UserID)"/>
   <postfield name="Password" value="$(Password)"/>
</go>
```

And encode the two name-value pairs in the request message body.

Try It Out — Sending Data in an HTTP Request using WML

Let's create a WML file that uses this code and try it out. For now we won't create an ASP file to receive the data we send – we'll do that in the next section.

1. Enter the following WML deck using your text editor, and save it in inetpub\wwwroot\ login.wml:

```
<%@ Language = "JScript"; %><% Response.ContentType = "text/vnd.wap.wml";
%><?xml version="1.0"?>
<!DOCTYPE wml PUBLIC "-//WAPFORUM//DTD WML 1.2//EN"
                     "http://www.wapforum.org/DTD/wml_1.2.xml">
<wml>
   <card id="login" title="Log In">
      <p>
         Name = $(UserID)<br/>
         Password = $(Password)<br/>
         <a title="Edit" href="#details">Edit Details</a><br/>
         Send data via:<br/>
```

```
        <anchor title="GET">
            GET
          <go href="login.asp">
              <postfield name="UserID" value="$(UserID)"/>
              <postfield name="Password" value="$(Password)"/>
          </go>
        </anchor><br/>
        <anchor title="POST">
            POST
          <go href="login.asp" method="post">
              <postfield name="UserID" value="$(UserID)"/>
              <postfield name="Password" value="$(Password)"/>
          </go>
        </anchor>
    </p>
 </card>
 <card id="details" title="Edit Details">
    <p>
        Enter name:
        <input name="UserID" title="Name"/><br/>
        Enter password:
        <input name="Password" title="Password"/>
        <a href="#login" title="Done">Done</a>
    </p>
 </card>
</wml>
```

2. Load this file in the UP.Simulator, follow the Edit Details link, and enter a name and password:

3. Follow the GET link, and look at the Phone Information window:

```
Phone Information                                                    _□×
cache miss: {
                <HTTP://LOCALHOST/Login.asp?UserID=Weimeng&Password=S
                  ecret>
            }
net request: {
                <HTTP://LOCALHOST/Login.asp?UserID=Weimeng&Password=S
                  ecret>
            }
HTTP GET Request: HTTP://LOCALHOST/Login.asp?UserID=Weimeng&Password=Secret
```

4. Go back, follow the POST link and look at the Phone Information window again:

```
Phone Information                                              _ | □ | x |
cache miss: <HTTP://LOCALHOST/Login.asp?0oc=106>
net request: <HTTP://LOCALHOST/Login.asp?0oc=106>

HTTP POST Request: HTTP://LOCALHOST/Login.asp
POST Data:
UserID=Weimeng&Password=Secret
```

How It Works

When we follow either the GET or POST links, we are sending two name-value pairs to the server as part of a request for Login.asp. If we use the GET method, we can see the values as part of the URL requested by the browser, which is displayed in the status window:

```
HTTP://LOCALHOST/Login.asp?UserID=Weimeng&Password=Secret
```

The URL of the ASP file is followed by a "?" then each "name=value" pair separated by "&" characters. This string, which contains the data and is appended to the URL, is known as a **query string**.

For the POST method, the status window shows this URL:

```
HTTP://LOCALHOST/Login.asp?0oc=106
```

Don't worry about the "?0oc=106"; the important part is the section below, where the data transmitted as part of the request is detailed:

```
POST Data:
UserID=Weimeng&Password=Secret
```

Of course, both methods ended up with the HTTP Error 404, because Login.asp doesn't yet exist. We'll build that file after we've looked at how we can get at this data from ASP.

Retrieving Data in ASP Files

To retrieve the values sent via an HTTP request, we can use the Request object. Data sent using GET can be retrieved using the Request object's QueryString() method; if data has been sent using POST, we can retrieve it using the Form() method.

The syntax for Request.QueryString() is:

```
value = Request.QueryString("name");
```

While the syntax for using Request.Form() is:

```
value = Request.Form("name");
```

In either case, *value* will hold the value associated with the *name*, if one exists. *value* will contain an empty string if there is no value associated with it, or *name* does not exist.

To test whether a given name-value pair exists, we can look at the `Count` property of the object returned by `QueryString()` or `Form()`:

```
NameNumber = Request.QueryString("name").Count;
```

or:

```
NameNumber = Request.Form("name").Count;
```

But wait: this is new syntax – there are *two* periods in those expressions on the right hand side! What's happening here is that we're requesting the value of the `Count` property of the *object* returned by `Request.Form()`. But why does this work?

In the previous example, `Request.Form()` appeared to returned a string, which we assigned to a variable called *value*. In reality, however, this method (and `Request.QueryString()`) returns not a string, but a new object with a **default property** that contains a string. When we 'store' the object in a variable, what actually gets stored is the value of the default property. In order to store the value of the `Count` property, we have to specify it by name.

NameNumber will contain 0 if *name* doesn't exist, and 1 if it does. If the value is greater than 1, then there is more than one name-value pair with the same name. If this is the case, then the value returned by `QueryString()` or `Form()` will be a comma-separated list of the values.

Try It Out — Retrieving Data Sent in an HTTP Request Using ASP

Let's put this code into action and create an ASP file that receives the data sent by our last example.

1. Enter the following code using your text editor, and save it in `inetpub\wwwroot\login.asp`:

```
<%@ Language = "JScript"; %><% Response.ContentType = "text/vnd.wap.wml";
%><?xml version="1.0"?>
<!DOCTYPE wml PUBLIC "-//WAPFORUM//DTD WML 1.2//EN"
                     "http://www.wapforum.org/DTD/wml_1.2.xml">

<wml>
    <head>
        <meta forua="true" http-equiv="Pragma"
                           content="no-cache"/>
        <meta forua="true" http-equiv="Cache-Control"
                           content="no-cache, must-revalidate"/>
    </head>
<%
    if (Request.QueryString("UserID").Count == 1)
    {
        UserID = Request.QueryString("UserID");
        Password = Request.QueryString("Password");
        methodUsed = "GET";
    }
```

```
      if (Request.Form("UserID").Count == 1)
      {
         UserID = Request.Form("UserID");
         Password = Request.Form("Password");
         methodUsed = "POST";
      }

      if (UserID == "")
      {
%>
   <card id="result" title="Error!">
      <p>
         You must enter a user name!
      </p>
<%
      }
      else
      {
         if ((UserID == "Weimeng") && (Password == "Secret"))
         {
%>
   <card id="result" title="Welcome!">
      <p>
         Hello Weimeng!<br/>
<%
         }
         else
         {
%>
   <card id="result" title="Sorry!">
      <p>
         Sorry <% Response.Write(UserID); %>, your password was not
         recognized. Please try again.<br/>
<%
         }
%>
         You sent information using HTTP <% Response.Write(methodUsed); %>.
      </p>
<%
      }
%>
      <do type="prev" label="Back">
         <prev/>
      </do>
   </card>
</wml>
```

2. Once again, open `login.wml` in your UP.Simulator, and type a name and password:

427

3. Select the GET or POST link. This time, you'll see:

How It Works

The code starts off with the standard ASP language and content type declaration. Next, we ensure that caching is prevented on the client by using the <meta> tag, as covered in Chapter 16, to prevent the browser from loading data from memory. If we don't do this, we'll get the same result for every subsequent request, regardless of the request type.

In this next section of code, we check whether the data was sent via POST or GET, using the technique we outlined earlier. In either case, data is extracted and placed in two variables: UserID and Password. We also set a third variable which stores the request method used.

```
<%
    if (Request.QueryString("UserID").Count == 1)
    {
        UserID = Request.QueryString("UserID");
        Password = Request.QueryString("Password");
        methodUsed = "GET";
    }
    if (Request.Form("UserID").Count == 1)
    {
        UserID = Request.Form("UserID");
        Password = Request.Form("Password");
        methodUsed = "POST";
    }
```

Next we check to see if a UserID was entered in login.wml. If the user has failed to enter a user name, we create an error message to that effect:

```
    if (UserID == "")
    {
%>
    <card id="result" title="Error!">
        <p>
            You must enter a user name!
        </p>
<%
    }
```

Notice that the WML code here is embedded in the `if` code block. This kind of conditional structure allows us to write WML easily, without hundreds of `Response.Write()` lines. The problem with having too many `Response.Write()` calls is that they can obscure the intention of the ASP file.

If a `UserID` exists, then we proceed to validate it. If the username and password match our criteria, we greet the user:

```
    else
    {
        if ((UserID == "Weimeng") && (Password == "Secret"))
        {
%>
    <card id="result" title="Welcome!">
        <p>
            Hello Weimeng!<br/>
<%
        }
```

And likewise if they do not. As you can see, we're free to insert blocks of ASP code almost wherever we choose to do so:

```
    else
    {
%>
    <card id="result" title="Sorry!">
        <p>
            Sorry <% Response.Write(UserID); %>, your password was not
            recognized. Please try again.<br/>
<%
    }
%>
```

Whether we know the user or not, we display the HTTP method used:

```
            You sent information using HTTP <% Response.Write(methodUsed); %>.
        </p>
```

Finally, we add a **Back** link to the card that has been created, and complete the deck:

```
<%
    }
%>
        <do type="prev" label="Back">
            <prev/>
        </do>
    </card>
</wml>
```

Of course, this only works with one username and one password. You could hardcode extra users and corresponding passwords into this code, but it would be far better to store information in a database, and check against that. We'll take a look at how we might do this later in the chapter.

Advanced ASP Techniques

The things we've seen so far, given a proper understanding of JScript, would allow us to create quite complex interactive WAP sites by dynamically generating WML code using ASP. Before we jump into database access with ADO, let's look at some of the other techniques we can use in ASP, which apply to two more of the built-in objects: `Application` and `Session`. Respectively, these objects allow us to consolidate multiple ASP files into a single application, and to enhance usability with user sessions.

We will also fulfill a promise that we've made a number of times over the course of the book: we'll look at how to detect what type of WAP browser is viewing your ASP files, allowing you to customize pages appropriately.

The Application Object

The `Application` object in ASP allows additional communication between ASP files, helping them to function together as an application. One key capability that this object provides is to allow multiple users to share common information, using application-level variable storage.

Try It Out — Using Application Level Variables

To illustrate this, let's take a look at an example.

1. Enter the following code using your text editor, and save it in `inetpub\wwwroot\reset.asp`:

```
<%@ Language = "JScript"; %><% Response.ContentType = "text/vnd.wap.wml";
%><?xml version="1.0"?>
<!DOCTYPE wml PUBLIC "-//WAPFORUM//DTD WML 1.2//EN"
                     "http://www.wapforum.org/DTD/wml_1.2.xml">

<wml>
   <head>
      <meta forua="true" http-equiv="Pragma"
                         content="no-cache"/>
      <meta forua="true" http-equiv="Cache-Control"
                         content="no-cache, must-revalidate"/>
   </head>

   <card id="card1" title="PageCount">
      <p>
<%
   Application("pageCount") = 0;
%>
         pageCount reset.<br/>
         <a href="pagecount.asp" title="Cont">Continue</a>
      </p>
   </card>
</wml>
```

Now enter this code and save it as `pagecount.asp` in the same location:

```
<%@ Language = "JScript"; %><% Response.ContentType = "text/vnd.wap.wml";
%><?xml version="1.0"?>
<!DOCTYPE wml PUBLIC "-//WAPFORUM//DTD WML 1.2//EN"
                     "http://www.wapforum.org/DTD/wml_1.2.xml">

<wml>
   <head>
      <meta forua="true" http-equiv="Pragma"
                        content="no-cache"/>
         <meta forua="true" http-equiv="Cache-Control"
                        content="no-cache, must-revalidate"/>
   </head>

   <card id="card1" title="PageCount">
      <p>
<%
   Application("pageCount") = Application("pageCount") + 1;
%>
         This page has been accessed
<%
   Response.Write(Application("pageCount"));
%>
         time(s)
      </p>
   </card>
</wml>
```

Open `reset.asp` in the UP.Simulator:

Follow the **Continue** link, taking you to `pagecount.asp`, and reload the page a couple of times (hit *F9* when the simulator is in use):

How It Works

When we load `reset.asp`, an application-level variable called `pageCount` is created and initialized to zero:

```
<%
    Application("pageCount") = 0;
%>
```

Then, every time we load `pagecount.asp`, `pageCount` will be incremented by 1 and displayed:

```
<%
    Application("pageCount") = Application("pageCount") + 1;
%>
        This page has been accessed
<%
    Response.Write(Application("pageCount"));
%>
        time(s)
```

The point here is that any other clients using this application will see the *same* `Application` object, and the *same* application-level variables, which can be a powerful way of sharing or pooling information between your users.

The Session Object

As well as the capacity for application-level storage provide by the `Application` object, there are times when we'd also like information to be stored on a user-by-user basis – in an e-commerce application, for example. To do this, we need to track the visitors to our WAP site, and be able to identify them uniquely when they return. However, as web servers will not 'remember' the user that was last connected, there is no easy way for the server to keep track of each user's purchases.

ASP provides the `Session` object as a means of maintaining information about a particular user session. Every user that connects to the web server will create a **session** on the server. The web server can then make use of this information to perform processing that is related to this particular user.

Data can be stored in a session, and it can be accessed by ASP files other than one that put it there in the first place. This is a great advantage over 'normal' variables in ASP, which do not 'persist' between files – they are destroyed when the ASP file completes its work.

Cookies

The `Session` object in ASP makes use of **cookies**. These are small pieces of information that are set by web servers, and sent to browsers. Often, cookies hold a unique ID that identifies an individual user, so that the next time the user browses to the site, the browser sends the cookie back to the web server, which provides enough information for the web server to identify the user.

In web development, this functionality is well established: almost all web browsers support cookies, and will happily store them on the computer being used. Unfortunately, this is not the case with WAP browsers, which are not well endowed when it comes to memory. Whereas a PC can store a large number of cookies without a problem, WAP devices can't – at least, not yet. For this reason, you cannot expect current devices to support cookies.

There is, however, a solution to this problem that is rapidly coming into fashion: storing cookies at the WAP gateway. Currently, only Phone.com has a working implementation, and so using the `Session` object is only possible through a Phone.com gateway to a real device, or by using a PC-based simulator. However, support is improving, and it is likely that WAP developers will have wider access to this technique in the near future. Luckily for us, the UP.Simulator supports cookies, allowing us to use them in our ASP files.

Try It Out — Cookies in the UP.Simulator

The first thing to remember about cookies in ASP is this: a cookie will be sent to the browser *when a user first accesses a given WAP site*. We can check this out for ourselves by looking at the cookies stored in the UP.Simulator.

1. If it is currently running, quit the UP.Simulator.

2. Delete the `CookieCache` file that is stored in the `UPSDK40` subdirectory of the Phone.com SDK's installation directory (if you followed the default installation, this will be in `C:\Program Files\Phone.com\UPSDK40\`).

3. Start the UP.Simulator again, and select the Info | Cookies menu option (or hit *F11*). You should see the following output in the Phone Information window:

4. Open the first example from the last section, `reset.asp`, or any other ASP-generated WML file.

5. Select the Info | Cookies menu option (or hit *F11*) again. This time, you'll see the following output:

The cookie on your machine is likely to have different values from this one, but it will look similar.

How It Works

The UP.Simulator stores its cookies in the `CookieCache` file, so by deleting this file we effectively cleared out any cookies that may have been stored. We confirmed this by reloading the simulator and viewing the cookies stored in memory – there was none.

433

Next, we created a cookie by browsing to `reset.asp` (which in this case was stored on the local computer). If we navigate to any other ASP file *in the same domain* (that is, under the control of the same web server), no further cookies are created. Having received this cookie, the web server will always be able to identify us, as it will be sent to the server on each subsequent visit.

This particular cookie is called `ASPSESSIONID` (plus some other characters that aren't important to us), and it contains a unique value and an expiry time (37 years – an eternity in computing terms). It is also possible to set an expiry date, which specifies the same thing by a different means. Either way, when time runs out, the cookie is deleted from the browser automatically.

If you used a different browser to access the same ASP file – perhaps using the UP.Simulator on a different PC – that browser would also receive an `ASPSESSIONID` cookie, but with its own unique value. This would enable the web server to identify users (or at least, browsers) uniquely.

Using the Session Object

When users first visit an ASP-driven WAP site, a **session** is created, identified by a cookie. This session can be used to store information that will be available for as long as the user is connected.

> *Note that this storage is not achieved* using *cookies – the information stored in a session is not stored in the client browser, but on the web server. The cookie is used to identify the information on the server as belonging to a particular user.*

Storing data in a session works in much the same way as storing information using the `Application` object, except that (sensibly enough) we use the `Session` object. For example, we could store a username and a password in a session using the following code:

```
<%
    Session("UserName") = "Mitch";
    Session("Password") = "secret";
%>
```

This code creates two session variables – `UserName` and `Password` – to store the login information of a user. Let's put this into action in an example.

Try It Out — Storing User Data in a Session

1. Enter the following code using your text editor, and save it in `inetpub\wwwroot\session1.asp`:

```
<%@ Language = "JScript"; %><% Response.ContentType = "text/vnd.wap.wml";
%><?xml version="1.0"?>
<!DOCTYPE wml PUBLIC "-//WAPFORUM//DTD WML 1.2//EN"
                     "http://www.wapforum.org/DTD/wml_1.2.xml">

<wml>
    <card id="card1" title="Welcome">
        <p>
            Tell us your name, please: <input type="text" name="UserName" />
```

```
                    <do type="accept" label="Next">
                       <go href="session2.asp#card2" method="post">
                          <postfield name="UserName" value="$(UserName)"/>
                       </go>
                    </do>
                 </p>
              </card>
</wml>
```

2. Having retrieved the user's name, we can start to personalize the questions we ask. This file's called session2.asp:

```
<%@ Language = "JScript"; %><% Response.ContentType = "text/vnd.wap.wml";
%><?xml version="1.0"?>
<!DOCTYPE wml PUBLIC "-//WAPFORUM//DTD WML 1.2//EN"
                     "http://www.wapforum.org/DTD/wml_1.2.xml">

<wml>
   <card id="card2" title="Age">
      <p>
<%
   Session("UserName") = String(Request.Form("UserName"));
%>
         Hello,
<%
   Response.Write(Session("UserName") + "<br/>");
%>
         Now, tell us your age: <input name="age" />
         <do type="accept" label="Next">
            <go href="session3.asp#card3" method="post">
               <postfield name="age" value="$(age)"/>
            </go>
         </do>
      </p>
   </card>
</wml>
```

3. Finally, we can use the information we've gathered in the two cards so far to tailor some output. Here's session3.asp:

```
<%@ Language = "JScript"; %><% Response.ContentType = "text/vnd.wap.wml";
%><?xml version="1.0"?>
<!DOCTYPE wml PUBLIC "-//WAPFORUM//DTD WML 1.2//EN"
                     "http://www.wapforum.org/DTD/wml_1.2.xml">

<wml>
   <card id="card3" title="Comments">
      <p>
<%
   Response.Write(Session("UserName") + ",");
   if (Number(Request.Form("age")) < 20)
   {
%>
      you are young!
```

```
<%
   }
   else
   {
      if (Number(Request.Form("age")) < 50)
      {
%>
         you are mature, huh...
<%
      }
      else
      {
%>
         life has just started, hasn't it?
<%
      }
   }
%>
      </p>
   </card>
</wml>
```

4. Open `session1.asp` in your browser, input data as requested, and observe the results:

How It Works

`session1.asp` passes the user name entered by the user to `session2.asp` using the HTTP POST method:

```
<go href="session2.asp#card2" method="post">
   <postfield name="UserName" value="$(UserName)"/>
</go>
```

In the following line of code, `session2.asp` retrieves this value and stores the user name in a session variable:

```
Session("UserName") = String(Request.Form("UserName"));
```

We know that the data will be passed to us using POST, so we don't need to check which method has been used. The String() method ensures that the returned value *is* a string, ready for storage in the Session object.

Once stored in the Session object, UserName is accessible in other ASP files – for example, in session3.asp. The following line of code retrieves this session variable, adds a comma, and displays it:

```
Response.Write(Session("UserName") + ",");
```

One further thing to note in the code for session3.asp is the use of the Number() method to format the age variable for processing. This code makes sure that the value is *not* in string format:

```
if (Number(Request.Form("age")) < 20)
```

The UserName session variable is accessible for the duration of the session – a definite advantage over other ASP variables, which are valid only for individual ASP files. When the session terminates (which can be forced, but also happens when the user has been disconnected or inactive for a long period), the information is lost.

Sending Data to ASP Files using Dynamically Generated URLs

As mentioned earlier, the current support for cookies in WAP applications is not extensive. This is a shame, because the kind of processing we've just been talking about would be very handy for WAP-enabled devices – when user input is awkward, anything that can help to reduce the amount of data entry is well worth pursuing.

In the absence of cookies, there is another technique that we can use to pass data to the server, which is to write session information into the query strings that we saw earlier in this chapter. In this scheme, every URL is dynamically rewritten to include data that must be available to other ASP files, such that when the user navigates to the next file, the information is transmitted to the server again.

If we mean to do this properly, we have to do it for *all* data we collect – even data that the 'current' ASP file doesn't need. If we want to make sure that the data is available for any files that the user may navigate to in the future, we must retrieve and pass on every name-value pair regardless. It also means that we cannot have any non-ASP files in our application: static WML files do not have the facility to capture data passed in the Request object, so the information would be lost and files that required it would be forced to ask for it to be entered again. To understand this more clearly, we will illustrate the technique with an example.

In the following code, we assume that the user's username has already been entered (perhaps using login.asp), and that the user has been browsing our site, adding items for purchase at some point:

```
<card id="menu">
    <p>
        Choose an option:
        <a href="checkout.asp?username=<% = username
                    %>&amp;books=<% = bookIDs
                    %>&amp;cds=<% = cdIDs%>">
            Check Out
        </a>
```

```
                    <a href="checkout.asp?username=<% = username
                              %>&amp;books=<% = bookIDs
                              %>&amp;cds=<% = cdIDs%>">
                  Browse Catalog
               </a>
               <a href="checkout.asp?username=<% = username
                              %>&amp;books=<% = bookIDs
                              %>&amp;cds=<% = cdIDs%>">
                  Cancel purchases
               </a>
               <a href="checkout.asp?username=<% = username
                              %>&amp;books=<% = bookIDs
                              %>&amp;cds=<% = cdIDs%>">
                  Shopping Cart
               </a>
         </p>
   </card>
```

The file above would generate the following WML code (or something very like it):

```
<card id="menu">
   <p>
         Choose an option:
         <a href="checkout.asp?username=Mitch&books=4583,4656&cds6812">
            Check Out
         </a>
         <a href="checkout.asp?username=Mitch&books=4583,4656&cds6812">
            Browse Catalog
         </a>
         <a href="checkout.asp?username=Mitch&books=4583,4656&cds6812">
            Cancel purchases
         </a>
         <a href="checkout.asp?username=Mitch&books=4583,4656&cds6812">
            Shopping Cart
         </a>
   </p>
</card>
```

This code represents a fictitious online book and CD vendor that implements a 'shopping cart' facility not unlike those currently offered by web sites. In the example above, the bookIDs and cdIDs variables represent the book and CD purchases made so far. Most of the work is done by the following lines of code, which are repeated for every URL in the WML file:

```
         <a href="checkout.asp?username=<% = username
                        %>&amp;books=<% = bookIDs
                        %>&amp;cds=<% = cdIDs%>">
```

The code is adding a query string that represents the username, together with the books and CDs chosen so far, to a URL. We've used the fact that ASP removes all data between the <%...%> delimiters (including white space) to format the code so that it is more readable.

As ever, there are disadvantages with this technique. Unless we are prepared to add passwords to the URL, which is not advisable for security reasons, there is no way to authenticate users. In addition, this technique does not allow us to 'expire' the user session in the way that cookies can 'expire'. Unless some kind of check is made against values stored on the server, if a user bookmarks this URL or the browser caches this menu, the user will be presented with stale data. Our application will attempt to process old or cancelled purchases. Lastly, it can lead to very long URLs, and we risk adding to the transmission time significantly, as well as to the size of the deck.

Writing session information as a query string on every URL is fine for some purposes, but not as elegant as using the `Session` object. There are ways of working around these problems and mimicking the `Session` object's functionality more accurately, but such techniques are beyond the scope of this book. If you're interested, refer to one of the many resources available on this subject.

Detecting WAP Browsers

We have now looked at many of the techniques that we can use to identify *users* and store information pertaining to them. In this section, we will look at ways of tailoring content generation to individual *browsers*, which may have differing support for WML, and will therefore benefit from WML files that are designed specifically for them.

When a web server receives an HTTP request from a browser – any browser, web or WAP – one of the headers received identifies the browser. This header is called `HTTP_USER_AGENT`, and it's easy to access from within ASP, using the `Request.ServerVariables()` method.

The following code could be used to examine this header:

```
<%@ Language="JScript"%><% Response.ContentType = "text/vnd.wap.wml";
%><?xml version="1.0"?>
<!DOCTYPE wml PUBLIC "-//WAPFORUM//DTD WML 1.2//EN"
                        "http://www.wapforum.org/DTD/wml_1.2.xml">
<wml>
    <head>
        <meta forua="true" http-equiv="Pragma"
                            content="no-cache"/>
        <meta forua="true" http-equiv="Cache-Control"
                            content="no-cache, must-revalidate"/>
    </head>

    <card id="card1" title="Type">
      <p>
         Browser Type:<br/>
<%
    useragent = new String(Request.ServerVariables("HTTP_USER_AGENT"));
    Response.Write(useragent);
%>
      </p>
    </card>
</wml>
```

This code produces the following results on the Phone.com UP.Simulator and the Nokia Toolkit 2.0 (simulating the Nokia 7110):

This means straight away that we *can* differentiate between browsers. The user agent strings above include information that is specific to the user agent version number, and some other data that we don't actually need to identify the browser. All we need to recognize the UP.Browser, for example, is that the user agent header includes the string "UP.Browser". For the Nokia, we can look for the string "Nokia".

Programmatically, we can do this by using the `indexOf()` method. Look at the following code:

```
<card id="card1" title="Type">
    <p>
        Browser Type:<br/>
<%
    useragent = new String(Request.ServerVariables("HTTP_USER_AGENT"));
    if (useragent.indexOf("Nokia") != -1)
    {
%>
        Nokia browser detected.
<%
    }
    if (useragent.indexOf("UP.Browser") != -1)
    {
%>
        UP.Browser detected.
<%
    }
%>
    </p>
</card>
```

`indexOf()` returns -1 if the specified substring *doesn't* occur in the string, and the position in the string where the substring is to be found if it does. When we run the code again, we get the following results:

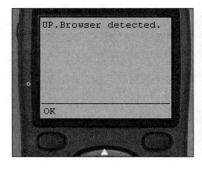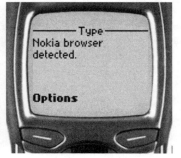

A list of user agent strings for a large number of microbrowsers can be found at
http://amaro.g-art.nl/useragent/. You can use this list to check for patterns in the browsers you want to
target, and structure your code accordingly.

Another possibility is to determine, in general, whether a WAP or a web browser is being used, so that
you could make the same URL work for both types of browser. Some texts will advise you to do this by
searching for the string Mozilla in the HTTP_USER_AGENT header, but don't believe them! Although
this string does appear in many web browser headers, it doesn't appear in all of them, and it also
appears in Microsoft Mobile Explorer.

A better choice is to look at the HTTP_ACCEPT header, which lists the content types supported by the
requesting browser. If this header contains the string wml, then the request is from a WAP-enabled
browser; otherwise it is a traditional HTML browser. The code for doing this is very similar to that
shown above – change the method call to Request.ServerVariables("HTTP_ACCEPT"), and
you're almost there.

The question that remains is: What do we do *after* we've detected which browser is being used to access
our site?

Redirecting Pages

It would be possible to use a single, enormous ASP file to generate content conditionally for the array of
different browsers that might come knocking on our door. This is an extension of the simple example
above. Alternatively, we can **redirect** the browser – that is, send the browser to a different URL from
the one it originally requested. This might be to an HTML page for a web browser, to separate WML
files for different WAP browsers, to various ASP files, or to a combination of the above. Whichever you
choose, redirecting pages uses the Redirect() method of the Response object:

```
Response.Redirect(location);
```

In order for this code to work properly, it must be *executed* before any part of the content is sent to the
browser. However, we can still *use* it anywhere in an ASP file, provided we **buffer** the Response
object – in other words, we delay sending anything back to the browser until the ASP file has finished
its work completely. If we then use the Redirect() method, any content is dumped, and a redirection
order is sent to the browser.

Try It Out — Sending Data in an HTTP Request using WML

Let's see a quick example that redirects Nokia browsers.

1. Here's the ASP file for this application, which you should save in inetpub\wwwroot\
    redirect.asp:

```
<%@ Language = "JScript"; %><%
    Response.ContentType = "text/vnd.wap.wml";

    // Enable buffering
    Response.Buffer = true;
    useragent = new String(Request.ServerVariables("HTTP_USER_AGENT"));
```

```
      if (useragent.indexOf("Nokia") == -1)
      {
          Response.Redirect("notnokia.wml");
      }
%><?xml version="1.0"?>
<!DOCTYPE wml PUBLIC "-//WAPFORUM//DTD WML 1.2//EN"
                        "http://www.wapforum.org/DTD/wml_1.2.xml">

<wml>
    <card id="main" title="Menu">
        <p>
            You'll only see this if you have a Nokia browser!
        </p>
    </card>
</wml>
```

2. This WML deck, which may be the target of navigation from the ASP file, should be stored as `inetpub\wwwroot\notnokia.wml`:

```
<?xml version="1.0"?>
<!DOCTYPE wml PUBLIC "-//WAPFORUM//DTD WML 1.2//EN"
                        "http://www.wapforum.org/DTD/wml_1.2.xml">

<wml>
    <card id="main" title="Menu">
        <p>
            You won't see this if you have a Nokia browser!
        </p>
    </card>
</wml>
```

3. Load `redirect.asp` in the Phone.com and Nokia simulators, and you will see the following results:

How It Works

We set up the buffer, checked for `Nokia` in the `HTTP_USER_AGENT` header, and redirected accordingly:

```
      Response.Buffer = true;
      useragent = new String(Request.ServerVariables("HTTP_USER_AGENT"));
      if (useragent.indexOf("Nokia") == -1)
      {
          Response.Redirect("notnokia.wml");
      }
```

Only browsers with this string will be unaffected; all others (including the UP.Simulator) will be redirected to the specified WML file.

Database Access using ActiveX Data Objects (ADO)

Our next task in this chapter is to take a look at how we can use ASP to access databases, using Microsoft's **ActiveX Data Objects** (**ADO**). We certainly won't cover the subject comprehensively – for that, you should refer to a book such as *Beginning ASP Databases* (Wrox Press, 1-861002-72-6), which provides an excellent tutorial and reference for ASP database developers. What we *will* do in this chapter is to illustrate the use of ADO to access a database, and cover the essential concepts required to get you started.

What is ADO?

ADO is a relatively simple way of accessing databases from ASP files. It can be used from other languages as well, but it has become particularly popular among ASP developers.

Apart from its ease of use, ADO is also convenient in that it is capable of connecting to many different kinds of databases. In this chapter, we'll use it to read from a Microsoft Access database, but modifying your code to work with SQL Server or Oracle, for example, usually requires very little work.

> *You* won't *need to have Microsoft Access on you computer to use these examples – simply downloading the database (*.mdb*) files from the Wrox web site is enough. Microsoft Access is only required to* edit *these files, and it has been used to obtain some of the screenshots in this chapter.*

As its name suggests, ADO relies on a number of objects to provide its functionality. However, when you've seen how to use objects from ASP once, you've seen pretty much all that you need to see, and there won't be a great deal of new programming to learn here.

ADO is shipped with ASP, so you'll almost certainly have a version of ADO on your system already. However, it's well worth downloading version 2.5, or the latest version (2.6) that's part of Microsoft Data Access Components (MDAC) and can be obtained for free at http://www.microsoft.com/data.

Detecting the Version of ADO on your System

In order to run the examples in this chapter, you should ideally have version 2.1 (or later) of the Microsoft Data Access Components (MDAC), which enable what Microsoft calls "Universal Data Access". Broadly speaking, Universal Data Access means the ability to access various kinds of database with the same set of objects and methods. This ability is provided by MDAC, of which ADO is a part.

There are two ways of checking the version of MDAC that's currently installed on your machine. First, you can perform a search for the file msdadc.dll on your hard disk – it can usually be found at c:\Program Files\Common Files\System\Ole DB. Once you've found this file, right click on it, select **Properties** from the context menu, and click on the **Version** tab to locate the version number. The first two digits are the important ones; the diagram overleaf shows the version number as 2.50.4403.0, which means MDAC 2.5.

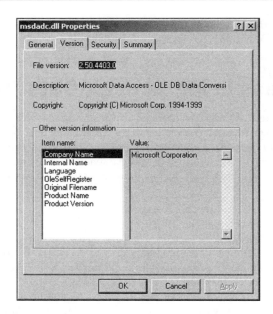

Alternatively, you can download the MDAC Component Checker from Microsoft's web site at http://www.microsoft.com/data/download.htm. Once the checker is downloaded and unzipped to your hard disk, launching it (double click c:\comcheck\comcheck.exe) will list the following options:

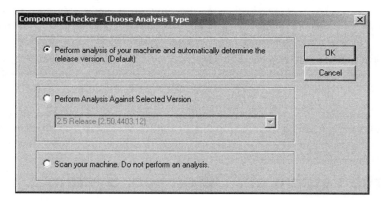

Select the first item, and click OK. The component checker will then determine the version of MDAC installed on your system – be aware that this process may take a few minutes, so don't worry!

The screenshot above shows the result returned by the component checker on a machine that has MDAC version 2.5 installed.

ADO Basics

The objects supplied by ADO for database access and manipulation include:

- ❏   `Connection` – contains details about a specific connection to a database.

- ❏   `Command` – allows the execution of Structured Query Language (SQL) commands (also known as queries).

- ❏   `Recordset` – a container for the set of database records returned as a result of executing a query.

- ❏   `Fields` – contains the individual items in a record, or the 'columns' of a database.

- ❏   `Errors` – a list of the errors that occurred during the processing of commands (if any).

- ❏   `Parameter` – used to pass extra information to queries, used by the `Command` object.

However, while we were able to use ASP's built-in objects by name, we'll need to use a slightly different technique when accessing these objects. The ADO objects don't just 'exist' – we have to create them when we need them, and store them in variables. Then, when we want to call their methods or access their properties, we'll identify the objects by the names of the variables storing them, rather than by their own names.

In general, the procedure for database access involves creating a `Connection` to a database, executing a query against it, and working with the returned `Recordset` if necessary. Alone, this is enough to read values from a database for display in a WML card.

To store the `Connection` and `Recordset` objects, we need to initialize two variables using the ASP `Server` object, which allows us to create, among other things, the ADO objects. We do this using the `CreateObject()` method:

```
conn = Server.CreateObject("ADODB.Connection");
rs   = Server.CreateObject("ADODB.Recordset");
```

`conn` and `rs` now contain ADO `Connection` and `Recordset` objects respectively. At the moment, however, these objects are empty, and we need to make a connection to a database before we can go any further. This is achieved using the `Connection` object's `Open()` method, although the precise syntax will vary according to the database being connected to. The syntax of the `Open()` method is as follows:

```
conn.Open("ConnectionString", UserID, Password);
```

`UserID` and `Password` are used to identify the user to the database specified in `ConnectionString`, which may take one of a number of forms. We'll limit this discussion to connecting to a Microsoft Access .mdb file. Of course, all good databases can (and should) be set up to require user authentication so that the information they hold is protected. In this example, however, we have chosen not to require a user name and password, so we can omit the second and third parameters, and connect using:

```
conn.Open("DRIVER={Microsoft Access Driver (*.mdb)};DBQ=filename.mdb;");
```

Where, predictably, `filename` points to the database we want.

Once the connection to the database is open, we can execute a query on the `Connection` object, returning a `Recordset` object with the results:

```
rs = conn.Execute("QueryString");
```

`QueryString` can be a SQL statement, the name of a table in the database, or a more complex entity. We'll learn a little more about SQL shortly, as we'll need to use it quite a lot, but for now it's enough to know that SQL is the language we use to execute queries on an Access database. There other ways of achieving finer control, but again, we won't need those here.

Once we've called `Execute()` we can use the `Recordset` object that it returns to output data. (We'll have a lot more to say about this later.) Finally, we close the connection using the `Connection` object's `Close()` method.

Try It Out — Simple Database Access

Before we move on to any more specifics, let's take a look at an example that illustrates everything we've talked about so far.

1. Either place the `travel.mdb` file from the code download into the `inetpub\wwwroot` directory or, if you prefer (and have the tools to do so), create an Access database called `travel.mdb` that contains the following data in a table called `Destination`:

DestinationID	Country
Chi	China
Hk	Hong Kong
Ind	Indonesia
Jap	Japan
Mal	Malaysia
Sin	Singapore

Record: 1 of 6

2. To use this database, enter the following code, and save it as `inetpub\wwwroot\destination.asp`:

```
<%@ Language = "JScript"; %><% Response.ContentType = "text/vnd.wap.wml";
%><?xml version="1.0"?>
<!DOCTYPE wml PUBLIC "-//WAPFORUM//DTD WML 1.2//EN"
                     "http://www.wapforum.org/DTD/wml_1.2.xml">

<wml>
   <card id="card1" title="Destinations">
      <p>
         List of Destinations<br/>
<%
   conn = Server.CreateObject("ADODB.Connection");
   rs   = Server.CreateObject("ADODB.Recordset");

   conn.Open("DRIVER={Microsoft Access Driver (*.mdb)};DBQ=" +
             Server.MapPath("travel.mdb") + ";");
```

```
      // Execute the query on the database
      rs = conn.Execute("Destination");

      while (!rs.EOF)
      {
         Response.Write(rs("Country") + "<br/>");
         rs.MoveNext();
      }
      conn.Close();
   %>
      </p>
   </card>
</wml>
```

3. Load destination.asp in the UP.Simulator:

How It Works

We create two objects – a Connection and a Recordset – and then connect to the database:

```
   conn.Open("DRIVER={Microsoft Access Driver (*.mdb)};DBQ=" +
             Server.MapPath("travel.mdb") + ";");
```

The Open() method of the Connection object requires the complete path of the file, which we're able to specify easily by making use of the Server object's MapPath() method, which maps the relative path of our access file (travel.mdb) to the complete path (c:\inetpub\wwwroot\Travel.mdb, if you've installed everything in default locations).

Next, we pass the name of the database table we want to access to the Connection object, so that the records can be retrieved and passed to the Recordset object. This gives us a way of accessing all the data in the table:

```
   // Execute the query on the database
   rs = conn.Execute("Destination");
```

Once the records are retrieved, we can use our Recordset object to step through each of them until the EOF (end of file) marker is reached, writing out the value of the Country column for each record:

```
while (!rs.EOF)
{
    Response.Write(rs("Country") + "<br/>");
```

The next line requires a little more understanding of recordsets. When a Recordset object is first created, it 'points' to the first record in the set. A reference to the Recordset such as the following:

```
rs("Country")
```

refers to the Country column of a particular record, until the record being 'pointed to' is changed. The MoveNext() method moves the RecordSet object's pointer along, so that it points at the next record in the set:

```
    rs.MoveNext();
}
```

If you omit the call to rs.MoveNext(), your machine will slow to a crawl as the loop never ends and WML is output continuously, based on the content of a single record. The ASP process will time out after 900 seconds (by default), but that's still a long time to wait!

Finally:

```
conn.Close();
```

We close the Connection object, which also closes all associated objects (including our Recordset object).

A Crash Course in SQL

You've now seen a basic example of using ADO for data access, but before we can go much further, we need to take a quick look at SQL, the language we used for our database query.

SQL, the Structured Query Language, was designed to allow database developers to **query** a database – although the term hardly does the language justice. As well as simply requesting information, SQL can be used to define a database, create and destroy tables within it, modify records, and much more.

> *SQL has many 'flavors', because different vendors have extended the language for their own purposes. What we present here is standard SQL that most databases can understand.*

In this section, we're going to provide a very short description of how to write SQL statements – just enough to enable us to retrieve, add, delete and modify records. Once again, we're not trying to supply an exhaustive reference, so we'll only need the following SQL keywords:

Keyword	Function
SELECT	Retrieves a set of records
FROM	Specifies table(s) to obtain records from

Keyword	Function
WHERE	Allows us to filter out records we don't want
LIKE	Allows database searches
INSERT INTO	Adds a group of records to a table
UPDATE	Sets the value of field(s) in a table
SET	Used to specify data to update with UPDATE
DELETE	Removes a set of records from a table

Let's look at some simple examples. To retrieve information about a particular item of stock in a table called `Inventory` with a `StockID` of `S3823`, we have:

```
SELECT * FROM Inventory WHERE StockID='S3823'
```

The `*` character specifies that we want all the fields for the records obtained, although we could specify individual fields here if we desired. To add new stock (`StockID=S1234`, `Price=34`, and `Qty=100`) to the `Inventory` table, we have:

```
INSERT INTO Inventory (StockID, Price, Qty) VALUES ('S1234', 34, 100)
```

To change the price of a stock item (`StockID=S8735`) to `250`, we have:

```
UPDATE Inventory SET Price=250 WHERE StockID='S8735'
```

To remove a stock item (`StockID=S6543`) from the `Inventory` table, we have:

```
DELETE FROM Inventory WHERE StockID='S6543'
```

Believe it or not, that's about as much as we need to say about SQL for now. Let's take a look at some more database access techniques, adding extra explanation where new SQL techniques are used.

ADO Techniques

It's time to look at some more advanced data access techniques. The first thing we'll examine is using the `Open()` method of the `Recordset` object (instead of the `Connection.Execute()` method) as a way of performing a query and obtaining a recordset. As we'll see, this method gives us greater flexibility and more options – and once we've mastered it, we'll look at inserting new records, deleting records, and performing searches on a database.

Database Queries using the Recordset Object

Earlier we used the following syntax to perform a query:

```
conn = Server.CreateObject("ADODB.Connection");
rs   = Server.CreateObject("ADODB.Recordset");
conn.Open("ConnectionString");
rs = conn.Execute(Query);
```

As an alternative, we can use the `Recordset` object's `Open()` method, in the following way:

```
conn = Server.CreateObject("ADODB.Connection");
rs   = Server.CreateObject("ADODB.Recordset");
conn.open("ConnectionString");
rs.Open(Query, conn, CursorType, LockType, Options);
```

Here, we can use the `CursorType`, `LockType`, and `Options` parameters for additional control over the properties of the recordset. Each of these takes values from sets that are predefined in `adojavas.inc`, a plain text file that can be found in `c:\Program Files\Common Files\System\ADO\` on systems that have ADO installed. To simplify access to this file, copy it into the `inetpub\wwwroot\` directory; we can then use these values in an ASP file by adding the following line of code:

```
<!-- #include file="adojavas.inc" -->
```

Note that this file contains white space outside the <% and %> delimiters, so if you place it before the XML declaration in your ASP file, you'll need to remove that white space from your copy of `adojavas.inc`. Alternatively, just make sure it is included after *the XML declaration, as we have done in the rest of the chapter.*

Let's take a look at these three parameters, and suggest what values would be necessary to modify the code we saw earlier to use this method of accessing a database.

CursorType

The 'pointer' that identifies a single record in the recordset, which we manipulated earlier with the `MoveNext()` method, is more formally called the **cursor**. When we used `Recordset.MoveNext()`, we were actually advancing the cursor through the records in the recordset, allowing us to access them one at a time.

The `CursorType` parameter can take one of the following values:

- ❑ `adOpenForwardOnly` – the default option, which allows you to move forwards in a recordset, but not backwards.

- ❑ `adOpenKeyset` – allows you to move forwards and backwards in a recordset. If a record in the database is deleted or modified by another user, you will see the changes immediately. However, if another user *adds* a new record to the database, it will not immediately be visible to you.

- ❑ `adOpenDynamic` – is similar to `adOpenKeyset`, except that you can see *all* changes made by other users.

- ❑ `adOpenStatic` – does not allow you to see the changes made by other users. It does, however, allow you to move forwards and backwards in a recordset.

The choice of cursor also has more subtle effects on what `Recordset` objects are capable of. We'll see an example of this later in the chapter, where we are forced to use `adOpenStatic`.

For our simple example, where we simply need to look at a list of database entries and write out one field for each record, `adOpenForwardOnly` is sufficient.

LockType

This parameter specifies what **locking** is necessary on records. Locking is necessary in dynamic databases, where multiple users may be accessing records simultaneously – without the ability to 'lock' a record for exclusive access, a situation could arise where two users attempt to make changes to one record at the same time, with potentially unpredictable results. To solve this we can specify that records become locked in certain circumstances, thereby preventing other users from modifying them.

The values that this parameter can take are the following:

- ❑ `adLockReadOnly` – no locking is performed, but that doesn't matter because you simply can't modify records in the recordset.

- ❑ `adLockPessimistic` – records are locked as soon as you start editing them, and unlocked when you commit changes. This is the safest form of locking.

- ❑ `adLockOptimistic` – you only lock records during updating, not while you edit them. This assumes that no one else will try to edit the data at the same time – if they do, then whoever commits changes first will 'win', other updates will fail.

- ❑ `adLockBatchOptimistic` – you update the records in batches, only locking each record when committing changes.

Our simple example doesn't make any updates to the database, so we can use `adLockReadOnly`.

Options

This parameter specifies what format the `Query` parameter takes, and can be:

- ❑ `adCmdTable` – `Query` is a table name.

- ❑ `adCmdText` – `Query` is a SQL statement.

- ❑ `adCmdStoredProc` – `Query` is a stored procedure or a stored query (an advanced method of database access involving setting up queries as part of the database, which we won't use in this chapter).

- ❑ `adCmdUnknown` – the `Query` type is not specified. This is the default value.

We'll use `adCmdText` in our example, as we'll be using a SQL Query.

Try It Out — Using the RecordSet.Open() Method

1. Reopen `destination.asp` in your text editor, make the following changes, and save it back as `destination2.asp`:

```
<%@ Language = "JScript"; %><% Response.ContentType = "text/vnd.wap.wml";
%><?xml version="1.0"?>
<!-- #include file="adojavas.inc" -->
<!DOCTYPE wml PUBLIC "-//WAPFORUM//DTD WML 1.2//EN"
                     "http://www.wapforum.org/DTD/wml_1.2.xml">

<wml>
    <card id="card1" title="Destinations">
        <p>
            List of Destinations<br/>
```

```
<%
   conn = Server.CreateObject("ADODB.Connection");
   rs   = Server.CreateObject("ADODB.Recordset");

   conn.Open("DRIVER={Microsoft Access Driver (*.mdb)};DBQ=" +
             Server.MapPath("travel.mdb") + ";");

   // Create a string to hold the SQL query
   sqlQuery = "SELECT Country FROM Destination";

   // Execute the query on the database
   rs.Open(sqlQuery, conn, adOpenForwardOnly, adLockReadOnly, adCmdText);

   while (!rs.EOF)
   {
      Response.Write(rs("Country") + "<br/>");
      rs.MoveNext();
   }
   conn.Close();
%>
      </p>
   </card>
</wml>
```

2. Load destination2.asp into the UP.Simulator:

How It Works

This example involved a few minor changes to our earlier application in order to use the Recordset object's Open() method. We added this line to get access to the ADO constants:

```
<!-- #include file="adojavas.inc" -->
```

And we removed the old call to Execute(), replacing it with some new code:

```
   // Create a string to hold the SQL query
   sqlQuery = "SELECT Country FROM Destination";

   // Execute the query on the database
   rs.Open(sqlQuery, conn, adOpenForwardOnly, adLockReadOnly, adCmdText);
```

The example produced exactly the same results as our earlier effort, although it used a slightly different method.

Inserting a New Record

We can insert a new record into a database using either the `Connection.Execute()` method, or the `Recordset.Open()` method. The first method relies on a SQL command, the second on manipulating a recordset after specifying that we want this capability with the options discussed earlier.

As an example, let's consider adding a new entry, `Taiwan`, into our `Destination` table. We can open a connection using the same code as in previous examples:

```
conn = Server.CreateObject("ADODB.Connection");
rs   = Server.CreateObject("ADODB.Recordset");
conn.Open("DRIVER={Microsoft Access Driver (*.mdb)};DBQ=" +
          Server.MapPath("travel.mdb") + ";");
```

Using the `Connection` object requires the following extra lines of code:

```
// Create a string holding the SQL query
sqlQuery = "INSERT INTO Destination (DestinationID, Country)
            VALUES ('Tw','Taiwan')";

// Execute the query on the database
conn.Execute(sqlQuery);
```

We can also use the `Recordset` object:

```
// Select all the data in the Destination table
sqlQuery = "SELECT * FROM Destination";

// Open recordset with a forward only-cursor and optimistic record locking
rs.Open(sqlQuery, conn, adOpenForwardOnly, adLockOptimistic, adCmdText);

// Add a new record, set a DestinationID field and a Country field
rs.AddNew();
rs.Fields("DestinationID") = "Tw";
rs.Fields("Country") = "Taiwan";

// Update the database
rs.Update();
```

Let's put this second method into practice, and then discuss what is happening.

Try It Out — Adding a Record

1. Open `destination2.asp` in your text editor, make the following changes, and save it back as `destination3.asp`:

```
<%
    conn = Server.CreateObject("ADODB.Connection");
    rs   = Server.CreateObject("ADODB.Recordset");

    conn.Open("DRIVER={Microsoft Access Driver (*.mdb)};DBQ=" +
              Server.MapPath("travel.mdb") + ";");
```

```
    // Select all the data in the Destination table
    sqlQuery = "SELECT * FROM Destination";

    // Open recordset with a forward only cursor and optimistic record locking
    rs.Open(sqlQuery, conn, adOpenForwardOnly, adLockOptimistic, adCmdText);

    // Add a new record, set a DestinationID field and a Country field
    rs.AddNew();
    rs.Fields("DestinationID") = "Tw";
    rs.Fields("Country") = "Taiwan";

    // Update the database
    rs.Update();

    // Refresh the recordset and move to the first record
    rs.Requery();
    rs.MoveFirst();

while (!rs.EOF)
{
    Response.Write(rs("Country") + "<br/>");
    rs.MoveNext();
}
conn.Close();
%>
```

2. If you're using Internet Information Server, you'll need to ensure that you have the correct permissions to write to the database. To do this, right click on `travel.mdb` and select **Properties**. In the **Security** tab, make sure that **Everyone** has **Full Control**:

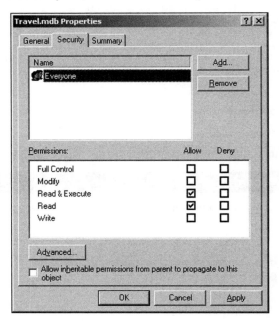

3. Load `destination3.asp` into the UP.Simulator, and scroll to the bottom of the list of destinations – Taiwan will now appear:

How It Works

We started by selecting all fields from the `Destination` table and storing them in our recordset, `rs`:

```
// Select all the data in the Destination table
sqlQuery = "SELECT * FROM Destination";

// Open recordset with a forward only cursor and optimistic record locking
rs.Open(sqlQuery, conn, adOpenForwardOnly, adLockOptimistic, adCmdText);
```

Note that we've opened our database using the `adLockOptimistic` option – using `adLockReadOnly` would lead to an error when we attempt to change the database.

We then use the `AddNew()` method of the `Recordset` object to add a new record to our recordset:

```
// Add a new record, set a DestinationID field and a Country field
rs.AddNew();
```

When we add this record, the cursor jumps to it, allowing us to add information to it by field name:

```
rs("DestinationID") = "tw";
rs("Country") = "Taiwan";
```

The changes we have made so far have updated our recordset; to update the database itself we must call the `Update()` method:

```
// Update the database
rs.Update();
```

Just to make sure, we should re-query the database, refreshing our recordset with the latest records and ensuring that we haven't missed any additions due to other users. This needs the `Requery()` method, so the code we add is:

```
// Refresh the recordset and move to the first record
rs.Requery();
rs.MoveFirst();
```

If you're using the `travel.mdb` file downloaded from the Wrox web site, try running this code a second time. You will get an error (HTTP Error: 500), because we are then trying to add a duplicate record, and the downloadable database specifies that the `DestinationID` values should be unique. If you want to run the code again, you will have to delete the new record first, which is what we'll do in the next section.

Deleting a Record

As with adding records, we can use methods from both the `Connection` and `Recordset` objects to delete records. The following SQL statement deletes the newly added `Taiwan` record from the database:

```
sqlQuery = "DELETE FROM Destination WHERE DestinationID='Tw'";

// Execute the SQL statement
conn.Execute(sqlQuery);
```

Notice in particular the `WHERE` clause, which specifies the record to delete. Make sure that you double-check this before executing your code, because if you omit it and just use:

```
sqlQuery = "DELETE FROM Destination";
```

You could destroy your entire database table!

To delete a record using the `Recordset` object, we can navigate to the record we want to delete, and then call the `Delete()` method. Alternatively, we can save time by acquiring a recordset that contains only the record we want to delete in the first place:

```
// Select all records whose DestinationID is Tw
sqlQuery = "SELECT * FROM Destination WHERE DestinationID='Tw'";

// Execute the query
rs.Open(sqlQuery, conn, adOpenForwardOnly, adLockOptimistic, adCmdText);

// Delete the record from the database
rs.Delete();
```

Let's try it out.

Try It Out — Deleting a Record

1. Open `destination3.asp` in your text editor, make the following changes, and save the result as `destination4.asp`:

```
<%
    conn = Server.CreateObject("ADODB.Connection");
    rs   = Server.CreateObject("ADODB.Recordset");

    conn.Open("DRIVER={Microsoft Access Driver (*.mdb)};DBQ=" +
              Server.MapPath("travel.mdb") + ";");

    // Select all records whose DestinationID is Tw
    sqlQuery = "SELECT * FROM Destination WHERE DestinationID='Tw'";
```

```
      // Execute the query
      rs.Open(sqlQuery, conn, adOpenForwardOnly, adLockOptimistic, adCmdText);

      // Delete the record from the database
      rs.Delete();

      // Close the current recordset
      rs.Close();

      // Retrieve all the data from the Destination table
      sqlQuery = "SELECT * FROM Destination";
      rs.Open(sqlQuery, conn, adOpenForwardOnly, adLockReadOnly, adCmdText);

   while (!rs.EOF)
   {
      Response.Write(rs("Country") + "<br/>");
      rs.MoveNext();
   }
   conn.Close();
%>
```

2. Load `destination4.asp` into the UP.Simulator and scroll to the bottom of the list of destinations – **Taiwan** has disappeared:

How It Works

This code uses the `Recordset` object to delete the entry for Taiwan in the database:

```
      sqlQuery = "SELECT * FROM Destination WHERE DestinationID='Tw'";

      // Execute the query
      rs.Open(sqlQuery, conn, adOpenForwardOnly, adLockOptimistic, adCmdText);

      // Delete the record from the database
      rs.Delete();
```

Note that no call to `Update()` is necessary here: `Delete()` changes both our recordset and the database itself.

To check that things have worked, we close the recordset, create a new query to return all records in the database, and execute it to return a new recordset. We then go ahead and view the individual records using our standard technique.

```
rs.Close();

// Retrieve all the data from the Destination table
sqlQuery = "SELECT * FROM Destination";
rs.Open(sqlQuery, conn, adOpenForwardOnly, adLockReadOnly, adCmdText);
```

Performing Searches

Sometimes, users won't know exactly what records we have in a database, and it would be a service to them to provide search capabilities. This is surprisingly simple, because we can do it all with SQL, using the LIKE keyword.

Let's say that we wanted to search our Destination table for countries beginning with "Ind". We could assemble this into a SQL statement like this:

```
SELECT * FROM Destination WHERE Country LIKE 'Ind*'
```

*Using the * character as a wildcard, as we've done in 'Ind*', works for Access databases. Other databases have different wildcards for use with the LIKE keyword.*

Similarly, we could search for countries containing the letter 'k' using:

```
SELECT * FROM Destination WHERE Country LIKE '*k*'
```

Access is case-insensitive when searching like this, so the above query would return Hong Kong.

Displaying Recordsets over Multiple Cards

When we generate code to display recordsets in a microbrowser, we have to be careful about how much data we put in any one deck. We are limited both by memory and usability – not only can we not fit many records in memory, but also it would be a nuisance to scroll through more than a few records at a time.

There will be times, however, when you have a long list of items to display. The best solution then is to split items over multiple cards, or even multiple decks. As this is likely to be a common problem, it's worth looking at some sample code that achieves this. In addition, we'll add some extra formatting to the display, automatically generating anchor links for further information (although we won't look at the destinations for these links).

Try It Out — Displaying Recordsets Over Multiple Cards

To use this example, you need the travel2.mdb database, which contains a much longer list of destinations.

1. Enter the code on the next page in your text editor, and save it as inetpub\wwwroot\destination5.asp:

```
<%@ Language = "JScript"; %><% Response.ContentType = "text/vnd.wap.wml";
%><?xml version="1.0"?>
<!-- #include file="adojavas.inc" -->
<!DOCTYPE wml PUBLIC "-//WAPFORUM//DTD WML 1.2//EN"
                     "http://www.wapforum.org/DTD/wml_1.2.xml">

<wml>
<%
    conn = Server.CreateObject("ADODB.Connection");
    rs   = Server.CreateObject("ADODB.Recordset");

    conn.Open("DRIVER={Microsoft Access Driver (*.mdb)};DBQ=" +
              Server.MapPath("travel2.mdb") + ";");

    // Return all data in Destination
    sqlQuery = "SELECT * FROM Destination";

    // Execute query
    rs.Open(sqlQuery, conn, adOpenStatic, adLockReadOnly, adCmdText);

    // If PageNo exists load it, otherwise PageNo is 1
    if (Request.QueryString("PageNo").Count == 1)
    {
        PageNo = Number(Request.QueryString("PageNo"));
    }
    else
    {
        PageNo = 1;
    }
%>
    <card id="dest" title="Destinations">
        <p>
            List of Destinations<br/>
<%
    rs.PageSize = 5;
    rs.AbsolutePage = PageNo;
    Counter = 1;
    while ((!rs.EOF) && (Counter <= rs.PageSize))
    {
        Response.Write((PageNo - 1) * rs.PageSize + Counter + ". ");
        Response.Write("<a href=\"" + rs("Country") + ".wml\"");
        Response.Write(" title=\"" + rs("DestinationID") + "\">");
        Response.Write(rs("Country") + "</a><br/>");
        Counter++;
        rs.MoveNext();
    }
    if (!rs.EOF)
    {
%>
        <do type="options" label="Next">
            <go href="destination5.asp?PageNo=<% = PageNo + 1 %>"/>
        </do>
```

```
<%
   }
   if (PageNo > 1)
   {
%>
         <do type="accept" label="Prev">
            <go href="destination5.asp?PageNo=<% = PageNo - 1 %>"/>
         </do>
<%
   }
   conn.Close();
%>
      </p>
   </card>
</wml>
```

2. Load `destination5.asp` into the UP.Simulator, and try navigating forwards and backwards through the list of destinations (note that the **Prev** softkey only appears when no link is selected):

How It Works

ADO provides for the possibility of wanting to do something like this by providing a paging system: it uses the concept of a 'page' to mean a set number of records, such that a given recordset will be divided up into several pages, each containing `PageSize` records. This is a purely artificial division, and not based on any logical grouping of records.

This is useful to us, because we can use it to dictate how many records we want in a card. For the UP.Simulator, five records seems a good choice, as they will all fit on a single screen. Once we've set the `PageSize` property, we can move the cursor to the start of any page by setting the `AbsolutePage` property. For example, if we were to set `PageSize` to 5 and `AbsolutePage` to 4, the cursor would be positioned on the 20th record.

One consequence of making use of these properties is that we are forced to use `adOpenStatic` when we obtain our recordset:

```
rs.Open(sqlQuery, conn, adOpenStatic, adLockReadOnly, adCmdText);
```

`AbsolutePage` isn't supported if we use `adOpenForwardOnly` or `adOpenDynamic`.

The page to be displayed is determined by a name-value pair sent via the HTTP GET method. The first time we look at the page, though, this value won't be set, so we check for that eventuality and set PageNo to 1 if it occurs:

```
if (Request.QueryString("PageNo").Count == 1)
{
    PageNo = Number(Request.QueryString("PageNo"));
}
else
{
    PageNo = 1;
}
```

Next, we write out the beginning of our deck, and tell the Recordset object how many records we want to fit in the card using the PageSize property, and move the cursor to page PageNo:

```
%>
    <card id="dest" title="Destinations">
        <p>
            List of Destinations<br/>
<%
    rs.PageSize = 5;
    rs.AbsolutePage = PageNo;
```

We then loop through all the records in the current page, and format them as <a> elements:

```
Counter = 1;
while ((!rs.EOF) && (Counter <= rs.PageSize))
{
    Response.Write((PageNo - 1) * rs.PageSize + Counter + ". ");
    Response.Write("<a href=\"" + rs("Country") + ".wml\"");
    Response.Write(" title=\"" + rs("DestinationID") + "\">");
    Response.Write(rs("Country") + "</a><br/>");
    Counter++;
    rs.MoveNext();
}
```

Here, the first line sets a link number (China 1, Indonesia 2, Japan 3, etc) that's calculated using the following formula:

```
((PageNo - 1) * rs.PageSize + Counter
```

The remainder of the code sets the title attribute of the hyperlink to the DestinationID of the record currently under consideration. The hyperlink text is set to the country name, while the target URL is set to a WML file whose name is that of the country (plus the .wml extension), all of which results in code such as the following:

```
11. <a href="Australia.wml" title="Aus">Australia</a>
```

After displaying the records, we determine whether we need to provide a **Next** button (which we do if there are more records to display), and whether a **Prev** button should be provided (which will be the case for all but the first page).

```
    if (!rs.EOF)
    {
%>
        <do type="options" label="Next">
           <go href="destination5.asp?PageNo=<% = PageNo + 1 %>"/>
        </do>
<%
    }
    if (PageNo > 1)
    {
%>
        <do type="accept" label="Prev">
           <go href="destination5.asp?PageNo=<% = PageNo - 1 %>"/>
        </do>
<%
    }
```

Finally, we close the connection and complete the WML code:

```
    conn.Close();
%>
      </p>
    </card>
</wml>
```

Wrox Travel Case Study

In this section, we'll use our newly acquired ASP knowledge to improve the Wrox Travel WAP application that we've been developing throughout this book. Specifically, we will:

- ❑ Dynamically generate vacation information using data stored in a database.
- ❑ Implement the promised booking form by recording customer bookings to a database.

The database we will use (again, a Microsoft Access database) is called `wroxtravel.mdb`, and is available as part of the code download for this book.

The Database

Before we begin, let's take a brief look at the structure of our database. The database consists of two tables – one to store vacation information, and one to store bookings – called `Vacations` and `Bookings` respectively.

The Vacations Table

The Vacations table contains the following fields:

Field Name	Data Type
ID	AutoNumber
ShortName	Text
Description	Text
Price	Currency
Accomodation	Text
Days	Number
Wintersports	Yes/No
Sun	Yes/No
Accesible	Yes/No
Kids	Yes/No
Watersports	Yes/No
Adventure	Yes/No
Cruise	Yes/No
Luxury	Yes/No
Sports	Yes/No
Relaxing	Yes/No
Cheap	Yes/No
Healthy	Yes/No
Party	Yes/No
Beach	Yes/No

This data is sufficient for us to be able create the vacation cards we used earlier in this book, such as andorra.wml and london.wml.

The downloadable version of the database contains information on six vacations, as we will see when we implement our dynamically generated vacation pages.

The Bookings Table

The Bookings table is structured as follows:

Field Name	Data Type
ID	AutoNumber
DepartureDay	Number
DepartureMonth	Text
DepartureYear	Number
Places	Number
Email	Text
VacationRef	Number
Done	Yes/No

The only field here that does not directly relate to one of the details we had users enter earlier in the book is Done. This field is included so that employees of the Wrox Travel organization can search the database for bookings, and respond to any that aren't flagged as 'done'. (That's what the user's e-mail address is for!) The database will keep a record of all bookings, past and present.

Generating Vacation Details Dynamically

To start off with, let's create the ASP files that will generate vacation details dynamically. This will involve:

❑   Modifying the offers.wml file and turning it into an ASP file (offers.asp) that extracts vacation names from the database and generates a list.

❑   Creating a new file, vacation.asp, which provides details of individual vacations when selected from offers.asp.

❑   Modifying wroxtravel.wml to point at our new offers.asp file.

To start off with, then, let's build offers.asp.

offers.asp

offers.asp needs to provide the user with a list of vacations, just like offers.wml does. On this occasion, though, we're getting the information from a database. To do this, we can use the standard database access code we had above, this time accessing wroxtravel.mdb:

```
<%@ Language = "JScript"; %><% Response.ContentType = "text/vnd.wap.wml";
%><?xml version="1.0"?>
<!-- #include file="adojavas.inc" -->
<!DOCTYPE wml PUBLIC "-//WAPFORUM//DTD WML 1.2//EN"
                      "http://www.wapforum.org/DTD/wml_1.2.xml">
<%
   conn = Server.CreateObject("ADODB.Connection");
   rs   = Server.CreateObject("ADODB.Recordset");

   conn.Open("DRIVER={Microsoft Access Driver (*.mdb)};DBQ=" +
             Server.MapPath("wroxtravel.mdb") + ";");
```

For the vacation listings, we need the following data:

❑   The name of the vacation

❑   The price of the vacation

❑   The ID number of the vacation (used to generate unique URLs for each vacation)

In turn, this means that we only need to acquire a recordset with the ShortName, Price, and ID fields. We'll also sort the recordset by price, listing the cheapest vacation first:

```
   sqlQuery = "SELECT ID, ShortName, Price FROM Vacations ORDER BY Price";
   rs.Open(sqlQuery, conn, adOpenForwardOnly, adLockReadOnly, adCmdText);
%>
```

Next, we start to construct our WML deck:

```
<wml>
    <card id="offers" title="Special Offers">
        <p>
            Wrox Travel is pleased to be able to offer you the following
            amazing deals:
        </p>
        <p mode="nowrap">
            <select title="Vacations">
```

We'll place our vacation details in a `<select>` field, with onpick events pointing at `vacation.asp`. To identify the vacation selected, we'll pass the ID of the vacation in the query string part of the URL, with the name VID. The code below iterates through every record in the recordset, writing an `<option>` element for each vacation:

```
<%
    while (!rs.EOF)
    {
        Response.Write("<option onpick=\"vacation.asp?VID=")
        Response.Write(rs("ID"));
        Response.Write("\">");
        Response.Write(rs("shortName"));
        Response.Write(", $$");
        Response.Write(rs("Price"));
        Response.Write("</option>");
        rs.MoveNext();
    }
```

The code above will generate entries such as the following:

```
<option onpick="vacation.asp?VID=3">Cairo, $$400</option>
```

After we've written the vacation entries, we close the connection (and the associated recordset object) and write out the remainder of our deck:

```
    conn.close();
%>
        </select>
    </p>
    <do type="prev" label="Back">
        <prev/>
    </do>
    </card>
</wml>
```

We'll see this code in action once we've finished the rest of our Wrox Travel files.

vacation.asp

The `vacation.asp` file takes the VID query string parameter, and uses it to write out full vacation details for the chosen vacation. As usual, we start off by opening a connection – this code is exactly the same as that in `offers.asp`, so we won't reproduce it here. Instead, we'll move straight on to using VID to build a SQL query and obtain the vacation details.

As the ID field is unique, we know that this will return a single record with the requested details:

```
sqlQuery = "SELECT * FROM Vacations WHERE ID=" + Request.QueryString("VID");
rs.Open(sqlQuery, conn, adOpenForwardOnly, adLockReadOnly, adCmdText);
```

We now build our deck, using the information retrieved in the recordset to output the details:

```
%>
<wml>
    <card id="vacation" title="<% Response.Write(rs("shortName")); %>">
        <p>
<%
    Response.Write(rs("shortName") + "- $$" + rs("Price"));
%>
        </p>
        <p>
            <% Response.Write(rs("Description")); %>
            <br/><br/>
            <b>Accommodation type:</b><br/>
            <% Response.Write(rs("Accommodation")); %>
            <br/><br/>
```

To place the informational icons, we check each applicable field. For every field that is set to true, we place the associated icon in the card:

```
            <b>Details:</b><br/>
<%
    if (rs("Wintersports") == true)
    {
        Response.Write("<img src=\"cat01.wbmp\" localsrc=\"snowflake\" " +
                        "alt=\"Wintersports\"/>");
    }
    if (rs("Sun") == true)
    {
        Response.Write("<img src=\"cat02.wbmp\" localsrc=\"sparkle\" " +
                        "alt=\"Sun\"/>");
    }
    if (rs("Accessible") == true)
    {
        Response.Write("<img src=\"cat03.wbmp\" localsrc=\"plus\" " +
                        "alt=\"Accessible\"/>");
    }
    if (rs("Kids") == true)
    {
        Response.Write("<img src=\"cat04.wbmp\" localsrc=\"family\" " +
                        "alt=\"Kids\"/>");
    }
    if (rs("Watersports") == true)
    {
        Response.Write("<img src=\"cat05.wbmp\" localsrc=\"baseball\" " +
                        "alt=\"Watersports\"/>");
    }
```

```
if (rs("Adventure") == true)
{
    Response.Write("<img src=\"cat06.wbmp\" localsrc=\"bolt\" " +
                        "alt=\"Adventure\"/>");
}
if (rs("Cruise") == true)
{
    Response.Write("<img src=\"cat07.wbmp\" localsrc=\"boat\" " +
                        "alt=\"Cruise\"/>");
}
if (rs("Luxury") == true)
{
    Response.Write("<img src=\"cat08.wbmp\" localsrc=\"dollar\" " +
                        "alt=\"Luxury\"/>");
}
if (rs("Sports") == true)
{
    Response.Write("<img src=\"cat09.wbmp\" localsrc=\"football\" " +
                        "alt=\"Sports\"/>");
}
if (rs("Relaxing") == true)
{
    Response.Write("<img src=\"cat10.wbmp\" localsrc=\"moon1\" " +
                        "alt=\"Relaxing\"/>");
}
if (rs("Cheap") == true)
{
    Response.Write("<img src=\"cat11.wbmp\" localsrc=\"downtri2\" " +
                        "alt=\"Cheap\"/>");
}
if (rs("Healthy") == true)
{
    Response.Write("<img src=\"cat12.wbmp\" localsrc=\"heart\" " +
                        "alt=\"Healthy\"/>");
}
if (rs("Party") == true)
{
    Response.Write("<img src=\"cat13.wbmp\" localsrc=\"present\" " +
                        "alt=\"Party\"/>");
}
if (rs("Beach") == true)
{
    Response.Write("<img src=\"cat14.wbmp\" localsrc=\"sun\" " +
                        "alt=\"Beach\"/>");
}
```

Next we finish the deck, adding information to be passed to book.wml by setting browser variables:

```
%>
        <br/><br/><anchor title="Book">
          <go href="book.wml">
            <setvar name="H" value="<% Response.Write(rs("ShortName")); %>"/>
            <setvar name="P" value="$$<% Response.Write(rs("Price")); %>"/>
            <setvar name="I" value="<% Response.Write(rs("ID")); %>"/>
          </go>
```

```
            Book now!
          </anchor>
      </p>
      <do type="options" label="Icons">
        <go href="icons.wml"/>
      </do>
      <do type="options" label="Book">
        <go href="book.wml">
            <setvar name="H" value="<% Response.Write(rs("ShortName")); %>"/>
            <setvar name="P" value="$$<% Response.Write(rs("Price")); %>"/>
            <setvar name="I" value="<% Response.Write(rs("ID")); %>"/>
        </go>
      </do>
      <do type="prev" label="Back">
          <prev/>
      </do>
    </card>
</wml>
```

Finally, we close the connection:

```
<%
  conn.close();
%>
```

wroxtravel.wml

The last thing to change is the reference in `wroxtravel.wml`, which only involves a couple of lines:

```
        <p>Check out our new unbeatable
            <a href="offers.asp" title="Offers">offers</a>,
            our full vacation listings,
            and our competitive vacation
            <a href="insure.wml" title="Insure">insurance</a> scheme.<br/>
            You can also read reviews of our vacations in
            our features section.
        </p>
```

and

```
        <do type="options" label="Offers">
            <go href="offers.asp"/>
        </do>
```

Now, if we open `wroxtravel.wml`:

Follow the **Offers** link:

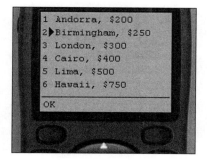

And select a vacation:

We're using two ASP files to do the job of what could be a large number of WML files.

Storing Booking Details

Now it's time to fill in the gap we left at the end of `book.wml`. You may recall that this file allowed the user to enter a departure date, a number of places to book, and an e-mail address. These parameters were stored in five browser variables: D, M, and Y for the date, N for places booked, and E for e-mail address. At the end of the `vacation.asp` file, we also have the vacation name stored in H, vacation price stored in P, and vacation ID stored in I.

Currently, the **Confirm** link in `book.wml` looks like this:

```
<a href="details.wml" title="Confirm">Confirm</a>
```

We just navigate to `details.wml`, where the details chosen are displayed. Now, however, we are in a position to change this link to an ASP file that will take the details entered, and place them in our database.

Looking back at our Bookings table structure, we can see that we require the variables D, M, Y, N, E, and I to be placed in our database. We can pass these to our booking ASP page (let's call it `book.asp`) by modifying the **Confirm** link in `book.wml`, as shown overleaf.

469

```
        <anchor title="Confirm">
           <go href="book.asp">
              <postfield name="day" value="$(D)"/>
              <postfield name="month" value="$(M)"/>
              <postfield name="year" value="$(Y)"/>
              <postfield name="places" value="$(N)"/>
              <postfield name="email" value="$(E)"/>
              <postfield name="VID" value="$(I)"/>
           </go>
           Confirm
        </anchor>
```

`book.asp` starts off in precisely the same way as our other database-accessing files, because we're still using `wroxtravel.mdb`. After that beginning, however, we need to build the SQL query that will insert a new record. This is the most complicated query we've seen so far, but it isn't too bad if you break it up into pieces. Basically, it takes the form:

```
INSERT INTO table (field1, field2) VALUES (value1, value2)
```

This will add a new record into *table*, where *field1* will become *value1*, and so on. The query we'll use is built up as follows:

```
sqlQuery = "INSERT INTO Bookings (DepartureDay, DepartureMonth, " +
           "DepartureYear, "Places, Email, VacationRef, Done) VALUES (" +
           Request.QueryString("day") + ", '" +
           Request.QueryString("month") + "', " +
           Request.QueryString("year") + ", " +
           Request.QueryString("places") + ", '" +
           Request.QueryString("email") + "', " +
           Request.QueryString("VID") + ", False)";
```

A lot of code, but it's really quite straightforward. The only slightly odd thing here is that text fields need to be enclosed in single quotes, but numeric fields don't.

Next, we execute the query:

```
conn.Execute(sqlQuery);
```

In order to give the user some feedback, we'll search the database for *all* bookings for the e-mail address entered, corresponding to all the vacation bookings for that user, and display the dates (displaying destinations is possible, but requires more complex database access – this will do fine for us). First, we run a second query:

```
sqlQuery = "SELECT * FROM Bookings WHERE Email='" +
           Request.QueryString("email") + "'";
rs.Open(sqlQuery, conn, adOpenForwardOnly, adLockReadOnly, adCmdText);
```

Then we write out our deck, including the dates as specified above:

```
%>
<wml>
    <card id="vacation" title="Booking">
        <p>
            Thank you. Current vacation dates booked for
<%
    Response.Write(rs("Email") + ":<br/>");
    while (!rs.EOF)
    {
        Response.Write(rs("DepartureDay") + ", " + rs("Departuremonth") +
                    ", " + rs("DepartureYear") + "<br/>");
        rs.MoveNext();
    }
```

Finally, we close the connection and finish the deck:

```
    conn.close();
%>
            <a href="WroxTravel.wml">Done</a>
        </p>
    </card>
</wml>
```

Let's test it out. Open `wroxtravel.wml`, follow the **Offers** link, and choose **Andorra**. Then, select the **Book Now!** link, add a date (let's say the 3rd of June 2002), and request two places. Finally, add the e-mail address joebloggs@somewhere.com, and select the **Confirm** link. You should get the following display:

If you have a copy of Microsoft Access you can verify that this data has been added to the database. When you look at the Bookings table, you should see something like:

ID	DepartureDay	DepartureMonth	DepartureYear	Places	Email	VacationRef	Done
25	3	Jun	2002	2	joebloggs@somewhere.com	3	☐
(AutoNumber)	0		0	0		0	☐

If you booked another vacation using the same e-mail address, you would see the departure dates for each booking in the confirmation screen on the browser.

Summary

Although the tutorials in Active Server Pages and ActiveX Data Objects were rather brief, you should now have a fair idea of the possibilities that are opened up to us through these technologies. In ASP, we have covered the dynamic generation of WML content, and the relevant declarations and syntax related to it.

We have also covered transmitting and receiving data between ASP files, using the GET and POST methods, and some uses to which such information might be put. In addition, we have examined the use of the objects that are provided in ASP in order to maintain application and session level information. Cookies are an important part of this technique, although due to inconsistent support it may be necessary to use other mechanisms, such as encoding query strings with relevant information.

You should also now be familiar with basic database access using ADO. You can add and delete records in a database, and request data from it with some confidence. To summarize, we have explored the following:

- ❑ ASP internals, and accessing the methods and properties of the built-in objects.

- ❑ Using the Session and Application objects in ASP to store data.

- ❑ Detecting browser types, and redirection using the Redirect() method of the Response object. Note that this requires buffering to be enabled.

- ❑ We looked briefly at ADO and had a crash course in SQL – we learned the SQL commands that are used in the majority of HTTP applications.

- ❑ We put this knowledge into practice through several examples: inserting and deleting records in a database, and performing searches.

- ❑ Finally, we learned some more advanced database techniques, using the paging functionality of the Recordset object to stagger data over multiple decks.

The last part of the chapter included a case study that brought new functionality to our Wrox Travel application. We put all of these new skills to the test with this application, and learned how the concepts translate to real life solutions.

The next chapter will be our final detour from the main line of examining increasingly complex techniques for creating more powerful WML applications. In it, we will learn XSLT, an XML language that can be used to *transform* XML. When we come to the last chapter in this book, the techniques learned in the next chapter will be used to create WML code that is tuned to different browsers, for improved usability of our applications.

XML and XSLT

One of the biggest problems with publishing content on the Internet is making sure that it remains current and accurate, and doing so when it is a part of an HTML or WML document can be particularly time consuming. The difficulty is concerned with the fact that the data content is mixed up with information that is devoted to telling browsers how to *present* the data, making editing a tedious process, especially if your content is used in several different places. The primary motivation for **XSLT**, or **Extensible Stylesheet Language Transformations**, is that it allows us to separate content and presentation completely, so that developers can concentrate on their job, and editors can focus on theirs.

XSLT is a technology that can be used to transform XML into any other text-based format, including other XML documents. Put simply, if we can persuade the editors always to place content in XML documents of our devising, we can use XSLT to process the content so that it's suitable for print, the Web, a WML browser – just about anything we want. When the content is later updated, we could use XSLT to transform it again, updating all of our target files in one go and ensuring consistency.

In this chapter, you will learn:

- ❑ What XSLT is
- ❑ How XSLT works
- ❑ What capabilities XSLT has
- ❑ How we can use XSLT to generate simple text, XML, and WML files

Note that XSLT is a complex subject, and we're not going to attempt to cover everything in depth here. We have, however, included plenty of examples for you to build on. For a more thorough tutorial in XSLT, see Beginning XML *(Wrox Press, 1-861003-41-2).*

What is XSLT?

In order to answer the question, "What is XSLT?" we must first deal with, "What is XSL?" We have to do this because XSLT is actually one half of the **Extensible Stylesheet Language** (**XSL**), the aim of which is to provide a standard way of expressing how the information in an XML document should be presented. The constructs of the language are such that page-based output is implicit, so if you wish you can think about XSL as a way of producing documents that contain the same *kind* of information as, say, PostScript files, or Adobe's PDF format.

Essentially, the process of creating such documents from XML files requires two things. First, there is the syntax we must use to describe the appearance of our documents, and second, there is the means of applying that syntax to our existing XML data. In XSL, the former is the domain of **XSL-FO** (**XSL Formatting Objects**) – a set of XML elements that (broadly) define the regions of a page, and the appearance of content within those regions. The latter is where **XSLT** (**XSL Transformations**) comes in: it's a means of writing **stylesheets** that specify how an XML document should change to use these formatting objects in place of its original elements.

Cutting to the chase, XSLT has applications beyond those we have just discussed. We've defined it as a way of specifying the transformation from one kind of XML document (the one containing the data we want to display, using custom elements) to another (the one that contains the same data in formatting objects), but in general it's possible to write XSLT stylesheets that define the transformation from *any kind* of XML document to *any other kind* of XML document. This is an extremely powerful idea with a number of uses, and we'll be seeing just a few of these over the next two chapters.

As an example of the sort of thing that's possible, consider the following XML document that contains details about a regular customer of a high street store:

```
<?xml version="1.0"?>
<customers>
   <customer>
      <name>
         <firstname>Mark</firstname>
         <lastname>Erpen</lastname>
      </name>
      <creditlimit currency="dollars">2000</creditlimit>
      <address>
         <line1>Ink House</line1>
         <line2>Street 32</line2>
         <line3>Magentaville</line3>
      </address>
   </customer>
</customers>
```

Now imagine that, for cross-marketing purposes, a business partner of the store wants to integrate its customer information into a larger database. Unless both parties developed their XML storage in the same way, it's highly likely that the partner will require the information to be formatted differently. They might want the same data as in the above document, but in the following form.

```
<?xml version="1.0"?>
<customers>
    <customer firstname="Mark" lastname="Erpen">
        <creditlimit currency="dollars">2000</creditlimit>
        <address>
            <line1>Ink House</line1>
            <line2>Street 32</line2>
            <line3>Magentaville</line3>
        </address>
    </customer>
</customers>
```

Both of these documents contain the same data, but in the second, the customer name appears in attributes, rather than elements. Using XSLT, we can write a stylesheet that describes how to change between these two representations, and then apply it to the first document to create the second programmatically.

What Does XSLT Look Like?

XSLT is written in XML – it consists of a set of elements that have special meanings, which we can use to achieve almost any transformation we may desire. XSLT stylesheets are made up of **templates** that identify patterns of elements to look for in the source document, and describe what should happen to these patterns in the document being created. The names of XSLT elements all begin with `xsl:`, followed by a word that says something about their function. Here's a simple example:

```
<xsl:template match="//customer">
    I've found a customer element
</xsl:template>
```

Templates are defined using the XSLT `<xsl:template>` element. The `match` attribute specifies a pattern in the source document, also called the source **tree**. The template will be applied to every **node** in the source tree that matches the pattern – in this case, it would be applied to any elements named `<customer>` that appear in the XML document.

> *Throughout this chapter, we'll talk about XML files in terms of **trees** and **nodes**. An XML document has a hierarchical structure: it begins with a single element that has several elements inside it, which each have elements inside them, and so on. This can be seen as resembling the way a tree splits into ever-finer branches, each large branch spawning several smaller ones. A node is any part of the document structure: an element, an attribute, the content of an element, etc. We'll discuss this idea at greater length later on.*

You specify what should go into the output (the result tree) in the content of the `<xsl:template>` element – here, we've simply used some text. If this template were to be included in a stylesheet and applied to an XML document, then every time a `<customer>` element appeared in the source tree, the text "`I've found a customer element`" would appear in the result tree.

All XSLT documents begin with these two lines:

```
<?xml version="1.0"?>
<xsl:stylesheet xmlns:xsl="http://www.w3.org/1999/XSL/Transform">
```

Given what you already know about XML from Chapter 3, this isn't too tricky. The XML declaration certainly shouldn't come as a surprise by now, while the second line, which is the opening tag of the document's root element (`<xsl:stylesheet>`), defines the namespace that all XSLT elements use.

The XSLT elements are defined within a namespace for at least two reasons. First, by specifying a namespace we can see by inspection that a document is an XSLT stylesheet, and not some other XML language. Second, we can check that a document complies with the XSLT specification by looking up the rules that match this namespace. Of course, it also removes any danger of the names of XSLT elements becoming confused with the names of elements in the source or result trees.

Running Transformations

In order to carry out transformations using XSLT, we need an **XSLT engine**. This is a program that takes an XSLT stylesheet and an XML document as input, and applies the former to the latter to produce the desired output. In this chapter, we'll be using an XSLT engine called **xt**, which was written by James Clark. This is the engine of choice for many developers, and it's available without charge from http://www.jclark.com, under the subheading **XML**.

To install xt on your machine, download it (you'll want "XT packaged as a Win32 executable"), unzip it, and save the single file xt.exe in the directory where you'll be working. You then can run the examples in this chapter from the MS-DOS prompt (under Windows 9x) or the Command Prompt (Windows NT/2000) using syntax like this:

```
> xt document.xml stylesheet.xsl output
```

document.xml is the XML document that we are transforming, stylesheet.xsl is the stylesheet we are applying to it, and output is the name of the document you would like xt to save the output to. If you don't specify one, xt will send its output to the screen, which is the option we'll use most of the time.

Try It Out — Transforming XML using XSLT and XT

Let's try this out to make sure that everything's working properly, and to show some of the possibilities we'll be discussing throughout this chapter.

1. Type the following XML document into your favorite editor, and save it as books.xml in the same directory where you placed xt.exe. This is our source file, which will be used to construct the source tree in XSLT:

```
<?xml version="1.0"?>
<Books>
    <Book ISBN="1-861004-58-3">
        <Title>Beginning WAP</Title>
        <Authors>
            <Author>Karli Watson</Author>
            <Author>Soo Mee Foo</Author>
            <Author>Wei Meng Lee</Author>
            <Author>Ted Wugofski</Author>
        </Authors>
        <Price>39.99</Price>
        <PublicationDate>2000</PublicationDate>
```

```
        <Synopsis>
            This book is for those who want to learn WAP,
            and specifically its markup and scripting
            languages: WML and WMLScript.
        </Synopsis>
    </Book>
</Books>
```

2. Next comes the XSLT file. Obviously, you're unlikely to take much from this just yet, but explanation of all the elements here is coming in due course! Call this file books.xsl:

```
<?xml version="1.0"?>
<xsl:stylesheet xmlns:xsl="http://www.w3.org/1999/XSL/Transform">
    <xsl:output method="text" indent="no"/>
    <xsl:template match="/">
        <xsl:for-each select="Books/Book">
            <xsl:value-of select="@ISBN" />:
            <xsl:value-of select="Title" />
            <xsl:value-of select="Synopsis" />
        </xsl:for-each>
    </xsl:template>
</xsl:stylesheet>
```

3. Now, open up a command prompt, navigate to the directory that contains these files, and type the following instruction at the command line:

```
> xt books.xml books.xsl
```

4. If all has gone well, this should give you the following output:

```
1-861004-58-3:
        Beginning WAP
        This book is for those who want to learn WAP,
        and specifically its markup and scripting
        languages: WML and WMLScript.
```

5. Let's try a different transformation. Enter the following code, and save it as books2.xsl:

```
<?xml version="1.0"?>
<xsl:stylesheet xmlns:xsl="http://www.w3.org/1999/XSL/Transform">
    <xsl:output method="xml" version="1.0" indent="yes"/>
    <xsl:template match="/">
        <Books>
            <xsl:for-each select="Books/Book">
                <Book>
                    <ISBN>
                        <xsl:value-of select="@ISBN" />
                    </ISBN>
                    <Title>
                        <xsl:value-of select="Title" />
                    </Title>
```

```
        </Book>
      </xsl:for-each>
    </Books>
  </xsl:template>
</xsl:stylesheet>
```

6. Now run this, using the following command:

```
> xt books.xml books2.xsl
```

7. This should give you the following output:

```
<?xml version="1.0" encoding="utf-8"?>
<Books>
<Book>
<ISBN>1-861004-58-3</ISBN>
<Title>Beginning WAP</Title>
</Book>
</Books>
```

8. One last transformation: enter this code, and save it as books3.xsl:

```
<?xml version="1.0"?>
<xsl:stylesheet xmlns:xsl="http://www.w3.org/1999/XSL/Transform">
   <xsl:output method="xml"
               version="1.0"
               indent="true"
               doctype-system="http://www.wapforum.org/DTD/wml_1.2.xml"
               doctype-public="-//WAPFORUM//DTD WML 1.2//EN" />
   <xsl:template match="/">
      <wml>
         <card id="books" title="Books">
            <p>
               <xsl:for-each select="Books/Book">
                  <b>
                     <xsl:value-of select="Title" />
                  </b><br/>
                  Authors:<br/>
                  <xsl:for-each select="Authors/Author">
                     <xsl:value-of select="." />
                     <br/>
                  </xsl:for-each>
               </xsl:for-each>
            </p>
         </card>
      </wml>
   </xsl:template>
</xsl:stylesheet>
```

9. And run it from the command line:

```
> xt books.xml books3.xsl books.wml
```

10. This time, we've created a WML deck called `books.wml` that you can view using the UP.Simulator:

How It Works

Before we begin to learn some of the concepts that are vital to an understanding of XSLT stylesheets, we can briefly look into how the three sections of this example work. In Step 1, we wrote an XML file that describes this book. It gives the ISBN number, the title of the book, a list of the authors, the price, and a short synopsis. The XML file is structured such that further books could be added at a later date.

Each of the XSLT stylesheets we applied performed different transformations on this XML file, resulting in different types of output. The key variations in the three XSLT stylesheets in the example occur in the `<xsl:output>` element – the first used `method="text"` to output plain text, while the other two used `method="xml"` to output XML. The last one also included the document type declaration for WML.

> *We'll examine this element, and how it can be used to affect output, in more depth later in the chapter. You've now seen, though, that XSLT can be used in the generation of non-XML output, and that we're able to choose just how much of the data in the source tree ends up in the result tree.*

The `<xsl:template>` element that we use in each stylesheet is something we've already looked at. In each case here, the pattern we specify is `"/"`, which matches the whole document – in XSLT's terms, it matches the **document root**, which we'll discuss shortly:

```
<xsl:template match="/">
```

The three stylesheets then used various XSLT elements, combined with plain text, to build up the result trees. In all three cases, we used the following line to specify that the engine should look for any `<Book>` elements inside `<Books>` elements in the document:

```
<xsl:for-each select="Books/Book">
```

The code contained in this element dealt with the specifics of the transformation for each type of output. For example, the stylesheet that caused plain text output used the following:

```
<xsl:value-of select="@ISBN" />:
<xsl:value-of select="Title" />
<xsl:value-of select="Synopsis" />
```

The above lines instruct the XSLT engine to copy the content of the ISBN *attribute*, the <Title> *element*, and the <Synopsis> *element* to the output. It also specifies adding a colon after the content of the ISBN attribute – and that's exactly what we saw.

Understanding XPath

The values we supplied to the match attribute of the <xsl:template> element, and to the select attribute of the <xsl:for-each> element, were written in a language called **XPath**. The primary use of this language is to enable XSLT to locate nodes in an input document – if you like, you can think of it as a set of directions in the document. Using XPath, we can describe a section of an XML document either by its name, or by its relationship with other parts of the document. The first thing that we should understand, then, is how each part is named.

The Document Tree

The **document tree** is the term that we use to describe the whole document: *everything* within an XML file falls under this heading. The first node in a document tree – the one that contains all the others – is called the **document root**. For example, we could represent books.xml like this:

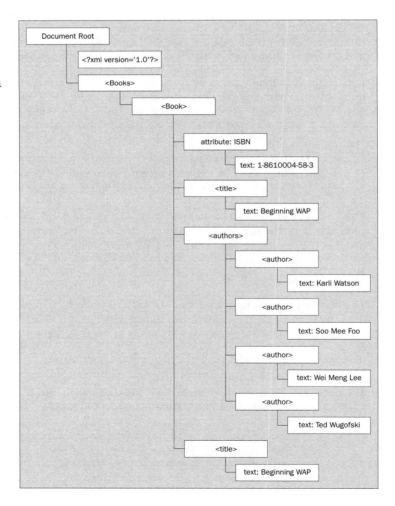

You should be careful not to confuse the *document root* with the *root element*. The latter is the topmost element that contains all other elements, while the former comprises the root element plus the XML declaration, any special instructions, and any other information that is not part of the data stored in the document.

> Notice in particular that the above diagram shows not only elements, but also attributes and text content being represented as nodes. This is how XPath 'sees' the content to be arranged — and explains how we have to navigate through it to get to the node that we want.

XPath Semantics

XSLT depends on us using XPath to state where in the document we want our templates to be applied – this is called setting the **context node**, which is the formal term for what's going on in this line:

```
<xsl:template match="/">
```

In Chapter 3, we talked about XML elements forming a grandparent-parent-child hierarchy, but here we can generalize that idea to include nodes as well. Using XPath, the document root is specified by "/", and all the other parts of the document are **child nodes** of the document root.

The template that we have defined above sets the context node to be the document root. By doing this, we ask the XSLT engine to start at the document root, and on that basis to carry out the transformation described in the rest of the template. If we had specified the following:

```
<xsl:template match="/Books/Book">
```

xt would read this as: "Starting at the document root, go to the Books child node, and select any Book child nodes of the Books node." (Strictly, the above refers to <Books> and <Book> *elements* – slightly different syntax is required for other types of node, as we will see.)

Once we've set the context of an <xsl:template> element, any use of XPath inside the element is taken to be relative to that context. For example, any transformations specified for Authors once the context has been set in this way would be translated as being relevant to "/Books/Book/Authors".

XPath Syntax

As we've seen, elements are referred to in XPath by their names: the <Books> element is referred to as Books. The names of child nodes are separated from their parents by a forward slash – the same character that refers to the document root node when it appears at the beginning of an XPath expression. This much you had probably gathered from the examples presented so far, but there are several more ways of referring to nodes that we might find useful.

To refer to the *parent* node of the context node, we use "..". So, if we're in "/Books/Book/Title", then "../Price" refers to the <Price> element of <Title>'s parent – or in full, "/Books/Book/Price".

To select all the element child nodes of the context node, we use "*". Furthermore, if you need to indicate that the transformation you want to carry out should be done on the current context node, you can do so by using ".". This will tell the XSLT engine to transform the contents of the current node.

So: we now know how to refer to any *element* within the document, but we should also look at how to refer to *attribute* nodes, such as the ISBN attribute of the <Book> element. As you may have spotted in our example, we do this by using the "@" character, so "/Books/Book/@ISBN" would match the ISBN attribute nodes of all <Book> element nodes contained in <Books>.

We can also use attributes to be more specific in our choices, by specifying only elements with certain attribute values. For example, "/Books/Book[@ISBN='1-861004-58-3']" refers to the <Book> in <Books> whose ISBN attribute is 1-861004-58-3. The brackets here act as a filter to select only the elements that meet the criteria specified inside them.

There's just one more way of referring to parts of the document that you need to know about before we continue. It's "//", known as the **recursive descent operator**, and best explained through an example. We could use "//" to refer to *every* <Book> element in a document, regardless of what other elements they might be contained in. Alternatively, we could match every <Book> element that had an ISBN attribute by using "//Book[@ISBN]". Finally, we could select all attribute nodes of a certain name, regardless of the elements they apply to, using (say) "//@id". If we then looked at the parent nodes of these attribute nodes, we would be able to perform some processing on any element with an id attribute.

> *Although this technique is potentially very versatile, it's only recommended if you absolutely need it. Because the whole document must be checked for attributes with the name you supply, it can be a very slow, processor-intensive task.*

Now we're getting somewhere! The references that we can construct using the syntax we have learned allow us to refer to almost any part of an XML document. Very soon, we'll see just what opportunities have been opened up.

XPath Functions

In order to make XPath more useful, it includes a number of functions to help you perform some of the tasks that cannot easily be achieved using normal XPath expressions. To mention just two, name() returns the name of the node specified as a parameter, while position() returns the position of the node in a set of sibling nodes, so in the following section of books.xml:

```
<Authors>
    <Author>Karli Watson</Author>
    <Author>Ted Wugofski</Author>
    <Author>Lee Wei Meng</Author>
    <Author>Foo Soo Mee</Author>
</Authors>
```

if we were to specify:

```
"Author[position() = 3]"
```

where the context node is Authors, this would return the third Author in the list: Lee Wei Meng. Because this is such a common requirement, there's even a shorthand form of this expression: "Author[3]".

There are many functions defined within XPath, and they range in functionality from those concerned with nodes, through logical functions, to those for carrying out other mathematical and numeric operations. There are also several that are concerned with strings and string manipulation. Explaining how each function works is beyond the scope of this book, but we will illustrate how useful some of them can be with an example. For the remainder of the chapter, we will explain any XPath functions that we use as we go along.

Try It Out — Using XPath Functions

Consider a situation in which you're writing XSLT stylesheets to extract information about a range of office stationery that's sold by the company you work for. They have asked you to calculate the cost of buying one item of each of the products they sell. They also want to know how many products they sell.

1. This is the file you have been given. Enter the following XML document into your text editor, and save it as `products.xml`. This will be used to create our source tree.

```xml
<?xml version="1.0" ?>
<Products>
    <Product ID="S123456">
        <Name>Eraser</Name>
        <Price>0.20</Price>
    </Product>
    <Product ID="S455456">
        <Name>Ruler</Name>
        <Price>1.20</Price>
    </Product>
    <Product ID="S785436">
        <Name>Marker</Name>
        <Price>2.00</Price>
    </Product>
    <Product ID="S432344">
        <Name>Pen</Name>
        <Price>0.50</Price>
    </Product>
    <Product ID="S456775">
        <Name>Stapler</Name>
        <Price>3.50</Price>
    </Product>
</Products>
```

2. We can use an XPath function to add up the prices of all the products. Enter the following stylesheet, and save it as `products.xsl`:

```xml
<?xml version="1.0"?>
<xsl:stylesheet xmlns:xsl="http://www.w3.org/1999/XSL/Transform">
    <xsl:output method="text" indent="no"/>
    <xsl:template match="/Products">
        Total Price for the
        <xsl:value-of select="count(Product)"/>
        products in our range is
        <xsl:value-of select="sum(Product/Price)"/>
    </xsl:template>
</xsl:stylesheet>
```

3. Carry out the transformation with the following command:

```
> xt products.xml products.xsl
```

4. You should see the following output:

```
Total Price for the
5
products in our range is
7.4
```

How It Works

The XML file we have used contains a list of products and their prices. In a real application, the number of products will probably be greater, but as far as the XSLT stylesheet is concerned, this is irrelevant. In the stylesheet, we've started by saying that we are carrying out our operation on the contents of the <Products> element that is a child node of the document root:

```
<xsl:template match="/Products">
```

The next line of the stylesheet should be output as-is, since it doesn't have any XSLT tags in it. The following line then calls the count() XPath function, which counts the number of occurrences of the item specified as a parameter. In this case, we have asked it to count the number of <Product> elements that are child nodes of the context node.

```
<xsl:value-of select="count(Product)"/>
```

The next line is again output as-is, and then we add together the prices of each product – the sum() function adds the values of the contents of the nodes passed to it. We have asked that the contents of every <Price> element that's a child of a <Product> element in the current context should be totaled.

```
<xsl:value-of select="sum(Product/Price)"/>
```

And that's all there is to it! We've now looked at all the XPath we need in order to be able to use XSLT, so in the remainder of this chapter we will at last explain each XSLT element in turn, giving examples where we can. By the end, you will have a good working knowledge of XSLT, ready for the challenges of the next and final chapter.

XSLT Elements

Now that we have seen how we can describe, filter, and navigate around an XML document using XPath, we are ready to manipulate and transform its content with XSLT. We have already seen the <xsl:template> element, and we've used <xsl:value-of>, <xsl:for-each>, and <xsl:output>. However, to make full use of XSLT, there are many more elements that we should learn. Let's start again, explaining each XSLT element from the beginning.

Structural XSLT Elements

The following XSLT elements are all concerned with the *structure* of our XSLT documents, and with the format of the output they're used to create. We will begin with `<xsl:stylesheet>`:

<xsl:stylesheet>

Quite simply, `<xsl:stylesheet>` is the outermost or root element of *every* stylesheet. For example:

```
<?xml version="1.0"?>
<xsl:stylesheet xmlns:xsl="http://www.w3.org/1999/XSL/Transform">
    <xsl:output method="text" version="1.0" indent="no"/>
    <xsl:template match="/">
        ...
    </xsl:template>
</xsl:stylesheet>
```

Within the `<xsl:stylesheet>` element, we define the namespace, and it's important that you specify it exactly as given here. Subsequent versions of XSLT, as and when they appear, will have new namespaces that differ only by this string. To demonstrate how important this is, xt uses the XSLT version whose namespace is given above – if any other is given, it will simply output the whole XSLT stylesheet as though it were text!

<xsl:output>

The `<xsl:output>` element can give us fine control over the result of applying the stylesheet. It has several attributes, but here we'll just discuss the ones that are relevant to this chapter. The syntax for this element is:

```
<xsl:output method="type"
            version="number"
            indent="yes|no"
>
```

Here, `method` specifies the type of output, which can be `html`, `text`, `xml`, or something specified by the XSLT processor being used. `version` is ignored unless `method` is `xml`, in which case it specifies the XML version number to be output. `indent` specifies whether the XSLT engine is allowed to add white space to the output in order to improve readability. The difference can be seen in the following two samples.

This output was generated using `indent="no"`:

```
<?xml version="1.0" ?>
<Products><Product
ID="S123456"><Name>Eraser</Name><Price>0.20</Price></Product><Product
ID="S455456"><Name>Ruler</Name><Price>1.20</Price></Product><Product
ID="S785436"><Name>Marker</Name><Price>2.00</Price></Product><Product
ID="S432344"><Name>Pen</Name><Price>0.50</Price></Product><Product
ID="S456775"><Name>Stapler</Name><Price>3.50</Price></Product></Products>
```

You can see that for human consumption, the following output (`indent="yes"`) is more pleasing:

```
<?xmlversion="1.0"?>
<Products>
<ProductID="S123456">
<Name>Eraser</Name>
<Price>0.20</Price>
</Product>
<ProductID="S455456">
<Name>Ruler</Name>
<Price>1.20</Price>
</Product>
<ProductID="S785436">
<Name>Marker</Name>
<Price>2.00</Price>
</Product>
<ProductID="S432344">
<Name>Pen</Name>
<Price>0.50</Price>
</Product>
<ProductID="S456775">
<Name>Stapler</Name>
<Price>3.50</Price>
</Product>
</Products>
```

The `<xsl:output>` element also includes the `doctype-system` and `doctype-public` attributes that we can use to specify a document type declaration. The following XSLT excerpt creates a document type declaration for a WML deck:

```
<?xml version="1.0"?>
<xsl:stylesheet xmlns:xsl="http://www.w3.org/1999/XSL/Transform">
   <xsl:output method="xml"
               version="1.0"
               indent="true"
               doctype-system="http://www.wapforum.org/DTD/wml_1.2.xml"
               doctype-public="-//WAPFORUM//DTD WML 1.2//EN" />
   <xsl:template match="/">
      <wml>
         <!-- Rest of stylesheet -->
```

This will produce the following output, which is formatted for readability's sake:

```
<?xml version="1.0" encoding="utf-8"?>
<!DOCTYPE wml PUBLIC "-//WAPFORUM//DTD WML 1.2//EN"
                     "http://www.wapforum.org/DTD/wml_1.2.xml">
<wml>
   <!-- Rest of stylesheet output -->
```

<xsl:template>

`<xsl:template>` defines a template for producing output, and despite the examples you've seen so far, there may be any number of templates in a single XSLT stylesheet. For example:

```xml
<?xml version="1.0"?>
<xsl:stylesheet xmlns:xsl="http://www.w3.org/TR/WD-xsl">
    <xsl:output method="text" indent="no"/>
    <xsl:template match="/">
        ...
    </xsl:template>

    <xsl:template match="/Products">
        ...
    </xsl:template>
</xsl:stylesheet>
```

The `<xsl:template>` element has the `match` attribute to specify a pattern in the source XML document. In the first template here, the `match` attribute refers to the document root of the source tree. The second template specifies any `<Products>` elements that are children of the document root.

<xsl:apply-templates>

The `<xsl:apply-templates>` element is used to invoke other templates within the current template. It has an attribute called `select` that can be used to select the current context, but it's optional – if it is omitted, the template called will use the current context. Let's have an example to see what all this means.

Try It Out — Using <xsl:apply-templates>

1. We will use the following XML document to build our source tree. Enter it into your text editor, and save it as `customer.xml`:

```xml
<?xml version="1.0"?>
<customers>
    <customer>
        <name>
            <firstname>Mark</firstname>
            <lastname>Erpen</lastname>
        </name>
        <creditlimit currency="dollars">2000</creditlimit>
        <address>
            <line1>Ink House</line1>
            <line2>Street 32</line2>
            <line3>Magentaville</line3>
        </address>
    </customer>
</customers>
```

2. In this example, we will extract the customer's name and address. Save the following stylesheet as `customer.xsl`:

```xml
<?xml version="1.0"?>
<xsl:stylesheet xmlns:xsl="http://www.w3.org/1999/XSL/Transform">
    <xsl:output method="text" indent="yes"/>
    <xsl:template match="customer">
        <xsl:apply-templates select="name"/>:
        <xsl:apply-templates select="address"/>
    </xsl:template>
```

```
    <xsl:template match="name">
       <xsl:value-of select="lastname"/>, <xsl:value-of select="firstname"/>
    </xsl:template>

    <xsl:template match="address">
          <xsl:value-of select="line1"/>,
          <xsl:value-of select="line2"/>,
          <xsl:value-of select="line3"/>.
    </xsl:template>
 </xsl:stylesheet>
```

3. Run the example using the following instruction at the command line:

> **xt customer.xml customer.xsl**

4. We get the following output:

```
Erpen, Mark:
     Ink House,
        Street 32,
        Magentaville.
```

As usual, the presentation of the information leaves something to be desired, but let's not worry about that for now.

How It Works

Our first template looks for the `<customer>` element, and sets it as the context node:

```
    <xsl:template match="customer">
```

The next line calls the template that matches and transforms the `<name>` child element of the context node:

```
       <xsl:apply-templates select="name"/>:
```

The engine looks for this template, and processes it:

```
    <xsl:template match="name">
       <xsl:value-of select="lastname"/>, <xsl:value-of select="firstname"/>
    </xsl:template>
```

This template outputs the content of the `<lastname>` child element of `<name>`, followed by a comma and the content of the `<firstname>` element. When this has been done, the first template continues with its processing; the next line calls the template that matches the `<address>` element:

```
       <xsl:apply-templates select="address"/>
```

This template simply outputs the contents of the first, second and third lines of the address (separated by commas), adds a period to the last line, and then ends. The first template will then continue processing once more.

```
<xsl:template match="address">
   <xsl:value-of select="line1"/>,
   <xsl:value-of select="line2"/>,
   <xsl:value-of select="line3"/>.
</xsl:template>
```

The next line completes the first template, and stops the output. On their own, the other two templates in the stylesheet don't match any elements – there are no `<name>` or `<address>` elements at document root level.

```
</xsl:template>
```

XSLT Elements Concerned with Content

The next set of elements that we will investigate is concerned with the content of elements, and in controlling the way that content is output. In particular, the `<xsl:text>` element is provided as a way of outputting content while preserving white space, and of disabling output escaping.

Output escaping allows us to display characters that are reserved in XML, such as < and >. We can make sure that they are included in the output by substituting their entity references, < and > for the < and > characters above.

<xsl:text>

The `<xsl:text>` element is used to write literal text to the output. We can use this element to output reserved characters through the use of the `disable-output-escaping` attribute. For example:

```
Some output
<xsl:text disable-output-escaping="yes">
   An example of an XML element is &gt;Book&lt;
</xsl:text>
More output
```

Notice that we have to encode the reserved characters, but when this is used to transform an XML document, the resulting output will have the following line in it.

```
Some output

   An example of an XML element is <Book>

More output
```

The `<xsl:text>` element can also be useful in situations where we need to guarantee white space. The above result also includes two new lines and several spaces that the `<xsl:text>` element has preserved. This can be especially useful in formatting plain text output, although it may result in messy code.

For example, adding a single line break would require:

```
Some output
<xsl:text>
</xsl:text>
More output
```

This is all very well when there's no indentation, but if this were in the middle of an XSLT file, we would end up with very ugly looking code:

```
        Some output
        <xsl:text>
</xsl:text>
        More output
```

A better way to add a line break using this element is to use the numeric character entities for the line feed (
) and carriage return () characters:

```
        Some output
        <xsl:text>&#10;&#13;</xsl:text>
        More output
```

We will see further use of this element, including an example of the technique above for adding line breaks, as we continue with our examples.

<xsl:value-of>

We have already seen the <xsl:value-of> element in action: it outputs the contents of the element or attribute given in the XPath expression. We can specify elements by name, by their position number, or using any other XPath expression we care to construct. For example, in the case where we had the following XML source code:

```
<address>
    <line1>Ink House</line1>
    <line2>Street 32</line2>
    <line3>Magentaville</line3>
</address>
```

It would have been quite reasonable to use the following structure instead:

```
<address>
    <line>Ink House</line>
    <line>Street 32</line>
    <line>Magentaville</line>
</address>
```

With the information presented in this fashion, the only way of differentiating between the lines is by their position. We could have output each line by using the following XSLT fragment:

```
<xsl:for-each select="address">
    <xsl:value-of select="line[1]" />
    <xsl:value-of select="line[2]" />
    <xsl:value-of select="line[3]" />
</xsl:for-each>
```

Or even:

```
<xsl:for-each select="address/line">
   <xsl:value-of select="." />
</xsl:for-each>
```

When included in an XSLT stylesheet, both of the above fragments will give the following output:

```
Ink HouseStreet 32Magentaville
```

By now, it's probably becoming apparent that for every result tree you wish to obtain, there are a number of ways of using XSLT stylesheets to do it. The one you choose will depend on your style and taste, and to some extent on what you are trying to achieve. To place commas *between* lines of the address here, for example, we'd have to choose the first option, as the second carries out the same actions on *every* line.

`<xsl:value-of>` also has the `disable-output-escaping` attribute, which can be used in much the same way as for `<xsl:text>`, provided that you're using the XML output method. You must remember to escape XML reserved characters wherever they occur, as the XSLT engine will object if you do not.

Looping and Decision-making Elements

Like other languages, XSLT includes constructs that can be used to loop, and to carry out specified operations conditionally. We have already seen one of these elements – `<xsl:for-each>` – in previous examples, but here we will discuss it in more detail, along with the other elements in this category.

<xsl:for-each>

The `<xsl:for-each>` element carries out the transformation it contains on each element that meets the criteria laid out in its `select` attribute:

```
<xsl:for-each select="Books/Book">
   <xsl:value-of select="@ISBN" />:
   <xsl:value-of select="Title" />
   <xsl:value-of select="Synopsis" />
</xsl:for-each>
```

The `select` attribute selects all the `<Book>` elements that are child nodes of the `<Books>` element, and transforms them accordingly. In this case, that means outputting the value of the `ISBN` attribute, and the contents of the `<Title>` and `<Synopsis>` child nodes.

<xsl:if>

The `<xsl:if>` element is similar to the `if` statement found in conventional programming languages (such as WMLScript). For example, the following stylesheet:

```
<?xml version="1.0"?>
<xsl:stylesheet xmlns:xsl="http://www.w3.org/1999/XSL/Transform">
   <xsl:output method="xml" version="1.0" indent="yes"/>
```

```
    <xsl:template match="/Products">
        <xsl:for-each select="Product/*">
            <xsl:if test="name()='Price'">
                <price>
                <xsl:value-of select="."/>
                </price>
            </xsl:if>
        </xsl:for-each>
    </xsl:template>
</xsl:stylesheet>
```

will give the following output if applied to the `products.xml` file we saw earlier:

```
<?xml version="1.0" encoding="utf-8"?>
<price>0.20</price>
<price>1.20</price>
<price>2.00</price>
<price>0.50</price>
<price>3.50</price>
```

The first highlighted line selects any `<Products>` elements that are child nodes of the document root. We then iterate through every `<Product>` child node. The `<xsl:if>` element checks whether the name of the child node is `'Price'`, and outputs its content if so.

<xsl:choose>

The `<xsl:choose>` element allows processing similar to if...else structures (or the `switch` statement) in conventional programming languages. It can contain two child elements, `<xsl:when>` and `<xsl:otherwise>`, that help it to achieve this. More powerful than `<xsl:if>`, this element allows us to select from one of several choices, and to ensure that there is also a default action associated with this operation.

Each `<xsl:when>` element specifies a possible condition. If none of the conditions has been met, whatever is specified within `<xsl:otherwise>` will be carried out instead. Let's see this in action.

Try It Out — The <xsl:choose> Element

For this example, we're going to use `products.xml` once again. Our fictitious company wants a report on the purchase price of its goods. It has decided that a price lower than 50 cents constitutes very good value, and that these items are 'cheap'. Items that cost more than 50 cents but less than $1 are considered 'good value', and finally items over $1 each are 'expensive'. We have been asked to print out a report showing each item, listed by name, and its value rating.

1. The XSLT file we will use is shown below. Enter this stylesheet, and save it as `value.xsl`.

```
<?xml version="1.0"?>
<xsl:stylesheet xmlns:xsl="http://www.w3.org/1999/XSL/Transform">
    <xsl:output method="text" indent="yes"/>
    <xsl:template match="/">
        <xsl:for-each select="Products/Product">
            <xsl:value-of select="Name"/>
            <xsl:text>: </xsl:text>
```

```
            <xsl:choose>
                <xsl:when test="Price[.&lt;0.5]">Cheap</xsl:when>
                <xsl:when test="Price[.&lt;1.0]">Good Value</xsl:when>
                <xsl:otherwise>Expensive</xsl:otherwise>
            </xsl:choose>
            <xsl:text>&#10;&#13;</xsl:text>
        </xsl:for-each>
    </xsl:template>
</xsl:stylesheet>
```

2. Now run the following command at the DOS prompt:

```
> xt products.xml value.xsl
```

3. You should get the following output:

```
Eraser: Cheap
Ruler: Expensive
Marker: Expensive
Pen: Good Value
Stapler: Expensive
```

How It Works

By now, you're probably getting a fair idea of what these stylesheets are going to do before we use them, but we'll go through this one line by line. First, we are outputting text, and the transformation will be carried out on the whole document:

```
<xsl:output method="text" indent="yes"/>
<xsl:template match="/">
```

This `<xsl:for-each>` element matches all of the `<Product>` elements that are children of `<Products>` child elements of the document root. Essentially, we're looping through every product the company stocks:

```
<xsl:for-each select="Products/Product">
```

The next two lines output the name of the product to the result tree, followed by a colon and a space:

```
<xsl:value-of select="Name"/>
<xsl:text>: </xsl:text>
```

Now we get to the `<xsl:choose>` element. The first test checks whether the contents of the current `<Price>` element is less than 0.5. If this is the case, the resulting output is "Cheap", and no more conditions are checked.

```
<xsl:choose>
    <xsl:when test="Price[.&lt;0.5]">Cheap</xsl:when>
```

Notice that we have had to escape the < character, and that even though it has been escaped, it acts in its numeric form as a comparison operator. All products with prices over 0.5 are then checked against the next condition, which tests whether the price is less than 1:

```
<xsl:when test="Price[.&lt;1.0]">Good Value</xsl:when>
```

In this case, the output is "Good Value", and once again no more conditions are checked if this one is met. If it *isn't* met, however, the contents of the <xsl:otherwise> element are evaluated, and the result is that "Expensive" is output.

```
            <xsl:otherwise>Expensive</xsl:otherwise>
        </xsl:choose>
```

The <xsl:otherwise> element is not required in this construct, although it's usually a good idea to put one in. Finally, we use the <xsl:text> element to insert a line break, and complete the stylesheet:

```
            <xsl:text>&#10;&#13;</xsl:text>
        </xsl:for-each>
    </xsl:template>
```

Element Manipulation Elements

The last group of XSLT elements to look at are used to manipulate, insert, and copy elements from the source tree into the result tree. These can be very useful when large sections of the output are identical to the input document, or for simple rearrangement of XML files. The elements concerned with element manipulation include <xsl:copy> and <xsl:copy-of>, which (as their names suggest) are used to copy elements in the source tree to the output, and <xsl:element> and <xsl:attribute> that can be used to insert element and attribute nodes into the result tree respectively. Let's begin by investigating <xsl:copy>.

<xsl:copy>

<xsl:copy> simply copies the context node. The following template:

```
<xsl:template match="/">
    <copy>
        hello
    </copy>
</xsl:template>
```

when transforming the following XML fragment:

```
<Products>
    <Product>
        <Name>Eraser</Name>
    </Product>
</Products>
```

would result in this output:

```
<Products>hello</Products>
```

As you can see, the <xsl:copy> element *only* copies the context node, and doesn't include child elements or any content. If you wish to do more, you can use an <xsl:value-of> element that outputs the contents of <Products>, or use the <xsl:copy-of> element that we'll look at next.

<xsl:copy-of>

The `<xsl:copy-of>` element simply copies the element specified in its `select` attribute to the output. It can be used to copy whole sections of the source tree:

```
<xsl:copy-of select="*"/>
```

The above line will copy all of the child nodes of the context node, plus any of *their* child nodes, etc.

<xsl:element>

As you've begun to see, XSLT has a variety of tricks up its sleeve, but we wouldn't be interested if it weren't for its ability to specify the creation of XML from other XML, and `<xsl:element>` is concerned entirely with that process: it creates a new element node in the result tree. Here's an example.

Try It Out — Using <xsl:element>

Let's continue the thread using `products.xml` as our source file. Until now, we haven't specified how many of each product must be bought in any one transaction, and the trouble is that selling each item in just *any* quantity is uneconomical. Instead, we are going to offer our products in packs, and we need to add elements that specify the number of items in each pack to the file.

1. Here is the XSLT file we will use, which you should save as `packs.xsl`:

```
<?xml version="1.0"?>
<xsl:stylesheet xmlns:xsl="http://www.w3.org/1999/XSL/Transform">
    <xsl:output method="xml" version="1.0" indent="yes"/>
    <xsl:template match="/">
        <Products>
            <xsl:apply-templates select="Products/Product"/>
        </Products>
    </xsl:template>

    <xsl:template match="Products/Product">
        <Product>
            <xsl:for-each select="*">
                <xsl:copy-of select="."/>
            </xsl:for-each>
            <xsl:element name="Pack-size">10</xsl:element>
        </Product>
    </xsl:template>
</xsl:stylesheet>
```

2. Try this out with the following command:

```
> xt products.xml packs.xsl
```

3. You should get the output on the next page.

```
<?xml version="1.0" encoding="utf-8"?>
<Products>
<Product>
<Name>Eraser</Name>
<Price>0.20</Price>
<Pack-size>10</Pack-size>
</Product>
<Product>
<Name>Ruler</Name>
<Price>1.20</Price>
<Pack-size>10</Pack-size>
</Product>
<Product>
<Name>Marker</Name>
<Price>2.00</Price>
<Pack-size>10</Pack-size>
</Product>
<Product>
<Name>Pen</Name>
<Price>0.50</Price>
<Pack-size>10</Pack-size>
</Product>
<Product>
<Name>Stapler</Name>
<Price>3.50</Price>
<Pack-size>10</Pack-size>
</Product>
</Products>
```

We have added a pack size that, in all cases, is 10.

How It Works

For this example, we are outputting XML to the result tree, we've turned indentation on, and the version is (as ever) 1.0. The first interesting action is that the context is set to the document root, and we begin a <Products> element:

```
<xsl:template match="/">
   <Products>
```

At this point, we call the second template in the stylesheet:

```
<xsl:apply-templates select="Products/Product"/>
```

This next template looks for any elements that match the pattern Products/Product, and for every match adds a <Product> element:

```
<xsl:template match="Products/Product">
   <Product>
```

It then copies all of the child nodes of any matches, and their content, to the output tree. Remember that "*" returns *all* the child nodes of the context node:

```
<xsl:for-each select="*">
    <xsl:copy-of select="."/>
</xsl:for-each>
```

And finally, we add an element that specifies the pack size, which is the same for all products in this version of the code. We add the closing `</Product>` tag, and the template is done:

```
        <xsl:element name="Pack-size">10</xsl:element>
    </Product>
</xsl:template>
```

To finish off the transformation, we add the closing `</Products>` tag back in the first template:

```
    </Products>
</xsl:template>
```

`<xsl:element>` has an attribute called `use-attribute-sets` that we'll see in action shortly. As suggested above, we could also have set the pack values to different amounts, depending perhaps on the unit price. You may wish to try this yourself; the code you'd need would be something like:

```
<xsl:if test="Price[.&lt;0.50]">
    <xsl:element name="Pack-size">20</xsl:element>
</xsl:of>
```

This code snippet checks whether the price is less than 0.50 (dollars), and if so sets the pack size to 20.

<xsl:attribute>

`<xsl:attribute>` adds an attribute node to the current node, and we can demonstrate how it works with another example from our stationery company.

The company is going global, and we need to add an attribute to the price of each item that states it's in dollars – it is important that errors are not made in charging. The following XSLT fragment shows one way of adding this attribute:

```
<xsl:for-each select="*">
    <xsl:if test="name()='Price'">
        <xsl:copy select=".">
            <xsl:attribute name="currency">dollars</xsl:attribute>
        </xsl:copy>
    </xsl:if>
</xsl:for-each>
```

Through this code, a `currency` attribute is added to the `<Price>` element, which would now look like this:

```
<Price currency="dollars">0.20</Price>
```

<xsl:attribute-set>

Last but one, `<xsl:attribute-set>` defines and names a set of attributes that always go together. The syntax for this element is:

```
<xsl:attribute-set name="NameAttributeSet">
    <xsl:attribute name="first">first value</xsl:attribute>
    <xsl:attribute name="middle">second value</xsl:attribute>
    <xsl:attribute name="last">third value</xsl:attribute>
</xsl:attribute-set>
```

If we were to define an element with the `use-attribute-sets` attribute set to *NameAttributeSet*, the three attributes listed above would be added. For example, the following fragment:

```
<xsl:element name="Element" use-attribute-sets="NameAttributeSet">
    content
</xsl:element>
```

Would result in `<Element>` being output in the result tree as follows:

```
<Element first="first value" second="second value" third="third value">
    content
</Element>
```

<xsl:sort>

To finish our discussion of XSLT elements, we will illustrate the use of `<xsl:sort>`. This element is used to specify the sort order for the `<xsl:apply-templates>` and `<xsl:for-each>` elements. Consider the following stylesheet fragment:

```
<xsl:for-each select="Products/Product">
    <xsl:sort select="@ID"/>
    ProductID: <xsl:value-of select="@ID"/>
</xsl:for-each>
```

When applied to our `products.xml` file, this will produce the following output in sorted order (that is, ascending order by ID):

```
ProductID: S123456
ProductID: S432344
ProductID: S455456
ProductID: S456775
ProductID: S785436
```

A WAP Application with XML and XSLT

Before we finish this chapter, let's have a look at a practical example of a WAP application that uses XML and XSLT. Imagine that your company asks you to make the names and addresses of its customers available to its sales team, who may need to check these details before appointments. We know that the sales team all have WAP phones, so we decide to write an XSLT stylesheet that will extract the names and addresses of our customers, and present them in WML format.

Try It Out — Outputting Names and Addresses

1. In order to make this example a little more interesting, we'd better add at least a couple more names and addresses to our database file. Load in `customer.xml`, make the following changes, and save it as `customers.xml` (note the plural):

```xml
<?xml version="1.0"?>
<customers>
    <customer>
        <name>
            <firstname>Mark</firstname>
            <lastname>Erpen</lastname>
        </name>
        <creditlimit currency="dollars">2000</creditlimit>
        <address>
            <line>Ink House</line>
            <line>Street 32</line>
            <line>Magentaville</line>
        </address>
    </customer>
    <customer>
        <name>
            <firstname>Peter</firstname>
            <lastname>Jones</lastname>
        </name>
        <creditlimit currency="dollars">3500</creditlimit>
        <address>
            <line>17 Arley Terrace</line>
            <line>LEEDS</line>
            <line>Great Britain</line>
        </address>
    </customer>
    <customer>
        <name>
            <firstname>Shmuel</firstname>
            <lastname>Levi</lastname>
        </name>
        <creditlimit currency="dollars">2800</creditlimit>
        <address>
            <line>Kfar Chittim</line>
            <line>Tvirya</line>
            <line>ISRAEL</line>
        </address>
    </customer>
</customers>
```

2. We will now construct the XSLT stylesheet. We want to output a menu card that allows the user to choose which customer they wish to find, so they can then navigate to the appropriate card where the customer's name and address will be shown. Enter the stylesheet on the following page, and save it as `addresses.xsl`.

```
<?xml version="1.0"?>
<xsl:stylesheet xmlns:xsl="http://www.w3.org/1999/XSL/Transform">
    <xsl:output method="xml"
                version="1.0"
                indent="yes"
                doctype-system="http://www.wapforum.org/DTD/wml_1.2.xml"
                doctype-public="-//WAPFORUM//DTD WML 1.2//EN" />
    <xsl:template match="/">
        <wml>
            <card id="menu">
                <p>Please choose a customer:<br/>
                <xsl:for-each select="customers/customer/name">
                    <a><xsl:attribute name="href">
                            <xsl:text>#</xsl:text>
                            <xsl:value-of select="lastname"/>
                        </xsl:attribute>
                        <xsl:value-of select="lastname"/>
                        <xsl:text>, </xsl:text>
                        <xsl:value-of select="firstname"/>
                    </a><br/>
                </xsl:for-each>
                </p>
            </card>
        <xsl:apply-templates name="customers/customer"/>
        </wml>
    </xsl:template>

    <xsl:template match="customers/customer">
        <xsl:for-each select="name">
            <card><xsl:attribute name="id">
                    <xsl:value-of select="lastname"/>
                </xsl:attribute>
            <p><xsl:value-of select="lastname"/>
                <xsl:text>, </xsl:text>
                <xsl:value-of select="firstname"/><br/>
            </p>
            <p><xsl:for-each select="../address/line">
                    <xsl:value-of select="."/><br/>
                </xsl:for-each>
            </p>
            </card>
        </xsl:for-each>
    </xsl:template>

</xsl:stylesheet>
```

3. Run the transformation using the following command:

```
> xt customers.xml addresses.xsl customers.wml
```

4. The output file, formatted here for readability's sake, is shown below:

```
<?xml version="1.0" encoding="utf-8"?>
<!DOCTYPE wml PUBLIC "-//WAPFORUM//DTD WML 1.2//EN"
                     "http://www.wapforum.org/DTD/wml_1.2.dtd">
<wml>
    <card id="menu">
```

```
        <p>Please choose a customer:<br/>
           <a href="#Erpen">Erpen, Mark</a><br/>
           <a href="#Jones">Jones, Peter</a><br/>
           <a href="#Levi">Levi, Shmuel</a><br/>
        </p>
     </card>

     <card id="Erpen">
        <p>
           Erpen, Mark<br/>
        </p>
        <p>
           Ink House<br/>
           Street 32<br/>
           Magentaville<br/>
        </p>
     </card>

     <card id="Jones">
        <p>
           Jones, Peter<br/>
        </p>
        <p>
           17 Arley Terrace<br/>
           LEEDS<br/>
           Great Britain<br/>
        </p>
     </card>

     <card id="Levi">
        <p>
           Levi, Shmuel<br/>
        </p>
        <p>
           Kfar Chittim<br/>
           Tvirya<br/>
           ISRAEL<br/>
        </p>
     </card>
  </wml>
```

5. Load this file into the UP.Simulator:

6. Choose and follow one of the links:

How It Works

This stylesheet contains two templates, the second of which is called by the first. After the usual preliminaries, the first template begins a WML deck by including the document type declaration, and opening with the <wml> tag. The first WML card is called "menu", and it starts with a section of text that asks the user to choose a customer from the list provided.

```
<xsl:output method="xml"
            version="1.0"
            indent="yes"
            doctype-system="http://www.wapforum.org/DTD/wml12.dtd"
            doctype-public="-//WAPFORUM//DTD WML 1.2//EN"
/>
<xsl:template match="/">
   <wml>
      <card id="menu">
         <p>Please choose a customer:<br/>
```

The next line selects every occurrence of a <name> element that's a child of a <customer> element that's a child of a <customers> element. Practically, this means that every customer with a name is listed.

```
<xsl:for-each select="customers/customer/name">
```

After that, we begin a hyperlink and assign it an href attribute whose value is a # character followed by the last name of the customer.

```
<a><xsl:attribute name="href">
        <xsl:text>#</xsl:text>
        <xsl:value-of select="lastname"/>
   </xsl:attribute>
```

The text of each hyperlink is the full name of the customer. Notice that we've included an <xsl:text> element to make the output more pleasing:

```
<xsl:value-of select="lastname"/>
<xsl:text>, </xsl:text>
<xsl:value-of select="firstname"/>
```

The result of this section of the stylesheet is that we will have a menu card with a hyperlink for each customer in our list. The target of each hyperlink is a card with an ID corresponding to the last name of the customer. After finishing off the card:

```
            </a><br/>
        </xsl:for-each>
        </p>
    </card>
```

We will get the following WML:

```
<card id="menu">
    <p>Please choose a customer:<br/>
        <a href="#Erpen">Erpen, Mark</a><br/>
        <a href="#Jones">Jones, Peter</a><br/>
        <a href="#Levi">Levi, Shmuel</a><br/>
    </p>
</card>
```

We now write a card, setting its id to the last name of the customer, and its contents to the customer's full name and address details. To do this, we call the second template in the stylesheet:

```
<xsl:apply-templates name="customers/customer"/>
```

The second template matches and returns all the `<customer>` elements in our XML file. It then loops through every customer using the following line:

```
<xsl:for-each select="name">
```

For each customer, we start a new card and give it an id attribute with the customer's last name as a value. We have now linked the menu card to the customer cards.

```
<card><xsl:attribute name="id">
        <xsl:value-of select="lastname"/>
    </xsl:attribute>
```

Each card then lists the name and address of the customer. Again, we've included an `<xsl:text>` element to make the output more pleasing.

```
<p>
    <xsl:value-of select="lastname"/>
    <xsl:text>, </xsl:text>
    <xsl:value-of select="firstname"/><br/>
</p>
```

The address is output using another `<xsl:for-each>` element that iterates through every line of the customer's address:

```
<p>
    <xsl:for-each select="../address/line">
        <xsl:value-of select="."/><br/>
    </xsl:for-each>
</p>
```

You can see that we're looping through every element that matches the following XPath expression:

```
../address/line
```

The reason why we must start the expression with the parent node, "..", is that the previous `<xsl:for-each>` element has changed the context node to "/customers/customer/name". We want to loop through every line of the `<address>` element, which is a child of `<name>`'s *parent* node, and so we must first change the context to /customers/customer/address/line.

We then finish the card, and when all cards have been written the WML deck is ended and the transformation stops.

```
        </card>
      </xsl:for-each>
    </xsl:template>
```

Of course, there are several improvements that could be made to this output. Currently, only browsers with a fixed 'back' button can navigate back to the menu card, but that could easily be fixed. The other problem is the deck size limitation: it wouldn't be too much of a stretch to imagine that we might have several hundred customers, if not more. We will need to think of a way of splitting this data, and perhaps allowing users to search under a name or letter – but for now, we need to move on again.

Summary

This chapter has provided a whirlwind tour of XSLT. In order to understand it, we illustrated an important technology that is part of the XSLT specification – XPath – and how XPath is used to locate the elements and attributes in an XML document. We also examined the XSLT elements and their uses. In summary, we saw:

❑ What XSLT is, and how can it be used.

❑ The XPath language and its functions, including the document root, child nodes and parent nodes. We learned that in XSLT, source files are called source trees, and output files are called result trees.

❑ We covered the core XSLT elements, and their most-used attributes

❑ We put this into practice by developing an XSLT-driven WML application

This chapter has laid the foundations for the next one, where we will integrate all of our dynamic content generation and XML transformation techniques to generate WML files dynamically, and customize them for specific browsers using XSLT transformations.

Dynamic WML Generation with ASP and XSLT

The last two chapters have shown two things. We have seen how we can use ASP and ADO to generate WML dynamically, and how we can use XSLT to manipulate XML files. In this final chapter, it is time to put these techniques together, combining the benefits we get from these technologies.

We will begin by looking at how we can manipulate XML data with ASP, using XSLT and direct control of the node tree. We will then use this knowledge to generate WML that's customized for the user agent requesting the resource – the process involved here is to identify the user agent, and then to generate the 'right kind' of WML by applying different XSLT stylesheets accordingly.

Last of all, we will look at some performance issues, since XSLT transformations can be processor and memory intensive. If we are expecting our WAP site to have a lot of users, we'll have to take that into account.

XML Manipulation in ASP

ASP has no built-in functionality for handling and manipulating XML, so in order to use it to do so, we'll need to use an 'add-on'. Handily, Microsoft provides just such a thing: the **MSXML Parser**. This piece of software provides us with a collection of objects that we can use to manipulate XML from within ASP files, just like the ADO objects we used to manipulate databases in Chapter 18.

> **If you have Internet Explorer, you'll almost certainly have a version of this parser installed on your system, but it's well worth downloading the latest version, for free, from the Microsoft web site at http://msdn.microsoft.com/xml. The version we used for this chapter is the September 2000 'beta' release of MSXML 3.0. Microsoft is committed to releasing the latest XML parser every alternate month, so it is likely that a more up to date version will be available by the time you read this.**

The MSXML parser allows us to perform XSLT manipulations, but before that we should look at the **DOM manipulation** that it makes possible.

DOM Manipulation

The **Document Object Model** (**DOM**) is a way of representing XML documents programmatically as a hierarchical set of objects. If that seems like an alien concept, it shouldn't, because we talked about exactly this idea in the previous chapter. It's just that then, we didn't use the term "DOM". We called it a tree of nodes.

We've seen how XPath allows us to navigate through a node tree in order to specify nodes for XSLT manipulation. The MSXML parser allows us to manipulate the node tree in a similar way: we can navigate through it, adding and removing nodes as required.

It sounds quite simple, but in fact we could construct a whole WML document in this fashion, if we wanted to. We might start off by adding a <wml> element, then a <card> element inside the <wml> element, and a <p> element inside the <card> element, then the content of the <p> element, and so on. In this section, we'll look at:

❑ Using the MSXML parser

❑ Traversing the DOM tree

❑ Modifying nodes

❑ Inserting nodes

❑ Deleting nodes

Using the MSXML Parser

In order to perform any manipulation of XML files using the MSXML parser in ASP, we first need to create the object that will represent the whole XML document. The object we create is called DOMDocument, and it's one of the objects supplied with the MSXML download. Using JScript, we create this object with the following code:

```
XMLDocument = Server.CreateObject("MSXML2.DOMDocument.3.0");
```

The parameter passed to the CreateObject() method is called the **programmatic identifier** of the object we want to create (compare it with things like ADODB.Recordset, which we saw in Chapter 18), and it must be entered exactly as shown. After execution of this statement, we have a DOMDocument object with which we can load an existing XML document from a file, build an XML document from scratch, or a mixture of the two.

If we want to load an existing XML document, we must first set the async (asynchronous) property of our new DOMDocument object to false. This halts execution of the ASP file until the whole document has been loaded. If we don't do this, our code may continue executing even though the XML document is still *being* loaded (a large file can take some time), and trying to access the object while the document is in this state is unlikely to yield the correct result. Once this property has been set, we can load the document using the load() method, which takes the name of the XML file as its one and only parameter. When the document is loaded, the parser will check that it is well formed.

```
XMLDocument.async = false;
XMLDocument.load(Server.MapPath("customers.xml"));
```

Here, as in Chapter 18, we've used the ASP `Server` *object's* `MapPath()` *method to generate the full pathname of this file. This will work provided that* `customers.xml` *is in the* `inetpub\wwwroot` *directory.*

Note that in this version of the `DOMDocument` *object, the* `load()` *method doesn't work for* `.wml` *files. For some reason, it only loads the XML and document type declarations, and ignores the rest of the WML. Later in the chapter, you'll see how we work around this little problem.*

The `DOMDocument` object has another method called `loadXML()` that can be used to parse and load an XML document passed as a string, as the following code shows:

```
XMLString = "<cds><cd><title>Autogeddon</title></cd></cds>";
XMLDocument.loadXML(XMLString);
```

However we begin, and whether we have an empty, partial, or full XML document in our `DOMDocument` object, there are many methods for modifying its contents. We can add elements, remove elements, move elements, copy elements, add attributes, add text, and so on – and we will see many of these in action later. For now, probably the simplest thing we can do with the document is to write it into the output stream. The `xml` property of the `DOMDocument` object returns its XML content:

```
Response.Write(XMLDocument.xml);
```

We can also save the XML document to disk, using the `save()` method:

```
XMLDocument.save("result.xml");
```

The above code saves the XML document to the file "`result.xml`" Let's see an example of a WML file generated using the `DOMDocument` object.

Try It Out — Generating WML by DOM Manipulation

1. Type the following code into your text editor and save it as `inetpub\wwwroot\domexample1.asp`:

```
<%@ Language = "JScript"; %><%
    Response.ContentType = "text/vnd.wap.wml";

    XMLDocument = Server.CreateObject("MSXML2.DOMDocument.3.0");

    wmlNode = XMLDocument.createElement("wml");
    cardNode = XMLDocument.createElement("card");

    // Add an attribute called id whose value is card1
    cardNode.setAttribute("id", "card1");

    // Create a paragraph element and add its text content
    paraNode = XMLDocument.createElement("p");
    paraNode.text = "We generated this WML using DOM Manipulation in ASP!";
```

```
    // Attach the paragraph element to the card element
    cardNode.appendChild(paraNode);

    // Attach the card element to the wml element
    wmlNode.appendChild(cardNode);

    // Attach the wml element to the document
    XMLDocument.appendChild(wmlNode);

%><?xml version="1.0"?>
<!DOCTYPE wml PUBLIC "-//WAPFORUM//DTD WML 1.2//EN"
                     "http://www.wapforum.org/DTD/wml_1.2.xml">
<%
    Response.Write(XMLDocument.xml);
%>
```

2. Load this file into the UP.Simulator:

How It Works

We start by setting the content type, as usual, and creating the DOMDocument object:

```
<%@ Language = "JScript"; %><%
    Response.ContentType = "text/vnd.wap.wml";

    XMLDocument = Server.CreateObject("MSXML2.DOMDocument.3.0");
```

Next, we create elements to add to the DOMDocument object, specify their relationships, attributes, and content, and then place them into our document:

```
    wmlNode = XMLDocument.createElement("wml");
    cardNode = XMLDocument.createElement("card");

    // Add an attribute called id whose value is card1
    cardNode.setAttribute("id", "card1");

    // Create a paragraph element and add its text content
    paraNode = XMLDocument.createElement("p");
    paraNode.text = "We generated this WML using DOM Manipulation in ASP!";
```

```
// Attach the paragraph element to the card element
cardNode.appendChild(paraNode);

// Attach the card element to the wml element
wmlNode.appendChild(cardNode);

// Attach the wml element to the document
XMLDocument.appendChild(wmlNode);
```

Even before we've given a formal explanation of these methods (as we will shortly), reading it line by line should give you a fairly clear idea of what's going on here. Finally, we write out the XML and document type declarations, followed by the XML document we've just created:

```
%><?xml version="1.0"?>
<!DOCTYPE wml PUBLIC "-//WAPFORUM//DTD WML 1.2//EN"
                    "http://www.wapforum.org/DTD/wml_1.2.xml">
<%
    Response.Write(XMLDocument.xml);
%>
```

This code actually generates the following WML document:

```
<?xml version="1.0"?>
<!DOCTYPE wml PUBLIC "-//WAPFORUM//DTD WML 1.2//EN"
                    "http://www.wapforum.org/DTD/wml_1.2.xml">
<wml>
    <card id="card1">
        <p>
            We generated this WML using DOM Manipulation in ASP!
        </p>
    </card>
</wml>
```

Traversing the DOM Tree

The example above looked at how a DOM tree can be constructed from scratch using ASP. Before we explain exactly how that was done, though, let's take a look at how to move around an *existing* tree, by loading an XML document and examining its contents. To illustrate this section, we will use an XML file from the previous chapter, books.xml:

```
<?xml version="1.0"?>
<Books>
    <Book ISBN="1-861004-58-3">
        <Title>Beginning WAP</Title>
        <Authors>
            <Author>Karli Watson</Author>
            <Author>Soo Mee Foo</Author>
            <Author>Wei Meng Lee</Author>
            <Author>Ted Wugofski</Author>
        </Authors>
```

```
            <Price>39.99</Price>
            <PublicationDate>2000</PublicationDate>
            <Synopsis>
                This book is for those who want to learn WAP,
                and specifically its markup and scripting
                languages: WML and WMLScript.
            </Synopsis>
        </Book>
    </Books>
```

We can load this XML file into a `DOMDocument` object using code we've already seen:

```
XMLDocument.async = false;
XMLDocument.load(Server.MapPath("books.xml"));
```

Again, this code will work if we place `books.xml` *in the* `inetpub\wwwroot\` *directory.*

We've seen that we can output the XML contained in this file simply by outputting the `xml` property of the `DOMDocument` object. If we want to get programmatic access to the DOM tree contained in this object, we need to use some of the other methods and properties that it possesses. A good starting point is to look at the `documentElement` property, which contains the root node:

```
node = XMLDocument.documentElement;
```

After execution of this statement, `node` contains an `XMLDOMNode` object, which is another of the objects contained in the MSXML library. Node objects have various properties to allow you gain access to their details (such as the node type, the node name, etc.) and contents (including child nodes). The table below shows some of the more useful ones:

Property	Description
`nodeName`	The name of the node, for example `"Book"`.
`nodeTypeString`	The type of the node, such as `"element"`, `"text"`, or `"attribute"`.
`text`	The text contained in the node, including the text contained by child elements (if any). This text is formatted to *exclude* the start and end tags of any child elements.
`attributes`	A collection of attribute nodes (if any exist).
`childNodes`	A collection of child nodes (if any exist), excluding attribute nodes.

With regard to the `attributes` and `childNodes` properties, we can discover how many nodes there are in these collections by using the `length` property, and access individual nodes by using the `item` property. The following code snippets show this syntax in more detail, first obtaining the collections:

```
attributes = node.attributes;
childNodes = node.childNodes;
```

Then obtaining the number of nodes in each:

```
attNum = attributes.length;
childNum = childNodes.length;
```

As `item` is the default property for both of these collections, we can use a convenient shorthand notation to get access to an individual node. Since numbering begins at zero, the following statements could be used to obtain attribute number 3 and child node number 4 respectively:

```
attribute = attributes[2];
child = childNodes[3];
```

Before we even look at a node's `childNodes` collection, we can first check to see if any exist by using the `hasChildNodes()` method, which returns `true` if they do:

```
if (node.hasChildNodes())
{
    childNodes = node.childNodes;
}
```

Unfortunately, there's no equivalent method to see if a node has attributes, although it is worth checking the *type* of the node, as only `element` type nodes are capable of having attributes:

```
if (node.nodeTypeString == "element")
{
    attributes = node.attributes;
}
```

At this stage, we can check to see if the node has any attributes by testing whether `attributes.length` is greater than zero.

Try It Out — Traversing the DOM

Let's put these properties into an example that will dissect an XML file, and display information about it in a WML card. Since we already have it around, we will use `books.xml` again.

1. Type the following code into your text editor and save it as `inetpub\wwwroot\domexample2.asp`:

```
<%@ Language = "JScript"; %><% Response.ContentType = "text/vnd.wap.wml";
%><?xml version="1.0"?>
<!DOCTYPE wml PUBLIC "-//WAPFORUM//DTD WML 1.2//EN"
                    "http://www.wapforum.org/DTD/wml_1.2.xml">

<wml>
    <card id="nodelist">
        <p>
<%
    XMLDocument = Server.CreateObject("MSXML2.DOMDocument.3.0");
    XMLDocument.async = false;
    XMLDocument.load(Server.MapPath("books.xml"));
```

```
    // Call PrintNodes function for root node
    PrintNodes(XMLDocument.documentElement);

    // PrintNodes function definition
    function PrintNodes(node)
    {
        Response.Write("'<br/>" + node.nodeName + "' node found, type is '")
        Response.Write(node.nodeTypeString + "'");

        // Check if node type is element. If so, output its name and attributes
        if (node.nodeTypeString == "element")
        {
            var attributes = node.attributes;
            var attNum;
            for (attNum = 0; attNum < attributes.length; attNum++)
            {
                Response.Write("<br/><br/>'" + node.nodeName + "' attribute ");
                Response.Write((attNum + 1) + " of " + attributes.length + ": ");
                Response.Write("'" + attributes[attNum].nodeName + "', ");
                Response.Write("value = '" + attributes[attNum].text + "'");
            }
        }

        // Check if the node is of type text. If so, output its content
        if (node.nodeTypeString == "text")
        {
            Response.Write(", text contents: '" + node.text + "'");
        }

        // Check if the node has child nodes. If so, call this
        // function for every child node.
        if (node.hasChildNodes)
        {
            var childNodes = node.childNodes;
            var childNum;
            for (childNum = 0; childNum < childNodes.length; childNum++)
            {
                Response.Write("<br/>'" + node.nodeName + "' child node ")
                Response.Write((childNum + 1) + " of " + childNodes.length + ": ");
                PrintNodes(childNodes[childNum]);
            }
        }
    }
%>
    </p>
    </card>
</wml>
```

2. Load this file into the UP.Simulator:

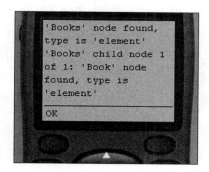

Since this code creates a card with too much content to see comfortably, here's a formatted transcript of the text:

'Books' node found, type is 'element'

'Books' child node 1 of 1: 'Book' node found, type is 'element'
'Book' attribute 1 of 1: 'ISBN', value = '1-861004-58-3'

'Book' child node 1 of 5: 'Title' node found, type is 'element'
'Title' child node 1 of 1: '#text' node found, type is 'text', text contents: 'Beginning WAP'

'Book' child node 2 of 5: 'Authors' node found, type is 'element'
'Authors' child node 1 of 4: 'Author' node found, type is 'element'
'Author' child node 1 of 1: '#text' node found, type is 'text', text contents: 'Karli Watson'

'Authors' child node 2 of 4: 'Author' node found, type is 'element'
'Author' child node 1 of 1: '#text' node found, type is 'text', text contents: 'Soo Mee Foo'

'Authors' child node 3 of 4: 'Author' node found, type is 'element'
'Author' child node 1 of 1: '#text' node found, type is 'text', text contents: 'Wei Meng Lee'

'Authors' child node 4 of 4: 'Author' node found, type is 'element'
'Author' child node 1 of 1: '#text' node found, type is 'text', text contents: 'Ted Wugofski'

'Book' child node 3 of 5: 'Price' node found, type is 'element'
'Price' child node 1 of 1: '#text' node found, type is 'text', text contents: '39.99'

'Book' child node 4 of 5: 'PublicationDate' node found, type is 'element'
'PublicationDate' child node 1 of 1: '#text' node found, type is 'text', text contents: '2000'

'Book' child node 5 of 5: 'Synopsis' node found, type is 'element'
'Synopsis' child node 1 of 1: '#text' node found, type is 'text', text contents: 'This book is for those who want to learn WAP, and specifically its markup and scripting languages: WML and WMLScript.'

How It Works

The code begins by writing out the start of our WML deck and loading the `books.xml` document:

```
<%@ Language = "JScript"; %><% Response.ContentType = "text/vnd.wap.wml";
%><?xml version="1.0"?>
<!DOCTYPE wml PUBLIC "-//WAPFORUM//DTD WML 1.2//EN"
                     "http://www.wapforum.org/DTD/wml_1.2.xml">

<wml>
   <card id="nodelist">
      <p>
<%
   XMLDocument = Server.CreateObject("MSXML2.DOMDocument.3.0");
   XMLDocument.async = false;
   XMLDocument.load(Server.MapPath("books.xml"));
```

Then we begin processing the `documentElement` property of our `DOMDocument` object by passing it to a function that we'll look at in a moment, `PrintNodes()`:

```
   PrintNodes(XMLDocument.documentElement);
```

Next we define our `PrintNodes()` function. The idea of this function is that it will take a node object, write out any details about this object, and then process any child nodes. It begins by writing the `nodeName` and `nodeTypeString` properties of the `node` object it is working on:

```
function PrintNodes(node)
{
   Response.Write("'<br/>" + node.nodeName + "' node found, type is '")
   Response.Write(node.nodeTypeString + "'");
```

This will output the node's name, and its type. After that, we want to write out the attributes of the current node, if any exist, so we check to see if the node is an element (since text and attribute nodes don't have attributes) and then iterate through each attribute, writing out its name, position, and value:

```
   if (node.nodeTypeString == "element")
   {
      var attributes = node.attributes;
      var attNum;
      for (attNum = 0; attNum < attributes.length; attNum++)
      {
         Response.Write("<br/><br/>'" + node.nodeName + "' attribute ");
         Response.Write((attNum + 1) + " of " + attributes.length + ": ");
         Response.Write("'" + attributes[attNum].nodeName + "', ");
         Response.Write("value = '" + attributes[attNum].text + "'");
      }
   }
```

If the node we are looking at is a text node, then it will have text content, which we output using the `text` property:

```
if (node.nodeTypeString == "text")
{
   Response.Write(", text contents: '" + node.text + "'");
}
```

Next we look at child nodes. If any exist, we write out a message to indicate that we are processing them, and pass each child node in turn to `PrintNodes()`.

> *PrintNodes() is a **recursive** function, which means that it calls itself during execution. This can be a tricky idea to follow, and we'll return to this subject after we've finished looking at the code. Note, though, that using a recursive function has compelled us to declare the variables we use with* var. *Doing this ensures that we get a new set of 'local' variables every time the function is called – if we didn't, the same variables would be reused, and the function would not work.*

The code to process child nodes is as follows:

```
if (node.hasChildNodes)
{
   var childNodes = node.childNodes;
   var childNum;
   for (childNum = 0; childNum < childNodes.length; childNum++)
   {
      Response.Write("<br/>'" + node.nodeName + "' child node ")
      Response.Write((childNum + 1) + " of " + childNodes.length + ": ");
      PrintNodes(childNodes[childNum]);
   }
}
```

We assign the child nodes to a variable named `childNodes`, and iterate through every node in the collection. Finally, we close the function, the script, and the deck:

```
   }
%>
      </p>
   </card>
</wml>
```

Let's turn now to the output, as this is representative of the way the code works, and will help to explain the recursion that is essential to its operation. When the code first executes, `PrintNodes()` is called with the `documentElement` property of the `DOMDocument` object, which contains `books.xml`. The `documentElement` property encapsulates the `<Books>` element of our XML document, in the form of a node object. `PrintNodes()` proceeds to output the following:

'Books' node found, type is 'element'

<Books> has no attributes and is not of type "text", so PrintNodes() moves on to look at its child nodes. It has one, and the following is output:

'Books' child node 1 of 1:

It's at this point that recursion kicks in. We call PrintNodes() again, this time with the *child node* of the documentElement node that we started with. PrintNodes() restarts, and outputs details for the <Book> element it has been passed:

'Book' node found, type is 'element'

This time it finds an attribute, and writes out its details:

'Book' attribute 1 of 1: 'ISBN', value = '1-861004-58-3'

Five child nodes are also found, and recursion moves to the next level: for every child node we call PrintNodes() yet again. After outputting some text signifying that child nodes have been found and that the first one will now be processed,

'Book' child node 1 of 5:

PrintNodes() is passed the first child node of <Book>, the <Title> element. Details are again output:

'Title' node found, type is 'element'

The <Title> element has one child (remember that text contained by elements is also classed as a node), so again we write out some status information,

'Title' child node 1 of 1:

and pass PrintNodes() our next node, the text child of <Title>:

'#text' node found, type is 'text'

This time the type is "text", so we write out the contents:

, text contents: 'Beginning WAP'

This node has no children, and here that recursion is key. This time, the function completes its execution *without* calling itself again. If you recall, this version of the function was called during the processing of the <Title> element node, so control returns to the child node processing routine for that node. In this case, no more child nodes are returned, so that function ends too. Control returns to the child node processing for the <Book> element node, and since we haven't finished looking at the child nodes of that node, the loop continues:

'Book' child node 2 of 5:

`PrintNodes()` is now called again, this time with the node object representing the `<Authors>` element. It carries on processing here:

> 'Authors' node found, type is 'element'

And so on, through the whole file. Eventually, when all child nodes have been processed, we will return to our top-level function and execution will end.

This kind of recursion is essential for moving through DOM trees because in the general case, the number and depth of child nodes will vary and conventional looping will not work. We can use recursive techniques to move through the tree, checking for the names of elements as we go, and processing them as we find them.

Addressing DOM Contents

With an in-depth knowledge of a specific XML file, we can specify an exact path for greater efficiency, but we still have to identify nodes by their position in the DOM tree structure. This can involve long and confusing statements, as you're about to see. Consider the following XML document, `members.xml`:

```xml
<?xml version="1.0"?>
<Members>
    <Member ID="1234567">
        <FirstName>Lee</FirstName>
        <LastName>Wei Meng</LastName>
        <Type>Ordinary</Type>
        <Address>Ang Mo Kio</Address>
        <Address>Ave 3</Address>
        <Address>Singapore</Address>
        <Postal>123456</Postal>
    </Member>
    <Member ID="7654321">
        <FirstName>Tan</FirstName>
        <LastName>Edward</LastName>
        <Type>Student</Type>
        <Address>Bukit Timah Street 27</Address>
        <Address>Singapore</Address>
        <Postal>654321</Postal>
    </Member>
</Members>
```

If we load this document into a `DOMDocument` object stored in a variable named `XMLDocument`, we can access any part of it using a single statement, through combinations of the properties we saw earlier. Let's look at a few examples:

- ❑ `XMLDocument.documentElement` refers to the root element, `<Members>`.

- ❑ `XMLDocument.documentElement.childNodes[0].nodeName` refers to the name of the first child of the root element, which is `"Member"`.

- ❑ `XMLDocument.documentElement.childNodes[1].childNodes[2].childNodes[0].text` refers to the text `"Student"`.

As you can see, this is hardly easy to read, but it *does* have its uses, as we will see in the next section.

Modifying Nodes

Of the node properties we've looked at so far, only one allows us to edit its contents: `text`. We can set this value using:

```
node.text = "text";
```

However, you need to be very careful with this property! If we were to write, for example:

```
XMLDocument.documentElement.text = "text";
```

We would overwrite all contents of the root element, effectively destroying all the elements it contains! The `text` property of the `documentElement` includes any text content of child elements, *plus* their child elements, etc. We should only really modify this property for "`text`" type nodes, where we can be sure that no data will be lost.

For example, using `members.xml`, we might want to change the way we denote members. Currently we use the text "`Ordinary`" and "`Student`". At some point we might change our categorization, and employ codes such as "`O`" for ordinary members and "`OS`" for students. We could replace the text of the `<Type>` elements for all members using the following code:

```
XMLDocument = Server.CreateObject("MSXML2.DOMDocument");
XMLDocument.async = false;
XMLDocument.load(Server.MapPath("members.xml"));
XMLDoc = XMLDocument.documentElement;

for (mem = 0; mem < XMLDoc.childNodes.length; mem++)
{
   if (XMLDoc.childNodes[mem].childNodes[2].childNodes[0].text == "Ordinary")
   {
      XMLDoc.childNodes[mem].childNodes[2].childNodes[0].text = "O";
   }
   if (XMLDoc.childNodes[mem].childNodes[2].childNodes[0].text == "Student")
   {
      XMLDoc.childNodes[mem].childNodes[2].childNodes[0].text = "OS";
   }
}
```

The above code changes the content of the "`text`"-type nodes contained by `<Type>` elements in the XML document. We can also rewrite this as:

```
for (mem = 0; mem < XMLDoc.childNodes.length; mem++)
{
   if (XMLDoc.childNodes[mem].childNodes[2].text == "Ordinary")
   {
      XMLDoc.childNodes[mem].childNodes[2].text = "O";
   }
   if (XMLDoc.childNodes[mem].childNodes[2].text == "Student")
   {
      XMLDoc.childNodes[mem].childNodes[2].text = "OS";
   }
}
```

Here, we are looking at the text property of the `<Type>` element nodes. Accessing this property for an element is equivalent to accessing the same property for "text"-type children – which can save us a bit of typing! Of course, we could add to the logic here, replacing other values if our XML document contained more data.

Inserting a Node into a DOM Tree

Having looked at the limited potential for modification, let's focus now on how to insert a new node into an XML document, which is the process you saw at work in this chapter's first example. Inserting a node consists of three stages:

- ❑ Creating the node
- ❑ Configuring the node
- ❑ Positioning the node

Creating the Node

The `DOMDocument` object that we've been using to store our DOM tree also provides methods for creating new nodes. There are several of these for different types of nodes; we'll look at the following for creating element, attribute, and text nodes respectively:

- ❑ createElement(*elementName*)
- ❑ createAttribute(*attributeName*)
- ❑ createTextNode(*textContents*)

Each of these methods returns a node of the required type, for you to store in a variable. Note that a node created this way does not yet belong to the XML document – it merely exists in our code. We must place the element at an appropriate position in the document later on.

When creating element and attribute nodes, we need to supply a name. nodeName is a read-only property, so this is the one and only chance we have to name our nodes – we can't change their names once created. Text nodes don't have a name, so the function that creates them just takes the value of the node as a parameter. As we've seen, we *can* change this value later on.

The following lines of code create one of each type of node:

```
newElement = XMLDocument.createElement("Description");
newAttribute = XMLDocument.createAttribute("Color");
newText = XMLDocument.createTextNode("High quality eraser!");
```

Configuring the Node

Configuring nodes involves assigning values to their properties. For the three types of node we are looking at, we will generally want to do the following:

- ❑ Element nodes – set any attributes and text content for the element
- ❑ Attribute nodes – set the value of the attribute
- ❑ Text nodes – set content (if not set at creation time)

523

Let's start with attribute nodes. When we create these, we give them a name, but no value. Setting their value, however, is simple: we assign a value to the text attribute. For example:

```
newAttribute.text = "Blue";
```

We can also use the text attribute to set the content of element or text nodes:

```
newElement.text = "High quality eraser!";
newText.text = "An eraser of dubious quality.";
```

There are two ways of assigning attributes to elements. We can use an existing attribute node object, such as the newAttribute we configured above, or we can automatically create an attribute node belonging to the element node. For the former, we use the setAttributeNode() method:

```
newElement.setAttributeNode(newAttribute);
```

Whereas to create an attribute node implicitly and attach it to the element, we use setAttribute():

```
newElement.setAttribute("Color", "Blue");
```

Where the two parameters are attribute's name and value respectively.

Positioning the Node

Node objects also have methods for attaching new nodes:

- ❑ appendChild(*newChild*)
- ❑ insertBefore(*newChild, refChild*)

In both cases, we call the methods of the node object that is to be the parent of the inserted node, and we specify the new node in the *newChild* parameter. *refChild* is an optional parameter that allows you to specify the location of the new child with respect to existing children. If, for example, you want your new node to be the third child of a parent, you need to pass the fourth child as the *refChild* parameter.

We might use these in the following way:

```
XMLDoc.childNode[2].appendChild(newElement);
XMLDoc.insertBefore(anotherElement, XMLDoc.childNode[2]);
```

This will give XMLDoc two new child elements, anotherElement and newElement, in that order.

Note that we can use these same methods to build up a collection of nodes before inserting them into the tree contained in our DOMDocument element. This, for example:

```
newElement.appendChild(newText);
newElement2.appendChild(newElement);
XMLDoc.appendChild(newElement2);
```

gives the following node tree:

```
<newElement2>
    <newElement>
        Text value of newText
    </newElement>
</newElement2>
```

In the following example, we'll insert a new node into the DOM tree, and at the same time set an attribute for the newly added node. For this, we will use another of the sample XML documents from the last chapter, products.xml, which you should ensure is located in inetpub\wwwroot:

```xml
<?xml version="1.0" ?>
<Products>
    <Product ID="S123456">
        <Name>Eraser</Name>
        <Price>0.20</Price>
    </Product>
    <Product ID="S455456">
        <Name>Ruler</Name>
        <Price>1.20</Price>
    </Product>
    <Product ID="S785436">
        <Name>Marker</Name>
        <Price>2.00</Price>
    </Product>
    <Product ID="S432344">
        <Name>Pen</Name>
        <Price>0.50</Price>
    </Product>
    <Product ID="S456775">
        <Name>Stapler</Name>
        <Price>3.50</Price>
    </Product>
</Products>
```

Try It Out — Inserting a Node

1. Make the following changes to domexample2.asp, and save it back in the same directory with the name domexample3.asp:

```
<%@ Language = "JScript"; %><% Response.ContentType = "text/vnd.wap.wml";
%><?xml version="1.0"?>
<!DOCTYPE wml PUBLIC "-//WAPFORUM//DTD WML 1.2//EN"
                     "http://www.wapforum.org/DTD/wml_1.2.xml">

<wml>
    <card id="nodelist">
        <p>
<%
    XMLDocument = Server.CreateObject("MSXML2.DOMDocument.3.0");
    XMLDocument.async = false;
```

```
        XMLDocument.load(Server.MapPath("products.xml"));

        newNode = XMLDocument.createElement("Description");
        newNode.text = "High quality eraser!";
        newNode.setAttribute("Color", "Blue");

        refNode = XMLDocument.documentElement.childNodes[0].firstChild;
        XMLDocument.documentElement.childNodes[0].insertBefore(newNode, refNode);

        Response.Write("Product ID=\"S123456\" now contains:<br/>");
        PrintNodes(XMLDocument.documentElement.childNodes[0]);

function PrintNodes(node)
    {
        ... rest of code as before
```

2. Load this file into the UP.Simulator, and scroll down to the portion showing the first child node of the first <Product> element:

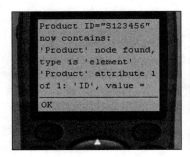

Once again, the result is too long to fit on the screen, so here's a formatted transcription:

Product ID="S123456" now contains:

'Product' node found, type is 'element'
'Product' attribute 1 of 1: 'ID', value = 'S123456'

'Product' child node 1 of 3:
'Description' node found, type is 'element'
'Description' attribute 1 of 1: 'Color', value = 'Blue'
'Description' child node 1 of 1:
'#text' node found, type is 'text', text contents: 'High quality eraser!'

'Product' child node 2 of 3:
'Name' node found, type is 'element'
'Name' child node 1 of 1:
'#text' node found, type is 'text', text contents: 'Eraser'

'Product' child node 3 of 3:
'Price' node found, type is 'element'
'Price' child node 1 of 1:
'#text' node found, type is 'text', text contents: '0.20'

How It Works

After the standard code for starting a deck and loading `products.xml`, we create a new element (a new node) using the `createElement()` method:

```
newNode = XMLDocument.createElement("Description");
```

Next, we set the text content for the new `<Description>` element:

```
newNode.text = "High quality eraser!";
```

And we create an attribute called `Color` for this element, and assign it the value `"Blue"`:

```
newNode.setAttribute("Color", "Blue");
```

Now that the new node is created, we need to insert it into the correct position in the tree. To do so, we will need to set a reference node:

```
refNode = XMLDocument.documentElement.childNodes[0].firstChild;
```

This selects the `<Name>` element highlighted below:

```
<Products>
    <Product ID="S123456">
        <Name>Eraser</Name>
        <Price>0.20</Price>
    </Product>
    ...
</Products>
```

Then we use the `insertBefore()` method to add our new node before the reference node:

```
XMLDocument.documentElement.childNodes[0].insertBefore(newNode, refNode);
```

Finally, we output the results, using the `PrintNodes()` method from the last example:

```
Response.Write("Product ID=\"S123456\" now contains:<br/>");
PrintNodes(XMLDocument.documentElement.childNodes[0]);
```

The tree stored in `XMLDocument` now includes the following new element:

```
<Products>
    <Product ID="S123456">
        <Description Color="Blue">High quality eraser!</Description>
        <Name>Eraser</Name>
        <Price>0.20</Price>
    </Product>
    ...
</Products>
```

Deleting a Node from a DOM Tree

Deleting a node from the DOM tree is easier than adding one. Again, we have a couple of methods at our disposal:

❑   removeChild(*oldChild*)

❑   removeAttribute(*oldAttribute*) (element node only)

removeAttribute() requires you to name the attribute you want to delete. From our previous example, we could use (albeit somewhat pointlessly):

```
newNode.setAttribute("Color", "Blue");
newNode.removeAttribute("Color");
```

Or:

```
XMLDocument.documentElement.childNodes[0].childNodes[0].removeAttribute("Color")
```

removeChild() is slightly awkward to use, as lengthy references may be required to delete nodes a long way down in the tree structure:

```
XMLDocument.documentElement.childNodes[0].removeChild(
    XMLDocument.documentElement.childNodes[0].childNodes[0]);
```

Because of this, it can be helpful to use an intermediate variable to store a reference to the parent of the node to delete:

```
refNode = XMLDocument.documentElement.childNodes[0];
refNode.removeChild(refNode.childNodes[0]);
```

Note that when nodes are deleted, all their child nodes are deletes as well, so be careful when you do this!

XSLT Manipulation

In the previous chapter, we used the xt parser to transform XML documents into other forms, including WML documents. In this chapter, we have already seen that we can use the MSXML DOMDocument object to store XML data. It turns out that we can also transform XML data in a DOMDocument object using XSLT, which means that we are able to transform XML in an ASP page.

In order to do this we need just two more steps:

❑   Loading the XSLT document into a separate DOMDocument object.

❑   Performing the transformation.

Performing the transformation uses the transformNode() method, and since both whole DOMDocument objects and individual nodes have this method, we can transform *portions* of a DOM tree if necessary. Let's look at an example of this.

Try It Out — Using the MSXML Parser for XSLT Transformations

1. Copy the files `customers.xml` and `addresses.xsl` from the previous chapter into `inetpub\wwwroot`.

2. Enter the following code, and save it as `domexample4.asp`:

```
<%@ Language = "JScript"; %><%
   Response.ContentType = "text/vnd.wap.wml";

   XMLDocument = Server.CreateObject("MSXML2.DOMDocument.3.0");
   XSLStyleSheet = Server.CreateObject("MSXML2.DOMDocument.3.0");

   XMLDocument.async = false;
   XMLDocument.load(Server.MapPath("customers.xml"));

   XSLStyleSheet.async = false;
   XSLStyleSheet.load(Server.MapPath("addresses.xsl"));

   Response.Write(XMLDocument.transformNode(XSLStyleSheet));
%>
```

3. Load `domexample4.asp` into the UP.Simulator:

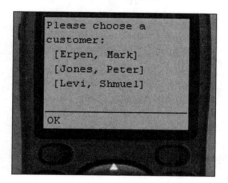

4. Choose and follow one of the links:

529

How It Works

The ASP file will be outputting a WML file, so we set the content type straight away:

```
<%@ Language = "JScript"; %><%
    Response.ContentType = "text/vnd.wap.wml";
```

However, we don't need to start by outputting a WML deck – the transformation includes the required WML code. So, we create DOMDocument objects to hold our source tree and XSLT transformation:

```
XMLDocument = Server.CreateObject("MSXML2.DOMDocument.3.0");
XSLStyleSheet = Server.CreateObject("MSXML2.DOMDocument.3.0");
```

Then we load in our XML and XSLT files:

```
XMLDocument.async = false;
XMLDocument.load(Server.MapPath("customers.xml"));

XSLStyleSheet.async = false;
XSLStyleSheet.load(Server.MapPath("addresses.xsl"));
```

And then we perform the transformation: transformNode() returns a string containing the transformed XML. As this transformation results in a complete WML document, we can simply write out this string, generating our WML deck:

```
    Response.Write(XMLDocument.transformNode(XSLStyleSheet));
%>
```

When the ASP file is requested, it generates a complete WML deck via an XSLT transformation of an XML file.

Important Note

The version of the MSXML parser used at the time of writing has a slight problem. If you look at the source code that reached the UP.Simulator in the status window, you may notice the following line:

```
<?xml version="1.0" encoding="UTF-16"?>
```

The encoding attribute here specifies the character encoding for the document, and while you don't need to understand how this works, you do need to know that UTF-16 causes problems for a number of WML microbrowsers – and the parser adds it to *all* transformations. The setting does not harm the UP.Simulator, but other browsers require this attribute either not to be included, or to be set to UTF-8.

In theory, this should be correctable by modifying the <xsl:output> element in the following way:

```
<xsl:output method="xml"
            version="1.0"
            encoding="UTF-8"
            indent="true"
            doctype-system="http://www.wapforum.org/DTD/wml_1.2.dtd"
            doctype-public="-//WAPFORUM//DTD WML 1.2//EN"
/>
```

However, this version of the MSXML parser ignored the change, presenting us with a problem: how do we use MSXML to generate WML for other browsers via XSLT transformations?

The solution we've used is not particularly elegant, but it does work. It relies on the fact that the XML declaration shown above is always created, and that JScript allows string manipulation in much the same way as WMLScript. Instead of outputting the generated WML using:

```
Response.Write(XMLDocument.transformNode(XSLStyleSheet));
```

We instead place the result in an intermediate string:

```
ResultString = new String(XMLDocument.transformNode(XSLStyleSheet));
```

And cut out the offending attribute when we output the WML:

```
Response.Write(ResultString.slice(0, 19) +
               ResultString.slice(37, ResultString.length));
```

The `slice()` method simply returns a string that starts at the character specified in the first parameter (zero is used for the first character), and is as many characters long as specified by the second parameter. The above code simply concatenates the WML code *before* the attribute with the WML code *after* the attribute, converting:

```
<?xml version="1.0" encoding="UTF-16"?>
```

to:

```
<?xml version="1.0"?>
```

We stress again that this is an intermediate solution, and should you find that the version of the MSXML parser you're using doesn't have this problem, you don't need to use this method! Hopefully, the problem will be resolved soon, but in the meantime we will use this technique in the remainder of the chapter.

Styling for Different Browsers

In Chapter 18, you saw how we can detect different WAP browsers by looking at the `HTTP_USER_AGENT` header. In Chapter 17, you saw how different browsers handle WML in different ways. In this chapter, we've seen how we can generate WML from XML documents. Why not put all this together, and generate WML files customized for different browsers, using the same XML source but different XSLT transformations? That's what we're going to do in this section.

When starting to think about solutions of this kind, two questions immediately spring to mind:

❑   What differences should we cater for in different browsers?

❑   What format should we store the 'uncustomized' data in?

Considering the first question, there are many differences in WML interpretation between different browsers, and you could specialize transformations to deal with all manner of things. In this section, we'll concentrate on:

❑ Formatting lists of links – the UP.Browser's implementation of the `<select>` element is ideal for lists of links, but other browsers are better suited to lists of anchor links. Browsers handle anchor links in different ways too, which is something else to take into account.

❑ Going back – even though a specific type of `<do>` element (`type="prev"`) is defined for creating 'back' links, we have seen that different browsers handle this in different ways. Some don't even display softkeys, making the 'back' option hard to select, so we should cater for this too – we can simply put the Back link in an anchor.

We could equally have focused on image formatting, tables, and so on, but that would have made this chapter excessively large, and once you've got the basic principles, you'll be able to design your own transformations for cases such as these.

As for the second question, what form *should* our XML source data take? This is a tricky one, and it could be solved in a number of ways. If you were targeting non-WAP browsers as well as WAP browsers, you might choose a data-centric system, where you ignore cards and decks and handle such things in your transformations. Because we're not tackling that issue here, we've been able to adopt a simpler format that's more obviously targeted toward WML.

Source XML

In our solution, we've invented two new elements, but we've kept the basic WML structure. The two new elements are `<CARD>` and `<LINK>`, using capital letters to make them easily distinguishable from WML elements. The reasoning behind and meanings of these elements are as follows:

❑ `<CARD>` – looks just like its WML counterpart, `<card>`, and is also responsible for holding individual WML cards. It supports all of the attributes that `<card>` does, but it can also be assigned additional ones to denote browser-specific behaviors. In the example that follows, we'll use just one extra attribute: `backlink`. Setting this attribute to `true` means, "Add a 'back' link to this card," while setting it to `false` means the opposite.

❑ `<LINK>` – is intended to be used in each place where a series of related links should be inserted. A series of these elements can then be used to build a `<select>` element or a series of anchor links, depending on the transformation. This element has three attributes: `href` for link destination, `text` for display text, and `label` to give the link a title in browsers that support this functionality.

Let's look at the example document we'll be transforming, `rawdeck.xml`:

```
<?xml version="1.0"?>
<wml>
    <CARD id="menu" title="Menu" backlink="false">
        <p>
            Select a food:<br/>
            <LINK href="#pizza" text="Pizza" label="Pizza"/>
            <LINK href="#curry" text="Curry" label="Curry"/>
```

```
            <LINK href="#pasta" text="Pasta" label="Pasta"/>
            <LINK href="#fryup" text="Fry-up" label="Fryup"/>
        </p>
    </CARD>
    <CARD id="pizza" title="Pizza" backlink="true">
        <p>
            Crispy bread base with cheese, tomatoes, etc.
        </p>
    </CARD>
    <CARD id="curry" title="Curry" backlink="true">
        <p>
            Spicy stew with bits in. Great with lager.
        </p>
    </CARD>
    <CARD id="pasta" title="Pasta" backlink="true">
        <p>
            White floppy stuff. Al dente if you want.
        </p>
    </CARD>
    <CARD id="fryup" title="Fry-up" backlink="true">
        <p>
            A heart attack waiting to happen - but the grease
            is good for hangovers!
        </p>
    </CARD>
</wml>
```

The syntax is so similar to WML that you shouldn't have any problem working out what this deck does: it is simply a menu of foodstuffs pointing to description cards. The list of foods in the first card uses the new <LINK> element, and all cards use the <CARD> element to specify whether they require a Back link (all except the first card do).

ASP Processing

The ASP file that we'll use to perform our user agent based transformations doesn't contain anything we haven't seen before, but let's break it down and examine it. The statements broken up below all join together to form style.asp.

First of all, we set the MIME type and the scripting language:

```
<%@ Language = "JScript"; %><%
    Response.ContentType = "text/vnd.wap.wml";
```

Next, we obtain the user agent type

```
    userAgent = new String(Request.ServerVariables("HTTP_USER_AGENT"));
```

Now we set a transformation file depending on this type. We've chosen to support the UP.Browser, Nokia, and R320 user agents directly, but we've also supplied a default transformation, default.xsl, which will be used if none of these applies. (It's actually just a copy of the Nokia stylesheet.)

```
styleSheet = Server.MapPath("default.xsl");
if (userAgent.indexOf("UP.Browser") != -1)
{
    styleSheet = Server.MapPath("phone.xsl");
}
if (userAgent.indexOf("Nokia") != -1)
{
    styleSheet = Server.MapPath("nokia.xsl");
}
if (userAgent.indexOf("R320") != -1)
{
    styleSheet = Server.MapPath("R320.xsl");
}
```

Then we create our DOMDocument objects...

```
XMLDocument = Server.CreateObject("MSXML2.DOMDocument.3.0");
XSLStyleSheet = Server.CreateObject("MSXML2.DOMDocument.3.0");
```

...load both XML and XSLT files...

```
XMLDocument.async = false;
XMLDocument.load(Server.MapPath("rawdeck.xml"));

XSLStyleSheet.async = false;
XSLStyleSheet.load(styleSheet);
```

...perform the transformation...

```
ResultString = new String(XMLDocument.transformNode(XSLStyleSheet));
```

...and finally, remove the encoding attribute:

```
Response.Write(ResultString.slice(0, 19) +
               ResultString.slice(37, ResultString.length));
%>
```

And that's all there is to it. Creating our XSLT stylesheets, however, isn't quite so simple.

Browser-specific XSLT Files

We can simplify things slightly by noting that none of the browser-specific changes occurs at the deck level, and that the XML declaration and output method will be the same for each transformation. We can therefore start each XSLT file in the following way:

```
<?xml version="1.0"?>
<xsl:stylesheet xmlns:xsl="http://www.w3.org/1999/XSL/Transform" version="1.0">
    <xsl:output method="xml"
                version="1.0"
                indent="yes"
                doctype-system="http://www.wapforum.org/DTD/wml_1.2.dtd"
                doctype-public="-//WAPFORUM//DTD WML 1.2//EN"
    />
```

And use identical root-matching templates:

```
<xsl:template match="/">
   <wml>
      <xsl:apply-templates select="/wml/CARD"/>
   </wml>
</xsl:template>
```

This template writes out our `<wml>` root element, and calls the template required to process each `<CARD>` element.

We can also process each `<CARD>` attribute in the same way for each transformation – except for the `backlink` attribute. To further simplify the beginning of each file, we'll process this attribute later, and keep the card templates identical (this assumes that each `<CARD>` has only one `<p>` element; if they have more then shifting the processing of `backlink` out of this template would cause problems):

```
<xsl:template match="CARD">
   <card>
      <xsl:attribute name="id">
         <xsl:value-of select="@id"/>
      </xsl:attribute>
      <xsl:attribute name="title">
         <xsl:value-of select="@title"/>
      </xsl:attribute>
      <xsl:apply-templates select="p"/>
   </card>
</xsl:template>
```

Note that as it stands, this transformation only supports the `id` and `title` attributes of `<card>` elements, but this is because the sample XML file we'll transform only uses these two attributes (and the `backlink` attribute) – it would be simple to expand this template to add other elements, in the form:

```
<xsl:attribute name="attname">
   <xsl:value-of select="@attname"/>
</xsl:attribute>
```

This simply copies the attribute *attname* from the `<CARD>` element to the `<card>` element we're creating.

The rest of the code is browser-specific, and will be different in each of:

- ❑   `phone.xsl`
- ❑   `nokia.xsl`
- ❑   `R320.xsl`

Let's look at each of the transformations in turn.

phone.xsl

Picking up from where we left off, the next template to be called matches the <p> element. Again, this transformation hasn't been written to support attributes of <p>, but it would be simple to add the required code to do this, using the same code structure as shown in the last section.

We start off by opening our <p> element:

```
<xsl:template match="p">
    <p>
```

And then writing out the text content as-is:

```
<xsl:value-of select="."/>
```

Next, we check for the presence of <LINK> element children. If we find any, we know that a list of links is required, and since we're targeting the UP.Browser, we know that we require a <select> element. We simply write out this element, and call the LINK template from inside it:

```
<xsl:if test="LINK">
    <select>
        <xsl:apply-templates select="LINK"/>
    </select>
</xsl:if>
```

Let's take a look at the LINK template, and come back to the p template in a moment. We need to format each <LINK> element as an <option> element. Each of these elements needs an onpick attribute specifying the destination (we stored this in the <LINK> element's href attribute), a title attribute (we use the label attribute here), and some text (using the text attribute). The following code transforms a <LINK> into an <option>:

```
<xsl:template match="LINK">
    <option>
        <xsl:attribute name="onpick">
            <xsl:value-of select="@href"/>
        </xsl:attribute>
        <xsl:attribute name="title">
            <xsl:value-of select="@label"/>
        </xsl:attribute>
        <xsl:value-of select="@text"/>
    </option>
</xsl:template>
```

Returning to the p template, the next thing we need to add is our **Back** link. Previously, we've noted that the best way to do this on the UP.Browser is to provide a <do> element of type options, and a label reading **Back**. We simply test to see if the backlink attribute of the current <CARD> element is true, and if so add the <do> element (remembering to finish the <p> element we started earlier first):

```
      </p>

      <xsl:if test="../@backlink='true'">
         <do type="options" label="Back">
            <prev/>
         </do>
      </xsl:if>
   </xsl:template>
```

And that's it. We've been right through the code for `phone.xsl` (except, if you're being pedantic, for the closing tag for the stylesheet), which of course you'll find in the code download for this book. If we now use the UP.Simulator to load `style.asp` (and assuming that all files are stashed away in a single directory on the web server), we should get the following results:

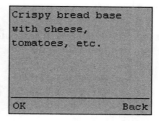

The first screenshot shows the first page of links, formatted as a `<select>` list, while the second shows one of the destination cards, including a 'back' option.

nokia.xsl

The stylesheet for Nokia browsers has a simpler `<p>` template. We know that each link simply requires a separate anchor element, so we don't need to enclose our LINK template call in a `<select>` element. We also know that the Nokia browser is quite happy with an ordinary 'back' link specification:

```
<xsl:template match="p">
   <p>
      <xsl:value-of select="."/>
      <xsl:if test="LINK">
         <xsl:apply-templates select="LINK"/>
      </xsl:if>
   </p>
   <xsl:if test="../@backlink='true'">
      <do type="prev">
         <prev/>
      </do>
   </xsl:if>
</xsl:template>
```

537

Converting a <LINK> into an <a> requires copying the href attribute, creating a title attribute with the value of the label attribute, and placing the text attribute as text inside the <a> element:

```
<xsl:template match="LINK">
   <a>
      <xsl:attribute name="href">
         <xsl:value-of select="@href"/>
      </xsl:attribute>
      <xsl:attribute name="title">
         <xsl:value-of select="@label"/>
      </xsl:attribute>
      <xsl:value-of select="@text"/>
   </a>
</xsl:template>
</xsl:stylesheet>
```

Testing this code out with the Nokia 7110 simulator yields the following:

As you can see, there's a list of links on the first page, and a standard Back button on all the rest.

R320.xsl

The R320 transformation is similar to the Nokia one, but it has two differences. First, we place the Back link as an anchor link, as softkeys are hidden on this device:

```
<xsl:template match="p">
   <p>
      <xsl:value-of select="."/>
      <xsl:if test="LINK">
         <xsl:apply-templates select="LINK"/>
      </xsl:if>
   </p>
   <xsl:if test="../@backlink='true'">
      <p>
         <anchor title="Back">Back<prev/></anchor>
      </p>
   </xsl:if>
</xsl:template>
```

Next, we add line breaks after each <a> link, to place the options in a column:

```
<xsl:template match="LINK">
   <a>
      <xsl:attribute name="href">
         <xsl:value-of select="@href"/>
      </xsl:attribute>
      <xsl:attribute name="title">
         <xsl:value-of select="@label"/>
      </xsl:attribute>
      <xsl:value-of select="@text"/>
   </a><br/>
</xsl:template>
</xsl:stylesheet>
```

This time, the results are as follows:

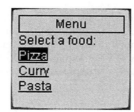 

Styling Summary

Hopefully, this section has illustrated some of the potential of using XSLT to style for different browsers. This is by no means a perfect solution, as it requires you to write non-WML source code, and to format it in specific ways (<LINK> elements will always occur at the end of card text in this example, which isn't necessarily a bad thing, but could be seen to be restrictive). It is also quite tricky to get the stylesheets to work properly, and may require a lot of effort before you are up and running. However, when you compare it with alternatives like writing completely separate decks for all the different browsers, it's not an unattractive option. The more data you have, and the more frequently it changes, the more the investment will pay off.

Performance Issues

The browser styling in the last section, and indeed the XSLT transformations earlier in the chapter, require a fair amount of processing power and memory. Loading XML documents into the MSXML parser, for example, requires much more memory than the XML documents themselves take up, as the information is placed in a (potentially large) number of different objects. Transforming documents using XSLT isn't a quick process either.

What this boils down to is that you don't want to perform DOM manipulation and XSLT transformation for every user that accesses your site, every time they want to download a file.

But before you cry, "What did we do all that for?" there *is* light at the end of the tunnel. It's possible to perform these transformations preemptively, without users requesting them, and doing so is remarkably simple. Depending on the frequency with which your site is updated, you simply run the transformations whenever necessary, either by creating a maintenance ASP page that runs each transformation and saves the result, or by using the xt parser we saw in the last chapter.

The end result is the same: you'll have a whole set of WML (or perhaps ASP) files that won't require transforming. You can still redirect different user agents to different places, but you won't need to perform browser-specific transformations at request time. Instead, you can just use the redirection techniques from Chapter 18. Every time your data changes, you can run the transformations, and the decks will be ready for the next user who visits your site.

Summary

This chapter has linked together many of the techniques that you have learned over the course of this book. In particular, we've seen how we can combine ASP and XSLT to tailor content for multiple devices using a common source file written in XML. The syntax used in this chapter for the XML source file is designed to be very similar to WML, but capable of being transformed for different browsers in a relatively simple way. This syntax is also very expandable, and if you decide to experiment with it you should end up with a remarkably streamlined delivery system for WAP content on multiple browsers.

In addition, we've seen how we can manipulate XML in simpler ways: adding, deleting, and modifying nodes using the DOM. Although not as powerful as XSLT, this can be a useful tool to make minor modifications to content before delivery.

If you're interested in areas for further research, one such is alternative ways of *storing* XML, which becomes an issue when data volume gets large. This can be complex because XML files in general do not map smoothly into database structures, and there are whole books devoted to this subject if you're keen to find out more. Another interesting topic is the other methods of dynamic content generation, such as Java Server Pages (JSP) and Perl, which have their own strengths and weaknesses.

Both of these subjects are given increased coverage in Professional WAP, *also from Wrox Press.*

To finish – we, the authors, hope that this book has been an interesting journey for you. You should now be equipped with the tools to strike out on your own and create enthralling WAP applications, and to delve into new uses for interactive wireless communication. If you do succeed in creating the 'killer' WAP application and becoming rich and famous, remember us poor authors who helped you get started, won't you?

Developing WAP Applications Using Emulators

As with any form of application development, one of the most important steps is testing. Only by exposing our applications to the real world can we hope to know that our applications are market ready. The problem with WAP applications, as you will know if you have read the book already, is that the number of devices is large and diverse, and it is increasing all the time.

There are, however, two distinct phases of testing: testing the logic of the application, and testing its performance on the various browsers. Assuming that your design has been done with due care, you will have an idea of how it should perform on the various browsers it is aimed for. This does not exempt you from testing your application as mistakes creep in. In the current climate, however, it is not cost effective to test the code logic on a real handset.

It is for this reason that several phone manufacturers have provided emulators to mimic the real handsets, with varying success, and they can be very useful for debugging your WAP applications. Chapter 1 covers the installation and use of the UP.Simulator, Phone.com's contribution to this area. We will examine some of the other emulators here.

Unfortunately, non-Windows users have been somewhat neglected in this field, and most of the available options are for Microsoft operating systems (although emulators for alternate operating system are beginning to appear). In this appendix, we will focus on the emulators that you can use if you are using Microsoft Windows as your operating system. We will take a look at the following:

- ❑ Nokia Toolkit – http://www.forum.nokia.com
- ❑ Ericsson WapIDE SDK – http://www.ericsson.se/wap
- ❑ Microsoft Mobile Explorer Emulator – http://www.benefon.com
- ❑ Motorola MADK – http://www.motorola.com/developers/wireless/tools

In particular, we will walk through the steps required to download and install them. We will also show you how to use the emulators and the various debugging aids provided by the toolkits.

Nokia WAP Toolkit v2.0

Nokia WAP Toolkit v2.0 provides a development environment for writing, testing, and debugging WAP applications on a PC platform running Windows NT (with at least Service Pack 3), or Windows 95/98/Me. It comprises the following main components:

- ❏ Nokia 7110 Phone Simulator, which supports WAP version 1.1.

- ❏ Blueprint Phone Simulator, which supports WAP version 1.2. This phone is currently a concept phone with no real equivalent product in the market.

- ❏ WAP Server emulator, which supports WAP 1.1.

- ❏ A toolkit that provides an integrated development environment, and supports both WAP version 1.1 and 1.2.

Downloading and Installing the Nokia WAP Toolkit

As the finding and downloading of the installation file is not very straightforward, we will take this a step at a time. The first step is downloading the toolkit from the Nokia web site.

Downloading the Nokia WAP Toolkit

At the time of writing, the Nokia WAP Toolkit v2.0 could be downloaded for free from Nokia's web site at http://www.forum.nokia.com/. When you enter the above URL, you will come to the following main page:

Follow the following steps for download:

- ❏ Click the **WAP Developers** link in the main display area, or **WAP** from the menu on the right of the browser window. Either link will lead you to the WAP Developers page.

❑ You will need to register at the Nokia Developers site before you can proceed. Choose **Registration Form** to do so.

❑ After you have sucessfully registered, go back to the **WAP Developer** page and choose the **Nokia WAP Developer Section** option, where you will be presented with a login page.

❑ Log in using your ID and password.

❑ For the next two pages, follow the links indicated in the right hand menu by **Nokia WAP Toolkit** and **Download**, at which stage you will be presented with the option to download the toolkit:

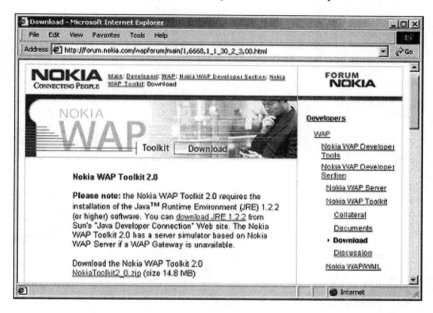

Notice that a requirement for running the Nokia WAP Toolkit 2.0 is a Java Runtime Environment (JRE) 1.2.2 (or higher). You may download the JRE software from the following web site, or simply follow the link from Nokia's site to http://java.sun.com/products/jdk/1.2/jre/.

The file for download is named `Nokia Toolkit2_0.zip`, and it has a file size of about 14.8 MB. You will need to *unzip* (that is, uncompress) the file using compression software such as WinZip, which you can buy or download from http://www.winzip.com/download.htm

If you have WinZip installed, you can simply double-click the downloaded file, and extract the files `ReleaseNotes.txt` and `setup.exe`, into a directory of your choice. Most compression software comes with instructions; consult the user manual if you have difficulty.

Installing the Nokia WAP Toolkit

To install the toolkit, simply double-click the `setup.exe` file. Note that the Java Runtime Environment will be installed along the way if you have not installed it before (and provided you have downloaded the proper version of JRE prior to starting the setup procedure).

To launch the toolkit, click Start | Programs | Nokia WAP Toolkit 2.0 | WAP Toolkit.

Configuring for the Nokia 7110

When the toolkit is first launched, the main toolkit window and the Blueprint phone will appear:

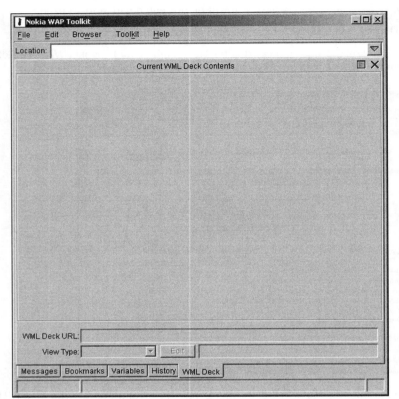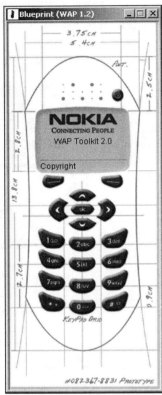

In this appendix, we will show you how to configure the Nokia 7110 phone simulator to load a simple WML deck. In addition to loading content from the file system, the Nokia 7110 simulator can be configured to load content from a web server in two ways. Connection to an HTTP server can be made via a WAP gateway, or using the WAP Server Simulator that comes with the toolkit. The first configuration more truly simulates the configuration of a real WAP phone.

To configure the Nokia 7110, click the Toolkit menu and select Nokia 7110 (WAP 1.1):

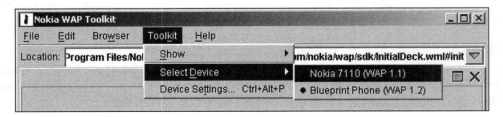

When the Nokia 7110 is selected, the default Blueprint phone simulator is changed to the following:

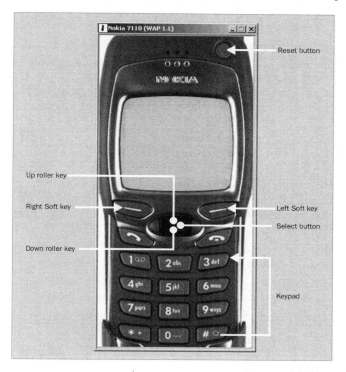

Under the same Toolkit menu, choose the Device Settings... option to set the connectivity configuration to a server. While many of the first examples in this book are possible without a web server, the more advanced examples, and especially those concerned with dynamic generation of WML, require it. The following display concerning general settings will then appear. These are concerned with caching, which specifies whether previously visited sites are reloaded from the Internet or from memory, and resetting of the phone simulator.

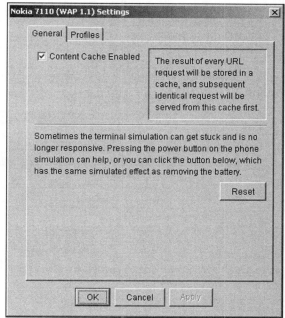

Choose the Profiles tab, and the following default settings are shown:

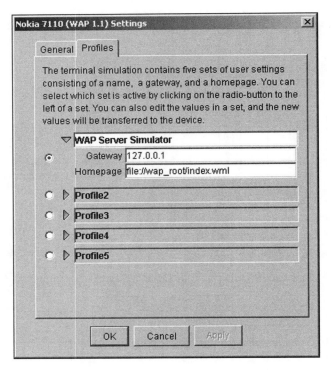

The above screenshot indicates that the WAP Server Simulator that comes with the toolkit is to be used as the intermediary between the simulated phone and your content. The IP address, 127.0.0.1, refers to the computer where the toolkit is installed. As it stands, the first automatically loaded file is file://c:/wap_root/hello.wml, set automatically at installation.

To display the home page in the phone simulator, simply click the Browser menu, followed by the Home option:

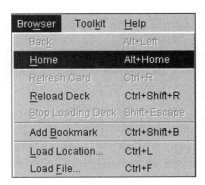

If the default is used, the following will be loaded as the homepage:

Notice in the device profile dialog window that there are up to four other profile options that you can set. For example, if you have set up a separate WAP gateway at IP address 153.20.248.166 using port 9201, then you may set Profile2 to this gateway and select the radio button next to it to indicate that you wish to use that setting for loading your WAP applications:

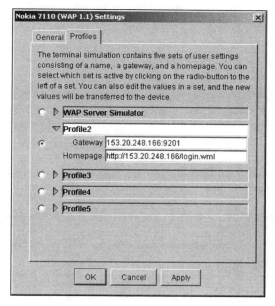

The connectivity between the simulated phone, the WAP gateway and the origin server implied by the above setting is as shown below:

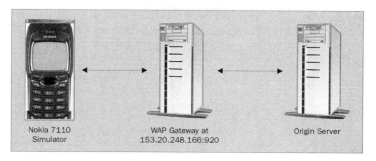

Loading WML Decks

Choose File | New | WML Deck, and key in the following WML deck, naming it `hello.wml`. You will need to delete the content that is automatically placed there by the toolkit:

```
<?xml version="1.0"?>
<!DOCTYPE wml PUBLIC "-//WAPFORUM//DTD WML 1.2//EN"
                     "http://www.wapforum.org/DTD/wml_1.2.dtd">
<wml>
   <card id="start" title="Hello">
      <p>
         Hello, WAPians!!
      </p>
   </card>
</wml>
```

Save the deck somewhere on your computer. If you have a web server, you can set up a virtual site or directory from which you can serve all of the code you write as a result of this book. The Nokia WAP Toolkit v2.0 then provides three ways to load a deck:

❑   Through the Location input box in the main toolkit window. To load the above deck from the local host, type in the following URL for `hello.wml` as shown below:

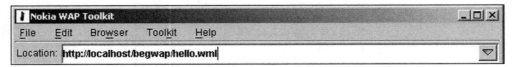

If you have deposited your deck in a remote web server (say, `someserver.com`), the URL might look like this:

❑   Choose Load Location from the Browser menu. Type the URL in a new dialog box that appears:

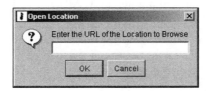

❑ Selecting Load File from the Browser menu. This option presents a dialog box where you can open the WML document via the selection of drive and folder. This is fine as long as the WML document resides in the local storage or a network drive accessible to the machine where the toolkit is installed. The following shows that we have stored the hello.wml in the \Inetpub\wwwroot folder of the C drive:

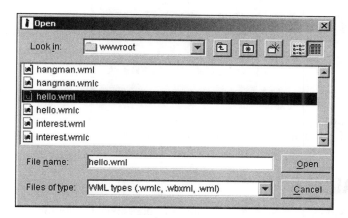

If all went well, regardless of which of the three methods you used, you should see the following screen display:

Possible Errors at Loading

Assuming that the installation went well, there are two main possibilities for errors. If your chosen WAP gateway requires a secure communication, you may get the following error message. Since the Nokia 7110 simulator does not support setting a secure communications channel for testing, you will not be able to fetch the requested deck through secure WAP gateways.

Sometimes, you may find that when specifying a localhost URL, the browser will complain, as shown in the diagram below (alternatively, nothing will appear on the phone):

In this case, you may be able to correct the problem by replacing references to localhost with the actual IP address of your machine, or the DNS name for your machine host as specified by your network.

Debugging Aids

In this section we will explore some useful features of the Nokia Toolkit for debugging. These features are easily accessible via the tabs at the bottom of the main toolkit window.

Alternatively, you can switch to the relevant feature through the Toolkit menu:

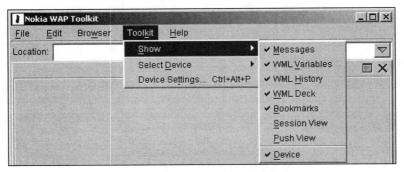

The Session View and Push View options are not checked, and are therefore not shown as tabs. This is because the Nokia 7110, which only claims WAP 1.1 compliance, does not support viewing of sessions or listening to push messages.

We will briefly discuss each of the views presented here. For this, we will write a new WML file that can illustrate the use of each tab. Start a new WML deck from the File menu and enter the following, saving it as login.wml. Notice that we have deliberately referred to the DTD for WAP 1.1, as several of the emulators only support WAP 1.1 and will complain if asked to refer to the 1.2 DTD.

```
<?xml version="1.0"?>
<!DOCTYPE wml PUBLIC "-//WAPFORUM//DTD WML 1.1//EN"
                     "http://www.wapforum.org/DTD/wml_1.1.xml">
<wml>
   <card id="card1" title="Login">
      <p>
         Name :<input type="text" name="ID" />
         Password :<input type="password" name="Password" />
         <do type="accept" label="Login">
            <go method="post" href="logon.asp">
               <postfield name="ID" value="$(ID)" />
               <postfield name="Password" value="$(Password)" />
            </go>
         </do>
      </p>
   </card>
</wml>
```

Save login.wml in the same directory as hello.wml. Load login.wml into the simulator:

Use the select button to edit the **Name** field and enter wrox:

Select **OK** (the left hand softkey) and repeat the same process for the **Password** input field, using secret for the password. When you have done that, you will have the following screen:

If you choose the Variables tab now, you will see that these two values can be checked under this view. This allows you to monitor values, checking that they hold the expected values. The majority of your debugging is likely to involve this view, as incorrectly set variables are the main cause, or visible effect, of non-syntax related errors.

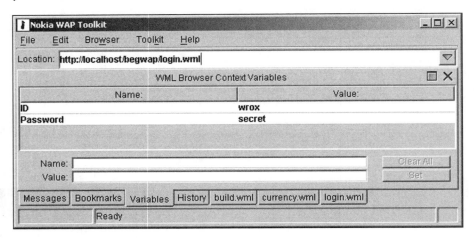

Unlike the Blueprint concept phone, the Nokia 7110 simulator does not seem to support setting variables to new values, a feature that can be helpful in debugging.

Next, load hello.wml and change to the History view to see the previous cards visited (also called the history stack) in the current context of the browser:

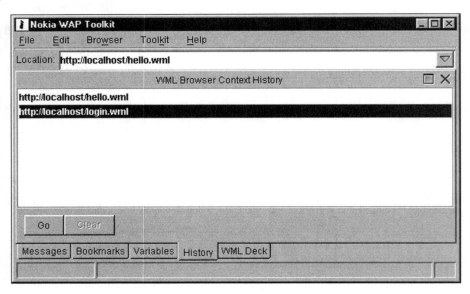

If you toggle back to the Variables view at this point, you will se that the variables and their corresponding values still exist, even though we have navigated to a different deck. This will be the case until newcontext is called, or the phone is switched off.

You may navigate to any of the documents listed in the history stack by highlighting the corresponding entry and clicking on the Go button.

To add the `login.wml` deck as a bookmark, which is especially convenient during debugging, choose Browser | Add Bookmark. You can easily load bookmarked documents by toggling to the Bookmarks view and selecting the document you wish to load via the Go button:

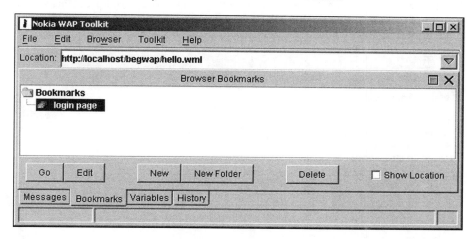

If you need to modify the content of a deck, you can open it via the Open option from the File menu. The `login.wml` file is shown below as an example. You should not have too much difficulty with these file-related functions, as they are identical to most other Windows programs.

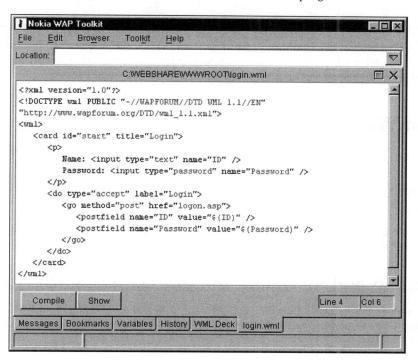

You can click the Compile button to compile a `.wml` document into a `.wmlc` document, or a `.wmls` script into a `.wmlsc` compiled version. Clicking the Show button will perform the compilation, and then cause the browser to show the edited deck on the phone simulator. Some browsers require WML and WMLScript in compiled format only and this is one way to do so. (Although it has some problems associated with it, as you will see later.)

Finally, let's take a look at the Messages view. If you haven't encountered problems so far, you'll most likely see an empty window. Enable the Debug message level option and you should see something similar to the following, showing the messages logged by the browser:

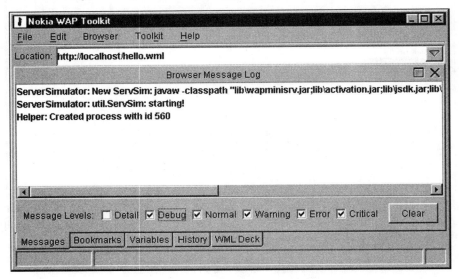

The Detail option switches the toolkit into verbose form, where each key press and process is logged. This is mainly for advanced debugging, and you may choose to turn it off as it will tend to clutter the window and could cause you to overlook error messages and important warnings.

Ericsson WapIDE SDK v2.1

The Ericsson WapIDE SDK is an integrated development environment for developing WAP applications. It consists of three main components: WAP Browser, Application Designer and Server Toolset.

The WapIDE SDK 2.1 release supports WML 1.1 and WML Script 1.1, as proposed in the specifications from the WAP Forum.

The SDK comes with a mandatory installation of a web server called Xitami that may cause a conflict with existing web servers you have set up. Don't worry: we will show you how to uninstall it if you wish to do so.

Downloading and Installing the Ericsson WapIDE v2.1

You can download the Ericsson WapIDE v2.1 from http://www.ericsson.com/wap. You need to register for a free developer account. Once you have registered, you can enter the developer zone and download the emulator.

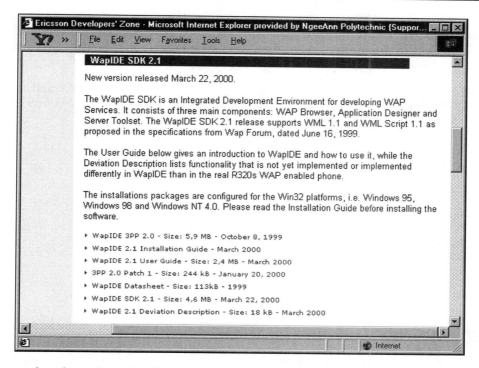

The screenshot above shows the files available for download at the Ericsson web site. You should download the following files:

❑ WapIDE 3pp 2.0

❑ WapIDE SDK 2.1

❑ 3PP 2.0 Patch 1 (optional)

The Ericsson WapIDE SDK is compiled to run on the Win32 platforms: Windows 95/98/Me, and Windows NT 4.0/2000.

Installation of the SDK involves two stages:

❑ First, install the WapIDE Runtime Environment

❑ Next, install the WapIDE SDK

To install the WapIDE runtime environment, double-click on `WapIDE_3PP_2_0.exe` to start the installation of WapIDE/3PP.

557

Accept all the defaults, and installation will take a few moments. When it has finished, installation of Xitami will begin. Do not abort this, as doing so also aborts the runtime environment installation. Again, accept all the defaults, making sure that automatic execution is not enabled. You may uninstall Xitami when you have finished the IDE SDK installation.

To install the WapIDE SDK, double-click on `WapIDE_SDK_2_1.exe` to start unpacking and installation of WapIDE/SDK. This installation uses the usual Wizard with which most users of Windows will be familiar.

The order of installation is important, but you can now uninstall Xitami if you wish. Go to Start | Settings | Control panel | Add/Remove Programs and select it. Scroll down the list of programs on your system until you find the Xitami icon, and click on the Change/Remove button. Choose automatic uninstallation, and the server will be removed. You should now restart your computer so that changes can be registered before starting the WapIDE.

To launch the WapIDE, click on Start | Programs | Ericsson | WapIDE | WapIDE 2.1.

Configuring the Ericsson WapIDE

Once the Ericsson WapIDE is installed successfully, launching it will display the following screen:

The Ericsson WapIDE consists of three components:

❑ Browser

❑ App Designer

❑ Server Toolset

The Browser is the component that emulates the Ericsson R320 handset.

The App Designer is an Integrated Development Environment (IDE) for managing WAP projects. It is somewhat similar to Microsoft Visual Studio (though not nearly as powerful!).

The Server Toolset contains various tools and library functions to support the development of WAP applications. It includes WML and WMLScript compilers, and a Perl function library. The server toolset is useful for developer who wants to compile WML decks into WML bytecode. We will focus here on the user of the browser component of the WapIDE

To launch the Browser component, simply click on the Browser icon and the following browser window will appear:

The R320 comes 'switched off' when it is first launched. To switch it on, press the No button on the right hand side and hold it for a few seconds, and the R320 will be 'switched on'.

When the R320 is switched on, you should see the default screen:

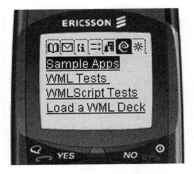

The Ericsson WapIDE offers a few configuration options through the Options menu item:

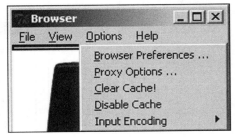

Browser Preferences

This option includes several advanced features that you are unlikely to need to change. The Browser engine port and IP address are used by the browser to communicate with the Communication Stack. The next entry is the shortcut to the browser to launch for the help files. This seems to be Netscape by default. The final entry allows simulation of WTA in tandem with a modem. WTA is the telephony functionality of WAP, and is designed to allow automatic dialing from a WML deck.

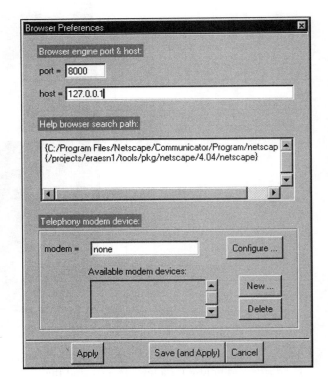

Proxy Options

If you are operating behind a proxy server, you can configure the Ericsson WapIDE to use it.

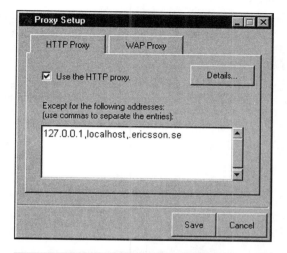

To connect the Ericsson WapIDE using a WAP gateway, click on the **WAP Proxy** tab. You can also configure the simulator to bypass the proxy and WAP gateway for certain servers. This normally includes the localhost and loopback address, 127.0.0.1.

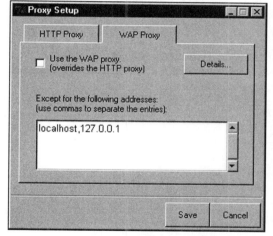

Clicking on the **Details...** button will reveal a screen for configuring the WAP gateway, the port number, and the bearer. You can choose the different ports available (with or without WTLS), and the bearer. The currently supported bearer is IPv4. You can also set the timeout for the proxy to return the requested resource.

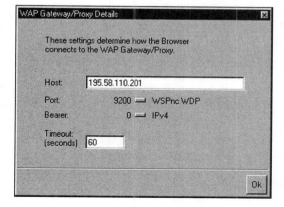

Clear Cache

Once a deck has been loaded, it will be cached in memory. If you want to reload the deck, you need to clear the cache. The Clear Cache option allows you to do that.

Disable Cache

If you do not wish to clear the cache every time you load an old deck, you can simply disable the cache. This option is useful during the development stage where you need to modify a deck and see the changes on the emulator on a regular basis.

Input Encoding

The input encoding option allows you to choose a language other than English and those with English-based character sets, and includes support for Greek, Turkish, and Japanese, among others. For the examples in this book, the default will be sufficient.

Loading WML Decks

There are two ways to load a WML deck:

❑ From the menu (File | Load URL...)

❑ Right-clicking on the browser window and then selecting File | Load URL... from the context menu.

In either case, the Load URL into Browser window will appear.

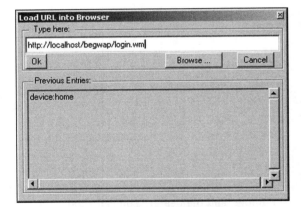

You can quickly navigate to previously visited decks from the window at the bottom. Key in the URL to the login.wml deck we wrote earlier, in the section on installing the Nokia toolkit. Once the URL is keyed in, the deck will be loaded:

To key in the user ID, press the Yes key and the following screen should appear:

You can key in your ID, or alternatively you can type it using the keyboard by right clicking on the browser, at which point the Browser Text Entry window will open. Type in your ID using the keyboard and select OK:

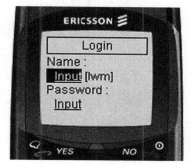

To enter the Password, simply press the 'down' arrow key and repeat the previous process.

When both user ID and password have been entered, we can pass the information to the server for authentication. To do that, press the Yes button and hold on to it. The following 'menu' should appear:

Selecting Login will send the information to the server, but since we have not written the destination file, it will currently give an error message: WAP ERR-404. Object not found.

Debugging Facilities

The Ericsson WapIDE offers some debugging facilities that aim to make your life as a WAP developer easier. There are two view options that can be used to examine what's going on behind the scenes:

❑   Log window

❑   WML variable viewer

Log Window

The log window allows the developer to create a log detailing the operations performed by the emulator.

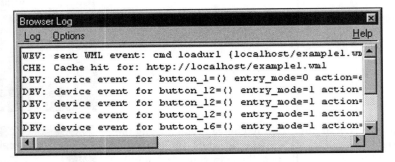

The log window logs the following operations:

Operations	Option Code	Description
Cache	CHE	Caching by the emulator
Request	REQ	Request for WML decks
Reply	RPY	Response from the server
Source	SRC	The source code for the loaded deck is recorded in the log.
WML/WAP	WEV	WAP events
Timer	TEV	Timer events
Device	DEV	Device event

WML Variable Viewer

You can also use the WML variable viewer to display the values of WML variables. For example, the previous entry has generated the following entries:

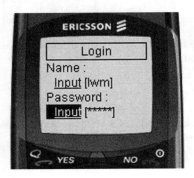
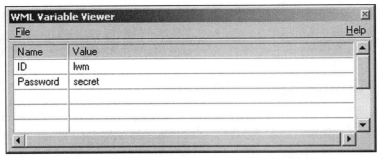

You can display the values of the WML variables by clicking on View | WML Variables.

Using the Application Designer

The application designer allows you to build your WAP application within an IDE. It is project based:

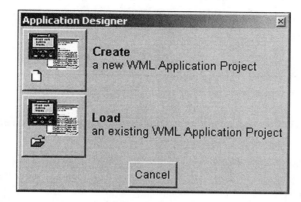

To create a new project, give it a name. You will also need to specify a target browser. At the moment, there is only one device, so this decision should be fairly straightforward. Select the Browse... button and choose r320s.dev.

Let's now enter the following WML deck into the IDE, saving it as `Example1.wml`:

```
<?xml version="1.0"?>
<!DOCTYPE wml PUBLIC "-//WAPFORUM//DTD WML 1.1//EN"
"http://www.wapforum.org/DTD/wml_1.1.xml">
<wml>
    <card id="card1" title="Card 1">
        <p>
         Hello, WAP!!!
        </p>
    </card>
</wml>
```

To test the WML deck on the R320s emulator, click on the **Toggle Project Test Mode** button to switch to test mode:

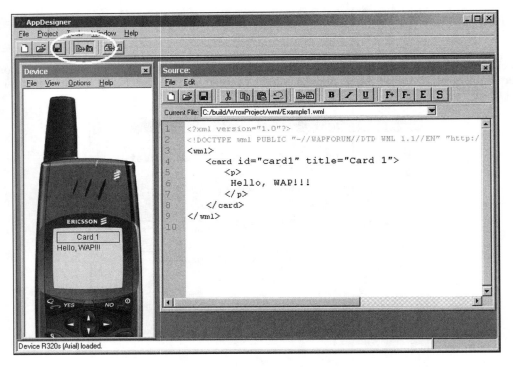

Once the deck is loaded onto the emulator, you cannot edit the WML unless you switch back to edit mode by clicking on the **Toggle Project Test Mode** button again. If there is an error in your deck, the error message will be shown on the emulator, as in the following example:

Ericsson R380 Emulator

The R380 WAP emulator is used for testing WML applications developed for the WAP browser in the Ericsson R380 Smartphone. This emulator mimics the real device very well, except that functionality that is not relevant to WAP application testing has been disabled.

The configuration of the emulator is a little tricky, but we will try to make it clear.

Downloading and Installing the R380 Emulator

You can download the Ericsson R380 emulator from the same URL as that of the R320, at http://www.ericsson.com/wap.

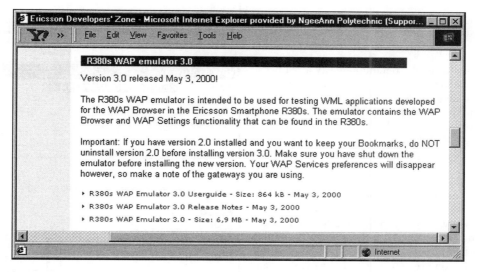

The above screenshot shows the files available for download at Ericsson's web site. You should download the **R380 WAP Emulator 3.0** file. Double click the file to install the program, and accept the defaults. The emulator can be launched from an icon placed on your desktop. The files can be found in a folder called Epoc32.

Configuring the R380 Emulator

To configure your R380 emulator, click on the Extras tab at the top right hand side, and from the menu click on the System icon.

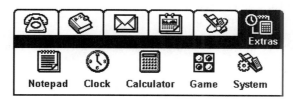

The System menu is then displayed:

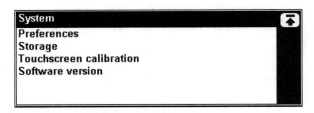

Select the Preferences item and from this submenu choose WAP services. Now select Gateway:

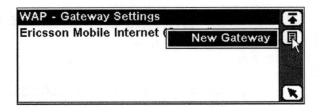

You should see the default gateway already configured for you. In our case, we want to create a new gateway, which we do by clicking on the Menu icon and select New Gateway, as shown above. Click on <Enter Gateway Name>:

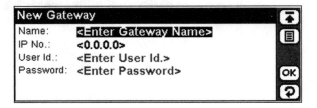

Name your gateway ("LocalHost" is a good choice). When you have done so, press the down arrow and key in the IP address of the local machine (The IP address 127.0.0.1 is called the loopback address, and refers to the machine you are working on.) Oddly, you can use the yen sign to enter a period.

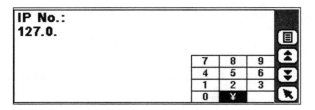

If you have a WAP gateway running, you may also key in the IP address of the machine running the gateway. If you are using a gateway that requires authentication, you will need to enter a user ID and password. When you've finished, press the icon in the bottom right hand corner. To use the newly added gateway, click on the menu icon and select Set Current.

Click on the OK button to complete the configuration process. That's it! You are now ready to test your R380 emulator.

Loading WML decks

To load a WML deck using the R380 emulator, simply invoke the WAP browser by clicking on the Browser icon from the WAP services tab:

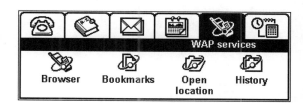

Then, click on the Menu option and select Open Location:

This emulator requires a gateway, but once you have installed the Nokia toolkit, the R380 emulator will use that (unless you have another one installed). Key in the URL for the WML deck that we wrote in a previous section, and click OK:

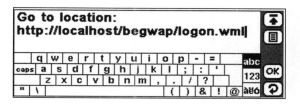

You should see the following WML deck:

As before, the ASP file that the hyperlink sends the result of the form to has not been implemented, so this is only for the purposes of this example.

Microsoft Mobile Explorer Emulator Rev. 6

You can get the Microsoft Mobile Explorer Emulator from http://www.benefon.com. Choose the Developers & Partners link, at which stage you will again need to register for an account. When you have done so, download MMEforBenefonQ.exe, which is about 3.5 MB in size. To install it, double click on the file. The emulator comes in three parts: the Mobile Explorer Emulator, the Mobile Explorer Configurator, and a user's guide.

Select the emulator, and you will get the following screen:

Switch the phone on using the green phone icon, and you will be able to choose from Refresh, Home, Add to Favorites, and Exit the Browser. Selecting Home and Browse the Web in sequence will give you the following screen, from which you can head for the URL of your choosing.

A word of caution here: the emulator only accepts compiled content, which means that you must use a real gateway of some sort. You should also remember that while we can pre-compile decks using the Nokia toolkit (for example), the links they contain will still refer to uncompiled decks and WMLScript files, so without a gateway this technique will be impractical. Both Nokia and Phone.com offer access to gateways, but this will mean testing online and requires that your server will have to be accessible on the Internet, with its own IP address and/or DNS.

The simulator contains several other features that you may like to experiment with, including the ability to set bookmarks and to display HTML content. If these appeal, you may wish to consult the manual.

The Configurator gives us some fine-tuning capabilities, some of which are available from the Simulator in submenus. Loading it gives the following screen:

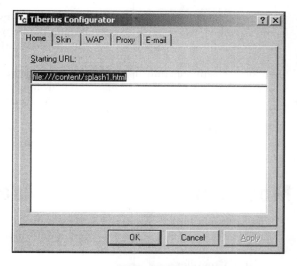

This allows us to specify the **Starting URL**, which (as you can see) can be HTML or WML. The **Skin** tab allows you to change the skin to the following:

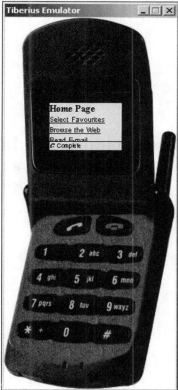

You will need to restart the emulator for any changes to take effect. It is expected that future releases will allow further 'skin' options – in this one, the * and # keys act as scroll keys, and 0 as the select button.

The next tab allows you to specify a WAP gateway to use – the options include the server's IP address, port number (this is 9201 by default), and the network bearer. This information is specific to the gateway, and should provided by your gateway provider.

If you are within a company LAN, you may need to configure the MME to go through a proxy server. Again, this depends on your setup and you should consult your network administrator for the information you require. They may need to adjust the configuration of the firewall to open the relevant port.

The final tab allows you to use the emulator as an e-mail client. You will need to enter your ISP's POP3 and SMTP server addresses, together with your name, password, and e-mail address.

Motorola MADK 2.0 Simulator

The Motorola Mobile Application Development Kit (MADK) is a tool for developing WAP and VoxML/VoiceXML applications. It contains the following components:

❏ Compiler

❏ Debugger

❏ Simulator

❏ Syntax Checker

❏ Microsoft Agent

❏ VoxML/VoiceML and WML sample applications

Downloading and Installing the MADK Simulator

To download the MADK 2.0 Simulator, point your web browser at http://www.motorola.com/developers/wireless/tools

You need to register at the web site. Once you have done so, the serial number for the MADK, which you need in order to install it, is sent to you via e-mail.

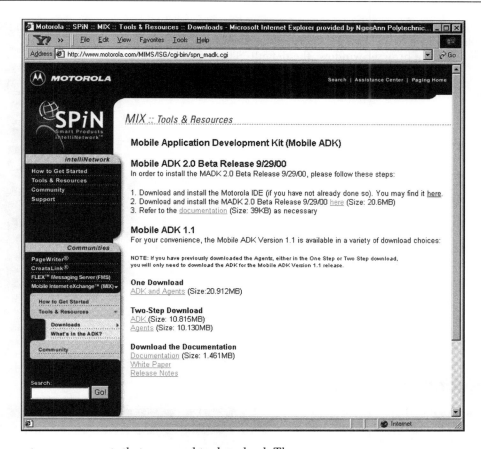

There are two components that you need to download. They are:

❑ Motorola IDE

❑ MADK 2.0 Beta Release

The Motorola IDE contains an IDE for developing WAP applications, while the MADK 2.0 contains the device emulators. You need to install the Motorola IDE before installing the MADK.

To install the two components mentioned, you need to have Microsoft's Java Virtual Machine (build 5.00.3186 or higher) installed on your system. To download the latest copy of the Java VM, you can point your web browser to http://www.microsoft.com/java

Once the MADK is installed, launch it by clicking on Start | Programs | Motorola Wireless IDE | Madk2_0 | MADK 2.0 Simulator. You should see the following browser window (the default "TimePort" model):

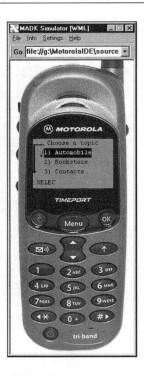

Configuring the MADK simulator

In our test of the MADK 2.0 beta, we found that the MADK is not very stable when it comes to connecting to a WAP gateway. As such, we advise you to connect using the direct HTTP method. To select the connection method, click on Settings | Mobile Settings...

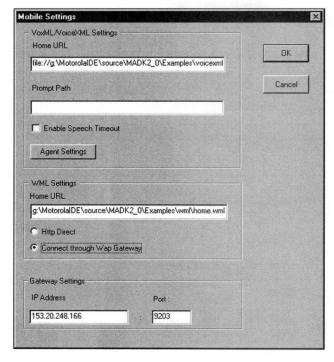

To connect using a WAP gateway, supply the IP address of the machine running the gateway, as well as the port to connect to.

Like Phone.com's UP.Simulator, the MADK offers browser 'skins' for emulating different devices. Unlike the UP.Simulator, however, it does not emulate the different behaviors of the different devices. It simply adjusts its appearance for each model.

Here are some of the 'skins' available in the MADK:

User navigation is largely through trial-and-error for the various phone emulators. (This is especially true for the V8160 model.) In our testing, the favorite is the TimePort model, which is the default device.

Loading WML Decks

To load a WML deck, simply key in the URL at the top of the browser window. Let's try http://localhost/begwap/logon.wml as usual.

Using the default TimePort model, you should see the following:

Using the Motorola IDE

Like the Ericsson WapIDE, the Motorola IDE also allows developers to manage their WAP application within an integrated environment. To launch the Motorola IDE, select Start | Programs | Motorola Wireless IDE | IDE.

When the Motorola IDE is launched for the first time, you have the option to open an existing project or create a new project.

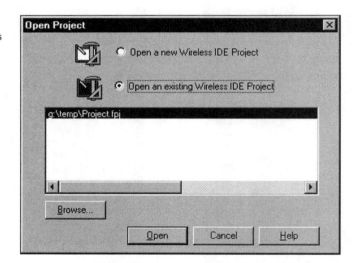

To create a new project, check Open a new Wireless IDE Project, and click Open.

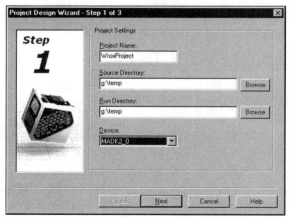

Enter a project name,
and click Next.

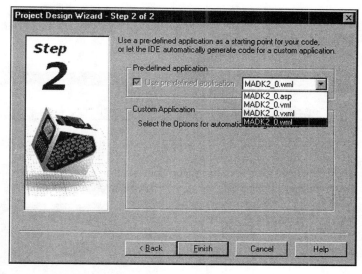

You can get the assistance of the IDE to pre-create templates for your application. You can have the following templates:

- ❑ ASP document
- ❑ VML document
- ❑ VXML document
- ❑ WML document

For this example, select WML, and click Finish. A default WML deck is then created for you:

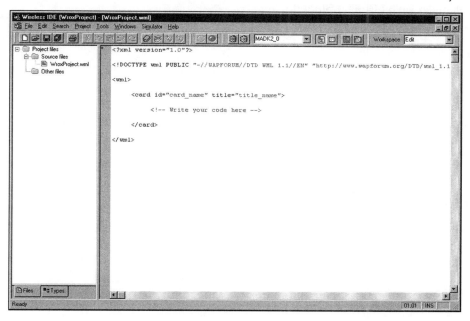

Let's now replace the default WML deck with `login.wml`: Select File | Open | File, and select `login.wml`. To load the WML deck onto the MADK emulator, you must first compile it by clicking on the Compilation button:

When the compilation is done, click on the Run button to load the deck onto the MADK emulator:

That's it! The WML deck is loaded onto the MADK emulator. If you want to find out more about this IDE, look under Help | Getting Started.

B

WML Elements

This appendix lists all of the WML elements in alphabetical order, along with all their attributes (where relevant), and a description of the function of each.

The last section of the appendix deals with some specialized elements that are specific to the UP.Browser, and consequently won't be recognized by other microbrowsers. It is strongly recommended that you bear this in mind when considering interoperability issues of your WML decks.

We have included the document type definition for WML 1.2 at the end. If you wish to find out more about DTDs, further information can be found at http://www.w3.org/xml

Common Attributes

One more thing before we plunge into the list: there are three attributes that can be applied to nearly every single element, so to save writing them out hundreds of times, we will detail them here:

`xml:lang`	Specifies the natural language for the element and its contents
`id`	Specifies the name of the element
`class`	Specifies the class name for the element

Unless specified otherwise in the individual element description, these attributes can be applied to any element.

One additional attribute that appears in user interaction elements `accesskey`, which can be used to specify a single key from the keypad of the device that corresponds to the activation of the event or action. Thus, assigning the 9 key to a hyperlink would mean that if the user was to press 9 on their keypad, the browser would navigate to the destination of the hyperlink.

<a>

Specifies a link to another card, deck, or other resource.

Attributes

href	Specifies the destination URL – the location of the resource.
title	Specifies a brief text string identifying the link. This text is displayed to the user.
accesskey	Maps a single keypad key to the action represented by this element, namely navigation to a hyperlink.

<access>

Allows the writer of the card to limit access to the document to decks originating from the specified domain name and path. It is contained within <head> tags. There can be any number of <access> elements.

Attributes

domain	Sets the domain that can access the card.
path	Sets a path within the domain of decks that can access the card.

<anchor>

Specifies the anchor to a link to another card, deck or other resource.

Attributes

title	Specifies a brief text string identifying the link.
accesskey	Maps a single keypad key to the action represented by this element.

<b>

Specifies bold text.

<big>

Specifies large text.

Tells the browser to add a line break to the text at the point the element is written.

<card>

A card is the display unit in WML, and is contained by a <wml> element. Each card contains content that is presented to the user in a browser specific way. A card logically specifies an interaction between the user and the device.

Attributes

title	Specifies a label for the card.
newcontext	Default is false, but if set to true, the current browser context is reinitialized upon entry to this card. This clears the navigational history state, and resets the implementation specific state to a default value (which may vary with browser).

ordered   This attribute gives an indication to the user agent about how the card content is organized.

If ordered="true", the card is naturally organized as a linear sequence of field elements, for example, a set of questions or fields which are naturally handled by the user in the order in which they are specified in the group.

If ordered="false", the card is a collection of field elements without a natural order.

`<do>`

Specifies a general mechanism for the user to act on the current card. The action performed when a `<do>` element has been activated is specified by the elements `<go>`, `<prev>`, `<noop>`, or `<refresh>`. See relevant sections.

Attributes

type   Specifies a hint to the microbrowser about the author's intended use of the element.

The table below shows the predefined `<do>` types.

Do type	Description
accept	Acknowledgement
prev	Backward history navigation
help	Request for help
reset	Clearing or resetting state
options	Request for options or additional operations
delete	Delete item or choice
unknown	Generic type
"" (empty string)	Equivalent to unknown
x–*, X–*	Experimental type
vnd.*, VND.*	Vendor or user agent specific type of the kind vnd.*co-type*, where co is a company name and type is the do type.

label   Specifies a text string suitable for dynamically labeling a UI component.
optional   If this attribute value is true, the microbrowser can ignore the element, otherwise it is set to false (the default), and it must not ignore the element.
name   Specifies a name for the element. If a card level and a deck level `<do>` element have the same name, the card level element will override the deck level element.

`<em>`

Specifies that text should be emphasized. The way this is represented will depend on the specific browser implementation.

<fieldset>

When <fieldset> brackets are put around sections of paragraph content it informs the browser to separate each section out, to structure the information in a logical way. At the moment, browsers do not support it very well. Most either completely ignore the element, or don't display the text inside the tags.

Attributes

title	A descriptive title of the section.

<go>

Specifies a task that navigates to a URI. xml:lang is not an associated attribute.

Attributes

href	Specifies the destination URI.
sendreferer	Defaults to false. If set to true, the user agent needs to specify the URI of the deck containing this task in the server-bound request.
method	Specifies the HTTP request method. get and post are currently supported.
enctype	Specifies the content type of the form when submitted using post. The default is application/x-www-form-urlencoded.
accept-charset	Must be followed by a list of character encodings for data that the origin server must accept for processing input.

<head>

This element specifies an optional header for the WML document. It is used to contain <access> and <meta> information that relates to the whole document.

<i>

Specifies italicized text.

<img>

Specifies an image to be displayed.

Attributes

You may find that the behavior of these attributes may differ on the emulators as compared to the real phones. For example, it was found that that the height and width attributes caused the Nokia 7110 toolkit to crash, but worked on the actual phone.

src	Specifies the URI of the image to display. If the localsrc attribute (see below) specifies a valid built-in image, this attribute is ignored.
alt	Specifies the alternative text to display if the device does not support images or neither the localsrc attribute or src attribute point to a valid image.
localsrc	Specifies a predefined icon. If this attribute specifies a valid icon, the src attribute and alt attributes are ignored.
align	Specifies how the image is aligned relative to the current line of text. It takes one of three values, top, middle, or bottom.
vspace	Specifies the amount white space to allocate above and below the image. This can be in pixels or as a percentage of the overall screen size.

hspace	Specifies the amount white space to allocate to the left and right of the image. This can be in pixels or as a percentage of the overall screen size.
height	Specifies the suggested height for the image.
width	Specifies the suggested width for the image.

<input>

Specifies a point at which the user is prompted to enter text.

Attributes

name	The name of the variable to store the user input in. If there is a variable of this name, its value will be overwritten, otherwise a new variable will be created.
value	Default value for the entry.
type	Sets the type of text entry. The default is text, which will allow normal text entry. The other option is password. When this is chosen, text entered will be starred out – a simple security option. Note that the values will be stored in plain text in memory.
title	Suggests a title for the text entry screen, may be displayed when entering text.
maxlength	Maximum length for entered strings.
format	Sets a format that the entered text is forced to stick to. See Chapter 10 for more details on this code system.
emptyok	Simply states that it is acceptable for the user to leave this empty.
tabindex	Sets the order in which the form components are tabbed through.
size	Specifies the width, in characters, of the input area.
accesskey	Input box can be mapped to a keypad key.

<meta>

The <meta> element is contained by the <head> element and is used to specify general information about the deck. This may include author and copyright detail, expiration date of the content, etc. If the browser doesn't understand this data, it simply ignores it.

Attributes

content	Specifies the property value.
name	gives the meta data a name.
http-equiv	Specifies the HTTP header name. Meta data named with this attribute is converted to a WSP or HTTP response header if the content is tokenized before arrival at the user agent.
forua	Specifies whether the meta data is intended to reach the user agent. If true, it must do. If false, then it must be removed at an intermediate stage.
scheme	Specifies a form or structure that may be used to interpret the data value.

<noop>

Specifies that nothing should be done. Can be used to disable functionality in the browser.

<onevent>

Declares that, when the specified event occurs, the action(s) contained within the tags will be taken.

Attributes

type   Sets the type of event associated with the code. The types are:
onenterbackward – specifies navigation with the use of the history stack.
onenterforward – specifies any navigation *except* through the history stack.
ontimer – will execute the specified action on timer expiration.

`<option>`

A set of `<option>` tags is needed to specify each individual item in a list (see `<select>`).

Attributes

value   Gives the option a shorthand value, for example, an initial for a name. This value can be given to a variable, or be used to set its option as the default choice, using the `<select>` attributes name and value respectively.

title   A name can be given to each option in the list for the browser to display.

onpick   Related to some of the `<onevent>` attributes, this attribute allows you specify the id of a card to navigate to when the user picks an option in a list.

`<optgroup>`

Sets of `<optgroup>` tags can be put around `<options>` in a `<select>` list. The effect of this is to break the options into submenus.

Attributes

title   Gives a title to each submenu.

`<p>`

Specifies a paragraph of text with alignment and line wrapping properties.

Attributes

align   The three available values, "left", "center", and "right" specify line alignment. If you do not specify an alignment it will take on the alignment of the previous paragraph.

mode   Has two possible values, "wrap" and "nowrap", used to specify the line wrapping mode. If you do not specify the mode value, the device uses the last specified mode value.

`<postfield>`

Specifies name-value pairs to transmit to origin server.

Attributes

name   Specifies the name of the name-value pair.

value   Specifies the variable whose value is assigned to the name-value pair.

`<prev>`

Specifies navigation to the previous URI in the history. xml:lang is not an associated attribute.

<refresh>

Specifies a refresh task, stating a need for an update of the user agent context as specified by the contained <setvar> elements (see relevant section). User visible effects of the update can occur during the processing of the <refresh>. This element may be used to update the screen so that it reflects changes in variables. These changes may occur as a result of entities outside of the <refresh> element or as a result of <setvar> elements within the <refresh> element itself.

<select>

Allows the definition of a limited set of option values for input.

Attributes

name	The name of the variable whose value will be the option chosen.
iname	You can also specify a variable whose value will be the index value of the option chosen.
value	Allows a default selection to be specified.
ivalue	Allows a default selection to be specified using the default option's index number.
title	A title for the browser to display.
multiple	Has two values, true and false. If true, the user will be able to select multiple entries from the list. The default is false.
tabindex	Allows you to set the order of movement between selection boxes, so that the user can 'tab' between them, using specialized control keys.

<setvar>

Sets a variable's value. If the variable already exists its value will be overwritten, otherwise a new variable will be created. Can only be included inside <refresh> and <go> tags.

Attributes

name	The name of the variable.
value	The value of the variable.

<small>

Specifies a smaller font than the default.

<strong>

Specifies strongly emphasized text.

<table>

This is the top-level table element. Tables structure data as columns and rows. This element can contains multiple row elements, see <tr>.

Attributes

title	Specifies the title of the table; this value may be used by the browser in the presentation of the table.

587

align   Specifies the layout of text and images within the columns of the table. The available settings are L, C, and R, which represent left-alignment, center-alignment and right-alignment respectively. The default is L. You can specify an alignment value for each column in the table. As an example, a three column table with left, right, left alignment would take the form `align="LRL"`. These attribute values only work in WML 1.2 devices. Previous devices only took a table wide value of `left`, `right`, or `center`.

columns   Specifies the number of columns in the table.

\<td>

Used to define individual cells in each row of a defined table. The content of this element is the content of a cell in a table.

\<template>

Specifies a template for all cards in the deck. Event binding (specifying an action for a specific event) will apply to all cards in the deck. May also specify \<do> elements that will apply to all cards. Cards may override this behavior by providing alternate \<do> elements with the same name as those defined here. See Chapter 14 for more information.

\<timer>

Sets a timer that will raise a timer event when it expires. This event can be bound using an \<onevent> element that specifies the name of the timer.

Attributes

name   The name of the timer. The timer event handler references this name.
value   Sets the length of time to count, in tenths of seconds.

\<tr>

Defines each row in a table.

\<u>

Specifies underlined text.

\<wml>

Top or Root level element of a WML deck. This element defines the limits of the deck.

UP.Browser specific elements

If you want to use these elements, you must change the DOCTYPE header to the following line:

```
<!DOCTYPE wml PUBLIC "-//PHONE.COM//DTD WML 1.1//EN"
                 "http://www.phone.com/dtd/wml11.dtd" >
```

<catch>

Specifies an exception handler.

Attributes

name   Specifies which exception is to be handled in this particular instance. If no name is specified, then any exception will be handled by this <catch>.

onthrow   Tells the engine what to do if and when the exception occurs.

<exit>

Declares an exit task; the current context is then stopped.

<link>

Carries out a very similar task to that of <a>; it declares a hyperlink

Attributes

href   Specifies the URL for the link to navigate to.

sendreferer   Defaults to false. If set to true, the user-agent must specify the URL of the deck containing this task in the server-bound request.

rel   Specifies what relationships exist between the deck containing the link, and the card to be navigated to.

<receive>

Receives data sent from another context.

Attributes

name   Specifies the name of the variable whose value will be assigned with the data received.

<reset>

Clears all the variables declared in the current context.

<send>

Specifies a single variable to be sent to the relevant parameter block position.

Attributes

value   Specifies the value to send.

<spawn>

Declares a spawn task; creates a child context, and spawns a URL.

Attributes

href   Specifies the URL to be navigated to.

sendreferer   Defaults to false. If set to true, the user agent needs to specify to URI of the deck containing this task in the server-bound request.

589

accept-charset	Must be followed by a list of character codes for data that the origin server must accept when processing input.
method	Specifies the HTTP request method, get or post.
onexit	Specifies the URL to navigate to, upon completion of the child context, through the performing of an exit action.

<throw>

Declares that an exception should be raised at the current context.

Attributes

name	Specifies the name of the exception to be raised.

WML 1.2 DTD

```
<!--

Wireless Markup Language (WML) Document Type Definition.
WML is an XML language. Typical usage:
<?xml version="1.0"?>
<!DOCTYPE wml PUBLIC "-//WAPFORUM//DTD WML 1.2//EN"
                     "http://www.wapforum.org/DTD/wml12.dtd">
<wml>
      …...
</wml>

-->

<!ENTITY % length "CDATA">
<!-- [0-9]+ for pixels or [0-9]+"%" for percentage length -->

<!ENTITY % vdata "CDATA">
<!-- attribute value possibly containing variable references -->

<!ENTITY % HREF "%vdata;">
<!-- URI, URL or URN designating a hypertext node.
     May contain variable references -->

<!ENTITY % boolean "(true|false)">

<!ENTITY % number "NMTOKEN">
<!-- a number, with format [0-9]+ -->

<!ENTITY % coreattrs "id ID #IMPLIED class CDATA #IMPLIED">

<!ENTITY % ContentType "%vdata;">
<!-- media type. May contain variable references -->

<!ENTITY % emph "em | strong |b |i |u |big |small">
```

```
<!ENTITY % layout "br">

<!ENTITY % text "#PCDATA | %emph;">
<!-- flow covers "card-level" elements, such as text and images -->

<!ENTITY % flow "%text; | %layout; | img | anchor |a |table">

<!-- Task types -->
<!ENTITY % task "go | prev | noop | refresh">

<!-- Navigation and event elements -->
<!ENTITY % navelmts "do | onevent">

<!--================ Decks and Cards ================-->
<!ELEMENT wml ( head?, template?, card+ )>
<!ATTLIST wml xml:lang NMTOKEN #IMPLIED %coreattrs;>

<!-- card intrinsic events -->
<!ENTITY % cardev
     "onenterforward %HREF; #IMPLIED
      onenterbackward %HREF; #IMPLIED
      ontimer %HREF; #IMPLIED"
>

<!-- card field types -->
<!ENTITY % fields "%flow; | input | select | fieldset">

<!ELEMENT card (onevent*, timer?, (do |p |pre)*)>
<!ATTLIST card
     title %vdata; #IMPLIED
     newcontext %boolean; "false"
     ordered %boolean; "true"
     xml:lang NMTOKEN #IMPLIED
     %cardev;
     %coreattrs;
>

<!--================ Event Bindings ================-->
<!ELEMENT do (%task;)>
<!ATTLIST do
     type CDATA #REQUIRED
     label %vdata; #IMPLIED
     name NMTOKEN #IMPLIED
     optional %boolean; "false"
     xml:lang NMTOKEN #IMPLIED
     %coreattrs;
>

<!ELEMENT onevent (%task;)>
<!ATTLIST onevent
     type CDATA #REQUIRED
     %coreattrs;
>
```

```
<!--================= Deck-level declarations =================-->
<!ELEMENT head ( access | meta )+>
<!ATTLIST head
    %coreattrs;
>

<!ELEMENT template (%navelmts;)*>
<!ATTLIST template
    %cardev;
    %coreattrs;
>

<!ELEMENT access EMPTY>
<!ATTLIST access
    domain CDATA #IMPLIED
    path CDATA #IMPLIED
    %coreattrs;
>

<!ELEMENT meta EMPTY>
<!ATTLIST meta
    http-equiv CDATA #IMPLIED
    name CDATA #IMPLIED
    forua %boolean; "false"
    content CDATA #REQUIRED
    scheme CDATA #IMPLIED
    %coreattrs;
>

<!--================= Tasks =================-->
<!ELEMENT go (postfield | setvar)*>
<!ATTLIST go
    href %HREF; #REQUIRED
    sendreferer %boolean; "false"
    method (post|get) "get"
    enctype %ContentType; "application/x-www-form-urlencoded"
    accept-charset CDATA #IMPLIED
    %coreattrs;
>

<!ELEMENT prev (setvar)*>
<!ATTLIST prev
    %coreattrs;
>

<!ELEMENT refresh (setvar)*>
<!ATTLIST refresh
    %coreattrs;
>
```

```
<!ELEMENT noop EMPTY>
<!ATTLIST noop
     %coreattrs;
>


<!--=============== postfield ================-->
<!ELEMENT postfield EMPTY>
<!ATTLIST postfield
     name %vdata; #REQUIRED
     value %vdata; #REQUIRED
     %coreattrs;
>


<!--=============== variables ================-->
<!ELEMENT setvar EMPTY>
<!ATTLIST setvar
     name %vdata; #REQUIRED
     value %vdata; #REQUIRED
     %coreattrs;
>


<!--=============== Card Fields ================-->
<!ELEMENT select (optgroup|option)+>
<!ATTLIST select
     title %vdata; #IMPLIED
     name NMTOKEN #IMPLIED
     value %vdata; #IMPLIED
     iname NMTOKEN #IMPLIED
     ivalue %vdata; #IMPLIED
     multiple %boolean; "false"
     tabindex %number; #IMPLIED
     xml:lang NMTOKEN #IMPLIED
     %coreattrs;
>

<!ELEMENT optgroup (optgroup|option)+ >
<!ATTLIST optgroup
     title %vdata; #IMPLIED
     xml:lang NMTOKEN #IMPLIED
     %coreattrs;
>

<!ELEMENT option (#PCDATA | onevent)*>
<!ATTLIST option
     value %vdata; #IMPLIED
     title %vdata; #IMPLIED
     onpick %HREF; #IMPLIED
     xml:lang NMTOKEN #IMPLIED
     %coreattrs;
>
```

```
<!ELEMENT input EMPTY>
<!ATTLIST input
      name NMTOKEN #REQUIRED
      type (text|password) "text"
      value %vdata; #IMPLIED
      format CDATA #IMPLIED
      emptyok %boolean; "false"
      size %number; #IMPLIED
      maxlength %number; #IMPLIED
      tabindex %number; #IMPLIED
      title %vdata; #IMPLIED
      accesskey %vdata; #IMPLIED
      xml:lang NMTOKEN #IMPLIED
      %coreattrs;
>

<!ELEMENT fieldset (%fields; | do)* >
<!ATTLIST fieldset
      title %vdata; #IMPLIED
      xml:lang NMTOKEN #IMPLIED
      %coreattrs;
>

<!ELEMENT timer EMPTY>
<!ATTLIST timer
      name NMTOKEN #IMPLIED
      value %vdata; #REQUIRED
      %coreattrs;
>

<!--================ Images ==================-->
<!ENTITY % IAlign "(top|middle|bottom)" >

<!ELEMENT img EMPTY>
<!ATTLIST img
      alt %vdata; #REQUIRED
      src %HREF; #REQUIRED
      localsrc %vdata; #IMPLIED
      vspace %length; "0"
      hspace %length; "0"
      align %IAlign; "bottom"
      height %length; #IMPLIED
      width %length; #IMPLIED
      xml:lang NMTOKEN #IMPLIED
      %coreattrs;
>

<!--================ Anchor ==================-->
<!ELEMENT anchor ( #PCDATA | br | img | go | prev | refresh )*>
<!ATTLIST anchor
      title %vdata; #IMPLIED
      accesskey %vdata; #IMPLIED
      xml:lang NMTOKEN #IMPLIED
      %coreattrs;
>
```

```
<!ELEMENT a ( #PCDATA | br | img )*>
<!ATTLIST a
      href %HREF; #REQUIRED
      title %vdata; #IMPLIED
      accesskey %vdata; #IMPLIED
      xml:lang NMTOKEN #IMPLIED
      %coreattrs;
>


<!--================ Tables =================-->
<!ELEMENT table (tr)+>
<!ATTLIST table
      title %vdata; #IMPLIED
      align CDATA #IMPLIED
      columns %number; #REQUIRED
      xml:lang NMTOKEN #IMPLIED
      %coreattrs;
>

<!ELEMENT tr (td)+>
<!ATTLIST tr
      %coreattrs;
>

<!ELEMENT td ( %text; | %layout; | img | anchor |a )*>
<!ATTLIST td
      xml:lang NMTOKEN #IMPLIED
      %coreattrs;
>

<!--================ Text layout and line breaks =================-->
<!ELEMENT em (%flow;)*>
<!ATTLIST em
      xml:lang NMTOKEN #IMPLIED
      %coreattrs;
>

<!ELEMENT strong (%flow;)*>
<!ATTLIST strong
      xml:lang NMTOKEN #IMPLIED
      %coreattrs;
>

<!ELEMENT b (%flow;)*>
<!ATTLIST b
      xml:lang NMTOKEN #IMPLIED
      %coreattrs;
>

<!ELEMENT i (%flow;)*>
<!ATTLIST i
      xml:lang NMTOKEN #IMPLIED
      %coreattrs;
>
```

```
<!ELEMENT u (%flow;)*>
<!ATTLIST u
     xml:lang NMTOKEN #IMPLIED
     %coreattrs;
>

<!ELEMENT big (%flow;)*>
<!ATTLIST big
     xml:lang NMTOKEN #IMPLIED
     %coreattrs;
>

<!ELEMENT small (%flow;)*>
<!ATTLIST small
     xml:lang NMTOKEN #IMPLIED
     %coreattrs;
>

<!ENTITY % TAlign "(left|right|center)">

<!ENTITY % WrapMode "(wrap|nowrap)" >

<!ELEMENT p (%fields; | do)*>
<!ATTLIST p
     align %TAlign; "left"
     mode %WrapMode; #IMPLIED
     xml:lang NMTOKEN #IMPLIED
     %coreattrs;
>

<!ELEMENT br EMPTY>
<!ATTLIST br
%coreattrs;
>

<!ELEMENT pre "(#PCDATA |a |br |i |b |em |strong | input | select )*">
<!ATTLIST pre
     xml:space CDATA #FIXED "preserve"
     %coreattrs;
>

<!ENTITY quot "&#34;"> <!-- quotation mark -->

<!ENTITY amp "&#38;#38;"> <!-- ampersand -->

<!ENTITY apos "&#39;"> <!-- apostrophe -->

<!ENTITY lt "&#38;#60;"> <!-- less than -->

<!ENTITY gt "&#62;"> <!-- greater than -->

<!ENTITY nbsp " "> <!-- non-breaking space -->

<!ENTITY shy "&#173;"> <!-- soft hyphen (discretionary hyphen) -->
```

C

WMLScript Reference

This appendix outlines the syntax of the WMLScript language:

- ❑   Operators:
    - ❑   Arithmetic
    - ❑   Logical
    - ❑   Bitwise shift
    - ❑   Bitwise logical
    - ❑   Assignment
    - ❑   Comparison
    - ❑   Miscellaneous

- ❑   Operator precedence
- ❑   WMLScript statements
    - ❑   Declarations
    - ❑   Loops
    - ❑   Execution control statements

- ❑   Pragmas
- ❑   Comments
- ❑   Escape codes

WMLScript Operators

Arithmetic Operators

Name	Example	Result
Addition	v1 + v2	Sum of v1 and v2.
		Concatenation of v1 and v2, if they are strings.
Subtraction	v1 - v2	Difference of v1 and v2
Multiplication	v1 * v2	Product of v1 and v2
Division	v1 / v2	Quotient of v2 into v1
Integer Division	v1 div v2	Integer quotient of v2 into v1 (that is, ignoring the remainder)
Modulus	v1 % v2	Integer remainder of dividing v1 by v2
Prefix Increment	++v1	++ v1 * v2 = (v1 + 1) * v2
Postfix Increment	v1++	v1++ * v2 is equal to (v1 * v2). v1 is then incremented by 1
Prefix Decrement	--v1	--v1 * v2 = (v1 - 1) * v2
Postfix Decrement	v1--	v1-- * v2 is equal to (v1 * v2). v1 is then decremented by 1

Logical Operators

These operators should return one of the Boolean literals, true or false. However, this may not happen if either v1 or v2 is neither a Boolean value nor a value that easily converts to a Boolean value, such as 0, 1, null, the empty string, or undefined.

Name	Example	Result
Logical AND	v1 && v2	Returns true if both v1 and v2 are true, false otherwise. Will not evaluate v2 if v1 is false.
Logical OR	v1 || v2	Returns false if both v1 and v2 are false, true otherwise. Will not evaluate v2 if v1 is true.
Logical NOT	!v1	Returns false if v1 is true, true otherwise.

Bitwise Shift Operators

These operators work by converting the value in v1 to a 32 bit binary number and then moving the bits in the number to the left or the right by the number of places specified by v2.

Name	Example	Result
Left Shift	`v1 << v2`	Shifts v1 to the left by v2 places, filling the new gaps with zeros.
Right Shift	`v1 >> v2`	Shifts v1 to the right by v2 places, the v2 right hand bits are lost. 1s are inserted for negative numbers, 0s for positive, in the left hand side.
Zero-fill Right Shift	`v1 >>> v2`	Shifts v1 to the right by v2 places, the right hand bits are lost, and v2 zeros are added to the left of the number.

Bitwise Logical Operators

These operators work by converting the values in both v1 and v2 to 32 bit binary numbers and then comparing the individual bits of these two binary numbers. The result is returned as a normal decimal number.

Name	Example	Result
Bitwise AND	`v1 & v2`	ANDs each pair of corresponding bits
Bitwise OR	`v1 | v2`	ORs each pair of corresponding bits
Bitwise XOR	`v1 ^ v2`	XORs (that is, exclusive ORs) each pair of corresponding bits
Bitwise NOT	`~v1`	Inverts all the bits in the number

Assignment Operators

Name	Example	Meaning
Assignment	`v1 = v2`	Setting v1 to the value of v2
Shorthand Addition *or* Shorthand Concatenation	`v1 += v2`	v1 = v1 + v2
Shorthand Subtraction	`v1 -= v2`	v1 = v1 – v2
Shorthand Multiplication	`v1 *= v2`	v1 = v1 * v2
Shorthand Division	`v1 /= v2`	v1 = v1 / v2
Shorthand Integer Division	`v1 div= v2`	v1 = v1 div v2

Table continued on following page

Name	Example	Meaning
Shorthand Modulus	v1 %= v2	v1 = v1 % v2
Shorthand Left Shift	v1 <<= v2	v1 = v1 << v2
Shorthand Right Shift	v1 >>= v2	v1 = v1 >> v2
Shorthand Zero Fill Right Shift	v1 >>>= v2	v1 = v1 >>> v2, adding a padding zero after assignment.
Shorthand AND	v1 &= v2	v1 = v1 & v2
Shorthand XOR	v1 ^= v2	v1 = v1 ^ v2
Shorthand OR	v1 |= v2	v1 = v1 | v2

Comparison Operators

These operators return the Boolean literal values, true and false. If v1 = 1 and v2 = 2, the following statements are all true.

Name	Example	Description
Equal	v1 == 1	True if two operands are strictly equal.
Not Equal	v1 != v2	True if two operands are not strictly equal.
Greater Than	v2 > v1	True if LHS operand is greater than RHS operand
Greater Than Or Equal	v2 >= v2	True if LHS operand is greater than or equal to RHS operand
Less Than	v1 < v2	True if LHS operand is less than RHS operand
Less Than Or Equal	v1 <= v1	True if LHS operand is less than or equal to RHS operand

Miscellaneous Operators

The following operators do not easily fit into any other category.

Name	Example	Description
Conditional Operator	evalquery ? v1 : v2	If evalquery is true, the operator returns v1, else it returns v2.
Comma Operator	eval1, eval2	Evaluates both eval1 and eval2 while treating the two as one expression. Can also be used to declare or set multiple variables at the same time.

Name	Example	Description
typeof	typeof v1 typeof (v1)	Returns a number representing the type of v1, which is not evaluated. The numbers 0, 1, 2, 3, 4 represent the types integer, floating point, string, Boolean and invalid respectively.
isvalid	isvalid x	Returns a Boolean: true if x is of a valid type, and false otherwise.

Operator Precedence

The table shows precedence from highest to lowest (top to bottom), with like operators grouped together. Evaluation order for like elements is from left to right.

Operator type	Operators
Postfix	[] () expr++ expr--
Unary	++expr --expr +expr -expr ~ !
Type	typeof isvalid
Multiplicative	* / div %
Additive	+ -
Shift	<< >> >>>
Relational	< > <= >=
Equality	== !=
Bitwise AND	&
Bitwise Exclusive OR	^
Bitwise Inclusive OR	|
Logical AND	&&
Logical OR	||
Conditional	? :
Assignment	= += -= *= /= div= %= &= ^= |= <<= >>= >>>=
Comma	,

WMLScript Statements/Functions

The following tables describe WMLScript statements

Declarations

Statement	Example	Description

var	`var Number;`
	`var Number = 6;`
	`var N1, N2, N3 = 6;`
		Used to declare a variable. Initializing it to a value is optional at the time of declaration.

function	`extern function doItNow()`
	`{`
	   `statements`
	`};`
	
	`extern function doThis(p1,p2,p3)`
	`{`
	   `statements`
	`};`
		Used to declare a function with the specified parameters.
		
		To return a value the function must use the `return` statement.
		
		`extern` is used so that the function is available outside of where it is defined.

use	`use url script2`
	`"http://www.somewhere.com/`
	`WMLScripts/script2.wmls";`
		`use` is used to enable the script to use pragmas (see table below)

Loops

Statement	Example	Description

for	`for (var i=0; i<15; i++)`
	`{`
	   `var x += i;`
	   `doSomething(x);`
	`}`
		Creates a loop controlled according to the three optional expressions enclosed in the parentheses after the `for` and separated by semicolons. The first of these three expressions is the initial-expression, the second is the test condition, and the third is the increment-expression.

Statement	Example	Description
if...else	```if (x <= y)` `{` ` thing += x;` ` x++;` `}` `else` ` thing += y;```	Executes a block of statements if the condition evaluates to true. If the condition evaluates to false, another block of statements can be executed using else (this is optional).
while	```while(y < 3)` `{` ` doSomething();` `}```	Executes a block of statements if a test condition evaluates to true. The loop then repeats, testing the condition with each repeat, ceasing if the condition evaluates to false.

Execution Control Statements

Statement	Example	Description
break	```var x = 0;` `while (x < 20)` `{` ` if (10 == x)` ` break;` ` x++;` `}` `return x*b;```	Used within a while or for loop to terminate the loop and transfer program control to the statement following the loop.
continue	```var count = 0;` `while (count < 16)` `{` ` if (0 == (++count %` `2))` ` continue;` ` return count*c;` `}```	Used to stop execution of the block of statements in the current iteration of a while or for loop; execution of the loop continues with the next iteration.
return	```extern function` `returnSthg(x, y)` `{` ` return x/y;` `}```	Used to specify the value to be returned by a function, or simply to exit from the current function.

Pragmas

Pragma	Example	Description
url	use url *ID* "*URL*"	Used to specify the URL of the WMLScript file containing the functions we want to use in *URL*, and can then access these functions using the name specified in *ID*.
access	use access domain "*domain*" path "*path*";	Used to specify the *domain* and *path* from which access is allowed to functions in the current WMLScript.
meta	use meta *type property content scheme*	Used to supply additional information. *type* represents the type of pragma, *property* the name of the header you wish to set, *content* the value you want to set the header, and *scheme* the formatting of the header.

Comments

Comments are notes that the script engine ignores, and which can be used to explain the code.

```
// This is the syntax for a one line comment...
```

```
/* And this is the syntax for a multiple line comment. The comment can be of any
length, as long as it is contained within the delimiters */
```

Escape Codes

The following table lists all the literal string escape codes.

Escape Code	Represents
\'	Single quote
\"	Double quote
\\	Backslash
\/	Frontslash
\b	Backspace
\f	Form feed
\n	Newline
\r	Carriage return
\t	Horizontal tab
\x*hh*	Character *hh* from the Latin-1 character set (ISO 8859-1), specified in hexadecimal format as two digits
ooo	Character *ooo* from the Latin-1 character set (ISO 8859-1), specified in octal format as three digits
\u*hhhh*	Character *hhhh* from the Unicode character set, specified in hexadecimal format as four digits

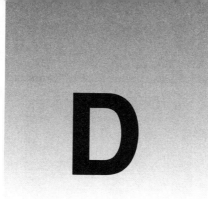

Standard WMLScript Library Functions

The following function libraries are listed here, in this order:

- ❑ Dialogs – user interaction functions.
- ❑ Float – functions relating to floating-point numbers.
- ❑ Lang – functions that relate closely to the WMLScript language core.
- ❑ String – string related functions.
- ❑ URL – functions for handling relative and absolute URLs.
- ❑ WMLBrowser – functions that allow scripts to access the current context.

Dialogs

This library contains functions used to produce simple user interface cards.

alert

Usage:　　　alert(message)

Parameters:　message – of type string, to be displayed to the user

Comments:　This function displays the message passed to it, and when the user confirms they have read the message returns them to the previous card

Example: `Dialogs.alert("There has been an error");`

confirm

Usage: confirm(message, ok, cancel)

Parameters: message – of type string, the question to ask the user
ok – of type string, the positive option to offer the user
cancel – of type string, the negative option to offer the user

Returns: a Boolean, `true` if the user chooses ok, `false` if they choose cancel

Comments: This function is used to prompt the user when a question, and in particular a confirmation, is required.

Example: `strResult = Dialogs.confirm("Are you sure you wish to do this", "Yes", "Not really");`

prompt

Usage: prompt(message, default)

Parameters: message – of type string, the text to display prompting the user for input.
default – of type string, the default text to fill the input box with.

Returns: a string, the text the user has entered.

Comments: This function presents the user with an input box to fill.

Example: `strResult = Dialogs.prompt("Enter your name", "Bob");`

Float

This library contains functions for the manipulation and conversion of floating-point numbers.

ceil

Usage: ceil(value)

Parameters: value – a floating-point number

Returns: an integer, which is nearest in size to the value, but not smaller than it.

Comments: Be careful when using negative numbers, ceil(-2.7) = -2 and *not* -3.

Example:
```
x = Float.ceil(4.1);
// x is assigned the value 5
```

floor

Usage: floor(value)

Parameters: value – a floating-point number

Returns: An integer, which is nearest in size to the value, but not greater than it

Comments: Be careful when using negative numbers, floor(-4.1) = -5 and *not* -4.

Example:
```
x = Float.floor(1.9);
// x is assigned the value 1
```

int

Usage: int(value)

Parameters: value – a floating-point number

Returns: the integer part of the floating-point value

Comments: This simply returns the integer part of the value; it doesn't round the number.

Example:
```
x = Float.int(2.9);
// x is assigned the value 2
```

maxfloat

Usage: maxFloat()

Parameters: none

Returns: The maximum size floating-point number that can be represented.

Comments: This will typically be 3.4028235E38.

Example:
```
x = Float.maxFloat();
// x is assigned the value 3.4028235E38
```

minfloat

Usage: minFloat()

Parameters: none

Returns: The smallest non-zero floating-point number that can be represented.

Comments: This will typically be 1.17549435E-38.

Example:
```
x = Float.minFloat();
// x is assigned the value 1.17549435E-38
```

pow

Usage: pow(number1, number2)

Parameters: number1 – a floating-point number.
number2 – a floating-point number.

Returns: The result of raising number1 to the power of number2. If number1 is a negative value, number2 must be an integer or the return value will be invalid.

Comments: This function performs the calculation $(number1)^{number2}$.

Example:
```
x = Float.pow(2.5, 3);
// x is assigned value 15.625
```

round

Usage: round(value)

Parameters: value – a floating-point number

Returns: An integer as a result of rounding the value

Comments: The normal mathematical rules for rounding apply.

Example:
```
x = Float.round(3.7);
// x is assigned value 4
```

sqrt

Usage: sqrt(value)

Parameters: value – a floating-point number

Returns: The result of taking the square root of the number.

Comments: If an attempt is made to take the square root of a negative number, it returns invalid.

Example:
```
x = Float.sqrt(31.36);
// x is assigned value 5.6
```

Lang

This library contains core WMLScript functions.

abort

Usage: abort(message)

Parameters: message – an error message of type string.

Returns: None.

Comments: This function stops the current execution of WMLScript and hands control back to the browser.

Example:
```
Lang.abort("Calculation failed");
```

abs

Usage: abs(number)

Parameters: number – number of any number type

Returns: The absolute value of the number.

Comments: The return type is of the same type as the parameter passed to the function.

Example:
```
x = Lang.abs(-3)
// x is assigned value 3
```

characterSet

Usage: characterSet()

Parameters: none

Returns: An integer that gives the MIBEnum value from IANA.

Comments: See `ftp://ftp.isi.edu/in-notes/iana/assignments/character-sets` for list of character sets.

Example:
```
x = characterSet();
// x is assigned an integer representing the present char set
```

exit

Usage: exit(value)

Parameters: value – a number of any type

Returns: None. This function ends the interpreter session.

Comments: This function stops the execution of the script and returns control to the WMLScript interpreter.

Example:
```
Lang.exit(3);
x = 6;
// The script is exited with return value of 3
// The assignment never takes place
```

float

Usage: float()

Parameters: none

Returns: A Boolean indicating whether the interpreter supports floating-point numbers.

Comments: The result of this function will obviously vary from one browser to another.

Example:
```
x = Lang.float();
// If the interpreter supports floating-point numbers then
// x is true, otherwise it is false
```

isFloat

Usage: isFloat(value)

Parameters: value – a value of any type

Returns: A Boolean indicating whether the value can be successfully converted to a floating-point number.

Comments: If the interpreter doesn't support floating-point numbers then the return value is invalid.

Example:
```
x = Lang.isFloat("3.53322");
// x is assigned the value true
```

isInt

Usage: isInt(value)

Parameters: value – a value of any type

Returns: A Boolean representing whether the value can be successfully converted to an integer.

Comments:

Example:
```
x = Lang.isInt("1243");
// x is assigned the value true
```

max

Usage: max(number1, number2)

Parameters: number1 and number2 are numbers of any type

Returns: The larger of the two numbers.

Comments: If the numbers are the same, the first is returned.

Example:
```
x = Lang.max(8, 12.4);
// x is assigned 12.4
```

maxInt

Usage: maxInt()

Parameters: none

Returns: The largest integer supported by the browser.

Comments: 2147483647 is the largest integer.

615

Example:
```
x = Lang.maxInt();
// x is an integer and has the largest value that an
// integer can be
```

min

Usage: min(number1, number2)

Parameters: number1 and number2 are numbers of any type

Returns: The smaller of the two numbers.

Comments: If the numbers are the same, the first is returned.

Example:
```
x = Lang.min(4.5, 9)
// x is assigned 4.5
```

minInt

Usage: minInt()

Parameters: none

Returns: The smallest integer supported by the browser.

Comments: -2147483648 is the smallest integer.

Example:
```
x = Lang.maxInt();
// x is an integer and has the smallest value that an
// integer can be
```

parseInt

Usage: parseInt(value)

Parameters: value – which is the string to be converted

Returns: The result of converting the value to an integer.

Comments: If this cannot be done, the function returns invalid.

Example:
```
x = Lang.parseInt("5");
// x is an integer with value 5
```

random

Usage: random(value)

Parameters: value – the maximum value to be returned.

Returns: An integer randomly chosen from the range 0-value.

Comments: The value parameter must be a positive number.

Example:
```
x = Lang.random(5);
// x is an integer anywhere in the range 0-5
```

seed

Usage: seed(value)

Parameters: value – a value to seed the random number generator

Returns: An empty string if the function succeeds.

Comments: This function should be used before the random function for best results.

Example:
```
Lang.seed(7);
// The random number generator is seeded with the number 7!
```

String

The string library contains functions for the manipulation and conversion of strings.

charAt

Usage: charAt(string, number)

Parameters: string – a string.
number – an integer offset for the string

Returns: The character from the string at the position given by the number.

Comments: The index numbering starts at 0.

Example:
```
x = String.charAt("Hello world", 6);
// x is assigned "w"
```

compare

Usage: compare(string1, string2)

Parameters: string1 and string2 – both of type string

Returns: -1 if string1 < string2.
1 if string1 > string2.
0 if string1 = string2.

Comments: The result of this calculation is dependent upon the character set that is used. The comparison is based on the indexing of the strings according to character positioning within the characters set. This usually means that A is before Z, a is before z, etc.

Example:
```
x = String.compare("a string", "a string");
// x is assigned the value 0
```

elements

Usage: elements(string, separator)

Parameters: string and separator are both strings

Returns: The number of elements in the given string where an element is defined as a substring separated by the given separator.

Comments: The separator should not be an empty string or the return value will be of invalid type.

Example:
```
x = String.elements("This has, three, elements", ",");
// x is assigned the number 3
```

elementAt

Usage: elementAt(string, index, separator)

Parameters: string and separator – of type string.
index – an integer index.

Returns: The element in the string at the given index where an element is a section divided by the separator.

Comments: The indexing of the elements starts from 0.

Example:
```
x = String.elementAt("This has, three, elements", 1, ",");
// x is assigned " three"
```

find

Usage: find(string, sub)

Parameters: string – a string.
sub – a substring to find in the string.

Returns: An integer index number of the first occurrence of the substring in the string.

Comments: The indexing starts from 0.

Example:
```
x = String.find("this is a string", is");
// x is assigned the number 5
```

format

Usage: format(format, value)

Parameters: format – a formatting string.
value – value to be converted to a string using the formatting string parameter.

Returns: The result of formatting the value using the format parameter.

Comments: A formatting string is a string that can contain a format specifier. This format specifier begins with a % and can then be followed by a width and an optional precision before its type is given. The three formatting types are d – integer, f – floating-point and s – string. So, to give a format parameter that means "seven characters wide with an integer" use: %7d. To give a format parameter that means "seven characters wide, with a precision of four" and using an integer, use: %7.4d.

Example:
```
x = String.format("Number-%7.4d", 12);
// x is assigned "Number-   0012"
```

insertAt

Usage: insertAt(string, element, index, separator)

Parameters: string – the string into which the new element is to be inserted.
element – the new string element that is to be inserted.
index – the index in the string where the element is to be inserted.
separator – the string that is used to separate the different elements.

Returns: A string that comprises of the given string with the element inserted at the index, where elements are sections separated by the given separator.

Comments: The indexing starts at 0.

Example:
```
x = String.insertAt("one, two, three", " one and a half", 1, ",");
// x is assigned "one, one and a half, two, three"
```

length

Usage: length(string)

Parameters: string – the string to calculate the length of.

Returns: The length of the string passed as a parameter.

Comments:

Example:
```
x = String.length("Hello");
// x is assigned 5
```

isEmpty

Usage: isEmpty(string)

Parameters: string – the string to be tested.

Returns: A Boolean as to whether the string has length 0 or not.

Comments:

Example:
```
x = String.isEmpty("");
// x is assigned true
```

removeAt

Usage: removeAt(string, index, separator)

Parameters: string – the string to remove an element from.
                index – the position of the element to be removed.
                separator – the string that is used to separate the elements.

Returns: A string with the element at the given index removed.

Comments: Indexing starts from 0, an element is defined as a section of the string separated by the
                given separator.

Example:
```
x = removeAt("zero, one, two", 1, ",");
// x is assigned "zero, two"
```

replace

Usage: replace(string, old, new)

Parameters: string – a string, which will have some of its substrings replaced.
                old – a string which is to be replaced.
                new – a string to replace the old string with.

Returns: The result of substituting the new substring into the string for every old substring.

Comments:

Example:
```
x = String.replace("Hello, world!", "world", "goodbye");
// x is assigned the value "Hello, goodbye!"
```

replaceAt

Usage: replaceAt(string, element, index, separator)

Parameters: string – a string of elements.
element – an element to be inserted into the string at the given index.
index – the position within the string of the element to be replaced.
separator – the string which divides the elements.

Returns: The result of replacing the element at the index in the string with the string given by the element parameter, where elements in the string are divided by the given separator.

Comments: The index starts from 0.

Example:
```
x = String.replaceAt("zero, one, two", " 1", 1, ",");
// x is assigned "zero, 1, two"
```

squeeze

Usage: squeeze(string)

Parameters: string – the string to be squeezed.

Returns: A string where all white spaces have been reduced to a single space character.

Comments:

Example:
```
String.squeeze("Hello,       goodbye   !");
// x is assigned the value "Hello, goodbye !"
```

subString

Usage: substring(string, index, length)

Parameters: string – the string to take the substring from.
index – the position in the string to take the substring from.
length – the number of characters to take from the string for the substring.

Returns: A substring, formed by taking a string of the given length from the given string at the position given by the index.

Comments:

Example:
```
x = String.subString("Hello world!", 6, 5);
// x is assigned "world"
```

trim

Usage: trim(string)

Parameters: string – the string to be trimmed.

Returns: The string with all leading and trailing white space removed.

Comments:

Example:
```
x = String.trim("   Hello, world!    ");
// x is assigned "Hello, world!"
```

toString

Usage: toString(value)

Parameters: value – the value to be converted to a string

Returns: The result of converting the value to its string representation

Comments:

Example:
```
x = String.toString(27);
// x is assigned the string "27"
```

URL

This library contains functions for the manipulation and validation of URLs.

escapeString

Usage: escapeString(string)

Parameters: string – the string to be escaped.

Returns: A string as the result of using normal URL escaping rules on the given string.

Comments: URL escaping is the process of taking characters that are illegal or have special meaning in a URL and replacing them with %xx, where xx is a character code representing the character.

Example:
```
x = URL.escapeString("The # character must be escaped");
// x is assigned "The %23 character must be escaped"
```

getBase

Usage: getBase()

Parameters: none

Returns: The current URL but without the details of the present WMLScript function being called.

Comments: If you call a script using
`http://www.companyname.com/testscript.wmls#function`, the base is
`http://www.companyname.com/testscript.wmls`.

Example:
```
x = URL.getBase();
// x is assigned the current URL but without the details of the
// present WMLScript function
```

getFragment

Usage: getFragment(string)

Parameters: string – a URL

Returns: The fragment part of the URL given as the string parameter.

Comments: The fragment part of URL is the part following the # that is used to determine the specific WMLScript function or WML card.

Example:
```
x = URL.getFragment("http://www.companyname.com/test.wml#main ");
// x is assigned the value "main"
```

getHost

Usage: getHost(string)

Parameters: string – an URL

Returns: The host part of the URL given as the string parameter

Comments: In a URL of the form
`http://www.companyname.com/testscript.wmls#function`, the host part is
`www.companyname.com`.

Example:
```
x = URL.getHost("http://www.companyname.com/test.wml#main");
// x is assigned the value "www.companyname.com"
```

getParameters

Usage: getParameters(string)

Parameters: string – a URL

Returns: A string of parameters from the URL given as the string parameter.

Comments: Parameters are given at the end of a URL and are separated by semicolons.

Example:
```
x = URL.getParameters("http://www.companyname.com/test.wml;10;12");
// x is assigned "10;12"
```

getPath

Usage: getPath(string)

Parameters: string – a URL

Returns: A string of the path from the URL.

Comments: The path is the location of the card on the current host.

Example:
```
x = URL.getPath("http://www.companyname.com/wap/test.wml#main ");
// x is assigned "/wap/test.wml"
```

getPort

Usage: getPort(string)

Parameters: string – a URL

Returns: The port as a string from the URL.

Comments: The port number is given at the end of the domain and is separated from it by using a colon.

Example:
```
x = URL.getPort("http://www.companyname.com:8080/test.wml#main ");
// x is assigned the value "8080"
```

getQuery

Usage: getQuery(string)

Parameters: string – a URL

Returns: The query part of the URL as a string.

Comments: The query part of a URL is placed at the end of a URL and its beginning is marked by a question mark (?), each parameter assigned is separated with an ampersand (&).

Example:
```
x = URL.getQuery("http://www.companyname.com/test.wmls#main?x=10&y=43");
// x is assigned "x=10&y=43"
```

getReferer

Usage: getReferer()

Parameters: None

Returns: The relative URL of the resource that called the current WMLScript.

Comments: If there was no referrer, then the function returns an empty string ("").

Example:
```
x = URL.getReferer()
// x is assigned a relative URL to the resource that called the
// present WMLScript unit
```

getScheme

Usage: getScheme(string)

Parameters: string – a URL

Returns: The scheme as a string of the URL given as the string parameter.

Comments: The scheme is the protocol given at the front of a URL.

Example:
```
x = URL.getScheme("http://www.companyname.com/test.wmls#main ");
// x is assigned the string "http"
```

isValid

Usage: isValid(string)

Parameters: string – a URL

Returns: A Boolean indicating whether the URL given as the string parameter is in a valid form for a URL.

Comments:

Example:
```
x = URL.isValid("http://www.companyname.com/test.wmls#main ");
// x is assigned the Boolean value true
```

loadString

Usage: loadString(url, type)

Parameters: url – a string representation of a URL
type – a string giving the MIME type of the URL which is to be loaded

Returns: If the document at the location given by the URL parameter is of the same type as the type parameter, then this document is returned as a string – otherwise the function returns an integer to signal an error.

Comments: The type of the URL to be loaded as a string must be a text type, that is, the MIME type must start "text/".

Example:
```
x = URL.loadString("http://www.companyname.com/test.wml
","text/vnd.wap.wml");
// x is a string which is the full contents of the WML text file
// located at http://www.companyname.com/test.wml
```

625

resolve

Usage:	resolve(base, relative)
Parameters:	base– a string representing a base URL
	relative – a string representing a relative path to a resource
Returns:	The result of embedding the relative URL into the base URL.
Comments:	

Example:
```
x = URL.resolve("http://www.company.com", "test.wml");
// x is assigned the string "http://www.company.com/test.wml"
```

unescapeString

Usage:	unescapeString(string)
Parameters:	string – the string that is to be unescaped
Returns:	A string as a result of applying unescaping rules to the string given as a parameter.
Comments:	The process of unescaping involves finding escape codes, which are of the form %xx (where xx is the number representing a character), and converting them back to their actual characters.

Example:
```
x = URL.unescapeString("The %23 character has been unescaped");
// x is assigned "The # character has been unescaped"
```

WMLBrowser

This library contains functions for controlling the WML browser. These functions have an effect when the script has finished executing and returns control back to the WML browser.

getCurrentCard

Usage:	getCurrentCard()
Parameters:	none
Returns:	A string giving a relative URL to the card that is presently being displayed by the browser.
Comments:	

Example:
```
x = WMLBrowser.getCurrentCard()
// x is assigned a string that gives a relative URL to the card
// currently being displayed
```

getVar

Usage: getVar(variable)

Parameters: variable – a string containing the name of a WML variable

Returns: The value of the WML variable whose name is given as a parameter.

Comments: If the variable doesn't exist then an empty string ("") is returned.

Example:
```
x = WMLBrowser.getVar("wmlVar1");
// x is assigned the value of the WML variable with name wmlVar1
```

go

Usage: go(string)

Parameters: string – a URL

Returns: An empty string ("").

Comments: When the execution of the current script finishes and control is returned to the browser, the card at the location given in the string parameter will be loaded by the browser.

Example:
```
WMLBrowser.go("http://www.company.com/test.wml#main");
// When the present script has finished executing, the card at the
// location http://www.company.com/test.wml#main will be loaded
```

newContext

Usage: newContext()

Parameters: None

Returns: An empty string ("")

Comments: This function clears the history stack and all WML variables; it has the same effect as using the newcontext="true" attribute in a WML <card> element.

Example:
```
WMLBrowser.newContext();
// When control is returned to the WML browser all WML variables
// have been destroyed and the history lost
```

prev

Usage: prev()

Parameters: None

Returns: An empty string ("")

Comments: When returning control to the browser, the `prev` task will be called. This will cause the browser to return to the previous card.

Example:
```
WMLBrowser.prev();
// when control returns to the browser, the previous card will be
// displayed
```

refresh

Usage: refresh()

Parameters: None

Returns: An empty string ("")

Comments: When returning control to the browser, the refresh task will be called. This will cause the browser to refresh the display of the card – this is particularly useful if the card displays some WML variables that have been altered in the script.

Example:
```
WMLBrowser.refresh();
// when returning to the browser, the display will be refreshed
```

setVar

Usage: setVar(variable, value)

Parameters: variable – the name of a WML variable
value – the new value to assign to the WML variable

Returns: A Boolean, `true` if it succeeds, `false` otherwise.

Comments: This function sets the value of the WML variable, named in the variable parameter, to the value given as the value parameter – if the value is not a string then it is converted to a string first.

Example:
```
WMLBrowser.setVar("WMLvar1", 12);
// The WML variable WMLvar1 is assigned the string "12"
```

Support, Errata, and p2p.wrox.com

We try hard to ensure no mistakes sneak out into the real world, but we won't promise that this book is 100% error free. What we can do is offer the next best thing by providing you with immediate support and feedback from experts who have worked on the book and eliminate these gremlins from future editions. We are also committed to supporting you while you read this book and beyond, as you begin to develop you applications, through our online forums where you can put your questions to the authors, reviewers, and peers.

In this appendix we'll look at how to:

- ❏ Enroll in the peer to peer forums at `http://p2p.wrox.com`
- ❏ Post and check for errata on our main site, `http://www.wrox.com`
- ❏ e-Mail our technical support a query or feedback on our books in general

Between all three of these support procedures, you should get a speedy answer to your problem.

The Online Forums at p2p.wrox.com

Join one or more of the three mobile mailing lists for author and peer support. Our system provides Programmer to Programmer™ support on mailing lists, forums and newsgroups, in addition to our one-to-one e-mail system, which we'll look at in a minute. You will be glad to know that your query is not just being examined by a support professional, but by the many Wrox authors and other industry experts present on our mailing lists.

How To Enroll For Support

Just follow these simple steps:

1. Go to http://p2p.wrox.com in your favorite browser. This first page includes the latest information concerning P2P – new lists created, any removed, and so on.

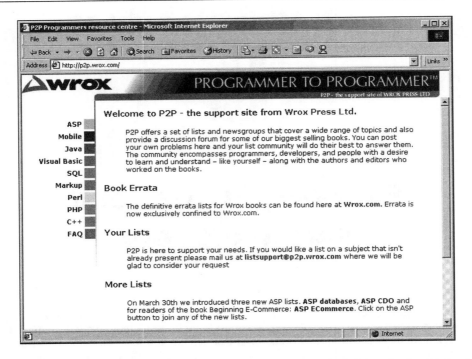

2. Choose the topic you are interested in from the menu on the left hand side; this book comes under the topic Mobile.

3. Choose the relevant list from the available options (wrox_wap and wrox_wml and several others all come under this category).

4. You can view a list without joining it, but if you wish to contribute, you will need to join. To do so select the relevant button.

5. You will be presented with a form that requests your e-mail address, name and a password (of at least 4 characters). Choose how you would like to receive messages from the list, and then hit Save.

6. Congratulations. You're now a member of one of the Wrox p2p mailing lists.

Why This System Offers the Best Support

You can choose to join the mailing lists, or you can receive them as a weekly digest. If you are wary of being inundated with e-mail, you can also choose not to receive e-mail submissions at all and instead get help by searching our online archives. You'll find the ability to search on specific subject areas or keywords. As these lists are moderated, you can be confident of finding good, accurate information quickly. Mails can be edited or moved by the moderator into a logical place, making this a most efficient resource. Junk and spam mail are deleted, and your own e-mail address is protected by the unique Lyris system from web-bots that can automatically hoover up newsgroup mailing list addresses.

Online Errata at www.wrox.com

The following section will take you step by step through the process of posting errata to our web site and getting help with known errata. The sections that follow, therefore, are:

- ❏ Wrox Developer's Membership
- ❏ Finding a list of existing errata on the web site
- ❏ Adding your own errata to the existing list
- ❏ What happens to your erratum once you've posted it

So that you only need view information relevant to yourself, we ask that you register as a Wrox Developer Member. This is a quick and easy process that will save you time in the long-run. If you are already a member, just update membership to include this book.

Wrox Developer's Membership

To get your *free* Wrox Developer's Membership, click on Membership in the top navigation bar of our home site – http://www.wrox.com. This is shown in the following screenshot:

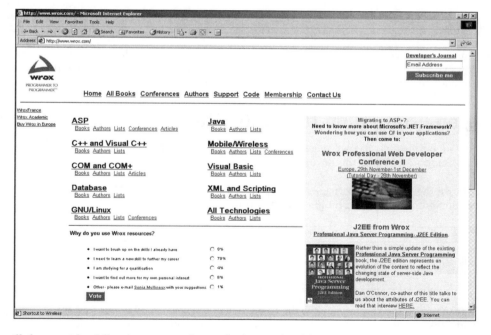

You will then get the following screen, from which you should click on New User. This will display a form. Fill in the details on the form, submit the details using the Register button at the bottom, and you will be returned to this screen:

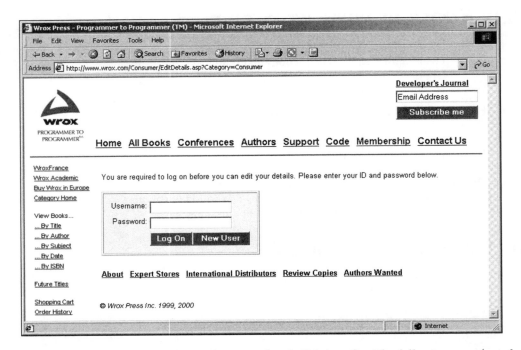

You can now type in your user name and password and click Log On. The following page (not shown here) allows you to change your details if you need to, but you are now logged on and have access to the source code, downloads, and errata for the entire Wrox range of books.

Finding an Erratum on the Web Site

Each book we publish has its own page and its own errata sheet. You can get to any book's page by clicking on Support from the top navigation bar.

Halfway down the main support page is a drop down box called Title Support. Simply scroll down the list, select Beginning WAP, and hit the Errata button.

This will take you to the errata page for the book. Select the criteria by which you want to view the errata, and click the Apply criteria button. This will provide you with links to specific errata. For an initial search, you are advised to view the errata by page numbers. If you have looked for an error before, you can filter out the messages you have read by specifying dates. We update these pages daily to ensure that you have the latest information on bugs and errors.

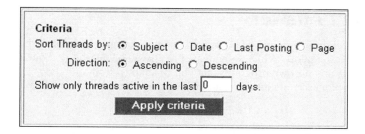

Submitting an Erratum: e-Mail Support

If you wish to point out an erratum, so that we can correct it in future editions, or directly query a problem in the book with an expert who knows the book in detail, then e-mail support@wrox.com. A typical mail should include the following things:

❑   The title and last four digits of the ISBN of the book, and the page number of the problem, should be placed in the subject field of your message.

❑   Your name, contact information, and as detailed a description of the problem as you can provide should be included in the body of the message.

We won't send you junk mail. We need the details to save your time and ours. When you send e-mail, it will go through the following chain of support:

Customer Support

Your message is delivered to one of our customer support staff, who are the first people to read it. They have files on most frequently asked questions, and will answer many problems immediately. They answer general questions about the book and the web site.

Editorial

More complex queries are forwarded to the technical editor responsible for the book. They have experience with the programming language or particular product, and are able to answer detailed technical questions on the subject. Once an issue has been resolved, the editor can post the erratum to the web site.

The Authors

Finally, in the unlikely event that the editor can't answer your problem, you message will be forwarded to the author. We try to protect the author from distractions, but we are quite happy to forward specific requests to them. All Wrox authors help with the support on their books. They'll mail you and the editor with their response, and again all readers should benefit.

What We Can't Answer

Obviously, with an ever-growing range of books and an ever-changing technology base, there is an increasing volume of data requiring support. While we endeavor to answer all questions about the book, we can't provide help with bugs in your own programs that you've adapted from our code. The best place for those types of queries is the p2p lists mentioned earlier, where people will happily pick apart your code for you.

How to Tell Us Exactly What You Think

We understand that without your input we can't improve our books, so please tell us why you like or loathe this book. Or you might have ideas about how this whole process could be improved. In either case, e-mail feedback@wrox.com. You'll always find a sympathetic ear, no matter what the problem is. Above all we do care about what you have to say, and we will do our utmost to act upon it!

Index

A Guide to the Index

The index is arranged hierarchically, in alphabetical order, with any symbols preceding the letter A. Most second-level entries and many third-level entries also occur as first-level entries. This is to ensure that users will find the information they require however they choose to search for it.

X

wrox
PROGRAMMER TO PROGRAMMER™

Wrox writes books for you. Any suggestions, or ideas about how you want information given in your ideal book will be studied by our team. Your comments are always valued at Wrox.

Free phone in USA 800-USE-WROX
Fax (312) 893 8001

UK Tel. (0121) 687 4100   Fax (0121) 687 4101

Beginnning WAP - Registration Card

Name _____

Address _____

_____

_____

_____

City_____ State/Region _____

Country_____ Postcode/Zip _____

E-mail _____

Occupation _____

How did you hear about this book? _____

☐ Book review (name) _____

☐ Advertisement (name) _____

☐ Recommendation _____

☐ Catalog _____

☐ Other _____

Where did you buy this book? _____

☐ Bookstore (name)_____ City _____

☐ Computer Store (name)_____

☐ Mail Order _____

☐ Other _____

What influenced you in the purchase of this book?

☐ Cover Design

☐ Contents

☐ Other (please specify) _____

What did you find most useful about this book? _____

_____

What did you find least useful about this book? _____

_____

Please add any additional comments. _____

_____

What other subjects will you buy a computer book on soon? _____

_____

What is the best computer book you have used this year?

_____

How did you rate the overall contents of this book?

☐ Excellent   ☐ Good

☐ Average   ☐ Poor

Note: This information will only be used to keep you updated about new Wrox Press titles and will not be used for any other purpose or passed to any other third party.

wrox
PROGRAMMER TO PROGRAMMER™

NB. If you post the bounce back card below in the UK, please send it to:

Wrox Press Ltd., Arden House, 1102 Warwick Road,
Acocks Green, Birmingham B27 6BH. UK.

———— *Computer Book Publishers* ————